The Law of Contract

Third Edition

HUGH COLLINS
Professor of English Law
London School of Economics and Political Science

Butterworths
London, Edinburgh,Dublin
1997

United Kingdom	Butterworths a Division of Reed Elsevier (UK) Ltd, Halsbury House, 35 Chancery Lane, LONDON WC2A 1EL and 4 Hill Street, EDINBURGH EH2 3JZ
Australia	Butterworths, SYDNEY, MELBOURNE, BRISBANE, ADELAIDE, PERTH, CANBERRA and HOBART
Canada	Butterworths Canada Ltd, TORONTO and VANCOUVER
Ireland	Butterworth (Ireland) Ltd, DUBLIN
Malaysia	Malayan Law Journal Sdn Bhd, KUALA LUMPUR
New Zealand	Butterworths of New Zealand Ltd, WELLINGTON and AUCKLAND
Singapore	Reed Elsevier (Singapore) Pte Ltd, SINGAPORE
South Africa	Butterworths Publishers (Pty) Ltd, DURBAN
USA	Michie, Charlottesville, VIRGINIA

Any Crown copyright material is reproduced with the permission of the Controller of Her Majesty's Stationery Office.

© Hugh Collins 1997

A CIP Catalogue record for this book is available from the British Library.

ISBN 0 406 89121 4

Printed by Redwood Books, Trowbridge, Wiltshire

THE LAW OF CONTRACT

LAW IN CONTEXT

Editors: William Twining (University College, London) and
Christopher Mc Crudden (Lincoln College, Oxford)

Ashworth: *Sentencing and Criminal Justice*
Barton & Douglas: *Law and Parenthood*
Bercusson: *European Labour Law*
Birkinshaw: *Freedom of Information: The Law, the Practice and the Ideal*
Cane: *Atiyah's Accidents, Compensation and the Law*
Cranston: *Legal Foundations of the Welfare State*
Davies and Freedland: *Labour Law: Text and Materials*
Detmold: *Courts and Administrators: A Study of Jurisprudence*
Doggett: *Marriage, Wife-Beating and the Law in Victorian England*
Dummett and Nicol: *Subjects, Citizens, Aliens and Others: Nationality and Immigration Law*
Elworthy & Holder: *Environmental Protection: Text and Materials*
Goodrich: *Languages of Law*
Hadden: *Company Law and Capitalism*
Harlow and Rawlings: *Law and Administration: Text and Materials*
Harris: *An Introduction to Law*
Lacey, Wells and Meure: *Reconstructing Criminal Law: Text and Materials*
Lewis: *Choice and the Legal Order: Rising above Politics*
Moffat: *Trusts Law: Text and Materials*
Norrie: *Crime, Reason and History*
Page and Fergusson: *Investor Protection*
Picciotto: *International Business Transaction*
Ramsay: *Consumer Protection: Text and Materials*
Richardson: *Law, Process and Custody*
Snyder: *New Directions in European Community Law*
Stapleton: *Product Liability*
Turpin: *British Government and the Constitution: Text, Cases and Materials*
Twining and Anderson: *Analysis of Evidence*
Twining and Miers: *How to do Things with Rules*
Ward: *A Critical Introduction to European Law*
Zander: *Cases and Materials on the English Legal System*
Zander: *The Law-Making Process*

Preface to the Third Edition

Perhaps no other subject in the standard canon of legal education can claim such an august tradition, such rigour of analysis, and such sublime irrelevance, as the law of contract. The multitude of textbooks typically repeat an interpretation of the subject which has remained unaltered for a century or more in its categorization and organization of the legal materials. The latent values which inform these works include a priority attached to personal liberty, minimal regulation of market transactions, and a profound divide between private economic transactions and public control over the social order. This fidelity to nineteenth-century *laissez-faire* ideals, which is unmatched in other fields of legal studies, often remains concealed behind a presentation of the law which emphasizes the formal, technical, and ahistorical qualities of legal reasoning.

The result of this fidelity to tradition is that students learn in their early years a misleading and almost entirely irrelevant set of rules. It is doubly misleading, for the values which support the law have altered, and the emphasis upon the formal qualities of legal reasoning tends to exclude any appreciation of how the law rests upon policy choices at all. The attempt to repeat the past guarantees the irrelevance of the subject, since it can only have rare practical applications, because most contractual relations will be governed by different rules from those stated in the books. My interpretation of the law of contract distances itself from these standard accounts of the subject in two ways.

The book defines the field of study by reference to the context of market transactions, rather than the traditional confines of the legal conceptual category of contracts. It delineates the subject as those rules which regulate trading practices and shape the permitted forms of market transactions. As well as compelling discussion of relevant parts of other aspects of private law, such as tort and unjust enrichment, this frame of reference also requires the introduction of statutory and regulatory materials. In particular, it requires an examination of how membership of the European Community and its Single Market is beginning to shape the rules which provide the basis for market transactions throughout Europe. By emphasizing the social context of market transactions, and identifying those rules and legal principles which have an important bearing on this context, the relevance of the subject to legal practice and social action becomes more assured. There remains a problem of generality, for most contracts are subject to particular regimes of law. But what a general introduction to the subject must achieve is an understanding of the criteria by which market transactions are differentiated from each other.

The second contrast with traditional accounts of the subject derives from the focus on these criteria of differentiation between contracts, which prompts a fundamental revision of the description of the values which underlie the modern law of contract. My interpretation of the legal materials emphasizes the way the law both establishes market transactions as an important site for citizens to acquire meaning for their lives, and controls the market for the sake of establishing and protecting public goods. I have referred to these goals compendiously as a conception of the 'social market'.

In the third edition, most of the text has been rewritten, with some reorganization of the material, and the introduction of new topics. The main themes in their essentials remain unaltered, but their development and elaboration has evolved. Although the contextual focus of the book compels the introduction of material which does not usually figure in the traditional canon, wherever possible I have made reference to familiar case-law to bring out the possibility of contrasting interpretations. Perhaps the most significant contrast between this edition and previous ones concerns the greater inclusion and discussion of the implications of recent empirical enquiries into the nature and practices of making contracts. As far as legal developments are concerned, the most important is undoubtedly the Unfair Terms in Consumer Contracts Regulations 1974.

The primary focus of the book remains upon English law. But to understand the current regulation of market transactions in England, some aspects of European and international law have to be considered. I have also introduced frequent comparisons with jurisdictions from elsewhere in the common law world, either where these countries have addressed problems yet to be considered in England, or where their reasoning points to the future direction which English law is likely to take.

To avoid any misunderstanding of my purpose in writing this book, let me make a few concluding observations about its objectives. It is primarily a study of legal rules and doctrines, not an attempt to discover the way some aspect of society works through a study of the law. An examination of legal doctrine is interesting and important in its own right, for the law frequently supplies the location for conclusive settlement of debates about social justice, and so lawyer's interpretations of social phenomena and the values built into their analyses constitute a vital focus of study for anyone interested in how a society is constituted and how it may be reformed. This work offers an interpretation of the law which tries to make the best moral sense of these materials, to fit them into a coherent picture of the social policies which the law pursues in its regulation of market transactions. It is no part of my purpose to bring out contradictions and incoherence in the legal doctrine, though in formulating a sustained interpretation no doubt I brush over local difficulties of internal coherence in the law.

Lawyers trained in the traditional canon of contract law may find some of the concepts and categories of my interpretation unfamiliar, and they may be concerned that because the courts do not use exactly the same terminology, then my interpretation of the law must be misleading. But given that my interpretation suggests that the traditional account conceals more than it reveals about legal regulation of market transactions, some novelty in the terminology becomes essential. It serves the purpose of better expressing the principles which guide the legal reasoning.

A restatement of the law of contract has considerable potential importance, because students throughout the common law world learn from the subject many of their elementary legal skills. The way the subject is taught, described, and examined shapes most students' perception of how legal reasoning works, and what objectives the law normally tries to achieve. As long as students continue to receive the implicit message from traditional texts that legal reasoning comprises the formal application of rules gleaned from ancient precedents which embrace nineteenth-century *laissez-faire* values, their legal education commences on the wrong foot and never really recovers. Students should learn instead that contemporary moral and political values decisively shape each branch of the law, that legislation provides the key element in the legal regulation of social life, and that disputes about the law reveal conflicting interpretations of social values and how they should be realized.

Acknowledgements
One's debts in writing a work of this kind multiply over the years, so one cannot hope to mention everyone who has assisted me by contributions and criticism. Special mention, however, should be made of Roberto Unger, who first inspired the project, to Nick McBride and Colin Scott for the comments on the second edition, and to Anna Edwards for her assistance on the current edition.

Hugh Collins
April 1997
London School of Economics

Contents

Preface to the Third Edition   v
Acknowledgements   vii
Table of statutes   xiii
Table of cases   xvii

Chapter 1   **Contract and Market**   1
    1   The Classical Law of Contract   3
    2   Towards a New Conception   7
    3   The Market Order   10
    4   The Constitution of the Market   15

Chapter 2   **The Transformation of the Law of Contract**   21
    1   The Social Market   22
    2   Materialization and Differentiation   36
    3   Globalization and Sources of Law   41

Chapter 3   **Tests of Enforceability**   46
    1   Purposes of Tests of Enforceability   46
    2   Evidence and Formalities   49
    3   Illegality and Public Policy   51
    4   Public and Private   53
    5   The Contractualization of Social Life   55

Chapter 4   **Consideration and The Exchange Model**   56
    1   The Concept of Consideration   56
    2   Intention to Create Legal Relations   64
    3   Rationale of Consideration   66

Chapter 5   **Estoppel and the Reliance Model**   71
    1   The Concept of Reliance   71
    2   The Classification of the Reliance Model   80
    3   Rationale of the Reliance Model   85

Chapter 6   **The Contractualization of Social Life**   89
    1   The Faith in Markets   89

	2	Legal Techniques for Controlling the Scope of Contracts	90
	3	Justifications for Limits on Contractual Obligations	96
	4	The Purpose of Markets	101

Chapter 7 **Ascription of Contractual Responsibility** 108
1 The Idea of Consent 108
2 Objective Test of Consent 111
3 Common Mistake 116
4 Consent by Remote Parties 119
5 The Boundaries of Contract 125

Chapter 8 **Coercion and Competitive Markets** 128
1 Voluntary Consent 131
2 Duress 132
3 Undue Influence 136
4 Affirmation and Bars to Rescission 142
5 Protection of Competitive Markets 143

Chapter 9 **The Moment of Responsibility** 148
1 Offer and Acceptance 150
2 Instrumentalism 159
3 Pre-Contractual Responsibility 165

Chapter 10 **The Duty to Negotiate with Care** 168
1 Misleading Statements 171
2 Failure to Disclose Information 185
3 Abuse of Positions of Trust 195
4 Misuse of Confidential Information 197
5 Misleading Implied Promises 198
6 Rationale for the Duty to Negotiate with Care 202

Chapter 11 **Terms** 206
1 Incorporation 208
2 Oral Agreements 209
3 Interpretation 212
4 Implied Terms 221

Chapter 12 **Mandatory Obligations** 229
1 The Social Dimension of Markets 229
2 The Use of Compulsory Obligations 231
3 Compulsory terms 233
4 Statutory Invalidity 235
5 Judicial Discretion over Exclusion Clauses 237
6 Agency Discretion 245
7 Negotiated Regulation 247

Chapter 13 **Fairness**   251
    1 Three Concepts of Fairness   252
    2 Fairness in the Common Law   253
    3 Statutory Controls   265
    4 Judicial Revision   273

Chapter 14 **The Range of Liability**   283
    1 Privity of Contract   283
    2 Parties to the Contract   289
    3 Rationale of Privity   291
    4 Objections to Privity   296
    5 Reform   302

Chapter 15 **Co-operation**   306
    1 Performance   309
    2 Modification   315
    3 Termination for Breach of Contract   331

Chapter 16 **Agreed Remedies**   338
    1 Freedom and Control   339
    2 Fixed Measure of Compensation   341
    3 Security   352
    4 Guarantees and Indemnities   364
    5 Forum   366

Chapter 17 **Judicial Remedies**   368
    1 Settlements   369
    2 Considerations Shaping Judicial Remedies 370
    3 Damages   376
    4 Compulsory Performance   394

    Index   403

Table of statutes

	PAGE
Agricultural Holdings Act 1948	234
Arbitration Act 1996	94
s 67	366
91	367
Bills of Exchange Act 1882	50
Bills of Sale Act (1878) Amendment Act 1882	355
Carriage of Goods by Sea Act 1992	50
Children Act 1989	
s 2(9)	51
Common Law Procedure Act 1852	
s 210–212	361
Companies Act 1985	
Pt XII (ss 395–424)	355
s 35	110
35A	110, 121
Companies Act 1989	110, 121, 355
Competition Act 1980	130
Consumer Credit Act 1974	
s 60–64	189
65	50, 189
67–68	141
87–89	361
90	363
99–103	349
105–113	366
114–121	354, 366
122	366
127	50, 189
129	282, 361
132	363
136	363
137	268, 349, 363
138	349
(1)	268
139	349
(2)	268
140	349
192(3)	340, 356

	PAGE
Consumer Protection Act 1987	8
Pt I (ss 1–9)	299
s 20	172, 173
21	194
39	178, 179
43–47	190
Contracts (Applicable Law) Act 1990	42
Courts and Legal Services Act 1990	
s 58	52
Criminal Law Act 1967	
s 5(1)	52
14(2)	52
Defective Premises Act 1972	193
Employment Rights Act 1996	
s 1	189
94	230
203	234
Equal Pay Act 1970	
s 1	234
Fair Trading Act 1973	130
s 124	248
Financial Services Act 1986	
s 47	193
Hire-Purchase Act 1964	
s 27	340, 356
Honours (Prevention of Abuses) Act 1925	52
Human Organ Transplants Act 1989	100
s 1	51
Industrial Relations Act 1971	249
Industrial Tribunals Act 1996	
s 18–19	372
Insolvency Act 1985	355
Insolvency Act 1986	368
s 238	58
423	58
Landlord and Tenant Covenants Act 1995	290
Land Registration Act 1925	355
Law of Property Act 1925	
s 49(2)	363

PAGE

Law of Property Act 1925–*contd*
s 146 361
Law of Property (Miscellaneous Provisions) Act
  1989
  s 1 53
  2 210
  (1), (3), (5) 49
Law Reform (Contributory Negligence) Act
  1945
  s 1(1) 386
Law Reform (Miscellaneous Provisions) Act
  1970 51
Matrimonial Causes Act 1973
  s 34 99
Minors' Contracts Act 1987 110
Misrepresentation Act 1967
  s 2 178
  (1) 181, 182, 183, 184, 392
  (2) 180
  3 192
Property Misdescriptions Act 1991 171
  s 2 178
Restriction of Offensive Weapons Act 1959
  s 1 51
Road Traffic Act 1988
  s 148(7) 302
Sale and Supply of Goods Act 1994
  s 4 335
Sale of Goods Act 1893 .... 117, 333
Sale of Goods Act 1979 .... 117, 333
  s 3 110
  7 277
  8 .... 62, 224
  13 239
  14 .... 192, 225, 236, 239, 387
  15 239
  15A(1) 335
  19 356
  28 342
  39 354
  48(2) 344
  49(1) 342
  (2) 342
  53(2) 382
Sale of Offices Act 1551 52
Sale of Offices Act 1809 52
Statute of Frauds (1677) 49
  s 4 .... 50, 365
Sunday Trading Act 1994 14
Supply of Goods and Services Act 1982
  s 13 .... 224, 309
  15 .... 62, 224
Surrogacy Arrangements Act 1985 106
Third Party (Rights Against Insurers) Act
  1930 302
Torts (Interference with Goods) Act 1977
  s 3 368
  12 .... 344, 354

PAGE

Trade Descriptions Act 1968
  s 1 .... 176, 236
  2 176
  3 194
  14 178
  24 .... 178, 179
Trade Union and Labour Relations (Consoli-
  dation) Act 1992
  s 152 392
  156-158 392
  236 400
Unfair Contract Terms Act 1977 .... 237, 246,
                                        343, 392
  s 2(1) 235, 236
  (2) 239
  3 239
  (2)(b) 269
  4 366
  6 .... 193, 236, 239, 240
  11(1) 240
  (4) 240
  12(1) 236
  13 239
  (1) 269
  (b) 346
  Sch 2 240
Uniform Laws on International Sales Act 1967
  Sch 2
  art 7 151

United Kingdom Statutory Instruments

Business Advertisements (Disclosure) Order
    1977, SI 1977/1918 194
Consumer Credit (Agreements) Regulations
    1983, SI 1983/1553 189
Consumer Protection (Cancellation of Contracts
    Concluded away from Business
    Premises) Regulations 1987, SI
    1987/2117 141
Consumer Protection (Code of Practice for
    Traders on Price Indications) Approval
    Order 1988, SI 1988/2078 173
Control of Misleading Advertisements Regula-
    tions 1988, SI 1988/915 185
General Product Safety Regulations 1994, SI
    1994/2328 8
  r 8 194
Mail Order Transactions (Information) Order
    1976, SI 1976/1812 194
Price Marking Order 1991, SI 1991/1382 188
Property Misdescriptions (Specified Matters)
    Order 1992, SI 1992/2834 171
Unfair Terms in Consumer Contracts Regu-
    lations 1994, SI 1994/3159 .... 237, 240,
                                        351, 367
  r 4 270

PAGE

Unfair Terms in Consumer Contracts Regulations
   1994–*contd*
r 4(4) 239
  6 .... 188, 213,
  214, 216
  8 .... 185, 246
Sch 2 271
Sch 3 .... 239, 271
  para 1(b) 343, 346
        (d) 361
        (e) 350, 361
        (i) 220
        (j) 315
        (n) 122
        (o) 342

European Community

Treaty of Rome
  art 30 14

PAGE

Treaty of Rome–*contd*
  art 36 14
     86 .... 130, 145
    100 14
    100A 14
Directives
68/151 110
84/450 185
85/374 .... 8, 299
85/557 141
87/102 189
88/314 188
88/315 188
91/533 189
92/49 42
92/59 8
93/13 .... 44, 188,
  231, 270
  art 2 237
    3 .... 239, 252
    4 252

Table of cases

PAGE

A

AMEV-UDC Finance Ltd v Austin (1986) 162 CLR 170, 68 ALR 185, 60 ALJR 741
(Aust HC) 351
Adams v Lindsell (1818) 1 B & Ald 681, 106 ER 250 158
Addis v Gramophone Co Ltd [1909] AC 488, 78 LJKB 1122, [1908-10] All ER Rep 1,
101 LT 466, HL 389
Aerial Advertising Co v Batchelors Peas Ltd (Manchester) [1938] 2 All ER 788, 82
Sol Jo 567 390
Ailsa Craig Fishing Co Ltd v Malvern Fishing Co Ltd and Securicor (Scotland) Ltd
[1983] 1 All ER 101, [1983] 1 WLR 964, [1983] 1 Lloyd's Rep 183n, 127 Sol Jo
508, [1983] LS Gaz R 2156, 1982 SLT 377, HL 346
Alaska v First National Bank of Ketchikan 629 P 2d 78 (1981) 299
Alaskan Trader, The. See Clea Shipping Corpn v Bulk Oil International Ltd, The
Alaskan Trader
Albacruz (Cargo Owners) v Albazero (Owners), The Albazero [1977] AC 774, [1976]
3 All ER 129, [1976] 3 WLR 419, [1976] 2 Lloyd's Rep 467, 120 Sol Jo 570, 126
NLJ 953, HL 286, 379
Alexander v Home Office [1988] 2 All ER 118, [1988] 1 WLR 968, [1988] ICR 685,
[1988] IRLR 190, 132 Sol Jo 1147, CA 392
Allcard v Skinner (1887) 36 Ch D 145, 56 LJ Ch 1052, 36 WR 251, [1886-90] All ER
Rep 90, 57 LT 61, 3 TLR 751, CA 143
Allied Marine Transport Ltd v Vale do Rio Doce Navegacao SA, The Leonidas D
[1983] 3 All ER 737, [1984] 1 WLR 1, [1983] 2 Lloyd's Rep 411, 127 Sol Jo 729;
revsd [1985] 2 All ER 796, [1985] 1 WLR 925, [1985] 2 Lloyd's Rep 18, 129 Sol
Jo 431, [1985] LS Gaz R 2160, CA 322
Aluminium Co of America v Essex Group 499 F Supp 53 (WD Pa 1980) 337
Aluminium Industrie Vaassen BV v Romalpa Aluminium Ltd [1976] 2 All ER 552,
[1976] 1 WLR 676, [1976] 1 Lloyd's Rep 443, 120 Sol Jo 95, CA 356, 357
Amalgamated Investment and Property Co Ltd v John Walker & Sons Ltd [1976] 3
All ER 509, [1977] 1 WLR 164, 120 Sol Jo 252, 239 Estates Gazette 277, CA 281
Amalgamated Society of Railway Servants v Osborne [1910] AC 87, 79 LJ Ch 87, 54
Sol Jo 215, 101 LT 787, 26 TLR 177, HL 47
Anglia Television Ltd v Reed [1972] 1 QB 60, [1971] 3 All ER 690, [1971] 3 WLR
528, 115 Sol Jo 723, CA 377
Anna, The. See Port Caledonia, The and The Anna
Arcos Ltd v EA Ronaasen & Son [1933] AC 470, 45 Lloyd's Rep 33, 102 LJKB 346,
38 Com Cas 166, [1933] All ER Rep 646, 77 Sol Jo 99, 149 LT 98, 49 TLR 231,
HL 334
Armour v Thyssen Edelstahlwerke AG [1991] 2 AC 339, [1990] 3 All ER 481, [1990]
3 WLR 810, [1991] 1 Lloyd's Rep 95, [1991] BCLC 28, [1990] BCC 925, 134 Sol
Jo 1337, 1990 SLT 891, HL 358

PAGE

Associated British Ports v Palmer [1995] 2 AC 454, [1995] 2 All ER 100, [1995] 2
   WLR 354, [1995] ICR 406, [1995] IRLR 258, [1995] 17 LS Gaz R 48, [1995]
   NLJR 417, HL 104
Associated Japanese Bank (International) Ltd v Crédit du Nord SA [1988] 3 All ER
   902, [1989] 1 WLR 255, 133 Sol Jo 81, [1989] 8 LS Gaz R 43, [1988] NLJR 109 .. 118,
                                                                                              276
Associated Newspapers Ltd v Wilson [1995] 2 AC 454, [1995] 2 All ER 100, [1995] 2
   WLR 354, [1995] ICR 406, [1995] IRLR 258, [1995] 17 LS Gaz R 48, [1995]
   NLJR 417, HL 104
Atlantic Baron, The. See North Ocean Shipping Co Ltd v Hyundai Construction Co
   Ltd, The Atlantic Baron
Atlas Express Ltd v Kafco (Importers and Distributors) Ltd [1989] QB 833, [1989] 1
   All ER 641, [1989] 3 WLR 389, 133 Sol Jo 977, [1989] NLJR 111 327
Attica Sea Carriers Corpn v Ferrostaal Poseidon Bulk Reederei GmbH, The Puerto
   Buitrago [1976] 1 Lloyd's Rep 250, CA 345
A-G of Hong Kong v Humphreys Estate (Queen's Gardens) Ltd [1987] AC 114,
   [1987] 2 All ER 387, [1987] 2 WLR 343, 54 P & CR 96, 131 Sol Jo 194, [1987]
   LS Gaz R 574, PC 114, 126
Avon Finance Co Ltd v Bridger [1985] 2 All ER 281, 123 Sol Jo 705, CA 139
Aylesford (Earl) v Morris (1873) 8 Ch App 484, 37 JP 227, 42 LJ Ch 546, 21 WR 424,
   [1861-73] All ER Rep 300, 28 LT 541 .... 140, 256
Ayres v Hazelgrove (9 February 1984, unreported) 140, 257

B

BICC plc v Burndy Corpn [1985] Ch 232, [1985] 1 All ER 417, [1985] 2 WLR 132,
   [1985] RPC 273, 128 Sol Jo 750, [1984] LS Gaz R 3011, CA 360, 362
Balfour v Balfour [1919] 2 KB 571, 88 LJKB 1054, [1918-19] All ER Rep 860, 63 Sol
   Jo 661, 121 LT 346, 35 TLR 609, CA 47, 65, 91, 98, 103
Banco Exterior Internacional v Mann [1995] 1 All ER 936, [1995] 2 FCR 282, [1995]
   1 FLR 602, [1995] Fam Law 297, 27 HLR 329, [1995] NLJR 179, CA 142
Bank of Credit and Commerce International SA v Aboody [1990] 1 QB 923, [1992] 4
   All ER 955, [1989] 2 WLR 759, [1990] 1 FLR 354, [1989] Fam Law 435, 132 Sol
   Jo 1754, [1989] 2 LS Gaz R 37, CA 137, 257
Bank of Nova Scotia v Hellenic Mutual War Risks Association (Bermuda) Ltd, The
   Good Luck [1992] 1 AC 233, [1991] 3 All ER 1, [1991] 2 WLR 1279, [1991] 2
   Lloyd's Rep 191, [1991] NLJR 779, HL 314
Banque Keyser Ullmann SA v Skandia (UK) Insurance Co Ltd [1990] 1 QB 665,
   [1989] 3 WLR 25, 133 Sol Jo 817, [1989] 26 LS Gaz R 33, [1988] NLJR 287, sub
   nom Banque Financière de la Cité SA v Westgate Insurance Co Ltd [1989] 2 All
   ER 952, [1988] 2 Lloyd's Rep 513, CA; affd sub nom Banque Financière de la
   Cité SA (formerly Banque Keyser Ullmann SA) v Westgate Insurance Co Ltd
   (formerly Hodge General and Mercantile Co Ltd) [1991] 2 AC 249, [1990] 2 All
   ER 947, [1990] 3 WLR 364, [1990] 2 Lloyd's Rep 377, 134 Sol Jo 1265, [1990]
   NLJR 1074, HL 196, 314, 315
Barclays Bank plc v Fairclough Building Ltd [1995] QB 214, [1995] 1 All ER 289,
   [1994] 3 WLR 1057, 39 Con LR 86, 68 BLR 1, [1994] BLM (June) 1, CA 387
Barclays Bank plc v O'Brien [1994] 1 AC 180, [1993] 4 All ER 417, [1993] 3 WLR
   786, [1994] 1 FCR 357, [1994] 1 FLR 1, [1994] Fam Law 78, 26 HLR 75, [1993]
   46 LS Gaz R 37, [1993] NLJR 1511, 137 Sol Jo LB 240, HL 139, 140, 142
Barton v Armstrong [1976] AC 104, [1975] 2 All ER 465, [1975] 2 WLR 1050, 119 Sol
   Jo 286, 3 ALR 355, [1973] 2 NSWLR 598, PC 133
Basham, Re [1987] 1 All ER 405, [1986] 1 WLR 1498, [1987] 2 FLR 264, [1987] Fam
   Law 310, 130 Sol Jo 986, [1987] LS Gaz R 112 83
Bates (Thomas) & Son Ltd v Wyndham's (Lingerie) Ltd [1981] 1 All ER 1077, [1981]
   1 WLR 505, 41 P & CR 345, 125 Sol Jo 32, 257 Estates Gazette 381, CA 214, 215
Beckham v Drake (1849) 2 HL Cas 579, 13 Jur 921 347
Bell v Lever Bros Ltd [1932] AC 161, 101 LJKB 129, 37 Com Cas 98, [1931] All ER
   Rep 1, 76 Sol Jo 50, 146 LT 258, 48 TLR 133, HL 117, 314

PAGE

Bentley (Dick) Productions Ltd v Harold Smith (Motors) Ltd [1965] 2 All ER 65,
[1965] 1 WLR 623, 109 Sol Jo 329, CA 179
Bentsen v Taylor Sons & Co (No 2) [1893] 2 QB 274, 63 LJQB 15, 7 Asp MLC 385, 4
R 510, 42 WR 8, 69 LT 487, 9 TLR 552, CA 333
Bentworth Finance Ltd v Lubert [1968] 1 QB 680, [1967] 2 All ER 810, [1967] 3
WLR 378, 111 Sol Jo 272, CA 312
Beswick v Beswick [1968] AC 58, [1967] 2 All ER 1197, [1967] 3 WLR 932, 111 Sol
Jo 540, HL 285, 293, 297, 378, 396
Birch v University of Liverpool [1985] ICR 470, [1985] IRLR 165, 129 Sol Jo 245,
CA 234
Bisset v Wilkinson [1927] AC 177, 96 LJPC 12, [1926] All ER Rep 343, 136 LT 97,
42 TLR 727, PC 175
Black King Shipping Corpn and Wayang (Panama) SA v Massie, The Litsion Pride
[1985] 1 Lloyd's Rep 437, 134 NLJ 887 314
Blackburn Bobbin Co Ltd v TW Allen & Sons Ltd [1918] 2 KB 467, 87 LJKB 1085,
119 LT 215, 34 TLR 508, CA 273, 278, 280
Blackpool and Fylde Aero Club Ltd v Blackpool Borough Council [1990] 3 All ER 25,
[1990] 1 WLR 1195, 88 LGR 864, [1990] 26 LS Gaz R 37, CA 115, 199
Bliss v South East Thames Regional Health Authority [1987] ICR 700, [1985] IRLR
308, CA 389
Boardman v Phipps [1967] 2 AC 46, [1966] 3 All ER 721, [1966] 3 WLR 1009, 110
Sol Jo 853, HL 196
Bodger v Nicholls (1873) 37 JP 397, 28 LT 441 192
Bolton v Madden (1873) LR 9 QB 55, 38 JP 118, 43 LJQB 35, 22 WR 207, 29 LT 505 .. 37,
64
Bolton v Mahadeva [1972] 2 All ER 1322, [1972] 1 WLR 1009, 116 Sol Jo 564, CA 312,
342, 377
Bolton v Stone [1951] AC 850, [1951] 1 All ER 1078, 59 LGR 32, 95 Sol Jo 333,
[1951] 1 TLR 977, HL 224
Borden (UK) Ltd v Scottish Timber Products Ltd [1981] Ch 25, [1979] 3 All ER 961,
[1979] 3 WLR 672, [1980] 1 Lloyd's Rep 160, 123 Sol Jo 688, CA 357
Boustany v Pigott (1993) 69 P & CR 298, PC 140, 257
Box v Midland Bank Ltd [1979] 2 Lloyd's Rep 391; revsd [1981] 1 Lloyd's Rep 434,
CA 174
Bradford City Metropolitan Council v Arora [1991] 2 QB 507, [1991] 3 All ER 545,
[1991] 2 WLR 1377, [1991] ICR 226, [1991] IRLR 165, CA 392
Bridge v Campbell Discount Co Ltd [1962] AC 600, [1962] 1 All ER 385, [1962] 2
WLR 439, 106 Sol Jo 94, HL 347, 349
Brinkibon Ltd v Stahag Stahl und Stahlwarenhandel GmbH [1983] 2 AC 34, [1982]
1 All ER 293, [1982] 2 WLR 264, [1982] 1 Lloyd's Rep 217, [1982] Com LR 72,
126 Sol Jo 116, HL 161
British Crane Hire Corpn Ltd v Ipswich Plant Hire Ltd [1975] QB 303, [1974] 1 All
ER 1059, [1974] 2 WLR 856, 118 Sol Jo 387, CA 208
British Steel Corpn v Cleveland Bridge and Engineering Co Ltd [1984] 1 All ER
504, [1982] Com LR 54, 24 BLR 94 167
Brogden v Metropolitan Rly Co (1877) 2 App Cas 666, HL 151, 152, 154, 157, 158
Bunge Corpn v Tradax SA [1981] 2 All ER 513, [1981] 1 WLR 711, [1981] 2 Lloyd's
Rep 1, 125 Sol Jo 373, HL 333
Butler Machine Tool Co Ltd v Ex-Cell-O Corpn (England) Ltd [1979] 1 All ER 965,
[1979] 1 WLR 401, 121 Sol Jo 406, CA 151, 156
Byrne & Co v Leon Van Tienhoven & Co (1880) 5 CPD 344, 44 JP 667, 49 LJQB 316,
42 LT 371 163

C

C and P Haulage (a firm) v Middleton [1983] 3 All ER 94, [1983] 1 WLR 1461, 127
Sol Jo 730, CA 380
CCC Films (London) Ltd v Impact Quadrant Films Ltd [1985] QB 16, [1984] 3 All
ER 298, [1984] 3 WLR 245, 128 Sol Jo 297 380

PAGE

CIBC Mortgages plc v Pitt [1994] 1 AC 200, [1993] 4 All ER 433, [1993] 3 WLR 802,
  [1994] 1 FCR 374, [1994] 1 FLR 17, [1994] Fam Law 79, 26 HLR 90, [1993] 46
  LS Gaz R 37, [1993] NLJR 1514, HL 137, 142, 257
CTN Cash and Carry Ltd v Gallaher Ltd [1994] 4 All ER 714, CA 136
Cadbury Ltd v Halliday [1975] 2 All ER 226, [1975] 1 WLR 649, 73 LGR 256, 139 JP
  428, [1975] Crim LR 249, 119 Sol Jo 219, DC 176
Caparo Industries plc v Dickman [1990] 2 AC 605, [1990] 1 All ER 568, [1990] 2
  WLR 358, [1990] BCLC 273, [1990] BCC 164, 134 Sol Jo 494, [1990] 12 LS Gaz
  R 42, [1990] NLJR 248, HL 181, 288, 299
Car and Universal Finance Co Ltd v Caldwell [1965] 1 QB 525, [1964] 1 All ER 290,
  [1964] 2 WLR 600, 108 Sol Jo 15, CA 180, 195
Carlill v Carbolic Smoke Ball Co [1893] 1 QB 256, 57 JP 325, 62 LJQB 257, 4 R 176,
  41 WR 210, [1891-4] All ER Rep 127, 67 LT 837, 9 TLR 124, CA 4, 37, 60, 75, 81,
                                                                     115, 152, 155
Casey's Patents, Re, Stewart v Casey [1892] 1 Ch 104, 61 LJ Ch 61, 9 RPC 9, 40 WR
  180, 36 Sol Jo 77, 66 LT 93, CA 63
Cehave NV v Bremer Handelsgesellschaft mbH, The Hansa Nord [1976] QB 44,
  [1975] 3 All ER 739, [1975] 3 WLR 447, [1975] 2 Lloyd's Rep 445, 119 Sol Jo
  678, CA 335, 385
Cellulose Acetate Silk Co Ltd v Widnes Foundry (1925) Ltd [1933] AC 20, 101 LJKB
  694, 38 Com Cas 61, [1932] All ER Rep 567, 147 LT 401, 48 TLR 595, HL 345
Central London Property Trust Ltd v High Trees House Ltd [1947] KB 130, [1956] 1
  All ER 256n, [1947] LJR 77, 175 LT 332, 62 TLR 557 .... 321, 324
Centrovincial Estates plc v Merchant Investors Assurance Co Ltd [1983] Com LR
  158, CA 214
Chapelton v Barry UDC [1940] 1 KB 532, [1940] 1 All ER 356, 38 LGR 149, 104 JP
  165, 109 LJKB 213, 84 Sol Jo 185, 162 LT 169, 56 TLR 331, CA 208
Charnock v Liverpol Corpn [1968] 3 All ER 473, [1968] 1 WLR 1498, [1968] 2
  Lloyd's Rep 113, 112 Sol Jo 781, CA 122
Chess (Oscar) Ltd v Williams [1957] 1 All ER 325, [1957] 1 WLR 370, 101 Sol Jo
  186, CA 179
Cityland and Property (Holdings) Ltd v Dabrah [1968] Ch 166, [1967] 2 All ER 639,
  [1967] 3 WLR 605, 111 Sol Jo 518 268
Clark v Marsiglia 1 Denio 317 (NY 1845) 344
Clarke v Earl of Dunraven and Mount-Earl, The Satanita [1897] AC 59, 66 LJP 1, 8
  Asp MLC 190, 75 LT 337, 13 TLR 58, HL 159
Clea Shipping Corpn v Bulk Oil International Ltd, The Alaskan Trader [1984] 1 All
  ER 129, [1983] 2 Lloyd's Rep 645 344
Clough Mill Ltd v Martin [1984] 3 All ER 982, [1985] 1 WLR 111, [1985] BCLC 64,
  128 Sol Jo 850, [1985] LS Gaz R 116, CA 357
Clydebank Engineering and Shipbuilding Co Ltd v Don Jose Ramos Yzquierdo y
  Castaneda [1905] AC 6, 74 LJPC 1, [1904-7] All ER Rep 251, 91 LT 666, 21
  TLR 58, 7 F 77, HL 348
Colburn v Patmore (1834) 1 Cr M & R 73, 4 Tyr 677, 3 LJKB Ex 317 52
Coldunell Ltd v Gallon [1986] QB 1184, [1986] 1 All ER 429, [1986] 2 WLR 466, 130
  Sol Jo 88, CA 141
Coleman v Myers [1977] 2 NZLR 225 197
Combe v Combe [1951] 2 KB 215, [1951] 1 All ER 767, 95 Sol Jo 317, [1951] 1 TLR
  811, CA 62, 91, 254, 325
Commercial Bank of Australia Ltd v Amadio (1983) 151 CLR 447, 46 ALR 402, HC
  of A 256
Commercial Solvents Corpn v EC Commission: 6, 7/73. See Istituto Chemioterapico
  Italiano SpA and Commercial Solvents Corpn v EC Commission: 6, 7/73.
Commission for the New Towns v Cooper (Great Britain) Ltd [1995] Ch 259, [1995]
  2 All ER 929, [1995] 2 WLR 677, 72 P & CR 270, [1995] NPC 34, [1995] 2
  EGLR 113, [1995] 26 EG 129, 139 Sol Jo LB 87, CA 215, 220
Commonwealth of Australia v Verwayen (1990) 170 CLR 394, 95 ALR 321, 64 ALJR
  540 .... 77, 83, 85

PAGE

Compaq Computers Ltd v Abercorn Group Ltd [1993] BCLC 602, [1991] BCC 484 357

Cook v Wright (1861) 1 B & S 559, 30 LJQB 321, 7 Jur NS 1121, 121 ER 822, 4 LT 704 369

Cooper v Phibbs (1867) LR 2 HL 149, 15 WR 1049, 16 LT 678, [1861-73] All ER Rep Ext 2109, HL 117

Co-operative Insurance Society Ltd v Argyll Stores (Holdings) Ltd [1996] Ch 286, [1996] 3 All ER 934, [1996] 3 WLR 27, 72 P & CR 130, [1996] 1 EGLR 71, [1996] 09 EG 128, CA; revsd [1997] 2 WLR 898, [1997] NLJR 845, [1997] 23 EG 141, 141 Sol Jo LB 131, HL 286, 399

Cornish v Midland Bank plc (Humes, third party) [1985] 3 All ER 513, 1985 FLR 298, [1985] NLJ Rep 869, CA 173, 178, 188

Cornwall v Henson [1900] 2 Ch 298, 69 LJ Ch 581, 49 WR 42, 44 Sol Jo 514, 82 LT 735, 16 TLR 422, [1900-3] All ER Rep Ext 1734, CA 364

Coulls v Bagot's Executor and Trustee Co Ltd (1967) 119 CLR 460, [1967] ALR 385, 40 ALJR 471, HC of A 286, 289

Courtney and Fairbairn Ltd v Tolaini Bros (Hotels) Ltd [1975] 1 All ER 716, [1975] 1 WLR 297, 119 Sol Jo 134, 2 BLR 97, CA 162

Couturier v Hastie (1856) 5 HL Cas 673, 25 LJ Ex 253, 2 Jur NS 1241, 10 ER 1065, [1843-60] All ER Rep 280, 28 LTOS 240 117

Crabb v Arun District Council [1976] Ch 179, [1975] 3 All ER 865, [1975] 3 WLR 847, 119 Sol Jo 711, CA 72, 75, 77, 79, 81, 125, 166, 200

Cresswell v Potter (1968) [1978] 1 WLR 255n 139, 257

Crossan v Ward Bracewell [1986] NLJ Rep 849 .... 126, 191

Cundy v Lindsay (1878) 3 App Cas 459, 42 JP 483, 14 Cox CC 93, 26 WR 406, [1874-80] All ER Rep 1149, 38 LT 573, sub nom Lindsay & Co v Cundy 47 LJQB 481, HL 195

Curtis v Chemical Cleaning and Dyeing Co Ltd [1951] 1 KB 805, [1951] 1 All ER 631, 95 Sol Jo 253, [1951] 1 TLR 452, CA 173, 219

D

D & C Builders Ltd v Rees [1966] 2 QB 617, [1965] 3 All ER 837, [1966] 2 WLR 288, 109 Sol Jo 971, CA 329

Dagenham (Thames) Dock Co, Re, ex p Hulse (1873) 8 Ch App 1022, 38 JP 180, 43 LJ Ch 261, 21 WR 898 359

Darlington Borough Council v Wiltshier Northern Ltd [1995] 3 All ER 895, [1995] 1 WLR 68, [1994] 37 LS Gaz R 49, 69 BLR 1, 11 Const LJ 36, 138 Sol Jo LB 161, CA 286

Daulia Ltd v Four Millbank Nominees Ltd [1978] Ch 231, [1978] 2 All ER 557, [1978] 2 WLR 621, 36 P & CR 244, 121 Sol Jo 851, CA 164

Davies v Sumner [1984] 3 All ER 831, [1984] 1 WLR 1301, 83 LGR 123, [1985] RTR 95, 149 JP 110, 128 Sol Jo 814, [1985] LS Gaz R 45, 4 Tr L 1, HL 236

Davis Contractors Ltd v Fareham UDC [1956] AC 696, [1956] 2 All ER 145, [1956] 3 WLR 37, 54 LGR 289, 100 Sol Jo 378, HL 276, 277

Decro-Wall International SA v Practitioners in Marketing Ltd [1971] 2 All ER 216, [1971] 1 WLR 361, 115 Sol Jo 171, CA 331

Derry v Peek (1889) 14 App Cas 337, 54 JP 148, 58 LJ Ch 864, 1 Meg 292, 38 WR 33, [1886-90] All ER Rep 1, 61 LT 265, 5 TLR 625, HL 181

Dies v British and International Mining and Finance Corpn Ltd [1939] 1 KB 724, 108 LJKB 398, 160 LT 563 354

Dillon v Baltic Shipping Co, The Mikhail Lermontov [1991] 2 Lloyd's Rep 155, CA ... 252, 327, 392

Director General of Fair Trading v Tobyward Ltd [1989] 2 All ER 266, [1989] 1 WLR 517, 133 Sol Jo 184, [1989] 11 LS Gaz R 44 185

Division of Labor Law Enforcement v Transpacific Transportation Co 69 Cal App 3d 268, 137 Cal Rptr 855 (1977) 78

Doyle v Olby (Ironmongers) Ltd [1969] 2 QB 158, [1969] 2 All ER 119, [1969] 2 WLR 673, 113 Sol Jo 128, CA 183

Drennan v Star Paving Co 51 Cal 2d 409, 333 P 2d 757 (1958) 86, 164, 166

PAGE

Dunlop Pneumatic Tyre Co Ltd v New Garage and Motor Co Ltd [1915] AC 79, 83
LJKB 1574, [1914-15] All ER Rep 739, 111 LT 862, 30 TLR 625, HL 348

E

East v Maurer [1991] 2 All ER 733, [1991] 1 WLR 461, CA 182
Elpis Maritime Co Ltd v Marti Chartering Co Inc, The Maria D [1992] 1 AC 21,
[1991] 3 All ER 758, [1991] 3 WLR 330, [1991] 2 Lloyd's Rep 311, 135 Sol Jo LB
100, HL 121, 365
Entores Ltd v Miles Far East Corpn [1955] 2 QB 327, [1955] 2 All ER 493, [1955] 3
WLR 48, [1955] 1 Lloyd's Rep 511, 99 Sol Jo 384, CA 157
Errington v Errington and Woods [1952] 1 KB 290, [1952] 1 All ER 149, 96 Sol Jo
119, [1952] 1 TLR 231, CA 164
Esso Petroleum Co Ltd v Mardon [1976] QB 801, [1976] 2 All ER 5, [1976] 2 WLR
583, [1976] 2 Lloyd's Rep 305, 120 Sol Jo 131, 2 BLR 85, CA 175, 181, 182
Euro-Diam Ltd v Bathurst [1990] 1 QB 1, [1988] 2 All ER 23, [1988] 2 WLR 517,
[1988] 1 Lloyd's Rep 228, 132 Sol Jo 372, [1988] 9 LS Gaz R 45, CA 51
Evans (J) & Son (Portsmouth) Ltd v Andrea Merzario Ltd [1976] 2 All ER 930,
[1976] 1 WLR 1078, [1976] 2 Lloyd's Rep 165, 120 Sol Jo 734, CA 181, 210
Evans Marshall & Co v Bertola SA [1973] 1 All ER 992, [1973] 1 WLR 349, [1973] 1
Lloyd's Rep 453, 117 Sol Jo 225, CA 390, 396
Export Credits Guarantee Department v Universal Oil Products Co [1983] 2 All ER
205, [1983] 1 WLR 399, [1983] 2 Lloyd's Rep 152, 127 Sol Jo 408, 23 BLR 106,
133 NLJ 662, HL 347

F

Faccini Dori v Recreb Srl: C-91/92 [1994] ECR I-3325, [1995] All ER (EC) 1, [1995] 1
CMLR 665, ECJ 141
Falcke v Gray (1859) 4 Drew 651, 29 LJ Ch 28, 5 Jur NS 645, 7 WR 535, 33 LTOS
297 396
Federal Commerce and Navigation Co Ltd v Molena Alpha Inc, The Nanfri [1978]
QB 927, [1978] 3 All ER 1066, [1978] 3 WLR 309, [1978] 2 Lloyd's Rep 132, 122
Sol Jo 347, CA; affd [1979] AC 757, [1979] 1 All ER 307, [1978] 3 WLR 991,
[1979] 1 Lloyd's Rep 201, 122 Sol Jo 843, HL.. 343
Feinberg v Pfeiffer Co 322 SW 2d 163 (1959) 73
Felthouse v Bindley (1862) 11 CBNS 869, 31 LJCP 204, 10 WR 423, 142 ER 1037;
affd (1863) 1 New Rep 401, 11 WR 429, 7 LT 835 .... 113, 153
Ferguson v Davies [1997] 1 All ER 315, CA 369
First Energy (UK) Ltd v Hungarian International Bank Ltd [1993] 2 Lloyd's Rep
194, [1993] BCLC 1409, [1993] BCC 533, CA.. 271
First National Bank plc v Syed [1991] 2 All ER 250, [1991] CCLR 37, 10 Tr LR 154,
CA 282, 361
Foakes v Beer (1884) 9 App Cas 605, 54 LJQB 130, 33 WR 233, [1881-5] All ER Rep
106, 51 LT 833, HL 318
Foley v Interactive Data Corpn 47 Cal 3d 654 (1988) 391
Forsikringsaktieselskapet Vesta v Butcher, Bain Dawles Ltd and Aquacultural
Insurance Services Ltd [1989] AC 852, [1988] 2 All ER 43, [1988] 3 WLR 565,
[1988] 1 Lloyd's Rep 19, 132 Sol Jo 1181, CA; affd [1989] AC 852, [1989] 1 All
ER 402, [1989] 2 WLR 290, [1989] 1 Lloyd's Rep 331, 133 Sol Jo 184, [1989] 11
LS Gaz R 42, HL 387
Frostifresh Corpn v Reynoso 54 Misc 2d 119, 281 NYS 2d 264 (1967) 140
Fry v Lane (1888) 40 Ch D 312, 58 LJ Ch 113, 37 WR 135, [1886-90] All ER Rep
1084, 60 LT 12, 5 TLR 45 256

G

Gator Shipping Corpn v Trans-Asiatic Oil Ltd SA and Occidental Shipping
Establishment, The Odenfeld [1978] 2 Lloyd's Rep 357 345
General Cleaning Contractors Ltd v Christmas [1953] AC 180, [1952] 2 All ER 1110,
[1953] 2 WLR 6, 51 LGR 109, 97 Sol Jo 7, HL 314

PAGE

Gibbons v Proctor (1891) 55 JP 616, 64 LT 594, 7 TLR 462, DC 156
Gibson v Manchester City Council [1978] 2 All ER 583, [1978] 1 WLR 520, 76 LGR
 365, 122 Sol Jo 80, CA; revsd [1979] 1 All ER 972, [1979] 1 WLR 294, 77 LGR
 405, 123 Sol Jo 201, HL 114, 151, 164, 165
Gill (Stewart) Ltd v Horatio Myer & Co Ltd [1992] QB 600, [1992] 2 All ER 257,
 [1992] 2 WLR 721, CA 343
Good Luck, The. See Bank of Nova Scotia v Hellenic Mutual War Risks Association
 (Bermuda) Ltd, The Good Luck
Gran Gelato Ltd v Richcliff (Group) Ltd [1992] Ch 560, [1992] 1 All ER 865, [1992] 2
 WLR 867, [1992] 1 EGLR 297, [1992] 18 LS Gaz R 36, [1992] NLJR 51 387
Greasley v Cooke [1980] 3 All ER 710, [1980] 1 WLR 1306, 124 Sol Jo 629, CA 76
Great Western Rly Co v Sutton (1869) LR 4 HL 226, 33 JP 820, 38 LJ Ex 177, 18
 WR 92, 22 LT 43, HL 135
Green v All Motors Ltd [1917] 1 KB 625, 86 LJKB 590, [1916-17] All ER Rep 1039,
 116 LT 189, CA 354
Greenwood v Greenwood (1863) 2 De GJ & Sm 28, 46 ER 285 197
Griffith v Brymer (1903) 47 Sol Jo 493, 19 TLR 434 .... 118, 279
Griffith v Spratley (1787) 1 Cox Eq Cas 383, 2 Bro CC 179n 263
Grist v Bailey [1967] Ch 532, [1966] 2 All ER 875, [1966] 3 WLR 618, 110 Sol Jo 791 259,
 281

H

Hadley v Baxendale (1854) 23 LJ Ex 179, 9 Exch 341, 18 Jur 358, 2 WR 302, [1843-
 60] All ER Rep 461, 2 CLR 517, 23 LTOS 69 382
Haigh v Brooks (1839) 10 Ad & El 309, 9 LJQB 99, 2 Per & Dav 477; affd sub nom
 Brooks v Haigh (1840) 10 Ad & El 323, 4 Per & Dav 288, Ex Ch 369
Haley v London Electricity Board [1965] AC 778, [1964] 3 All ER 185, [1964] 3 WLR
 479, 63 LGR 1, 129 JP 14, 108 Sol Jo 637, HL 224
Hannah Blumenthal, The. See Wilson (Paal) & Co A/S v Partenreederei Hannah
 Blumenthal, The Hannah Blumenthal
Hansa Nord, The. See Cehave NV v Bremer Handelsgesellschaft mbH, The Hansa
 Nord
Harbutt's Plasticine Ltd v Wayne Tank and Pump Co Ltd [1970] 1 QB 447, [1970] 1
 All ER 225, [1970] 2 WLR 198, [1970] 1 Lloyd's Rep 15, 114 Sol Jo 29, CA 387
Harlingdon & Leinster Enterprises Ltd v Christopher Hull Fine Art Ltd [1991] 1
 QB 564, [1990] 1 All ER 737, [1990] 3 WLR 13, [1990] NLJR 90, CA 259
Hart v Emelkirk Ltd [1983] 3 All ER 15, [1983] 1 WLR 1289, 9 HLR 114, 127 Sol Jo
 156, 267 Estates Gazette 946 368
Hart v O'Connor [1985] AC 1000, [1985] 2 All ER 880, [1985] 3 WLR 214, 129 Sol Jo
 484, [1985] LS Gaz R 2658, PC 140, 257
Hartog v Colin and Shields [1939] 3 All ER 566 214
Harvela Investments Ltd v Royal Trust Co of Canada (CI) Ltd [1986] AC 207, [1985]
 2 All ER 966, [1985] 3 WLR 276, 129 Sol Jo 522, [1985] LS Gaz R 3171, [1985]
 NLJ Rep 730, HL 2115, 199
Hedley Byrne & Co Ltd v Heller & Partners Ltd [1964] AC 465, [1963] 2 All ER 575,
 [1963] 3 WLR 101, [1963] 1 Lloyd's Rep 485, 107 Sol Jo 454, HL 181
Henrik Sif, The. See Pacol Ltd v Trade Lines Ltd and R/I Sif IV, The Henrik Sif
Henry, The (1851) 15 Jur 183, 16 LTOS 553 136
Heron II, The. See Koufos v C Czarnikow Ltd, The Heron II
Heywood v Wellers [1976] QB 446, [1976] 1 All ER 300, [1976] 2 WLR 101, [1976] 2
 Lloyd's Rep 88, 120 Sol Jo 9, CA 389
Hill v C A Parsons & Co Ltd [1972] Ch 305, [1971] 3 All ER 1345, [1971] 3 WLR 995,
 12 KIR 135, 115 Sol Jo 868, CA 401
Hirachand Punamchand v Temple [1911] 2 KB 330, 80 LJKB 1155, 55 Sol Jo 519,
 105 LT 277, 27 TLR 430, [1911-13] All ER Rep Ext 1597, CA 288
Hoenig v Isaacs [1952] 2 All ER 176, [1952] 1 TLR 1360, CA 342, 343
Hoffman v Red Owl Stores Inc 26 Wis 2d 683, 133 NW 2d 267 (1965) 77, 126,
 166, 298

PAGE

Hoffmann-La Roche & Co AG v EC Commission: 85/76 [1979] ECR 461, [1979] 3
    CMLR 211, ECJ... 146
Hollier v Rambler Motors (AMC) Ltd [1972] 2 QB 71, [1972] 1 All ER 399, [1972] 2
    WLR 401, [1972] RTR 190, 116 Sol Jo 158, CA.. 187
Holwell Securities Ltd v Hughes [1974] 1 All ER 161, [1974] 1 WLR 155, 26 P & CR
    544, 117 Sol Jo 912, CA 152, 158
Hong Kong Fir Shipping Co Ltd v Kawasaki Kisen Kaisha Ltd [1962] 2 QB 26,
    [1962] 1 All ER 474, [1962] 2 WLR 474, [1961] 2 Lloyd's Rep 478, 106 Sol Jo 35,
    CA... 332
Horcal Ltd v Gatland [1984] IRLR 288, [1984] BCLC 549, CA 314
Horwood v Millar's Timber and Trading Co Ltd [1917] 1 KB 305, 86 LJKB 190,
    [1916-17] All ER Rep 847, 61 Sol Jo 114, 115 LT 805, 33 TLR 86, CA 52
Household Fire and Carriage Accident Insurance Co v Grant (1879) 4 Ex D 216, 44
    JP 152, 48 LJQB 577, 27 WR 858, 41 LT 298, CA 158
Howard Marine and Dredging Co Ltd v A Ogden & Sons (Excavations) Ltd [1978]
    QB 574, [1978] 2 All ER 1134, [1978] 2 WLR 515, [1978] 1 Lloyd's Rep 334, 122
    Sol Jo 48, 9 BLR 34, CA 178
Howe v Smith (1884) 27 Ch D 89, 48 JP 773, 53 LJ Ch 1055, 32 WR 802, [1881-5]
    All ER Rep 201, 50 LT 573, CA 354
Hughes v Metropolitan Rly Co (1877) 2 App Cas 439, 42 JP 421, 46 LJQB 583, 25
    WR 680, [1874-80] All ER Rep 187, 36 LT 932, HL 322
Hughes v Southwark London Borough Council [1988] IRLR 55 398
Hugin Kassaregister AB v EC Commission: 22/78 [1979] ECR 1869, [1979] 3 CMLR
    345, ECJ 146
Hurley v Dyke [1979] RTR 265, HL 192
Hyde v Wrench (1840) 3 Beav 334, 4 Jur 1106, 49 ER 132 151
Hyman v Hyman [1929] AC 601, 27 LGR 379, 93 JP 209, 98 LJP 81, [1929] All ER
    Rep 245, 73 Sol Jo 317, 141 LT 329, 45 TLR 444, HL 99
Hyundai Heavy Industries Co Ltd v Papadopoulos [1980] 2 All ER 29, [1980] 1 WLR
    1129, [1980] 2 Lloyd's Rep 1, 124 Sol Jo 592, HL.. 354

I

Igbo v Johnson Matthey Chemicals Ltd [1986] ICR 505, [1986] IRLR 215, 130 Sol Jo
    524, [1986] LS Gaz R 2089, CA.. 234
Initial Services Ltd v Putterill [1968] 1 QB 396, [1967] 3 All ER 145, [1967] 3 WLR
    1032, 2 KIR 863, 111 Sol Jo 541, CA 52
Interfoto Picture Library Ltd v Stiletto Visual Programmes Ltd [1989] QB 433,
    [1988] 1 All ER 348, [1988] 2 WLR 615, [1988] BTLC 39, 132 Sol Jo 460, [1988]
    9 LS Gaz R 45, [1987] NLJ Rep 1159, CA 169, 188, 202, 216, 255, 347
Istituto Chemioterapico Italiano SpA and Commercial Solvents Corpn v EC
    Commission: 6, 7/73 [1974] ECR 223, [1974] 1 CMLR 309, ECJ 146

J

Jackson v Chrysler Acceptances Ltd [1978] RTR 474, CA 383
Jackson v Horizon Holidays Ltd [1975] 3 All ER 92, [1975] 1 WLR 1468, 119 Sol Jo
    759, CA.. 285, 293, 379
Jacob and Youngs v Kent 230 NY 239, 129 NE 889 (1921) 388
Jaggard v Sawyer [1995] 2 All ER 189, [1995] 1 WLR 269, [1995] 1 EGLR 146,
    [1995] 13 EG 132, [1994] EGCS 139, CA 393
Jarvis v Swans Tours Ltd [1973] QB 233, [1973] 1 All ER 71, [1972] 3 WLR 954, 116
    Sol Jo 822, CA 389, 392
Jobson v Johnson [1989] 1 All ER 621, [1989] 1 WLR 1026, 4 BCC 488, CA 347, 349,
    350, 362
Johnson v Agnew [1980] AC 367, [1979] 1 All ER 883, [1979] 2 WLR 487, 39 P & CR
    424, 123 Sol Jo 217, 251 Estates Gazette 1167, HL... 385
Johnstone v Bloomsbury Health Authority [1992] QB 333, [1991] 2 All ER 293, [1991]
    2 WLR 1362, [1991] ICR 269, [1991] IRLR 118, [1991] 2 Med LR 38, CA 221, 227,
    235, 259

PAGE
Jones v Lee and Guilding (1980) 78 LGR 213, [1980] ICR 310, [1980] IRLR 67, 123
    Sol Jo 785, CA 401
Jones v Padavatton [1969] 2 All ER 616, [1969] 1 WLR 328, 112 Sol Jo 965, CA 65
Junior Books Ltd v Veitchi Co Ltd [1983] 1 AC 520, [1982] 3 All ER 201, [1982] 3
    WLR 477, [1982] Com LR 221, 126 Sol Jo 538, [1982] LS Gaz R 1413, 21 BLR
    66, 1982 SLT 492, HL 301

K

KH Enterprise v Pioneer Container, The Pioneer Container. See Pioneer Container,
    The, KH Enterprise v Pioneer Container
Kendall (Henry) & Sons (a firm) v William Lillico & Sons Ltd [1969] 2 AC 31, [1968]
    2 All ER 444, [1968] 3 WLR 110, [1968] 1 Lloyd's Rep 547, 112 Sol Jo 562, HL 208
Ketley (A) Ltd v Scott [1981] ICR 241 269
Kilmer v British Columbia Orchard Lands Ltd [1913] AC 319, 82 LJPC 77, 57 Sol
    Jo 338, 108 LT 306, 29 TLR 319, PC 359
Kleinwort Benson Ltd v Birmingham City Council [1997] QB 380, [1996] 4 All ER
    733, [1996] 3 WLR 1139, CA 378
Kleinwort Benson Ltd v Malaysia Mining Corpn Bhd [1989] 1 All ER 785, [1989] 1
    WLR 379, [1989] 1 Lloyd's Rep 556, 5 BCC 337, 133 Sol Jo 262, [1989] 16 LS
    Gaz R 35, [1989] NLJR 221, CA 99
Kleinwort Benson Ltd v Sandwell Borough Council [1994] 4 All ER 890, 91 LGR 323 ... 378
Koufos v C Czarnikow Ltd, The Heron II [1969] 1 AC 350, [1967] 3 All ER 686,
    [1967] 3 WLR 1491, [1967] 2 Lloyd's Rep 457, 111 Sol Jo 848, HL 382, 383
Kpohraror v Woolwich Building Society [1996] 4 All ER 119, [1996] 01 LS Gaz R 22,
    140 Sol Jo LB 28, CA 390
Krell v Henry [1903] 2 KB 740, 72 LJKB 794, 52 WR 246, [1900-3] All ER Rep 20,
    89 LT 328, 19 TLR 711, CA 276, 279

L

LAC Minerals Ltd v International Corona Resources Ltd [1990] FSR 441, 44 BLR 1,
    [1989] 2 SCR 574, 101 NR 239, 69 OR (2d) 287, 35 ETR 1, 61 DLR (4th) 14, 26
    CPR (3d) 97, 36 OAC 57, 6 RPR (2d) 1, Can SC 197, 198, 393
Lambert v Co-operative Insurance Society [1975] 2 Lloyd's Rep 485, CA 195
Lancashire County Council v Municipal Mutual Insurance Ltd [1996] 3 All ER 545,
    [1996] 3 WLR 493, [1996] 21 LS Gaz R 27, 140 Sol Jo LB 108, CA 213
Lasky v Economy Grocery Stores 319 Mass 224, 65 NE 2d 305 (1946) 160
Lauritzen (J) AS v Wijsmuller BV, The Super Servant Two [1990] 1 Lloyd's Rep 1,
    CA 280
Lazenby Garages Ltd v Wright [1976] 2 All ER 770, [1976] 1 WLR 459, 120 Sol Jo
    146, CA 85, 382
Leaf v International Galleries [1950] 2 KB 86, [1950] 1 All ER 693, 66 (pt 1) TLR
    1031, CA 180
Lee v Jones (1864) 17 CBNS 482, 34 LJCP 131, 11 Jur NS 81, 13 WR 318, 12 LT
    122, 144 ER 194 191
Lemenda Trading Co Ltd v African Middle East Petroleum Co Ltd [1988] QB 448,
    [1988] 1 All ER 513, [1988] 2 WLR 735, [1988] 1 Lloyd's Rep 361, 132 Sol Jo
    538 52
Leonidas D, The. See Allied Marine Transport Ltd v Vale do Rio Doce Navegacao
    SA, The Leonidas D
L'Estrange v F Graucob Ltd [1934] 2 KB 394, 103 LJKB 730, [1934] All ER Rep 16,
    152 LT 164, DC 111, 217
Levett v Barclays Bank plc [1995] 2 All ER 615, [1995] 1 WLR 1260 197
Lewis v Averay [1972] 1 QB 198, [1971] 3 All ER 907, [1971] 3 WLR 603, 115 Sol Jo
    755, CA 195
Lewis v Motorworld Garages Ltd [1986] ICR 157, [1985] IRLR 465, CA 225
Lexmead (Basingstoke) Ltd v Lewis [1982] AC 225, 268, [1981] 2 WLR 713, [1981]
    RTR 346, [1981] 2 Lloyd's Rep 17, 125 Sol Jo 310, sub nom Lambert v Lewis
    [1981] 1 All ER 1185, HL 386

PAGE

Linden Gardens Trust Ltd v Lenesta Sludge Disposals Ltd [1994] 1 AC 85, [1993] 3
   All ER 417, [1993] 3 WLR 408, 36 Con LR 1, [1993] 45 LS Gaz R 39, [1993]
   NLJR 1152, 137 Sol Jo LB 183, HL 286, 379
Lipkin Gorman (a firm) v Karpnale Ltd [1991] 2 AC 548, [1992] 4 All ER 512, [1991]
   3 WLR 10, [1991] NLJR 815, 135 Sol Jo LB 36, HL 378
Lister v Romford Ice and Cold Storage Co Ltd [1957] AC 555, [1957] 1 All ER 125,
   [1957] 2 WLR 158, [1956] 2 Lloyd's Rep 505, 121 JP 98, 101 Sol Jo 106, HL 225
Litsion Pride, The. See Black King Shipping Corpn and Wayang (Panama) SA v
   Massie, The Litsion Pride
Liverpool City Council v Irwin [1977] AC 239, [1976] 2 All ER 39, [1976] 2 WLR
   562, 74 LGR 392, 32 P & CR 43, 13 HLR 38, 120 Sol Jo 267, 238 Estates
   Gazette 879, 963, HL 226, 228, 258, 310
Lloyds Bank Ltd v Bundy [1975] QB 326, [1974] 3 All ER 757, [1974] 3 WLR 501,
   [1974] 2 Lloyd's Rep 366, 118 Sol Jo 714, CA 137, 138, 197
Lobb (Alec) (Garages) Ltd v Total Oil GB Ltd [1985] 1 All ER 303, [1985] 1 WLR
   173, 129 Sol Jo 83, [1985] 1 EGLR 33, [1985] LS Gaz R 45, 273 Estates Gazette
   659, CA 141
Lombard North Central plc v Butterworth [1987] QB 527, [1987] 1 All ER 267,
   [1987] 2 WLR 7, [1986] BTLC 382, 130 Sol Jo 681, [1986] LS Gaz R 2750, CA 362,
                                                                                          363
Lusk-Harbison-Jones Inc v Universal Credit Co 164 Miss 693, 145 So 623 (1933) 78
Lutetian, The. See Tradax Export SA v Dorada Compania Naviera SA, The Lutetian
Luxor (Eastbourne) Ltd v Cooper [1941] AC 108, [1941] 1 All ER 33, 110 LJKB 131,
   46 Com Cas 120, 85 Sol Jo 105, 164 LT 313, 57 TLR 213, HL 311, 313

M

McClaren v Home Office [1990] ICR 824, [1990] IRLR 338, CA 401
McDonald v Dennys Lascelles Ltd (1933) 48 CLR 457, 39 ALR 381, 7 ALJ 95,
   HC of A 364
McEntire v Crossley Bros Ltd [1895] AC 457, 64 LJPC 129, 2 Mans 334, 11 R 207,
   [1895-9] All ER Rep 829, 72 LT 731, [1895] 1 IR 308, HL 356
McMaster University v Wilchar Construction Ltd (1971) 22 DLR (3d) 9; affd (1973)
   69 DLR (3d) 400 214
McRae v Commonwealth Disposals Commission (1950) 84 CLR 377, [1951] ALR
   771, 25 ALJ 425, HC of A 119, 377, 381
Mahkutai, The [1996] AC 650, [1996] 3 All ER 502, [1996] 3 WLR 1, [1996] 2 Lloyd's
   Rep 1, [1996] NLJR 677, 140 Sol Jo LB 107, PC 291
Malik v BCCI SA (in liquidation) [1995] 3 All ER 545, [1995] IRLR 375, [1995]
   NLJR 593, CA; revsd [1997] 3 All ER 1, [1997] NLJR 917, HL 390
Manchester Diocesan Council for Education v Commercial and General Investments
   Ltd [1969] 3 All ER 1593, [1970] 1 WLR 241, 21 P & CR 38, 114 Sol Jo 70 152
Maria D, The. See Elpis Maritime Co Ltd v Marti Chartering Co Inc, The Maria D
Martinez v Socoma Companies Inc 11 Cal 3d 394, 521 P 2d 841 (1974) 294
Mechanical and General Inventions Co Ltd and Lehwess v Austin and Austin Motor
   Co Ltd [1935] AC 346, 104 LJKB 403, [1935] All ER Rep 22, 153 LT 153, HL 197
Melody Home Manufacturing Co v Barnes 741 SW 2d 349 (Tex 1987) 235
Mendelssohn v Normand Ltd [1970] 1 QB 177, [1969] 2 All ER 1215, [1969] 3 WLR
   139, 113 Sol Jo 263, CA 122
Midland Electric Manufacturing Co Ltd v Kanji [1980] IRLR 185, EAT 234
Mikhail Lermontov, The. See Dillon v Baltic Shipping Co, The Mikhail Lermontov
Mitchell (George) (Chesterhall) Ltd v Finney Lock Seeds Ltd [1983] 2 AC 803,
   [1983] 2 All ER 737, [1983] 3 WLR 163, [1983] 2 Lloyd's Rep 272, [1983] Com
   LR 209, HL 241, 242, 346
Mona Oil Equipment and Supply Co Ltd v Rhodesia Railways Ltd [1949] 2 All ER
   1014, 83 Ll L Rep 178 313
Moorcock, The (1889) 14 PD 64, 58 LJP 73, 6 Asp MLC 373, 37 WR 439, [1886-90]
   All ER Rep 530, 60 LT 654, 5 TLR 316, CA 223

PAGE

Morgan Crucible Co plc v Hill Samuel & Co Ltd [1991] Ch 295, [1991] 2 WLR 655,
    [1991] BCC 82, [1990] NLJR 1605, sub nom Morgan Crucible Co plc v Hill
    Samuel Bank Ltd [1991] 1 All ER 148, [1991] BCLC 178, CA 300
Morris v Baron & Co [1918] AC 1, 87 LJKB 145, 118 LT 34, HL 319
Morris v C W Martin & Sons Ltd [1966] 1 QB 716, [1965] 2 All ER 725, [1965] 3
    WLR 276, [1965] 2 Lloyd's Rep 63, 109 Sol Jo 451, CA 122, 284
Moschi v Lep Air Services Ltd [1973] AC 331, [1972] 2 All ER 393, [1972] 2 WLR
    1175, 116 Sol Jo 372, HL 364

N

Nanfri, The. See Federal Commerce and Navigation Co Ltd v Molena Alpha Inc,
    The Nanfri
National Westminster Bank plc v Morgan [1985] AC 686, [1985] 1 All ER 821,
    [1985] 2 WLR 588, [1985] FLR 266, 17 HLR 360, 129 Sol Jo 205, [1985] LS Gaz
    R 1485, [1985] NLJ Rep 254, HL 32, 138, 256, 257
New York Star, The. See Port Jackson Stevedoring Pty Ltd v Salmond & Spraggon
    (Australia) Pty Ltd, The New York Star
New Zealand Shipping Co Ltd v AM Satterthwaite & Co Ltd [1975] AC 154, [1974] 1
    All ER 1015, [1974] 2 WLR 865, 118 Sol Jo 387, sub nom The Eurymedon
    [1974] 1 Lloyd's Rep 534, PC 38, 59, 121, 159, 290, 298
North Ocean Shipping Co Ltd v Hyundai Construction Co Ltd, The Atlantic Baron
    [1979] QB 705, [1978] 3 All ER 1170, [1979] 3 WLR 419, [1979] 1 Lloyd's Rep
    89, 123 Sol Jo 352 .... 143, 327, 329
Norwich City Council v Harvey [1989] 1 All ER 1180, [1989] 1 WLR 828, 133 Sol Jo
    694, [1989] 25 LS Gaz R 45, [1989] NLJR 40, 45 BLR 14, CA 288, 301
Nottingham Patent Brick and Tile Co v Butler (1886) 16 QBD 778, 55 LJQB 280, 34
    WR 405, [1886-90] All ER Rep 1075, 54 LT 444, 2 TLR 391, CA 191

O

Odenfeld, The. See Gator Shipping Corpn v Trans-Asiatic Oil Ltd SA and Occidental
    Shipping Establishment, The Odenfeld
Olley v Marlborough Court Ltd [1949] 1 KB 532, [1949] 1 All ER 127, [1949] LJR
    360, 93 Sol Jo 40, 65 TLR 95, CA 187
O'Sullivan v Management Agency and Music Ltd [1985] QB 428, [1985] 3 All ER
    351, [1984] 3 WLR 448, 128 Sol Jo 548, CA 143
Overbrooke Estates Ltd v Glencombe Properties Ltd [1974] 3 All ER 511, [1974] 1
    WLR 1335, 118 Sol Jo 775 121

P

Pacol Ltd v Trade Lines Ltd and R/I Sif IV, The Henrik Sif [1982] 1 Lloyd's Rep 456,
    [1982] Com LR 92, 126 Sol Jo 312 83
Palmateer v International Harvester Co 421 NE 2d 876 (Ill 1981) 235
Pan Atlantic Insurance Co Ltd v Pine Top Insurance Co Ltd [1995] 1 AC 501, [1994]
    3 All ER 581, [1994] 3 WLR 677, [1994] 2 Lloyd's Rep 427, [1994] 36 LS Gaz R
    36, [1994] NLJR 1203, 138 Sol Jo LB 182, HL 195
Panoutsos v Raymond Hadley Corpn of New York [1917] 2 KB 473, 86 LJKB 1325,
    22 Com Cas 308, [1916-17] All ER Rep 448, 61 Sol Jo 590, 117 LT 330, 33 TLR
    436, CA 211, 317
Pao On v Lau Yiu Long [1980] AC 614, [1979] 3 All ER 65, [1979] 3 WLR 435, 123
    Sol Jo 319, PC 59, 327
Parker v Camden London Borough Council [1986] Ch 162, [1985] 2 All ER 141,
    [1985] 3 WLR 47, 84 LGR 16, 17 HLR 380, 129 Sol Jo 417, [1985] LS Gaz R
    2334, CA 368
Parker v Great Western Rly Co (1844) 3 Ry & Can Cas 563, 13 LJCP 105, 8 Jur 194,
    7 Man & G 253, 7 Scott NR 835, 2 LTOS 420 135
Parsons (H) (Livestock) Ltd v Uttley Ingham & Co Ltd [1978] QB 791, [1978] 1 All
    ER 525, [1977] 3 WLR 990, [1977] 2 Lloyd's Rep 522, 121 Sol Jo 811, CA 384

PAGE

Pascoe v Turner [1979] 2 All ER 945, [1979] 1 WLR 431, 123 Sol Jo 164, CA 79, 82
Patel v Ali [1984] Ch 283, [1984] 1 All ER 978, [1984] 2 WLR 960, 48 P & CR 118,
    128 Sol Jo 204, [1984] LS Gaz R 1285 401
Payzu Ltd v Saunders [1919] 2 KB 581, 89 LJKB 17, [1918-19] All ER Rep 219, 121
    LT 563, 35 TLR 657, CA 385
Pearce v Brooks (1866) LR 1 Exch 213, 30 JP 295, 4 H & C 358, 35 LJ Ex 134, 12
    Jur NS 342, 14 WR 614, [1861-73] All ER Rep 102, 14 LT 288 52
    Penarth Dock Engineering Co Ltd v Pounds [1963] 1 Lloyd's Rep 359 393
Pharmaceutical Society of Great Britain v Boots Cash Chemists (Southern) Ltd
    [1953] 1 QB 401, [1953] 1 All ER 482, [1953] 2 WLR 427, 117 JP 132, 97 Sol Jo
    149, CA.. 161
Photo Production Ltd v Securicor Transport Ltd [1980] AC 827, [1980] 1 All ER 556,
    [1980] 2 WLR 283, [1980] 1 Lloyd's Rep 545, 124 Sol Jo 147, 130 NLJ 188, HL 244,
    331
Pioneer Container, The, KH Enterprise v Pioneer Container [1994] 2 AC 324, [1994]
    2 All ER 250, [1994] 3 WLR 1, [1994] 1 Lloyd's Rep 593, [1994] 18 LS Gaz R 37,
    PC 123
Port Caledonia, The and The Anna [1903] P 184, 72 LJP 60, 9 Asp MLC 479, 52 WR
    223, 89 LT 216 .... 134, 256
Port Jackson Stevedoring Pty Ltd v Salmond & Spraggon (Australia) Pty Ltd, The
    New York Star [1980] 3 All ER 257, [1981] 1 WLR 138, [1980] 2 Lloyd's Rep
    317, 124 Sol Jo 756, PC 291
Posner v Scott-Lewis [1987] Ch 25, [1986] 3 All ER 513, [1986] 3 WLR 531, 130 Sol
    Jo 14, [1986] 1 EGLR 56, 277 Estates Gazette 859 400
Post Chaser, The. See Société Italo-Belge pour le Commerce et l'Industrie SA v
    Palm and Vegetable Oils (Malaysia) Sdn Bhd, The Post Chaser
Pound (A V) & Co Ltd v M W Hardy & Co Inc [1956] AC 588, [1956] 1 All ER 639,
    [1956] 2 WLR 683, [1956] 1 Lloyd's Rep 255, 100 Sol Jo 208, HL 313
Powell v Brent London Borough Council [1988] ICR 176, [1987] IRLR 466, CA ... 398, 401
Price v Strange [1978] Ch 337, [1977] 3 All ER 371, [1977] 3 WLR 943, 36 P & CR
    59, 121 Sol Jo 816, 243 Estates Gazette 295, CA... 401
Public Works Comr v Hills [1906] AC 368, 75 LJPC 69, 94 LT 833, PC 363
Puerto Buitrago, The. See Attica Sea Carriers Corpn v Ferrostaal Poseidon Bulk
    Reederei GmbH, The Puerto Buitrago

Q

Queensland Electricity Generating Board v New Hope Collieries Pty Ltd [1989] 1
    Lloyd's Rep 205, PC 199
Quinn (or Quin) v Burch Bros (Builders) Ltd [1966] 2 QB 370, [1966] 2 All ER 283,
    [1966] 2 WLR 1017, 110 Sol Jo 214, CA.. 386
Quinn v Williams Furniture Ltd [1981] ICR 328, CA 34

R

R v Lord Chancellor's Department, ex p Nangle [1992] 1 All ER 897, [1991] ICR
    743, [1991] IRLR 343 95
R v Warwickshire County Council, ex p Johnson [1993] AC 583, [1993] 2 WLR 1, 91
    LGR 130, 157 JP 249, [1993] Crim LR 940, [1993] 6 LS Gaz R 41, [1993] NLJR
    127, 137 Sol Jo LB 37, sub nom Warwickshire County Council v Johnson [1993]
    1 All ER 299, HL 173, 179
R & B Customs Brokers Co Ltd v United Dominions Trust Ltd (Saunders Abbott
    (1980) Ltd, third party) [1988] 1 All ER 847, [1988] 1 WLR 321, [1988] RTR
    134, [1988] BTLC 52, 132 Sol Jo 300, [1988] 11 LS Gaz R 42, CA 237
Radford v De Froberville [1978] 1 All ER 33, [1977] 1 WLR 1262, 35 P & CR 316,
    121 Sol Jo 319, 7 BLR 35... 385, 388
Raffles v Wichelhaus (1864) 2 H & C 906, 33 LJ Ex 160, 159 ER 375 216
Ramsden v Dyson and Thornton (1866) LR 1 HL 129, 12 Jur NS 506, 14 WR 926,
    HL.. 126
Ratzlaff v Franz Foods 250 Ark 1003, 468 SW 2d 239 (1971) 296

PAGE

Record v Bell [1991] 4 All ER 471, [1991] 1 WLR 853, 62 P & CR 192 210

Reid v Rush & Tompkins Group plc [1989] 3 All ER 228, [1990] 1 WLR 212, [1990]
RTR 144, [1989] 2 Lloyd's Rep 167, [1990] ICR 61, [1989] IRLR 265, CA 226, 313

Rewe-Zentral AG v Bundesmonopolverwaltung für Branntwein: 120/78 [1979] ECR
649, [1979] 3 CMLR 494, CMR 8543, ECJ 14

Rich (Marc) & Co AG v Bishop Rock Marine Co Ltd, The Nicholas H [1996] AC 211,
[1995] 3 All ER 307, [1995] 3 WLR 227, [1995] 2 Lloyd's Rep 299, [1995] 31 LS
Gaz R 34, [1995] NLJR 1033, 139 Sol Jo LB 165, HL 288

Rigby v Ferodo Ltd [1988] ICR 29, [1987] IRLR 516, HL 315, 336

Riverlate Properties Ltd v Paul [1975] Ch 133, [1974] 2 All ER 656, [1974] 3 WLR
564, 28 P & CR 220, 118 Sol Jo 644, 231 Estates Gazette 1287, CA 212

Robb v Hammersmith and Fulham London Borough Council [1991] ICR 514, [1991]
IRLR 72 401

Robertson v Dicicco (1972) 70 LGR 589, [1972] RTR 431, [1972] Crim LR 592, 116
Sol Jo 744, 122 NLJ 680 .... 176, 194

Robinson v Harman (1848) 18 LJ Ex 202, 1 Exch 850, [1843-60] All ER Rep 383, 13
LTOS 141 381

Robophone Facilities Ltd v Blank [1966] 3 All ER 128, [1966] 1 WLR 1428, 110 Sol
Jo 544, CA 152

Rogers v Parish (Scarborough) Ltd [1987] QB 933, [1987] 2 All ER 232, [1987] 2
WLR 353, [1987] RTR 312, [1987] BTLC 51, 131 Sol Jo 223, [1987] LS Gaz R
905, CA 259

Rolled Steel Products (Holdings) Ltd v British Steel Corpn [1986] Ch 246, [1985] 3
All ER 52, [1985] 2 WLR 908, [1984] BCLC 466, [1984] BCLC 466, 128 Sol Jo
629, [1984] LS Gaz R 2357, CA 110

Rose and Frank Co v JR Crompton & Bros Ltd [1925] AC 445, 94 LJKB 120, 30 Com
Cas 163, [1924] All ER Rep 245, 132 LT 641, HL 99

Rose (Frederick E) (London) Ltd v William H Pim Jnr & Co Ltd [1953] 2 QB 450,
[1953] 2 All ER 739, [1953] 3 WLR 497, [1953] 2 Lloyd's Rep 238, 97 Sol Jo 556,
CA 211

Royscott Trust Ltd v Rogerson [1991] 2 QB 297, [1991] 3 All ER 294, [1991] 3 WLR
57, 135 Sol Jo 444, [1991] NLJR 493, CA 182, 183

Ruxley Electronics and Construction Ltd v Forsyth [1996] AC 344, [1995] 3 All ER
268, [1995] 3 WLR 118, [1995] 31 LS Gaz R 33, [1995] NLJR 996, 73 BLR 5,
139 Sol Jo LB 163, HL 388, 389

S

SS & O Corpn v Township of Bernards Sewerage Authority 62 NJ 369, 301 A 2d 738
(1973) 134

St John Shipping Corpn v Joseph Rank Ltd [1957] 1 QB 267, [1956] 3 All ER 683,
[1956] 3 WLR 870, [1956] 2 Lloyd's Rep 413, 100 Sol Jo 841 51

Sancho-Lopez v Fedor Food Corpn 211 NYS 2d 953 (City Court, New York, 1961) 160

Satanita, The. See Clarke v Earl of Dunraven and Mount-Earl, The Satanita

Saunders v Edwards [1987] 2 All ER 651, [1987] 1 WLR 1116, 131 Sol Jo 1039,
[1987] LS Gaz R 2193, 2535, [1987] NLJ Rep 389, CA 51

Scally v Southern Health and Social Services Board [1992] 1 AC 294, [1991] 4 All
ER 563, [1991] 3 WLR 778, [1991] ICR 771, [1991] IRLR 522, 135 Sol Jo LB
172, HL 314

Scandinavian Trading Tanker Co AB v Flota Petrolera Ecuatoriana, The Scaptrade
[1983] 2 AC 694, [1983] 2 All ER 763, [1983] 3 WLR 203, [1983] 2 Lloyd's Rep
253, 127 Sol Jo 476, HL 359

Scaptrade, The. See Scandinavian Trading Tanker Co AB v Flota Petrolera
Ecuatoriana, The Scaptrade

Schroeder (A) Music Publishing Co Ltd v Macaulay [1974] 3 All ER 616, [1974] 1
WLR 1308, 118 Sol Jo 734, HL 28, 260

Schuler (L) AG v Wickman Machine Tool Sales Ltd [1974] AC 235, [1973] 2 All ER
39, [1973] 2 WLR 683, [1973] 2 Lloyd's Rep 53, 117 Sol Jo 340, HL 210, 334

Scriven Bros & Co v Hindley & Co [1913] 3 KB 564, 83 LJKB 40, 109 LT 526 ..... 187, 215

PAGE

Scruttons Ltd v Midland Silicones Ltd [1962] AC 446, [1962] 1 All ER 1, [1962] 2
WLR 186, 106 Sol Jo 34, sub nom Midland Silicones Ltd v Scruttons Ltd [1961]
2 Lloyd's Rep 365, HL 287
Sears Roebuck & Co v Jardel 421 F 2d 1048 (3d Cir 1970) 301
Secretary of State for Employment v Associated Society of Locomotive Engineers
and Firemen (No 2) [1972] 2 QB 455, [1972] 2 All ER 949, [1972] 2 WLR 1370,
[1972] ICR 19, 13 KIR 1, 116 Sol Jo 467, CA 310
Shadwell v Shadwell (1860) 9 CBNS 159, 30 LJCP 145, 7 Jur NS 311, 9 WR 163,
142 ER 62, 3 LT 628 .... 60, 76
Shanklin Pier Ltd v Detel Products Ltd [1951] 2 KB 854, [1951] 2 All ER 471, [1951]
2 Lloyd's Rep 187, 95 Sol Jo 563 59
Shell UK Ltd v Lostock Garage Ltd [1977] 1 All ER 481, [1976] 1 WLR 1187, 120 Sol
Jo 523, CA 226
Sherwood v Walker 33 NW 919, 66 Mich 568 (1887) 260, 277
Shiloh Spinners Ltd v Harding [1973] AC 691, [1973] 1 All ER 90, [1973] 2 WLR 28,
25 P & CR 48, 117 Sol Jo 34, HL 359, 400
Shirlaw v Southern Foundries (1926) Ltd [1939] 2 KB 206, [1939] 2 All ER 113, CA;
affd sub nom Southern Foundries (1926) Ltd v Shirlaw [1940] AC 701, [1940] 2
All ER 445, 109 LJKB 461, 84 Sol Jo 464, 164 LT 251, 56 TLR 637, HL 222
Sidaway v Board of Governors of the Bethlem Royal Hospital and the Maudsley
Hospital [1985] AC 871, [1985] 1 All ER 643, [1985] 2 WLR 480, 129 Sol Jo 154,
1 BMLR 132, [1985] LS Gaz R 1256, HL 314
Sindall (William) plc v Cambridgeshire County Council [1994] 3 All ER 932, [1994]
1 WLR 1016, 92 LGR 121, [1993] NPC 82, CA 181
Sky Petroleum Ltd v VIP Petroleum Ltd [1974] 1 All ER 954, [1974] 1 WLR 576, 118
Sol Jo 311 397
Smith v Eric S Bush [1990] 1 AC 831, [1989] 2 All ER 514, [1989] 2 WLR 790, 87
LGR 685, 21 HLR 424, 17 Con LR 1, 133 Sol Jo 597, [1989] 1 EGLR 169, [1989]
NLJR 576, [1989] 17 EG 68, 18 EG 99, HL 238, 241,
300
Smith v Hughes (1871) LR 6 QB 597, 40 LJQB 221, 19 WR 1059, [1861-73] All ER
Rep 632, 25 LT 329 .... 111, 207
Smith v Kay (1859) 7 HL Cas 750, 30 LJ Ch 45 138
Smith v Land and House Property Corpn (1884) 28 Ch D 7, 49 JP 182, 51 LT 718,
CA 175
Smith v William Charlick Ltd (1924) 34 CLR 38 135
Société des Industries Métallurgiques SA v Bronx Engineering Co Ltd [1975] 1
Lloyd's Rep 465, CA 396
Société Italo-Belge pour le Commerce et l'Industrie SA v Palm and Vegetable Oils
(Malaysia) Sdn Bhd, The Post Chaser [1982] 1 All ER 19, [1981] 2 Lloyd's Rep
695, [1981] Com LR 249 .... 322, 336
Solholt, The. See Sotiros Shipping Inc and Aeco Maritime SA v Sameiet Solholt, The
Solholt
Sotiros Shipping Inc and Aeco Maritime SA v Sameiet Solholt, The Solholt [1983] 1
Lloyd's Rep 605, 127 Sol Jo 305, CA 331
Spencer v Harding (1870) LR 5 CP 561, 39 LJCP 332, 19 WR 48, 23 LT 237 114
Sport International Bussum BV v Inter-Footwear Ltd [1984] 2 All ER 321, [1984] 1
WLR 776, 128 Sol Jo 383, [1984] LS Gaz R 1992, 134 NLJ 568, HL 360
Staffordshire Area Health Authority v South Staffordshire Waterworks Co [1978] 3
All ER 769, [1978] 1 WLR 1387, 77 LGR 17, 122 Sol Jo 331, CA 330, 336
Starside Properties Ltd v Mustapha [1974] 2 All ER 567, [1974] 1 WLR 816, 28 P &
CR 95, 118 Sol Jo 388, CA 359
Steele v Williams (1853) 17 JP 378, 22 LJ Ex 225, 8 Exch 625, 17 Jur 464, 1 CLR
258, 21 LTOS 106 135
Stilk v Myrick (1809) 2 Camp 317, 6 Esp 129, 170 ER 851 .... 318, 320,
324
Stockloser v Johnson [1954] 1 QB 476, [1954] 1 All ER 630, [1954] 2 WLR 439, 98
Sol Jo 178, CA 364

PAGE

Stoke-on-Trent City Council v B & Q plc: C-169/91 [1993] AC 900, [1993] 1 All ER
    481, [1993] 2 WLR 730, [1992] ECR I-6635, [1993] 1 CMLR 426, 91 LGR 237,
    ECJ; affd sub nom Stoke-on-Trent City Council v B & Q plc [1993] AC 900,
    [1993] 2 All ER 297n, [1993] 2 WLR 730, [1993] 2 CMLR 509, 91 LGR 237, 137
    Sol Jo LB 120, HL 14
Strand Electric and Engineering Co Ltd v Brisford Entertainments Ltd [1952] 2 QB
    246, [1952] 1 All ER 796, 96 Sol Jo 260, [1952] 1 TLR 939, CA 393
Strathcona (Lord) SS Co v Dominion Coal Co [1926] AC 108, 95 LJPC 71, 16 Asp
    MLC 585, 31 Com Cas 80, [1925] All ER Rep 87, 134 LT 227, 42 TLR 86, PC 124
Super Servant Two, The. See Lauritzen (J) AS v Wijsmuller BV, The Super Servant
    Two
Surrey County Council v Bredero Homes Ltd [1993] 3 All ER 705, [1993] 1 WLR
    1361, [1993] 1 EGLR 37, [1993] 25 EG 141, 137 Sol Jo LB 135, CA 393
Swiss Bank Corpn v Lloyds Bank Ltd [1979] Ch 548, [1979] 2 All ER 853, [1979] 3
    WLR 201, 123 Sol Jo 536; revsd [1982] AC 584, [1980] 2 All ER 419, [1980] 3
    WLR 457, 124 Sol Jo 741, CA; affd [1982] AC 584, [1981] 2 All ER 449, [1981] 2
    WLR 893, 125 Sol Jo 495, HL 124
Sybron Corpn v Rochem Ltd [1984] Ch 112, [1983] 2 All ER 707, [1983] 3 WLR 713,
    [1983] ICR 801, [1983] IRLR 253, [1983] BCLC 43, 127 Sol Jo 391, CA 314

T

Tamplin (F A) SS Co v Anglo-Mexican Petroleum Products Co [1916] 2 AC 397, 85
    LJKB 1389, 21 Com Cas 299, [1916-17] All ER Rep 104, 32 TLR 677, sub nom
    Re F A Tamplin SS Co Ltd and Anglo-Mexican Petroleum Products Co Ltd 13
    Asp MLC 467, 115 LT 315, HL 280
Tamplin v James (1880) 15 Ch D 215, 20 WR 311, [1874-80] All ER Rep 560, 43 LT
    520, CA 213
Tanner v Tanner [1975] 3 All ER 776, [1975] 1 WLR 1346, 119 Sol Jo 391, CA 92, 102
Taylor v Caldwell (1863) 27 JP 710, 3 B & S 826, 32 LJQB 164, 2 New Rep 198, 11
    WR 726, 122 ER 826, [1861-73] All ER Rep 24, 8 LT 356 276
Tesco Supermarkets Ltd v Nattrass [1972] AC 153, [1971] 2 All ER 127, [1971] 2
    WLR 1166, 69 LGR 403, 135 JP 289, 115 Sol Jo 285, HL 179
Thake v Maurice [1986] QB 644, [1986] 1 All ER 497, [1986] 2 WLR 337, 129 Sol Jo
    894, [1986] LS Gaz R 123, [1986] NLJ Rep 92, CA 314
Thompson v T Lohan (Plant Hire) Ltd (JW Hurdiss Ltd, third party) [1987] 2 All ER
    631, [1987] 1 WLR 649, [1987] IRLR 148, [1987] BTLC 221, 131 Sol Jo 358,
    [1987] LS Gaz R 979, CA 236, 365
Thornton v Shoe Lane Parking Ltd [1971] 2 QB 163, [1971] 1 All ER 686, [1971] 2
    WLR 585, [1971] RTR 79, [1971] 1 Lloyd's Rep 289, 115 Sol Jo 75, CA 187
Tinn v Hoffman & Co (1873) 29 LT 271 152
Tinsley v Milligan [1994] 1 AC 340, [1993] 3 All ER 65, [1993] 3 WLR 126, [1994] 2
    FCR 65, [1993] 2 FLR 963, HL 51
Tito v Waddell (No 2) [1977] Ch 106, [1977] 3 All ER 129, [1977] 2 WLR 496, 121 Sol
    Jo 10 .... 388, 400
Toker v Westerman 13 NJ Super 452, 274 A 2d 78 (1970) 263
Tradax Export SA v Dorada Compania Naviera SA, The Lutetian [1982] 2 Lloyd's
    Rep 140, [1982] Com LR 130 315
Trident General Insurance Co Ltd v McNiece Bros Pty Ltd (1988) 165 CLR 107, 80
    ALR 574, 62 ALJR 508, HC of A 297, 302
Tudor Grange Holdings Ltd v Citibank NA [1992] Ch 53, [1991] 4 All ER 1, [1991] 3
    WLR 750, [1991] BCLC 1009 392

U

Ultramares Corpn v Touche 255 NY 170, 174 NE 441 (1931) 294
Union Eagle Ltd v Golden Achievement Ltd [1997] 2 All ER 215, [1997] 2 WLR 341,
    141 Sol Jo LB 56, PC 360
Universal Corpn v Five Ways Properties Ltd [1979] 1 All ER 552, 38 P & CR 687,
    123 Sol Jo 33, 250 Estates Gazette 447, CA 363

PAGE

Universe Tankships Inc of Monrovia v International Transport Workers Federation,
   The Universe Sentinel [1983] 1 AC 366, [1982] 2 All ER 67, [1982] 2 WLR 803,
   [1982] 1 Lloyd's Rep 537, [1982] ICR 262, [1982] IRLR 200, 126 Sol Jo 275, HL 133

V

Vandepitte v Preferred Accident Insurance Corpn of New York [1933] AC 70, 102
   LJPC 21, [1932] All ER Rep 527, 76 Sol Jo 798, 148 LT 169, 49 TLR 90, PC 302
Victoria Laundry (Windsor) Ltd v Newman Industries Ltd [1949] 2 KB 528, [1949] 1
   All ER 997, 93 Sol Jo 371, 65 TLR 274, CA 383

W

Wade v Simeon (1846) 2 CB 548, 3 Dow & L 587, 15 LJCP 114, 10 Jur 412, 6 LTOS
   346 369
Waldron-Kelly v British Rlys Board [1981] CLY 303 .... 241, 242, 245
Walford v Miles [1992] 2 AC 128, [1992] 1 All ER 453, [1992] 2 WLR 174, 64 P & CR
   166, [1992] 1 EGLR 207, [1992] NLJR 123, [1992] 11 EG 115, HL 199
Walker v Boyle [1982] 1 All ER 634, [1982] 1 WLR 495, 44 P & CR 20, 125 Sol Jo
   724, [1982] LS Gaz R 954, 261 Estates Gazette 1090 250
Waltons Stores (Interstate) Ltd v Maher (1988) 164 CLR 387, 76 ALR 513, 62 ALJR
   110 (Aust HC) 74, 75, 77, 81, 159, 201
Ward v Byham [1956] 2 All ER 318, [1956] 1 WLR 496, 100 Sol Jo 341, CA 58, 93, 102
Ward v Hobbs (1878) 4 App Cas 13, 43 JP 252, 48 LJQB 281, 27 WR 114, 40 LT 73,
   HL 192
Warner Bros Pictures Inc v Nelson [1937] 1 KB 209, [1936] 3 All ER 160, 106 LJKB
   97, 80 Sol Jo 855, 155 LT 538, 53 TLR 14 400
Watteau v Fenwick [1893] 1 QB 346, 56 JP 839, 5 R 143, 41 WR 222, [1891-4] All
   ER Rep 897, 37 Sol Jo 117, 67 LT 831, 9 TLR 133 121
Watts v Morrow [1991] 4 All ER 937, [1991] 1 WLR 1421, 23 HLR 608, [1991] 2
   EGLR 152, [1992] 1 LS Gaz R 33, 54 BLR 86, [1991] 43 EG 121, CA 378, 389
Webb v McGowin 168 So 196, 27 Ala App 82 (1935) 63
Weisz v Parke-Benet Galleries Inc 67 Misc 2d 1077, 325 NYS 2d 576 (1971) 221
West v AGC (Advances) Ltd (1986) 5 NSWLR 610, CA 252
Westdeutsche Landesbank Girozentrale v Islington London Borough Council [1994]
   4 All ER 890, [1994] 1 WLR 938, [1994] 8 LS Gaz R 38, 138 Sol Jo LB 26, CA;
   revsd [1996] AC 669, [1996] 2 All ER 961, [1996] 2 WLR 802, 95 LGR 1, [1996]
   NLJR 877, 140 Sol Jo LB 136, HL 378
White v Jones [1995] 2 AC 207, [1995] 1 All ER 691, [1995] 2 WLR 187, [1995] 3
   FCR 51, [1995] NLJR 251, 139 Sol Jo LB 83, HL 34, 300, 379
White and Carter (Councils) Ltd v McGregor [1962] AC 413, [1961] 3 All ER 1178,
   [1962] 2 WLR 17, 105 Sol Jo 1104, HL 344, 345
Wiley v Berg 282 Or 9, 578 P 2d 384 (1978) 292
Wilkie v London Passenger Transport Board [1947] 1 All ER 258, 45 LGR 170, 111
   JP 98, [1947] LJR 864, 177 LT 71, 63 TLR 115, CA 149
Williams v Bayley (1866) LR 1 HL 200, 30 JP 500, 35 LJ Ch 717, 12 Jur NS 875,
   [1861-73] All ER Rep 227, 14 LT 802, HL 139
Williams v Roffey Bros & Nicholls (Contractors) Ltd [1991] 1 QB 1, [1990] 1 All ER
   512, [1990] 2 WLR 1153, [1990] 12 LS Gaz R 36, [1989] NLJR 1712, 48 BLR 75,
   CA 59, 68, 255, 324, 329
Williams v Walker-Thomas Furniture Co 350 F 2d 445 (DC Circ 1965) 140
Willmott v Barber (1880) 15 Ch D 96, 49 LJ Ch 792, 28 WR 911, 43 LT 95; on appeal
   (1881) 17 Ch D 772, 45 LT 229, CA 126
Willson v Love [1896] 1 QB 626, 65 LJQB 474, 44 WR 450, [1895-9] All ER Rep 325,
   74 LT 580, CA 347
Wilson v Best Travel Ltd [1993] 1 All ER 353 224
Wilson (Paal) & Co A/S v Partenreederei Hannah Blumenthal, The Hannah
   Blumenthal [1983] 1 AC 854, [1983] 1 All ER 34, [1982] 3 WLR 1149, [1983] 1
   Lloyd's Rep 103, 126 Sol Jo 835, HL 114, 322, 323

PAGE

With v O'Flanagan [1936] Ch 575, [1936] 1 All ER 727, 105 LJ Ch 247, 80 Sol Jo
  285, 154 LT 634, CA 191
Wood v Lucy, Lady Duff-Gordon 222 NY 88, 118 NE 214 (1917) 61
Woodar Investment Development Ltd v Wimpey Construction (UK) Ltd [1980] 1 All
  ER 571, [1980] 1 WLR 277, 124 Sol Jo 184, HL 286, 333, 379
Woodman v Photo Trade Processing Ltd (7 May 1981, unreported) 242
Woods v WM Car Services (Peterborough) Ltd [1982] ICR 693, [1982] IRLR 413,
  [1982] Com LR 208, CA 225
Woolcott v Sun Alliance and London Insurance Ltd [1978] 1 All ER 1253, [1978] 1
  WLR 493, [1978] 1 Lloyd's Rep 629, 121 Sol Jo 744 196
Woolwich Equitable Building Society v IRC [1993] AC 70, [1992] 3 WLR 366, [1992]
  STC 657, 65 TC 265, [1992] 32 LS Gaz R 38, 136 Sol Jo LB 230, sub nom
  Woolwich Building Society v IRC (No 2) [1992] 3 All ER 737, HL 378
Workers Trust and Merchant Bank Ltd v Dojap Investments Ltd [1993] AC 573,
  [1993] 2 All ER 370, [1993] 2 WLR 702, 66 P & CR 15, [1993] 1 EGLR 203,
  [1993] 14 LS Gaz R 44, [1993] NLJR 616, 137 Sol Jo LB 83, PC 363
Wroth v Tyler [1974] Ch 30, [1973] 1 All ER 897, [1973] 2 WLR 405, 25 P & CR 138,
  117 Sol Jo 90 385
Wrotham Park Estate Co v Parkside Homes Ltd [1974] 2 All ER 321, [1974] 1 WLR
  798, 27 P & CR 296, 118 Sol Jo 420, 229 Estates Gazette 617 .... 393, 400

1

Contract and Market

The law of contract states the fundamental legal rules governing market transactions. In most societies markets serve as the principal mechanism for the production and distribution of wealth. This part of the law reveals some of the basic organising principles of their economic arrangements. It describes the elementary regulation of such key economic institutions as sale of goods, employment relations, arrangements for credit, and the provision of professional services. Individuals enter these market transactions for a variety of motives. The law of contract supports these practices by making transactions legally enforceable, but at the same time it places restraints on conduct, shapes the types of obligations which can be created, and limits the extent to which the parties may enforce their agreement by means of self-help or coercion from legal institutions.

A study of the legal regulation of the market system as a whole would require an examination of every branch of private law and other aspects of state regulation of the economy. Such an investigation would encompass the law of private ownership of property and the rules of tort law which require the observance of obligations to respect the economic and personal interests of others. Although no sharp distinction can be drawn, the law of contract focuses on the practices of entering transactions or exchanges, and of making binding commitments with respect to future economic behaviour. But this focus covers an enormous variety of market practices, ranging from consumer purchases in shops to international business transactions, or from the supply of a professional service to a major construction project.

These market practices may be examined from a variety of perspectives. An economic perspective analyses how transactions create wealth. A sociological perspective examines the patterns of behaviour of the parties to market transactions. A moral perspective might evaluate the conduct of the parties and the justice of the economic system. The legal perspective, like the others, serves to organise and rationalize our understanding of events. The objective of legal analysis differs, however, for its purpose lies ultimately in a determination of how these market practices should be governed by state regulation. The law of contract contains a set of legal concepts which are employed simultaneously to analyse the events of economic transactions and then to regulate the conduct of the parties.

Although the legal analysis of market transactions is distinct, it must be informed by the other perspectives. In order to achieve effective regulation, the law must take into account the likely response to its rules. It must also beware of regulation which damages the prospects of the market system for the production of wealth. For these reasons the legal analysis must be guided by sociological and economic perspectives. But this endeavour proves difficult, for each perspective tends to operate within its own closed system of analysis and evaluation. The concepts used in the legal analysis of contracts do not embrace economic or sociological ideas, so that the significance and effects of legal regulation cannot be immediately comprehended. The law of contract therefore constantly runs the risk of what Teubner calls 'the regulatory trilemma': either the legal rules may fail to have an impact on social practice, or they may subvert the desirable social practices by impractical demands, or the law may lose the coherence of its own analytical framework by seeking to incorporate sociological and economic perspectives in its reasoning.[1]

The legal analysis of market transactions may only represent a partial perspective, but it holds great interest because it displays the detailed ramifications of ideological debates within a society. Since the law can rely in the last resort upon a legitimate claim to the monopoly of violence in order to insist upon behaviour according to its vision, it becomes a principal site of disputes about the justice of the market order. The law's link to state power requires that its doctrines conform to shifts in the claims for legitimacy on which effective state power rests.

The legal analysis of market transactions holds particular interest, of course, for practising lawyers, who may be brought in to advise businesses on how best to organise their transactions. Lawyers observe the legal rules and then devise contractual arrangements which give their clients the maximum advantage. This establishes a recursive process under which the courts and legislature then observe how the lawyers have reformulated contracts to escape restrictions on the pursuit of their clients' interests, and then seek to reregulate the contractual practice in order to restore the original policy decision.

The principal effect of the use of lawyers in drafting contract clauses is that quickly the lawyers seek to routinise their work by formulating standard form contracts. In a business context, such a standard form contract preserves the wisdom of the firm of lawyers about the best way in which to handle recurrent problems of negotiation and performance. In the context of mass production of goods and services, this use of standard forms gives rise to the most significant new phenomenon in the practice

---

1   Teubner, 'After Legal Instrumentalism? Strategic Models of Post-Regulatory Law', in G Teubner (ed), *Dilemmas of Law in the Welfare State* (New York/Berlin, 1988) 299, at p 309.

of making contracts in the twentieth century, the application of mass contracts to consumer transactions. For a business dealing with consumers, the lawyers devise a printed contract which purports to govern exclusively the business relation between the parties. The contracts are issued on a take-it-or-leave-it basis, which has earned them the soubricet of 'adhesion contracts'. One of the major challenges for legal regulation of markets during the twentieth century has been the requirement to restrict the advantages which businesses can obtain against consumers by deploying standard form contracts. This regulation has reached the stage where in simple retail sales there remains little or no scope for manipulating legal rights through the written contract, so in this context the standard form may gradually fall into disuse.[2]

The legal concept of contract law constantly evolves by expanding or contracting its scope, further differentiating its rules, and revising its basic principles. This evolution is prompted by changes in the social practices of the economy, the reception of new social policies and political ideals, and interactions with other fields of law. Despite this permanent evolutionary trajectory, we can discern in retrospect that during the nineteenth century lawyers in Europe and North America devised a new, radical system of contract law with which to interpret and regulate economic practices. This powerful vision persists in its influence today by providing the basic framework of the legal analysis of market transactions. Having considered the principal elements of this concept of contract law, however, I shall argue that it structures our thoughts about the market order in a way which once seemed so illuminating, but now seems to obscure, distort, and impede understanding and practical reasoning.

1. The Classical Law of Contract

The new law of contract in the nineteenth century possessed two striking features. It was simultaneously sparse in content and imperialist in its ambitions of interpretation and regulation. These features have subsequently earned it the title of the classical law of contract.

The simplicity and rigour of the doctrinal system of thought betrayed its dependence upon a relatively small set of fundamental principles. The nineteenth-century conception of contract law plundered highly selectively the antecedent intellectual traditions, thus abandoning their rich moral texture for a sparse group of organizing principles.[3] This impoverishment of the law then permitted its restatement in a few terse rules.

A second distinctive characteristic of the nineteenth-century conception of contract law was the extent to which lawyers conceived so

---

2 Micklitz, 'Directive 93/13 in Action: A Report on A Research Project on Unfair Terms in Consumer Sales Contracts', in C Willett (ed), *Aspects of Fairness in Contract* (London, 1996) 77, at p 78.

3 J Gordley, *The Philosophical Origins of Modern Contract Doctrine* (Oxford, 1991).

many different types of social relationships as falling within the conceptual framework of contracts. Together with the law of private property, the law of contract supplied most of the key principles through which lawyers sought to interpret and thence regulate every aspect of economic social relations. Obligations based upon status, trust, and economic dependence were reinterpreted as contractual arrangements to be governed by the new organizing classification of contract law. The potential scope of this classification stretched from marriage to business companies and employment, and from sales of private property to the provision of public services by governments. The new category of contract law threatened to subject nearly every kind of social and economic relation to its logic. The empire of the law of contract expanded in tandem with what Marx decried as the commodification of social life.[4]

We can discern both these features of the law of contract developed in the nineteenth century in a case familiar to many law students: *Carlill v Carbolic Smoke Ball Co*.[5] The defendant manufacturer of these carbolic smoke balls placed an advertisement in a number of magazines which claimed that the product would cure all sorts of ailments including coughs, hay fever, loss of voice, asthma, influenza and many others. The defendant added that it would pay £100 in compensation to anyone who contracted influenza despite using the smoke ball according to the printed directions supplied with the ball, and, to demonstrate its sincerity, the defendant deposited £1,000 in a bank. Needless to say, the plaintiff caught influenza despite having purchased this quack remedy in a shop and having used it faithfully according to the directions. The Court of Appeal upheld the plaintiff's claim for £100, asserting that she had formed a contract with the manufacturer on the terms of the advertisement.

The amusing circumstances of the case should not obscure the surprising extent to which the court was prepared to conceive social relations in terms of contracts. The parties to the alleged contract had never met or communicated with each other directly. Nor had they exchanged goods, money or services between themselves. The law of contract is used by the court as an instrument for discouraging misleading and extravagant claims in advertising, and deterring the marketing of unproven and perhaps dangerous pharmaceuticals. The court protects the gullible and confused consumer by interpreting the events in the form of a contractual relationship giving rise to reciprocal obligations. In so doing it ignores alternative interpretations of these events, such as the idea that the misleading advertisement might constitute a civil wrong in itself, or that consumers who are ignorant of the properties of goods put on the market should be protected against any harmful consequences.

At the same time, the reasoning of the Court of Appeal towards the conclusion that the plaintiff could succeed in her claim for £100 displays

---

4   K Marx, *Capital*, Vol 1 (London, 1867), ch 1.
5   [1893] 1 QB 256, CA; Simpson, 'Quackery and Contract Law: The Case of the Carbolic Smoke Ball' (1985) 14 *Journal of Legal Studies* 345.

considerable analytical rigour based upon a terse set of rules. The court operates a check-list for determining whether an enforceable contract has been made. The judges run through a shopping-list of questions. Was there a promise? Was the promise serious and intended to be acted on? Was the promise sufficiently definite and certain? Was the promise accepted by the plaintiff? Did the plaintiff perform some action in exchange for the promise? If these questions, and others, could be answered affirmatively, then the court held itself bound to find the existence of a legally enforceable contract. The legal reasoning thus takes the form of a brief and finite set of rules which must be applied to the facts of the case. The rules establish binary oppositions: either the test is satisfied, or it is not. No questions of degree, apportionment of blame, compromise of interests, or social policy imperatives will be considered.

This case illustrates both the extensive province of the category of the nineteenth-century law of contract and its logical and formal reasoning process. The court employs its simple checklist of rules to interpret and regulate any kind of economic relationship. The generality and abstraction of the rules permit both the extensive utilization of this category of law and its application to the case, without any discussion of such matters as the moral claims of the parties, the nature of the market for pharmaceuticals and the problems generated by misleading advertising. The new textbooks on the law of contract in the nineteenth century both helped to create and to reinforce the construction of this category in the law.[6] The writers performed a crucial role in organizing the legal materials, individuating the rules and tests, and carving out this branch of the law from other categories such as the law of property rights, status, and civil wrongs. Books on contract law have altered little in their organization of the materials, their chapter headings, their identification of the rules, and their conceptions of the scope of the subject. Although some significant challenges have been mounted against this system of thought,[7] the law of contract as it was constructed in the nineteenth century survives with an assurance and even complacency which renders it a daunting target for criticism.

The timing of the origins of this conception of the law of contract provides an important clue to the success of this structure of thought. This category of the law provided an essential tool for lawyers to understand the social and economic relations which were formed in the course of the explosion of a market economy. As markets became the dominant instrument for the production and allocation of wealth, the

---

6 Eg W Anson, *Principles of the Law of Contract* (Oxford, 1879); F Savigny, *System des heutigen Romischen Rechts* (Berlin, 1840–48).

7 Eg G Gilmore, *The Death of Contract* (Columbus, Ohio, 1974); Macneil, 'The Many Futures of Contract' (1974) 47 *Southern California Law Review* 691; Slawson, 'The New Meaning of Contract: The Transformation of Contracts Law by Standard Forms' (1984) 46 *University of Pittsburgh Law Review* 21; Feinman, 'Critical Approaches and Contract Law' (1983) *UCLA Law Review* 829; P Atiyah, *Essays on Contract* (Oxford, 1988); T Wilhelmsson (ed), *Perspectives of Critical Contract Law* (Aldershot, 1993).

nineteenth-century conception of contract law supplied the tool by which these market relations could be understood and regulated. Such an understanding could perhaps have been achieved by a reworking of other categories of law concerning property and status. But the powerful attraction for lawyers of the law of contract as a fundamental system of thought for understanding the social relations thrown up by a market economy lay in its theory of legitimacy for the exercise of the power of the law.

The latent social ideal of the nineteenth-century law of contract embodies a libertarian state, in which the law maximizes the liberty of individual citizens, encourages self-reliance, and adopts an avowedly neutral stance with regard to permissible patterns of social life. The law of contract secures these goals perhaps more effectively than any other category of the law by facilitating the creation of legal obligations on any terms which individuals freely choose. We should recognize, therefore, that not only was the law of contract a convenient way of understanding the social relations of a market economy, but also it represented a particular theory of the legitimacy of state power, one which limited the exercise of such power in the name of respecting the liberty of citizens.[8]

The fundamental analytical framework of the law of contract became one which focused upon the voluntary choices of individuals. The role of the law of contract was conceived principally as the facilitation of voluntary choices by giving them legal effect. To achieve this purpose, however, the law had to protect this social facility by identifying and declining to enforce those undertakings which were not truly voluntary. The textbooks described exhaustively what kinds of choices would be regarded as sufficiently voluntary to justify the imposition of legal obligations. The shopping-list of rules used by the court in *Carlill v Carbolic Smoke Ball Co* illustrates clearly how all the crucial questions were directed to ascertaining the choices of the parties concerned. The court ostensibly awarded a contractual remedy, not because the manufacturer of the smoke ball deserved to be made to pay up for its lies, but because it had voluntarily chosen to undertake that obligation. As a necessary corollary to this conception of the law of contract, the books excluded from consideration those instances where the law imposed obligations regardless of, or for reasons independent of, choice, such as those branches of law described today as Tort and Unjust Enrichment (Restitution), even though these sources of obligations have profound effects on the regulation of market transactions.

The unity and simple analytical framework of the law of contract, which was provided by the cardinal principle of respecting and enforcing voluntary choices, established a closed system of thought which necessarily excluded inconsistent rules and doctrines. There could be no place, for example, for a rule which insisted upon the fairness of the exchange between the parties, because that would contradict the fundamental

---

8   P Atiyah, *The Rise and Fall of Freedom of Contract* (Oxford, 1979).

assumption of this system of doctrinal thought that it was designed to facilitate and enforce the voluntary choices of individuals regardless of the wisdom or prudence of such choices. Nor could the traditional conception of contract law acknowledge the possibility of imposed contracts without the consent of the parties, for again that would contradict the basic tenets of the system. In some instances, of course, a court may have wanted to refuse to enforce a contract because of its shocking unfairness, or may have wanted to impose a contract regardless of consent for some instrumental purpose. In these cases, the integrity of the traditional doctrine prohibited any express recognition of such possibilities. The courts had to justify the results within the logic of the traditional doctrine. They had to argue in the case of unfairness that the choice was not truly a voluntary one; and in order to impose a contract, the court had to claim that the circumstances in fact revealed an agreement, as occurred in *Carlill v Carbolic Smoke Ball Co.*

This traditional conception of contract law persists in part because of the need to preserve the integrity and hence the legitimacy of this closed doctrinal system of thought.[9] Its doctrinal integrity helps to achieve legitimacy, because the law can be presented as objective and neutral, not a matter of politics or preference, but a settled body of rules and principles, legitimated by tradition and routine observance, and applied impartially and fairly to all citizens.

Even in modern accounts of the law of contract, therefore, one cannot ignore the traditional conception of contract law based upon the idea of facilitating voluntary choices. Its presence in the origins of the subject, the continuity of the tradition for more than a century, and its power as an analytical tool for understanding market relations and legitimating legal decisions, seem to render it almost immune from challenge. But challenge it we must. Whilst the evolutionary trajectory of the law of contract may have stalled, the market system and other aspects of private law have altered at an ever increasing pace. The classical concept of contract law now prevents us from understanding the significance of these developments by treating them as irrelevant or distorting their implications.

2. Towards a New Conception

We have already glimpsed typical defects in the traditional conception of contract law in our discussion of *Carlill v Carbolic Smoke Ball Co.* Such an event, were it to occur today, would almost certainly be understood through the spectacles of the law in a radically different way. We would first note that legal regulation attempts to proscribe the marketing of dangerous or ineffective drugs through licensing systems and bans

---

9 For this sense of integrity, see R Dworkin, *Law's Empire* (Cambridge, Mass, 1986).

supported by criminal sanctions. These laws set limits to ranges of products and services which can be offered in the market, and confine the number and type of persons who may engage in such transactions. There are also more general criminal regulations which prohibit unsafe products from being put on the market, and permit government agencies to intervene to prevent such products from being marketed.[10] Next we would note the formidable array of criminal regulations which control marketing strategies such as false and misleading advertising.[11] We might also discover that the relevant trade association insists upon certain standards of conduct from its members, and these Codes of Practice might be given legal sanctions. Furthermore, the events of the case would have to be considered in the light of legislation and judicial decisions which have increasingly recognized that consumers need to be protected from their free choices, since these are so often based upon inadequate information and lack of expertise. Finally, we might observe that the economic relation between manufacturer and consumer has become the subject of mandatory laws which establish strict liability for defects resulting in personal injuries irrespective of the choice of the parties.[12] From this perspective, the relation between Mrs Carlill and the manufacturer might be regarded as one based not on voluntary choice but economic dependence, which in turn justifies the imposition upon the producer of compulsory duties of care with respect to the quality of the product and the information supplied about it. To interpret the events of the case as a voluntary choice to undertake an obligation was at the time regarded as stretching the category of contracts, but within the framework of today's laws and regulations it seems to provide a perverse understanding of the issues and problems to be addressed.

We need to construct a new conception of the law of contract.[13] It should provide a system of thought that illuminates present concerns of government, and that helps to analyse issues within an intellectual framework which has a place for all the relevant rules and doctrines. It should also provide a key for an interpretation of law's past, which simultaneously reconstructs the law and enables further transformations to take place.

The place to start no doubt, as did the Victorians before us, is with a desire to understand the market order. We still require legal systems of

---

10 General Product Safety Regulations 1994, SI 1994/2328, implementing EC Product Safety Directive 92/59.

11 See chapter 10.

12 Consumer Protection Act 1987, implementing EC Directive on Liability for Defective Products 1985, 85/374.

13 For other critical reformulations, see: Friedman and Macaulay, 'Contract Law and Contract Teaching: Past, Present and Future' (1967) *Wisconsin Law Rev* 805; Leff, 'Contract as Thing' (1970) 19 *American University Law Review* 131; Lewis, 'Criticisms of the Traditional Contract Course' (1982) 16 *Law Teacher* 111; Summers, 'Collective Agreements and the Law of Contracts' (1969) 78 *Yale Law Journal* 525; P Birks (ed), *Examining the Law Syllabus* (Oxford, 1992); Frug, 'Re-reading Contracts: A Feminist Analysis of a Contracts Casebook' (1985) 34 *American University Law Review* 1065.

thought for interpreting, analysing, and guiding events and relations in the marketplace. The difference between our enterprise and theirs springs not from the site of the inquiry, but rather from the alteration in both the market order itself, and the nature of political and moral justifications for its legal regulation.

During this century, the state has intervened to devise new principles to govern the operation and outcomes of the market. With respect to outcomes, the evidence is incontrovertible. Instead of permitting the distribution of wealth to be determined by voluntary choices to enter market transactions, the social security system which relieves poverty and all the other dimensions of the Welfare State, funded largely through progressive taxation, clearly affect the eventual outcomes of the distribution of wealth. What seems to be less generally perceived is that at the same time similar ideals of social justice have justified the channelling and regulation of market transactions. The purpose of these limits upon the exercise of voluntary choices lies in the realization of a compatible scheme of social justice.[14] The persistence of traditional descriptions of the law of contract no doubt contributes to this failure to perceive how the ground rules for the establishment of obligations in economic relations have been substantially altered in order that they may fit better with contemporary ideals of social justice.

How, therefore, should we conceive the law of contract today? It comprises those rules, standards, and doctrines which serve to channel, control, and regulate the social practices which we can loosely describe as market transactions. This branch of the law certainly facilitates the growth of the social practice of making economic transactions, especially those transactions where performance is not instantaneous; but it also sets limits to the exercise of voluntary choice. By emphasizing how modern ideals of social justice channel market transactions into approved patterns, this conception of contract removes the assumption that the law provides an open-ended facility for making binding commitments. Although some flexibility persists, especially with regard to the price, this freedom should be regarded as a privilege granted on stringent conditions, rather than a general licence to enter contractual obligations of one's choice. This perspective reduces the facilitative role of the law of contract to a vestigial role, leaving the detailed regulations which define the model contracts as the core of the subject.

As a consequence, the traditional contrast between imposed and voluntary obligations ceases to provide a crucial characteristic of the scope of the law of contract. Within the conception of the subject to be pursued here, we should define the field of inquiry by considering all those rules which serve to mould the form and content of market transactions, whether they be criminal offences, civil obligations of compensation imposed by the law, administrative regulations, or legislation which fixes the terms of obligations. It should be apparent that this conception of the subject

---

14 T Wilhelmsson, *Critical Studies in Private Law* (Dordrecht, 1992).

incorporates many aspects of the law traditionally excluded from the classification of contract, because those topics cannot be derived from the concept of voluntary consent.

In one respect, however, this revised conception of contract law narrows the focus of study. Because the traditional conception offered to analyse so many types of relation within its logic, it lacked any determinate boundaries. Indeed, the subject became almost incoherent, because its expansive generality had to be constrained artificially by excluding such matters as marriage and property transactions in order to prevent it from occupying nearly all of private law. At the same time, the necessary generality of the traditional conception rendered it increasingly irrelevant to contractual disputes, where almost invariably some particular rules of law governed the transaction, such as the law governing sales, credit arrangements, and employment. In order to counter this incoherence and redundancy, the conception of contract law employed here focuses on the social context of market transactions, that is where people seek to acquire property or services by dealing with others. Whilst acknowledging that the law regulates these transactions by classifying them into particular types, this conception of contract law seeks to understand the general principles and social policies which inform and guide the legal classifications and regulation. The discussion tends to exclude those market transactions which establish an economic organization such as a firm, a trade association, or a partnership.

In the remaining sections of this chapter, we will examine the nature of the market transactions which the law seeks to regulate, the significance of market transactions in the social system, and the complex relation between the social system and legal regulation. In the following chapter, the values which inform the modern law of contract will be explored in greater detail by contrasting them with the traditional libertarian ideals briefly described above. We shall note how these changes have forced a modification in the form of the law and have drawn upon new sources of law.

3. The Market Order

Every society creates an order of wealth and power. It establishes rules and institutions which direct the means for the creation and distribution of wealth and allocate power to certain individuals to control others. In modern western societies, market transactions play a central role in establishing the order of wealth and power. Consequently, the law of contract, which regulates these transactions, plays a leading role in determining the order of wealth and power.

Where considerable social division of labour exists in a market economy, wealth is normally created and distributed through the actions of selling, hiring, and lending. These transactions tend to move commodities, services, and capital towards those persons who value them most and who can exploit these factors of production efficiently. The bulk of most people's assets are purchased with income from contractual productive relations such as employment. Distributive relations reallocate this wealth through trade in commodities, securities, and other forms of property. As well as the willingness to take risks with the resource of capital, superior information and expertise permit advantageous trading, resulting in a redistribution of wealth. Since the law of contract regulates both productive and distributive relations, it supplies a key ingredient in the determination of the distribution of wealth, though of course such laws as inheritance, taxation, social security payments, and obligations of status (such as a parent's duty to care for a child) alter this pattern.

Not only does the market provide a principal mechanism for the distribution of wealth, it also establishes some of the significant relations of power in modern society.[15] Contracts provide the basis for the construction of many institutional arrangements which operate in the market. These institutions, be they firms, trade unions, or trade associations, can exert power over members of the organization, according to the licence of the contractual constitution.

Many market transactions comprise a fragment of the vertically integrated production scheme known as the firm. The firm, which normally takes the legal form of a company, acquires capital through a mixture of contracts with shareholders and loans from banks. The firm acting through its directors, who are its contractual agents, employs managers to organize production. Employees of the firm accept the managers' contractual right to direct and control their efforts during working hours in return for the payment of wages. The firm enters into numerous agreements with suppliers and customers for the purchase of raw materials and the sale of the finished product. Suppliers often undertake a requirements contract, which obliges them to satisfy the needs of the firm for a raw material at a fixed price. Similarly, through franchise agreements with retailers and distributorships with wholesalers, the firm secures reliable outlets for its product and the right to control price and exclude competition. Within this matrix of production relations established by a variety of contractual relations, each party necessarily becomes heavily dependent upon the others for the proper performance of contracts: a franchisee can be driven out of business by a failure to supply the finished product, and a supplier or an employee can easily halt production, unless alternative raw materials and employees are readily obtainable. These comprise symbiotic contracts,[16] where the economic interests of the parties are so closely tied together that the contract provides the occasion for the construction of power relations between them. The contractual rights and duties regulate the allocation and legitimate exercise of these powers, both in the case of transactions with persons internal to the firm, such as employees and

---

15   I Macneil, *The New Social Contract* (New Haven, 1980), pp 32–35.
16   Schanze, 'Symbiotic Contracts: Exploring Long-Term Agency Structures between Contract and Corporation', in C Joerges (ed), *Franchising and the Law* (Baden-Baden, 1991).

shareholders, and external ones such as those with suppliers and distributors.

These familiar power relations established in production relations require no further elaboration, but we frequently overlook the dimension of power which permeates distribution relations, even in the most humble consumer purchases. It is tempting to regard such purchases as momentary transactions, a simple exchange of goods for money, which raise no questions about the distribution of power in society. But even in these momentary, discrete transactions, we should recognize that social relations with power dimensions have been established. Disparities of knowledge and expertise normally place the seller at an advantage over the consumer. If the consumer can compel the retailer or manufacturer to remedy defects or to disclose information about the product, some equalization of relative power occurs. The absence of such consumer rights also evidences a power relation, though one where the consumer's control and influence terminate abruptly at the moment of delivery of the goods. It is a mistake, therefore, to think that power relations are only established by long-term contractual relations such as employment and franchises, for the presence or absence of contractual rights and immunities after a discrete transaction such as a sale of goods also signifies a power relation.

Standing back from these dimensions of power and wealth located in production and distribution relations, we can glimpse the main outlines of the market order. Every stable social system possesses an order of power and wealth but, unlike historically prior distributive schemes, the market order avoids the imposition of a detailed pattern. Instead of a structure of rank and privilege fixing entitlements to wealth and power, the distributive mechanism of the market allocates resources to those persons both able and willing to pay the highest price for them. Thus anyone with sufficient money may purchase a Rolls-Royce, or employ someone as a servant, or set himself or herself up in a country seat. The market order avows blindness to claims of privilege or force, so it recognizes no claims of an inherent right to govern or to possess superior wealth. Each transaction creates its own power relation and exerts an independent effect upon the distribution of wealth. In an employment relation, for instance, the level of wages and the employer's measure of control depend upon many factors, including the type of work, the effectiveness of union organization, and the scarcity of labour. Each employment relation potentially differs from the next in its distribution of wealth and the range and oppressiveness of managerial control. Although certain patterns and regularities emerge in the course of the myriad of market transactions, their contingency upon the vector of market forces renders them always subject to renegotiation. The market order lets fly the centrifugal forces of radical individualism, permitting philosophers to celebrate the relative fluidity of its distributive outcome, and to legitimate it by appeals to the impervious mask of market forces. No other order so successfully disguises the fact that it constitutes an order at all.[17]

17   O Kahn-Freund 'Introduction', in K Renner, *The Institutions of Private Law and Their Social Functions* (London, 1949).

In what sense should we regard the market as constituting an order of power and wealth? Under a regime of contract law which facilitates all types of voluntary transactions, it can be argued that individual choices determine distributive outcomes and the law does not impose any particular pattern of the distribution of wealth and power. The justice of this distributive scheme can be defended either on the ground that each individual has chosen his or her lot, or on the ground that no justification is called for because the state does not seek to impose any pattern of distribution at all.[18] Both arguments resist the claim that the market constitutes an order of wealth and power in any strong sense. But these arguments are gravely flawed.

Even supposing that the law of contract might permit all voluntary transactions to take place, the effects of such a free market on the distribution of wealth and power are predictable. The decisions of the legislature and the courts to allow those predictable consequences to occur by abstaining from intervention in the market call for justification, just as much as attempts to control distributive outcomes.[19]

Moreover, the law of contract cannot avoid taking a stand on which distributive consequences should be permitted. In the legal rules which determine whether a voluntary transaction has taken place, as opposed to some coercive taking of property, the law necessarily takes a stand on the question of which bargaining chips may be used to a person's advantage in the market-place. The law must determine what kinds of pressure may be used to secure better terms. It must determine the limits of fair dealing, so that certain types of lying and cheating cannot be used to gain advantage. Although all these rules may be described in the traditional understanding of the law of contract as rules designed to distinguish between voluntary and involuntary transactions, whatever rules may be chosen will inevitably have distributive consequences. They will determine the extent to which both natural advantages, such as intelligence, strength, and a facility in lying, and acquired advantages such as ownership of resources and a monopoly position in the market, can be used to win further advantageous transactions and so redistribute wealth. Because the law cannot avoid taking a stand on these questions, the rules of contract law, even if conceived solely in terms of facilitating voluntary choices, have necessary and foreseeable distributive consequences.[20] Market transactions regulated by law can never be free.

---

18 F von Hayek, *Law, Legislation and Liberty*, Vol 2 (London, 1976), pp 65–69; R Nozick, *Anarchy, State, and Utopia* (Oxford, 1974), p 159.
19 Collins, 'Distributive Justice Through Contracts' (1992) 45(2) *Current Legal Problems* 49; R Plant, *Modern Political Thought* (Oxford, 1991), pp 80–97.
20 Kronman, 'Contract Law and Distributive Justice' (1980) 89 *Yale Law J* 472; Alexander and Wang, 'Natural Advantages and Contractual Justice' (1984) 3 *Law and Philosophy* 281; Lucy, 'Contract as a Mechanism of Distributive Justice' (1989) 9 *Oxford Journal of Legal Studies* 132; Richardson, 'Contract Law and Distributive Justice Revisited' (1990) 10 *Legal Studies* 258; Ramsay, 'Consumer Credit Law, Distributive Justice and the Welfare State' (1995) 15 *Oxford Journal of Legal Studies* 177.

But of course the modern law of contract goes much further than simply distinguishing between voluntary and involuntary choices. It imposes compulsory terms on certain kinds of contractual relations, such as landlord and tenant, employment, and consumer purchases. The law controls the remedies which the parties may enjoy to vindicate their contractual rights, which in turn determines the strength and effectiveness of those rights. Modern legislative interventions cannot conceal their distributive motives. All these rules shape the market order and produce foreseeable distributive outcomes.

The existence of all these rules alerts us, however, to the point that in one sense there is no such thing as the market order.[21] Market systems flourish under a considerable variety of regulatory strategies. The degree and scope of regulation does not prevent the market from functioning as an efficient provider of goods and services, or at least as a system which proves more efficient than the alternative of state bureaucratic control. But each of these market systems shaped by different regulatory strategies imply different judgements about acceptable distributive outcomes. One legal system may, for example, fix a minimum wage for employees in order to alleviate poverty and provide an incentive for the efficient use of labour, whereas another system leaves wage levels alone but promotes the efficient use of labour by giving employees other rights to job security and profit-sharing. The market order does not have a single fixed content or a pure paradigm. Competition between markets to attract trade may compel a degree of harmonization, and this movement may be buttressed by legal measures in free trade areas such as the European Community. But these legal constraints do not rule out significant national divergence in the regulation of markets,[22] so that ultimately each legal system devises its own scheme for how the market should be permitted to operate.

An interpretation of the law of contract therefore becomes an interpretation of a particular distributive order contained in a legal system. A study of this branch of the law reveals the distributive principles which govern the allocation of rights and duties in the market-place. The contests between different interpretations of the law of contract should therefore be understood as rival interpretations of the market order.

---

21   R Unger, *False Necessity* (Cambridge, 1987).
22   EC law imposes a degree of harmonization under the Treaty Articles 30, 36, 100, 100A, as interpreted in *Rewe-Zentral v Bundesmonopolverwaltung für Branntwein* (the *Cassis de Dijon* case) [1979] ECR 649, ECJ, but this does not prevent variations in trading conditions, as in the case concerning the opening of shops on Sundays: *Stoke-on-Trent City Council v B & Q plc* [1993] 1 All ER 481, ECJ. See Weatherill, '1992 and Consumer Law: Can Free Trade be Reconciled with Effective Protection?' (1988) 6 *Trading Law* 175. Now the position is regulated by Sunday Trading Act 1994; Maher, 'The New Sunday: Reregulating Sunday Trading' (1995) 58 *Modern Law Review* 72.

4. The Constitution of the Market

What role does the law play in constituting the market order? What place does the law of contract have in influencing behaviour in the market on a day-to-day basis? Two polar opposite views often dominate reflection on these questions. On the one side, it is argued that without the secure, calculable framework provided by the law of contract, then a market order could not exist. This is the Hobbesian presupposition that the indispensable function of the law of contract is to provide the necessary insurance against breach of promise, for without a legal sanction, each party might seek to cheat and renege on the transaction.[23] On the other side, however, it is observed that the vast majority of transactions are 'self-enforcing' in the sense that both parties will complete their side of the bargain out of self-interest. People do not think about the legal aspects, but simply get on with their business. The truth lies between these extreme positions.

Markets can certainly flourish in the absence of a legal framework and effective sanctions. A withholding of performance or an insistence upon payment in advance normally suffices to discourage sharp practice. A person who examines fruit on a market-stall simply declines to purchase the goods if he or she suspects poor quality or excessive price. A carpenter will be discouraged from performing shoddy work by the threat of a deduction from the agreed payment. Studies of business contractors reveal that the most important implicit threat which they have at their disposal consists of a refusal to trade in the future with a particular person or business.[24] As consumers, defection is also our only realistic threat, which is a hazard that shops which depend upon volume sales and repeat contracting such as supermarkets and chain stores take seriously enough to lead them to adopt policies of accepting returns of goods with no questions asked. In his study of the Trobriand Islanders, Malinowski describes how farmers and fishermen establish working trading partnerships without courts and recognizable legal sanctions; if a farmer fails to deliver fruit or yams, the fisherman simply declines to hand over a portion of the day's catch.[25] Stewart Macaulay recounts how there 'was

---

23 Thomas Hobbes, *Leviathan*, (Oxford, 1955) (first published 1651) at pp 89–90 '..he that performeth first, has no assurance the other will perform after; because the bonds of words are too weak to bridle men's ambition, avarice, anger, and other Passions, without the fear of some coercive power; which in the condition of her Nature, where all men are equal, and judges of the justness of their own fears cannot possibly be supposed..'

24 Beale and Dugdale, 'Contracts Between Businessmen: Planning and the Use of Contractual Remedies', (1975) 2 *British J of Law and Society* 45, p 48; Deakin, Lane, and Wilkinson, '"Trust" or Law? Towards an Integrated Theory of Contractual Relations between Firms' (1994) 21 *Journal of Law and Society* 329, 335; Klein and Leffler, 'The Role of Market Forces in Assuring Contractual Performance' (1981) 89 *Journal of Political Economy* 615.

25 B Malinowski, *Crime and Custom in Savage Society* (London, 1926).

a time when courts in the United States refused to enforce a contract in which the seller agreed to supply all of the buyer's requirements of particular goods'.[26] But the commercial community continued to make such requirements contracts regardless, no doubt because this form of commitment was commercially useful and adequately sustained by non-legal means. Even in more complex transactions, the parties may dispense with legal institutions if private organizations such as unions and trade associations arbitrate disputes and discipline their members. In the chartering of vessels through shipbrokers in London, for instance, the 'fix' is arranged by phone, the ship sails, and the 'paperwork' follows in the shape of a standard form charterparty, a practice sustained by the rules and standards established by membership of the Baltic Exchange. The diamond merchants of the Jewish community in New York City enter transactions of enormous value on the basis of a handshake, a practice sustained by the intense social ties of an immigrant community and supported by membership of a bourse and a system of private arbitration which relies on the risk of harm to business reputation for its effectiveness.[27] But do these observations support entirely the view that market transactions proceed independently of legal regulation, with the discipline of self-interest bringing the parties together and discouraging opportunism, leaving the law trailing along behind like the tail of a dog wagging in response to the stimuli of events?

If attention is turned to more complex transactions, such as the establishment of a partnership, a joint venture, or a long-term supply contract, then the role of the legal framework appears more central. In these transactions the parties are creating an institutional arrangement to govern their business dealings for the future. The law appears crucial in the process of constructing, refining, and enforcing that institution, so that both parties can count upon it as the foundation for their business relation in the future. The law of contract provides some of the essential tools for the construction of private institutions of governance between the parties. Yet it does not follow that once such institutions have been created that the legal framework will exclusively govern the business relation between the parties. On the contrary, the real dynamic of business co-operation in such relations will spring from the visible commitments of the parties to the success of the transaction such as specific investments, and the willingness to sacrifice immediate self-interest in favour of co-operation for the sake of maximizing joint gains and protecting business reputation in the long term.

In market transactions we can observe that the parties will orient their conduct towards a variety of sources of norms. In close, long-term business relations, the parties may well emphasise ideas of loyalty and

---

26   Macaulay, 'Elegant Models, Empirical Pictures, and the Complexities of Contract', (1977) 11 *Law and Society*, 507, at p 524.

27   Bernstein, 'Opting Out of the Legal System: Extralegal Contractual Relations in the Diamond Industry' (1992) 21 *Journal of Legal Studies* 115; Williamson, 'Calculativeness, Trust, and Economic Organization' (1993) 34 *Journal of Law & Economics* 453, 465.

co-operation, so that they expect from each other high moral standards of good faith in dealings. These norms are not legal requirements, but derive from social and moral discourses such as friendship and mutual respect.

> Businessmen often prefer to rely on 'a man's word' in a brief letter, a handshake, or 'common honesty and decency' – even when the transaction involves exposure to serious risks.[28]

Reference to the legal norms in this context might be interpreted as a betrayal of trust or a form of sharp practice. In other contexts, where the parties contemplate a single transaction with a distant stranger, they may discuss their relations and regulate their conduct exclusively according to legal norms specifying strict entitlements and obligations. In the social practice of market transactions, we should therefore expect to discover a variety of normative standards to which the parties refer in discussing their relation and considering their actions. These norms may compete for attention and the parties vacillate in their observance of different normative standards, at one time valuing co-operation and long-term business interests, and at others insisting upon their strict legal entitlements.[29] The move to insist upon a strict legal analysis of the relation or the dispute is likely to close down any further reference to norms of goodwill or co-operation between the parties, for it carries the implicit threat of a recourse to the power of the state to force observance of the contractual relations.[30] We should therefore expect that in many contexts that the parties will pay scant attention to their precise legal rights and obligations, a prediction which is often confirmed by observation of business practice.[31]

It is a mistake, however, to conclude from these findings that a market may exist independently of law. Although the parties to a transaction may refer to different sources of norms to guide their behaviour, these norms are influenced in their content by each other. The legal norms help to refine traditional or customary standards of trade, and equally the legal discourse seeks to accommodate accepted business standards of behaviour within its standards for regulating conduct. At the market-stall, the standards governing such issues as when performance is due and the quality of the goods to be provided depend upon both customary expectations and legal refinements. The law requires the goods to be of 'satisfactory quality', a standard which simultaneously reflects and endorses customary expectations, and yet depends upon those expectations

28 Macaulay, 'Non-contractual Relations in Business: A Preliminary Study' (1963) 28 *American Sociological Rev* 55, 58.
29 Collins, 'Competing Norms of Contractual Behaviour', in D Campbell and P Vincent-Jones, *Contract and Economic Organisation* (Aldershot, 1996) 67.
30 Macaulay, 'Organic Transactions: Contract, Frank Lloyd Wright and the Johnson Building' (1996) *Wisconsin Law Review* 75, 114.
31 Macaulay, 'Non-contractual Relations in Business: A Preliminary Study' (1963) 28 *American Sociological Review* 55; Beale and Dugdale, 'Contracts between Businessmen: Planning and the Use of Contractual Remedies' (1975) 7 *British Journal of Law and Society* 141.

for greater specificity in particular cases. On this view, the law becomes an essential ingredient in the market order, not because transactions could not take place without it, but because it supplies an authoritative determination of the standards to be observed in case of dispute, and supplies a discourse in which the detailed specification of standards can be articulated.

Even though the law constitutes the market order in this sense, it does not follow that legal sanctions play an important part in policing the market.[32] The parties may choose to disclaim legal obligations because they believe that the non-legal sanctions will be more appropriate and efficient in holding each other to commitments and resolving disputes.[33] Furthermore, few enjoy the time and resources to litigate, and most lack an incentive in view of the potential for self-help by simple refusals to perform. Commercial contractors will guide their actions by their business interests, which may rarely indicate the need to invoke legal sanctions rather than seek an accommodation of interests. Even here, the potential legal sanctions will probably not be employed, but rather provide the bargaining positions from which the parties can negotiate a settlement. If the suit is brought and proves successful, then unless the claim is for a simple money debt, the remedy of compensatory damages will normally fall short of any deterrent against breach, since the courts only compensate for the net unavoidable losses. A buyer of goods can only claim the difference between the contract price and the prevailing market price, which, if the market is competitive, should be minimal. The seller of goods can only claim the loss of the bargain if the goods cannot be sold to another at a similar price. 'The "net loss" approach also means that it is usually much cheaper for the defendant to break his contract than to perform it.'[34] Attempts to increase the level of the threat through penalty clauses will be defeated by the courts invalidating such terms. For most contracts, therefore, the legal sanction presents no credible threat.

Does the law of contract therefore serve little purpose when people seek to enter binding commitments towards each other? Must self-help in the form of a refusal to enter transactions in the future be regarded as the principal tool for binding people together in economic relations? The law of contract can supply other tools apart from brute sanctions. It can help the parties to make their commitments towards each other more credible despite the weakness of ordinary legal sanctions, and it can strengthen the threat posed by opportunities for self-help.[35]

The law plays a supplementary role in constructing mechanisms for self-help. It provides techniques for taking hostages against defective

32   Llewellyn, 'What Price Contract? – An Essay in Perspective' (1931) 40 *Yale Law Journal* 704.
33   Charney, 'Nonlegal Sanctions in Commercial Relationships' (1990) 104 *Harvard Law Review* 373.
34   Harris, 'Incentives to Perform, or Break Contracts' (1992) 45(2) *Current Legal Problems* 29, at p 34.
35   Collins, 'The Sanctimony of Contract' in R Rawlings (ed), *Law, Society, Economy* (Oxford, 1997) 63.

performance, and then, in the event of breach, the hostage can be executed. The hostages are called security: that is property rights such as a mortgage, a reservation of title clause, or a deposit. These property rights can be asserted unilaterally, without the co-operation of the party in breach of contract, in order to punish or compensate for default.[36] The law also supports the use of alternative dispute resolution mechanisms, such as arbitration, which lower the cost of litigation, and therefore can increase the likelihood of a legal sanction for breach of contract. The most important alternative dispute resolution technique is simply one of discipline provided by the rules of the contract, such as dismissal for employees, and acceleration clauses for debtors.

The law can also assist in constructing credible commitments. It produced the technique of guarantees provided by a wealthy third person, which more than doubles the chance of performance. International trade relied from the earliest times on transfers of money through negotiable Bills of Exchange, that is an offer of payment from a nominee trusted by the seller.[37] Attempts to enhance business reputation through misleading advertising or deceptive accounting can be policed and prohibited, so that the consumer can place greater confidence in information disseminated by businesses. Yet these devices and regulations amount to no more than marginal interventions in the market, for the law cannot confer a reputation for honesty and integrity on particular traders.

In relation to sanctions, therefore, the law of contract may not play a significant role in constituting the market order. Its principal function in this context will often be to permit the parties to establish arrangements under which there is no need to rely upon judicial sanctions at all. But the law of contract appears more important in its contribution to discourses governing the normative standards which the parties observe during negotiation and performance of contracts. It provides an authoritative point of reference for the resolution of disputes over the standards, and contributes to the specification of those standards. In so doing, the law articulates a detailed ideal of social justice in market relations by which people judge their behaviour and criticize others.

An interpretation of these legal ground-rules setting standards of behaviour during market transactions provides a representation of the scheme of distributive justice embedded in the market order. A fresh interpretation of those legal standards, the doctrinal expressions of fair trading and of justice in economic exchange, which alters our understanding of the market order and its implicit scheme of distributive justice, can claim in a sense to amount to a reconstitution of the market order itself. By altering our system of thought, thereby facilitating a new understanding of the economic sphere of social life, we can restate the legal doctrines, which in turn will serve to consolidate this new vision of

36 Llewellyn, 'What Price Contract? An Essay in Perspective' (1931) 40 *Yale Law Journal*, 704, at p 724.
37 F Braudel, *Civilization and Capitalism*, Vol ii, *The Wheels of Commerce*, trans S Reynolds (London, 1982), p 142.

the market order and its favoured distributive outcomes. This book will, I hope, make a contribution to the development of a new interpretation of the law's standards of fair trading and justice in economic exchange, for the traditional interpretation born in the nineteenth century, with its root understanding of the law of contract as facilitating voluntary choices, seems to me to provide only a blinkered and distorted vision of the composition of those standards today.

2

The Transformation of the Law of Contract

This chapter briefly describes the interpretation of the law of contract presented in this book. The claim advanced suggests that the modern law of contract differs from the classical tradition in its motivating ideals, in its methods of legal reasoning, and in its sources of law. When these differences are considered together, these developments amount to a transformation of the law of contract.

This discontinuity has been masked by the evolutionary pattern of legal developments. Change occurs through reinterpretation and differentiation rather than the invention of new principles of law. Reinterpretation of the law results from either redefinitions of basic legal concepts or the attribution of greater weight to principles which were occluded in the past. Traditional concepts such as consideration acquire new meanings rather than being abandoned or replaced. Alternatively, legal doctrines such as estoppel or undue influence acquire much greater force, so that they override traditional rules. Differentiation involves the exclusion of innovations from the canon of contract law, such as hiving off developments in consumer law or employment contracts. The transformation of the law of contract can only be perceived if the formal continuity of principle is examined in its practical applications and the process of differentiation is resisted. The perception of transformation can be enhanced by reorganizing the elaboration of the legal principles by reference to concepts which emphasize the themes of the modern law. The chapters of the book therefore invoke untraditional concepts such as fairness and co-operation which serve to highlight the thematic unity of the changes in the law.

The transformation thesis is controversial both as to its occurrence and as to its details. Most texts on the law of contract persist in an attachment to the organizing categories of the classical law. Changes in legal principle are described as refinements or qualifications. Differentiation of legal rules becomes rife, so that the most common types of market transactions such as a sale of goods to consumer are attributed with marginal significance. This denial of change has received a boost from the methodology of economic analysis of law, which both supplies a new rationale for the traditional principles of law in terms of efficiency and provides plausible accounts of the justifications for the modern qualifications in terms of market failure. Even for those interpreters of the law who acknowledge the case for transformation, there is marked disagreement about the themes which underlie the evolution of the law.[1] For some authors the alterations reflect merely a greater concern for the protection of consumers,[2] whereas others detect a more fundamental reorientation of the values expressed by the law moving from an emphasis on rights and freedom to a concern for needs and economic dependence.[3] In arguing the case for a particular interpretation of the transformation thesis, therefore, this book encounters critics on all sides.

1. The Social Market

A central element of the transformation thesis concerns the values which underlie the interpretation and application of the legal principles. A contrast can be drawn between the importance attached to the slogan 'freedom of contract' in the nineteenth-century law and the search in modern law to regulate the market so that it offers worthwhile opportunities and satisfies needs. Whereas the former value system emphasized the importance of individual choice, the modern law conceives markets as a collective good which requires steering, channeling, and supplementation. This contrast leads to different conceptions of contracts: the former regards contracts as a creation of individuals which is facilitated by the law; the latter regards contracts as structured obligations imposed by the law on people participating in markets.

(1) The Justice of Exchange
The governing ideal of the nineteenth-century law of contract is usually described as 'freedom of contract'.[4] This slogan was certainly a crucial political banner. It signified both a resistance to state interference in the economy and a desire to augment each individual's freedom of choice. It summarizes well some of the cardinal principles of the law: citizens enjoy a broad discretion to make contracts; the law routinely respects their choice of terms; and the voluntariness of their choices is protected against coercion and fraud. Yet respect for individual liberty comprises only one element in the ideals embedded in the Victorians' interpretation of the market order. In many respects, the ideal of individual liberty plays second fiddle to a deeper faith in the justice of an order of wealth and power established through exchange relations. This faith stems from the belief

---

1   T Wilhelmsson (ed), *Perspectives of Critical Contract Law* (Aldershot, 1993).
2   J Adams and R Brownsword, *Understanding Contract Law* (London, 1987).
3   T Wilhelmsson, *Critical Studies in Private Law* (Dordrecht, 1992).
4   P Atiyah, *The Rise and Fall of Freedom of Contract* (Oxford, 1979); L Friedman, *Contract Law in America* (Madison, 1965); M Horwitz, *The Transformation of American Law 1780–1860* (Cambridge, Mass, 1977), ch 6; D Miller, *Social Justice* (Oxford, 1976).

that the market order establishes both equality in place of social hierarchy and reciprocity instead of exploitation.

Equality
Unlike social orders which distribute wealth and power by reference to such criteria as social status, political power, physical force, or moral worth, the market order claims to respect the ideal of equality. Each person enjoys the same opportunity to enter any kind of transaction, and through trade to improve his or her lot in life. This market order achieves a great social levelling, since the distribution of wealth and power depends upon success in trading under the regime of contract law, not upon social rank or military might. People transfer commodities according to voluntary agreements, not under imposed laws of political fealty. The market mechanism for the allocation of wealth and power is therefore fit for a democratic republic.

The ideal of equality which lies at the root of this conception of the market order is not, of course, one which insists upon an egalitarian distribution of wealth and power. It is not concerned with the ultimate distributive consequences of trade. It is concerned rather with formal equality and a narrow view of equality of opportunity. Formal equality requires that each person enjoys the same set of rights to enter contracts and to own property. The narrow view of equality of opportunity insists that each person in principle should be permitted to enter into any branch of trade and thereby to improve his or her position without limit. The law recognized some exceptions to formal equality with respect to children and the insane, and, more controversially, married women, but in general the rhetoric of the law admitted no distinctions of rank and privilege in determining contractual rights and duties.

Within this perspective there seems to be no serious concern that freedom of contract might be used, in combination with ownership of scarce resources and superior technical knowledge, to achieve relations of domination which subvert the equality of citizens. The belief seems to be that, provided that a person has freely consented to the terms of the contract, then there could be no danger that the contract established unjustifiable positions of power. Under this analysis, for example, an employer's right to give orders to his employees and demand obedience on pain of dismissal rests upon consent at the moment of hiring and is restricted to the scope of the duties envisaged in the contract. Such a limited, consensual obligation apparently runs little risk of establishing unjustifiable domination. Questions about the effects of inequality of bargaining power upon the terms of contracts, and thus upon the nature of social relations established by contracts, seem to be ignored or suppressed. It is as if positions of unjustifiable power over others simply cannot arise within the framework of freely chosen agreements.

Distributive Justice
It is often overlooked that the nineteenth-century interpretation of the market order also proclaimed its fairness. The law insisted that only those

transactions which involved an exchange could be enforceable. Both parties should give up something of value in return for something which was desired. This requirement of reciprocity, as defined by the doctrine of consideration (which will be examined in Chapter 4), established a distinction between, on the one hand, enforceable market transactions which had to be bargains or exchanges, and, on the other hand, instances of expropriation, domination, and exploitation. The nineteenth-century lawyers perceived a vital difference between an employment relation where wages are paid and one where no remuneration is given; the former constitutes a bargain struck between equals from which both parties expect to benefit, whereas the latter smacks of slavery and extortion. From this perspective, the presence of reciprocal rights and duties guarantees the fairness of productive and distributive relations.

This idea of fairness does not ensure an exact equivalence in the value of the performance supplied by each party to the contract. The courts did not believe that it was either possible or desirable to test the balance of the bargain. It was impossible because value depends upon a subjective appreciation by each individual, which differs from one person to the next, so the court could only assume that parties entering a contract had accepted at that time the fairness of the exchange. Any such interference would also be undesirable, for it would undermine the reliability of bargains which had been struck and pose a threat to freedom of contract. But above all, such intervention was unnecessary, because the presence of a freely chosen exchange ensured that the bargain was fair. No one enters a transaction voluntarily unless he or she expects to benefit from it, so that every voluntary bargain must be fair, because it leaves each party better off than before.

Some limited intervention was necessary, however, to ensure the preservation of competitive markets. It is readily apparent that someone holding a monopoly over a scarce and valuable item of commerce might use that bargaining position to impose contracts which were scarcely distinguishable from expropriation. Legislation against combinations and cartels, combined with the judges' development of the doctrine of restraint of trade, tried to preserve a competitive market. In addition, some legislation prevented owners of monopolies such as railways from charging unfair prices. But these were limited and necessary interventions in order to uphold the general ideal that contractual exchanges established fair economic relations and distributive outcomes.

Absent from this conception of fairness in the market order is the possibility that the distributive consequences of freely chosen agreements could be unjust in any but a few isolated instances of foolishness and carelessness. The idea that large groups of people entering transactions in competitive markets might all suffer a diminution of their resources from concluding bad bargains is simply dismissed as absurd. Tenants who pay high rents, borrowers who accept exorbitant rates of interest, workers who settle for wages below subsistence levels, all have only themselves to blame for errors of judgement. Nor does this concept of the market order recognize any need for a distribution of wealth which protects people against poverty and hardship. In particular, the law of contract should not concern itself with the ultimate distributive consequences of the market order.

Freedom of Contract

The slogan of freedom of contract both summarized vital elements of these ideals of equality and fairness, and then added to them an interpretation of the kind of freedom which the state should establish and protect. This idea of freedom insisted that individuals should be given the choice whether to enter contracts or not, which ruled out compulsory contracts and other legally imposed duties, and that individuals should also enjoy the freedom to choose the terms of their agreements. This idea of freedom contains a negative element, which rejects the interference of the state in the terms of market transactions, but also a positive element, for it sees in the general licence to enter binding contracts an enhancement of freedom, because this facility permits new forms of co-operative endeavours which last over a period of time.

The adherence to the negative aspect of liberty could not be absolute without endangering the justice of the market order. Parties entering into contracts had to be protected against threats of violence and fraudulent misrepresentations, but this could be justified as an intervention designed to protect the genuineness of the choice to enter the contract. It also seemed possible, though unlikely, that a person might freely choose to enter a contract which permanently circumscribed liberty, as in the example of a contract of slavery, and in such instances the courts insisted that such contracts would be unenforceable. The courts also declined to enforce certain transactions on the grounds that they exhibited gross immorality or criminal behaviour; liberty of contract could not be permitted to become a licence to misbehave. But the limited nature of these exceptions to the general ideal of freedom of contract reveals how strongly this ideal informed interpretations of the just market order in the nineteenth century.

Liberty, equality, and fairness in reciprocity: these ideals make up the conception of the just market order expressed by the law of contract as it was originally conceived in the nineteenth century. For convenience, this interpretation of the market order which informed the values embedded in the law may be called 'the justice of exchange'.

(2) Efficiency and Market Failure

In contemporary legal writing, a similar interpretation of the law of contract is presented using rather different concepts and values drawn from economics.[5] The central value is efficiency, or, more precisely, wealth

---

5   V Goldberg, *Readings in the Economics of Contract Law* (Cambridge/New York, 1989); A Kronman and R Posner, *The Economics of Contract Law* (Boston/Toronto, 1979); R Posner, *Economic Analysis of Law* 4th edn (Boston/Toronto, 1992), ch 4; M Trebilcock, *The Limits of Freedom of Contract* (Cambridge, Mass, 1993).

maximization. The virtue of contracts is described as the opportunity presented by exchanges for both parties to enhance their wealth. If a transaction is freely chosen, then the motivation for the exchange in obtaining something of greater value to the purchaser will ensure that both parties will be better off. For the purpose of maximizing the wealth of society, the law of contract should respect and enforce the choices of parties to enter exchanges. Although the modern rhetoric differs, it supports the traditional interpretation of the law of contract. Freedom of contract is essential in order to ensure that the transaction does maximize wealth, though freedom of contract is now regarded as an instrumental value rather than a value in itself.

It is recognized in economic theory, however, that in many circumstances this ideal cannot be realized in practice. Individuals and businesses simply do not have the time or the resources to acquire all the necessary information and to plan every aspect of their economic arrangements through detailed agreements. Within these constraints, which may generically be called 'transaction costs', we should expect that in many instances agreements will be left seriously incomplete. Moreover, the impediment of transactions costs may lead to market failure in the sense that the parties may not enter into a wealth maximizing transaction by mistake. This result can occur, for example, where one party lacks vital information about market conditions or is unable to process the available information.

From this economic perspective, the law serves the useful regulatory function of overcoming the obstructions of transactions costs and preventing or reducing the occurrence of market failure. For incomplete contracts, the law can set 'default' rules to govern market relations to which the parties would have agreed themselves but for the impediment of transactions costs. To remedy market failure, the law can impose duties to disclose information or make it more accessible. In a consumer purchase of food, for instance, the law can establish 'default rules' about liability for food which is unhygienic, and can improve access to information for the consumer by requiring clear labelling of contents on the packaging. Far from interfering with freedom of contract, these interventions can be presented in economic analysis as facilitating freedom of contract for the purpose of wealth maximization.

This economic interpretation of the law of contract can, at a pinch, provide a plausible account of modern developments in the law. Although at first sight rules which impose compulsory terms in contracts, such as the duty on a seller to supply goods of satisfactory quality to a consumer, appear to impede freedom of contract and restrain wealth maximization, such rules can be explained as a necessary response to transactions costs and market failure. The consumer lacks the expertise to judge the quality of the product and can only obtain the necessary information and expertise at considerable expense. This results in market failure in consumer purchases of complex products, so that consumers acquire products which do not satisfy their preferences. The remedy lies in the compulsory term which restricts choice in order to protect the satisfaction of preferences.

These arguments always work as explanations of the interventionist character modern law both because transactions costs are omnipresent and unquantifiable, and because market failure is endemic. But they are weak explanations, because the economic arguments can always support lesser regulation or no regulation at all.

Advocates of this economic interpretation of the law of contract do not in fact support all modern restrictions on freedom of contract. On the contrary they identify certain interventions as undesirable and unjustifiable infringements of the market order. Price controls, for example, as occur sometimes in rented accommodation and minimum wages, will normally be rejected on the ground that these do not respond to a market failure, but in fact create a market failure themselves. By artificially lowering the price of rented accommodation, the law will reduce the supply, thereby creating a problem of homelessness. Similarly, by artificially raising the price of wages, the law reduces employers' demand for labour, which in turn creates the market failure represented by unemployment. By analogy, the desirability and justice of many other types of interference in free contracts may be questioned, such as the imposition of compulsory terms in leases and contracts of employment, on the ground that they cause a market failure which in the long run leaves everyone worse off than before. In short, compulsory terms, though occasionally justifiable as a last resort to handle market failures, often create a market failure themselves, so should normally be avoided.

Furthermore, market failure is always a matter of degree. It is only when it seriously undermines the wealth maximizing properties of exchanges that intervention is required. On this view, there can rarely be a case for intervention in contracts between businesses. In the absence of a market monopoly, we should assume that any disparities of knowledge and expertise between the parties have been acquired by diligence and investment. To disallow a party to benefit from such investments by making favourable transactions will seriously reduce the incentives to make such investments, which in the long run will make markets less efficient and reduce general welfare. Once the justification for legal intervention rests upon the degree of market failure, in the absence of any way of calibrating the degree of failure which will trigger intervention, then the economic analysis degenerates into a series of idiosyncratic assessments of how best wealth maximization may be achieved.

What adds particular bite to this economic interpretation of the modern law is the perception of a tension between the market order and the institutions of the Welfare State. It alleges that an excessive tax burden and the crowding-out effect of the state budget deficit needed to fund the welfare functions lead to disincentives to invest, employ, and work, and cause labour market rigidities and a psychology of dependence. This in turn stifles economic growth, which in the long run actually detracts from the welfare of society. The economic interpretation of the modern law of contract therefore claims not only to describe the values and principles of the market order, but also insists that they are necessary to achieve the maximum welfare of society.

(3) The Value of Autonomy

Like the paradigm of the justice of exchange, the market failure approach shares a disregard for problems of power, distributive fairness, and the need to encourage co-operation in the realization of market opportunities. Its system of understanding the market order confines attention to the process of economic exchange and an assessment of how best to facilitate its efficient operation as a mechanism for the generation of wealth. This represents a vital perspective on the market order, but this system of understanding seems to me to be impoverished in its appreciation of the issues raised by disputes.

Consider, for example, the case of the unknown songwriter in *Schroeder Music Publishing Co Ltd v Macaulay*.[6] This young composer agreed to give all his songs to a publisher for a period of five years, renewable at the option of the publisher, in return for royalties on published work but no promise to publish the work. The House of Lords declared the agreement void under the doctrine of restraint of trade, arguing that the weak bargaining position of the composer had led to an unfair agreement under which the publisher undertook minimal obligations in return for total commitment by the composer. If one considers this decision from the perspective of market failure, then it seems hard to justify. As Trebilcock argues,[7] there seems to have been a competitive market operating in this instance, with many music publishers competing for young talent. Nor can it be seriously suggested that the composer did not understand the terms of the agreement because they were too complex. In the absence of such grounds to suspect market failure, then the contract should be enforced, for any interference may disrupt the market opportunities for young composers in the future.

But these arguments, though sound in themselves, miss the real objections to this contract, which concern the dimensions of power, fairness, and co-operation, not the efficiency of the market. Because the composer's career was completely dependent upon the publisher's discretion for a period up to ten years, his degree of subordination to another represented an unjustifiable form of domination. The absence of an undertaking on the part of the publisher to publish any of his songs rendered the exchange too one-sided to be fair. In addition, because the composer could not terminate the agreement during its fixed period, he had no effective sanction against the publisher to ensure that at least it made reasonable efforts to bring the venture to fruition by publishing and promoting his work.

These three themes – the concern about unjustifiable domination, the equivalence of the exchange, and the need to ensure co-operation – which seem to me to motivate the decision in *Schroeder Music Publishing Co Ltd v Macaulay*, form the core of the interpretation of law of contract presented in this book. The emphasis upon these values in the modern

---

6   [1974] 1 WLR 1308, [1974] 3 All ER 616, HL.
7   Trebilcock, 'An Economic Approach to Unconscionability' in B Reiter and J Swan (eds), *Studies in Contract Law* (Toronto, 1980), p 379.

law signifies a new understanding and justification of the market order. It may be thought that the law's endorsement of those values represents the adoption of a socialist or communitarian political philosophy and a rejection of the market order, but this does not seem to me to be the case. The constitution of the market by reference to these values, as well as the traditional concerns for liberty and competitive markets, merely represents a new understanding of the market order and its justificatory principles, not a wholesale rejection of markets as the most efficient system for the satisfaction of wants.

The question of what political philosophy underpins this conception of the market order is more troublesome to answer. It cannot be the libertarian philosophies which underpin the justice of exchange paradigm, nor the wealth-maximization goal which seems to provide the main justification for the market failure interpretation. On the other hand, these values do not seem to be incompatible with certain liberal ideals, which seem to be sensible to attribute to legislators and judges as the basis for their unarticulated political assumptions.

Perhaps the core principle in this interpretation of the market order consists in a revised notion of liberty or autonomy.[8] Whilst one should celebrate the liberating potential of a market order, because it offers considerable choices of occupation and consumption, we should recognise that not all choices seem so worthwhile and deserving of approbation. For instance, choices to harm the environment, to injure one's own body, to sell one's property at far less than its market value, and to enter into economic relations which give others discretionary power over major aspects of one's well-being, do not seem to be valuable choices which the law should respect and protect. If so, then although the law should continue to support the facility of entering into binding commitments by voluntary choice, it should limit this facility to choices which are likely to prove worthwhile ways of pursuing one's life. The law can tolerate a considerable range of economic transactions and give the benefit of the doubt to activities which seem of little worth to most people, but the law sets limits to freedom of contract when the choices made do not appear worthwhile on any reckoning. In other words, the positive side of liberty, the ability to enter into binding commitments, is interpreted not as a general licence, but a power to be exercised for worthwhile purposes; and the negative aspect of liberty relaxes the constraints upon state intervention in the market to place limits on the types of contractual obligations which may be undertaken.[9]

Another way in which to make the same point is to interpret the modern law of contract as not regarding the market merely as a source of

---

8 Perhaps closest to J Raz, *The Morality of Freedom* (Oxford, 1986). For similar views, see Brownsword, 'Liberalism and the Law of Contract' (1988) 36 *Archives for Philosophy of Law and Social Philosophy* 86; Smith, 'Future Freedom and Freedom of Contract' (1996) 59 *Modern Law Rev.* 167.

9 Sunstein, 'Disrupting Voluntary Transactions', in J Chapman and J Pennock (eds), *Markets and Justice* (New York, 1989), ch 10.

preference satisfaction, but as an opportunity to augment and contribute to the meaning of a person's life.[10] The purchase of a house, for example, though certainly sharing a dimension of preference satisfaction, will often mean so much more to an individual, for it offers security, a home, and a base from which the rest of life may be organized. Similarly, the entry into a contract of employment will often mean more than simply the opportunity to earn cash for purchasing goods; it marks the entry into a career, the acquisition of status, and an opportunity to gain dignity and respect. To understand the realm of the market order merely in terms of preference satisfaction, as the sophisticated economic models tend to do, seriously misunderstands the significance of many market transactions.

When contracts have these qualities of contributing in important ways to meaning in a person's life, then the modern law of contract responds by securing that person's reasonable expectations. The concept of the social market appreciates how the market must be channeled and controlled to preserve its quality as an opportunity for the construction of meaning in a person's life. To perform this function so that the law can reflect in its standards the different meanings which may be derived from economic transactions, the unity of the law of contract must be sacrificed. Each type of transaction must be governed by its own distinctive standards, which seek to preserve and enhance the opportunities afforded by that type of transaction for the establishment of meaning.

Unjustifiable Domination

One derivation from this more complex notion of liberty or autonomy concerns the power relations developed through contractual relations. Under the principles of the justice of exchange, with its idol of freedom of contract, the potentialities of ownership and knowledge can be realized into oppressive forms of domination to the extent that lawyers can devise complex organizational structures in the form of exchange relations. The main constraint upon the facility for domination lies in the limits of one's ability to persuade others to bind themselves by way of contract. But here the discipline of economic necessity operates to provide compelling inducements to contract. Since the principal source of wealth lies in the market in the form of wages and profits, few can afford to remain aloof. Consequently, the law of contract lies at the intersection of the market and state power, and it uses the coercion of the latter to reinforce the discipline of the former.

One response to this risk of domination through contract is to limit freedom of contract to prevent persons from making such binding commitments. In some instances contractual rights will be superseded by a statutory framework of rights. For example, under English law an employee is granted a statutory right to challenge unfair dismissal from employment, which circumscribes the power of management to coerce

10   D Levine, *Needs, Rights and the Market* (Boulder, 1988).

the worker, and this right cannot normally be given up by contractual agreement. Although these rules still permit the individual to choose his occupation unfettered by law, they ensure that any choice will not be one which in effect establishes an unjustifiable level of subordination. In other instances mandatory terms shape the reciprocal obligations of the parties. Indeed, with little exaggeration, we can say that in most standard types of contracts made by ordinary persons, apart from the price, the parties have little choice over the terms of the agreement. The law adopts a number of model contracts, such as purchases, loans, employment, and leases, and describes a pattern for these economic relations which is imposed by a set of compulsory terms. For example, the seller of goods to a consumer must guarantee their quality and fitness for their normal purpose, and any attempt to limit or qualify this guarantee in the terms of the contract will be void. Although businesses still enjoy a greater measure of freedom when contracting amongst themselves, even here the courts have powers to control unreasonable terms inserted in standard form contracts, and through their interpretation of the terms of the contracts the courts may more subtly ensure conformity to unarticulated model agreements.

Another way in which to counter domination through contracts is to introduce a more substantive conception of equality. Although an ordinary consumer and a large business such as a retail chain store enjoy the formal equality to own property and enter bargains, it is clear that a business can often call upon much greater technical knowledge and legal expertise in order to secure favourable transactions. These disparities become particularly noticeable in complex transactions, as where the consumer requires a credit arrangement or a loan in order to complete the purchase, or when the item purchased involves complex technology as in the case of a car or electrical goods. But disparities appear in even a simple purchase of a can of beans at the supermarket, where the business is likely to have a much better understanding of the quality of the goods and the exact contents of the tin, which may include, besides the beans, various sauces, preservatives, colourings and so forth. The modern law recognizes these differentials in knowledge and expertise by introducing measures of consumer protection, and in so doing drops the presumption that citizens enter the market on equal terms. The credit arrangement must follow a prescribed explanatory form and cannot be extortionate; the seller of the car or electrical appliance must guarantee its quality, and the manufacturer will be liable for any injury caused to the purchaser; and the contents of the can of beans must be clearly labelled. The modern law replaces the commitment to formal equality by a recognition that each person enters the market from a different situation, and that to ignore those differences in knowledge, expertise, needs and command over resources is not to treat people equally but to treat unlike cases alike.

Behind these responses to unjustifiable domination lies a perception that the traditional separation between public and private spheres has become inadequate. Under the classical law, problems of power and domination were regarded as problems presented exclusively by the state.

The role of public law was to combat state power by subjecting government bodies to controls over the exercise of discretionary power. Once it is recognised that similar problems of power arise in the context of contractual relations, especially those contracts which establish organizations such as firms, trade unions, and trade associations, then the case for extending controls over discretionary power to such private relations becomes pressing. We therefore discover the courts and the legislature inserting rules into such organizations which require them to follow fair procedures, to exercise discretion rationally and for lawful purposes, and to respect the rights of individuals. In other words, concepts and values formerly present exclusively in public law are applied to market relations where the contracts establish the potential for domination.[11]

Fairness
A second derivation from this complex notion of liberty concerns the fairness of the price of exchanges. Although the law tolerates considerable disparity of prices, for this reflects the different values which people choose to place on opportunities, it is sceptical about choices which amount to contracts which set a price significantly above or below comparable market prices or under which most of the reciprocal promises seem illusory. Such a choice does not amount to a worthwhile exploration of market opportunities, unless, of course, it signifies that an outright gift was intended. Statutes also give the courts the power to revise or invalidate unfair transactions, either explicitly as in the case of extortionate credit bargains, or indirectly by monitoring whether the quality of the goods supplied lives up to the expected standard in the light of the price paid for them. The statutory power to invalidate unreasonable exemption clauses which limit or exclude liability for defective performance also contributes to equivalence in exchange, for it is no longer possible for one party to reduce drastically his or her obligations without a commensurate reduction in the price paid. Under the common law the courts deploy a battery of legal doctrines which tend to ensure an equivalence in exchange. When the circumstances surrounding the formation of contract signify the possibility of pressure or exploitation of a necessitous position or person's weak understanding of business, then the court will rely upon the unfairness of the terms of the contract, judged by reference to other similar market transactions and the degree of disadvantage to the weaker party, in order to impugn the validity of the contract under the doctrines of duress and undue influence. For example, in *National Westminster Bank plc v Morgan*,[12] in order to stave off repossession by a lender of a house jointly owned by

---

11   Blades, 'Employment at Will vs. Individual Freedom: On Limiting the Abusive Exercise of Employer Power', (1967) 67 *Columbia Law Review* 1404; H Collins, *Justice in Dismissal*, (Oxford, 1992) pp 185–192; Black, 'Constitutionalising Self-Regulation', (1996) 59 *Modern Law Review* 24.
12   [1985] AC 686, [1985] 1 All ER 821, HL.

husband and wife, which was threatened because the husband was unable to make loan repayments as his business was failing, the wife agreed to a new mortgage on the matrimonial home in return for a loan to pay off the existing debts. At the husband's request, the bank manager visited her at home, where she expressed the worry that the new mortgage would secure her husband's business liabilities to the bank. The manager reassured her, incorrectly, that this would not be the case, and she signed the documents. When the husband failed to repay instalments on the new loan, the bank foreclosed on the mortgage and sought possession of the house. The wife sought to have the transaction set aside on the ground of undue influence. This claim was ultimately rejected by the courts, for the judges doubted whether the manager had exercised sufficient influence over the wife or whether she had placed trust in him. But even supposing that she had, the court reasoned that the transaction was not to her manifest disadvantage, so there was no evidence that a relation of confidence had been abused. This decision makes it abundantly clear that in transactions where the parties are not dealing at arm's length, but where one party reposes confidence in the advice and judgement of the other, then serious unfairness in the transaction will provoke the avoidance of the contract. These developments in the law of contract signify an abandonment of the presumption of fairness in exchanges.

Co-operation

A third derivation from this complex notion of liberty concerns the relation between the individual and others. The underlying image of the individual in the ideals of the justice of exchange was one who was antagonistic towards others and who entered transactions solely for the sake of his or her own interests. Indeed, from this perspective, it is hard to find adequate justification for the enforcement of contracts against the will of the individual in the absence of clear economic harm to others. If, however, one regards the law of contract as offering an opportunity for entering into binding long-term commitments with others, an opportunity which augments the freedom of the individual, then one can argue that precise calculations of self-interest at every stage in the transaction should not be permitted to subvert the value of the institution of contracts. Instead, the law must impose certain duties of co-operation in the formation and performance of contracts, which reflect the need to secure reliable and worthwhile opportunities for market exchanges. These duties both expand and articulate the reciprocal duties implicit in a contractual relation.

Furthermore, this new interpretation of the relation between the individual and others introduces two kinds of limitations on the freedom to choose whether or not to enter a contract. In the first place, this freedom has been curtailed in order to ensure better equality of opportunity in the market. For this purpose, sex and race discrimination legislation deters refusals to enter contracts on the grounds of sex, marital status, race, nationality, and other motives which display a lack of respect for the equality of others. In *Quinn v Williams Furniture Ltd*,[13] a married woman agreed to purchase a three-piece suite of furniture, paid a deposit, and then requested a loan arrangement for the balance of the price. The shop assistant said that the loan could not be made without her husband signing a collateral personal guarantee for the loan as well. The Court of Appeal decided that, since a similar guarantee from a spouse would not have been demanded by the shop in the case of a loan to a married man, this constituted discrimination. This simple case illustrates how the modern law, though not requiring entry into contracts, does limit freedom by insisting, for the sake of equality of opportunity in the market, that offers should not discriminate between persons on grounds which signify a denial of the formal equality of citizens.

Secondly, the choice whether or not to undertake an obligation, though still a characteristic of contractual obligations, has in practice been significantly diminished by the expansion of alternative grounds for the imposition of obligations. The law of tort, for instance, implies a duty of care between manufacturers and ultimate consumers regardless of their choice. This liability for negligence may extend to many kinds of relations of economic dependence, which, though not established by agreement between the parties, nevertheless are regarded as entailing an obligation to take care. For example, the decision in *White v Jones*[14] illustrates how a solicitor who negligently fails to draft a Will with the consequence that the testator's intentions are frustrated, will be held liable to the intended beneficiaries to the extent of their expected inheritance. Although the solicitor never entered a contract with these beneficiaries, he or she nevertheless owes them a similar duty to take care as that established in the contractual relation with the testator. The precise ambit of such tortious duties of care between parties who have not made agreements or bargains remains controversial, but the possibility of liability in tort in order to protect economic interests represents a major invasion of the freedom of individuals from obligations without their consent.

The above argument claims that the modern themes in the law of contract which I have identified as constituting a transformation in the market order may be derived from a sophisticated version of liberalism which relies upon a perfectionist conception of liberty or autonomy. It suggests that the modern law of contract should be understood by an examination of themes such as restrictions on the scope of contracts, mandatory terms, fairness, co-operation, and imposed duties of care and responsibility. Yet this interpretation fails to account for all the dimensions of the transformation. A second element of the values underlying the transformation turns its attention to collective interests.

13   [1981] ICR 328, CA.
14   [1995] 2 AC 207, [1995] 1 All ER 691, HL.

(4) Collective Interests and Public Goods

By delegating to individuals the choice of how to lead their lives, the market seeks to realize the value of autonomy, but at the same time the market risks both itself and collective interests.

The market creates a risk to its own competitiveness by permitting business practices and contracts which seek to insulate traders from competition. To combat that risk the law must regulate market practices in order to eliminate deceptive and misleading practices, to assist the transparency of the variety of market opportunities, and to discourage the formation of cartels. To this extent the market failure analysis of the modern law has to be accepted. Where my interpretation of the law differs is in its understanding of the extent to which legal intervention for this purpose is necessary. Once the purpose of competitive markets is conceived not merely in terms of preference satisfaction, but also as the potential site for the construction of meaning, then the nature and scope of practices which harm the market broadens. With respect to requirements to disclose information, for instance, the absence of a duty to disclose information about a particular product applied across the board to all traders could be regarded as establishing a fair competitive market. But the absence of information could seriously disadvantage consumers who wish to understand the properties of the goods in question in order to evaluate their worth to them. A competitive market in this sense is one which makes available all the information necessary for meaningful choices to be made by consumers. This requirement expands the scope of regulation by broadening the concept of deceptive practices in contracting and insisting upon greater transparency in the identification and explanation of market opportunities.

A free market in which the only binding norms are those created by contracts also creates the risk of destructive competition. For example, although employers all require employees with training and skills, it is usually cheaper for each employer to acquire employees with the necessary education already rather than to pay for the costs of training. Interventions in contractual relations can prevent these kinds of risks. Indeed, the establishment of standards for products and services, training boards to improve the skills of the workforce, quality assurance methods for ensuring efficient management, and the dissemination of expertise provide vital ingredients for a dynamic economic system.[15] The establishment of such collective standards helps to create the necessary trust on which to found an innovative economy. It requires complementary restrictions on freedom of contract to prevent the subversion of collective standards by individualized transactions.

The market also runs the danger that the system of individualized transactions will fail to take sufficient account of other kinds of social

---

15 Deakin, Lane, and Wilkinson, '"Trust" or Law? Towards an Integrated Theory of Contractual Relations between Firms', (1994) 21 *Journal of Law and Society* 329, 345; Zucker, 'Production of Trust: Institutional Sources of Economic Structure, 1840–1920', (1986) 8 *Research in Organizational Behaviour* 53.

goals, such as a collective interest in a healthy environment or the safety of individuals. To protect such collective interests, the law may have to forbid certain types of contracts or terms in contracts, or it may have to render other contracts obligatory or insist that certain terms should become compulsory in contracts of a particular type. The manipulation of contracts in these ways is often designed to transfer the risk of harm back onto one of the contracting parties, which should either deter unjustifiable risks, or at least secure adequate compensation for those harmed. This reallocation of risk therefore challenges the freedom to enter contracts and to select the terms.

One of the major social goals of twentieth-century western societies has been the relief of hardship and poverty through the Welfare State. Can the transformation in the law of contract be attributed in part to a concordance with the distributive aims of the Welfare State?[16] The provisions of the Welfare State are designed primarily to reduce the possibility that, under a market order, many members of society will fail to achieve the economic conditions under which individual liberty can be a worthwhile experience. For this purpose the state tries to satisfy everyone's basic needs, such as food, clothing, and shelter, in order to establish the basic conditions for human dignity and flourishing. In place of a negative concept of liberty which requires the state to minimize its regulation of social life to protect individual freedom, modern societies place greater emphasis upon fairness in the distribution of wealth, in order to provide the necessary conditions for the positive enjoyment of that freedom. These concerns have influenced the development of the law of contract, giving greater impetus to the themes of control of unjustifiable power and fairness in exchange. But there is little sign that the major doctrines of contract law have bent much further towards responding to social needs as opposed to their normal concern to protect entitlements.[17] The Welfare State used as its primary instruments the law of taxation and social security, not the law of contract, and the law of contract has not been used to construct a market order which avoids the risk of poverty. At most we may discover a concordant pattern in these two spheres of politics, so that developments in the law of contract were perceived as compatible with and supportive of the goals of the Welfare State.

2. Materialization and Differentiation

The second element of the transformation of the law of contract concerns the method of legal reasoning. Of course the basic elements of legal reasoning have remained constant. The courts follow precedent, apply

---

16   Rehbinder, 'Status, Contract, and the Welfare State', (1971) 23 *Stanford Law Rev.* 941; R Brownsword, G Howells, and T Wilhelmsson (eds), *Welfarism in Contract Law* (Aldershot, 1994).
17   Compare: T Wilhelmsson, *Critical Studies in Private Law* (Dordrecht, 1992).

statutes, and distinguish cases on their facts. Nevertheless, there has been a shift in the scope of reasoning and the complexity of the system of classification. The scope becomes broader as the courts acknowledge the relevance of a greater diversity of considerations. The system of classification becomes complex as different types of contractual relation receive differentiated treatment. In short, the formalism and unity of the classical law is replaced by contextual legal reasoning.

(1) Formalism and Unity

We observed in Chapter 1 that in the nineteenth century the common law defined its conception of the law of contract in a simple set of rules. These rules comprised categories with logical relations between themselves. The application of these categories with their logical implications to the facts of a dispute determined the result. For example, for an enforceable contract the law required an agreement, comprised of an offer by one party and an acceptance by the other, so that the absence of either element prevented a binding agreement from arising.

We examined this rule-governed and conceptual style of reasoning in the case of *Carlill v Carbolic Smoke Ball Co*.[18] Recall how in that case the court's reasoning towards the conclusion that the promise to pay £100 was enforceable proceeded by listing the requirements of an enforceable contract, and then ticking them off as each was satisfied on the facts. Similarly, the general test of enforceability for contracts, the doctrine of consideration, received an abstract statement in the form of a rule:

> The general rule is, that an executory agreement, by which the plaintiff agrees to do something on the terms that the defendant agrees to do something else, may be enforced, if what the plaintiff has agreed to do is either for the benefit of the defendant or to the trouble or prejudice of the plaintiff. If it be either, the adequacy of the consideration is for the parties to consider at the time of making the agreement, not for the court when it is sought to be enforced.[19]

The formalism of the law of contract probably contributed to its certainty and predictability, which were desirable features for the law governing an expanding market economy.[20]

As a style of legal reasoning, legal formalism does not prevent the insertion of moral and political values into law. On the contrary, the technical rules are but clues to the submerged principles of the law, and it is these principles which express the governing ideologies of the legal control over the market order. Moreover, in the application of the rules to the particular facts of cases, the courts could manipulate the results for instrumental purposes. The *Carlill v Carbolic Smoke Ball Co* case itself illustrates this, for the court had to strain the requirements of offer and

---

18   [1893] 1 QB 256, CA.
19   Blackburn J, *Bolton v Madden* (1873) LR 9 QB 55, 56.
20   M Weber, *Economy and Society* (G Roth and C Wittich (eds), Berkeley, 1968), Vol 2, ch 8, esp pp 687-688; Cotterrell, 'The Development of Capitalism and the Formalisation of Contract Law' in B Fryer et al (eds), *Law, State and Society* (London, 1981).

acceptance in order to conclude that, even in the absence of direct communication by the plaintiff with the manufacturer, they had in fact reached an agreement. Nevertheless, the underlying values and purposes of the rules and their manipulation for instrumental purposes was rarely acknowledged by the courts. They preferred to dispose of a case by reference to a narrow technical rule, without venturing into the field of basic principle or considering openly the consequences of the decision. This method conformed to a narrow conception of the political authority of judges under the Rule of Law, in which their job is, in principle, to enforce the law, not to create it. The judiciary seeks to appear neutral between conflicting interest groups and competing conceptions of the good life. This conception of the judicial role in developing the law of contract leads the courts to refer extensively to precedent, to present the law as a logical elaboration of ancient principles, and to frame the rules in terms avoiding reference to group interests.

During the development of this classical scheme of rules, the courts were not confronted with the whole range of contractual disputes. For the most part, these technical rules were designed to cope with disputes between persons who actually litigate, which generally means businesses in the course of a series of commercial transactions rather than private individuals. The character of this site for the development of the classical rules had a number of consequences. The language of the technical rules savours of the world of commerce rather than consumer purchases. The categories of the law, such as offer and acceptance, presuppose a situation where the parties negotiate the details of their contract and reach a firm conclusion, rather than the more casual, everyday contracts, such as boarding a bus or purchasing a can of beans. As Lord Wilberforce has observed:

> It is only the precise analysis of this complex of relations into the classical offer and acceptance, with identifiable consideration, that seems to present difficulty, but this same difficulty exists in many situations of daily life, e.g. sales at auction; supermarket purchases; boarding an omnibus; purchasing a train ticket; tenders for the supply of goods; offers of rewards; acceptance by post; warranties of authority by agents; manufacturers' guarantees; gratuitous bailments; bankers' commercial credits. These are all examples which show that English law, having committed itself to a rather technical and schematic doctrine of contract, in application takes a practical approach, often at the cost of forcing the facts to fit uneasily into the marked slots of offer, acceptance and consideration.[21]

More importantly, the common context of the decisions in business disputes permitted the insistence upon a unified law of contract. No matter what the substance of the transaction, nor the nature of the parties concerned,

---

21   Lord Wilberforce, *New Zealand Shipping Co Ltd v A M Satterthwaite & Co Ltd (The Eurymedon)* [1975] AC 154, [1974] 1 All ER 1015, PC.

the general rules applied. The doctrine of consideration was the test of enforceability, for instance, regardless of whether the dispute concerned a transaction for the import of a valuable commodity, a loan from a bank, a claim of a reward offered in a newspaper, or an informal social agreement. The law of contract was conceived as an abstract and general set of rules applicable to all transactions.

If we tie together these strands of the classical form of the law of contract, we find an unusual legal knot. The law comprises a unified set of formal rules which eschews any claims to a moral vision and which systematically suppresses as irrelevant questions about the distribution of wealth and power. The rules are technical, tied to precedent, and can be expanded by appeals to logic and rationality. Judges express the rules in the discourses of commerce and tend to describe all obligations in monetary values. This combination indubitably possesses a peculiar fascination for lawyers, particularly professors of law, for it presents a challenge for which raw intellect suffices. To write a classical treatise on contracts apparently involved no political or moral judgements; instead, the patient application of logic to the learning generated by reading precedents would reveal the majesty of the law of contract. The subject became the ideal instrument for acquainting students with the desired autonomous modes of legal reasoning and the sparring ground for the most talented lawyers of the age.

(2) Materialization and Differentiation
In contrast, legislatures have often provided the decisive innovations which constitute the modern law of contracts. Legislators can select openly between competing distributions of wealth and power. A legislature may treat types of contracts distinctly and is capable of discriminating between persons. It can identify consumers, employees, and tenants as categories of persons which deserve protection from the relations of domination established by freedom of contract. This differentiation between types of contracts and the character of the parties to contracts is incompatible with the unity of classical contract law.[22] Many texts therefore limit their discussion of legislation to footnotes or tailpieces to chapters, and in the classroom the legislative interventions usually produce separate courses altogether on such matters as consumer law, landlord and tenant, and employment law. But these methods of accommodating legislative innovations ignore their real impact on the general principles of the law of contract, for they demand a reconsideration of the fundamental assumptions of the classical model.

The novel legislative standards often delegate considerable discretion to the courts, because the laws often employ imprecise concepts such as reasonableness, fairness, good faith, and unconscionability, the meaning

22   J Wightman, *Contract: A Critical Commentary* (London, 1996) ch 8.

of which must be elaborated in the ordinary run of cases.[23] Judges often find this task uncomfortable for it requires them to regulate market practices and to impose moral judgments on the behaviour of the parties. To avoid this difficulty, judges tend to appeal to normal practices in the market-place to define standards of reasonableness and fairness. This weakens the impact of legislation, for it restricts the proscriptions of legislation to unconventional practices and perhaps indirectly legitimizes those standard practices which the legislation was designed to reform.

In order to overcome this judicial inhibition, legislatures sometimes vest the task of interpretation in special courts such as rent tribunals, labour courts and trade commissions, though this technique enjoys only limited success in altering the behaviour of adjudicators. Perhaps of greater significance for the regulation of markets, legislation commonly vests agencies with considerable powers to fix the terms of contracts on which monopoly industries may deal with others. In addition, under the Fair Trading Act 1973 the Director General of Fair Trading has the power to initiate a legislative process to establish regulations to govern the contractual practices of particular trades and professions, and to initiate court procedures against the conduct of business in a manner which is detrimental to the interests of consumers. Many trading and professional sectors also acknowledge the authority of self-regulatory bodies to determine the content of their contracts and to regulate practices.

To a limited extent the courts have also participated in the elaboration of common law principles which fit better the modern values presaged by legislation. Their contribution has been limited, however, because they remain committed to the unity of the law of contract. They have resisted differentiation of the law according to context, so they have deprived themselves of a crucial tool in legal reasoning. For example, they could not distinguish between exclusion clauses in consumer contracts and in commercial contracts, so that they failed to create any protection for consumers against the deprivation of legal rights in the small print of standard form contracts. On the whole, lawyers prefer their legal doctrines to be stirred but not shaken.

Despite these important changes in the form of the law of contract, it is fair to say that they can easily be overlooked because the features of the bulk of litigated cases remain similar to those which provided the forge for the classical law. If a study of the law of contract is confined to

---

23   Some authors suggest that there is a connection between the values of the modern law and its form, particularly this dimension of materialization: Kennedy, 'Form and Substance in Private Law Adjudication' (1976) 89 *Harvard Law Review* 1685; Adams and Brownsword, 'The Ideologies of Contract' (1987) 7 *Legal Studies* 205; Cockrell, 'Substance and Form in the South African Law of Contract' (1992) 109 *South African Law Journal* 40. Although there have been important concordances between changes in form and substance, these homologies seem to be contingent facts rather than logical relations: M Kelman, *A Guide to Critical Legal Studies* (Cambridge, Mass, 1987), ch 1. For example, our discussion of the case *Carlill v Carbolic Smoke Ball Co* in the previous chapter revealed that it was consumerist in orientation, but strictly formal, judge-made rules in its discourse.

the reported decisions of higher courts of appeal, then the cases usually involve commercial organizations locked into disputes over large sums of money. To resolve these disputes the courts still rely heavily on the classical rules of the law of contract. But, of course, this gives a misleading picture of the law of contract as a whole. Even in commercial litigation, however, we can discern significant adjustments to the style of legal reasoning employed by the courts. There is an unwillingness to apply the 'marked slots' of the classical categories without regard to the consequences of classification of the facts. Moreover, the relevant legislation often forces courts even in commercial disputes to have regard to looser terminology, such as standards of 'unconscionability' and 'reasonableness'.

Looking generally at the form of contract law we observe that, whereas the classical law assumes a style of autonomous legal reasoning, the modern law fails to draw a bright line between legal, political, and moral argument. Legal discourse has shifted from a rhetoric of entitlements determined by the application of general rules to the facts of a case, to one of consequentialist reasoning and a balancing of moral values. This 'materialization' of the modern law of contract[24] both breaks down the generality of the rules by devising norms appropriate to specific classes such as consumer and employee, and it challenges the closed quality of formal legal reasoning by compelling courts and regulators to confront the social and economic consequences of their decisions in their interpretation of the law. To grasp the transformation of legal thought and reasoning about contractual disputes which the modern law of contract engenders, we must abandon the old legal categories focused on entitlement and replace them with an articulation of the values and policies pursued by modern legal discourse. In order to capture the spirit of the modern law, instead of listing a set of rules which can be applied mechanically to resolve contractual problems, this book must present the dominant values which inform and direct legal reasoning.

3. Globalization and Sources of Law

The third aspect of the transformation of the law of contract concerns the sources of law. The classical law was linked to the nation state. Each nation developed its own closed system of doctrine using distinctive concepts and rules. This insularity is breaking down under the globalization of markets and the evolution of international political structures to regulate such markets. This expands the sources of the law of contract to encompass rules emanating from transnational legal orders. Furthermore it accelerates the development of legal orders which are to a considerable degree autonomous from any political origin.

---

24 R Unger, *Law in Modern Society* (New York, 1976), pp 192–216; G Teubner (ed), *Dilemmas of Law in the Welfare State* (New York/Berlin, 1988); J Habermas, *Between Facts and Norms* (Cambridge, 1996) ch 9.

(1) Sources in National Law

The insularity of the classical law did not prevent each legal system from having a rich set of sources of law. The rules could be derived from the variety of jurisdictions within the national legal order, such as specialist commercial courts. In common law jurisdictions, such as England and the United States, the rivalry between common law courts and Chancery permitted the evolution of contrasting legal principles. When the jurisdictions were fused in the late nineteenth century, the law of contract had to integrate into the doctrinal system both distinctive equitable doctrines such as undue influence, estoppel, and relief from penalties, and also special equitable remedies such as specific performance and rescission. The process of integration continues to this day, and provides judges occasionally with the opportunity to seize upon the fertile principles of equity to justify some modern departure from classical precedents.

As well as separate courts, the classical law drew upon the intellectual resources provided by historical antecedents and comparative studies. The common law judges transplanted many doctrines, like the ideas of mistake, frustration, and tests for the measurement of damages, from the scholarly tradition of natural law, whose own intellectual roots lay in Roman Law, but which culminated in the readily available Napoleonic Civil Code. These transplants overlapped with existing common law concepts, provoking some confusion and inconsistency.[25]

(2) Transnational Legal Orders

Despite this diversity, the law of contract remained tied to the political authority of the nation state. With the advent of greater international trade and the creation of free trading blocks such as the single market of the European Union, the source of legal regulation of markets now includes transnational legal orders.

A typical example concerns the rules governing the legal system applicable to contracts. For international transactions the question of which legal system applies to the contract is determined by the Contracts (Applicable Law) Act 1990. But this national statute merely incorporates the standards agreed in an international convention, the Rome Convention 1980 on the Law Applicable to Contractual Obligations. This convention is itself supplemented by European Community rules which create exceptions for particular kinds of contracts.[26] The English courts have to produce interpretations of this law which conform to the interpretations placed upon it by other courts. Although English commercial law has been slow to adopt such international conventions through legislation,[27] in the long term the globalization of the economic system is likely to compel accession.

---

25   Simpson, 'Innovation in Nineteenth-Century Contract Law' (1975) 91 *Law Quarterly Review* 247; Nicholas, 'Rules and Terms – Civil Law and Common Law' (1974) 48 *Tulane Law Review* 946.

26   Directive 92/49, 18 June 1992, OJ L 228/1, Art 31, which imposes a mandatory duty of express notification of choice of law clauses in insurance contracts.

27   Steyn, 'A Kind of Esperanto?' in P Birks (ed), *The Frontiers of Liability*, Vol 2 (Oxford, 1994) 11, discussing the Vienna Convention on Contracts for the International Sale of Goods to which most of the EU, North America, and Australasia are already signatories.

For English law, the most important development in transnational regulation of markets has been the creation of the single market of the European Community. The scope of European regulation has expanded from the elimination of obvious barriers to trade between member states to include more subtle impediments such as the diversity in the laws of contracts. If this diversity inhibits trade within the single market, as it may, then there is a case for devising a European uniform law of contract,[28] or at least to seek approximation of the laws. As a first step along such a road, a series of directives has sought the harmonization of the legal rules governing consumer transactions in member states. The need for harmonization is arguably the greatest in consumer transactions, for uniform laws prevent regulatory competition which causes each state to minimize the legal obligations imposed on businesses in order to attract investment and trade.[29] Directives of the European Community have to be implemented by each member state in national legislation, but the European source of the regulation will require the courts in each jurisdiction to ensure that their interpretations conform to the common pattern. For the future, therefore, European law will become a crucial determinant of the evolution of the law of contract in the United Kingdom. What effect will this transnational regulation have on the common law of contract?

Will the values contained in directives coincide with the ambitions of the social market described earlier in this chapter, or will the values differ? Since the driving force of the single market comprises the enhancement of competition by breaking down barriers to entry into markets, there is certainly a risk that laws which restrict choice in entering contracts and promote social goals will be regarded as obstructions to competition. For the time being, however, this danger has been avoided by framing directives as minimum standards rather than compulsory levels of

28 O Lando and H Beale, *Principles of European Contract Law, Part 1: Performance, Non-performance and Remedies,* (Dordrecht, 1995); Beale, 'Towards a Law of Contract for Europe: the Work of the Commission on European Contract Law', in G Weick (ed), *National and European Law on the Threshold to the Single Market,* European University Studies, Vol 1347 (Frankfurt am Main, 1993); Hartkamp et al (ed), *Towards a European Civil Code* (Nijmegen, 1994); O Lando, 'Principles of European Contract Law' (1992) 56 *RabelsZ* 261.

29 T Bourgoigne and D Trubeck, *Consumer Law, Common Markets and Federalism in Europe and the United States* (Berlin/New York, 1987); Community Consumer Action Programmes, OJ C92/1 (25 April 1975); OJ C133/1 (3 June 1981); European Commission, *A New Impetus for Consumer Protection Policy* (Luxembourg, 1985); Reich, 'Protection of Consumers' Economic Interests by the EC' (1992) 14 *Sydney Law Rev.* 23; Maastricht Treaty on European Union, 7 February 1992, Art 3(s), Titles XI, XVIII; Weatherill, '1992 and Consumer Law: Can Free Trade be Reconciled with Effective Protection?' (1988) 6 *Trading Law* 175; Reich, 'Competition between Legal Orders: A New Paradigm of EC Law?' (1992) 29 *Common Market Law Review* 861; R Buxbaum, G Hertig, A Hirsh, K Hopt (eds), *European Business Law: Legal and Economic Analysis on Integration and Harmonization* (Berlin, 1991); Trachtman, 'International Regulatory Competition, Externalization, and Jurisdiction' (1993) 34 *Harvard International Law Journal* 47; Collins, 'Good Faith in European Contract Law' (1994) 14 *Oxford Journal of Legal Studies* 229.

protection. There remains the deeper question whether the gradual replacement of common law by transnational regulation poses a challenge to the cultural identity of regions within the single market.[30]

The directives often include concepts drawn from other national legal orders, such as the reference to the concept of good faith in the Directive on Unfair Terms in Consumer Contracts 1993.[31] English courts must insert this concept into the common law, giving it the meaning which it acquires in the European legal order, yet at the same time reconciling it with the doctrines of the common law. Its meaning in many national legal orders such as Germany can only be expressed by broad concepts such as unconscionability or unfairness. We have noted that such standards were alien to the classical law of contract, and, though they are incipient standards in the modern law, they have not been accepted as governing principles. European regulation therefore promises the insertion of new doctrinal principles into the common law, which may prove a liberating and productive force for change.

Even more puzzling is the question whether the introduction of European regulation, which may even extend to a European Code of contract law,[32] poses a challenge to the form of legal reasoning? Since the common law lacks a codified law of contract, its method of reasoning has never attained the same level of formalism as civil law systems. The formulation of rules derives from generalizations about previous decisions, so the description of the rule can always be reconsidered and qualified. The canon of rules is never fixed in the common law, for earlier lines of authority can be permitted to atrophy or can be resuscitated. The challenge posed by European regulation is that these pragmatic and inductive qualities of common law legal reasoning will be inhibited under the influence of the formal deductive style of reasoning characteristic of legal systems governed by Codes.[33]

(3) Commercial Legal Order

Beyond transnational legal regulation, international business transactions have always forged their own miniature legal orders. The first step in this development was the creation of commercial standard form contracts, which through their elaborate provisions created a novel set of legal relations suited to international trade. These contracts such as Bills of Exchange and bankers' commercial credits often fitted uneasily into the traditional doctrinal fabric of national contract law. They were designed to bind together numerous parties and to create a system of credit, and these objectives could not always be achieved consistently with the ordinary rules of contract law such as the doctrines of consideration and

---

30   Collins, 'European Private Law and the Cultural Identity of States' (1995) 3 *European Review of Private Law* 353.
31   93/13, 5 April 1993, OJ L 95/29, 21 April 1993.
32   Resolution of the European Parliament on the Harmonization of Certain Sectors of the Private Law of the Member States, OJ C 205/518, 6 May 1994.
33   Legrand, 'Against a European Civil Code' (1997) 60 *Modern Law Review* 44.

privity of contract. Recognizing the utility of these types of documents, however, English courts routinely gave effect to the intentions of these documents, either brushing aside doctrinal difficulties or inventing special categories of exceptions such as 'negotiable instruments' which could transfer contractual rights with the minimum of formality. But these commercial contracts remained tied to the national legal order insofar as they required state courts to supply effective sanctions.

The connection with national legal orders becomes more attenuated once the contracts allocate jurisdiction to arbitration tribunals. In effect the parties select their own judges, and define the mechanism by which the arbitrators may enforce sanctions. This development permits the arbitrators to draw upon sources of law which are not tied to a particular legal order. The parties to the contract may instruct the arbitrator to use the guidance of a code of rules specially devised for international business transactions. As international arbitration of commercial disputes becomes more common, the practice is developing its own standards which supplement any rules selected by the parties, but which are not based upon any national legal system specifically.[34] In this context, it is only the final sanction which must be backed by state power, but the remaining sources of law regulating the transaction derive from non-state, depoliticized institutions and customs. Where the effective sanction is exclusion from a private association such as a particular exchange or trading market then even this tenuous connection with state law is sundered.

This form of private ordering is sometimes called a *lex mercatoria*. Whether or not it should be regarded as a separate source of law governing international contracts remains a controversial issue. Since its standards remain ultimately dependent upon state sanctions for their enforcement, it can be discounted as merely an elaborate form of contract regulated ultimately by state law. On the other hand, to the extent that the standards applicable to the contracts derive from other sources such as conventions, customs of business, rules of private associations, then it can be regarded as an independent source of legal regulation of contracts.

---

34   Teubner, 'Global Bukowina: Legal Pluralism in the World Society', in G Teubner (ed), *Global Law Without A State*, (Aldershot, 1997) 3; Mertens, 'Lex Mercatoria: A Self-applying System Beyond National Law?', in G Teubner (1997) *ibid* 31; B Cremades, 'The Impact of International Arbitration on the Development of Business law', (1983) 31 *American Journal of Comparative Law* 526.

3

Tests of Enforceability

Should the law enforce all transactions? In a market economy, which depends for its success upon the prolific exchange of goods and services, we expect the law of contract to enforce nearly every undertaking. Although this proves correct in general, the law requires the transaction to comply with both formal and substantive tests of legal enforceability. In this chapter we consider the purposes served by these tests of enforceability, before turning in subsequent chapters to an examination of the details of these tests.

1. Purposes of Tests of Enforceability

Tests of enforceability determine the scope of legally enforceable transactions. The tests play a role, therefore, in the legal constitution of markets. An agreement which does not satisfy the tests of enforceability might nevertheless be observed by the parties. They might conform to their agreement due to a sense of moral obligation, or from a fear of threats or a loss of reputation for fair dealing, or for some other kind of pragmatic reason. But failure to comply with the legal tests of enforceability removes the potential advantage of legal support for the transaction. Why does the law insist upon tests of enforceability which have the effect of excluding legal support for some voluntary undertakings?

Consider some illustrations which point to the need to confine the law of contract. In the first case a man agrees with his wife to wash up the dishes if she will go out and do the grocery shopping. On her return she discovers that her husband has failed to stir himself from in front of the television. Should she be able to sue her husband for breach of contract? In a second case, a politician agrees to cast his or her votes according to the instructions of a large multinational corporation in return for money to fund an expensive lifestyle. Should the multinational be permitted to sue the politician when he or she disobeys instructions? In both of these instances the persons concerned reach an agreement, one which has been freely chosen, and from which they expect to benefit. Yet it seems unlikely that any legal system would regard these agreements as legally enforceable. In the first illustration, a court would simply decline to become involved in this matrimonial dispute.[1] In the second instance, not only would the agreement be unenforceable on the grounds of illegality and public policy,[2] but also it would probably trigger the application of criminal penalties for corruption.

These examples reveal some cases when it is appropriate for the courts to set limits to the possibility of contractual obligations. They also demonstrate that it would be improper for the courts to delegate entirely to the parties themselves the question of whether their agreement should be legally enforceable. These tests of enforceability must therefore contain mandatory rules. If we examine the reasons for having tests of legal enforceability, we can distinguish four purposes which they serve.

In the first instance, tests of enforceability address a practical problem. A court will sometimes be faced with a dispute about whether any undertaking, promise, or agreement has occurred at all. To resolve this dispute, the court requires evidence to prove the existence of the transaction. A test of enforceability indicates what kind of evidence suffices to prove the transaction. Such a test may indicate that the form of proof must be a written, signed document, or an oath sworn in front of witnesses or a public official such as a notary, or the registration of the contract in a public registry. If the law adopts any of these formal requirements, then failure to satisfy the relevant formality will prevent the transaction from being legally enforceable. Provided that the formalities required are well-known and understood, this device immediately resolves most disputes about the existence of a contract.

Secondly, the law examines the content and purpose of agreements, for it will deny legal sanctions to transactions which it regards as improper on the ground that they involve activities which involve criminal or immoral conduct. This function requires an examination of the substantive content of the undertaking in order to determine whether or not it involves the kind of activity to which the law ought to lend its support. Easy cases where the law will deny a legal sanction involve blatant criminal activity such as a contract for the murder of an individual. The harder cases present facts where the actions may be generally regarded as immoral, but against which there is no specific legal prohibition.

The third purpose of tests of enforceability is to set limits to the intervention of the state in the private activities of individuals. Here the object of the agreement may be unobjectionable, but nevertheless the law determines that the voluntary undertaking should not be supported by the sanctions offered by the state. Should the law, for instance, be prepared to enforce an agreement to meet a financial consultant, or to comment on

---

1   *Balfour v Balfour* [1919] 2 KB 571, CA.
2   *Amalagmated Society of Railway Servants v Osborne* [1910] AC 87, HL.

a colleague's work? In an appropriate context, an agreement to attend a meeting or to give professional advice could be an appropriate field for the state to regulate. But if the agreement consists in a casual, informal arrangement, an intervention by the state in the form of sanctions for breach of contract would be regarded as an excessive intrusion in the private lives of its citizens. The agreement may be binding in morality or etiquette, but should not be the subject of state intervention. We might say in other words that these agreements are private rather than public matters. Disputes which arise from them should be settled by compromise or the deployment of informal social sanctions, rather than by coercion by the state in the form of awards of damages for breach of contract.

The final purpose of tests of enforceability is to govern the extent to which relationships may be reduced to a contractual form. In an agreement between a husband and wife over household jobs such as cleaning and shopping, the issue is whether contractual arrangements are appropriate to govern the obligations arising under the matrimonial relationship? To what extent should the law permit contractualization of social relations? The effect of permitting a contract to govern a relationship is that it tends to exclude any open-ended diffuse obligations arising from trust and friendship. The recognition of an enforceable contract suggests that the relationship can be created exclusively by express agreement and can be reduced to measurable obligations. Tests of enforceability police this boundary in order to exclude contractual obligations where these would subvert the values of the relationship.

Although these four purposes of the tests of enforceability are distinguishable, in a particular case before a court more than one of these issues might be raised. For example, if the agreement concerns an invitation to dinner at a friend's house, the legal enforcement of the transaction may be objectionable both on the ground that it would involve an undesirable contractualization of a relation of friendship and that it would lead to the imposition of a state sanction in an inappropriate private context.

Since the purposes of tests of enforceability are complex and overlapping, every legal system employs a number of legal doctrines to serve this function. These doctrines use both formal and substantive criteria. The substantive criteria examine the purpose of the agreement or the activities which it involves. These criteria include tests of whether the agreement involves illegality or acts contrary to public policy. The formal criteria examine the structure and form of the voluntary undertaking. With respect to the structure of the transaction, the test applies models of enforceable types of undertaking. In common law countries, the dominant structural model consists of the doctrine of consideration, which requires the transaction to consist of an exchange relationship under which each party undertakes an obligation requested by the other. The other type of formal requirement serves the evidentiary function of insisting upon a particular kind of documentary proof of the existence of the agreement.

2. Evidence and Formalities

A tension plainly exists between the exigencies of a flourishing market economy and the need for clear proof of voluntary undertakings. The desire for proof of transactions points in favour of a requirement of formalities, such as an official record of a transaction, or at least a written document signed by both parties to the alleged contract. Yet such formal requirements might tend to stifle commercial transactions, where often agreements are concluded orally, perhaps on the telephone, with paperwork only being transmitted subsequently. Similarly, ordinary consumer transactions such as purchasing goods in a shop would be hampered if the law required an agreement in writing for the transaction to be legally efficacious. Of course, prudential considerations often cause parties to a major transaction to reduce their agreement to a written document. But this wise precaution, which avoids problems of proof with regard to the existence of the contract and reduces disputes about the terms of the agreement, need not become a legal requirement, without which the transaction would be treated as invalid.

This tension has been resolved in favour of the exigencies of a fluid market economy. As the market system has intensified, so the legal requirements of formalities have declined. At one time, by virtue of the Statute of Frauds (1677) and other legislation, most major transactions required at least evidence in writing, but this increasingly proved to be a trap for the unwary and an unnecessary impediment to transactions.[3] These evidentiary conditions have therefore been dismantled. Problems of proof of the existence of undertakings usually have to be resolved by the courts by examining all the evidence including the actions and statements of the parties to the alleged contract. Two principal exceptions persist, one concerning transactions in land, and the other negotiable instruments, both of which must be in writing in order to be legally enforceable.

With respect to transactions involving land, the Law of Property (Miscellaneous Provisions) Act 1989, s 2(1) provides:

> A contract for the sale or other disposition of an interest in land can only be made in writing and only by incorporating all the terms which the parties have expressly agreed in one document or, where contracts are exchanged, in each.

The scope of this provision is broad, because it includes not only sales of land, but also the creation or transfer of an interest in land, such as a lease or a charge.[4] In addition, the contract must be signed by or on behalf of each party.[5] The effect of a failure to comply with these requirements

---

3 Law Revision Committee, *Sixth Interim Report (Statute of Frauds and the Doctrine of Consideration)*, Cmd 5449 (1937).
4 S 2(5) recognises some narrow exclusions to this requirement.
5 S 2(3).

in an appropriate case will be a failure to conclude an enforceable contract on the intended terms. But these formal requirements do not apply to claims based upon proprietary estoppel, so that informal promises concerning interests in land may still have some legal effects amounting in a few cases to the equivalent of enforcement of the contract.

With respect to negotiable instruments, the requirement of writing fits into their purpose, which cannot be achieved by other means. One of the objectives of such documents as bills of exchange, promissory notes and bills of sale is to permit a simple transfer of credit rights from one person to another. For example, bills of exchange provide a credit arrangement, used especially in international trade, but an ordinary cheque drawn on a bank account is a simple commonplace example, which provides the valuable facility that the credit may be transferred by endorsement of the document by a signature. This device only works, of course, if the bill is in writing and follows a specified form of identifying the creditors and debtors.[6] The observance of the particular form then prevents any doubts being raised about the validity, effectiveness, and meaning of the credit arrangement. Similar rules apply to bills of lading, which enable the transfer of ownership of goods by endorsement of a written document in a particular form. By virtue of the endorsement, the new owner enjoys all the rights and obligations of the previous owner, and the document serves as conclusive proof of transfer and shipment.[7]

Apart from these two exceptions, which require contracts to be in writing, the only other significant requirement of formalities to establish the existence of a contract concerns contracts of guarantee which require evidence in writing and signature.[8]

Modern consumer legislation also prescribes formal requirements for contracts, but the objective of the law is not so much to establish proof of the existence of the agreement, but to disclose to the consumer the nature of the transaction. In a consumer credit contract, for instance, a failure by the lender to comply with the formalities does not prevent the formation of a binding contract. Instead, the consumer may enforce the credit arrangement despite the absence of compliance with formal requirements, and the creditor may enforce the agreement if it can persuade a court that it would be unjust in the light of any prejudice and fault to refuse to enforce the contract in whole or in part.[9] The purpose of these formal requirements is not to determine the existence of the contract, but rather to provide information to the consumer concerning the terms of the transaction. These formalities are better considered in the context of duties of disclosure in Chapter 10.

---

6   Bills of Exchange Act 1882.
7   Carriage of Goods by Sea Act 1992.
8   Statute of Frauds (1677), s 4.
9   Consumer Credit Act 1974, ss 65, 127.

3. Illegality and Public Policy

The courts exercise general powers to refuse legal enforcement to contracts which involve illegality or conduct which is contrary to public policy. Most instances of the illegality of contracts by virtue of a statutory prohibition concern rules designed to secure fair trading conditions and to invalidate contracts which in whole or in part undermine competitive markets or create risks to personal safety and property. Apart from these rules which will be considered in subsequent chapters, in some instances the authority for exclusion of these agreements stems directly from statute,[10] such as gambling,[11] but more commonly the courts infer the exclusion on the ground that the agreements are contrary to public policy. Thus an agreement to commit a criminal offence, which itself amounts to the crime of conspiracy, will be unenforceable on the ground of public policy regardless of whether any statute expressly so provides.

The precise effects of the illegality of a contract may vary. Sometimes the courts regard the contract as void, but more usually the contract is said to be unenforceable. Formerly, the courts were extremely reluctant to permit either party to enforce a contract tainted by illegality in order to deter such conduct.[12] But in recent years the courts have been moving rapidly towards a more subtle and flexible position, which examines whether enforcement of the contract would in fact undermine public policy, and whether enforcement or some restitutionary remedy would prevent injustice between the parties.[13] Although the House of Lords in *Tinsley v Milligan*[14] ruled out the exercise of a broad discretionary power to enforce contracts tainted by illegality if the court believed justice so required, they recognised a broad power to permit restitution of proprietary rights provided that the entitlement could be established without reliance upon the plaintiff's own illegal conduct.

It is only possible here to illustrate some of the reasons for limiting the scope of markets on the ground of illegality. Some statutes control the entry of contracts into family relations. It is no longer possible to enforce an engagement to marry.[15] Parental responsibility for children cannot be surrendered or transferred by contract, but it is possible for a parent to arrange for parental responsibility to be met by another person acting on his or her behalf.[16]

---

10   Restriction of Offensive Weapons Act 1959, s 1 (sale of flick-knife); Human Organ Transplants Act 1989, s 1 (sale of body parts).
11   Gaming Act 1845, s 18.
12   Grodecki, 'In Pari Delicto Potior Est Conditio Defendentis' (1955) 71 *Law Quarterly Review* 254.
13   *Saunders v Edwards* [1987] 1 WLR 1116, [1987] 2 All ER 651, CA; *Euro-Diam Ltd v Bathurst* [1990] 1 QB 1, [1988] 2 All ER 23, CA; *St John Shipping Corpn v Joseph Rank Ltd* [1957] 1 QB 267, [1956] 3 All ER 683, QBD.
14   [1994] 1 AC 340, [1993] 2 All ER 65, HL.
15   Law Reform (Miscellaneous Provisions) Act 1970.
16   Children Act 1989, s 2(9).

Another common purpose of statutory illegality is to protect the proper administration of the state and the machinery of justice. Contracts to pervert the course of justice will in general be illegal. For example, a contract under which a person agrees to hide information which may help to secure the conviction of a criminal offender of an arrestable offence amounts to the crime of compounding and will be an illegal contract.[17] Public policy may also prevent the enforcement of contracts not to disclose information revealing breaches of regulatory offences.[18] Similarly, an agreement under which a person agrees to indemnify another against the consequences of criminal liability such as a fine will be illegal.[19] On the other hand, an agreement by a victim to accept compensation for loss or injury suffered in return for withdrawing information which may lead to a criminal conviction is probably not contrary to public policy.

Contracts involving corruption in governments will also be contrary to public policy. The sale of honours and offices will be illegal either under statute or at common law.[20] Bribery of officials will also violate public policy.[21]

Agreements under which one person agrees to fund another person's civil litigation in return for a share in the proceeds, often known as contingency fee agreements, are illegal in Britain though permitted in the USA.[22] But a recent statutory reform in Britain permits some agreements with lawyers under which payment for litigation may be conditional upon a successful outcome and set at a percentage of the amount recovered at a rate regulated by the Lord Chancellor.[23]

The courts have traditionally reserved to themselves a residual power to deny enforcement to a contract on the grounds that it involves immorality or contemplates actions contrary to the public interest. In the nineteenth century the moral scruples of judges led to the denial of enforcement to any agreement tainted with some type of immorality. In *Pearce v Brooks*,[24] the court declined to enforce a contract to hire out an ornate brougham to a prostitute, who planned to attract customers with it. Although extensive legislative control over contracts has considerably reduced the exercise of this residual moralistic power, it lies in wait as a resource for the courts to set the limits of the sphere of contracts.

A final strand of controls on the scope of markets worth noting concerns contracts which unduly restrict personal liberty. No doubt a contract which amounts to slavery will be contrary to public policy, but the limit on contracts extends to other severe restrictions on personal liberty. In *Horwood v Millar's Timber and Trading Co*,[25] a money lender extracted an agreement from

17   Criminal Law Act 1967, s 5(1).
18   *Initial Services Ltd v Putterill* [1968] 1 QB 396, [1967] 3 All ER 145, CA.
19   *Colburn v Patmore* (1834) 1Cr M & R 73.
20   Sale of Offices Acts 1551 and 1809; Honours (Prevention of Abuses) Act 1925.
21   *Lemenda Trading Co Ltd v African Middle East Petroleum Co* [1988] QB 448, [1988] 1 All ER 513, QBD.
22   Criminal Law Act 1967, s 14(2).
23   Courts and Legal Services Act 1990, s 58.
24   (1866) LR 1 Exch 213.
25   [1917] 1 KB 305, CA.

the borrower that he would not leave his job, borrow further money, dispose of his property or move house without the lender's consent. This agreement was illegal as it unduly restricted the borrower's freedom.

4. Public and Private

For the sake of privacy the law should not enforce every voluntary undertaking, even where the substance concerns matters otherwise appropriate for market transactions. The law will not simply endorse some elementary principle such as promises ought to be kept or that people should act in good faith towards each other, for this would involve the intrusion of the state into private and intimate relationships.[26] But how should this zone of private conduct, where voluntary undertakings do not give rise to legal obligations, be defined? What tests of enforceability does the law adopt to mark this boundary between public and private domains? Here the common law adopted formal and structural tests of enforceability rather than directly confronting the issue of defining the zone of unenforceable voluntary undertakings.

The oldest test of enforceability comprises the satisfaction of the requirements of a deed. This is a formal test of enforceability which describes a ritual. A ritual may comprise oaths, the signing of particular types of documents, or the presence of witnesses. All these elements are necessary, for example, to create a binding contract of marriage. A deed became the normal formal mechanism for entering enforceable contracts in a wide range of circumstances. Formerly a deed comprised a written document, signed by both parties, with a seal attached, and which was then delivered to the person who expected to acquire property under the contract. A valid deed no longer requires a seal under English law, but instead the document must be signed in the presence of a witness who attests the signature and the document must make it clear on its face that it is intended to be a deed.[27] The attraction of using a deed no doubt includes the prudential consideration of establishing proof of a particular transaction before a court. But here the important point to note is that whenever the formal test of the use of a deed is satisfied, a court will enforce the promises contained in the document, for the court assumes that the adoption of the formality provides a sufficient justification for the use of state sanctions.[28] The majority of jurisdictions in the USA have abolished this test of enforceability, perhaps because it is appreciated that the use of this formality should not be determinative of the province of the public sphere.[29]

---

26 Collins, 'Counsel to Philosophers' (1982) 45 *Modern Law Review* 225.
27 Law of Property (Miscellaneous Provisions) Act 1989, s 1.
28 Specific performance (an order of compulsory performance) may not be available if there is no consideration.
29 EA Farnsworth, *Contracts* (Boston, 1982), pp 83–85.

The second test of enforceability which has become firmly established in common law countries is the doctrine of consideration. This requires the parties to have agreed an exchange, such as the transfer of goods or the provision of services for money. An oral or informal agreement can therefore satisfy the doctrine of consideration. It excludes from enforcement, however, donative promises, that is promises to give or to do something without some bargained exchange in return. This doctrine therefore suggests that whenever the parties have agreed an exchange, rather than a donative promise, that the agreement is appropriate for legal sanctions. In practice this generalization has proved too sweeping, and the courts have supplemented the doctrine with an additional safeguard that in casual social contexts the courts will refuse to enforce bargains on the ground that the parties did not have an intention to enter legal relations.

A third test of enforceability is more controversial, for it has received only halting and partial recognition in English law. It leads to the enforcement of promises where the promise has induced detrimental reliance on the part of the promisee, even though the promise was not contained in a deed and nor was it part of a bargain under which the promisee undertook an obligation in exchange. Often this test for the enforceability of promises is described as promissory estoppel or reliance-based liability. Doubts persist whether or not this is a test of the enforceability of contracts. It may be regarded as an alternative species of liability, arising in equity, with a distinctive set of rules and remedies. Here it will be argued that reliance-based liability is better regarded as a species of contractual liability. Whatever the appropriate classification, the test of reliance justifies the application of state sanctions to a voluntary undertaking, and therefore draws another boundary between the public and private spheres.

The principal type of promise which these tests exclude from legal enforceability can be described as an informal donative promise. This is a gratuitous promise, not given in exchange for another, not contained in a deed, and not one which induces detrimental reliance. The exclusion of donative promises from the realm of legal enforceability makes sense, for normally such promises are given in informal social contexts. Promises to give another a lift to the station, or to give a particular book as a birthday present, are informal donative promises, and these promises characteristically fit into perceptions of the proper scope of the private sphere of promises where legal enforceability is inappropriate. In business contexts one of the three tests of enforceability will almost invariably be satisfied.

The hard cases that test the boundaries of the public realm of enforceability fall typically into two kinds of situation. In the first, the promise occurs in a social context, but there are aspects of the promise, such as its degree of seriousness and expectations of reciprocal undertakings, which indicate that this promise should be classified in the public realm of enforceability. The second type of case occurs in a business context, but superficially it appears to be no more than an informal donative promise, an indulgence or an act of goodwill offered by one business to another. In these cases the courts are asked to recognize either the implicit exchange taking place or the reasonableness of the reliance upon the undertaking, and so enforce the promise. But it should be stressed that, despite the theoretical interest of these hard cases, in the vast majority of commercial transactions the tests of enforceability are routinely satisfied. The details of the doctrine of consideration and the reliance model which determine the scope of the public realm of enforceability will be examined in Chapters 4 and 5.

5. The Contractualization of Social Life

The final purpose of tests of enforceability concerns the extent to which contractual obligations should be permitted to regulate and define all types of social relations. The issue is whether contracts should be permitted to rewrite other types of obligations such as those arising from status, as in the relation between parent and child. The problem here is not whether the obligation is fit for state regulation; there will be legal obligations in place already. The question is rather whether a contractual obligation can be created which in some way supplants or modifies the existing legal obligations.

No specific legal doctrine addresses this aspect of the test of enforceability. An attempt to govern a relationship through a contract can be defeated by the use of the doctrines which we have already mentioned, such as a finding of illegality or that the contract is contrary to public policy. More subtle approaches involve a finding that the contract was not supported by consideration, or that the reliance was not reasonable.

However the legal analysis may be framed, the underlying issue is whether or not the practices and legal regulation of market transactions should be extended to govern a particular kind of social relationship. This poses the issue of whether certain aspects of social life should be excluded from legal regulation through delegation to consensual arrangements. We examine how the modern law answers this question in Chapter 6.

4

Consideration and the Exchange Model

Although historians can trace the doctrine of consideration back to early common law, in the nineteenth century the courts devised a rigorous formulation of it, which has since predominated. The fundamental concept is that each party must promise to give up, or actually give up, some right or liberty specified by the other as the price of the reciprocal undertaking. In a simple transaction, such as a sale of goods, the parties satisfy the doctrine of consideration by one party promising to deliver the selected goods in return for the requested price, and the other promising to pay the stated price in return for delivery of the specified goods. Notice that each promise must be supported by consideration: the promisor must receive in return for the promise a reciprocal promise to perform the act requested as the price of the promise.

This concept of an exchange serves as the general criterion distinguishing between public enforceable transactions and private unenforceable agreements. It identifies the donative promise as the type of promise which should be regarded as a private arrangement which can be broken with only moral sanctions brought to bear. In practice this means that to ensure enforceability of donative promises, a particular type of formality should be adopted, such as a Will or a deed. At the same time, the doctrine of consideration requires only slender evidence of the existence and terms of a transaction.

1. The Concept of Consideration

Due to its remarkable degree of abstraction, the doctrine of consideration does not tie legal enforceability to particular kinds of transactions or subject matter. In principle, it seems possible to satisfy the doctrine with any kinds of promises and acts, such as promises to keep quiet, to stop pestering someone, or to give some token which has negligible market value. The doctrine of consideration serves as a general test of legal enforceability, because any human action or forbearance, from complex commercial deals to trivial consumer purchases, potentially satisfies the test. This degree of abstraction turns out to be the weakness of the doctrine, for it cannot cope with the subtleties of context which the distinction between the public and private spheres of conduct must examine.

(1) Benefit and Detriment

Although this formal structure of an exchange relation has constituted the predominant concept of consideration, another version of the doctrine couched in terms of benefit and detriment has also played a role in legal reasoning. In normal exchange relations both parties expect to acquire a benefit at the price of a detriment, so the language of benefit and detriment provides a loose model of the exchange relation. Yet the formulation of the doctrine in terms of benefit and detriment entails two crucial differences.

First, the language of benefit and detriment underplays the significance of the request: in the exchange concept the detriment to the promisee must be that requested by the promisor as the price of receiving the benefit. The conferral of a benefit which has not been requested, or the suffering of a detriment which has not been requested as the price of a promise, cannot count usually as consideration. In this respect, the exchange concept of consideration introduces as part of its definition the idea of consent to an obligation. When the courts switch to the language of benefit and detriment, they often seek to minimize the requirement of consent in order to create an obligation on the basis of the receipt of an unrequested but freely accepted benefit.

Secondly, the language of benefit and detriment suggests that the court will make a substantive evaluation of the promises to discover whether or not each party in fact suffered a detriment and received a benefit. Under the exchange concept, however, the law assumes that if the act has been requested, then it must confer some benefit. The formulation of the doctrine of consideration in terms of benefit and detriment tends to occur when the courts seek to deny legal force to an agreement where they perceive that there is no real exchange of economic value, and that the bargain smacks of extortion.

The common law thus contains two concepts of consideration, the exchange concept which predominates, but also the supplement in terms of benefit and detriment which can both extend and confine the scope of contractual obligations. Most of the puzzling decisions involving consideration represent instances where the courts are unwilling to pursue the logic of the concept of exchange, and have slipped into the language of benefit and detriment in order to alter the result. Yet the formulation in terms of benefit and detriment cannot become the dominant conception for it necessarily implies that the test of enforceability contains a substantive conception of fairness. As we have seen, however, the ideal of the justice of exchange expressly denied that it was part of the role of the courts to judge the fairness of consensual bargains.

(2) Adequacy of Consideration

Under the exchange concept of consideration, the courts do not investigate the fairness of the exchange. The sole question is whether the requested action in return for the promise has either been promised or in fact performed. Although the doctrine of consideration requires an exchange of something, it leaves it to the parties to determine what they value and the price which they are prepared to pay for any item. It is accepted, for example, that the hire of a car in return for a 'peppercorn' rent, that is either a nominal sum or even literally a peppercorn, will provide consideration to support enforcement of the contract.[1] This is usually stated as the rule that the courts will not test the adequacy of the consideration. This test of enforceability obviously fits closely an adherence to a free market philosophy.

It should follow from the rule against judging the adequacy of consideration that a promise to perform an act which the promisor is already under a legal duty to perform should constitute consideration. For example, if one person succeeds in making two agreements with different people under which he promises to perform exactly the same task, then both agreements amount to an exchange relation, though clearly the second agreement involves no additional cost to the promisor. Both agreements should be enforceable under the doctrine of consideration, because it is up to the promisee to determine the value of the promise or act requested. Yet for a long time the courts were loath to accept the logic of the concept of exchange in practice. They argued, using the supplementary concept of consideration in terms of benefit and detriment, that in the absence of any real detriment to the promisor, there was no consideration to support the second agreement. But this view which was called the 'pre-existing duty rule' has gradually been discarded. Now a promise to perform an existing duty in return for payment, such as a mother's promise to the father of an illegitimate child to look after a child in return for payment,[2] or a promise to perform duties which the promisor is already bound to perform under a contract with a third party,[3] will amount to good consideration. Such agreements may, however, fail some other test of enforceability by violating public policy, as in the case of a promise not to hurt someone in exchange for money.

The most difficult cases for the courts to accept the logic of the abstract concept of exchange concern modifications of existing contracts. One party may simply demand more money for performing the same service agreed under the original contract. Alternatively, one party may simply offer less in return for the agreed sum under the original contract. Under the subjective valuation of promises in the abstract concept of exchange, both of these types of modification should be supported by consideration if the change of terms is accepted. Yet the courts naturally baulked at the

---

1   But some statutes invalidate such transactions in order to protect creditors: eg Insolvency Act 1986, ss 238, 423.
2   *Ward v Byham* [1956] 1 WLR 496, [1956] 2 All ER 318, CA.

enforcement of such modifications, since they looked unfair and smacked of extortion. The courts demanded some 'fresh consideration', no matter how trivial, in return for the promise to pay more or to accept a lesser payment. But this does not prevent reversion to the exchange concept where the court perceives genuine commercial motives for the additional payment, such as when the payment is promised in return for an undertaking to complete a building project on time.[4] We will consider the whole issue of modification of contracts in Chapter 15.

(3) Promises, Actions and Omissions

In an exchange relation both parties must promise to sacrifice, or actually relinquish, some dimension of their freedom or their rights. This broad concept of exchange permits the doctrine of consideration to be satisfied by a wide variety of types of promises, actions or omissions.

In the normal exchange, the promise contains an offer to give something or to perform a service. But it is also possible to promise to forbear to act, in which case freedom of action is sacrificed as the consideration for a reciprocal promise. One party may promise, for example, to refrain from using a right of way in return for payment, or relinquish any rights to sue for damage caused to his property by a contractor in return for a cheaper job, and in either case the promise constitutes good consideration for the other's promise. Settlements of legal claims are an important example of this kind of agreement to forbear from action.

As well as promises to perform or refrain from actions, another type of promise which satisfies the idea of sacrifice consists in a guarantee or warranty that certain facts are true or that certain claims will turn out to be true. This involves an extension of the idea of sacrifice of rights, for what is sacrificed is merely the freedom not to offer a warranty. These warranties normally comprise part of the consideration for a wider transaction, such as a sale of goods where the seller promises not only to supply the goods but also warrants their good quality. Occasionally, however, warranties comprise the main consideration for a transaction, as in the case of manufacturer's guarantees. For example, in *Shanklin Pier Ltd v Detel Products Ltd*[5] the defendant assured the plaintiff that a certain paint manufactured by the defendant would have a life of at least seven years if it was applied to the plaintiff's pier. On the faith of this promise, the plaintiff instructed its contractors to purchase the paint and use it on the pier. When the paint lasted only three months, the plaintiff successfully claimed damages against the defendant on the ground of

---

3   *New Zealand Shipping Co Ltd v Satterthwaite & Co (The Eurymedon)* [1975] AC 154, [1974] 1 All ER 1015, PC; *Pao On v Lau Yiu Long* [1980] AC 614, [1979] 3 All ER 65, PC.

4   *Williams v Roffey Bros & Nicholls (Contractors) Ltd* [1991] 1 QB 1, [1990] 1 All ER 512, CA.

5   [1951] 2 KB 854, [1951] 2 All ER 471, KBD.

breach of warranty. The warranty constituted a promise in return for which the plaintiff acted by instructing the contractors to purchase the paint for use on the pier.

It has already been pointed out that exchanges may be constituted either by reciprocal promises or acts. The type of contract known as an unilateral contract consists of an exchange of a promise for an act.[6] The promisor offers to give up some right, if the promisee actually performs certain actions. For example, if I promise Pat that I will pay her £20 to tidy up my garden this afternoon, Pat may claim the money if she carries out the work even though she has made no formal promise to do so. The same analysis was applied to the facts in *Carlill v Carbolic Smoke Ball Co*,[7] so that Mrs Carlill's regular use of the smoke ball according to the instructions was the consideration for the promise to pay £100, since that was the action requested by the company in the advertisement. In unilateral contracts, no exchange of promises takes place; actual performance of the request by one party in exchange for a promise of payment by the other constitutes the consideration, and, until the promisee performs the requested task, the transaction is not legally enforceable, since reciprocity of sacrifice occurs only once the promisee has performed the action.

(4) Requests and Conditional Promises

Although unilateral contracts fit the concept of exchange, it will sometimes be difficult to distinguish them from conditional promises. In a conditional promise, there is a donative promise which is made contingent upon some event happening. In *Carlill v Carbolic Smoke Ball Co* there was both consideration, consisting of the requested action of using the smoke ball, but also a condition of the promise, namely on the event of Mrs Carlill catching influenza. If the court had construed the advertisement so that it merely declared a promise to pay a sum of money if anyone caught influenza whilst using the smoke ball, without in fact requesting use of the smoke ball, then there would have been no exchange relation, but simply a conditional donative promise which would have been unenforceable. The difference between unilateral contracts and conditional donative promises turns simply on the issue whether the condition can be construed as amounting to a request to perform an action in return for the promise.

Although the conceptual distinction between unilateral contracts based on exchange and conditional donative promises is clear, many promises may prove hard to categorize. Behind this problem of categorization lies the court's attempt to grapple with the distinction between public and private spheres. In *Shadwell v Shadwell*,[8] an uncle wrote to his nephew in the following terms. 'I am glad to hear of your

---

6   Pettit, 'Modern Unilateral Contracts' (1983) 63 *Boston University Law Review* 55.
7   [1893] 1 QB 256, CA.
8   (1860) 9 CBNS 159, 142 ER 62, Common Bench.

intended marriage with Ellen Nicholl; and, as I promised to assist you at starting, I am happy to tell you that I will pay to you £150 yearly during my life and until your annual income derived from your profession of a Chancery barrister shall amount to 600 guineas.' The uncle paid the money until his death, but the executors of his estate then declined to pay any further sums. This promise could only be regarded as an exchange, if it could be construed as either requesting the nephew to marry or requesting the nephew to proceed with his profession as a barrister. In the absence of such implied requests, then the promise had to be regarded as a conditional donative promise to pay an annuity until the nephew's income reached a certain level. A majority of the court upheld the nephew's claim, holding that the consideration for the promise of the annuity was the nephew's marriage. Byles J, dissenting, declined to find any request by the uncle for his nephew to marry or to practise at the Bar, so that the letter merely disclosed a conditional donative promise to pay an annuity until the nephew's income improved.

The case reveals how a degree of flexibility enters into the legal process of deciding which promises to enforce by virtue of the ability of the courts to interpret events as either including or omitting implied requests for reciprocal sacrifice. This flexibility is employed to fine tune the public/private boundary. The majority of the court in *Shadwell v Shadwell* regarded the uncle's promise as falling into the public realm of enforceable contracts, so they invented the implied request in order to satisfy the doctrine of consideration in that case.

(5) Implied Requests
What emerges most clearly from this examination of the doctrine of consideration is that it exhibits considerable flexibility as an instrument for policing the boundaries of enforceable contracts. The crucial device employed by the courts is to discover an implied request to perform an act whenever they wish to enforce a donative promise. They will almost invariably place such a construction on the circumstances of the case when it concerns business and commercial matters.

The courts will quickly infer the existence of such implied reciprocal promises in business contexts, where, in the notorious absence of free lunches, it seems likely that the parties would have intended the benefits of the transaction to flow in both directions. For example, in the famous New York case, *Wood v Lucy, Lady Duff-Gordon*,[9] a designer of fashions agreed an exclusive agency arrangement with the plaintiff, such that he had the right to market her designs (and styles which she endorsed) for a year, in return for giving her one-half of all profits. The designer broke this agreement by endorsing styles without the agent's knowledge and without sharing the profits. The defence that the agreement was unenforceable because the agent had not promised to market the designs,

---

9   222 NY 88, 118 NE 214 (1917).

but merely to share profits if he did, was rejected by a majority of the court. They inferred an exchange under which by implication the defendant promised to use reasonable efforts to market her designs, for without such an implication the exclusive agency agreement made little commercial sense for either party. Here we see the court discerning an implicit exchange relation, which both makes sense of the commercial transaction and serves the purpose of bringing the agreement into the public realm of enforceable contracts.

To discover an implicit exchange in a commercial context, a court may also have to overcome the problem of vagueness of the reciprocal undertakings. Questions may arise about the satisfaction of the doctrine of consideration in cases where the parties do not specify with precision the exact terms of their exchange. It may be argued in such cases that no real exchange was intended, so that no contract was formed. If one person asks another to deliver some goods, which he does, but no price was mentioned, then it may appear that no exchange was envisaged. The courts are likely to infer in such situations, however, that an implied promise to pay for the goods was understood between the parties. There must have been an understanding that the requested action was to be remunerated. Under statute a court is then empowered to fix a reasonable price as the consideration for sale or a reasonable charge for a service.[10]

But where the court regards the promises as falling outside the commercial sphere, we see a much greater reluctance to infer requests and to imply terms which specify the intended reciprocity of sacrifice. In *Combe v Combe*,[11] during divorce proceedings, a husband agreed to pay his wife an allowance of £100 per year. After several years the wife claimed arrears of payment, the husband never having paid the allowance. The Court of Appeal rejected the claim on the ground that the wife had given no consideration for the promise of an allowance. It would have been easy for the court to have implied a request from the husband that the wife should refrain from applying to the courts for maintenance. But the court declined to construct such an implied request, even though it would have been simple to do so in the context of a promise made during divorce proceedings. One reason for this reluctance may have been the court's sense that the husband's promise should be regarded as a private arrangement, which should not be legally enforceable. The court also observed that the wife's income exceeded that of her husband, so they hinted that in any case fairness considerations disinclined them to enforce the agreement.

The construction of implied requests has also proved useful as a device for determining when benefits which have been conferred on another should be paid for. If a friend fixes my broken bicycle without discussing the matter with me first, then despite the undoubted conferral of a benefit on me, the action will not create a contractual obligation to pay my friend

10   Sale of Goods Act 1979, s 8; Supply of Goods and Services Act 1982, s 15.
11   [1951] 2 KB 215, [1951] 1 All ER 767, CA.

because the service was not requested. The position might be different if the court could imply a request, as in the situation where I had asked my friend to mend my bicycle on previous occasions, so that a court might infer a kind of standing order under which I requested my friend to fix the bicycle whenever it was broken. Another way to achieve the same outcome is to apply the law of restitution for the value of services conferred, where instead of demanding a request the court searches for 'free acceptance of the benefit'.

A similar technique is employed in cases often described under the heading of 'past consideration'. Here the court discovers an implied request to perform the work, and then relies upon a later promise to pay a specific sum for the work in order to determine the content of the reciprocal obligation. On its face the subsequent promise looks like a donative promise, a promise to pay out of gratitude, but on closer inspection of the facts of the case the courts may reason that the subsequent promise merely renders concrete the reciprocal obligations envisaged in an exchange relation formed earlier. In *Re Casey's Patents*,[12] for instance, an employee provided his employer with several inventions. Later on, after the work was completed, the employer promised to give the employee a share in the intellectual property rights of the patents on the inventions. On the question whether this promise created any binding contract, the court decided that the promise was supported by consideration, for it concluded that both parties understood that the work would be paid for; so the later promise, though merely a donative promise in form, was in fact merely a way of giving greater precision to the earlier undertaking to enter an exchange relation.

Perhaps the most troubling instances of unrequested benefits concern those promises given out of gratitude for an important service such as a rescue. A few American courts have proceeded so far as to undermine the doctrine of consideration by enforcing donative promises to pay for work rendered where the court senses a strong moral obligation to recompense the rescuer. For example, in *Webb v McGowin*,[13] the plaintiff was crippled for life in the course of saving the defendant from serious injury, and a month later the defendant promised to pay the plaintiff a fixed sum every two weeks for the rest of the plaintiff's life. The Court of Appeals of Alabama was prepared to enforce this contract on the ground that the doctrine of consideration was satisfied by the motive of gratitude, though clearly the defendant neither expressly requested to be saved nor was there a prior understanding that the act of heroism would be rewarded. No doubt the fact that a benefit had been conferred was crucial in leading to the conclusion that the promise should be enforced. The orthodox analysis which prevails in English law, however, insists that such promises to pay merely represent donative promises made in response to, but not in exchange for, the prior gift.

12   [1892] 1 Ch 104, CA.
13   27 Ala App 82, 168 So 196 (1935).

The conclusion which emerges from this examination of the doctrine of consideration is that, although the abstract concept of exchange contains an internal rigour and logic, in its application to particular circumstances the courts enjoy the discretion to construct events in ways which suit their sense of how the private/public boundary should be drawn. In commercial contexts, the doctrine of consideration will seldom present an insuperable burden to a plaintiff in order to establish a contractual claim. A court will rely upon its understanding of the implicit exchange, in order to construct the necessary implied request, and to fashion detail to the reciprocal undertakings. We have also observed that, although the abstract concept of exchange should not be concerned with the fairness of the reciprocal undertakings, the courts have often defied the logic of the concept, in order to avoid the enforcement of what they regard as unfair contracts. The use of the language of benefit and detriment is often a sign that the court is engaging in either a diminution of the element of request or a substantive evaluation of the fairness of the transaction.

2. Intention to Create Legal Relations

As a test of enforceability designed to delineate the boundary between the public and private spheres, however, the doctrine of consideration suffers from one major defect. It assumes that all exchange relations should fall within the public sphere of legal enforceability. Yet it is readily apparent that casual social arrangements can often take the form of an exchange. This creates the difficulty that the test of consideration suggests disfunctionally that such agreements should be enforceable. In *Bolton v Madden*[14] the plaintiff and defendant subscribed to a charity, the objects of which were elected by the subscribers by casting votes in proportion to their contributions. The two friends agreed that, if at one election the plaintiff would direct his votes to the defendant's favoured object, at the next election the defendant would reciprocate the favour. The plaintiff sued to enforce the agreement when the defendant failed to keep his side of the bargain. On the question of whether this agreement was enforceable, the court reached the inevitable conclusion that it fitted the exchange model of the doctrine of consideration. Nor could the court refuse to enforce the agreement on the ground of public policy, for it could see nothing improper in the arrangement. What the court lacked was a way of explaining that perhaps this agreement between friends should not be legally enforceable, because it was intended to be binding in honour only, and not subject to the public realm of enforceability.

To deal with this problem of private arrangements which satisfy the doctrine of consideration, the courts have developed a subsidiary rule under which they refuse to enforce private agreements on the ground of

14   (1873) LR 9 QB 55.

an absence of an intention to create legal relations. The doctrine of no intention to create legal relations will be employed to avoid the enforcement of casual social arrangements, promises made as jokes, and informal domestic agreements. Pollock first suggested this test in English law when he wrote,

> If people make arrangements to go for a walk or to read a book together, there is no agreement in a legal sense. Why not? Because their intention is not directed to legal consequences, but merely to extra-legal ones; no rights or duties are to be created.[15]

After a period of gestation, courts accepted the rule that social arrangements are not binding because the parties do not intend to make a contract.

Atkin LJ's famous remarks in *Balfour v Balfour*[16] illustrate this concern to limit the province of state intervention in family relations, which in this case involved a promise of financial support between an estranged husband and wife.

> It would be the worst possible example to hold that agreements such as this resulted in legal obligations which could be enforced in the courts ... Agreements such as these are outside the realm of contracts altogether. The common law does not regulate the form of agreements between spouses. Their promises are not sealed with seals and sealing wax. The consideration that really obtains for them is that natural love and affection which counts for so little in these cold courts. The terms may be repudiated, varied or renewed as performance proceeds or as disagreements develop, and the principles of the common law as to exoneration and discharge and accord and satisfaction are such as to find no place in the domestic code ... In respect of these promises each house is a domain into which the King's writ does not seek to run, and to which his officers do not seek to be admitted.

Similarly, in *Jones v Padavatton*,[17] a mother promised her daughter that if the latter would give up her well-paid job in the United States, the mother would give her £200 a month until she completed her studies for the English Bar. A majority of the English Court of Appeal declined to enforce the agreement despite the presence of consideration, because the parties did not intend to create legal relations.

The requirement of an intention to create legal relations has been criticized, however, on a number of grounds.[18] One obvious objection points out that the references to intent are at best fictitious, since the parties probably did not consider the matter; and at worst are actually false, since in these cases which occur in the law reports at least one party has chosen to litigate, which suggests an original intention to make a legally binding contract. The rule also raises a more general question of principle, namely whether the realm of legal liability should depend exclusively

---

15 F Pollock, *Principles of Contract*, 1st edn, (London, 1876), p 2.
16 [1919] 2 KB 571, CA.
17 [1969] 1 WLR 328, [1969] 2 All ER 616, CA.
18 S Williston, *A Treatise on the Law of Contracts* (Mount Kisko, 3rd edn by Jaeger, 1967), section 21.

upon the wishes of the parties. If, for example, an invitation to dinner contained an express clause stating that failure to attend once the invitation had been accepted would give rise to legal liability, should the courts comply with the express intention of the parties and enforce the agreement? It seems unlikely that the courts would award damages for breach of this agreement, though the point has not been tested, for the reason that in the last resort the courts will insist upon the ultimate power to determine the scope of legally enforceable obligations.

Nevertheless, this resort to the intention of the parties neatly resolves the dilemma presented by some social arrangements for the doctrine of consideration. It preserves a realm of private conduct where legal obligations should not arise despite the presence of consideration.

3. Rationale of Consideration

Although the doctrine of consideration, supplemented by the test of intention to create legal relations, marks the boundary between the public and private spheres of conduct, it remains a puzzle to know why the concept of exchange has been adopted as the test for delimiting this boundary.[19] The puzzle begins with the abstract nature of the test: why use this proxy rather than assess directly the context of the agreement in order to determine whether the agreement should be accorded legal sanctions? Given the use of an abstract test, however, the question then becomes what policy is the law pursuing in determining that exchange relations almost invariably fall into the public sphere? The question can also be posed in the obverse way: why does the law regard donative promises almost invariably as falling into the private sphere?

It is clear that the doctrine of consideration does not comply with the idea that the state should enforce some elementary moral principle such as the principle that promises ought to be kept. Nor does the doctrine of consideration delegate to the parties the choice over whether or not the voluntary undertaking should be legally enforceable. Even when the doctrine is qualified by the test of intention to create legal relations, the courts are plainly not relying on the actual intentions of the parties but rather imposing some mandatory rules about the proper limits of the public sphere. The two most attractive explanations of the doctrine of consideration which we will consider, the harm principle and the goal of wealth maximization, both come close to an adequate justification for the doctrine, but neither fits the legal requirement precisely.

---

19   Cohen, 'The Basis of Contract', (1932) 46 *Harvard Law Review* 553; Patterson, 'An Apology for Consideration', (1958) 58 *Columbia Law Review* 929; Pound, 'Promise or Bargain?', (1959) 33 *Tulane Law Rev.* 455; J Dawson, *Gifts and Promises* (New Haven, 1980); G Gilmore, *The Death of Contract* (Columbus, Ohio, 1974); P Atiyah, *Essays on Contract* (Oxford, 1988), ch 8; Eisenberg, 'The Principles of Consideration', (1982) 67 *Cornell Law Review* 646; Gordon, 'A Dialogue About the Doctrine of Consideration', (1990) 75 *Cornell Law Review* 987.

(1) Harm Principle

In JS Mill's interpretation of the idea of liberty, the proper role of the state should be confined to the prevention of harm being caused by one person to another.[20] In the context of economic transactions, this harm principle may be interpreted to mean that the law should impose a legal obligation where, as a result of misplaced reliance upon an undertaking, promise or agreement, some economic detriment has been suffered. In the absence of such detriment, then the law has no justification for intervention. Although the harm principle may have influenced the development of the doctrine of consideration, especially in connection with the language of benefit and detriment, it is hard to explain every aspect of the doctrine by this rationale.

The major problem is simply that not every type of detriment induced by a promise or voluntary undertaking counts as consideration. It is only when the detriment has been requested by the promisor, that the test of consideration is satisfied. A donative promise may induce detrimental reliance, yet such a promise will not be enforceable under the test of consideration. We shall shortly see that perhaps the reliance model of enforceability fills this gap.

A second problem with this rationale is that consideration can be found even in the absence of any detriment. The outstanding instance is an executory contract, where agreement has been reached but neither party has commenced performance. If there has been any harm to the promisee in such a case, then it must consist merely in disappointment of expectations, which may not be a sufficiently serious harm to justify the imposition of state sanctions for breach of contract.[21] Alternatively, if the disappointment of business expectations is regarded as a sufficient harm,[22] then the question arises why this disappointment does not apply equally to donative promises in a commercial context.

To deal with the problem of the enforceability of executory contracts, it may be argued that the harm caused by breach is the damage to the social practice of entering agreements for future market transactions.[23] This explanation of how the harm theory accounts for the enforcement of executory contracts involves a degree of circularity: the potential harm arises from a failure to enforce the agreement when enforcement is expected and relied upon. If these agreements were not enforced in general, then no such harm would arise. What this version of the harm principle really establishes is simply the proposition that, once the law has adopted a test of enforceability, it should stick to it firmly, for otherwise the market system may be damaged. Furthermore, the argument assumes that the

20 JS Mill, *On Liberty and Considerations of Representative Government* (R McCullum (ed), London, 1946).
21 Fuller and Perdue, 'The Reliance Interest in Contract Damages' ,(1936) 46 *Yale Law Journal* 52, 373; Atiyah, 'Contracts, Promises and the Law of Obligations', (1978) 94 *Law Quarterly Review* 193.
22 G Treitel, *The Law of Contract*, 9th edn, (London, 1995) 66–67.
23 Raz, 'Promises in Morality and Law', (1982) 95 *Harvard Law Review* 916, at pp 933–938.

social institution of making voluntary undertakings is coterminous with the legal tests of enforceability. Unless this is the case, then we may find that the social institution is broader than that defined by the doctrine of consideration, so that harm to the social institution may occur through breaches of donative promises. If this is true, as seems likely because the moral principle of keeping promises extends beyond exchanges, then the theory is incomplete, since it must explain why only some harms to the social institution of voluntary undertakings are redressed by the law.

It may be correct, however, that the presence of detriment or benefit will incline a court towards discovery of consideration. We have observed this tendency in the contrast between a requested exchange and a conditional gift, and in the discovery of an implied request when a benefit has been conferred. Similarly, in cases concerning modification of contracts, a promise to pay a greater sum of money for the same original performance may cease to appear like a donative promise, if the court perceives that the additional promise to perform actually secured some tangible benefit to the promisor.[24] Atiyah uses this practice to imply that the doctrine of consideration rests on the harm principle,[25] but this step blurs the requirement of the doctrine of consideration that the detriment or benefit should be one which was requested by the promisor. Actions which involve detriment or which confer a benefit on the promisor cannot on their own give rise to contractual obligations under the doctrine of consideration. A person may foresee that as a result of a promise another may act to his or her detriment, but, unless those actions were requested by the promisor, the detriment cannot count as consideration to support the enforcement of the promise. It is to solve this problem that the reliance model of enforceability, to be considered in the next chapter, has been developed. For this reason, the liberal harm principle justification for the doctrine of consideration seems unsatisfactory, even though it may help to explain the considerations relevant to a court's interpretation of the facts of a case.

(2) Wealth Maximization

The economic analysis of law suggests that the boundary between the public and private spheres is drawn by the doctrine of consideration for the purpose of wealth maximization. The public sphere is coterminous with those agreements and voluntary undertakings which increase the total wealth of society. The doctrine of consideration serves this function well on the whole. It excludes from enforcement donative promises, which are usually sterile transactions because they do not necessarily transfer property to another person who values it more highly.[26]

---

24   *Williams v Roffey Bros & Nicholls (Contractors) Ltd* [1991 1 QB 1, [1990] 1 All ER 512, CA.
25   P Atiyah, *Essays on Contract* (Oxford, 1986), chs 2 and 8.
26   R Posner, *Economic Analysis of Law*, 4th edn (Boston, 1992), ch 4; Posner, 'Gratuitous Promises in Economics and Law' (1977) 6 *Journal of Legal Studies* 411; Eisenberg, 'Donative Promises', (1979) 47 *University of Chicago Law Review* 1; Farber, 'Contract Law and Modern Economic Theory', (1983) 78 *Northwestern University Law Review* 303.

Unfortunately, the test of consideration cannot distinguish with sufficient precision between sterile and value-enhancing transactions. Sometimes donative promises may move property to persons who value it more highly, as in the case of a promise by a rich man to give an annual donation to a charity which desperately requires funds, for the charity places much greater value on the money than the rich man. Equally, sometimes exchanges will not satisfy the value-maximizing criterion, where, for instance, one party to the exchange has made a mistake in his original valuation of the property. It is possible, of course, to preserve the economic explanation of the doctrine of consideration in the face of these examples by acknowledging that the doctrine only provides a rough guide to value-maximizing transactions. Since the law must employ rules which are general in nature, these exceptions are bound to occur. Any difficulties which arise from use of the general rule can be dealt with by supplementary rules and exceptions. Even so, this chip in the economic explanation casts some doubt on its validity.

When we add to this the observation that the courts rarely acknowledge that the aim of the law is to promote value-maximizing behaviour, the economic explanation looks more doubtful. The underlying problem here is that the complex moral judgement which determines the proper limits of state action cannot be reduced to the single issue of wealth enhancement.

(3) Conclusion

The doctrine of consideration thus presents a puzzle. None of the rationales which we might expect to justify a test of enforceability by describing the proper sphere of state intervention appears to fit exactly the established legal rules which comprise the doctrine. We might conclude from this discussion that the doctrine of consideration therefore should be abandoned as an historical anachronism without satisfactory justification. This is the view taken, for example, by Fried.[27] Alternatively, we might seek to redefine the doctrine of consideration so that it fits better one of the rationales for legal enforceability. Atiyah follows this course in some of his work, by maintaining according to the liberal rationale that benefit and detriment should suffice for enforceability without the element of request.[28]

My own view is that the harm principle underlies the distinction between the public and private spheres. But the law does not take a simple material or economic view of harm. In devising a scheme for the legal protection of the interests of individuals, the law can construct the interests to be protected without being confined to instances of economic harm. This approach to the construction of protected interests fits into the perspective of the social market, for it appreciates that the motives for entering contracts cannot be confined to wealth enhancement. The motives

27 C Fried, *Contract as Promise* (Cambridge, Mass, 1981), ch 4.
28 P Atiyah, *Essays on Contract* (Oxford, 1988), ch 8.

can include the potential of the agreement to contribute to a particular way of life and to assist in the planning and achievement of personal goals.

Once the concept of a protected interest is expanded in this way, then it becomes possible to justify a test of enforceability which sanctions executory contracts. Even though the breach of such agreements may not cause economic harm, it may disrupt plans and prevent the realisation of valued goals. If necessary, we can describe the loss in economic terms as an opportunity cost: that is by entering one agreement, which is broken, the opportunity to make another contract to achieve my objective may have been lost. It is better, however, to recognise that law is capable of constructing personal, non-material interests, which it then seeks to protect by the application of legal sanctions.

5

Estoppel and the Reliance Model

Is there a second general structural test of enforceability in addition to the doctrine of consideration? The reliance model, as I shall call it in contrast to the exchange model represented by the doctrine of consideration, has received halting recognition in common law courts. It encounters resistance because it subverts the orthodox classical analysis that all contracts must be supported by consideration. Many texts, especially in England, relegate the reliance model to the role of either an equitable doctrine, outside the law of contracts, concerned with the informal allocation of property rights, or a minor supplement used to enforce an anomalous collection of donative promises. Moreover, uncertainty about the rationale and limits of this model leads to cautious and reluctant application, and a judicial preference to ground decisions on the basis of consideration wherever possible. Nevertheless, I will suggest that in practice courts use this second model as a subsidiary test of enforceability in the arena of market transactions for the same purpose of demarcating the division between the public and private spheres of conduct.

1. The Concept of Reliance

The elements of the reliance model cannot be reduced to a brief set of rules. The modern style of legal reasoning prefers to establish the parameters of this test of enforceability by reference to broad standards which require further interpretation before application to particular cases. But these broad standards indicate that the English courts look for four main elements to establish an enforceable obligation.

The first requires a deliberate encouragement of reliance by means of a promise or some other form of express or implied undertaking. The second element requires proof that the other party has in fact relied upon that undertaking by acting to his detriment. The third element is the perception that the detrimental reliance was reasonable in all the circumstances. The fourth element considers whether it would be unfair, or 'unconscionable', to permit someone to go back on his or her original promise or undertaking. In practice, of course, these elements may prove hard to disentangle, for unreasonable detrimental reliance may not have been sufficiently encouraged under the first element, or alternatively it may not be unfair or unconscionable to go back on the promise in such circumstances.

A leading example of the application of this reliance model in English law is found in *Crabb v Arun District Council*.[1] The defendant council built a road along the boundary between its property and the plaintiff's land, and granted the plaintiff a point of access to the road. Later on the plaintiff decided to divide his land and sell one portion, but for this purpose he needed a second point of access to the road. During conversations with officers of the council, the plaintiff received the impression that he would be granted the second point of access. Subsequently, when the defendant council erected a fence along the road, it left two gates corresponding to the intended points of access. Although no legal grant of the right of way was ever completed, for that would have required the satisfaction of formalities and registration, the plaintiff proceeded to sell a portion of his land. The council then blocked the second gateway, leaving the plaintiff's land inaccessible, and asked the plaintiff for £3,000 for a right of access.

In seeking a remedy against the council, the plaintiff had to overcome the problem that he had not provided consideration for any alleged promise or undertaking to grant the right of way. During the conversations with the officers of the council, he had not promised to buy the right, so no exchange was contemplated. His detrimental reliance upon those conversations, though substantial because the sale of a portion of the land left the remainder inaccessible and useless, could not comprise consideration because, though it had been foreseen, it had not been requested by the council's officers. Nevertheless, the English Court of Appeal granted the plaintiff the right of way. Lord Denning MR expressed the principle which supported the plaintiff's claim in the following terms:

> Short of a binding contract, if he makes a promise that he will not insist on his strict legal rights – even though that promise may be unenforceable in point of law for want of consideration or want of writing – and if he makes the promise knowing or intending that the other will act on it, and he does act on it, then again a court of equity will not allow him to go back on that promise ... Short of an actual promise, if he, by his words or conduct, so behaves as to lead another to believe that he will not insist on his strict legal rights – knowing or intending that the other will act on that belief – and he does so act, that again will raise an equity in favour of the other, and it is for a court of equity to say in what way the equity may be satisfied.

This statement of the reliance model of enforceability reveals many of the hesitations surrounding its adoption by the English courts. Lord Denning

---

1   [1976] Ch 179, [1975] 3 All ER 865, CA.

emphasizes how the principle serves as a qualification to the doctrine of consideration. The principle does not replace consideration as the major test of enforceability of contracts, but represents an equitable exception which supplements consideration in certain situations. Nor is Lord Denning willing to describe the council's obligation to give the right of way as a contractual obligation. He reserves that title to agreements supported by consideration. He draws instead upon doctrines established by equity to establish by informal means certain kinds of proprietary rights. These have been conventionally called 'equitable estoppels', the central idea being that because of the defendant's misleading conduct, he or she is barred from insisting upon his strict legal rights. Nevertheless, Lord Denning is willing to enforce the council's undertaking in the same way as if it were a contractual undertaking, provided that the justice of the case requires that result. The decision thus supports in form the view of the classical law that binding contracts require consideration, but in substance acknowledges an exception to that view in appropriate cases.

Such hesitation in the reception of the reliance model as a second test of enforceability is less marked in other common law jurisdictions. Many jurisdictions in the United States routinely apply a similar principle which is called promissory estoppel.[2] Section 90 of the American Restatement (Second) of Contracts summarizes the principle applied by American courts thus:

(1) A promise which the promisor should reasonably expect to induce action or forbearance on the part of the promisee or a third person and which does induce such action or forbearance is binding if injustice can be avoided only by enforcement of the promise. The remedy granted for breach may be limited as justice requires.

In a typical application of this principle, in *Feinberg v Pfeiffer Co*,[3] the plaintiff claimed that she was entitled to a pension from her former employers. Her claim was based upon a resolution of the board of directors of the company which specified that she would receive $200 per month when she chose to retire. She retired a year and a half later at 57 years of age, and received this pension for nearly seven years. Following a change in the control of the company, however, it now sought to extricate itself from the promise. The Missouri Court of Appeals could find no consideration for the promise, because no action had been requested from the plaintiff in return for the promise. Nevertheless, the court enforced the promise on the ground of promissory estoppel. The court discovered ample detrimental reliance in the plaintiff's decision to retire and then

---

2 Boyer, 'Promissory Estoppel: Requirements and Limitations of the Doctrine', (1950) 98 *University of Pennsylvania Law Review* 459; Henderson, 'Promissory Estoppel and Traditional Contract Doctrine', (1969) 78 *Yale Law Journal* 343; Feinman, 'Promissory Estoppel and Judicial Method', (1984) 97 *Harvard Law Review* 678; G Gilmore, *The Death of Contract* (Columbus, Ohio, 1974); Knapp, 'Reliance in the Revised Restatement: The Proliferation of Promissory Estoppel', (1981) 81 *Columbia Law Review* 52.
3 322 SW 2d 163 (1959).

neither to seek employment nor secure her financial position in other ways. The reasoning of the American court differs, however, from the English cases in numerous minor respects, which all flow from a greater disposition to accept promissory estoppel as a species of contractual liability equivalent to consideration.

In Australia as well, the courts have recently moved towards an acceptance of the reliance model of liability. In the leading case of *Waltons Stores (Interstate) Ltd v Maher*,[4] the company entered into negotiations for lease of property with its owner under which the owner was to demolish a building and construct a new one to the company's specifications. During these negotiations the owner made it clear to the company's solicitor that the agreement needed to be concluded promptly, so that building supplies could be ordered in time, and also that he would not want to demolish the existing building until it was clear that there were no problems with the lease. The company's solicitor drafted a lease incorporating some suggested amendments by the owner, saying that the company had notified him orally that they approved of the amendments, and that if there were any objections they would be raised the following day. No such objections were made. The owner then signed the lease and sent it to the company's solicitor by way of exchange. The owner then demolished the building. A week later the company began to regret the transaction, and, having been advised by its solicitor that it was not legally bound to proceed until signed contracts had been exchanged, it took no further action, except to tell its solicitor to go slow on the negotiations, until a month later, after the new building was about forty per cent completed, when the company announced its intention not to proceed with the lease. The High Court of Australia accepted that no legally binding agreement had arisen because of the absence of the exchange of promises represented by the exchange of copies of the signed lease, but nevertheless held that the lease was binding on the ground of estoppel. Though differing slightly in their description of the relevant principle, the members of the court agreed that the company should be held to its implied promise to complete the contract because, knowing that the owner was exposing himself to detriment by acting on the basis of a false assumption, it was unconscionable for the company to adopt a course of inaction which served to encourage him in incurring that detriment.

At the outset, I divided the elements of the reliance model into four elements. These should be considered in turn, whilst remembering the warning that the elements are bound to overlap. Moreover, these four elements may not apply with equal force to the different jurisdictions mentioned above. In particular, as the description of the American doctrine of promissory estoppel in Restatement 90 revealed, the American courts tend to confine the reliance model to express promises and avoid references to such equitable terms as unconscionability. This results from the courts' greater confidence in regarding the reliance model as a species of

4   (1988) 164 CLR 387 (Aust HC).

contractual obligation. Whether this makes any substantive difference in the law is harder to judge, for of course promises may be implied from conduct and other statements, and the equitable considerations stressed by English and Australian courts may equally well surface in the American criterion of injustice. With these reservations in mind, we should now elaborate the four strands of the reliance model.

(1) Encouragement

The first element examines the initial actions of the person who has allegedly entered into a voluntary undertaking. An express promise satisfies this element, but also actions short of a promise which amount to the deliberate creation or encouragement of an expectation of future action. In *Crabb v Arun District Council*,[5] this element was satisfied by the combination of the discussions with the council officers and the subsequent action of installing two gates in the fence. This requirement was satisfied in *Waltons Stores (Interstate) Ltd v Maher*,[6] by the deliberate omission to inform the owner of the building of the change of heart in the knowledge that he was acting on the belief that the lease would be completed. The idea of encouragement which is central to these cases implies the requirement of actual knowledge or foresight of the reliance which the injured party will place upon the action.

This first element marks the crucial distinction between the exchange and the reliance models of enforceability. Although the difference between, on the one hand, encouraging someone to act in a particular way by promises and undertakings which create certain expectations, and, on the other, requesting him or her to act in a particular way as the price of a reciprocal promise which engenders expectations, may not appear great, it marks the boundary between the two models of enforceability. The difference may be summarized crudely by saying that unrequested detriment may generate liability under the reliance model but not the exchange model. In *Crabb v Arun District Council*, for instance, because the Council's officers had not requested the plaintiff to sell his land, this detriment could not count as consideration to support their alleged promise to grant the right of way.

Although this distinction is conceptually clear, it must be observed that the courts may often interpret a particular set of facts as falling under either model. The acts which amount to encouragement can be interpreted by a court as constituting an implied request that those acts should be performed. This style of interpretation of the facts may have been present in *Carlill v Carbolic Smoke Ball Co.*[7] The court construed the terms of the company's advertisement to amount to a request to use the smoke ball according to the instructions, but the action would have failed under the exchange model if the court had only found in the

---

5 [1976] Ch 179, [1975] 3 All ER 865, CA.
6 (1988) 164 CLR 387 (Aust HC).
7 [1893] 1 QB 256, CA.

advertisements an encouragement to use the smoke ball. The absence of a developed reliance model as a test of enforceability in the classical law indubitably led to the practice of the courts becoming ever more ingenious in discovering implied requests to perform actions, in order to bring a deserving case within the exchange model of consideration. The decision in *Shadwell v Shadwell*[8] illustrates this practice. Although not all the facts of the case were beyond dispute, it was clear that the uncle, on hearing of his nephew's engagement to be married, had promised his nephew in a letter £150 per annum for a certain period to assist him. Unless this promise contained an implied request to go ahead with the marriage, however, it seemed that the nephew had not supplied any consideration to bring it within the exchange model. The majority of the court was prepared to impose this artificial construction on the promise in order to render it enforceable, but it is clear that what influenced the court was the sense that the nephew had acted to his detriment in undertaking the support of a wife due to reliance on the promise. This strained process of discovering requests for detrimental reliance may become less frequent as the reliance model gains acceptance.

(2) Detrimental Reliance
The second element of the reliance model requires proof that the other party has in fact relied upon that undertaking by acting to his detriment. This strand in the reasoning can be subdivided into a causal test and a requirement of detriment. For causation to be established, it must be shown that the words and conduct of the other party were at least a substantial factor leading to the change of position, but the evidence of a promise followed by detrimental reliance creates a strong presumption of the causal connection.[9] The requirement of detriment is more controversial, since it is not always clear whether this constitutes a test of enforceability or merely the basis for the assessment of an appropriate remedy. Perhaps the best view is that detriment is necessary, provided that it is understood that the detriment can comprise not only out of pocket expenses and financial losses, but also the failure to safeguard a legal position caused by reliance upon the expectation generated by the promise, even though such reliance caused no financial loss in itself. In the latter instance, the absence of financial loss will defeat the claim eventually, either because it will not be unfair or unconscionable to go back on the promise, or because the remedy will be nil. In a case, for example, where a promise to give money induces the purchase of an extravagant item, the purchase itself may count as detrimental reliance in satisfaction of this element of the reliance model, but a remedy will not be forthcoming unless it was both unfair to revoke the promise and economic detriment can be shown resulting from reliance, as for example in the case of a forced resale of the item at a loss.

8   (1860) 9 CBNS 159.
9   *Greasley v Cooke* [1980] 1 WLR 1306, [1980] 3 All ER 710, CA.

The Australian case, *Commonwealth of Australia v Verwayen*[10] illustrates this point. A former member of the Navy sued for personal injuries caused twenty years earlier during combat exercises. As a result of a stated policy decision, the Commonwealth did not initially plead the defence that the action was barred by lapse of time, but, after a change of policy two years later, it sought to amend its pleadings. The High Court, by a narrow majority, held that the Commonwealth could not dispute its liability to the plaintiff on this ground at this late stage. The main issue which divided the court was the remedy available to the plaintiff. Given that the lapse of time defence was bound to succeed if pleaded, then unless the Commonwealth was held to its original decision not to plead the defence the plaintiff's only detriment comprised his legal costs over a period of two years. The minority members of the court accepted the majority's view that the reliance upon the Commonwealth's stated policy position for two years of litigation was sufficient to create an obligation under the doctrine of estoppel, but preferred to limit the remedy to the legal costs during this time. This case illustrates the point that a change of position, or a failure to safeguard a position, caused by a promise or encouraged by the other party, will suffice to amount to the relevant type of detrimental reliance, but that the remedy awarded will not necessarily coincide with the expectation, if the actual losses caused by the misplaced reliance can be compensated in some other way.

(3) Reasonable Reliance
The third element of the reliance model is the perception that the detrimental reliance was reasonable in all the circumstances. During negotiations for a commercial transaction, for example, the parties may incur substantial costs in preparing plans and providing estimates. Normally, businesses undertake the risk that these expenditures will be wasted if the negotiations break down, and the courts refer to this practice to raise a presumption that reliance in such situations is unreasonable. Yet this presumption can be rebutted, where one party encourages the other to incur unusual costs or change his position irretrievably, as in *Waltons Stores (Interstate) Ltd v Maher*.[11] Disparities of business sophistication probably influence the standard of reasonableness, such as where one party takes advantage of the other's naivety in business matters by stringing him along. This element of advantage-taking undermines the defendant's claim that the negotiations had not yet reached the stage where it was reasonable for legal obligations to be imposed.[12]

What the courts will regard as reasonable reliance can, of course, only be indicated by reference to certain themes. The notion of reasonable

10   (1990) 170 CLR 394 (Aust HC).
11   (1988) 164 CLR 387 (Aust HC).
12   *Crabb v Arun District Council* [1976] Ch 179, [1975] 3 All ER 865, CA; *Hoffman v Red Owl Stores Inc* 26 Wis 2d 683, 133 NW 2d 267 (1965).

reliance clearly functions to rule out the enforceability of undertakings which were not intended to be binding and could not reasonably be expected to be binding. Suppose that a person relies upon a published railway timetable to select a train which will take him to his destination in time to conclude a highly profitable business deal. The train runs late, the passenger misses the opportunity to clinch the deal, and the business is given to a competitor. It is reasonably foreseeable that passengers will place reliance upon timetables, but it is unlikely that a court would find the railway company liable to passengers for any loss arising from delays. The reason is surely that no one expects the publication of a train timetable to engender legal liability; it is a service offered to passengers without expectation of serious reliance. This interpretation of the requirement of reasonable reliance explains the result in the American case *Division of Labor Law Enforcement v Transpacific Transportation Co.*[13] For fifteen years an employer annually paid its employees a Christmas bonus, but a claim for a sixteenth bonus on the basis of an implied promise to pay derived from the settled practice was defeated. The court regarded the reliance as unreasonable, for employees were aware, or should have been aware, that the payment of future bonuses was conditional and uncertain, so any implied promise could not be reasonably relied upon.

In a similar way, the test of reasonable reliance functions like the test of 'no intention to create legal relations' to exclude legal liability in social and family contexts. English courts have also handled this aspect of the reliance model by focusing on the content of the promise itself. They insist that the promise should be directed towards a change of position which alters legal rights, such as a modification of an existing contract or an alteration in interests in property.

The test of reasonable reliance also serves to confine the range of liability to intended beneficiaries of the promise or undertaking. It would be unreasonable to rely upon a promise when it should have been clear that the promisor did not expect or intend a plaintiff who is not the promisee to be able to do so. This dimension of reasonableness parallels the requirement of privity of contract which rules out claims by persons who are not parties to the contract under the exchange model. But the test of reasonable reliance does not limit the range of responsibility to parties within an exchange relation. Under a complex division of labour in production or distribution, it will be possible to discover reasonable reliance upon promises outside the strict confines of actual or expected exchanges. This point can be illustrated by the American case, *Lusk-Harbison-Jones, Inc v Universal Credit Co.*[14] A retailer of cars repossessed them after a purchaser had missed payments on the credit arrangement provided by a finance company (which in this case was a subsidiary of the manufacturer). The dealer omitted to insure the repossessed automobiles in reliance on a pamphlet distributed by the finance company, which said

---

13   69 Cal App 3d 268, 137 Cal Rptr 855 (1977).
14   164 Miss 693, 145 So 623 (1933).

that the finance company would arrange insurance protection for the dealer's interest, and this would continue in force until the loan was liquidated. Unfortunately, after the cars were destroyed by fire, the dealer discovered that no insurance coverage had been arranged by the finance company. Notice that the relation between dealer and finance company was not based upon an exchange, even though they co-operated in securing sales, so there could be no contractual relation based upon consideration between them. Nevertheless, the Supreme Court of Mississippi held the finance company liable to the dealer to pay compensation for damage to the automobiles, because his failure to insure was caused by reasonable reliance upon the finance company. The case provides a commonplace illustration of how the division of labour in an advanced capitalist society cannot be grasped fully in terms of exchanges between autonomous traders, at least not without considerable artificiality and distortion of the exchange model. To fill this gap, the test of reasonable reliance permits the creation of binding obligations outside exchanges or contemplated exchanges.

(4) Unconscionability

The fourth element of the reliance model considers whether it would be unfair, or unconscionable, to permit someone to go back on his or her original promise or undertaking. This requirement looks at the situation which has arisen as a result of the reliance, rather than at the acts and omissions which caused the reliance. The question to be addressed is whether the promisor's attempt to enforce his strict legal rights which defeat the expectation engendered by the promise or undertaking should now be regarded as unjust. The normal source for this finding of unfairness or unconscionability will consist in the irretrievable economic harm which has resulted from misplaced reliance upon the undertaking, as in the case of the sterile land in *Crabb v Arun District Council*.[15]

This element goes beyond an identification of actual financial loss suffered, however, for it can amount to a moral judgement about the behaviour of the promisor in all the circumstances. One illustration of this requirement concerns those cases where the absence of conformity to requirements of formalities in sales of interests in land presents an additional obstacle to the recognition of any binding obligation. The revocation of a promise or a course of conduct which encouraged the belief that the formalities would be satisfied will be regarded as unconscionable here, if, to rely upon the requirement of formalities, would be to use the formal requirements as an instrument of unfairness to the injured party. The moral judgement will also extend to other dimensions of the conduct of the parties, such as the 'high-handedness' of Arun District Council. In *Pascoe v Turner*,[16] when a man deserted his mistress, he said, 'The house is yours and everything in it.' On the strength of this promise, the woman

15   [1976] Ch 179, [1975] 3 All ER 865, CA.
16   [1979] 1 WLR 431, [1979] 2 All ER 945, CA.

took no steps to secure her occupation of the property and spent £230 on improvements. In fact, he never arranged for a conveyance of the property, and he eventually brought an action for possession. The English Court of Appeal held that the woman had a defence to the action for possession, and, furthermore, ordered the man to execute a conveyance of the property. Here the 'ruthless' determination of the man to evict his former mistress from her home was added to the relatively meagre financial loss of the mistress to render the attempt to insist upon strict legal rights unconscionable or unjust.

2. The Classification of the Reliance Model

In contrast to most jurisdictions in the United States, the English, and, to a lesser extent, the Australian courts display a hesitation in regarding the enforcement of promises on the ground of reliance as equivalent to the enforcement of contractual obligations. This hesitation finds its sustenance in both good and bad reasons. It is worth considering these reasons further before examining the rationale for the reliance model of enforceability.

Let me commence my observations on this question of whether the reliance model constitutes an example of contractual obligations by doubting the significance and interest of this question. For those who wish to organize the law of obligations into a tidy scheme of tight conceptual classifications, no doubt the issue becomes of paramount importance. But with the more contextual approach adopted here, where the interest lies in examining the grounds and scope of legal obligations arising in market transactions, the question of proper classification fades into insignificance. What seems far more important in this contextual approach is the fact that the reliance model does generate obligations to transfer property, to refrain from certain courses of action, and to compensate others for their frustrated expectations during commercial dealings. It must be admitted that the issue does sometimes have some practical importance, where, for example, a statute insists upon certain formalities for the enforcement of contracts, and in order to avoid that requirement in the interests of justice courts have often found it convenient to deny that the reliance model counts as a contract. This instrumental reasoning, however, should not be permitted to elevate the question of classification into a matter of fundamental importance. The only significant aspect of this issue consists in the extent to which the courts are reluctant to classify these obligations based upon the reliance model as contractual, which leads to a deeper hesitation to acknowledge these obligations at all.

(1) Time-frame
The fundamental difference between contracts supported by consideration and those supported by reliance consists in the time-frame of the legal

analysis. Whereas in a bilateral contract, formed by an agreement, the contractual obligation comes into force immediately, in cases of reliance the obligation matures as a result of a series of actions referable to a relationship over a period of time. In the case of *Crabb v Arun District Council*,[17] for instance, it is hard to say at what point the council's obligation to grant a right of way arose. The discussions with the council's officers would not suffice in themselves, for at that stage no reliance had occurred. The source of the obligation lay rather in the combination of measures by the council which encouraged the owner's belief that he would be granted a right of way such as the erection of gates, the foreseen detrimental reliance of sale of part of the land leaving the remainder inaccessible, and the judgment that it would now be unjust for the Council to insist upon its strict legal rights. Similarly, in *Waltons Stores (Interstate) Ltd v Maher*,[18] the obligation did not arise at any fixed point of time, but matured as a result of the combination of detrimental reliance in the form of demolition and construction on the part of the owner and the awareness of these actions together with a decision not to disabuse the owner of his mistake. At the end of the day the court regarded this as rendering the company's attempt to deny the lease as unconscionable.

The classical model of contract law tends to stress the way contractual obligations come into existence at a fixed point in time through the satisfaction of the rules of consideration and agreement. The reliance model runs against the grain of this perception of how contractual relations must be conceived, but this in itself does not appear to justify the exclusion of the reliance model from the realm of contracts. Indeed, the classical model was always forced to qualify this assumption in the case of unilateral contracts, for there the contract only becomes binding following completion of the requested act of consideration. For instance, in *Carlill v Carbolic Smoke Ball Co*,[19] it was not until Mrs Carlill had used the smoke ball according to the instructions and had caught influenza that the company's contractual obligation to pay £100 arose. Once one accepts that contractual obligations may mature over a period of time in the manner of unilateral contracts, then there seems little reason to continue to insist, because the reliance model creates obligations out of a relationship because of conduct over a period of time, that it should not be regarded as the basis of contractual obligations.

(2) Consistency with Consideration

Another ground for hesitation at the inclusion of the reliance model in the fabric of contractual obligations concerns the worry that it tends to subvert the doctrine of consideration. It is true, of course, that acknowledgement of the reliance model prevents the apotheosis of consideration as the exclusive test of legal enforceability. But this does

17 [1976] Ch 179, [1975] 3 All ER 865, CA.
18 (1988) 164 CLR 387 (Aust HC).
19 [1893] 1 QB 256, CA.

not necessarily mean that the rationale of consideration is thereby frustrated. In particular, we have noted that one clear effect of the doctrine of consideration is to prevent enforcement of donative promises. The reliance model apparently threatens to alter that result, and as a consequence challenges a central purpose of the doctrine of consideration. But the reliance model only enforces a certain kind of donative promise, one that lacks consideration, but which has the other elements of encouragement of detrimental reliance, reasonable reliance, and unconscionable conduct by the promisor. These additional elements create grounds for the imposition of legal obligations, which may not conflict with the rationale underlying the doctrine of consideration's rejection of donative promises, but merely supplement and refine that rationale.

(3) Promises and Statements
Is there a fundamental difference between the two models of enforceability, under which only the test of consideration permits the enforcement of promises of future action? Some of the origins of the reliance model lie in the doctrine of estoppel, and this doctrine was primarily designed to prevent persons from denying that a state of facts which they had asserted to be true was in fact true. These origins lead to the claim that the reliance model can only create obligations arising from statements of present fact, not create obligations with respect to the future. It is clear, however, that whatever the legal source of the reliance model, recent cases in England and elsewhere have overstepped this alleged boundary. The decision in *Crabb v Arun District Council* clearly concerned a promise with respect to future action, namely the granting of a right of way, not a statement about the existing factual or legal situation. The High Court of Australia in *Waltons Stores (Interstate) Ltd v Maher* also did not disguise the point that it was enforcing an implied promise to complete the lease, not simply preventing the company from going back on any implied statement that it had already executed the lease.

It is perhaps possible to distinguish the cases which clearly enforce promises as to future conduct on the ground that they all concern dealings in interests in land. It is suggested that this species of estoppel, often called 'proprietary estoppel', does permit enforcement of promises for the future, but that, apart from dealings in land, such promises are unenforceable under the reliance model. This distinction seems highly improbable. No reason other than the certainty achieved by following scrupulously the limits of precedent decisions is given for treating the general grounds for enforceability of promises connected with interests in land any differently from those concerning goods and services. If applied systematically the proposed distinction might produce some strange anomalies. In *Pascoe v Turner*,[20] for instance, it will be recalled that the man's promise to his mistress referred to both the house and its contents.

20   [1979] 1 WLR 431, [1979] 2 All ER 945, CA.

It was not suggested in this case that the goods in the house did not belong to the woman as well, and, though this result may be explicable as a simple gift, it would surely have been an absurd result if, on the strength of the promise and the subsequent detrimental reliance, the woman had won the house but not its contents, because the latter do not comprise interests in land.

Unconvinced by the necessity for this limitation to proprietary interests, some English decisions trespass over this alleged boundary to the enforceability of promises under the reliance model. In *Re Basham (deceased)*,[21] the deceased had promised to give his stepdaughter his estate on his death, and this promise was enforced, despite the absence of a Will, even though the estate comprised both a house and a substantial sum of money in the bank. Similarly, in *Pacol Ltd v Trade Lines Ltd (The Henryk Sif)*,[22] following a breach of contract, the defendants encouraged the plaintiff to believe that the correct people to sue were themselves, whereas, in fact, due to complex commercial arrangements, they were not the party liable under the contract. By the time the plaintiff discovered the true position, the period of limitation for bringing legal actions against the correct party had expired. The court held the defendants responsible under the contract in view of their failure to disabuse the plaintiff of their reasonable misunderstanding and their subsequent detrimental reliance. Here the promise or undertaking which was enforced is unconnected with land, though the court also believed that the case could be decided the same way as a more traditional type of estoppel based upon a statement of fact.

The limitation of enforcement of promises to proprietary estoppel has never been part of the American doctrine. In recent years, the Australian courts have expressly dissented from the proposition. Casting aside most of the suggested limitations on the scope of the doctrine of estoppel, Mason CJ in *Commonwealth v Verwayen* summed up the principle in the following terms:

> The result is that it should be accepted that there is but one doctrine of estoppel, which provides that a court of common law or equity may do what is required, but no more, to prevent a person who has relied upon an assumption as to a present, past or future state of affairs (including a legal state of affairs), which assumption the party estopped has induced him to hold, from suffering detriment in reliance upon the assumption as a result of the denial of its correctness. A central element of that doctrine is that there must be a proportionality between the remedy and the detriment which is its purpose to avoid.[23]

It is surely only a matter of time before the English courts will also break down these artificial and unjustified limits on the application of the reliance model of enforceability.

21 [1987] 1 All ER 405, Ch.
22 [1982] 1 Lloyd's Rep 456, QB.
23 (1990) 170 CLR 394, at 413 (Aust HC).

(4) Remedies

One more substantial ground for hesitation at the introduction of the reliance model into the fabric of contract law concerns the type of remedies afforded by the courts. Whereas a contract supported by consideration will invariably, at the least, give a right to damages for breach of the agreement, the remedy for breach of undertakings under the reliance model appears to lie within a broad discretion of the court. As we saw in connection with *Crabb v Arun District Council*, English law insists that the remedy should be merely that which is necessary to satisfy equity in the case. Similarly, as in the statement of Mason CJ above, the Australian courts have stressed that the remedy should do what is required, but not more, to prevent a person who has relied upon a promise from suffering detriment.[24] The American Restatement also stresses the need to enforce the promise only to the extent that is necessary to avoid injustice.

Nor have English courts so far been willing to award damages for breach of promises under the reliance model, but have instead adopted equitable remedies such as ordering the conveyance of the right of way in *Crabb v Arun District Council*. This approach reflects the origins of these types of estoppel in equity, but, given the fusion of common law and equity, together with the power of equity courts to award damages, any possible denial of damages seems to be a historical anachronism. Australian courts have ignored this limitation, as in *Waltons Stores (Interstate) Ltd v Maher*, where the court eventually ordered payment of damages in lieu of specific performance.

Now the force of this undoubted contrast between remedies for breach of contracts, supported by consideration, and those obligations, arising under the reliance model, depends upon how closely one links the concept of contractual obligations to a particular remedial scheme. A close linkage inevitably leads to the reasoning that, if the remedies differ, then the type of obligation must differ also. It must follow on this view that the reliance model does not create contractual obligations, but some other species of equitable proprietary right. But this view seems riddled with inconsistencies. The logic of this position should also insist upon a sharp distinction between, on the one hand, contracts which can be specifically enforced (an equitable remedy entailing compulsory performance and sometimes the creation of equitable proprietary interests), and on the other, those where the sole remedy lies in damages at common law. Yet all these contracts, despite the difference in remedies available, are invariably classified as full contractual obligations. No reason is given for ignoring the differences created by the availability of equitable remedies in some cases, but then relying upon the practice of using equitable remedies in the reliance model in order to justify the exclusion of these cases from the realm of contractual obligations.

As well as the inconsistent treatment of the significance of equitable remedies, this focus on the remedies for breach of the obligations also produces some paradoxical conclusions. It is often asserted that the remedial difference reveals that, for contractual obligations supported by consideration, the courts will attempt to enforce the promise or undertaking, whereas for obligations under the reliance model the court will provide the minimum equitable protection necessary, which will be simply the measure of detrimental reliance or out of pocket expenses. In other words, contractual obligations protect expectations, but obligations under the reliance model merely compensate detrimental reliance. Yet it is readily apparent that in many instances of the reliance model, the court concludes that the equitable remedy must comprise enforcement of the promise or expectation. In *Pascoe v Turner*, for instance, the deserted mistress received a conveyance of the house. Similarly, in *Crabb v Arun District Council*, the plaintiff received the expected right of way over the road. In contrast, in contracts supported by consideration, the injured party may not receive enforcement of the promise, but merely nominal damages if his losses cannot be proven.[25] This suggests that the remedial contrast between the exchange model and the reliance model does not rest upon a difference of principle, in the form that only under contracts supported by consideration should the injured party receive his or her expected performance. Although remedial differences do exist between the two models, there seems no good reason arising from this divergence to deny that both represent species of contractual obligation.

In so far as this question of the proper classification of the reliance model as a species of obligation deserves attention, therefore, the arguments against regarding it as representing a species of contractual obligation seem overstated and confused. Without denying the important differences of emphasis between the exchange and reliance models, particularly the contrast between time-frames, it seems a mistake to insist upon a conception of the market order constituted by the law of contract which excludes these reliance model obligations.

3. Rationale of Reliance Model

The reliance model plainly draws a different line between the public and private spheres from the doctrine of consideration. This difference signals that it has a different conception of the appropriate sphere of state action. But this difference springs, I suggest, not from a radical departure in values, but merely a refinement of the harm principle.

(1) Good Faith
It seems wrong to attribute to the emergence of the reliance model a simple legal endorsement of moral standards such as the idea that promises ought to be kept.[26] Even if the reliance model is tied to express or implied promises, which seems doubtful from the cases on acts of encouragement,

---

24 *Commonwealth of Australia v Verwayen* (1990) 170 CLR 394 (Aust HC).
25 Eg *Lazenby Garages v Wright* [1976] 1 WLR 459, [1976] 2 All ER 770, CA.
26 C Fried, *Contract as Promise* (Cambridge, Mass, 1981).

the model does not require that all promises should be enforced, or even that all serious promises should give rise to legal liability. Instead, only where the promise has induced reasonable reliance will the courts insist that the promise be kept. Nevertheless, the emphasis placed by the courts upon the fourth element of unfair or unconscionable results, as a condition for intervention, suggests that moral standards play an important role in determining liability and shaping the remedy. In this context, however, the term unconscionability appears to contain two dimensions.

In the first place, it suggests a deliberate manipulation of another person's choices by provoking or not disabusing false impressions about future intentions. This is similar to fraud, but, instead of making statements of fact known to be false, the promisor in the reliance model encourages certain expectations with regard to his or her future conduct and these expectations are known by the promisor to be unfounded either at the outset or later on whilst the ensuing detrimental reliance is taking place. The moral ideal here seems to be a requirement of acting in good faith. But the law cannot be endorsing a moral requirement of conduct in good faith alone, for the reliance model insists upon the additional requirement of detrimental reliance.

The second dimension of the term unconscionability examines the exposed position of the person who has relied to his or her detriment on this false expectation. A denial that the expectation was justified becomes unconscionable if the promisee cannot revert to his or her former position without loss directly attributable to reliance upon the expectation. Stated in this manner, this second dimension of unconscionability is merely a restatement of the harm principle, making it clear that what is required is an irretrievable change of position which entails economic loss.

(2) Wealth Maximization

Can the reliance model of enforceability be explained as a technique for identifying value-enhancing transactions beyond the exchange model? Recall that the difficulty for the wealth maximization idea in connection with the doctrine of consideration was that some donative promises could increase wealth yet were excluded from the public sphere. Does the reliance model solve that problem by identifying those situations where a supplement is required in order to bring the tests of enforceability into line with the dictates of the principle of wealth maximization?

Many of the cases which employ the reliance model fit the pattern of grappling with complex economic associations between numerous parties which cannot be distilled into a series of discrete exchange transactions. This standard feature of the cases stands out in a common instance of the application of the reliance model in America in disputes between building contractors illustrated by *Drennan v Star Paving Co.*[27] A general contractor, in preparing a tender for building work, solicited bids from specialist sub-

---

27   51 Cal 2d 409, 333 P 2d 757 (1958).

contractors for portions of the work. The general contractor then computed all the costs of the work and submitted a bid for the whole job, which was accepted. One of the sub-contractors had made a mistake in the quotation for his specialized work and refused to carry it out. It was clear that the general contractor had not formally accepted the sub-contractor's bid, so the doctrine of consideration had not been satisfied, but all the parties were aware that the general contractor would rely upon the quotation in putting forward his tender. The California Supreme Court held that, despite the absence of reciprocal promises, the sub-contractor's bid was binding, because it was reasonably foreseeable that it would be relied upon by the general contractor and had in fact been relied upon. These practices of the construction industry involve complex arrangements between numerous independent contractors, and, for this system of production to work effectively, sometimes parties must be protected in their reliance upon others at a point earlier than the establishment of formal exchange relations. To obtain the general efficiency advantages of a competitive tendering system for construction work, the general contractors must be able to rely upon the accuracy of bids by sub-contractors. To this extent, the reliance model may display a response to concerns for economic efficiency and value-enhancing market transactions.

The difficulty with this interpretation lies in the problem of accounting for its application in cases where the facts reveal no more than a donative promise followed by reasonable detrimental reliance. In cases such as *Pascoe v Turner*, for instance, the enforcement of the promise to convey the house looks like a sterile transaction, not deserving of support as a value-enhancing exchange. We noted above, however, that not all donative promises are sterile, for it is possible that the recipient of the intended gift will value the property more highly than the donor. This opens up the possibility that the presence of unrequested detrimental reliance reveals that in fact the donee values the property more highly than the promisor. On this view, the fact that the deserted mistress in *Pascoe v Turner* made improvements to the house evidences the greater value which she placed upon the property. But even supposing that detrimental reliance does evidence the donee's greater valuation of the property, the argument must overcome the problem that the absence of detrimental reliance does not prove the contrary point that the donee places no greater value on the property. The presence or absence of detrimental reliance appears an inept test of the relative utilities of the property between the parties.[28]

(3) Harm principle
Lon Fuller[29] first suggested that the reliance model could be justified within the framework of the harm principle.[30] The harm is described as

28 Eisenberg, 'Donative Promises', (1979) 47 *University of Chicago Law Review* 1.
29 Fuller and Perdue, 'The Reliance Interest in Contract Damages', (1936) 46 *Yale Law Journal* 52, 373.
30 Collins, 'Contract Law and Legal Theory', in W Twining (ed), *Legal Theory and Common Law* (Oxford, 1986).

misplaced reliance upon another causing detriment. Indeed, Fuller suggested that this description of the nature of the harm which the law regarded as a protected interest fitted the whole of the law of contract and much of the law of tort.

Where the reliance model differs from the exchange model of consideration is in the absence of a request to incur the detriment. This is significant, for it indicates a diminution of the requirement of consent to contractual obligations. But the difference does not affect the application of the harm principle, which focuses on the fact of detrimental reliance as the reason for intervention. The reliance model is utilized when it seems impossible on the facts of the case to imply a request to incur the detriment, yet nevertheless the detriment has been encouraged by the promisor. In this respect the reliance model represents the mirror image of cases where benefits have been conferred without a request. If the court is unable to imply a request, then it must resort to the law of restitution or unjust enrichment to justify the imposition of a compensatory obligation.

In drawing the scope of the public realm of enforceability, therefore, the reliance model imitates the doctrine of consideration in adopting an interpretation of the harm principle. But instead of employing the abstract notion of exchange to determine when interests have been harmed, the reliance model examines the whole course of conduct of the parties in order to determine the extent and causes of the detrimental reliance.

6

The Contractualization of Social Life

This chapter examines the final purpose of tests of legal enforceability. This concerns the extent to which contractual obligations should be permitted to regulate and define all types of social relations. This issue does not raise the question of the proper limits of state regulation, but rather whether the form of regulation derived from the law of contract is the appropriate criterion of governance of the relation. In recent times, with the success of the market economy, it has become increasingly common to assume that contractual relations should enjoy priority over other obligations unless there is good reason to exclude them. Let us consider some of the reasons for the strength behind the belief in the virtue of freedom of contract, before considering in greater detail some of the justifications put forward for limiting markets and contracts.

1. The Faith in Markets

The contemporary resurgence of faith in markets springs from a number of sources. The success of markets in performing the task of efficient satisfaction of consumer wants is no doubt the major justification for the contractualization of social relations. This explains, for example, why public services have become increasingly approximated in their organization and financing to private contractual provision of services. Viewed in this light, any limit upon contracts and markets, such as a prohibition of the sale of parts of the body, or arrangements for prostitution, is likely to impede the efficient satisfaction of wants, and is therefore to be regarded as undesirable without strong justification. But there are deeper reasons for the strength of the faith in markets.

One attraction of markets is their seductive claim that they avoid any governmental choice with respect to the pattern of the distribution of wealth in society.[1] The stock of goods which a person possesses depends

---

1   F von Hayek, *Law, Legislation and Liberty*, Vol 2 (London, 1976), pp 65–69; R Nozick, *Anarchy, State, and Utopia* (Oxford, 1974), p 159. See ch 13 below.

upon a myriad of market transactions rather than any conscious human agency which engineers a particular distributive pattern. The 'invisible hand' of market forces as a distributive mechanism has the apparent attraction that it requires no political justification for its outcomes. The government can absolve itself from responsibility, and simply claim that poverty and wealth are the result of market choices by individuals. Once again this thesis strongly supports the absence of limits to markets, for those limits will necessarily interfere with this neutral mechanism for the distribution of wealth.

But the deepest attraction of markets and contracts is, I believe, that they provide a solution to a problem of loss of confidence in institutionalized structures giving direction to people's lives. The preference for markets is symptomatic of a scepticism with respect to any claim to know best how social relations should be organized, what standards they should observe, and perhaps a fear that any institutionalized power of control over social relations will be abused and employed to destroy individuality. By permitting contractual relations to flourish, the state effectively delegates to individuals as many choices as possible as to the nature of the social relations into which they may enter. Instead of determining in advance the reciprocal obligations in cohabitation, for instance, the law leaves the parties to select their own property settlement and distribution of assets and responsibilities. This scepticism about the role of institutionalized direction of social standards thus gives considerable impetus to the extension of contractual relations.[2]

When these three forces are combined – the efficiency of markets, the avoidance of responsibility for distributive patterns and the escape from scepticism about imposed social standards – then the question becomes not what relations should be governed by contracts, but rather why should there be any limits to contracts and markets at all. Before considering potential answers to this question, let us consider the variety of legal techniques available for policing the scope of markets and contractual obligations.

2. Legal Techniques for Controlling the Scope of Contracts

No particular legal doctrine serves as a general technique for confining the scope of contracts. The courts achieve this result by a combination of the legal doctrines which we have considered so far in previous chapters, especially the doctrines of illegality and public policy, consideration, and intention to create legal relations.

---

2   Collins, 'The Sanctimony of Contract' in R Rawlings (ed), *Law, Society, and Economy*, (Oxford, 1997) 63, 75.

(1) Contracts in the Family

Although the obligations between members of a family are determined in the first instance by obligations of status, such as the parental duty to support children, contracts have played an important supplementary role, especially in connection with the distribution of property entitlements. It was once common for the parties involved in a marriage and their parents to devise an elaborate settlement of the distribution of property by means of a legally enforceable contract. Parties to a marriage today normally leave the issue of the distribution of assets to be determined by statutory norms, either the provisions regarding spousal support in the event of separation or divorce, or the law of succession and inheritance with respect to death. Although the law often encourages the parties to agree a settlement in these cases, it will not tolerate agreements which violate the legislative standards of a fair distribution of assets.

One way the courts exclude contractual relations is to invoke a combination of the doctrine of consideration and the idea of intention to create legal relations. The court will argue that either there is no consideration to support the agreement, as in *Combe v Combe*,[3] or if there is consideration, then there was no intention to create legal relations. The famous decision in *Balfour v Balfour*[4] illustrates a court using both of these legal doctrines in order to establish a limit to the application of market justice to family relationships. Here the wife alleged that her husband, before leaving to resume his job abroad, promised her an allowance of £30 a month. Her action to recover the money under this agreement failed. One ground for the decision was the absence of consideration. The wife alleged that the consideration which she gave for her husband's promise was a reciprocal promise to refrain from enforcing her husband's legal obligation to maintain her. Warrington LJ denied that the wife had given any such promise, and nor could one be implied in the circumstances. Duke LJ agreed that there was no consideration, but on the ground that the wife's power to pledge her husband's credit was not a right but merely a permission granted by her husband, so that she was not giving up any right which it was in her power to dispose. In the same case, the court also relied upon the doctrine of intention to create legal relations. Warrington and Atkin LJJ agreed that there was no intention to enter a binding contractual arrangement. Atkin LJ insisted that even if consideration could be established, the court should not enforce this type of agreement.

> It is quite common, and it is the natural and inevitable result of the relationship of husband and wife, that the two spouses should make agreements between themselves, agreements such as are in dispute in this action, agreements for allowances by which the husband agrees that he will pay to his wife a certain sum of money per week or per month or per year to cover either her own expenses or the necessary expenses of the household

3   [1951] 2 KB 215, [1951] 1 All ER 767, CA.
4   [1919] 2 KB 571, CA.

> and of the children, and in which the wife promises either expressly or impliedly to apply the allowance for the purpose for which it is given. To my mind those agreements, or many of them, do not result in contracts at all, and they do not result in contracts even though there may be what as between other parties would constitute consideration for the agreement ... Nevertheless they are not contracts, and they are not contracts because the parties did not intend that they should be attended by legal consequences.

The underlying objective of the court in keeping contractual relations out of this case was to ensure that the wife benefited from the open-ended statutory duty of maintenance based upon need rather than be confined to a fixed sum.

The same objection to contracts determining fixed sums of maintenance does not apply outside marriage, for there is no statutory duty to support a partner after separation. The courts have enforced express and implied contracts between cohabiting couples, which distribute property and arrange financial affairs. These contracts often replicate the financial arrangements, which would have applied, had the parties been married. In *Tanner v Tanner*,[5] a married man persuaded his mistress (who took his name) to move with their children from her rent-controlled tenancy to a house which he had bought as more suitable accommodation. Later the man married another woman and sought to evict his former mistress, so that he might live there himself with his new wife and family. At no time had the man and his partner made a formal agreement with regard to ownership of the house. Nevertheless, the Court of Appeal concluded that she had a contractual licence to live there until the children left school, and for breach of this contract the court awarded damages as well as setting aside the order for repossession. Although the court took considerable pains to fit the circumstances into the normal positive requirements for enforcement of contracts, such as agreement (by implication) and consideration (by giving up previous accommodation on request), the judgments, particularly that of Lord Denning MR, are also coloured by rhetoric which reflects a social context other than a market.

> The man had a moral duty to provide for the babies of whom he was the father. I would go further. He had a legal duty towards them. Not only towards the babies. But also towards their mother. She was looking after them and bringing them up. In order to fulfill his duty towards the babies, he was under a duty to provide for the mother, too.

The court ignores the previous objection to the enforcement of these contracts that they involve a dimension of immorality, so that the court should not condone sexual relations outside marriage. This reflects, no doubt, a change in conventional moral standards under which cohabitation ceased to be an immoral arrangement akin to prostitution, and became instead a common basis for family life. Taking into account this alteration in moral standards, and in the absence of explicit legislative guidance on

5   [1975] 1 WLR 1346, [1975] 3 All ER 776, CA.

property distribution between cohabiting couples, the court permitted the enforcement of a contractual relation, which, in its effects on property entitlements, mirrored the standards applicable to marriage.

Even where explicit legislative guidance is available, the courts may sometimes use contractual techniques to permit family members to reach binding agreements which extend their legal commitments towards each other. Such agreements may seem on balance beneficial to the meanings established in the social sphere of the family, either because these agreements add to, rather than subtract from, the obligations of the family community, or because they permit the members of the family to mould the full dimensions of their commitment in perhaps an unconventional way, but which nevertheless provides valuable meaning to the parti-cipants.In *Ward v Byham*,[6] for instance, a father promised to pay £1 a week to the mother of his illegitimate child in return for her promise to keep the child well looked after and happy, and to allow the child to decide for herself whether she wished to live with her mother. Later the mother re-married and the father discontinued payments. Under the family law of the time, the mother but not the father was under an obligation to maintain the child. It was argued in defence to the mother's claim for arrears of payment that no consideration supported the father's promise, since the mother had only promised to do what she was already bound to do. Brushing aside this technical problem of satisfying the doctrine of consideration, the Court of Appeal held that all the positive conditions necessary for the formation of a contract were satisfied, and no public policy was violated, so it awarded the mother the arrears of payment. A technical consideration could be discovered either in the mother's promises which went beyond the public duty of support, or alternatively, as Lord Denning MR insisted, simply in the benefit conferred on the father from the mother's promise to care for the child.

Behind the formal grounds for the decision in this case, we may conjecture that the court found the scheme of distributive justice envisaged by family law in these circumstances (that is the absence of a duty of maintenance imposed on the father of an illegitimate child) unattractive, and, perceiving that the father had acknowledged greater responsibilities of support and care for his child, the court did not hesitate to translate those duties into contractual obligations. The case illustrates the paradox that contracts may be used instrumentally to remedy perceived defects in the existing scheme of family entitlements, so that the family is treated like the market for the purpose of limited interventions which add to, rather than subtract from, the independent meanings to be constructed in the family sphere of social life. The court was prepared to enforce the contract, because the obligation which it imposed on the father fitted into a particular meaning for the social relationship which the court approved and sought to foster.

With respect to contracts in the family, therefore, we can see the boundaries of the scope of enforceable agreements being constantly subject

6   [1956] 1 WLR 496, [1956] 2 All ER 318, CA.

to scrutiny and renegotiation. The limits to contracts spring from the concern to uphold public legislative standards of reciprocal obligations and fair distribution of assets, and from an unwillingness to condone contracts which contemplate breaches of conventional moral standards. But within this framework, the courts can permit enforceable contracts, provided that they do not upset the fair distributive scheme, and appear to give greater specificity to choices about how family obligations are to be constructed.

(2) Contracts with the State

We have already noted that the operations of government have also typically been insulated from the market. An agreement by a public official to distribute a benefit such as a construction contract to a particular contractor who in return has given lavish entertainment will be regarded as improper invasion of market principles into the sphere of government, and such agreements will be unenforceable and the actions treated as the criminal offences designed to deter bribery and corruption. The role of the judicial branch of government is also insulated from market transactions, where either the agreement amounts to a conspiracy to pervert the course of justice, such as a bribe to commit perjury, or an attempt to oust the jurisdiction of the courts over the agreement altogether. This latter rule does not prevent the important practice of private arbitration of disputes, which is often chosen to reduce the costs of litigation, but the exclusion of the courts is subject to statutory safegards.[7]

Aside from clear illustrations of contracts designed to corrupt the good administration of government, however, a more subtle difficulty arises with respect to contracts with the state. In pursuit of the common good, the state may enter into market relations in order to secure the efficient provision of services and supplies to the public. In recent years, the extent to which the operations of the state have been contracted out to private businesses has been enlarged, with, for example, franchises for the operation of prisons, refuse collection, and broadcasting. Yet, if for some reason these contracts turn out to be harmful to the common good, then should the contract be binding? It can be argued that the state should not make such binding commitments for fear that it may jeopardize its purpose. If so, then the principles of the law of contract and the scope of markets should be narrowed to exclude these transactions.

The dilemma need not be so sharp. It is possible for the state to insist in its contracts upon a term which permits withdrawal at any time, or upon a condition precedent to obligations arising which protects the common good. Such terms, however, run the risk of losing the advantage of acquiring the service or supplies with the maximum efficiency to be obtained by using the market mechanism. A contractor with the state

---

7   Arbitration Act 1996; see ch 16 below.

will naturally demand a higher price for services, if there is a risk that any investment will be lost by cancellation.

Consider, as an example of this problem, the nature of the legal relationship between civil servants and the Crown (for this purpose the legal identity of the state). The question is whether this relationship should be classified as a market transaction in the form of an ordinary contract of employment, or whether it should be conceived as an exercise of public power with special rules appropriate to the exercise of that power. The practical implications of these different interpretations of the legal position may be summarized by saying that if there is a contract of employment then its terms would be enforceable, whereas, in the absence of a contract, the public law rules which ensure government according to the Rule of Law would provide the relevant regulatory framework regardless of the terms of employment.

For example, in *R v Lord Chancellor's Department, ex p Nangle*,[8] an executive officer was disciplined following allegations of sexual harassment. He sought judicial review of the disciplinary decision on the ground that the Department had broken the standards of good government by violating the principles of fair procedure, the rules of 'natural justice'. The court dismissed this application, however, on the ground that the civil servant was employed under a contract of employment, a market relation, to which the standards of public law did not apply, so his remedy, if any, had to be damages for breach of contract. The problem with this conclusion is, however, that the terms of the contract might impede the government from exercising its power for the common good. The solution no doubt lies in a finding that the terms of the contract of employment provide scant protection to a civil servant whose continued employment in a post frustrates the common good.

The extent to which the state may enter contracts for the achievement of its purposes is thus a negotiable standard. The courts have gradually recognized that the state may enter into binding market commitments for the efficient provision of public services without jeopardizing the public good. In each particular case, however, it is a matter for discussion whether the sphere of market justice should be permitted to govern the state's agreements.

(3) *Inalienable Property*

A final illustration of the exclusion of contract on the ground that contractual obligations are inappropriate for regulating the relation can be described as inalienable property. Examples might include the sale of human organs, human sperm and ovaries, and endangered species of animals. The prohibition on such sales will be justified on the grounds of illegality or public policy.

8   [1991] IRLR 343, Div Ct.

3. Justifications for Limits on Contractual Obligations

These three illustrations of limits to the extent of contractual obligations and market relations raise the question of the purpose of these legal controls. Can we discern a pattern which explains why the market is excluded from certain kinds of relations and subject-matter in contracts? Although I believe that the best explanation requires a deeper understanding of the meaning of contractual relations, arguments have been put forward to explain these limits on the straightforward ground of efficiency and respect for individual liberty. We will consider those explanations before examining the deeper implications of the contractualization of social relations.

(1) Externalities and Market Failure [9]

In answer to the question of why such limits to markets should be imposed, it has been suggested that we should confine our attention to the potential defects of markets with respect to the efficient satisfaction of consumer preferences. Any limits to the sphere of contracts and markets would have to be justified within this framework on the grounds that for some reason the market has failed or that the agreement was not freely chosen. It is certainly possible to justify many limits to the sphere of markets and contracts on these grounds. Moreover, we can detect that these considerations have played a role in guiding the courts and the legislature towards setting the limits to contracts and markets. The economic or market failure explanation of the limits of the sphere of market justice begins with a strong presumption in favour of freedom of contract. It identifies free markets in all goods and services with liberty of the individual and the efficient satisfaction of human wants. Interferences with this freedom are undesirable as a general rule, because they normally create either shortages or black markets in order to evade prohibitions, which display undesirable properties of violence and fear to secure performance of undertakings. Yet the market mechanism has one systematic imperfection. It is likely to discount what are called externalities.

These externalities comprise costs to the parties not involved in the transaction. Such potential costs might include environmental damage, death to an endangered species of animals, injury to health or quality of human life, and disgust and offence. Two parties to an agreement may conclude a bargain which satisfies their own interests, but which incidentally imposes some of these externalities on others. These costs could only be taken into account if all affected parties were permitted to influence the terms of the transaction. But this is impracticable because of transaction costs. These are the costs of time and effort in bringing all

---

9   Calibresi and Melamed, 'Property Rules, Liability Rules, and Inalienability: One View of the Cathedral', (1972) 85 *Harvard Law Review* 1089; Epstein, 'Why Restrain Alienation?', (1985) 85 *Columbia Law Review* 970.

these persons together to haggle over the deal. The solution in these instances of market failure will be for the law to impose limits upon the freedom of two parties to a contract, so that their transaction reflects the externalities involved. Limits to the scope of contracts and markets should be devised such that, where non-participants in a transaction would have been prepared to pay the parties enough to stop the transaction from taking place, then the law should prohibit this type of contract altogether. This legal rule ensures that the market serves the purpose of wealth maximization despite the obstruction presented by transaction costs.

This reasoning can explain most instances where the law forbids contracts for certain types of goods and services. For example, the law may forbid the sale of certain types of drugs on the ground that these contracts will eventually impose costs on the rest of the community in terms of health care. Similarly, the law may prohibit trade in child labour, prostitution, slavery, and bodily organs, on the ground that others find such transactions shocking and offensive. The assumption here is that other members of the community would have been prepared to pay the contracting parties sufficient sums not to trade in such items, so that it would no longer be wealth maximizing for the parties to enter such contracts. The legal prohibition therefore achieves the efficient result, the one which would have occurred but for the problem of transaction costs which prevent the incorporation of externalities into the calculation of wealth maximization.

Notice that this market failure approach finds nothing intrinsically wrong in the legal enforcement of any of these types of transaction. Legal prohibition is triggered by the market functioning inefficiently, so that where the market seems to produce efficient results, even taking into account externalities, then the prohibition will be unjustified. Provided that other members of the community would not be prepared to pay enough to put an end to the transactions in slavery, ivory from elephant tusks, political votes, child labour, and so forth, then on this view the law should permit these transactions.

Like any argument based upon efficiency criteria, it is difficult to falsify its explanation of the limits of markets and contracts, since suitable configurations of externalities can warrant any or no legal limits to market transactions. What is striking about this explanation is the absence of moral criteria other than wealth maximization. Notice that under the market failure theory, the objection to the politician selling his or her votes to the highest bidder is not that the vote has been given on trust by the people to further the common good, but simply that not all persons were present at the auction, with the resulting risk of inefficiency that the electors as a whole would have been willing to pay more for the vote than the multinational corporation. Limits to markets and contracts are therefore set by reference to the presumed goal of markets in wealth maximization, without any concern to promote other kinds of social values.

It is the unequivocal feature of this theory of the limits of contracts which renders it unsatisfactory as an explanation of the law. Even if a concern for externalities sometimes motivates the courts in setting limits to contracts, it is clear that a wide range of other moral considerations and values lead to constraints being imposed as well. The court in *Balfour v Balfour*[10] was concerned about externalities, for it was worried about the potential cost of widespread litigation over domestic disputes, but far more important was its concern that the distributive pattern settled by law for deserted spouses should not be subverted by contractual agreement. As a rationalization of the law setting limits to contracts and markets, the efficiency explanation may work, but, as an interpretation of the motives which lie behind the courts' judgments, it is plainly inadequate, because it fails to take into account the diversity of reasons for setting those limits.

(2) Libertarian Considerations[11]

A libertarian explanation of the limits of markets shares the stance of doubting the intrinsic wrongfulness of transactions. It is prepared to allow the principles of market justice to operate wherever parties have genuinely chosen to make binding commitments, provided that the agreement does not interfere with the rights of others. This explanation relies upon the protection of individual rights as the key to setting the limits to markets. Enforceable contracts should not interfere with rights, including the right to choose whether or not to enter a binding contract.

At first sight the libertarian explanation accounts satisfactorily for many of the limits to markets set by the legal doctrines of illegality. Most criminal laws can be interpreted as protecting the rights of citizens, such as the rights to private property, freedom, and personal security. Agreements which invade these rights, or contemplate an invasion, should not be enforceable, and will be rejected by the courts on the ground of illegality.

But this strand in the libertarian explanation encounters a problem of accounting for the ranking of individual rights. Since freedom of contract is a right itself, the libertarian theory must be able to explain when this right succumbs to the force of superior rights. Perhaps the resolution of this issue is simple in the case of a conspiracy to steal property, for we can say that the right to freedom of contract must always give way to the right to private property. In the case of agreements entailing slavery, however, the libertarian explanation must address the conundrum that a prohibition on such contracts both interferes with a basic right, namely freedom of contract, and simultaneously protects that right in the future and other aspects of liberty. Indeed, the whole legal institution of enforceable contracts presents a difficulty for libertarian accounts, for they inevitably both secure freedom but also constrain it once the bargain becomes enforceable.[12]

In addition, the libertarian explanation places great weight on the intention of the parties, so that the limits of contract are set by reference

---

10   [1919] 2 KB 571, CA.
11   Kronman, 'Paternalism and the Law of Contracts', (1983) 92 *Yale Law Journal* 763, 774–786.
12   Collins, 'Contract and Legal Theory', in W Twining (ed), *Legal Theory and Common Law* (Oxford, 1986).

to the choice of the parties to enter a binding agreement. The crucial reasons for setting limits on the scope of contracts therefore comprise both the intention of the parties to enter a binding legal agreement, and the genuineness of the choice to consent to an agreement.

The libertarian explanation accounts for the presence of the doctrine of intention to create legal relations in the rhetoric of the courts. One of the reasons given in *Balfour v Balfour* for refusing to enforce the agreement was that the parties did not intend to enter a binding contract. In a few instances, the parties may have made it plain that they do not expect to be legally bound. It is a common practice in business, for instance, to issue 'letters of comfort' or 'letters of intent', which contain indications of likely future action and current business strategy, but these are not intended, without more, to create binding obligations, and the courts respect this choice not to enter the market sphere.[13] Similarly, it is normally stated expressly or implied by custom in the United Kingdom that the parties to a collective agreement between management and trade unions do not intend to create a legally enforceable agreement. Apart from these clear expressions of intent, however, the libertarian explanation seems to be fatally flawed.

In cases where the issue is litigated, it seems likely that one party intended a legal agreement and the other wanted the agreement to be merely morally binding. This contradiction removes any possibility of justifying the limits on contracts on the basis of the joint intent of the parties. We are forced to the conclusion that the courts must rely upon hidden policy considerations when determining the intent of the parties. The libertarian focus upon the choice of the parties to make contracts in a family context runs the risk of ignoring the obligations imposed by law, which are designed to support the family as a way of life insulated from market considerations. Even if both husband and wife in *Balfour v Balfour* had seriously intended to make a binding contract, the agreement would surely not have been enforceable, because it was likely to subvert the distributive principles of family law, such as depriving the wife of her needs-based right to maintenance.[14] If so, then this aspect of the libertarian explanation of how the courts set the limits to markets is plainly inadequate.

Another source of justifiable limits on the sphere of the market under the libertarian explanation springs from doubts about the genuineness of the choice to trade in a particular type of goods or services. It seems unlikely, for instance, that a person would really want to choose to be another's slave whatever the inducement offered. Similarly, it might be argued that a wife would not wish to sell her right to maintenance by her husband, or that a politician would not wish to restrict his or her freedom

---

13   *Kleinwort Benson Ltd v Malaysia Mining Corpn* [1989] 1 WLR 379, [1989] 1 All ER 785, CA; *Rose & Frank Co v JR Crompton & Bros Ltd* [1925] AC 445, HL.
14   *Hyman v Hyman* [1929] AC 601, HL; by statute the wife may now sue upon an express promise, but cannot undertake not to apply to a court for her right to maintenance as well: Matrimonial Causes Act 1973, s 34.

of action by selling his or her votes in advance. We have reason to suspect in many of these cases that the contract has been secured by coercion or some other form of unfair dealing.

But, of course, it is hard to discern as a practical matter whether or not such a genuine choice was made. As we shall see in the discussion of consent and coercion in Chapter 8, since every contract is entered into under certain constraints and motivated by needs, the dividing line between free choices and coerced invalid choices cannot be sharply drawn. Even in cases where elements of coercion are patent in the circumstances of the case, we should still need to draw the line between coercion sufficient to negative genuine consent and those ordinary pressures we must expect in life. Consider, for instance, the case of a poor man who sells a kidney in return for money to help his starving family. To doubt that this was a genuine choice requires one to believe that the man valued his kidney above the lives of his family, yet one could also argue that such a sale is plainly a desperate measure of last resort signifying the absence of any real choice.

This problem may be solved, admittedly with a certain degree of arbitrariness, by certain presumptions in the form of legal prohibitions against contracts which seem unlikely to be genuine choices. Recent statutes have certainly employed this technique of absolute prohibition. For instance, the Human Organs Transplants Act 1989 makes it a criminal offence for any person to make or receive payment for the supply of, or offer to supply, an organ removed or to be removed from any person, alive or dead. This rule against sale of bodily organs could be interpreted as an irrebutable presumption against such choices being genuine, and in this way reconciled with the libertarian explanation of the limits of markets and contracts.

But such presumptions enshrined in rules are normally an anathema to libertarians. They fear that such presumptions will disguise instances of paternalism, in which the state imposes on people particular views of how to lead their own lives on the ground that the state knows better what is in their own best interests. Such presumptions, therefore, can only establish suspect grounds for intervention from a libertarian perspective. To be consistent with the libertarian explanation, the law should always admit the possibility that a genuine choice has been made, in order to avoid the risk of unjustifiable paternalism, and this should leave the scope of the market unconfined. In this respect, the approach adopted in *Balfour v Balfour* of presuming the absence of an intent to create legal relations in agreements between spouses seems more consistent with libertarian principles, for it permits exceptions to be found in cases, for instance, where the breakdown of matrimonial relations may indicate a genuine choice to enter a market transaction. One weakness of the libertarian explanation of the limits of the market order therefore comprises its inability to explain satisfactorily the presence of fixed limits to the scope of market transactions.

The underlying weakness of the libertarian explanation of the limits of markets and contracts is that it attempts to rely upon a few simple criteria for fixing the boundaries. Even though these criteria may account for some of the limits to markets, such as an express agreement to avoid legal enforceability, these criteria are inadequate to account for the reasons justifying the limits of markets in a wide range of different examples. To rely upon the choice of the parties in order to account for the prohibition against bribery of public officials seems to fly in the face of common understandings of the problem here, which is that the parties concerned may genuinely have wished to make the bargain, but that it should be deterred for the sake of the integrity of the political system. This final weakness of the libertarian explanation, which is shared with the market failure analysis, points to the need for a theory of the limits of markets and contracts which is sensitive to the wide range of considerations which lead courts to set boundaries.

4. The Purpose of Markets

During my examination of the idea of the social market in Chapter 2, I suggested that markets and contracts should be regarded primarily as a facility for expanding valuable choices and as providing the necessary security for the pursuit of more detailed plans in life. This understanding of markets and contracts suggests that it is wrong to regard these institutions as simply mechanisms for satisfying preferences. The purpose of markets involves a selection between preferences, aiding those which contribute to the pursuit of valuable choices, but prohibiting or obstructing preferences which seem to involve an undesirable way of life.[15] Unlike the market failure and the libertarian explanations of the limits of the market, therefore, the idea of a social market does not commence with a basic disposition towards general freedom of contract, but instead regards freedom of contract as merely valuable within limits for the pursuit of worthwhile individual goals.

From this perspective, the limits upon contracts and markets, far from being potentially dangerous and undesirable infringements of liberty and efficiency, comprise some of the central features of the legal construction of markets as an institution through which individuals may pursue valuable choices in life. It is implicit that not every choice or agreement fits into a valuable way of life, so that these poor and unvaluable choices need to be identified and denied legal enforceability. An agreement involving slavery must be unenforceable, because the choice to subjugate oneself to another cannot lead to a valuable life plan in which one develops personal capacities to the full.[16] Similarly, an agreement for prostitution should not be enforced, because it cannot contribute to the development of worthwhile sexual relations. The important question thus becomes one

---

15   Radin, 'Market-Inalienability' (1987) 100 *Harvard Law Review* 1849.
16   Smith, 'Future Freedom and Freedom of Contract' (1996) 59 *Modern Law Review* 167.

of how should we ascertain those choices which the law should and should not support through the facility of binding contracts.

It is important to recognize fully what is at stake in this question. Contracts represent a delegation of power (or at least the acceptance of the rightful exercise of power) to individuals by which they can shape their lives. It is ultimately within the power of the state to expand or to narrow these delegated powers. In exercising this choice, the state must make a judgement about the relative advantages of granting individuals permission to shape their lives against the alternative of determining or shaping those aspects of life through regulation either by the state or intermediate institutions. The state can, for instance, exclude the education of children from the market, and replace it with administrative regulations which ensure the supply of the necessary quantity and quality of education desired. This measure which excludes the market from education of children might be justifed on such grounds as the need for an even provision of education across the population in order to ensure equality of opportunity, or a belief that professional teachers in fact understand better than parents what kind of education will equip children for life. Against this state control and exclusion of markets, it could be argued that it is best to leave to parents the choice of how to educate their children, for this will promote diversity in the culture, encourage efficiency through competition, and lead to greater preference satisfaction for the parents and possibly the children as well.

No simple answer will be available to such questions concerning the proper scope of markets. Not only will opinions vary over time with respect to the value of particular choices, but also it is a virtue of the market as an institution that it permits considerable experimentation in the kinds of life which people may choose to lead. It follows that the law of contract should recognize, as it does, the possibility of renegotiation of boundaries of enforceability, when it is the vehicle for interesting and potentially valuable new choices of the way to spend a life. It was in this spirit that the law of contract was allowed to govern the family relations in *Ward v Byam*[17] and *Tanner v Tanner*.[18]

But there are two principal dangers which may be provoked by experimentation through contracts. In the first place, law of contract analyses and evaluates social relations formed within its confines by reference to criteria which may lead to an undesirable distortion of the meaning of the social relation involved. Secondly, the seductive attraction of avoidance of explicit distributive decisions by delegating outcomes to the market mechanism can pose a threat to important principles of distributive justice.

(1) The Meaning of Contractualization
The significance of the contractualization of social relations can be elucidated in four dimensions.

17 [1956] 1 WLR 496, [1956] 2 All ER 318, CA.
18 [1975] 1 WLR 1346, [1975] 3 All ER 776, CA.

Valuation of Conduct

Contracts create a particular form of valuation of conduct. They purport to measure conduct narrowly by reference solely to the terms recorded for the transaction. The terms purport to set the exclusive point of reference, which inevitably confines or truncates the perception of the obligations owed between the parties.[19] This perception then creates the possibility of a conflict between the agreed bargain and the reasonable expectations of the parties based upon informal understandings regarding co-operation, give-and-take, and dealing in good faith. In some long-term business relations a strict insistence upon the terms of the contract will be regarded as a form of opportunism,[20] for this valuation of conduct contradicts the basis of the relation in good faith conduct which establishes a business reputation for fair dealing. Diffuse obligations of support, co-operation, reciprocity, and sharing, become harder to establish, with the effect that the dynamic and meaning of the social relation becomes altered. This was the fundamental reason which Atkin LJ gave for declining to enforce the agreement in *Balfour v Balfour*.[21] The problem becomes most striking in agency relations, such as employment, where the more that the employer seeks to control the employee's discretion about how to define and carry out tasks, the less the employer can call upon diffuse obligations of loyalty and professionalism to further the interests of the employer's business.

Currency of Exchange

Contracts also establish social relations with a currency of exchange which is quantifiable and measurable. This permits the introduction of what Max Weber called formal rational economic behaviour into any type of social relation contained in a contract.[22] The question asked about the relation is whether it increases the wealth of the parties or whether it satisfies their preferences. Other questions about the contribution of the relation to the meaning of the lives of the parties are rendered irrelevant because they cannot be incorporated into the measurement of success. In this vein, for instance, non-pecuniary losses such as vexation and disappointment caused by breach of contract cannot be the basis of a remedy in damages for they cannot be quantified. Similarly, to view an invitation to dinner with a friend as a contract would suggest that the value of the invitation can be reduced to a monetary price, whereas the point of the invitation is to reinforce the ties of friendship which are not the product of formal rational economic behaviour. The insertion of contracts into such relations as friendship does not destroy those relations,

19   P Goodrich, *Languages of Law* (London, 1990) at p 154.
20   Beale and Dugdale, 'Contracts Between Businessmen: Planning and the Use of Contractual Remedies' (1975) 2 *British Journal of Law and Society* 45, 47.
21   [1919] 2 KB 571, CA.
22   M Weber, *Economy and Society*, eds G Roth and C Wittich (Berkeley, 2 Vols, 1978) 85, 669.

but it does introduce a particular form of valuation of behaviour which may tend to exclude other types of measurement such as loyalty and trust.[23]

Atomization

A third feature of contractualization consists in the atomization of social relations, so that the effects of a transaction upon other people are regarded as irrelevant. For instance, if one employee of a business receives high pay, which compels the business to dismiss another for lack of funds, the connection between these two decisions is rendered opaque by separation of contractual relations. Similarly, the decision to permit employers to offer higher wages to workers who belong to one union as opposed to another can be justified as an aspect of freedom of contract, but it overlooks the effects on union membership and the potential for solidarity through unions for other employees.[24]

Discretionary Power

Finally, contractualization permits the formation of a particular type of power relation. Although the imagery of freedom of contract presents an egalitarian picture of two people negotiating the terms of their agreement, in practice most contracts constitute the opportunity for one party to create unilaterally a system of rules and governance structures for the relation.[25] The standard form consumer contract represents only the tip of an iceberg of these governance structures. Contracts can incorporate whole regulatory systems such as staff handbooks, works rules, railway by-laws, and quality assurance procedures. These codes simulate the form of a contract, but they really represent the exercise of discretionary economic power by one party to the contract over the other backed up by a system of economic sanctions specific to that relation, such as the discipline of the employee or the disqualification of a contractor.

The Meaning of Contractual Relations

These four features of contractual relations as a form of social relation – the valuation in delimited terms, the measurement by a precise currency of exchange, the externalization of social effects, and the unilateral rule-making power – reveal that the decision to delegate to individuals the power to construct their own social relations through the market mechanism is not such a neutral choice as it may appear at first. In the case of cohabitation agreements, for instance, we can welcome the empowerment to the parties concerned of being able to shape through

---

23   Duxbury, 'Do Markets Degrade?', (1996) 59 *Modern Law Review* 331.
24   *Associated Newspapers Ltd v Wilson, Associated British Ports v Palmer* [1995] 2 AC 454, [1995] ICR 406, HL.
25   Kessler, 'Contracts of Adhesion – Some Thoughts About Freedom of Contract' (1943) 43 *Columbia Law Review* 629.

contracts how their relation should be constructed. They may wish, for instance, to pool all their property, or alternatively to keep their financial affairs strictly apart with no assumption of maintenance obligations towards a partner. By permitting contracts to be made between the parties on such matters, the law facilitates this power of choice to construct social relations.[26] But it should be recognized that at the same time the contractualization of such social relations will have the tendencies described above of emphasizing the values of preference satisfaction and a monetary currency of exchange between the parties. If we wish to insist that cohabitation arrangements should entail more open-ended commitments of sharing, reciprocity and loyalty, then we may find that the intrusion of contracts subverts this goal.

At bottom, therefore, the proper scope of the market and contracts must turn on carefully balanced judgements on the question of whether the valuable freedom for individuals to construct their own social relations, which give meaning to their lives, should be restricted in particular instances, for the reason that, if the meanings are to be established through the market mechanism, it is unlikely that they constitute valuable and worthwhile choices in life. To prevent social relations with these undesirable properties from being constituted, it will be necessary to exclude markets and contracts. Just as the law must be wary about allowing the sphere of politics to intervene too meticulously in the market for fear of stifling its properties as an efficient satisfier of human wants, so too the law must prevent the market from infringing upon other social spheres such as politics and the family to their detriment as sites and opportunities for meaning. This explanation of the limits of the market order, unlike the libertarian one, therefore justifies mandatory limits to the field of contracts.

Nevertheless, it remains a difficult question of degree and calculation of probable effects to determine whether the market should be excluded from a particular kind of social relation. We might reject, for instance, a market in babies, for fear that these transactions would lead to a perception of babies as products to be evaluated in monetary terms by their characteristics, rather than as independent persons to whom the parents owe duties of care and nourishment. The case where a couple tried to exchange their baby for a used car raises the spectre that all children might become valued, and value themselves, according to their exchange value in the market, which might depend on colour, size, and likely inherited genetic traits, rather than being valued for themselves and their many qualities.[27] But the same fears might not extend to a surrogacy transaction by which a woman, in return for payment, agrees to bear and hand over a child to a childless couple. Although in form this

26 Olsen, 'The Family and the Market: A Study of Ideology and Legal Reform' (1983) 96 *Harvard Law Review* 1497; Dalton, 'An Essay in the Deconstruction of Contract Doctrine' (1985) 94 *Yale Law Journal* 997, 1095.
27 *Toronto Star*, 5 September 1980; E Landes and R Posner, 'The Economics of the Baby Shortage' (1978) 7 *Journal of Legal Studies* 323.

resembles the sale of a baby, it does not so much signify an economic valuation of the child but a valuation of the service of gestation in the womb. Again we may fear the commercialization of this dimension of motherhood, but against this we must recognize that the transaction is intended not to thwart the values of the social sphere of the family but to extend the opportunity to establish meaning in that sphere for a childless couple.[28] Under the Surrogacy Arrangements Act 1985 the practice of surrogacy is not prohibited, but it is a criminal offence to initiate or take part in any negotiations, or offering or agreeing to do so, with a view to the making a surrogacy arrangement on a commercial basis. The statute therefore excludes the market from establishing social relations of surrogacy, but permits them as an aspect of family life based upon gift and caring. This explanation of the limits of the market order cannot produce bright lines to define the limits of social spheres, for the boundaries depend in the final analysis upon uncertain predictions about the deleterious effects of the extension of contractualization to particular kinds of social relations.[29]

(2) *Distributive Justice*

A second major consideration which determines the scope of markets and contracts returns to the problem of social justice. We noted above the seductive attraction of the market mechanism as a distributive solution which avoids direct state intervention to fix a pattern for the distribution of wealth. Nevertheless, it has to be recognized that the market mechanism has foreseeable distributive effects. Those with strong bargaining power derived from wealth, special talents, and other resources, can usually employ the market mechanism to their relative advantage. Although perhaps not objectionable in general, in particular instances the use of bargaining power to achieve superior distributive outcomes may conflict with important distributive principles which we wish to protect from market manipulation.

By permitting markets to enter particular kinds of social relations, what becomes possible is the use of resources which are valuable in the commercial and economic spheres of social life in order to gain distributional advantages in other spheres of life. If, for example, a rich man is permitted to buy votes, then he is able to convert his wealth into political power by use of the market mechanism. Michael Walzer in his book *Spheres of Justice*[30] argues cogently that the limits to markets and contracts should be set in order to protect the integrity of the distributional

---

28   Hollinger, 'From Coitus to Commerce: Legal and Social Consequences of Noncoital Reproduction' (1985) 18 *University of Michigan Journal of Law Reform* 865; Note, 'Rumplestiltskin Revisited: The Inalienable Rights of Surrogate Mothers' (1986) 99 *Harvard Law Review* 1936.

29   Radin, 'Market-Inalienability' (1987) 100 *Harvard Law Review* 1849; Mack, 'Dominos and the Fear of Commodification' in J Chapman and JR Pennock (eds), *Markets and Justice* (New York, 1989).

30   (Oxford, 1983).

principles appropriate to different spheres of social life. Hence the rich man may use his wealth to acquire expensive goods, but should not be permitted to buy votes, because this practice interferes with the egalitarian principle for the distribution of political power envisaged in a democracy. To achieve this separation and integrity of different spheres of distributive justice, limits to contracts and markets must be established.

Once again, of course, the extent to which the market mechanism should be permitted to influence distributive outcomes will be controversial and constantly subject to revision. Indeed, this debate often lies at the heart of contemporary political disputes. Should access to health care for the sick, or education for children, be dependent upon ability to pay, or should some non-market distributive principle such as need or equality of opportunity be adopted to govern access to these scarce resources? Consider as another example the governance of the workplace. Ownership of the capital which creates a productive enterprise has traditionally brought with it the right of the owner to manage and regulate the workplace. But this power of governance in the workplace derived from the application of markets through the contract of employment might be thought to belong more properly to all those employed by the firm, or even to the community in which the business operates. To the extent that the latter view becomes dominant, then the owner's power to enter contracts which give him the right to manage the business must be constrained and replaced by institutions of government in the workplace which reflect the objective of worker or community control.

The presence of these distributive considerations is evident in some of the earlier examples. One of the reasons for the court's reluctance to enforce the agreement in *Balfour v Balfour* was the concern that the market might be employed to undermine the distributive scheme for families arranged through the law of maintenance. Similarly, the rejection of bribery and political influence obtained through contracts reflects a desire to keep the sphere of politics relatively immune from the distributive pattern established by markets. These distributive considerations, and in particular the desire to prevent the conversion of market power into other forms of favourable distributive outcomes in different social spheres, thus accounts for many of the significant limits on markets and contracts.

7

Ascription of Contractual Responsibility

How does a person become bound to a contractual obligation? This is the question of the ascription or attribution of contractual responsibility. The traditional principle insists that a person's consent or agreement is an essential prerequisite to the ascription of contractual responsibility. This requirement of consent derives from the idea that a contractual obligation constitutes a voluntary assumption of an obligation, which is additional to the general obligations imposed by the law upon everyone.

The foundation of contractual responsibility in consent also serves to provide a rough distinction between contractual obligations and those deriving from other branches of private law such as tort, restitution, and property. Although issues concerning consent may be relevant to those other sources of obligations, the law of contract is distinctive in the way in which it seeks to attribute the source of the obligation to the consent of the parties. In the law of tort, for instance, a duty to exercise reasonable care will be imposed by virtue of the relationship between the parties, and the role of consent may be confined to limiting the scope of that obligation. In the law of contract, however, the existence of a similar duty of care will be founded on the agreement of the parties to the creation of such an obligation. This contrast can never be drawn sharply, however, for, as we shall see, it is possible to infer consent from the nature of a relationship or a course of dealing, and equally other sources of obligation employ concepts which are closely analogous to consent, such as the idea of 'free acceptance' in restitution or the idea of 'voluntary assumption of responsibility' in tort.

1. The Idea of Consent

Nevertheless, the idea of consent is central to the attribution of contractual responsibility. Indeed, many of the complexities in the classical law of contract derived from the attempt to deal with a variety of issues by reference solely to the idea of consent. As a result, the law's concept of consent became muddled and at times contradictory.

The breathtaking range of issues which the classical law attempted to resolve by reference to the idea of consent included the following. How does a person become bound to a contractual obligation? – by consent to an agreement. When does a person become bound by a contractual obligation? – liability begins at the moment when both parties have consented to an agreement. What is the content of the contractual obligation? – the terms of the contract to which consent has been given. Who is bound by the contractual obligation? – only the persons who have consented to the agreement can obtain rights or incur obligations under the contract. When will the use of threats or lies by one party towards the other prevent a contractual obligation from arising? – when those threats or lies invalidate the apparent consent given to the contract. When will mental incapacity or immaturity prevent a person from entering a contractual obligation? – when that incapacity prevents consent from being given to the contract.

This emphasis upon the idea of consent contributed to the elegance and simplicity of the classical law of contract, but a brief reflection on the variety of issues handled by the idea reveals that they present rather different problems for the law to handle. For example, even though entry into a contractual obligation may require consent, there may be good reason to answer the question about the content of the obligation by reference to criteria other than by the consent of the parties, so that the content of the obligation may be either supplemented or confined by reference to considerations of fairness, efficiency, or social policy. Similarly, there may be good reasons of fairness or efficiency to extend the range of liability beyond the parties to the contract where third persons were intended to benefit from performance of the contract.

Indeed, as we consider these different issues, we will discover that despite the lip-service paid to the idea of consent, the law handles them effectively by other rules and standards. The absence or presence of consent tends to be the conclusion of a process of reasoning, in which the idea of consent has played no role at all. In the case of fraud, for instance, the law examines the kind of statement which was made, whether or not it was false, and whether it induced entry into the contract, and if these tests are satisfied then the contract will be avoided because fraud has vitiated consent. In this reasoning process, the lack of consent to the contract represents the conclusion of the argument, but serves no function in determining whether or not a valid contract has been created.

Similarly, the classical law analysed the incapacity of children and artificial bodies such as corporations and public authorities to enter contracts as a result of a lack of an ability to give consent. But the modern rules do not conform to the logic of consent at all. With respect to children, that is minors under the age of eighteen, the general rule is that the contract is not binding on the child, but the rule is severely qualified by exceptions designed to protect the trader who deals with a child in good faith and fairly, and where an incapacity would prevent the minor from making contracts which are necessary for his or her own welfare. In practice this has the effect that everyday contracts with children which are fair are binding.[1] For corporations, the traditional position denied the power to consent to contracts outside the capacity conferred by the constitutional documents which established the artificial entity.[2] This link between capacity and the ascription of contractual responsibility proved a trap for the unwary in dealings with corporations, so now they are presumed to have contractual capacity.[3] Limits on the capacity to contract may, however, still apply to government agencies and other statutory corporations under the doctrine of 'ultra vires'. The courts appear to assume that if a contract was outside the powers of a public authority, then it should be regarded as void for the sake of the public interest. Yet the public interest could be protected better by permitting those who have entered into contracts with public authorities in good faith to enforce their contracts, for this would avoid the deterrent to making contracts with public authorities which the doctrine of ultra vires creates, whilst devising appropriate sanctions for those public officials who act beyond the scope of their powers. The idea of consent gives a spurious unity and coherence to the legal doctrine concerning capacity, but on examination of how the law determines the particular issues it rarely performs any significant part. It might be better to abolish the doctrine of capacity altogether and replace it with appropriate rules governing the circumstances when contracts should be unenforceable against certain types of parties.

The emphasis upon the idea of consent is not only misleading but also confusing. As the law addresses the different issues, the concept of consent twists and turns in its meanings. The unity of the classical law therefore turns out to be a mirage, for the meaning of the requirement of consent alters according to the context of the problem and the relevant policy issues which the court must consider. As an example, consider two cases concerning the purchase of an automobile. In the first, the dealer lies about the qualities of the car, and the contract can be invalidated because the fraud negatives consent. Here the idea of consent suggests that the purchaser did not give consent to the contract because he did not know the full facts of the matter. In the second case, the car has a latent defect which is a breach of warranty by the dealer. If we applied the idea of consent in which the purchaser must have full knowledge of the facts of the case to this problem, we would conclude that no contract had been formed at all, since the purchaser would not have bought the car with a latent defect. The law will certainly conclude, however, that a contract was made in the second case despite the mistake, though the purchaser will be entitled to reject the car and receive back his money. The idea of consent therefore shifts radically according to the problem to be addressed.

---

1   Sale of Goods Act 1979, s 3; Minors' Contracts Act 1987.
2   *Rolled Steel Products (Holdings) Ltd v British Steel Corpn* [1986] Ch 246, [1985] 3 All ER 52, CA.
3   Companies Act 1985, ss 35, 35A, as amended by Companies Act 1989, and EC Directive 68/151.

In this chapter, the issue to be considered is how a person becomes bound by a contractual obligation. The simple answer is by consent to an agreement, but a more perceptive answer will include an examination of the idea of consent employed in this context and an investigation of the extent to which the idea of consent plays any real function in the determination of contractual responsibility. Since the idea of consent is regarded as the hallmark of contractual obligations, we will also take the opportunity to consider how far this idea of consent serves to distinguish contractual obligations from other sources of obligations in tort, restitution and property law.

2. Objective Test of Consent

It must be rare for parties entering a contract to make a declaration in the form 'I consent to this contract'. The shopper in a store simply presents the goods selected and a method of payment, and the sales assistant registers the sale on the till. When a person travels by public transport, (s)he simply purchases a ticket. In complex commercial transactions with reams of written documents, all that happens is a signature on a document and perhaps a handshake. In the normal case, therefore, the law must infer consent to a contract from the words and conduct of the parties.

A signature on a document, for example, will normally be regarded as an expression of consent to the contract.[4] But we should be aware that even in this case of clear evidence of consent, we must go through a process of inferring consent from conduct. The signature on a document is regarded as a sign that consent has been given to the undertaking of the contractual responsibility contained in the document. The meaning of a signature has been established by convention, a common practice which the law recognizes as effective to attribute contractual responsibility to the signatory. Outside such clear conventions, however, the law must examine the conduct of the parties to discover whether consent to a transaction may be inferred. The problem confronting the law is to decide which forms of words and conduct should be regarded as signifying consent to a contract.

Since the law infers consent from conduct, the approach is often described as an objective test. The law examines the evidence which is verifiable by observation rather than speculating upon the actual state of mind of the parties. The law must therefore cope with the problem presented by a person whose conduct indicates consent to a contract, yet who asserts that he had no intention to enter any contract. The objective test denies any strength to such secret reservations. Blackburn J summarized both aspects of this objective test in a celebrated statement of principle in *Smith v Hughes*:[5]

---

4   *L'Estrange v F Graucob Ltd* [1934] 2 KB 394, DC.
5   (1871) LR 6 QB 597.

> If, whatever a man's real intention may be, he so conducts himself that a reasonable man would believe that he was assenting to the terms proposed by the other party, and that other party upon that belief enters into the contract with him, the man thus conducting himself would be equally bound as if he had intended to agree to the other party's terms.

It follows from the objective test of consent that apparent consent to an agreement suffices to establish contractual responsibility, and that actual consent in the sense of an intention to enter a contract is not strictly necessary. It is no good, for instance, to fill up a car with petrol at a self-service petrol station, and then claim that no contract for the sale of the petrol was made because you did not intend to make the contract. A court will infer from the conduct of filling up the car with petrol that consent was given to a contract for the sale of petrol. Equally the court will infer from the conduct of the garage proprietor of permitting the tank to be filled that the proprietor consents to the sale of the petrol.

By permitting inferences of consent to be drawn from conduct, the law certainly facilitates transactions by avoiding unnecessary obstacles such as a requirement for contracts to be in writing or constituted by express statements. Inevitably, however, the courts will encounter situations where the conduct is ambiguous and could be regarded either as consent to a contract or a rejection of a contract. The test propounded by Blackburn J to cover these cases, that the court should examine the facts from the point of view of the other party, to see whether it was reasonable for that other party to infer consent, provides useful but incomplete guidance.

Standard Form Contracts
The most important practical effect of the objective test of consent concerns the validity of standard form contracts. In many consumer and business transactions, the contract will be concluded on the basis of a printed document which purports to contain all the terms of the contract. In some cases the printed document will be signed by both parties, but often it is merely handed over or posted at the time of the formation of the contract. Some doubt has been expressed about the validity of such standard forms to count as contracts.[6] The process often resembles an imposition of will rather than mutual consent to an agreement, so these transactions have been described as contracts of adhesion.

The use of standard forms responds to two economic pressures. They reduce the transaction costs of contracting by making available at no extra cost a suitable set of terms. In addition, the printed form permits senior management of a firm to control the contractual arrangements made by

---

6   Kessler, 'Contracts of Adhesion – Some Thoughts About Freedom of Contract' (1943) 43 *Columbia Law Review* 629; Slawson, 'Standard Form Contracts and Democratic Control of Lawmaking Power' (1971) 84 *Harvard Law Review* 529; Slawson, 'The New Meaning of Contract: The Transformation of Contracts Law by Standard Forms' (1984) 46 *University of Pittsburgh Law Review* 21; Johnson, 'Autonomy and Contractual Liability' (1983) 2 *Law and Philosophy* 271.

subordinate sales staff.[7] For these reasons, it makes sense to permit the use of standard forms, but to control the content of the terms of the contracts. The objective test of consent ensures that normally they count as a contractual agreement between the parties.

Inaction and Silence
The objective test helps to resolve cases where consent has been inferred from inaction or silence. If an offer is sent by post but the offeror receives no reply, then it is not reasonable to infer from that silence that consent has been given, for the silence might equally or even more probably signify a rejection of the offer. Evidence to the effect that the recipient of the letter did intend to agree to the proposed contract is irrelevant under this objective test, for unless this evidence had come to the attention of the offeror he could not reasonably infer consent from silence. Hence in *Felthouse v Bindley*,[8] following muddled and inconclusive negotiations for the sale of a horse, the plaintiff wrote to his nephew offering to buy the horse at a fixed price, adding, 'If I hear no more about him, I consider the horse is mine at £30 15s.' His nephew did not reply to this letter, but a few weeks later he informed an auctioneer of his stock that the horse had been sold. Unfortunately the horse was inadvertently sold by the auctioneer to another person, and the plaintiff claimed damages against the auctioneer for the loss of his property. The claim failed on the ground that no valid contract of sale for the horse had been concluded. One reason for invalidity was that the nephew's consent could not be inferred from his silence to the plaintiff, even though it was apparent that the nephew had intended to agree to the contract. This case can be interpreted under the objective test as making the point that the plaintiff could not reasonably infer consent from silence, though it leaves open the possibility that if the plaintiff had heard of the nephew's intentions in some other way, then consent might have been reasonably inferred.

The problem of determining consent from inaction becomes particularly acute when the alleged consent is to a contract which modifies an existing legal relation. In this context we can expect more informal dealings between the parties, so it becomes reasonable to infer consent from inaction. For example, if a buyer does not receive the promised goods on time, but raises no objection when they are delivered late, then it might be inferred from this conduct that the buyer has agreed to a modification of the contract. In this context of inaction in an existing contractual relation, Lord Brandon suggested that the test of consent should be that:

> the conduct of B, as evinced towards A, has been such as to lead A reasonably to believe that B has abandoned the contract, even though it has not in fact

---

7   Rakoff, 'Contracts of Adhesion: An Essay in Reconstruction' (1983) 96 *Harvard Law Review* 1174; Macneil, 'Bureaucracy and Contracts of Adhesion' (1984) 22 *Osgoode Hall Law Journal* 5.

8   (1862) 11 CBNS 869, 142 ER 1037.

been B's intention to do so, and that A has significantly altered his position in reliance on that belief.[9]

Express Reservations

It follows from the objective test that express reservations indicating an unwillingness to enter a contract will normally prevent an inference of consent. The presence of the express reservation renders it unreasonable to suppose that consent to the contract has been given. Thus a statement that any agreement should be regarded as provisional and will be 'subject to contract' negatives consent,[10] for this disclaimer makes the unwillingness to make a contract clear.

Less explicit statements will also suffice to negative the intention to enter a contract. In *Gibson v Manchester City Council*,[11] the Council sent to council tenants details of a scheme under which they might purchase their homes. The appellant filled in a form indicating interest in this opportunity. The city treasurer then sent him a letter which stated that 'the corporation may be prepared to sell the house to you at the purchase price of ... £2,180' and finished by saying, 'If you would like to make a formal application to buy your council house, please complete the enclosed application form and return it ... ' The appellant returned the completed application form (after some further communications) and claimed that a contract for the sale of the house had been concluded. But the House of Lords decided that the letter from the city treasurer did not indicate a willingness to consent to a contract. Their interpretation of the letter was to the effect that it expressly negatived an intention to enter a contract.

Implied Reservations

A court may be asked to draw a similar inference about a reservation to entering a contract from the context and the statements made by the parties. This inference will customarily be drawn, for instance, when construction work is put out for tender. Here the normal course of events consists of work being put out for tender, the competing bids for the work are received from different construction companies, and then finally one of these bids is accepted. In these cases a court will normally decide that no contractual responsibility arises until one of the bids has been accepted, for this bidding process is designed to facilitate a competitive market, and so no inference of consent to any particular contract should be drawn until a bid is accepted.[12]

Advertisements in newspapers and magazines often present a similar kind of problem. If a person responds to the advertisement in the terms

---

9   *Paal Wilson & Co A / S v Partenreederei Hannah Blumenthal (The Hannah Blumenthal)* [1983] 1 AC 854, [1983] 1 All ER 34, HL.
10   *A-G of Hong Kong v Humphreys Estate (Queen's Gardens) Ltd* [1987] AC 114, [1987] 2 All ER 387, PC.
11   [1979] 1 WLR 294, [1979] 1 All ER 972, HL.
12   *Spencer v Harding* (1870) LR 5 CP 561.

specified, such as placing an order, or, as in *Carlill v Carbolic Smoke Ball Co*,[13] using the smoke ball, should this suffice to create contractual responsibility? On the one hand it may be urged that the advertisement has all the appearance of consent to a contract on the terms specified, but on the other hand it may be argued that it is merely intended as a publicity exercise and that any contracts should be formed by express dealings between the parties. In accordance with the principle of the objective test propounded by Blackburn J, the answer must depend in each particular case on whether a reasonable person would infer from the terms of the advertisement that it evidenced consent to a contract on satisfaction of any conditions. For example, a typical small advertisement in a newspaper may read, 'Flat for rent, Camberwell, £70 p.w. tel: 123'; it would not be reasonable to construe this as consent to a contract with the first person who telephoned. It should be expected that the landlord will wish to interview the potential tenants or at least establish their suitability before agreeing to the contract. On the other hand, an advertisement which is sufficiently explicit and without reservation, as in *Carlill v Carbolic Smoke Ball Co*, may well be regarded as an expression of consent to a contract.

When examining these examples of inferences of consent and implied reservations or conditions, it is important to be alert to the possibility that several contracts may be contemplated between the parties. In the case of tendering, for example, although the tenderer may expressly or by implication reserve the right to decide whether or not to enter into any contract at all with any bidder, the tenderer may at the same time indicate consent to other contractual obligations, such as an obligation to award the job to the lowest bidder if the job is awarded to any bid at all,[14] or an obligation to consider all bids which have been submitted in proper form at the appointed time and place.[15] These subsidiary or collateral contracts can be formed by consent tested objectively, even though the main contract which is contemplated for the building works is never formed between the parties.

Consent or Reliance?

It is plain from this discussion of the objective test of consent, that a very thin theory of consent is applied by the law. Although in most instances no doubt the entry into a contract coincides with an intention to make a contract, such an intention is not required. Nor does the objective test of consent require a knowledge or understanding of the terms of the proposed contract. The signature on a document or the receipt of the standard form contract counts as conduct which evidences consent to the contract. The question arises whether the objective test of consent is really a test of consent at all.

---

13 [1893] 1 QB 256, CA.
14 *Harvela Investments Ltd v Royal Trust Co of Canada Ltd* [1986] AC 207, [1985] 2 All ER 966, HL.
15 *Blackpool and Fylde Aeroclub Ltd v Blackpool Borough Council* [1990] 1 WLR 1195, [1990] 3 All ER 25, CA.

We could say that in reality consent is irrelevant; what matters is whether it was reasonable for the other party to rely upon the existence of contractual responsibility in view of the observed conduct. This hypothesis translates the test for ascription of responsibility from one concerning consent by one party to another test of reasonable reliance by the other.

This reinterpretation of the cases raises a question of principle, for the reference to reasonable reliance reduces the respect paid by the law to freedom of contract and the choice whether or not to enter a contract. It also suggests that consent should not be regarded as the distinguishing quality of the source of contractual obligations. Instead, the origin of contractual responsibility appears to lie in a special type of reliance on another's conduct that indicates that the other has voluntarily undertaken a special obligation.

This view is strengthened by a comparison with the reliance model of the test of enforceability. It will be recalled that to satisfy the reliance model, one party must encourage the other to believe that rights have been granted or will be granted, and the other party must act to his detriment on the faith of that encouragement. This requirement is similar to the ordinary contractual idea of reliance on the other's conduct which indicates the voluntary undertaking of an obligation. In both cases attention shifts from the state of mind of the promisor, which is the emphasis in the traditional idea of consent, to the reasonableness of the reliance of the promisee in the light of the promisor's conduct. This parallel in the determination of the ascription of responsibility between the two structural models of enforceability adds weight to the view that the origin of contractual responsibility lies in special instances of reliance rather than consent.

3. Common Mistake

Can consent to a contract be negatived by a fundamental mistake about the circumstances surrounding the transaction?[16] If I agree to purchase a car, but shortly before the agreement and unknown to both parties the car was completely destroyed in an accident, is the agreement invalid? If the agreement is invalid, is this due to the absence of consent to the contract? The objective test of consent should rule out this latter possibility, for the evidence supports consent to a contract. The nature of my relief from the contract should depend upon the allocation of risk in the contract with regard to the destruction of the car. Nevertheless, there have been occasional suggestions that the contract is invalid due to the absence of consent.

---

16   Slade, 'The Myth of Mistake in the English Law of Contract' (1954) 70 *Law Quarterly Review* 385.

The logic behind this argument depends upon forging a link between the ideas of consent and intent. In the ordinary usage of the word intent, we usually recognize that a mistake about the facts will negative intent. If I take a raincoat from a hook, believing it to be my own, whereas in fact it is a similar one belonging to someone else, we would not say that I intended to take the other person's raincoat. The mistake about the ownership of the raincoat negatives my intent to take another's property. Similarly, it may be argued that a mistake about the circumstances surrounding a transaction may negative consent to the agreement, if the consent would have been withheld had the true state of affairs been known. Thus it might be argued that my mistake about the state of the car negatives my intention to make the contract, and therefore invalidates my consent. This argument overlooks the point that the objective test of consent sunders the connection between consent and intent in the context of the ascription of contractual responsibility. The actual intent of the parties is not crucial for the ascription of contractual responsibility. What matters is the appearance of consent to a contract, which may be inferred from words and conduct, regardless of the intentions of the parties.

Nevertheless, in a perplexing judgment in *Bell v Lever Bros*,[17] Lord Atkin claimed that there existed a narrow doctrine of mistake with regard to the subject-matter of a contract.

> In such a case a mistake will not affect assent unless it is the mistake of both parties and is to the existence of some quality which makes the thing without the quality essentially different from the thing as it was believed to be.

Having stated this principle, however, Lord Atkin was unable to find either authority from cases to support it, or examples to illustrate it. He was able to point to the Sale of Goods Act 1893 (now 1979), which declares in section 6 that a sale is void if the seller was ignorant of the fact that the goods had already been destroyed. This statutory provision was itself based upon a misreading of earlier cases, such as *Couturier v Hastie*,[18] which had not declared the contract void for mistake, but had simply denied the seller any remedy on the ground that the seller had failed to perform his side of the bargain. There is also authority which suggests that a sale to a buyer who already owns the property will be voidable,[19] but as Lord Atkin himself observed, normally a seller will be understood to warrant that he owns the goods or property, so the sale can be terminated for breach of this warranty, which suggests that a binding contract has been formed.

It is also possible to view these authorities as merely deciding that where a contract contains an express or implied term that it will only be enforceable if a particular circumstance or state of affairs exists, then the failure of this condition precedent will prevent a binding contract arising.

17   [1932] AC 161, HL.
18   (1856) 5 HL Cas 673.
19   *Cooper v Phibbs* (1867) LR 2 HL 149, HL.

Strictly speaking, however, on this analysis a contract has been entered into, but, one of its terms, which is enforceable, declares that certain events shall render the contract unenforceable and without any legal effect. There is ascription of contractual responsibility to a conditional contract, and, on failure of the condition, the contract provides that it should have no legal effect. This analysis has the potential to explain all the English cases which seem to give credence to the doctrine of mistake. For example, in *Griffith v Brymer*,[20] the plaintiff agreed to hire a room to view a coronation procession an hour after it was decided to operate on the King and therefore cancel the procession. The plaintiff recovered the rent he had paid. Although the decision can be interpreted as an application of Lord Atkin's principle of common mistake, Lord Atkin himself seems to have regarded the coronation cases as an example of an implied condition about a state of facts, so that on failure of the condition the contract had no legal effect. This analysis also fits coherently into the general principles governing ascription of responsibility, for it holds the parties bound to a contract by virtue of their apparent consent, but then out of respect for their autonomy permits the parties to determine the effects of their transaction in the event of mistakes being discovered.

The remaining illustrations of the doctrine of mistake offered by Lord Atkin all display the perverse characteristic that they invariably indicate that the doctrine has no application. For example,

> A buys a picture from B: both A and B believe it to be the work of an old master, and a high price is paid. It turns out to be a modern copy. A has no remedy in the absence of misrepresentation or warranty.

Nevertheless, Lord Atkin's statement of principle stands and may occasionally find some application.

A revealing recent application of the doctrine occurred in *Associated Japanese Bank (International) Ltd v Crédit du Nord SA*.[21] An engineering company arranged with the plaintiff bank a sale and leaseback transaction with respect to four precision machines. The defendant bank gave a guarantee to the plaintiff for the repayments by the engineering company under the leaseback. It turned out that the engineering company had perpetrated a fraud, for it never owned any such machines. The plaintiff tried to enforce the guarantee given by the defendant when the engineering company failed to keep up its repayments. The defendant, however, succeeded in arguing that the guarantee was subject to a condition precedent that the machines existed, so that it was unenforceable on failure of the condition. As an alternative ground for the decision, the court was also prepared to apply the doctrine of common mistake formulated by Lord Atkin. Steyn J held that the mistake about the existence of the machines rendered the nature of the guarantee essentially different. He added, however, that the defendant would not have been

20   (1903) 19 TLR 434.
21   [1989] 1 WLR 255, [1988] 3 All ER 902, QB.

able to rely upon the mistake if it had had no reasonable grounds for belief in the existence of the goods. This decision supports the earlier point that all cases on common mistake can be explained by means of construction of implied conditions precedent. But it also gives credence to the existence of a doctrine of common mistake.

The doctrine of common mistake is not only inconsistent with the objective test of consent and based upon little authority, but also the problems in such cases are better handled through construction of the express and implied terms of the contract. This latter approach is superior because it addresses more directly the question whether the parties have allocated the risk of mistakes in a particular way. The danger posed by the doctrine of common mistake is that it will upset a fair allocation of the risks made by the contracting parties. The doctrine was rejected for this reason in *McRae v Commonwealth Disposals Commission*.[22] The Commission sold the wreck of an oil tanker to the defendant for salvage, but after a fruitless search by the defendant, it emerged that no such wreck existed. The Commission tried unsuccessfully to defend an action for breach of contract on the ground that both parties were mistaken about the existence of the wreck. The High Court of Australia rejected the defence, arguing either that mistake could not be relied upon because it was entirely due to the Commission's negligence, or that the doctrine of mistake was excluded by the express warranty of the existence of the wreck made by the Commission.

4. Consent by Remote Parties

The problems of the ascription of contractual responsibility which we have considered so far involve two persons entering negotiations and contracts. In practice, however, it is extremely common for difficult issues of ascription of contractual responsibility to arise when three or more persons are involved. In a typical instance, a householder employs a builder to effect repairs, and the builder enters a subcontract with a specialist electrician to carry out part of the required works. Although there are plainly two contracts in this case, one between householder and builder, and another between builder and electrician, is there a third between householder and electrician? This issue might become important if the electrician is injured, or if the electrician is careless and burns down the house.

The application of the objective test of agreement to such cases normally results in the conclusion that no direct contract between householder and electrician has been formed. The evidence is likely to demonstrate that there was no direct contact between householder and electrician, or if they had conversations, then they were not about the

---

22   (1950) 84 CLR 377 (Aust HC).

terms of a contract. There is nothing from which an inference of consent to a contract could be drawn.

Another way of looking at the case, however, suggests the possibility of a contractual relation. It might be argued that a direct contract between householder and electrician was formed through the builder as an intermediary. This argument will be successful if it can be established that the builder acted as the householder's agent for the purpose of making the subcontract for electrical work. We consider the topic of agency next. But this does not necessarily exhaust the possibilities of discovering a direct contract between householder and electrician. Can an implied direct contract be inferred from evidence such as the fact that the householder knew and consented to the proposal that the builder should use a subcontractor for the electrical work, and from the fact that the electrician knew that the ultimate employer for whom the work was being performed was the householder?

By way of a preliminary remark to these topics, however, it is important to observe that as a general principle contractual responsibility will not attach to remote parties. At bottom, this principle concerns a respect for the liberty of the individual. A person should not have additional onerous obligations imposed without consent. It would be a gross infringement of liberty, for instance, if two persons were able by agreement to impose substantial contractual obligations upon another. That would permit, for instance, two persons to agree that another should perform an arduous task, and that third person then to be in breach of a contractual obligation for failure to do so. In our earlier example, it might suggest that the agreement between householder and builder imposed the obligation on the subcontractor to perform the work, or that the agreement between builder and electrician imposed an obligation on the householder to pay the agreed price to the electrician. Such conclusions will normally be rejected in principle as amounting to the imposition of a contract without consent. This general principle is often described as an aspect of the doctrine of privity of contract, which will be considered in Chapter 14, but in fact it flows directly from the requirement of consent to contracts. The principle only applies to contractual obligations, of course, so it does not rule out the possibility of tortious or proprietary obligations between remote parties, for these obligations can arise without consent.

(1) Agency
The major exception to this principle is the doctrine of agency. Here the third party authorizes one of the contracting parties to make the contract on his or her behalf. In our example, the householder would ask the builder to enter into a contract on behalf of the householder with the electrician. The third party is described as the principal and the authorized contracting party an agent. Because the agent is not making the contract for himself but for the principal, the legal analysis insists that the principal but not the agent is the party to the contract, and that consent by the principal to the contract is achieved through the authorized agent as an intermediary.

As a result, it is the principal but not the agent who incurs contractual responsibility.

It is extremely common for contracts to bind third parties as principals by virtue of agency relations. Every time a contract is made with a company the doctrine of agency applies. The company, as an artificial legal entity, must act through human agents, usually either directors or employees. The contracts made by these agents then bind the company as a principal to the contract. Within companies a wide doctrine of agency normally applies, so that directors and employees will be regarded as enjoying the authority to make those contracts, which by virtue of their positions in the company they possess ostensibly or apparently the authority to enter. To take a simple example, a shop assistant will have the ostensible authority to bind the shop to sales of its wares by virtue of his or her position, so such a sale will bind the shop as a principal. But if the transaction concerns the sale of the premises of the shop, then the assistant will lack ostensible authority; such a major transaction will normally require the authorization of the board of directors of the company, which can be presumed to have authority to bind the company on any matter.[23]

Although an agent entering a contract on behalf of a principal will not incur personal contractual liability, it is possible that a complex transaction will involve several contracts under which a person contracts both as agent and as principal. For example, a person may sign the main contract merely as an agent for another, but at the same time undertake a personal obligation under a collateral contract such as a contract of guarantee.[24] Thus a carrier of goods on a ship may both enter a contract with the owner of the goods as a principal to carry the goods, but at the same time act as an agent to make contracts on behalf of other persons such as the ship's crew and the stevedores who will load and unload the goods onto and from the ship.[25]

Although the details of the law of agency will not be examined here, one important limitation upon the ostensible authority of agents should be considered. The question arises whether the principal may limit the ostensible authority of an agent, such as the employee of a company. It is insufficient for the principal to prohibit the agent from making certain types of contract, for that will not diminish the agent's apparent authority.[26] But if the principal notifies the other contracting party in advance that the agent's ostensible authority is limited in certain respects, that can suffice to prevent ascription of contractual responsibility to the principal.[27] It is common, for instance, for employers to rely upon notices

---

23 Companies Act 1985, s 35A, as amended by Companies Act 1989.
24 *Elpis Maritime Co Ltd v Marti Chartering Co Inc (The Maria D)* [1991] 2 Lloyd's Rep 311, HL.
25 *New Zealand Shipping Co Ltd v Satterthwaite & Co Ltd (The Eurymedon)* [1975] AC 154, [1974] 1 All ER 1015, PC.
26 *Watteau v Fenwick* [1893] 1 QB 346.
27 *Overbrooke Estates Ltd v Glencombe Properties Ltd* [1974] 1 WLR 1335, [1974] 3 All ER 511, Ch.

or terms of printed contracts which contain a statement to the effect that their employees do not have any authority to vary or add to the terms and conditions. Such a statement should in principle suffice to negative the ostensible authority of the agent. In consumer standard form contracts, however, such disclaimers of ostensible authority will be regarded as unfair terms, not binding on the consumer under the Unfair Terms in Consumer Contracts Regulations 1994.[28] The consumer is therefore entitled to rely on promises given within the ostensible authority of employees of a company.

The application of the notion of ostensible agency therefore creates the possibility of contractual responsibility without express consent. Although in cases of actual authority, we may say that in effect the principal has consented to the contract by giving the agent the authority to make the contract on his behalf, it is quite possible in cases of ostensible authority that the principal did not wish to make the contract, or had indeed forbidden the making of the contract, yet will nevertheless be bound by it.

(2) Implied Consent

Aside from agency, the principle that contractual obligations cannot be incurred without consent normally prevents the ascription of contractual responsibility to remote parties. It may be possible, however, to imply consent to a contract in the circumstances of the case by reference to the conduct and knowledge of the remote party. An implication of consent may be drawn where the remote party is aware of the contract and has encouraged its making because it serves the remote party's interests. This may occur in a context where an employer encourages the main contractor to enter into a sub-contract in order to complete a particular job for the employer. In *Charnock v Liverpool Corpn*,[29] the plaintiff took his car to a garage for repairs which were to be paid for by his insurers. Although the main contract for repairs was between the insurance company and the garage, the Court of Appeal found an implied contract between the plaintiff and the garage under which the garage undertook to carry out the repairs in a reasonable time. The garage had consented to this contract by implication when it received the car delivered by the plaintiff.

This reasoning has been applied to cases involving work by a sub-contractor in relation to the employer's goods. In *Morris v CW Martin & Sons Ltd*,[30] the plaintiff instructed a furrier to clean her mink stole, but the furrier explained that he did not clean furs, so instead he undertook to send it to be cleaned by the specialist defendant cleaners, and the plaintiff agreed to this arrangement. One of the defendant's employees

---

28   SI 1994/3159, Sch 3, para 1(n). Decisions by the courts at common law had foreshadowed this regulation: *Mendelssohn v Normand Ltd* [1970] 1 QB 177, [1969] 2 All ER 1215, CA.
29   [1968] 1 WLR 1498, [1968] 3 All ER 473, CA.
30   [1966] 1 QB 716, [1965] 2 All ER 725, CA.

stole the fur, and the plaintiff sued the defendant for damages. As a defence to this claim, the defendant relied upon the terms of its contract with the furrier. These terms included a provision that the defendant should 'not be responsible for loss or damage however caused' to 'goods belonging to customers'. One question was whether the plaintiff could be bound by the terms of the sub-contract, even though she had never agreed to those terms or been a party to the agreement. There would be no difficulty, of course, if the furrier had acted as the plaintiff's agent, but it was clear in fact that two separate contracts had been made. Lord Denning MR held the plaintiff bound by the terms of the sub-contract, because she had impliedly consented to the furrier making a contract for cleaning on the terms usually current in the trade. Nevertheless, the plaintiff's claim for damages succeeded, because on a strict interpretation of the exclusion clause it only disclaimed liability for goods belonging to customers of the defendant, and the plaintiff was not the customer, but merely a customer of a customer, the furrier. The same argument has been applied to a contract for the international carriage of goods, where the carrier sub-contracted the work of transporting the goods to a shipowner, whose ship then sank causing the destruction of the goods. The owner of the goods was held to have consented by implication to the terms of the sub-contract between carrier and shipowner, for in the contract between owner and carrier the owner had consented to permit the carrier to sub-contract the work of handling, storage and carriage 'on any terms'.[31]

An interesting question is whether or not such reasoning could be extended to the context of construction, where the owner of the building consents to sub-contracts for specialist work. In principle, this argument should work provided that there is sufficient evidence either from conduct or in the main contract that the owner of the building has authorized the sub-contract and acquiesced to its terms.

The dilemma confronting the law is that, although it is contrary to principle to ascribe contractual responsibility without consent, an implied contract may appear to conform to the intentions of the parties and represent a fair allocation of the risk. In *Morris v CW Martin & Sons Ltd*, for instance, the subcontractor only agreed to perform the work of cleaning the fur on its standard terms. The price for the work no doubt reflected the content of these terms. Although these terms bound the main contractor, the furrier, they could not affect the employer, the owner of the mink stole, without stretching the normal principles for ascription of responsibility. Yet this result seems only fair because either all the parties would be forced into the costly procedure of making direct contracts with each other, or other sources of obligations, particularly the law of tort, would in effect circumvent and undermine carefully constructed contractual arrangements.

---

31 *KH Enterprise v Pioneer Container (The Pioneer Container)* [1994] 2 AC 324, [1994] 2 All ER 250, PC.

(3) Equitable Proprietary Interests

Remote parties may be bound by contracts when they receive property in the knowledge that under a contract another person has acquired rights over that property. A typical example arises where a tenant assigns a lease to another, and the new tenant or assignee is then bound by any rights of the landlord over the property created by the original lease of which he receives notice. In a loose way of speaking, the new tenant must respect the contractual rights of the landlord merely by virtue of his knowledge of those rights. In formal legal analysis, however, the argument is rather that the new tenant must respect the property rights of the landlord, which avoids a direct clash with the normal principles governing the ascription of contractual responsibility. This reasoning is not confined to interests in land.

A contract may establish a proprietary right in any kind of personal property, and, provided that this contract is specifically enforceable, then any subsequent purchaser of the property who has notice of the proprietary interest in it will be bound to respect that interest.[32] This principle was applied, for instance, to a ship in *Lord Strathcona SS Co Ltd v Dominion Coal Co Ltd*.[33] The purchaser of the ship bought it with knowledge that it had been chartered out already by the previous owner. The charterer was able to defend his contractual rights against the new owner, even though the new owner had not agreed to the contract. The case may not be a correct application of the principle, however, for it is unclear that the charter contract intended to confer a proprietary interest in the ship on the charterer, and it is unlikely that the contract was specifically enforceable.

Manufacturers have attempted to take advantage of similar legal reasoning in the absence of vertical integration of their distributive system, in order to prevent retailers at the end of a chain of supply selling their products at substandard quality or beneath recommended prices. By attaching obligations to the product in contracts with wholesalers or distributors, which purport to bind anyone who deals with it after notice of those conditions, the manufacturer seeks to protect its trading reputation and keep up the market price of its product. Though unable to draw a principled distinction between cases concerning obligations attached to goods from those of covenants attached to land, with few exceptions the courts rebuff manufacturers' attempts to gain the advantages of vertical integration without the financial risks entailed in ownership of retail outlets. Moreover, statutes outlaw attempts to establish minimum resale prices of goods in order to protect consumers.

---

32   *Swiss Bank Corpn v Lloyds Bank Ltd* [1979] Ch 548, [1979] 2 All ER 853, Ch; revs'd on other grounds [1982] AC 584, HL; Chafee, 'Equitable Servitudes on Chattels' (1928) 41 *Harvard Law Review* 945; Gardner, 'The Proprietary Effect of Contractual Obligations under *Tulk v Moxhay* and *De Mattos v Gibson*' (1982) 98 *Law Quarterly Review* 389.

33   [1926] AC 108, PC.

5. The Boundaries of Contract

The requirement of consent, as defined by the objective test, marks the traditional boundary of contractual responsibility. This boundary is by no means sharply defined, for the objective test permits inferences of consent to be drawn in circumstances where at least one party had no intention of consenting to a contract. In such borderline cases, where consent has to be constructed from slim evidence, the court may prefer to recognize the existence of another species of obligation drawn from unjust enrichment (restitution), equity, or tort. This approach has the advantage of doing less violence to the integrity of contract doctrine and its attachment to the idea of consent, and, at the same time, much the same result may be achieved. We should briefly illustrate these possibilities here and reflect upon their implications for the modern law's conception of contractual responsibility.

Unjust Enrichment
In the absence of conduct from which consent to a transaction may be inferred, it may be possible to impose liability on the basis of unjust enrichment. If, without my consent or request, a person performs a service, which necessarily enriches me, such as mending my broken bicycle, a court may impose liability to compensate the mender for the value of the service on the ground of unjust enrichment. There is a hazy borderline here between cases where a court is prepared to infer consent and thus contractual responsibility from such conduct as standing by watching the mechanic perform his work, and other cases where consent is not inferred so the cause of action is classified as unjust enrichment. Many restitutionary claims for unjust enrichment rest upon facts similar to unilateral contracts, except that no fixed remuneration for the service has been promised; the court simply adds a term providing for payment of a reasonable price. Hence a request to perform a task without any further terms being settled suffices to ascribe responsibility in restitutionary claims such as 'quantum meruit', so that it matters little whether or not contractual responsibility can be based upon inferred consent.

Reliance Model
Similarly, under the reliance model of liability discussed in Chapter 5, if these obligations are not considered to be part of contract law, their importance should nevertheless be recognized as an important qualification to the test for ascription of contractual responsibility. Under the reliance model of liability, a claim may be founded on conduct from which consent may not be inferred yet upon which it was reasonable to rely. In *Crabb v Arun District Council*[34] the English Court of Appeal

---

34   [1976] Ch 179, [1975] 3 All ER 865, CA.

granted the plaintiff a right of access to his property from the Council's adjacent road in the absence of an inference of agreement, because his land had become inaccessible as a result of a sale of part of it induced by reliance upon the statements of intent and conduct of the Council's officers, especially the fact that they had left a suitable gap in the road's fence in anticipation of the proposed right of access. Similarly, in the American case of *Hoffman v Red Owl Stores Inc*,[35] the parties never reached an agreement for a franchise, but, since the defendants had encouraged the plaintiff to incur expenses in the expectation that he would be granted a franchise, they were bound to compensate him for that wasted expenditure.

The conduct which engenders this kind of reliance-based liability will normally consist of words and positive acts, but it is possible for responsibility to arise from omissions to act where there is knowledge of the misplaced reliance upon the omission. When a landowner watches another build a house on his land, knowing that the builder labours under a mistake as to the ownership of the property or his permission to build there, the landowner cannot evict the builder without at least compensating him for his wasted expenditure.[36] An adequate warning from the landowner will, of course, negative this potential source of liability.[37]

Duty of Care in Tort

Finally, we should note the striking possibilities offered by the introduction of the law of negligence in tort into this field. Consider the case discovered by Atiyah: *Crossan v Ward Bracewell*.[38] Here the plaintiff, who had been charged with the criminal offence of reckless driving after having caused a serious road traffic accident, visited the defendant solicitor, who told him that he could either plead guilty, in which case he would not need a solicitor, or he could plead not guilty, but then the defendant would only provide the necessary legal advice on payment of £50 in advance against the defendant's costs. The plaintiff decided to plead guilty and to dispense with a lawyer's services. The plaintiff was subsequently sued for compensation for the damage which he had caused in the road accident, and under a term of the plaintiff's insurance policy the insurers disclaimed liability, because they had not been duly notified of the criminal charge of reckless driving. The plaintiff then sued the defendant solicitor for his failure to alert him to this risk of forfeiting his insurance cover against claims for civil liability. The court held the defendant liable in tort for failing to take reasonable care in advising the plaintiff. This liability was established despite the clear finding that no contractual responsibility

35 26 Wis 2d 683, 133 NW 2d 267 (1965).
36 *Ramsden v Dyson* (1866) LR 1 HL 129, HL; *Willmott v Barber* (1880) 15 Ch D 96, Ch.
37 *A-G of Hong Kong v Humphreys Estate (Queen's Gardens) Ltd* [1987] AC 114, [1987] 2 All ER 387, PC.
38 [1986] *New Law Journal* 849, discussed in P Atiyah, *Essays on Contract* (Oxford, 1990) at p 381.

had been created, because the defendant made it abundantly clear that he was not prepared to act without the prepayment. Yet the tortious duty of care was exactly the same duty as that which would have been owed if a contract had been concluded. Decisions such as this clearly eviscerate the principle of freedom of contract, for they indicate that, even in the absence of consent, liability in tort equivalent to contractual responsibility may arise from conduct.

Autonomy and Responsibility
This brief survey of alternative sources of responsibility draws out some vital points. Although the courts preserve the boundary of contractual responsibility by reference to the idea of consent, it has become clear that the objective process of inferring consent from conduct introduces considerable flexibility in that boundary, especially in cases of collateral contracts. The analysis also reveals that alternative sources of obligation may impose exactly the same or equivalent responsibilities to those founded in contract. It will often matter little, therefore, whether a court chooses to combat deceptive practices by manipulating the objective test of consent or by recognizing some alternative source of legal obligation.

Given the diversity and power of these alternative sources of liability, the boundary of the ascription of contractual responsibility on the basis of consent may have been shorn of any practical implications. The question of what theory lies behind the limitation of contractual responsibility therefore loses much of its interest. What we can usefully say is that, although one of the best justifications for compromising personal autonomy by imposing legal obligations remains an act of consent to an agreement, since that act of consent to an agreement is in itself an exercise of the freedom granted out of respect for personal autonomy, in the modern law personal autonomy can also be compromised by other types of conduct which can be regarded as a deceptive practice. The modern law expands the horizon of these deceptive practices, so that they go beyond secret reservations of unwillingness to contract. They include many forms of conduct which induce reasonable reliance, without there being any intention to deceive. To this extent we should interpret the modern law as reducing the importance of the value of freedom to choose to enter a contract, by qualifying this value with a demand to respect the interests of others in many circumstances.[39]

---

39   Collins, 'The Transformation Thesis and the Ascription of Contractual Responsibility' in T Wilhelmsson (ed), *Perspectives of Critical Contract Law* (Aldershot, 1993), 293.

8
Coercion and Competitive Markets

Coercion may negative consent to a contract. In order to protect the freedom to choose whether or not to enter a contract, the law must recognize that certain types of coercion effectively eliminate that freedom. If someone holds a gun to my head and says that unless I sign a contract then he will shoot, then clearly my freedom to choose whether or not to enter the contract is gravely impaired. In these circumstances the common law will hold that my consent is vitiated by duress, so that I can avoid the contract. To protect the institution of contracts as an exercise of autonomy, the law must distinguish between consensual transactions and coercive taking. It must do so both by prohibiting acts of coercive taking, such as criminal laws against theft and blackmail, but also by invalidating any apparent contracts produced by coercion.

The central difficulty confronting the law in this context is to determine the extent to which freedom to choose whether or not to enter a contract should be protected. To some extent every contract is the product of constrained choice. A consumer wishing to purchase a loaf of bread could in theory buy from any shop in the world, but the costs involved in travel effectively confine the choice to a purchase from a local trader. Similarly, someone seeking a job could in theory search throughout the European Community, but in practice the costs of search limit it to a locality or region. The constraints upon choice become even more severe when an effective monopoly dominates market supply, such as the transport authority which runs buses and trains, or utilities which supply water, gas, and electricity. Although the law must protect freedom to choose whether or not to enter a contract, it cannot permit every constraint upon freedom to negative consent, for otherwise few contracts could be enforced.

The nature of constraints upon freedom to choose whether or not to enter a contract comprise three distinct types. One sort of constraint derives from each person's shortage of resources when entering the market. Without unlimited finance to acquire information and advice, and to give time to search and consider market opportunities, each person must necessarily make contractual agreements without the freedom to choose between all the various possibilities. A second source of constraint derives from limits in the market itself originating from monopolies. Although few monopolies can persist in a market economy without government support, effective monopolies deriving from a combination with the first kind of constraint may be common. A village shop may be able to charge high prices, because in the absence of another shop in the village it will enjoy an effective monopoly, if it is expensive to travel to town to purchase goods elsewhere. The third source of constraint occurs when one person feels compelled to subordinate his wishes to another's. A parent may feel obliged to put the interests of the children first, or a member of a religious community may be held under oath to place the interests of the group above his own. No one can act entirely freely from all such constraints.

To recognize the effectiveness of all these types of constraints, however, would be to delegitimize the market order. It cannot be acknowledged, for instance, that poverty severely constrains choice, for this would render many common instances of contracting, such as employment, tenancies, and purchases of food, invalid. To a considerable extent the law must exclude from its evaluation of events in the market-place factors which constrain choice, for otherwise the consent to commonplace transactions will appear illusory or invalid. Support for a market order requires the law to start with the assumption that few of the constraints listed above can negative consent. It must regard the contracting parties for the most part as disembodied, unsituated persons, the abstract 'A's and 'B's of contract textbooks, ignoring the effective constraints upon action experienced in everyday life, in order to attribute to them true consent to transactions.

But the market order demands that some constraints must be acknowledged. At the least, it requires a distinction between voluntary transactions and coerced taking. Without such a distinction, then there would be no safeguard to ensure that market transactions are wealth enhancing in the long run. Moreover, unless coercion is prevented, then the law of contract would cease to be a legal institution for augmenting individual autonomy; it would be a cloak for oppression.

Is it possible to develop a sharp conceptual distinction between those types of coercion which negative consent and those which do not? Can we distinguish clearly those constraints upon freedom which are acceptable, in the sense of being necessary to tolerate for the sake of enjoying the fruits of the market order, from those constraints which negative the ascription of contractual responsibility?

The common law, following the civil law tradition, sought to answer these questions through a distinction between voluntary and involuntary consent to a contract. If consent was involuntary, then contractual responsibility could not arise. It developed two doctrines to identify cases of involuntary consent. The common law invalidated contracts under the doctrine of duress. This was supplemented, however, by the equitable doctrine of undue influence, which extended the definition of involuntary consent. I shall argue, however, that the conceptual distinction between voluntary and involuntary acts could never provide a coherent foundation for the law governing coercion, and that in practice it provides a poor interpretation of the doctrines of duress and undue influence.

I suggest on the contrary that the law is best understood as lacking any such clear conceptual distinction. Instead, it seeks to regulate markets in order to ensure that market competition prevails as far as possible. The freedom to choose whether or not to enter a contract is protected to the extent that it is possible to have a competitive market for products and services. The law cannot guarantee perfect competition, for that is rarely possible, but it can develop standards of fair competition so that markets function fairly. Impermissible coercion which prevents the ascription of contractual responsibility should therefore be understood as conduct which comprises an attempt to take advantage of a position of unfair competition in a market.

From this perspective the rules governing coercion in the private law of contract should be examined alongside the rules governing competition in markets more generally. Competition law empowers governments to intervene in order to prevent anti-competitive practices. The government may prevent mergers and take-overs of companies, if they might result in the creation of an effective monopoly of a market. It will also prevent trade practices designed to exclude competition in markets. For example, the device known as 'dumping' which involves flooding a market with cheap products temporarily in order to drive competitors out of business will be constrained. Under English law the government has extensive powers under the Competition Act 1980 and the Fair Trading Act 1973 to intervene through regulatory control to prevent such anti-competitive practices. But the most significant protection of competitive markets is located at the level of the European Community, for one of its prime objectives is to establish a competitive and free market for goods and services throughout Europe. Under Article 86 of the Treaty of Rome,

> Any abuse by one or more undertakings of a dominant position within the common market or in a substantial part of it shall be prohibited as incompatible with the common market in so far as it may affect trade between Member States.

The remedies which are available under Article 86 include both quasi-criminal proceedings conducted by the Commission of the European Community resulting in substantial fines, and the opportunity for individual businesses to seek injunctions against anti-competitive practices. Where a business discovers that it is effectively being excluded from a particular market, or being permitted to enter it only on unfavourable terms compared to its competitors, it may seek an injunction against these constraints upon competition. These aspects of competition law provide the major remedy against forms of economic pressure which can coerce businesses into unfavourable transactions, and it is here that we gain the clearest insight into the way in which the law draws the line between ordinary market forces and coercive economic pressure.

This chapter commences with an examination of the private law of contract, in order to examine the conditions under which courts invalidate individual contracts on the ground that some form of coercion invalidated consent to the contract. It then broadens the perspective to include the public control of anti-competitive practices in markets for the purpose of suggesting that private law and competition law share the aim of protecting competitive markets.

1. Voluntary Consent

The first step in this argument is to scrutinize the coherence of the distinction between voluntary and involuntary consent, which serves as the foundation for traditional accounts of the private law. My aim is to cast doubt on the idea that this distinction could provide a coherent foundation for the law governing the extent to which coercion invalidates contracts.

One way of distinguishing between voluntary and involuntary acts is to insist that voluntary acts require a conscious control over bodily movements by the mind. If one person A pushes another B into a third person, then we can say that B's action was involuntary on the ground that B's action was not consciously controlled by his mind. It is hard to see how this conception of involuntary acts could have any practical application to the formation of contracts. Perhaps it would negative B's contractual responsibility if A physically carried B against his will onto a train. But the distinction does not help to explain why a person has not acted voluntarily in signing a contract at the point of a gun, for the signature was an action controlled by the mind.

On the contrary, the signature extracted at gunpoint appears to be a voluntary action in a strong sense. In these circumstances, signing the contract is probably the action which the signatory most wishes to perform at that moment. The problem seems to be rather that options were severely constrained, so that no other course of action except death was available. It follows that, if the conceptual distinction between voluntary and involuntary action is to serve as the basic principle governing coercion negativing the ascription of contractual responsibility, then the distinction must serve to identify those cases of constrained choice which should be regarded as leading to involuntary actions.

This step in the reasoning switches attention away from the state of mind of the person who is alleged not to have consented to a contract due to coercion. It examines instead those conditions which will be held to negative voluntariness. We might say, for example, that threats of personal injury and death designed to induce consent to a contract count as conditions which negative voluntariness. But how should we distinguish those conditions which negative voluntariness from those which do not? How, for instance, should we decide whether those conditions have been satisfied in a case where a homeless family agrees to a high rent for a room for the night because they cannot find any other accommodation? Once the reasoning switches its attention away from the state of mind of the parties to the external conditions under which they reach an agreement, then the distinction between involuntary and voluntary acts ceases to assist us, for the problem becomes one of identifying external conditions which should be regarded as negativing consent.

This problem of how coercion negatives consent or voluntary acts is not unique to the law of contract. The criminal law recognizes the possibility of a defence on the ground that the mind did not control the acts of an individual under the doctrines of automatism and insanity. The criminal law also recognizes that duress may negative criminal responsibility except in the case of murder. But we cannot gain much assistance in defining the conditions which negative contractual responsibility from the law of crime. J L Austin points out that the excuses which negative voluntariness differ according to the obligation which might be imposed. For example, 'We may plead that we trod on the snail inadvertently but not on a baby – you ought to look where you're putting your great feet.'[1] Similarly, the content of legal excuses varies according to the kind of legal duty involved. Whilst a threat to cause serious bodily harm would certainly provide an excuse from contractual liability under the doctrine of duress, it would not exempt a person from the crime of murder though it might excuse theft or criminal damage. These examples indicate that coercive conditions which negative voluntary acts must be determined according to the obligation at stake. Because contractual obligations are voluntarily assumed, then it seems likely that this branch of the law will permit the most extensive range of conditions to negative consent.

This investigation of the concept of voluntary consent suggests the following conclusions. It is true that coercion negatives voluntary consent to a contract. But the concept of voluntary act cannot itself provide an adequate account of what forms of coercion will negative consent. The law requires a second premise. It needs a principle by which to identify those external conditions which will be deemed to negative consent. This principle must seek to draw a line between ordinary market constraints under which most contracts are reached, and those where some aberrational circumstances should be regarded as negativing consent.

2. Duress

The common law doctrine of duress has developed fairly precise criteria for determining which surrounding conditions negative consent. It requires an illegitimate act performed by one party which causes the other to consent to the contract. The scope of this doctrine depends crucially on the elements of causation and the illegitimate act.

The illegitimate act must be at least one reason why the contract was concluded in order to satisfy the requirement of causation, though other

---

1   Austin, 'A Plea for Excuses' (1956/57) 57 *Proceedings of the Aristotelian Society* 1, p 20.

considerations may play a part in the decision.[2] Duress is ineffective if another reasonable course of action short of making a contract was available. But the courts understand that commercial considerations such as business reputation and compliance with other contracts will often make it inadvisable for one party to decline to make a contract and seek other means of protection against the threatened unlawful act.

In its earliest formulations, the illegitimate act was confined to threats of unlawful violence. After a period of doubt, it has become clear that threats of damage to property or of unlawful seizure of it will also negative consent. Although examples in cases are sparse, it seems likely that any tortious act which is unlawful can satisfy the requirement of an unlawful act so that consent will be regarded as negatived.[3]

The importance of the criterion of illegitimate act was stressed in *Universe Tankships Inc of Monrovia v International Transport Workers' Federation (The Universe Sentinel)*.[4] The union organized industrial action so that a ship was immobilized. The plaintiff secured the release of the ship by reaching a collective agreement with the union, a term of which provided that the plaintiff should pay a sum of money into the union's welfare fund. The plaintiff later sought recovery of this money. The trial court determined that the collective agreement was reached under severe economic compulsion, because of the potentially disastrous effects of the industrial action upon the plaintiff's business. But a further obstacle which confronted this claim was the requirement of an illegitimate act. Although the union's action constituted under the ordinary law an unlawful interference with business, statute law protects a worker's right to strike by granting immunity from an action in tort under certain conditions. The House of Lords decided that the money was recoverable, but only because the statutory conditions had not been satisfied. If the industrial action had been lawful, so that the coercion was not actionable in tort, then the plaintiff could not have relied upon duress to negative consent.

But is the requirement of an illegitimate act confined to tortious acts? Can duress be established by other forms of illegitimate act? Lord Scarman suggested in *Universe Tankships Inc of Monrovia v International Transport Workers' Federation (The Universe Sentinel)* that the nature of the demand which the pressure is applied to support may render the act illegitimate. He had in mind the example of blackmail, where the threat may be to perform a lawful act such as to inform the police of criminal conduct unless money is paid. But it is far from clear that such instances of extortion will not themselves amount to unlawful conduct, either the crime of blackmail or the tort of intimidation. In which case, they will satisfy the requirement of a tortious act, so no exception need be established.

One exception has been clearly established, but this may be confined to instances of modifications of contract. Where one party threatens to

---

2   *Barton v Armstrong* [1976] AC 104, [1975] 2 All ER 465, PC.
3   Beatson, 'Duress as a Vitiating Factor in Contract' (1974) *Cambridge Law Journal* 97.
4   [1983] 1 AC 366, [1982] 2 All ER 67, HL.

breach an existing contract between them unless he is given some further advantage, then, although this does not amount to a tort, it will satisfy the requirement of an illegitimate act. The party subject to this pressure may rescind the modified agreement and insist upon performance of the contract according to the original terms of the contract. But as we shall see in Chapter 15, the law of duress in the context of modifications of contracts must be understood to be governed by particular policy considerations concerning the need to promote co-operation between the parties during performance of a contract. The existence of this exception to the requirement of a tortious act may not provide evidence that it does not apply during the formation of contracts.

The crucial question here is whether forms of coercion during the formation of a contract which do not involve the commission of a tortious act can satisfy the doctrine of duress.[5] Consider a case where a walker in the hills becomes lost and the night closes in and the weather turns sour. The walker stumbles across a remote road and flags down a car. The driver offers to take the walker to the nearest inn, but only in return for a payment of £100. The walker agrees to the fee reluctantly, but subsequently refuses to pay. If the law of duress requires a tortious act, then this agreement must be binding, for the driver of the car in offering a lift on certain terms has not committed a tort. The implicit threat not to make a contract cannot comprise a tort either, for this would undermine the general freedom to choose whether or not to enter contracts. The law established in the *Universe Tankships* case therefore suggests that this contract is binding and that the walker must pay £100.

To put the question more abstractly, does the law of duress extend to cases where one party to a contract has exploited an effective monopoly position, originating from the necessity of the other combined with the absence of other opportunities to satisfy the need in order to obtain a highly advantageous transaction? Some authorities suggest that duress may extend to such instances. In *The Port Caledonia and The Anna*,[6] a captain of a ship, which was about to hit another boat, agreed to the demand of a master of a tug-boat for a charge of £1,000 to tow the ship out of danger. The court permitted the captain of the ship to resist the claim for £1,000 on the ground that he was forced under compulsion to agree to an extortionate bargain, though he was required to pay a reasonable fee of £200. Here it was the costs of inaction, compounded by the state of necessity and the effective monopoly position of the master of the tug-boat, which vitiated the captain's consent. Perhaps a more typical example these days of exploitation of a monopoly position occurred in the American case of *S S & O Corpn v Township of Bernards Sewerage Authority*,[7] where the Supreme Court of New Jersey invalidated an agreement between a real estate developer and a municipal authority for

5   Dawson, 'Economic Duress – An Essay in Perspective' (1947) 45 *Michigan Law Review* 253.
6   [1903] P 184.
7   62 NJ 369, 301 A 2d 738 (1973).

payment of excessive charges for connecting new houses to the sewerage system exacted by threats of refusal to supply the service. Duress in the form of a threat to refuse to enter a contract imposed by persons clothed with official authority exacerbates the exploitation of a monopoly position in such cases.

Although these decisions lend support to the idea that duress can be satisfied without a tortious act, there is reason to doubt that they remove the requirement of an illegitimate act entirely. In the instances of public authorities demanding exorbitant payments, there is usually a violation of law, for the law establishing their powers, foreseeing the risk of exploitation of the monopoly powers, places limits on it. In *S S & O Corpn v Township of Bernards Sewerage Authority*, the law provided that all houses should be connected without discrimination, so it was unlawful under the terms of this power to demand higher rates of payment from one construction company than another. The statutory limits on the public monopoly power may forbid any demands for money,[8] require non-discrimination between citizens, or require that a reasonable rate be charged for the service.[9] These cases support the view that a tortious act is not required for duress, but at the same time they indicate that some other kind of illegal action is necessary to establish duress in the formation of contracts. For this reason, it may be suggested that in the Australian case of *Smith v Charlick*,[10] the exploitation of a public monopoly position did not constitute duress. The plaintiff was informed by the Wheat Harvest Board that unless he paid a premium on the wheat he had already bought from them, no further supplies of wheat would be forthcoming, which would have put the plaintiff out of business. The plaintiff failed in his claim for recovery of premium payments, the main ground for the decision being that the Wheat Harvest Board had not acted unlawfully but within its powers. These decisions therefore support the requirement of an illegitimate act, though it need not be a tortious one. This requirement would prevent the walker from avoiding his contract with the motorist.

On the other hand, the cases concerning salvage agreements, such as *The Port Caledonia and the Anna*, cannot be so distinguished, for there is no unlawful act in the master of the tugboat threatening not to make a contract. But a different interpretation of these cases may take them outside the doctrine of duress altogether. In the case of salvage, the admiralty courts developed doctrines governing agreements which sought to ensure that salvors always received a fair rate of remuneration for their services. Thus a contract could be set aside for being agreed at a price which was either too high or too low. In establishing a fair rate of remuneration, the court would take into account such factors as the danger to the cargo, the risk to the salvors, and the work involved, together with the general consideration that the rate must be set at a level sufficiently

8   *Steele v Williams* (1853) 8 Exch 625.
9   *Parker v Great Western Rly Co* (1844) 7 Man & G 253; *Great Western Rly Co v Sutton* (1869) LR 4 HL 226, HL.
10   (1924) 34 CLR 38 (Aust HC).

high to provide a general incentive for persons to enter the salvage business.[11] Similarly, the common law implied an obligation on common carriers, such as railways and other public transport services, to accept and convey all goods delivered to them according to their line of business on being paid a reasonable remuneration for their services. The emphasis in these doctrines upon a fair market price for services rendered suggests that the real ground for these decisions was not so much the exploitation of an effective monopoly position but rather the unfairness of the terms concluded. In which case, these cases would be better considered in connection with standards of fairness in general, and there might not be authority supporting the extension of duress beyond the requirement of an illegitimate act.

Although the authorities may be so limited, thereby placing the example of the walker paying a high price for a lift outside the scope of the law of duress, this conclusion seems unsatisfactory. The presence or absence of some technical illegality can often be the product of the accidents of legislation. If the legislators foresee the problems posed by monopolies, then they may enact appropriate qualifications on the powers to make contracts, but it is apparent from cases such as *Smith v Charlick* that controls may prove less than complete. Similarly, although the law may have developed adequate controls over price to regulate common situations such as salvage and common carriers, this should not mean in the unusual instance of exploitation of an effective monopoly position falling outside these established categories that the law is unable to intervene. This suggests that duress constituted by lawful acts should be possible in some cases, especially if the court detects bad faith.[12] Equity may provide relief in these circumstances, as we shall see below.

3. Undue Influence

Courts exercising an equitable jurisdiction have developed a more elaborate conception of the types of coercion which may negative ascription of contractual responsibility. Although the term 'undue influence' is the one most frequently employed to describe this jurisdiction, it has also been described as equitable or constructive fraud and unconscientious dealing. Viewed as a whole, the equitable jurisdiction encompasses many subtle forms of domination and pressure, which the common law of duress, confined by the requirement of illegitimate act, excludes from relief. Equity recognizes that choice can be impaired from all three types of constraint identified at the beginning of this section – shortage of resources, effective monopolies, and personal subordination.

The doctrine of undue influence intervenes both where subtle coercive techniques have been employed and where a stronger party has taken

---

11   *The Henry* (1851) 15 Jur 183.
12   *CTN Cash and Carry Ltd v Gallaher Ltd* [1994] 4 All ER 714, CA.

advantage of a relation of trust and confidence. The courts seek to identify aberrational cases where the unconscientious dealing removes the case from the normal market conditions of constraints upon choice. Although it is unwise to think that a complete list of such aberrational situations could ever be drawn up, four broad types where relief has been given will be identified below.

Having identified such a situation, the courts must then determine whether the stronger party has taken advantage of its position, either by inducing the weaker party to enter a contract which he would not otherwise have chosen, or by persuading the weaker party to agree to a contract on unfavourable terms. Although the courts do not require proof that the contract was unfair,[13] evidence of substantive unfairness or manifest disadvantage clearly provides excellent evidence that pressure or manipulation has been employed to the advantage of the stronger party. The terms of the transaction may evidence a harsh bargain, such as property being sold at far less than its market value, or the charging of an exorbitant interest rate on a loan which far exceeds comparable market rates. Alternatively, the disadvantage may arise from entry into the contract itself, because it was not a transaction which an ordinary businessperson would regard as prudent. In *Lloyds Bank Ltd v Bundy*,[14] a farmer mortgaged his home to a bank in return for a loan to his son's business, in circumstances where the prospects for his son's business were so poor that the risk amounted to an unsound commercial prospect which no businessperson would have recommended. In order to provide compelling evidence that the stronger party has taken advantage of its position, the disadvantage must be sufficiently great that, 'it would have been obvious as such to any independent and reasonable persons who considered the transaction at the time with knowledge of all the relevant facts'.[15]

Entrusting Choice to Another

The most common instance of undue influence concerns those forms of constraint over freedom of contract which arise from personal authority and subordination. Undue influence arises 'where influence is acquired and abused, where confidence is reposed and betrayed'.[16] The court requires proof that for some reason one party acquired a dominating influence over the other, such that in effect choices whether or not to enter into contracts were entrusted by the subordinate party to the other.

This requirement of a dominating influence can be established in many ways. In some cases a person may become a trusted commercial adviser, so that the subordinate party effectively permits himself to be guided in business transactions by the adviser. In many common instances of this

---

13   *CIBC Mortgages plc v Pitt* [1994] 1 AC 200, [1993] 4 All ER 433, HL.

14   [1975] QB 326, [1974] 3 All ER 757, CA.

15   *Bank of Credit and Commerce International SA v Aboody* [1990] 1 QB 923, [1992] 4 All ER 955, CA.

type of dominating influence, equity subjects the adviser to fiduciary duties and presumes that the first requirement is satisfied. This will be true in such relationships as solicitor and client, guardian and ward, and religious adviser and disciple. But the dominating influence may arise in special circumstances in many other commercial relationships. Although in general a bank manager will not have acquired such a dominating influence over a client, it is possible for such a relationship to develop. In *Lloyds Bank Ltd v Bundy*,[17] an elderly farmer relied upon a bank manager to advise him on business matters over a number of years. The farmer wanted to assist his son's ailing business, but the manager explained that the bank would only make a further loan to the son's business if the farmer secured it by a charge over his home. When agreeing to this loan, the farmer was relying on the bank manager for advice, and though the manager was aware of this, and also was aware that the son's business position was grave, the manager did not suggest that the farmer should obtain independent advice. Subsequently the bank sought to enforce the charge on the farmer's home, but the farmer succeeded in avoiding the transaction on the ground of undue influence. On these special facts, the necessary elements of a dominating influence were established. The manager was aware that the farmer was relying upon him to make the decision whether or not to enter the contract. But of course this is rarely the case in the relations between banks and their customers. Although the bank manager may be asked for advice on many occasions, as in *National Westminster Bank plc v Morgan*,[18] this in itself will not suffice to establish a dominating influence; equity looks for an instance when the decision to enter the contract has been entrusted to the other party.

It is always possible, however, to rebut the charge that advantage has been taken of a dominating position, by demonstrating that the position was not used to secure the agreement. If, for example, the farmer had obtained independent advice before making the contract, then the bank could not be said to have taken advantage of its dominating position. The court must be persuaded that, despite the dominating position and the apparently disadvantageous contract, the choice to enter it was a free exercise of will. Obviously, this is unlikely, so in practice it will have to be shown that the contract was concluded in pursuance of independent competent advice given on the basis of full knowledge of all the circumstances. Alternatively, it may be possible to rebut the charge that advantage was taken of a dominating position by proving that the transaction was entirely beneficial to the weaker party.

Pressure to Compel Choice
Short of a tortious act of intimidation which would satisfy the common law of duress, equity may recognize that pressure was exercised to such

16   *Smith v Kay* (1859) 7 HL Cas 750, 779.
17   [1975] QB 324, [1974] 3 All ER 757, CA.
18   [1985] AC 686, [1985] 1 All ER 821, HL.

an extent as to deprive the weaker party of any real freedom of choice whether or not to consent to a contract. Ordinary commercial pressures will not suffice; the court requires aberrational conduct which it can describe as wrongful, unfair, or unconscionable. This requirement might be satisfied in a case where a man bullies and cajoles his wife so persistently that she gives in to his instructions and permits him to manage her affairs. In *Williams v Bayley*,[19] a father agreed to pay his son's debts to a bank (by way of executing a mortgage) when the bank showed him documents which clearly exposed his son to a criminal charge of forgery. Here the father naturally subordinated his interests to those of his son, and consequently he enjoyed little control over the decision whether or not to meet the bank's demands, so the court rescinded the contract. This type of undue influence has become rarer as the scope of the law of duress has expanded.

Taking Advantage of Business Ignorance
In the early days of the equitable jurisdiction, the courts frequently came across instances of transactions with naive, often illiterate, people, who had been persuaded to part with property at greatly less than its market value. To give relief in these circumstances, the courts either inferred fraud, or stated that there had been unconscientious dealing with either a poor and ignorant person or a youthful and inexperienced one. This emphasis upon the type of shortage of resources stemming from ignorance of business matters could obviously apply to a large section of the population in modern society as well. But such an expansion would threaten the validity of many common market transactions.

The necessary limits on this type of equitable jurisdiction, however, remain obscure. In *Cresswell v Potter*,[20] a woman obtained rescission of a contract with her husband, under which she agreed to give him her interest in the matrimonial home in return for his promise to repay all outstanding debts on the property. But these debts were small in comparison to the value of her share in the house, so her advantage from the transaction was illusory. The court based rescission on the ground that the wife counted as a poor and ignorant person, because she had only a modest income and was ignorant of property transactions, and that the sale had proceeded without independent advice at considerable undervalue. Perhaps a better way of understanding the case, following *Barclays Bank plc v O'Brien*,[21] is to suggest that a husband may be able sometimes to take advantage of his wife's lack of adequate understanding of financial affairs and the nature and consequences of a proposed transaction. A similar argument might apply when a person takes advantage of his elderly parents' ignorance of business matters.[22]

19   (1866) LR 1 HL 200, HL.
20   (1968) [1978] 1 WLR 255n, Ch.
21   [1994] 1 AC 180, [1993] 4 All ER 417, HL.
22   *Avon Finance Co Ltd v Bridger* [1985] 2 All ER 281, CA.

The decision in *Cresswell v Potter* appears to dispense with any need to prove unconscientious dealing by the other party, such that he has deliberately taken advantage of the other's ignorance of business matters. That requirement was stressed, however, in *Hart v O'Connor*,[23] where an unfair transaction with a person of unsound mind was not rescinded on the ground that this lack of capacity was unknown to the other party to the transaction, so that he could not be said to have taken advantage of it. It should be possible in most cases, however, to infer from the manifestly disadvantageous nature of the transaction and the characteristics of the weaker party that such unconscientious dealing has taken place,[24] especially if there was no warning that independent advice should be obtained.[25] Alternatively, the stronger party may have sufficient knowledge of the circumstances that the court will find that the stronger party should have ascertained further details, and have taken reasonable steps to ensure that the weaker party entered the transaction with an adequate understanding of its nature and effects.[26]

Legislation has taken up this theme of invalidating contracts on the ground of shortage of resources concerning business skills. The technique differs from the doctrine of undue influence because of the legislature's authority to isolate particular kinds of transactions and parties which should routinely be granted protection. But in some codes of law, there is recognition of a broader ground for relief based upon the equitable doctrines. Under the unconscionability provision of the American Uniform Commercial Code s 2-302, courts decline to enforce contracts where the terms are grossly unfair in circumstances where the purchaser was illiterate or naive in business matters,[27] or on the broadest statement of the test of unconscionability, where there is 'an absence of meaningful choice'.[28]

Taking Advantage of Effective Monopoly

In the context of the law of duress, we noted that the common law does not give relief from contracts formed under conditions of effective monopoly, except where there is illegitimate conduct or the parties are purporting to modify an existing contract. But the equitable jurisdiction has strayed beyond these limits. It recognizes that some contracts should be set aside where there has been an unconscientious use of bargaining power arising out the necessitous circumstances of the weaker party. This type of situation for equitable relief arose in *Aylesford v Morris*.[29] A young

23   [1985] AC 1000, [1985] 2 All ER 880, PC.
24   *Boustany v Pigott* (1993) 69 P & CR 298, PC; *Ayres v Hazelgrove* (9 February 1984, unreported), Ch, discussed in P Birks, *Restitution – The Future* (Sydney, 1992) at p 50.
25   Green, 'Proof of Mental Incompetency and the Unexpressed Major Premise' (1944) 53 *Yale Law Journal* 272.
26   *Barclays Bank plc v O'Brien* [1994] 1 AC 180, [1993] 4 All ER 417, HL.
27   *Frostifresh Corpn v Reynoso*, 54 Misc 2d 119, 281 NYS 2d 264 (1967).
28   *Williams v Walker-Thomas Furniture Co* 350 F 2d 445, 449 (DC Circ 1965).
29   (1873) 8 Ch App 484.

nobleman, in need of cash to pay his debts, obtained a loan from a moneylender at sixty per cent interest on the security of his future inheritance. The young man had to conceal the transaction from his father, so was unwilling to seek independent advice or pursue other possible opportunities to borrow money. There was an effective monopoly in such circumstances, and the money lender had clearly taken advantage of the situation. The court rescinded the transaction on the ground that there was a kind of equitable fraud both against the young man and his father, though it ordered repayment of the debts with 5% interest. Although this case should be read in the context of the courts seeking to protect the fortunes of the aristocratic and governing families of the country against moneylenders, it can also be regarded as an instance where the equitable jurisdiction extends to give relief where advantage has been taken of an effective monopoly. It might apply in a modern context where a large multinational corporation can effectively insist upon extremely advantageous terms against a small business because under the prevailing business context the small business had no choice but to enter the contract with the multinational.[30]

Some legislation pursues this dimension of the equitable jurisdiction by identifying particular problem instances of taking advantage of effective monopolies. For example, most jurisdictions regulate door-to-door sales or contracts negotiated away from business premises,[31] because of evidence of the high pressure sales techniques employed which prevent the consumer from making price comparisons. The consumer is granted a 'cooling-off' period during which time the contract can be cancelled.

An interesting question is whether this dimension of the equitable jurisdiction might have a role to play in cases such as the lost walker who accepts a lift at a high price, for a court of equity might regard the conduct of the driver as an unconscionable taking advantage of the necessity of the walker, and so rescind the contract.

Constructive Notice
The effects of undue influence are not confined to the stronger and weaker party. In many cases the stronger party has exercised the influence in order to obtain credit from a bank secured on the weaker party's property. In these circumstances the bank will be unable to enforce the security against the weaker party either if the bank had authorised the stronger party to act as its agent,[32] or if it had actual or constructive notice of the undue influence.

---

30 *Lobb (Alec) (Garages) Ltd v Total Oil GB Ltd* [1985] 1 WLR 173, [1985] 1 All ER 303, CA; the argument was rejected on the facts in this case.
31 EC Directive 85/557, OJ L371/31, 31 December 1985; Consumer Protection (Cancellation of Contracts Concluded away from Business Premises) Regulations 1987, SI 1987/2117; Consumer Credit Act 1974, ss 67–68; *Faccini Dori v Recreb Srl* (Case C-91/92) [1995] All ER (EC) 1, ECJ.
32 *Coldunell v Gallon* [1986] QB 1184, [1986] 1 All ER 429, CA.

Constructive notice arises when the bank ought to have realised from the nature of the relationship between the parties and the unfavourable content of the transaction for the weaker party that there was a risk of undue influence. The nature of the relationship must be one where it is likely that the weaker party placed confidence in the business judgment of the other. This is likely to occur between husband and wife, other cohabiting couples, and parents and children, but it could also occur whenever emotional ties compel the weaker party to trust the stronger.[33] Other relations of subordination, such as between employer and employee also place the bank on notice that the relationship offered the opportunity for undue influence. In addition, the contract must be unfavourable to the weaker party on its face. This requirement will usually be satisfied where the weaker party is giving security for the stronger party's loan. But where the ostensible purpose of the agreement is to benefit the weaker party as well, this condition for constructive notice will not be satisfied. The bank in *CIBC Mortgages plc v Pitt*[34] did not receive constructive notice of the husband's fraud on his wife when he persuaded her to mortgage their home to the bank, for the bank was told falsely by the husband that the purpose of the loan was to purchase a family holiday home.

If the bank receives constructive notice of undue influence or other unconscientious dealing, then it must take reasonable steps to ensure that consent to the contract was properly obtained. These reasonable steps should normally include direct contact with the weaker party for the purpose of informing the weaker party of the exact nature of the transaction, the extent of liability which it entails, the risk of liability, and to advise the weaker party to take independent advice. The courts have accepted rather unsatisfactorily that provided a solicitor explains the transaction then the requirement of reasonable steps has been satisfied, even though the lawyer may not have expressed a view on the advisability of the transaction from a commercial perspective.[35] If the bank becomes aware that undue influence has actually been used, then it will have to insist that the transaction can only occur after independent advice has been given.[36]

4. Affirmation and Bars to Rescission

Through the doctrines of duress and undue influence, the law recognizes that coercion may vitiate consent to a contract. But the effect of these doctrines is not to prevent a contract from arising; rather they lead to a

---

33   *Barclays Bank plc v O'Brien* [1994] 1 AC 180, [1993] 4 All ER 417, HL.
34   [1994] 1 AC 200, [1993] 4 All ER 433, HL.
35   *Banco Exterior Internacional v Mann* [1995] 1 All ER 936, CA; Fehlberg, 'The Husband, the Bank, the Wife and Her Signature – the Sequel' (1996) 59 *Modern Law Review* 675, 685.
36   *Barclays Bank plc v O'Brien* [1994] 1 AC 180, [1993] 4 All ER 417, HL.

conclusion that the contract may be avoided by the weaker party, usually by an action for rescission of the contract.

The main reason for this rule must lie in the point that the coercion may dissipate after the contract has been formed. Once the coercion has been removed, the weaker party may nevertheless indicate a willingness to be bound by the contract. In these circumstances, a court may declare that the contract has been affirmed, so that the right to avoid it has been forfeited. In *North Ocean Shipping Co v Hyundai Construction Co (The Atlantic Baron)*,[37] a contract for the supply of a ship had been modified to increase the price at the insistence of the supplier, who threatened not to deliver without the increase. The court decided that this pressure amounted to economic duress, but nevertheless declined to void the contract on the ground that the buyer had subsequently affirmed the contract. The buyer had taken no steps to void the contract for seven months after delivery of the ship, and nor had it entered any protest at the time of making the final payments. The court judged the question of affirmation by the objective test of consent, finding that the buyer's conduct indicated to a reasonable man that it consented to the amended contract price.

Pragmatic considerations will also influence a court to resist an application for avoidance of a contract. If a substantial period of time elapses between the formation of the contract and the suit to avoid the contract, to upset the contract may have adverse effects on third parties and pose considerable problems in unravelling the transaction. For these reasons, actions to avoid a contract on the ground of coercion may be barred by reason of lapse of time, the impossibility of putting the parties back into the position which they held prior to the formation of the contract, and the necessity of protecting the interests of innocent third parties. The weaker party must seek relief within a reasonable time after the removal of the coercion.[38] Restitution must be possible to ensure that the parties are placed in more or less the same financial position as they enjoyed prior to the formation of the contract, but for this purpose it is acceptable to require payments of money to be made in order to compensate for property which cannot be returned and valuable services which have been rendered.[39] Third parties who have not knowingly taken advantage of the coercion will be protected by the court declining to avoid the contract if this would adversely affect them.

5. Protection of Competitive Markets

This analysis of the law of duress and undue influence reveals that various types of constraint on freedom to choose to enter a contract suffice to

---

37 [1979] QB 705, [1978] 3 All ER 1170, QB.
38 *Allcard v Skinner* (1887) 36 Ch D 145, CA.
39 *O'Sullivan v Management Agency and Music Ltd* [1985] QB 428 [1985] 3 All ER 351, CA.

negative consent and to prevent the ascription of contractual responsibility. The law must draw a line between the ordinary pressures and disadvantages experienced by people entering market transactions from aberrational cases when no transaction should be enforceable. Without this line, the commonplace inequalities of bargaining power between parties entering into contracts would suffice to invalidate contracts, which in turn would destroy the utility of the law of contract in providing a foundation for a market economy. The question to be addressed in concluding this chapter is whether or not the legal doctrines of duress and undue influence reveal a coherent basis for drawing this line.[40]

As we observed at the outset, it is unsatisfactory to claim that the line has been drawn on the basis of the concept of voluntary consent alone. The doctrines of duress and undue influence clearly introduce more specific criteria by which to distinguish those cases where consent is vitiated by coercion. The doctrine of duress insists upon an illegitimate act, and the equitable jurisdiction confines relief to recognizable patterns of aberrational situations where the weaker party has been exploited. On what basis is it possible to justify these particular criteria for intervention?

Illegality
It may be possible to synthesize the legal doctrines by suggesting that in their different ways both duress and undue influence require an illegitimate act on the part of the stronger party. On this argument, duress remains tied to cases of an illegitimate act under ordinary law such as tort, and equity also identifies a number of wrongful acts in various patterns of unconscientious dealing which are akin to fraud. Even granting that this loose synthesis is a permissible interpretation of the equitable jurisdiction, the question remains, why should illegality provide the basis for drawing the line governing intervention? It seems puzzling because the legality of the actions of the stronger party seems irrelevant to the fundamental question of whether the weaker party gave his voluntary consent to the contract.

A revised version of the traditional theory meets this objection by positing a realm of private autonomy, guarded by the normal rights of citizens under the common law, within which all actions are presumed to be voluntary. Interference with these rights necessarily results in unlawful behaviour, and then it can be assumed that a person lacks the voluntary choice required for contractual responsibility.[41]

The reasoning here is analytically suspect. In the terminology of Hohfeld,[42] from the interference with a claim-right of the weaker party, it

---

40   Kronman, Contract Law and Distributive Justice' (1980) 89 *Yale Law Journal* 472; Hale, 'Bargaining, Duress and Economic Liberty' (1943) 43 *Columbia Law Review* 603.
41   Epstein, 'Unconscionability: A Critical Reappraisal' (1975) 18 *Journal of Law and Economics* 293; Eisenberg, 'The Bargain Principle and its Limits' (1982) 95 *Harvard Law Review* 741; C Fried, *Contract as Promise* (Cambridge Mass, 1981), chapter 7.
42   W Hohfeld, *Fundamental Legal Conceptions as Applied in Judicial Reasoning* (ed W Cook, 1923).

assumes that the different privilege or liberty-right to enter contracts of one's choice has been removed as well. The false logic of this argument can be illustrated in the instance of a settlement of a valid claim. In a case where one party is guilty of committing a nuisance such as pollution against a neighbour's property, a settlement between the parties which provides compensation to the injured party will be binding despite the fact that rights were invaded. It is clearly essential that the illegality involves an invasion of rights which somehow destroys or weakens the right to choose whether or not to enter a contract directly. It is for this reason that the causation element in duress requires that the illegitimate act presents the weaker party with no reasonable choice but to make the contract.

Another weakness in this justification for controlling intervention by reference to the touchstone of illegality is the difficulty which it has in accounting for the breadth of the equitable jurisdiction. The grounds for invalidating contracts extend beyond ordinary examples of tortious or criminal conduct, and, though a loose analogy may be drawn with fraud in many of these instances, the normal tests for fraud will not necessarily be satisfied. At best, therefore, this explanation in terms of the interference with the rights of the weaker party will only account for the common law doctrine of duress, and we require another justification for the equitable jurisdiction.

Anti-Competitive Practices

A more promising justification for the scope of the doctrines of duress and undue influence links this branch of the law of contract to a more general legal policy of the protection of competitive markets. On this interpretation, it is recognized that many different kinds of constraints serve to limit the freedom to choose whether or not to enter contracts. But these constraints only become impermissible if they prevent the operation of a competitive market. The law has to address both structural flaws in market sectors and particular instances of behaviour which frustrate the operation of competitive markets. The law addresses structural flaws through the law of competition, so that measures are taken to ensure that in relation to any one product sector no one producer can obtain a near-monopoly position. But the law must also address particular types of behaviour which subvert the operation of a competitive market. The law of duress and undue influence serve to identify those types of behaviour, drawing a boundary for unacceptable anti-competitive practices. But they are supplemented by competition law, which also provides the possibility of injunctions against anti-competitive behaviour.

Under Article 86 of the Treaty of Rome, an abuse of a dominant market position occurs when a business practice has the effect of reducing or eliminating competition in a particular market. One example is price discrimination by a supplier between different distributors. If the supplier favours one distributor over others by offering lower prices or rebates, then this has the effect of reducing competition between distributors and is forbidden.[43] Similarly, a refusal to supply an existing customer, thereby making it difficult or impossible for the customer to trade in that market, will be unfair competition.[44] A glaring example will be the refusal by a manufacturer to supply spare parts to a particular distributor or retailer.[45] Notice that, in these instances, a competitive market for the benefit of consumers may not be prevented. EC law objects to practices which prevent particular businesses from entering markets on equal terms.[46]

This purpose establishes the link of complementary purpose with the private law governing coercion. The objective of the law is to protect businesses and individuals in their freedom to trade. When economic resources are deployed to prevent equal competition, then this anti-competitive practice will be prohibited. Competition law provides an active remedy which permits prevention of such practices. The private law of duress and undue influence serves to invalidate contracts which have been entered into under such conditions of unfair competition.

The strength of this interpretation of the law lies in its ability to account for the design and complexities of the legal doctrines. Firstly, it explains why the law focuses on the behaviour of the stronger party rather than the state of mind of the weaker. Although the state of mind of the weaker party should be the matter most relevant to the question of whether or not free consent was given to a contract, the emphasis of the law is always upon the behaviour of the stronger party. This can be explained as voicing a concern against anti-competitive trading practices. The protection for freedom of contract is therefore determined by the extent to which anti-competitive practices will be tolerated. Secondly, this interpretation explains why the equitable jurisdiction of undue influence extends beyond illegitimate acts. Unacceptable anti-competitive behaviour will include unlawful acts such as torts, but it can extend to more subtle forms of pressure. Thirdly, this interpretation explains why the equitable jurisdiction places such emphasis on the evidence of a manifest disadvantage. The equitable jurisdiction poses the hypothetical question of whether this contract could reasonably have been agreed under competitive conditions. If it could have been concluded on the same terms under competitive conditions, then despite the existence of pressures or abuse of confidence the contract does not evidence any advantage having been taken of the anti-competitive behaviour, so it should be permitted to stand as valid.

What this interpretation of the law cannot provide is any sharp line which identifies prohibited types of anti-competitive behaviour. As in the equitable jurisdiction, the law must examine all the facts of the case to determine whether the behaviour effectively secured the result that advantage was taken of an uncompetitive market. It is plainly not

---

43 *Hoffman-La Roche v EC Commission*, Case 85/76 [1979] ECR 461, [1979] 3 CMLR 211, ECJ.
44 *Commercial Solvents v EC Commission*, Case 6/73 [1974] 1 CMLR 309, ECJ.
45 *Hugin v EC Commission*, Case 22/78 [1979] ECR 1869, [1979] 3 CMLR 345, ECJ.
46 R Whish, *Competition Law*, 2nd edn (London, 1989) pp 310–311.

sufficient, however, that the parties enjoyed different degrees of bargaining power in the sense of better resources or an advantageous trading position due to possession of some scarce commodity. What is crucial is rather that the superior bargaining position was used to establish the situation of an uncompetitive market, and then that situation was exploited in order to impose a disadvantageous transaction on the other weaker party.

The interpretation of the doctrines of duress and undue influence in terms of the preservation of competitive markets marks a break from the classical law. Instead of attempting to account for the legal doctrines as an elaboration of the idea of the voluntary consent which generates contractual responsibility, the doctrines are perceived as serving the function of protecting competitive markets which only indirectly protects freedom of contract. [47]

---

47   Compare: Birks and Chin, 'On the Nature of Undue Influence', in J Beatson and D Friedmann (eds), *Good Faith and Fault in Contract Law* (Oxford, 1995) chapter 3; Bigwood, 'Undue Influence: "Impaired Consent" or "Wicked Exploitation"?' (1996) 16 *Oxford Journal of Legal Studies* 503.

9
The Moment of Responsibility

When does contractual responsibility arise? The answer under the classical law is that both parties must consent to the contract. In simple cases, this rule presents no problem. If two persons each sign a contract in the presence of each other, then the contract is formed at the moment of the second signature. When the consent must be inferred from conduct with less precise meaning than a signature on a document, however, the exact moment at which contractual responsibility arises may prove more difficult to determine.

Imagine that a person is waiting for a bus at a bus stop. The bus lumbers into view, and the intending passenger waves it down. The doors open, the passenger steps inside, pays the fare, and takes a seat in the interior. At what point in time was the contract of carriage completed? Payment of the fare clearly evidences consent to the contract, but it is arguable that boarding the bus, and even waving it down, also constitute acts of consent to the contract. Does it matter when the contract is formed? In most cases it does not, but it is not hard to invent problems where the precise timing of the formation of a contract makes a difference. Suppose, for example, that the bus driver failed to stop to pick up the passenger: if the contract was formed by waving the bus down, then the driver would have broken the contract of carriage. In another case, suppose that the passenger's shopping is damaged on boarding the bus, perhaps because the door suddenly shuts and squashes a bag of fruit, then the question of a possible claim for damages would be governed by the contract of carriage if the contract had been formed, or by the ordinary law of negligence in tort if it had not.

To decide when consent has been given by both parties to a contract, the authors of traditional contract textbooks devised an intricate set of rules employing the concepts 'offer and acceptance' to fix the moment of responsibility. These rules typify the formalist qualities of classical law: they are detailed, technical, and mysterious, yet claim logical derivation from the idea of agreement. Judges quickly appreciated the rigour of this analytical framework, and in the nineteenth century they adopted most of the terminology from the textbooks. They would approach the question of when the contract of carriage had been formed for instance in the above example, by asking whether the bus company had made an offer and when it had been accepted by the passenger. In some instances this formulation of the issue can be helpful, as in the case where one person offers to sell his car and the other says 'I accept your offer'. But in the example of the bus passenger, the words 'offer and acceptance' are not employed, so clearly a court must attach these concepts to the facts by reference to further criteria. Even if the words of 'offer and acceptance' are used, they will not inevitably prove determinative, if the court's analysis of the moment of contractual responsibility differs, and again this indicates that the courts use further criteria by which to determine the moment of the formation of the contract.

In this chapter we commence by examining the details of the rules of offer and acceptance as they have been developed by the courts and the treatise writers. These rules usually purport to constitute no more than an elaboration of the principle that both parties should consent to an agreement before it forms a contract. Yet the rules reveal a tension with this principle in many instances, which suggests that they are designed to serve other purposes as well.

Furthermore, we will quickly notice that even the formal rules of offer and acceptance are sometimes subverted and ignored. This suggests that, despite the conventional lip-service paid to the rules of offer and acceptance, a court will often determine the moment of contractual responsibility by reference to the practical implications of its decision. In other words, in the example of the bus passenger, the court will determine the moment of contractual responsibility by reference to the effects of its decision on the rights and liabilities of the parties. If the court wishes to discourage bus drivers from passing bus stops with passengers waiting, then it can hold that the contract is formed by the passenger waving down the bus. If the court wishes to permit the bus company to be able to rely on its standard term contract which excludes or limits liability for damage to personal possessions, then it can hold that the contract was formed when the passenger stepped onto the bus, and not later when he paid his fare. If, on the contrary, the court seeks to avoid the application of the bus company's standard terms of carriage, it can hold that the contract was formed on payment of the fare.[1] This chapter concentrates upon an exploration of the instrumental purposes which influence the courts' determinations of the moment of formation of contracts.

The chapter concludes with a brief discussion of the sources of legal liability which may arise prior to the formation of a contract. In the case of the bus passenger, for instance, the general duty of care owed under the law of tort can be relied upon as a basis for recovery of damage to goods before the contract has been formed. These sources of pre-contractual responsibility will be considered in greater depth in Chapter 10.

---

1   In *Wilkie v London Passenger Transport Board* [1947] 1 All ER 258, CA, Lord Greene MR suggested that the contract was concluded when the passenger was fully inside the bus and in a position to pay his fare, which had the effect of entitling the bus company to avoid liability for personal injuries.

It must be observed at the outset of this discussion, however, that the emphasis upon this issue of the moment of responsibility gives a misleading impression of its importance. In practice, informal understandings are likely to be observed even though the rules of offer and acceptance have not been satisfied. This is likely to occur for fear of damage to business reputation or loss of future contracts.[2] The withdrawal of an offer in circumstances where it has not yet been accepted though it has been acted upon in some respects may be regarded as bad faith conduct which will be sanctioned by a refusal to deal with that party in the future.[3] These non-legal sanctions will therefore establish a sense of obligation some time prior to the formation of the contract according to the legal analysis. Where this gap emerges between the application of the formal legal rules and the informal understanding, then we are likely to discern an attempt by the courts to bridge that gap by employing ideas of pre-contractual responsibility. Whether or not the courts should try to bridge that gap appears to be an issue which divides the classical law with its respect for autonomy and the modern law's commitment to the value of co-operation.[4]

1. Offer and Acceptance

The classical law determines when the parties reach an agreement by imagining that they enact a short scene in which one makes an offer which the other accepts. The parts may be either spoken or mimed, for the offer and acceptance can be written, spoken, or even inferred from conduct. The law requires no special incantations, so the parties may improvise the manner of expression. The climax of the drama unfolds when one person pronounces his acceptance, for at that moment, precisely, contractual responsibility makes its entrance and seizes both players. Classical theory writes this script as the logical denouement of the principle that an agreement, as the basis of responsibility, is the product of an exercise of will by two parties. When an exercise of will signifies acceptance of the terms of the offer, then there is a 'meeting of the minds' or an agreement.

We have already considered the question of what amounts to an act of consent to a contract. Under the objective test of agreement, the words or conduct must be reasonably understood by the other party to signify assent to the contract. The question to be considered here is when those manifestations of consent coalesce into a binding agreement. The answer lies according to classical analysis when an acceptance is given to an offer.

2   Lewis, 'Contracts Between Businessmen: Reform of the Law of Firm Offers' (1982) 9 *British Journal of Law and Society* 153.
3   Schultz, 'The Firm Offer Puzzle: A Study of Business Practice in the Construction Industry' (1952) 19 *University Chicago Law Review* 237.
4   Charney, 'Nonlegal Sanctions in Commercial Relationships' (1990) 104 *Harvard Law Review* 373, esp at p 449.

(1) The Test of Acceptance
Three key rules determine which significations of consent succeed in forming a contract. These rules define three qualities of an act of will, which are essential if it is to count as an acceptance.

Correspondence
An acceptance must correspond exactly to the terms of the offer. Accordingly, a purported acceptance containing terms which differ from the original offer fails to create contractual responsibility.

At most, the purported acceptance constitutes another offer, a counter-offer, to make a contract on different terms. A counter-offer also has the effect of terminating the original offer, so that it can no longer be accepted.[5] In *Gibson v Manchester City Council*,[6] it will be recalled that the city treasurer wrote to the plaintiff stating that the City may be prepared to sell his rented council house to the plaintiff for £2,180. The House of Lords decided that the treasurer's letter did not even constitute an offer of sale because of its guarded terms. In the Court of Appeal, the majority had decided that a binding contract had been formed because the parties were agreed on all material terms. In a dissenting judgment, Geoffrey Lane LJ held that no contract had been formed because the plaintiff, instead of accepting the treasurer's offer immediately, had in fact written a counter-offer of a lower price to take into account repairs needed to the house, which was rejected by the treasurer. It was only later that the plaintiff had purported to accept the treasurer's original offer, by which time the plaintiff's counter-offer had annulled it, so there was no subsisting offer from the treasurer for the plaintiff to accept.

This rule, stated bluntly, has the implication that under English law even a minor suggested alteration in the terms for the contract turns what purports to be an acceptance into a counter-offer, thereby preventing a contract from arising.[7] If, for example, the modification concerns not the price of goods, but merely an alteration by the buyer of the place where they are to be delivered, then a strict application of the rule would lead to the conclusion that no contract is formed unless the counter-offer is itself accepted. But this technicality might not be observed if the modification appears minor, unobjectionable, and immaterial to the seller of the goods. Some judges would certainly hold there to be a contract despite the absence of a formal acceptance of the counter-offer, provided that the modification was not so material that it would affect the price.[8] Alternatively, the seller's action of sending the goods to the buyer's chosen location could be treated as an act of consent to the modified terms to be inferred from conduct.[9]

---

5   *Hyde v Wrench* (1840) 3 Beav 334, 49 ER 132, Rolls Court.
6   [1978] 1 WLR 520, [1978] 2 All ER 583, CA; revsd [1979] 1 WLR 294, [1979] 1 All ER 972 , HL.
7   Compare: Uniform Laws on International Sales Act 1967, Sch 2, Art 7.
8   For example Lord Denning MR in *Butler Machine Tool Co Ltd v Ex-Cell-O Corpn (England) Ltd* [1979] 1 WLR 401, [1979] 1 All ER 965, CA.
9   *Brogden v Metropolitan Rly Co* (1877) 2 App Cas 666, HL.

Nexus

An acceptance must be in response to an offer. Unless the offeree knows that an offer has been made, and attempts to accept it, then no agreement takes place. For example, if a person supplies information to the police leading to the apprehension of a person for whom a reward has been offered, the reward may only be claimed by the informant if he is aware of the offer of the reward. Similarly, the balance of legal authority holds that two offers, identical in their terms, made at the same time or which cross in the post, will not create a contract, because neither offer counts as an informed acceptance of the other.[10] The justification for this rule commonly given is that, without an acceptance of a known offer, neither party can be sure whether the other regards himself as being bound.

Communication

An acceptance must be communicated to the offeror. Thus a mere intention to agree to an offer does not create responsibility; the offeror must be informed of the acceptance of his offer. This rule must be interpreted with two important qualifications in mind. First, because the courts will infer consent from conduct, an acceptance can be constituted by conduct which comes to the attention of the offeror, such as part performance of the contract.[11] Secondly, the offeror has the power to specify in the offer the manner in which acceptance must be made. This gives the offeror both the power to insist upon strict observance of an elaborate procedure, such as the requirement that any acceptance must be received by a particular method of transmission at a particular time and place,[12] but also the power to weaken the requirement of communication of acceptance to vanishing point. These qualifications were combined in *Carlill v Carbolic Smoke Ball Co.*[13] Under the terms of the offer in the newspaper, acceptance was constituted by the purchase and use of the smokeball according to the manufacturer's instructions. Compliance with this condition therefore counted as acceptance, for the performance evidenced consent, and the requirement of communication had been waived by the terms of the offer.

(2) *Justification of the Rules*

Whilst these three rules defining the concept of an acceptance purport to be derived from the principle that agreement generates responsibility, when we examine them closely, the connection between the rules and this justification appears weak. Although the first rule requiring correspondence does make sense as a requirement dictated by the need

10　*Tinn v Hoffman* (1873) 29 LT 271, Ct of Exch Ch.
11　*Brogden v Metropolitan Rly Co* (1877) 2 App Cas 666, HL; *Robophone Facilities Ltd v Blank* [1966] 1 WLR 1428, [1966] 3 All ER 128, CA.
12　*Holwell Securities Ltd v Hughes* [1974] 1 WLR 155, [1974] 1 All ER 161, CA; *Manchester Diocesan Council for Education v Commercial and General Investments Ltd* [1970] 1 WLR 241, [1969] 3 All ER 1593, Ch.
13　[1893] 1 QB 256, CA.

for agreement, since it ensures that the parties are intending to contract on the same terms, the second and third rules, concerning nexus and communication, make it abundantly clear that an agreement is not created by a shared intention, or a meeting of minds. The rules require not simply agreement in fact, and not only conduct evidencing consent, but also conduct which both evidences that the consent was induced by the offer of the other party and which has been drawn to the other party's attention.

What is the purpose of these additional rules, if it is not to ensure that the parties have reached agreement? The underlying purpose of the rules governing acceptance is to determine the moment at which both parties can rely upon the existence of a binding contract between them. On the basis of this reliance, either may then incur expenditure in preparing for, or actually performing, the agreement. They may also forgo other opportunities to make contracts, believing that they are now bound by the contract. Goods may be withdrawn from sale, or a person may desist in seeking employment for his or her services. The rules governing acceptance of contracts determine at which point it is reasonable to act in these various ways in reliance upon the binding contract. They also transfer the risk of that reliance to the other party, so that if that other party breaks the contract, he or she will incur liability for any wasted expenditure or forgone opportunities. On this analysis of the test of acceptance, therefore, the fundamental issue is not whether or not there is agreement between the parties, but whether or not the negotiations and conduct have reached such a point that both parties can reasonably suppose that the other is committed to the contract so that it can be relied upon.

This analysis explains why proof of agreement in fact is not crucial to the decision whether or not the moment of contractual responsibility has been reached. The courts can decline to find a contract in circumstances which indicate a shared intention to carry out a transaction without any observable action of acceptance. This is true in the instance of cross-offers. It is also true in the case where the offeree first makes a counter-offer, and then purports to accept the original offer: the parties may be in agreement, but, in the light of the history of the negotiations, the courts regard this as an unsafe basis on which to claim that reliance upon a binding contract was reasonable. Similarly, in *Felthouse v Bindley*,[14] the plaintiff wrote to his nephew offering to buy his horse for £30 15s, saying, 'If I hear no more about him, I consider the horse mine at that price.' The nephew failed to reply to this letter, though he instructed an auctioneer to withdraw the horse from a forthcoming sale of his stock. The Court of Common Pleas found that no contract had been formed, insisting that direct and unequivocal evidence of acceptance is essential for contractual liability. Although the facts of the case revealed that the parties were in fact in agreement, the court could not accept that it was reasonable for the uncle to assume so without a further communication from the nephew.

14   (1862) 11 CBNS 869.

The differing decisions of the courts in *Gibson v Manchester City Council* illustrate this function of the rules of offer and acceptance most clearly. Lord Denning MR in the Court of Appeal was probably correct to say that the parties were agreed on all the material terms of the proposed sale of the council house. But he was mistaken to infer from this agreement that the moment of contractual responsibility had been reached. He slipped into the error of thinking that the test of the moment of contractual responsibility is when the parties have reached agreement. But the test imposes additional hurdles such as communication of the acceptance, because its function is to determine at what point it is reasonable for both parties to rely upon the existence of a binding legal commitment. Mr Gibson had jumped the gun in believing that he had a binding legal commitment from the Council, for it had not formally accepted his offer, even though it no doubt intended to do so. What the technical rules governing acceptance seek to achieve is to determine the moment of time at which it is reasonable to act in reliance upon the existence of a binding legal contract, not merely to ascertain whether in fact the parties were in agreement.

Exponents of the classical theory of contracts were aware that the rules governing acceptance created a problem for their analysis of contract rules based upon agreement. The rules governing acceptance occasionally produced the result that, despite the parties being in agreement in fact, there was no contract. They attempted to explain this disparity by reference to the problem of proving intent or will. The need to communicate acceptance was regarded as a necessary element in the proof of consent, 'for the devil himself knows not the thought of man'.[15] As well as being theologically suspect, this response is unconvincing, for the rules about nexus and communication can prevent the formation of a contract, even though the evidence based upon proven observable facts points unambiguously towards the conclusion that the parties were in agreement. This was the position in *Felthouse v Bindley*, where the nephew had withdrawn the horse from auction and told the auctioneer that it had been sold, leaving little doubt that he believed himself to be bound by a contract with his uncle. This disparity between the tests of acceptance and the foundational principle of agreement in classical law therefore leads writers such as Anson to doubt decisions such as *Felthouse v Bindley*, insisting that 'there seems to be no convincing reason why a contract should not come into existence', given that intention could be proven.[16]

The function of the rules governing acceptance is therefore not to serve as an evidentiary device. This function is already performed by the rules governing consent and the inference of consent from conduct. The rules of acceptance mark the point at which reliance can be placed upon the existence of a binding contract between the parties. The requirement of

15   Per Brian CJ, Anon. (1477), YB Pasch 17 Edw IV, f 1, pl 2.; this dictum was frequently repeated in formation of contract cases in the nineteenth century: eg *Brogden v Metropolitan Rly Co* (1877) 2 App Cas 666, per Lord Blackburn.

16   A Guest, *Anson's Law of Contract* (Oxford, 26th edn, 1984), p 39.

nexus follows logically from that purpose, because it cannot be reasonable to rely upon the existence of a contract between the parties if one is unaware of the other's offer. The general requirement of communication of acceptance makes sense as marking the point in time when both parties are likely to be aware that the other is now reasonably relying upon the existence of a contract between them. But it is also clear that the offeror may dispense with the requirement of communication of acceptance, if he or she is content to assume the risk of liability under the contract without notification of acceptance, as in the case of *Carlill v Carbolic Smoke Ball Co.*[17] One can consistently claim, therefore, that the source of contractual responsibility lies in an exercise of will or an agreement, and at the same time maintain that the moment of responsibility is deferred until both parties know of the agreement. The classical lawyers, however, resisted this separation of the issues of ascription of responsibility and the moment of responsibility, and consequently failed to mount an adequate defence against the criticism that the rules defining the concept of acceptance do not conform to the principle that basis of responsibility lies in agreement or consent.

(3) Avoidance of the Rules
The problem which these well established rules governing acceptance present to the courts is that from time to time they will take the view that the moment of responsibility has been reached even though, under the normal tests of acceptance, some element is missing. To justify the conclusion that a contract was formed, the courts have two choices. Either they may subvert the three rules of acceptance, and maintain that a contract was formed despite the failure to comply with one or more of the rules. To achieve this result, they must adopt a surprising view of the facts of the case, in order to bring them into conformity with the rules. Alternatively, the courts may alter the category of the legal analysis, choosing to impose a different form of liability in order to compensate the misplaced reliance.

Twisting the Facts
Under the first method of judicial avoidance, the court pays lip-service to the rules of acceptance, but it is hard to see how the facts of the case can satisfy those rules. This has often been the problem, for instance, in cases known as the 'battle of forms', where the court must strive to fit the facts under the correspondence rule. Businesspersons prefer to make contracts on their own standard terms of business for the sake of simplicity and efficiency. Between two such persons, even after a number of exchanges of offers, quotations, tenders, invoices, orders and so forth, it is possible that they will have failed to achieve a coincidence of offer and acceptance because of the incompatibility of their respective standard terms.

---

17 [1893] 1 QB 256, CA.

Nevertheless, the courts strive to impose contractual responsibility once performance has commenced, since it seems reasonable at that point to transfer the risk of reliance upon the contract; but this result compels the court to ignore the first rule of correspondence.

Such a flaunting of the rule happened in *Butler Machine Tool Co v Ex-Cell-O Corpn (England) Ltd*.[18] The plaintiff offered to manufacture and deliver a machine tool for £75,535 on two conditions, which were that orders were accepted only on the terms set out in the quotation, and secondly that a price variation clause should apply whereby the defendant would be charged at the prices ruling at the date of delivery. The defendant then placed an order including its own terms and conditions which contained no price variation clause. The order had a tear-off acknowledgment for signature, which accepted the order on the terms it contained. The seller signed and returned the acknowledgment with a covering letter stating that delivery was to be in accordance with the terms of the original quotation. On delivery of the machine tool, the seller invoked the price variation clause and charged an extra £2,892. The English Court of Appeal denied the seller's claim for the extra sum, holding that the return of the signed acknowledgment form on the buyer's terms which excluded any price variation constituted the binding contract. Yet this conclusion is evidently artificial,[19] for the covering letter made it plain that the price variation clause contained in the original quotation was intended to remain part of the agreement. In truth, the parties never reached an agreement which satisfied the requirement of correspondence, for each purported acceptance really constituted a counter-offer. The court adeptly excluded a part of the written evidence in order to bring the facts under the established rules of acceptance. This achieved the result that a contract had been formed, a conclusion which the court no doubt believed warranted because of the extent of the reliance upon the contract by both parties.

The courts similarly manipulate facts to fit the rule concerning the nexus of agreement, and perhaps even ignore it. For example, many cases involving a claim for a reward succeed, even though the plaintiff cannot establish that he intended to accept the offer because he was unaware of it.[20] Sometimes courts will interpret the events in such a way that the informant is presumed to have heard of the reward moments before supplying the information. Another technique involves interpreting the terms of the offer to apply whether or not the informant was motivated by knowledge of the reward. Many judges simply ignore the nexus rule completely, motivated perhaps by the belief that an informant, who acted in an exemplary fashion and without mercenary motives, should be able to recover the reward as payment for his services even though he was ignorant of the offer. Of course, these decisions infuriate and torment the classical theorists. Listen to the outraged Anson:

18   [1979] 1 WLR 401, [1979] 1 All ER 965, CA.
19   P Atiyah, *An Introduction to the Law of Contract* (Oxford, 5th edn, 1995), p 67.
20   Eg *Gibbons v Proctor* (1891) 64 LT 594; Hudson, '*Gibbons v Proctor* Revisited' (1968) 84 *Law Quarterly Review* 503.

One who does an act for which a reward has been offered, in ignorance of the offer, cannot say either that there was a *consensus* of wills between him and the offeror, or that his conduct was affected by the promise offered. On no view of contract could he set up a right of action.[21]

Anson dismisses cases to the contrary as uncertain on their facts, or simply wrong. Other writers list a number of special cases or exceptions which do not fit the general rule. As the list of exceptions to the requirement of nexus lengthens, or the dogmatic assertions of judicial error multiply, one is entitled to doubt whether the courts really accept the importance of the nexus rule as a determinant of the formation of contractual responsibility.

Of the three rules, the last one concerning the requirement of communication of the acceptance retains perhaps the shakiest hold on judicial practice. The courts can infer that the acceptance has been communicated from any conduct which is referable to a concluded contract and comes to the notice of the offeror. In *Brogden v Metropolitan Rly Co*,[22] after negotiations between the parties, the railway company sent a requirements contract to the coal merchant. The latter signed the agreement after making some alterations and returned it. The company's agent then put the document in a drawer. Both parties subsequently acted upon the agreement by ordering and supplying coal. The coal merchant's alterations of the document turned it into a counter-offer, and so at first sight the company had never communicated its acceptance by simply putting it into a drawer. Nevertheless, the House of Lords held that a contract had been concluded by virtue of the subsequent orders for, and delivery of, coal. In effect the courts are prepared to look at subsequent events and the conduct of the parties in order to determine whether a contract was formed, sliding over the logical difficulty that subsequent conduct cannot prove that the original acceptance was ever communicated.

A celebrated source of difficulty with the requirement of communication of acceptance involves contracts concluded by post. Acceptance of a contract by post is permissible unless the offeror specifies a contrary method or it is not reasonable in the circumstances. It will not be reasonable usually if the offer is made by a method of instantaneous communication, such as telephone, fax, or electronic mail, in which case a court will normally regard it as only reasonable to reply by using a similar instantaneous medium. An acceptance by one of these instantaneous methods of communication will therefore only conclude the contract when it is received by the offeror.[23] Assuming, however, a postal acceptance is reasonable, at what point in time is the contract concluded? Under the third rule requiring communication of acceptance, one would expect the English rule to be that the letter has to be received by the offeror. Since the early part of the nineteenth century, however, the courts have followed

21 W Anson, *Principles of the Law of Contract* (Oxford, 10th edn, 1903), p 23; (Oxford, 26th edn, A Guest, 1984), p 30.
22 (1877) 2 App Cas 666, HL.
23 *Entores Ltd v Miles Far East Corpn* [1955] 2 QB 327, [1955] 2 All ER 493, CA.

the anomalous rule that the acceptance is complete when it is posted.[24] The justification for this anomaly was said to be that the post office acted as the agent for the offeror, so in effect the posting of the letter of acceptance simultaneously constituted receipt by the authorized agent of the offeror.[25] This fits the facts into the rule requiring communication of acceptance, but at the price of considerable distortion, for if the post office acts as an agent for sending and receiving communications at all, which seems improbable because it does not otherwise act like an employee of the parties, it is surely the agent of the offeree who pays for the service rather than the offeror.

The central difficulty in these cases of postal acceptance is to identify a moment at which it is reasonable for both parties to be able to rely upon a concluded contract. In favour of selecting the moment at the time of posting the letter, it can be said that from that time onward the offeree cannot alter his mind and will reasonably suppose that the letter will reach its destination and so conclude the contract.[26] Against this view it can be argued that until the offeror receives the letter, he cannot act in reliance upon the conclusion of the contract; moreover, if the letter goes astray or is misdirected, the offeror may only learn of the conclusion of the contract when he has irretrievably harmed his own position.[27] In favouring the former solution, the courts appear to have decided that an offeror who is prepared to accept the risk of a postal acceptance without protecting himself in the terms of the offer, should also take the risk of misdirection or loss of letters, which is a harsh conclusion given that the failure to communicate the acceptance may prove to be the offeree's fault. The lesson has, however, been learned by offerors, who normally specify a requirement of communication of the acceptance in the terms of an offer, which prevents the postal rule from operating.[28]

New Categories of Liability

The drama of offer and acceptance, as it is recounted in the classical texts, takes as its paradigm a series of oral negotiations leading to an express agreement between the parties. As the facts of cases move beyond this paradigm, as in the case of postal communications, or promises which induce reliance, then the courts are forced to make the choice between twisting the facts to fit them into the rules, or to recognize new categories of liability for which the formal rules of offer and acceptance do not apply.

The most important example of this latter technique concerns unilateral contracts. Living in a hybrid world between the exchange model and the reliance model of contractual enforceability, these contracts are

---

24 *Adams v Lindsell* (1818) 1 B & Ald 681.
25 Eg Thesiger LJ, *Household Fire Insurance Co v Grant* (1879) 4 Ex D 216, CA.
26 *Brogden v Metropolitan Rly Co* (1877) 2 App Cas 666, HL, per Lord Blackburn.
27 See Bramwell LJ in *Household Fire Insurance Co v Grant* (1879) 4 Ex D 216, CA.
28 Eg *Holwell Securities Ltd v Hughes* [1974] 1 WLR 155, [1974] 1 All ER 161, CA.

valid despite the absence of conduct which satisfies the rules of acceptance. Although it is possible to say that in *Carlill v Carbolic Smoke Ball Co* that the company waived its right to have acceptance of its offer communicated to it, this is an artificial way of reconciling unilateral contracts with the rules of acceptance. It is better to recognize that the courts can use the category of unilateral contract when they believe that the moment of contractual responsibility has been reached even though there was no communication of acceptance. This device is frequently employed in commercial contexts to overcome the problem that in networks of contracts between several parties there may not be any direct communication between the parties in dispute, or indeed any precise knowledge of the terms of any offer, with the effect under the rules of acceptance of preventing the conclusion of any contract. But a unilateral contract can be discovered between parties who have never communicated from an offer which is acted upon.[29] This device was used, for example, in *New Zealand Shipping Co Ltd v Satterthwaite & Co Ltd (The Eurymedon)*,[30] so that a contract was formed between the owner of goods and the stevedores who unloaded them, even though they had never communicated with each other, but in fact made separate contracts with the carrier of the goods.

As well as unilateral contracts, the courts can also rely upon clear examples of the reliance model of contractual liability, by holding the parties estopped from denying contractual responsibility. This can overcome the problem of the absence of a communication of an acceptance when one party is induced to act to his detriment by the acts of the other, even though those acts cannot be characterized as a communication of the acceptance. This was the technique employed by the High Court of Australia in *Waltons Stores (Interstate) Ltd v Maher*,[31] in order to overcome the problem that no formal acceptance of the contract had ever been sent, and no acceptance could be inferred from conduct. Nevertheless, there were acts and omissions which led the other party to believe that he could reasonably rely upon the contract being concluded.

2. Instrumentalism

Even in those cases where the analysis in terms of offer and acceptance potentially applies, we must observe from our earlier example of the bus passenger that the courts can so readily manipulate the facts in order to satisfy the formal rules that this possibility belies the classical theory that the facts are readily categorized in these terms. On the contrary, a hidden element of discretion permits the courts to label the facts with the

---

29 *Clarke v Earl of Dunraven* [1897] AC 59, HL.
30 [1975] AC 154, [1974] 1 All ER 1015, PC.
31 (1988) 164 CLR 387 (Aust HC).

terminology of offer and acceptance, whenever they believe it is fair and reasonable to impose contractual liability.

Consider, for example, the purchase of goods in a self-service store. At what point is an agreement completed by an acceptance? Does the customer accept the offer when he or she places the goods in the wire basket? Or does acceptance take place when the customers present the goods to the assistant at the cash register? Alternatively, we can even argue that the assistant accepts the offer to buy by ringing up the prices of the goods on the cash register. Or is that merely an offer, accepted by the customer by the presentation of the right amount of money? Since each interpretation is plausible, a court must make a discretionary choice between them, concealing the real grounds for the decision by the formalist reasoning of offer and acceptance. In this brief section we cannot hope to identify all the relevant considerations which a court takes into account. Instead we will illustrate the surprising variety of such considerations in order to alert us to the complexity of the issue.

The variety of potentially relevant considerations emerges with a brief review of the conflicting decisions from different jurisdictions concerning the moment of formation of a contract of sale in a self-service store. Sometimes the courts desire to make the moment of responsibility as late as possible, in order to avoid making the customer liable to pay for the goods before he or she has had a chance to inspect them and compare the price between different brands. Courts encourage this consumer circumspection by holding that the customer forms the contract by presenting the goods at the cash register.[32] In contrast, in other cases courts insist that the parties enter a contract when the customer places the goods in the wire basket, if for instance this result strengthens the legal position of a customer injured by a bottle exploding as it is placed in the basket.[33] The relative advantage to a customer of being allowed a contractual claim against the shopkeeper for personal injuries depends upon the state of the law of tort governing the liability of owners of premises towards those injured upon them, so courts in different jurisdictions react in the light of the background law applicable to personal injuries. Another reason for deferring the moment of acceptance emerges in cases involving charges of shoplifting. If the customer completes the contract when he or she removes goods from the shelf, then the shoplifter could defend himself or herself against a charge of theft by arguing that he or she had purchased the goods before taking them from the store. Of course, the shoplifter would in these circumstances be liable to pay the price of the goods, and might also be guilty of another criminal offence involving fraud. But the shoplifter would avoid liability for theft if the contract is formed by taking the goods from the shelf, for logically one cannot steal goods which belong to oneself as a result of a contractual purchase. For this reason, the court is likely to defer the moment of formation of the contract until the goods have been paid for.

---

32   *Lasky v Economy Grocery Stores* 65 NE 2d 305 (Supreme Court of Mass, 1946).
33   *Sancho-Lopez v Fedor Food Corpn* 211 NYS 2d 953 (1961)(City Court, New York).

These conflicting considerations which influence the determination of the moment of contractual responsibility in a simple case of supermarket purchases explain why courts reach such different results. They also illustrate how difficult it is to anticipate all the relevant considerations. Further complications are introduced in the leading English case, which illustrates how special statutory provisions give added legal significance to a particular result. In *Pharmaceutical Society of Great Britain v Boots Cash Chemists*,[34] the self-service store was required to demonstrate that it satisfied a statutory requirement that all sales of certain non-prescription drugs should be made under the supervision of a registered pharmacist. The store argued that it complied with the statute by posting a pharmacist in the vicinity of the cash register, as opposed to stationing one near all the display shelves. The Court of Appeal facilitated the development of self-service pharmacies, and incidentally reduced the need for registered pharmacists whose professional body had commenced the action, by concluding that customers made contracts of sale at the cash register and therefore the store complied with the law. The reason given by the court for its decision was simply one of permitting customers to inspect the goods and change their minds in the shop. But one wonders also how impressed the court was by the desire of the pharmacists to retain their restrictive practices, though this consideration was not explicitly acknowledged.

Although this discussion of the self-service store demonstrates how difficult it is to list in advance all the policy considerations which influence the determination of the moment of contractual responsibility, we can identify some of the factors which frequently weigh heavily in the exercise of judicial discretion. Lord Wilberforce has acknowledged the balancing process at the heart of this determination of the moment of contractual responsibility when he remarked that:

> No universal rule can cover all such cases: they must be resolved by reference to the intentions of the parties, by sound business practice and in some cases by a judgment where the risks should lie.[35]

The following list comprises the most popular considerations acknowledged by courts in commercial contexts.

Room for manoeuvre
Courts recognize that negotiations may be carried out over a considerable period of time without any binding commitment being assumed by either party. These exploratory discussions perform a valuable service, for the parties become better informed about the details of the transaction, and they resolve possible ambiguities. They also use this period of time to consider alternatives, and to check up on the reliability of the other party. In a typical building contract, for example, the investor seeks tenders

---

34   [1953] 1QB 401, [1953] 1 All ER 482, CA.
35   *Brinkibon Ltd v Stahag Stahl GmbH* [1983] 2 AC 34, [1982] 1 All ER 293, HL.

from a number of contractors, and only when all the bids have been considered will one particular contractor be selected. The investor will obviously be attracted to the least expensive bid, but on closer scrutiny may decide to select another more conscientious and skilled contractor. The courts examine these cases with a disposition towards granting both parties room for manoeuvre, though naturally this licence must not be abused by the kind of sharp practice where one party leads another on by letting the other believe that a binding commitment has been, or shortly will be, made.

The courts employ a variety of conceptual tools to effectuate this policy. At the simplest level, the court reaches a conclusion on the basis of whether or not an acceptance was made, though this determination will depend upon the court's judgment of whether the offeror was genuinely seeking room for manoeuvre. Sometimes the courts adopt a more elaborate conceptual structure. In the example of a building contract described above, courts normally characterize the investor's request for tenders as 'an invitation to treat' rather than an offer, and regard the tenders placed by building contractors as offers, leaving the selection of a contractor as the acceptance which forms the contract. A similar analysis works for the purchase of goods in a self-service store, where the courts preserve the customer's freedom for manoeuvre by characterizing the display of goods on the shelves not as an offer but as an invitation to treat. A third technique for delaying the moment of responsibility denies legal enforcement to uncertain agreements. A vague agreement can be valid provided that a court can infer that the parties intended to supplement their informal understanding according to the normal terms of the trade. But where the parties deliberately leave open terms for future negotiation, thereby exhibiting a desire to preserve their freedom for manoeuvre, a court will decline to enforce this uncompleted agreement on the ground of uncertainty.[36]

Discouragement of Opportunism
The courts prevent manipulation of the time at which the parties reach a contract in order to stop one party from exploiting alterations in market price to his or her advantage. In the simplest example, a seller may discover after making an offer to sell at a fixed price that the market price for the goods has risen. The policy of the courts is to disallow revocation of the offer where the purchaser has already taken steps to indicate completion of the bargain, in order to prevent the seller from gaining an advantage. Courts carry out this policy through the terminology of offer and acceptance, though at the cost of a further distortion of the underlying principles of responsibility.

The courts place obstacles in the way of revocation of offers, so that they may conclude that the acceptance was completed prior to the

---

36   *Courtney and Fairbairn Ltd v Tolaini Bros (Hotels) Ltd* [1975] 1 WLR 297, [1975] 1 All ER 716, CA.

revocation of the offer. In particular, the courts adopt the rule that the offeror must communicate any revocation of an offer to the offeree. In *Byrne & Co v Leon van Tienhoven & Co*[37] the defendant posted a letter from Cardiff to New York offering to sell 1,000 boxes of tinplates at a fixed price. Before the letter reached New York, the defendant posted a revocation of the offer, explaining that there had been, 'a regular panic in the tinplate market during the last few days, which has caused prices to run up about twenty-five per cent'. The plaintiff in New York accepted the offer by post when it arrived, and only later received the revocation of the offer. Lindley J held that the revocation of the offer was inoperative until it was communicated to the plaintiff, so the plaintiff had successfully accepted the offer according to the postal acceptance rule described above. This result prevented the offeror from waiting to see which way the market moved, in order to choose whether or not to go forward with the transaction.

The rule that a revocation of an offer must be communicated cannot be squared with the theory that contracts are created by agreement, for clearly the offeror no longer intends to make the agreement once he tries to withdraw his offer. In his judgment, Lindley J acknowledges this problem, but argues that under the principles of the common law, 'a state of mind not notified cannot be regarded in dealings between man and man'. Of course, he promptly ignores this justification by applying the rule that the letter of acceptance completes the transaction when it is posted, not when it arrives in the hands of the offeror. Given this inconsistency, it is better to admit that the policy behind the rule that revocations of offers have to be communicated is one which discourages offerors from taking advantage of market fluctuations retrospectively.

Partial Performance

The courts hesitate to conclude that no contract was ever formed when one party has partially performed his side of the bargain. This policy is even more insistent when performance has been completed. We have already noticed one example of this policy being applied in the battle of forms cases. The same policy applies to partial performance of unilateral contracts. In the classic statement of the problem, the offeror promises to pay a sum of money if another walks from London to York. Can the offeror revoke his offer once the walker has set out on his journey? According to the logic of the rules of offer and acceptance, performance of the contract constitutes acceptance by the offeree, but, until the walker completes performance, he has not accepted the offer, and so no contractual responsibility arises. This result causes injustice where the walker has travelled a substantial proportion of the journey. The courts therefore strive to find a means to invalidate the revocation of the offer. One way to achieve this result involves the finding of a collateral contract, under which the offeror promises to keep the offer open until the journey has been

---

37   (1880) 5 CPD 344.

completed or abandoned.[38] Another analysis suggests that the walker accepts the offer prior to setting out on his journey, thereby transforming a unilateral contract into a bilateral one. Sometimes courts simply insist that the offer cannot be revoked once the offeree has embarked upon performance,[39] which has the merit of being straightforward, though once again it creates an exception to the idea that contractual responsibility is based upon consent. Whichever method the courts adopt, however, the policy remains the same: to provide the protection of contractual rights to a party who partially performs an anticipated contract.

Protection of Ancillary Reliance

Ancillary reliance involves acts of expenditure incurred in anticipation of the formation of a contract, or as a result of a mistaken belief in the existence of a contract, where this expenditure does not count as partial performance of the anticipated contract. Where such detrimental reliance has taken place, the courts may lean towards the discovery of contractual responsibility. In *Gibson v Manchester City Council*[40] Lord Denning relied upon the ancillary reliance of the purchaser of the council house in order to justify his conclusion that a contract had been formed. The difficulty of this reasoning is that the court cannot easily infer acceptance of an offer from the conduct, since it does not comprise partial performance. For this reason, the protection of ancillary reliance will often have to be achieved by means of some different category of contractual liability such as estoppel under the reliance model.

In the leading American authority, *Drennan v Star Paving Co*,[41] a general contractor, in preparing a tender for building work, relied to his detriment upon a mistaken bid from a specialist sub-contractor for a portion of the work. The California Supreme Court held that, despite the absence of agreement, the sub-contractor's bid was binding, because it was reasonably foreseeable that it would be relied upon by the general contractor. Once this principle is admitted into the law, it provides a means for effecting the policy of protecting ancillary reliance without any distortion of the traditional rules of offer and acceptance. Whilst the American courts have followed this course, English courts have preferred to manipulate and distort the classical rules in order to achieve the same result.

By listing these policy considerations which influence the courts in determining the moment of contractual responsibility, we have inevitably touched upon only a small proportion of the relevant considerations. Our aim, however, has not been to supply a complete list, but rather to indicate some of the most common policy factors. We have also noticed that these policies often conflict and that the courts must balance the rival

38   *Errington v Errington and Woods* [1952] 1 KB 290, [1952] 1 All ER 149, CA.
39   *Daulia Ltd v Four Millbank Nominees Ltd* [1978] Ch 231, [1978] 2 All ER 557, CA.
40   [1978] 1 WLR 520, [1978] 2 All ER 583, CA.
41   51 Cal 2d 409, 333 P 2d 757 (1958).

considerations in each case. The important point to grasp is that the application of the rules of offer and acceptance involves a seldom acknowledged discretionary judgment in which the competing policies are weighed.

At a deeper level, these policy factors signal the presence of the balancing process between respect for private autonomy and the communitarian value of concern for the interests of another which runs through the modern law of contractual responsibility. On the one hand, the preservation of room for manoeuvre ensures respect for private autonomy, and, on the other, the discouragement of opportunism and the protection of partial performance and ancillary reliance reflect that limited form of altruism which we have called co-operation. The general trend of favouring the latter policies confirms the view that the path of the modern law of contract lies towards communitarian values. This movement finds additional impetus from another doctrinal development.

3. Pre-Contractual Responsibility

In many of the cases which we have considered in this chapter, the doctrinal analysis assumes that either contractual responsibility has arisen, or that the parties have no legal rights against each other at all. In the classical law, prior to the moment of acceptance, the parties owe no voluntarily undertaken duties towards each other. Yet in these cases an equitable solution might be to refuse to create contractual responsibility, but nevertheless provide a measure of compensation in deserving cases for misplaced reliance. This solution might have been appropriate in *Gibson v Manchester City Council*.[42] The plaintiff could have been compensated for the costs of his repairs to the property without being granted a contractual right to purchase his house. This result would respect the normal freedom of manoeuvre during negotiations, but at the same time satisfy the policy of protecting ancillary reliance. In short, all relevant policies would be satisfied by the adoption of pre-contractual liability, whereas the normal pattern of the common law tends to insist upon the triumph of one policy over the other.

A similar attractive solution presents itself for the problem of the revocation of offers during the course of performance of unilateral contracts. In the case of a man who has walked half-way to York on the strength of an offer to pay him £100 when he reaches the city, pre-contractual responsibility would require the offeror to compensate the walker for his time and trouble until the revocation of the offer, without requiring full payment of £100. Here the policy of compensating partial performance could be satisfied, without undermining the normal freedom to revoke offers entirely.

42   [1979] 1 WLR 294, [1979] 1 All ER 972, HL.

On the whole, however, the courts have ignored this attractive compromise. The main reason for their reluctance to accept a form of pre-contractual responsibility stems from the sense that such a step would subvert the basic value of freedom to contract which colours the whole theory of responsibility. By permitting liabilities to arise before agreement has been reached, the courts sense a danger that this would amount to the imposition of responsibility without consent. This fear is misplaced, for in effect the courts already subvert the value of liberty by determining the moment of responsibility by reference to such considerations as ancillary reliance and partial performance. Even so, the modern law has yet to achieve a coherent doctrinal basis through which the compromise of pre-contractual responsibility could be effectuated.

One possible legal category which could be nurtured towards establishing a legal basis for unilateral responsibility prior to the formation of a contract is liability for negligence in tort. Courts could impose a duty of care upon the parties during the course of negotiations. Whenever it could be demonstrated that, through the fault of one party, the other was induced to act to his detriment, then a duty to compensate wasted expenditure would arise. As we shall see in Chapter 10, the courts have been edging towards this position. Another possible source for pre-contractual responsibility lies in the development of the reliance model and the doctrine of estoppel. Here, instead of the fact of detrimental reliance grounding full contractual rights as it did in *Drennan v Star Paving Co*,[43] the estoppel technique would merely permit recovery for wasted expenditure. This method was used in the American case *Hoffman v Red Owl Stores Inc*,[44] where the plaintiff wasted large sums of money in anticipation of a franchise agreement which never materialized. His remedy was an award of damages commensurate with his wasted expenditure, not the award of the franchise agreement. No English case precisely replicates this use of estoppel to compensate pre-contractual reliance. But *Crabb v Arun District Council*[45] verges on this result, even though the plaintiff was awarded the right of access which he thought he had been promised, for in the circumstances, the only sensible way in which the plaintiff could be compensated for his inaccessible land was the award of a right of access, and the court indicated that they thought that the plaintiff's loss during the period of inaccessibility was roughly equivalent to the commercial value of the right of access.

Normally, however, common law courts impose pre-contractual responsibility through the law of restitution or unjust enrichment. Where one party confers a benefit upon the other in anticipation of a binding contract, he may recover the value of his work if the contract never materializes. For example, if it emerges after a battle of forms that the parties never reached an agreement prior to performance, each may

---

43   51 Cal 2d 409, 33 P 2d 757 (1958).
44   26 Wis 2d 683, 133 NW 2d 267 (1965).
45   [1976] Ch 179, [1975] 3 All ER 865, CA.

recover from the other in an action for *quantum meruit* the value of any property transferred or services performed.[46]

As we shall discover in the next chapter, these cases of tort, estoppel and restitution provide an embryonic form of pre-contractual responsibility for the common law to develop. It certainly makes sense to recognize this compromise source of liability, as many other legal systems do, for it permits a more satisfactory reconciliation of the relevant policies already entertained by the courts.

---

46   *British Steel Corpn v Cleveland Bridge & Engineering Co Ltd* [1984] 1 All ER 504, QB.

10

The Duty to Negotiate With Care

Prior to the formation of a contract, particularly in a commercial context, lengthy negotiations may take place. During these negotiations, the parties may give explicit or implicit undertakings, and may incur considerable expenditure in anticipation of the concluded contract. As we saw in the previous chapter, the law fixes the moment of contractual responsibility at the time when it is reasonable for the parties to rely upon the existence of a binding contract between them as a result of having reached agreement and having communicated their acknowledgment of the obligation. But prior to that moment, during the negotiations, the law also imposes obligations, which are the topic of this chapter.

The common law has exhibited a persistent reluctance to impose pre-contractual obligations. The main reason for this reluctance is a concern to protect the parties' freedom to choose whether or not to enter a contract. If obligations arose as soon as negotiations commenced, then parties would discover that they had undertaken obligations unexpectedly and without due deliberation. Moreover, as we discovered in Chapter 9, the law recognizes the need to protect the parties' room for manoeuvre. It permits, for instance, revocation of an offer at any time until the offeree has communicated an acceptance. Exploratory discussions serve many useful purposes, such as permitting individuals to discover all the market opportunities before making any commitment, which will assist the competitiveness of the market. For these reasons, pre-contractual obligations require a justification which has sufficient weight to overcome objections based on the protection of freedom of contract and the efficient operation of the market.

Such justifications can be established, however, in many instances. Where one party lies to another during the negotiations, or carefully conceals some vital information, then this misconduct can be regarded as forfeiting the protection of freedom to contract and as frustrating the operation of market competition. Similarly, where one party deliberately induces another to incur expenditure or to disclose confidential information, without any intention of making a contract, then again we can regard this conduct as an abuse of the freedom to negotiate without incurring obligations. Many other examples will be considered in this chapter where these and analogous reasons justify the imposition of pre-contractual obligations.

Do all these instances of pre-contractual obligations rest upon general principles, or do they represent minor, pragmatic exceptions to the general policy of declining to recognize pre-contractual liabilities? In some legal systems, the codes of contract law declare the existence of a general duty to bargain in good faith.[1] It can be argued that English law, and even more strongly US law, respects the same principle once all the different strands of pre-contractual obligations are gathered together.[2] But this argument encounters two difficulties. In the first place, the courts have been reluctant to acknowledge any such general principle, proceeding rather by reference to narrower doctrines such as misrepresentation, undue influence, collateral contracts and equitable estoppel. The results may be similar to other legal systems with an acknowledged principle of good faith in bargaining, but English lawyers have never systematized their particular doctrines under this principle.[3]

The second difficulty for English law concerns the idea of good faith itself. The meaning of the idea is obscure. It tends to function, as Summers suggests,[4] as a negative concept in practice, so that various sorts of conduct are labelled as negotiation in bad faith, without any clarity about the positive duty which is envisaged by the concept. But worse than obscurity, the idea of good faith implies a content to the duty which is far too narrow. In its ordinary legal usage, the standard of good faith requires honesty or conduct which does not deliberately deceive or harm another. It does not include negligent or careless behaviour which has the same effect. But many of the pre-contractual obligations arising under English law, such as the duty not to misrepresent facts, require more than honesty. They require carefulness in giving information, so that reasonable care must be taken to ensure its accuracy. For this reason, the terminology of good faith proves unsatisfactory as an indication of the reach of pre-contractual obligations.

This chapter argues that the sources of pre-contractual obligations can be usefully conceived as deriving from a general principle. The

1 Eg Italian Civil Code, Art 1337; Israeli Contracts (General Part) Law 1973, s 12(a).
2 Kessler and Fine, 'Culpa in Contrahendo, Bargaining in Good Faith, and Freedom of Contract: A Comparative Study' (1964) 77 *Harvard Law Review* 401; Finn, 'Equity and Contract', in P Finn (ed), *Essays on Contract* (Sydney, 1987), 104, at p 105; Reiter, 'Good Faith in Contract', (1983) 17 *Valparaiso University Law Review* 705.
3 Bingham LJ in *Interfoto Picture Library Ltd v Stiletto Visual Programmes Ltd* [1989] QB 433, [1988] 1 All ER 348, CA; Bridge, 'Does Anglo-Canadian Contract Law Need a Doctrine of Good faith?' (1984) 9 *Canadian Business Law Journal* 385; Farnsworth, 'Precontractual Liability and Preliminary Agreements: Fair Dealing and Failed Negotiations' (1987) 87 *Columbia Law Review* 217.
4 Summers, 'Good Faith in General Contract Law and the Sales Provision of the Uniform Commercial Code' (1968) 54 *Virginia Law Review* 195.

principle serves to bring coherence to a diverse collection of legal doctrines and to bring their weaknesses and anomalies to light. But the principle concerned should be described as a duty to negotiate with care, not to bargain in good faith. What English law requires of parties is carefulness towards each other during the period of negotiation. The modern law rejects the strong protection for freedom of contract afforded by the absence of pre-contractual obligations, and instead recognizes that some obligations of respect for the interests of others should be owed during negotiations. There are two principal justifications for the common law to adopt this limited duty of respect for the interests of others during negotiations.

In part these rules serve to protect the operation of a competitive market. False or misleading claims about products and the terms of contracts obstruct competitive markets, for they make it difficult to acquire accurate information about the merits of different opportunities. Moreover, such behaviour will place other traders at a competitive disadvantage unless they also employ deceptive practices, which would escalate the harm to the competitive market.

In addition, the duty of care during negotiations recognises that even in the absence of a concluded contractual relation, the parties may enter a relation of dependence during negotiations where the actions of one party may foreseeably cause economic harm to another unless care is taken. Promises, statements, and conduct may induce the dependent party to act to his detriment, and where this action was one of reasonable reliance upon the promises, statements or other conduct, then the law is likely to impose a duty to compensate for the losses incurred. This duty of care during negotiations fits into the broader scheme of the law of tort where obligations are owed to prevent harm to the interests of others, but it receives a specialized articulation in the context of negotiations towards a contract.

To complement these general justifications for a duty of care during negotiations, the modern law has sought to promote the social market by means of specialized legislative interventions. One important theme of this legislation is to develop duties imposed upon businesses during negotiations with consumers which aim to educate consumers about the nature of the transaction and the qualities of the products and services on offer. With the sale of a car, for instance, the manufacturer or retailer can be required to supply certain kinds of information about fuel consumption per mile in a standard form. This enables the consumer to become knowledgeable about a particular product, and thereby make a more rational choice about whether its acquisition fits harmoniously into his or her chosen plan of life.

This chapter considers the diverse doctrinal and legislative sources of this duty to negotiate with care before returning in the conclusion to an examination of the question whether they are united by this general principle. It organizes the materials under brief factual descriptions of the types of conduct which constitute a breach of the duty to negotiate with care.

1. Misleading Statements

The law imposes a duty of care on parties to negotiations for a contract when they make statements to each other. The duty requires that statements of fact are made with reasonable care in the light of the specialized knowledge and expertise of the representor. This duty is broken by making a statement which is false or misleading because insufficient care was taken. The breach of duty can be sanctioned both by an award of damages to compensate for losses arising from misplaced reliance upon the statement, and by rescission of any contract which is induced by reliance upon the representation. In addition, many such misleading statements constitute criminal offences if made by a person in the course of a trade or business.

This duty of care in making statements during negotiations qualifies to a considerable extent the freedom of parties to avoid obligations until the moment of formation of contract. Given that in practice most negotiations will involve the making of various representations about the quality and variety of products and services on offer, the duty will normally be triggered and circumscribe the parties' freedom to avoid obligations during the bargaining process. This duty provides a strong example of the more general principle of a duty to negotiate with care. But the duty of care in making statements is confined by numerous technical requirements, which betray the diverse sources of the duty in common law, equity and statute.

(1) Reasonable Reliance

The obligation to take care in making statements is confined to statements on which it is reasonable to place reliance. In developing the common law and interpreting statutes, the courts have attempted to define the types of statements on which it will not be reasonable to rely, excluding for instance statements of law, expressions of opinion and statements about future conduct. But these classifications can be misleading, unless one bears in mind the point of the classification, which is to limit the obligation to take care to statements on which it is reasonable to rely. The statutes governing criminal offences offer more specific lists of the kinds of statements made by traders on which it is reasonable for consumers to rely, but this leads to extensive, detailed, and confusing regulation, which itself creates problems for compliance by traders.[5]

These attempts to reduce to the form of rules the situations and contexts when it will be reasonable to rely upon pre-contractual statements look doomed to failure for two reasons. In the first place, the reasonableness of reliance must depend upon numerous features of the particular case, such as the relative expertise and knowledge of the parties,

---

5 I Ramsay, *Consumer Protection* (London, 1989) p 257. See also, Property Misdescriptions Act 1991, Property Misdescriptions (Specified Matters) Order 1992.

and the context in which a statement is made. For example, a statement about the legal effect of a document such as a Will might be reasonably relied upon if made by a qualified lawyer to a client, but not if made by someone without legal expertise, and nor perhaps if made by a lawyer in informal circumstances such as a casual conversation on a train. The common law attempts to distinguish these different cases by saying that some are statements of fact, others statements of law and opinion on which no reliance can be placed, but, since the statement remains identical in every case, it is clear that these distinctions merely represent conclusions of law about whether or not reliance was reasonable in the circumstances rather than an analysis of the words employed.

We should also be aware that the issue of whether it was reasonable to rely upon a statement is not simply a question of fact. It involves a normative judgement about which kinds of statements negotiating parties ought to be able to rely upon. For example, every consumer is familiar with misleading statements about the price of goods. Blaring notices proclaim that the goods are on special offer, their prices have been slashed, or there is extra value and a great bargain. It is doubtful whether most consumers place much trust in such claims, but will try to make their own price comparisons. Nevertheless, there is good reason for traders to be held to such claims if any substance can be given to them at all. The proliferation of such claims obstructs a competitive market for it is difficult to make price comparisons, and there is always a risk that an unsophisticated consumer will be genuinely misled and waste his money. For these reasons the Consumer Protection Act 1987, section 20 renders giving misleading price indications a criminal offence. We may not regard it as sensible to place much faith in such misleading price claims, but nevertheless the law deems it to be reasonable to rely upon such statements, in order to regulate the market towards competitive practices and to protect even instances of unreasonable reliance by consumers. This reveals that the question of whether or not reliance was reasonable not only depends upon all the circumstances of the case, but also requires a normative judgement about which statements should become reliable for the sake of improving market competition and protection of the weak from the unscrupulous. In the light of these general observations about the test of reasonable reliance, we should look more closely at the formal rules which the courts employ to draw these subtle distinctions.

Statements of Law and Contractual Terms

It is probably not reasonable to rely upon someone's opinion of the law in general, since it is advisable to seek one's own advice about legal rights and responsibilities. For this reason the common law holds that statements of law as opposed to statements of fact may not be relied upon. But there will be many special cases where reliance can be placed reasonably upon express and implied statements of law. For instance, a misleading statement about the law by a lawyer to a client as a result of carelessness will count as a statement on which it is reasonable to rely.

During negotiations for a contract one party may make misleading statements about the content and meaning of the terms of the contract. The precise interpretation of a contract is ultimately a question of law, so it might be supposed that such statements could not be relied upon. In addition, it may not be reasonable to rely upon such statements in general, for each party should read the terms of the contract for himself or herself.

Nevertheless, there will be many circumstances in which statements about the effects of a legal document can be relied upon. For instance, a statement about the legal effects of a document from a person who should understand those effects will be treated as a representation on which reliance can be placed. What is crucial is the difference in relative expertise between the parties. The person giving the statement may be relied upon because that person has greater legal expertise or business experience. In *Cornish v Midland Bank plc*,[6] a bank clerk gave advice to a customer about the effects of a mortgage upon her home which her husband wished her to sign. The advice was misleading in that it omitted to explain the full effects of the document. The customer obtained damages for losses resulting from this negligent advice. Similarly, a statement about the legal effects of a contract can be relied upon where the representation is made by a party seeking to rely upon a standard form contract. In *Curtis v Chemical Cleaning and Dyeing Co*[7] the plaintiff took her wedding dress to the defendant's shop to be cleaned. She was required to sign a contract, which, she was told by an assistant, disclaimed liability for certain specified risks to the beads and sequins which adorned the dress. In fact, the contract contained a clause which exempted the defendant from liability for any damage to the dress, howsoever arising. The plaintiff subsequently sued for damage to her dress comprising a stain of uncertain origin. The English Court of Appeal held that the defendant could not rely upon the full width of the exclusion clause on account of the misrepresentation by its employee of the meaning and content of the terms.

One of the most common kinds of misleading statement about the terms of the contract concerns the price of goods or services. These have been singled out for detailed regulation by the Consumer Protection Act 1987.[8] Section 20 makes it a criminal offence if a person in the course of a business of his gives by any means to a consumer a misleading indication of the price of goods, services, accommodation or facilities. The statute adopts a broad interpretation of such misleading statements by not requiring the statement to be false, but rather to ask whether consumers might reasonably be misled by the indication of price. The offence is committed, for instance, when a shop fails to honour an advertisement which claims that it will 'beat any TV Hi-fi and Video price by £20 on the spot'.[9]

---

6 [1985] 3 All ER 513, CA.
7 [1951] 1 KB 805, [1951] 1 All ER 631, CA.
8 See also Consumer Protection (Code of Practice for Traders on Price Indications) Approval Order 1988, SI 1988/2078.
9 *R v Warwickshire County Council, ex p Johnson* [1993] AC 583, [1993] 1 All ER 299, HL.

Statements of Future Intentions
It is also, in general, unreasonable to rely upon promises about future conduct. Such promises should be part of a binding contract before they can be relied upon. But that leaves open the question whether such promises themselves may constitute an independent or collateral contract or establish facts sufficient to ground an equitable estoppel. We will examine these possibilities below when we consider misleading implied promises.

Yet statements about future intentions can involve simultaneously implied statements of fact. The expression of intention may indicate that the representor has taken reasonable care to ascertain certain facts which are material to the negotiations. If the representee has reasonably relied upon these implied statements of fact, then an action for misrepresentation may succeed. In *Box v Midland Bank plc*[10] a businessman sought an overdraft facility in order to finance an export contract which would save the business. During discussions of the proposal, the bank manager advised the plaintiff businessman that, although he would require approval from head office for the loan, the process would be a mere formality. But the head office scrutinized the transaction and rejected it. As a result the plaintiff's business collapsed and he sought a remedy for misrepresentation against the bank. The court accepted that the bank manager had failed to take reasonable care in indicating that the loan would be forthcoming, for he ought to have realized that under the bank's rules there was never the slightest possibility of the overdraft facility being made available. Since the plaintiff would have sought a loan elsewhere if the bank manager had provided a careful prediction of the outcome, the bank was held liable for £5,000 to cover the plaintiff's additional costs of borrowing to finance the export sale at a late stage, though not for the whole cost of the collapse of the business. In this instance liability for misrepresentation comes close to holding the bank liable for its informal promise to make the overdraft facility available during negotiations, but the measure of damages makes it clear that the true basis of liability consists in the opportunity costs incurred as a result of misplaced reliance upon a statement.

Statements of Opinion
It will also be unreasonable to rely upon vague statements of opinion and inflated sales talk. Hence if I persuade someone to buy my car by claiming that it is the fastest red Peugeot 104 on the road, the purchaser can rely upon my statements of fact about the colour, make, and model of the car, but he or she should treat my claim about its speed with more circumspection, since a court would probably regard it as 'mere puff', like an advertising slogan which claims that a detergent will make clothes 'whiter than white', and therefore not a statement upon which reliance may be placed. But it is wrong to suppose that every statement of opinion

10   [1979] 2 Lloyd's Rep 391, QB.

will be excluded, or that every apparent statement of fact can be reasonably relied upon.

Some statements of opinion imply that the representor knows facts on which his opinion is based, and a failure to take reasonable care in ascertaining these facts which renders the opinion false will constitute a breach of the duty of care. When, in *Smith v Land and House Property Corpn*,[11] the landlord who was selling property declared that it was 'let to a most desirable tenant', knowing in fact that the tenant was in serious arrears with the rent, the court treated this as a statement of fact, because the landlord could know better than the purchaser the qualities of the tenant, and it was therefore reasonable for the purchaser to rely upon this vague statement. Moreover some statements of opinion will be given by experts who hold themselves out as being in a position to make reliable statements, and again these opinions will be treated as giving rise to the duty of care. This analysis will be applied for example to medical opinions. It was also applied in *Esso Petroleum Co Ltd v Mardon*,[12] where the defendant took on the tenancy of a petrol station on the basis of an opinion of an expert representative of the oil company as to the probable turnover of the station. The court rejected the oil company's defence that the forecast was merely an expression of opinion. It was a statement which could be relied upon because it was made by a person with special knowledge and skill, and, though in form it was an opinion, the statement implied that it was founded upon facts known to the representor. Lord Denning MR summarized the principle:

> If a man, who has or professes to have special knowledge or skill, makes a representation by virtue thereof to another – be it advice, information or opinion – with the intention of inducing him to enter into a contract with him, he is under a duty to use reasonable care to see that the representation is correct, and that the advice, information or opinion is reliable.

It follows, of course, that some apparent statements of fact cannot be relied upon, if they do not draw upon special expertise or knowledge. For example, in *Bisset v Wilkinson*,[13] the seller asserted that a piece of farm land was sufficiently fertile to support 2,000 sheep. The court decided that this was a statement of opinion which could not be reasonably relied upon, for the parties were both farmers who could make their own judgements about the fertility of the land.

These decisions reveal that the question of whether or not a statement which looks like an opinion rather than a statement of fact can be reasonably relied upon involves a complex determination of several factors. One important factor will be the relative expertise or knowledge of the parties, so that it will be more reasonable to rely on statements when the representor enjoys superior knowledge or expertise. The circumstances in which the representation is made will also colour the court's judgment,

---

11   (1884) 28 Ch D 7, CA.
12   [1976] QB 801, [1976] 2 All ER 5, CA.
13   [1927] AC 177, PC.

so that casual remarks or statements made on social occasions should not be relied upon, though the same statements made in a professional or commercial context could amount to a breach of the duty.

When devising the Trade Descriptions Act 1968, Parliament attempted to produce more specific regulations which would determine which statements involved a breach of duty and therefore a criminal offence. The Act is limited by section 1 to statements made by a person in the course of a trade or business. Section 2 lists the kinds of statements about products which are covered by the Act, which include such matters as quantity, composition, fitness for purpose, strength, performance, behaviour or accuracy, and the history of the product. Statements are caught by the Act even though they are not false, but merely misleading, that is to say, likely to be taken as an indication of some quality referred to in the list of kinds of statements covered by the Act. This provision permits the courts to punish broad statements which imply particular qualities for the goods. In *Robertson v Dicicco*[14] the defendant advertised a used car claiming that it was a 'beautiful car'. The court found that although the external appearance of the car was indeed attractive, the statement that the car was beautiful also implied that the car was fit for its normal purpose. In fact the car suffered from serious corrosion and was thoroughly unroadworthy. This is an example of a statement which, though literally true, could be understood to imply further statements of fact which were false.

This decision reveals how the determination of the statements on which reasonable reliance may be placed involves a complex policy determination. In formulating the Trade Descriptions Act 1968, Parliament sought to provide consumer protection against an extremely broad range of misleading statements. The legislation seems to take as its model an unsophisticated and credulous consumer, who is likely to be misled by 'sales talk'. The common law, however, developed a narrower picture of the circumstances in which reasonable reliance might take place, so that a statement that a car was 'beautiful' would almost certainly be treated as mere puff and therefore not a statement which could found a breach of duty. It is unfortunate that this divergence of statutory and common law standards may have developed. It is to be hoped that courts will view the 'mere puff' defence circumspectly in the context of consumer transactions in future.

Unfortunately, what may have happened occasionally is exactly the reverse. Steeped in the common law tradition of evaluating reasonable reliance, the courts may have ignored the point that the statutes aimed at consumer protection intended to include within their ambit even some instances of foolish reliance, in order to further the policies of consumer protection and enhance the competitive market. In *Cadbury Ltd v Halliday*[15] consumers could find in retail shops two types of bars of

14   [1972] RTR 431, DC.
15   [1975] 1 WLR 649, DC.

chocolate. One sort of bar bore a 'flash' sign on its wrapper stating that the bar was 'extra value'. Close inspection revealed, however, that the other sort of bar on sale in fact contained more chocolate and was cheaper. The company was prosecuted for a misleading price claim, but successfully appealed against conviction on the ground that the phrase 'extra value' conveyed no identifiable factual meaning. The court regarded the phrase as a matter of opinion, a mere puff, on which no reliance could reasonably be placed.

It may be true, of course, that prudent consumers place no reliance upon such statements, but to confine the legislation in this way defeats its objective. It is seeking to eliminate such confusing statements from the market, in order to foster genuine competition and at the same time to protect even the gullible consumer. The phrase 'extra value' could easily be attributed a more definite meaning, such as more chocolate for the same price, and in this sense it would have been misleading. By sticking to the common law standard of reasonable reliance, and not realizing that consumer protection measures will often take a broader view of which statements may reasonably be relied upon, the court managed to defeat the purpose of the legislation in this case.

(2) The Standard of Care
The standard of care required in making pre-contractual statements may be described as negligence. It requires reasonable care to be taken to ensure the accuracy of the statement and facts on which it is based. This standard may be contrasted with fraud and strict liability. In the case of fraud the statement is made either knowing that it is false or being aware that it is likely to be false. Of course, fraudulent statements will also involve a breach of the duty to negotiate with care. But the duty does not set the standard of strict liability under which a false or misleading statement is a breach of duty even though it was made honestly and as a result of reasonable care.

In defining the standard of care, however, the courts and the legislature have some latitude in raising or lowering the requirements experienced in practice by manipulating two factors. The first concerns the standards by which reasonable behaviour is set. These could range from the highest and most careful standards of any trader to the lowest practices. The second factor concerns the burden of proof of negligence. Since it will often be difficult to ascertain the facts on which it may be possible to assert that a statement was made carelessly, if the burden of proof is reversed, this will give the party who has relied upon a false or misleading statement an immense practical advantage in establishing a breach of the duty.

Burden of Proof
The common law traditionally requires a person alleging negligence to prove that lack of reasonable care was taken. But for most practical purposes this burden has been reversed in the context of statements made during negotiations. To obtain rescission of the contract at common law, a

party to the contract merely has to show that it was reasonable to rely upon the statement and that it was false, without the further need to prove negligence. To obtain damages for losses resulting from misplaced reliance upon the statement, the Misrepresentation Act 1967, section 2 requires the representor to prove that he had reasonable ground to believe and did believe up to the time when the contract was made that the facts represented were true. This reverses the normal burden of proof once the statement has been shown to be false and one which was reasonably relied upon.

The statutory offences offer a different framework, which in effect also reverses the burden of proof. Although the Trade Descriptions Act 1968 and the Consumer Protection Act 1987 impose strict liability upon traders for making false and misleading statements (except in the anomalous case of statements about services),[16] traders have open to them a number of special statutory defences, including the general one of 'due diligence'. This permits the evasion of liability, if the trader can show that he or she took all reasonable precautions and exercised all due diligence to avoid the commission of the offence by himself or herself or any person under his or her control.[17]

Reasonable Care

The question of what amounts to reasonable care, adequate precautions, or due diligence leaves the court considerable scope for adjusting the standard of the duty to negotiate with care. As in the ordinary law of negligence in tort, the courts are likely to rely upon standard trading and professional practices as a guide to what should be regarded as reasonable care. For example, in *Cornish v Midland Bank plc*,[18] on the question whether the bank clerk had taken reasonable care in describing the terms of the mortgage accurately, the court used the bank's own internal instructions to employees as a useful guide to standard banking practice. Similarly, the standard of care for doctors and surgeons will be set by the normal practices of the profession. But there is a danger in merely endorsing established trade practices, if these fall below what a court regards as reasonable.

The standard of care required will also be affected by the particular skill and knowledge of the representor. If the representor is in a special position to know the true facts or to ascertain them, then the care required will normally involve taking advantage of this special position. In *Howard Marine & Dredging Co Ltd v A Ogden & Sons (Excavations) Ltd*,[19] during negotiations for the hire of some barges, the owner's agent stated their freight capacity on the strength of an inaccurate entry in the Lloyd's

---

16   Trade Descriptions Act 1968, s 14; for criticism, see Director General of Fair Trading, *Review of the Trade Descriptions Act 1968* (London, 1976), pp 18–20.
17   Trade Descriptions Act 1968, s 24; Consumer Protection Act 1987, s 39; Property Misdescriptions Act 1991, s 2.
18   [1985] 3 All ER 513, CA.
19   [1978] QB 574, [1978] 2 All ER 1134, CA.

Register of ships, and omitted to check the owner's records of capacity. The agent was held liable for a negligent misrepresentation because he was in a position to check the accuracy of the registers, whereas other persons could have made the same statement without negligence, for normally the Lloyd's Register is a reliable guide. Similarly, special expertise in judging the accuracy of information is likely to heighten the precautions required. In the sale of used cars for example, statements about their qualities such as age made by a dealer will have to be made with considerable care, whereas an ordinary consumer selling a car with no special knowledge of the facts should be able to rely upon the appearance and records of the car.[20]

The most troublesome issue in determining the standard of care required concerns the liability of employers for negligent employees. The false statement may be made by an employee or an agent, even though the employer has taken care to instruct employees not to make such statements. Should the employer be held responsible for such statements? When the plaintiff's action concerns civil law remedies of rescission of the contract or damages, then the employee making the false statement will normally be regarded as an agent acting within the scope of his authority, so the employer will be vicariously responsible for the agent's statements. When the case involves a criminal prosecution, however, the legislature and the courts have proved reluctant to hold the employer strictly liable for the acts of employees.

Under the Trade Descriptions Act 1968 section 24, the employer may establish a defence that the statement was made by an employee even though the employer had exercised all due diligence to prevent the employee from making the false statement. The employer can escape conviction therefore, if it can impress the court with the elaborate details of its staff manuals and procedures for ensuring that consumers are given accurate information, even though, of course, the procedures failed in this particular case.[21] A similar position prevails with respect to misleading prices under the Consumer Protection Act 1987. Here criminal liability is confined to employers,[22] but the employer can avoid liability for a misleading price statement by employees by claiming that the employer took all reasonable steps and exercised all due diligence to avoid committing the offence.[23] No criminal offence will be committed if the employee makes an unauthorized misleading price statement which the employer had taken reasonable steps to prevent.

This reluctance to convict employers of criminal offences reveals how strongly the law remains attached to a requirement of blameworthiness

---

20 Compare: *Dick Bentley Productions Ltd v Harold Smith (Motors) Ltd* [1965] 1 WLR 623, [1965] 2 All ER 65, CA, with *Oscar Chess Ltd v Williams* [1957] 1 WLR 370, [1957] 1 All ER 325, CA.
21 *Tesco Supermarkets Ltd v Nattrass* [1972] AC 153, HL; T Ison, *Credit Marketing and Consumer Protection* (London, 1979) p 375; I Ramsay, *Consumer Protection* (London, 1989) p 249.
22 *R v Warwickshire County Council, ex p Johnson* [1993] AC 583, [1993] 1 All ER 299, HL.
23 Consumer Protection Act 1987, s 39.

in the criminal law. But this attachment may serve in this context to frustrate the operation of the legislation, for if the employer can succeed in this defence too easily, then little incentive remains to check upon employees to the benefit of consumers. It could be argued that any false statement by an employee represents a failure by the employing organization to establish procedures to ensure that due diligence is undertaken, so that employers should normally be held vicariously liable under criminal regulatory offences, as under civil law.[24]

(3) Remedies

Rescission
The remedy of rescission for a false or misleading statement aims to avoid the contract and to put the parties back into the position which they held prior to the formation of the contract. The remedy is available to the representee if the misrepresentation was a material inducement to entry into the contract, subject to a number of equitable bars. Until the contract has been rescinded, it is merely voidable, not void, so that it may transfer property rights. The contract may be rescinded either by a court declaration or by giving notice to the representor.[25]

The right to rescind a contract will be barred in four main circumstances. These rules apply generally whenever a contract is voidable. First, where the representee cannot make restitution of what he has received under the contract, he may be prevented from rescinding the contract. But precise restitution is not necessary. Rescission will be available provided that the subject-matter transferred under the voidable contract can be substantially restored, and that due allowance in the form of compensation can be paid for any deterioration and any profits obtained by dealing with the property. Secondly, third party interests will be protected by preventing rescission if property transferred under the contract has already been sold to an innocent third party. Thirdly, the right to rescind the contract can be lost by affirming it after the truth has been discovered. Finally, the right to rescind will be lost by the lapse of time,[26] except perhaps in the case of fraud where lapse of time after discovery of the truth will merely amount to evidence of affirmation.

Under the Misrepresentation Act 1967 section 2(2), a court also has a discretion to refuse rescission and award damages instead. This broad equitable discretion is likely to be exercised if the misrepresentation is not fraudulent, is relatively minor, and the losses likely to be caused to the representor by rescission far exceed the losses to the representee if

---

24   Cartwright, 'Defendants in Consumer Protection Statutes: A Search for Consistency' (1996) 59 *Modern Law Review* 225.
25   In the case of fraud where the representor has deliberately disappeared, it may be possible to rescind the contract by giving notice to the police and other affected parties: *Car & Universal Finance Co Ltd v Caldwell* [1965] 1 QB 525, [1964] 1 All ER 290, CA; criticized by Law Reform Committee 12th Report (1966) Cmnd 2958 para 16.
26   *Leaf v International Galleries* [1950] 2 KB 86, [1950] 1 All ER 693, CA.

the contract is upheld. The measure of damages will be the cost of curing the defect or the diminution of the value of the property.[27]

Damages
The slow and grudging acknowledgement by the courts of a pre-contractual duty to be careful in making statements led to an extraordinarily complex body of law governing the award of damages. Even today, after statutory reform, many doubts remain about the principles on which damages will be awarded for breach of the duty.

Most claims for damages for misrepresentation will today be brought under the Misrepresentation Act 1967, section 2(1). This statutory remedy has several advantages. It provides a clear basis for recovery, unlike the confusing common law position. Plaintiffs can take advantage of the reversal of the burden of proof in establishing negligence. Finally, recent cases indicate that the statute provides the most advantageous measure of recovery.

But the statutory claim for damages has not eliminated the common law, which still persists and may sometimes be employed. In particular, the statutory claim for damages only applies if the parties have entered a contract which subsequently causes loss, whereas the common law claims do not depend upon entry into a contract. At common law damages are available for fraudulent misrepresentation, but of course this requires proof of the defendant's knowledge of the falsity of the statement which will often not be practicable.[28] The law of tort also provides a remedy of damages for negligent misrepresentation, though the limitations and conceptual complexity of this claim render it less attractive than the statutory action.[29] Prior to the statute, the most common basis for a claim for damages consisted of an allegation of the existence of a collateral contract. Under this implied contract, the statement became a warranty and the consideration given for it was entry into the main contract.[30] Both the common law claim for negligent misrepresentation and the claim for a collateral warranty succeeded, for instance, in *Esso Petroleum Co Ltd v Mardon*.[31]

One difficult question is to know how these damages under the statute and the common law will be calculated. The courts have established that the measure of damages should not be the same as for breach of contract, in the sense that the plaintiff should not receive damages commensurate to the profits which the plaintiff expected from entry into the contract. The courts have insisted that a tort measure of damages is more

---

27 *William Sindall plc v Cambridgeshire County Council* [1994] 1 WLR 1016, [1994] 3 All ER 932, CA.
28 *Derry v Peek* (1889) 14 App Cas 337, HL.
29 *Hedley Byrne & Co Ltd v Heller & Partners Ltd* [1964] AC 465, [1963] 2 All ER 575, HL; *Caparo Industries plc v Dickman* [1990] 2 AC 605, [1990] 1 All ER 568, HL.
30 *Evans & Son (Portsmouth) Ltd v Andrea Merzario Ltd* [1976] 1 WLR 1078, [1976] 2 All ER 930, CA.
31 [1976] QB 801, [1976] 2 All ER 5, CA.

appropriate for misrepresentation, either for claims at common law,[32] or under the Misrepresentation Act 1967, section 2(1).[33] But that conclusion leaves open the question of how the tort measure should be calculated.

The losses in the situation of a pre-contractual misrepresentation which induce the formation of a contract can be described in three ways. First, the loss can be conceived as the original entry into the disadvantageous contract, so that the plaintiff should be put back into the position he held prior to the formation of that contract. In the case of a purchase of a hotel on the strength of a false statement about its occupancy rate, for instance, the purchaser would receive back any money paid for the hotel, a purely restitutionary remedy. Secondly, the loss can be described as the difference in the plaintiff's situation between the statement being true and false. Here the damages would amount to the difference between the actual value of the hotel at the time of purchase and its value if the statement had been true. Thirdly, the loss could be conceived as the difference between the plaintiff's situation in entering this contract and his likely situation if he had entered another similar contract, which might have been made but for the fraudulent misrepresentation. In the case of a purchase of a hotel, the losses would then include the profits which would have been made by the exploitation of an alternative hotel which had the qualities described in the misrepresentation, a measure of damages which includes opportunity costs. This third measure of damages could greatly exceed the others, for it encompasses the profits which would have been made under an alternative contract. It differs only slightly from the measure of damages for breach of contract, which would include in principle the profits which would have been made if the representation about the hotel had been true.

There is support in the decided cases for each of these approaches to the quantification of damages for misrepresentation, usually depending on what has been claimed and can be proven. The crucial point is that the third measure is a possibility. In *Esso Petroleum Co Ltd v Mardon*, for instance, the tenant of the garage which had a lower turnover than predicted by the landlord oil company received as his measure of damages, not only his capital loss from investment in the business and his operating losses, but also the return that he would have made from investment and work in another comparable business. Similarly, in *East v Maurer*,[34] in a claim for fraud at common law, the third measure of damages was awarded. Here the plaintiffs had purchased the business of a hairdresser for £20,000, on the faith of a fraudulent representation by the hairdresser that he would not continue a competing business in the town. The business was a failure as a result of the continuing competition, leading to trading losses,

32   *Esso Petroleum Co Ltd v Mardon* [1976] QB 801, [1976] 2 All ER 5, CA.
33   *Royscott Trust Ltd v Rogerson* [1991] 2 QB 297, [1991] 3 All ER 294, CA.
34   [1991] 1 WLR 461, [1991] 2 All ER 733, CA.

and eventually a sale of the business which realised only £5,000. As well as awarding compensation for the difference in value of the business between the purchase price and its true market value, and for the trading losses, the court awarded a further £10,000 for the loss representing the profits which would have been made if an alternative hairdressing business had been purchased in another town. Of course, this loss of profits is likely to be much the same as the expected profits from the business which was in fact purchased, so there is little difference, if any, between this measure of recovery and an ordinary action for breach of contract.

Section 2(1) of the Misrepresentation Act 1967 does not give any clear indication of the measure of damages to be awarded. But the section does suggest that the measure should be the same as the common law of fraud, since it states that the liability for damages for misrepresentation should arise as if the statement had been made fraudulently. This 'fiction of fraud' has been taken to mean that the measure of damages under the statute should be the tortious measure,[35] not a contractual measure, and the cases on fraud invariably apply the third, most generous, quantification of damages.

A second difficulty in determining the measure of damages is whether the ordinary limits on the types of loss recoverable in cases of breach of contract should apply to actions for misrepresentation. In particular, damages are not normally awarded in actions for breach of contract to cover disappointment and distress, but only for actual financial losses incurred by extracting oneself from a bad bargain. But this limitation has not been observed in claims for losses resulting from misrepresentation. In *East v Maurer*, for instance, the court awarded £1,000 as general damages for disappointment and inconvenience.

The third difficulty in calculating damages arises from the question of whether the rules should differ between fraudulent and negligent misrepresentations. In particular, some losses resulting from a misrepresentation may seem so remote and unforeseeable that compensation for those losses should be awarded, if at all, only in cases of deliberate fraud. Although the common law adopts this division,[36] the statutory claim for damages for negligent misrepresentation under section 2(1) of the Misrepresentation Act 1967 appears on its wording to insist upon identical treatment for cases of fraud and negligence, and it has been so interpreted by the courts.[37]

The strange result of these decisions concerning the quantification of damages is that often a person will gain a higher measure of damages for a claim for negligent misrepresentation during pre-contractual negotiations than could be obtained for a simple claim for breach of contract. Under the third version of the tort measure, which includes

---

35 *Royscott Trust Ltd v Rogerson* [1991] 2 QB 297, [1991] 3 All ER 294, CA.
36 *Doyle v Olby (Ironmongers) Ltd* [1969] 2 QB 158, [1969] 2 All ER 119, CA.
37 *Royscott Trust Ltd v Rogerson* [1991] 2 QB 297, [1991] 3 All ER 294, CA.

opportunity costs, in a competitive market this should always approximate to the profits which were expected under the contract which was undertaken. In addition, the plaintiff in an action for negligent misrepresentation under the Misrepresentation Act 1967, section 2(1) can also avoid the rules barring recovery in an action for breach of contract for claims concerning disappointment and inconvenience and for remote and unforeseeable losses. This strange conclusion results from the courts' adhesion to a sharp conceptual distinction between the measure of damages in contract and tort, and then the relentless application of the tort measure to pre-contractual representations. This conceptualism ignores the context of these claims, which is essentially one concerned with pre-contractual arrangements. What the law requires is the recognition of a distinct species of liability, which is neither precisely contract nor tort, but which addresses directly the proper measure of the sanction for breach of a duty to negotiate with care.

Regulatory Offences

We have noted how the duty of care in making statements during pre-contractual negotiations has been buttressed by criminal sanctions in many consumer contexts. The justification for this regulation, in addition to the sanctions of private law in rescission and damages, lies in the general problem of enforcement of private rights in small consumer transactions. The costs of obtaining a remedy such as damages for a misrepresentation with respect to a consumer purchase may well far exceed the likely measure of recovery and the value of the item purchased. The expense and trouble of litigation, combined with the likely unsatisfactory outcome, will deter most consumers from asserting their legal rights beyond a letter of complaint. The result will be that few traders will be deterred from making misleading claims about products and prices, and in turn this will harm consumers, and obstruct a competitive market. A number of possible solutions to this problems can be imposed.

Private law rights could be enhanced and made more effective. For this purpose the measure of compensation could be augmented and access to justice improved by provision for inexpensive means for enforcing rights.

Alternatively, and this is the route chosen in most jurisdictions, a criminal sanction is introduced as a deterrent. The criminal sanction has the advantage that the costs of policing the market are borne by state agencies and that the sanction, because it exceeds mere compensation, should eliminate the deceptive trade practices. But the effectiveness of such measures depends ultimately upon consumers passing along complaints to the public authority, and then the authority acting vigorously upon them through enforcement mechanisms. Studies of these procedures often reveal a marked lack of effective monitoring and enforcement of standards. The criminal penalties also can prove meagre and therefore lack any real deterrent force. A criminal sanction can be combined with a power vested in the courts to award damages to individuals adversely affected by a misleading trade practice, as in Australia.[38]

Administrative Injunction
The Control of Misleading Advertisements Regulations 1988[39] established a novel procedure under which complaints about misleading business advertising should be made to a public official, the Director General of Fair Trading. Unless the complaint can be settled by informal means, such as control by self-regulatory bodies, the Director may apply to a court for an injunction against any person concerned in the publication of the misleading advertisement. If the court agrees that the advertisement is misleading,[40] and likely to cause economic detriment to consumers, then it issues an injunction against publication. This procedure avoids the use of criminal penalties and emphasizes prospective prevention of misleading advertisements. The employment of the Director as a substitute litigator for the ordinary consumer overcomes many of the weaknesses of control of deceptive practices through private law. The same procedure has now been adopted by the Unfair Terms in Consumer Contracts Regulations[41] in order to prevent the use of unfair terms such as exclusion clauses in consumer contracts. This cumbersome procedure and its emphasis upon settlement and self-regulation, however, combine to weaken the Regulations' deterrent effect against misleading advertisements, and the same result is likely to occur with respect to unfair terms.

2. Failure to Disclose Information

To what extent are the parties to negotiations for a contract required to disclose information in their possession? The law's answer to this question draws a sharp distinction between two sorts of information. On the one hand, the law displays a reluctance to require disclosure of information about the circumstances surrounding the transaction, but on the other hand it provides considerable incentives to disclose information about the terms of the proposed transaction. This distinction can be justified by the need to protect and enhance a competitive market.

The efficiency of markets will be enhanced if the law provides incentives for the discovery of commercially valuable information. This information tends to ensure that goods will move to those who value them

---

38 Australian Trade Practices Act 1974, s 82. This law also differs from the English regulation by including a general regulation against misleading practices which is described as 'conduct that is unconscionable within the meaning of the unwritten law': s 51AA.
39 SI 1988/915; this implements EC Directive 84/450, OJ L250/17 of 19 September 1984.
40 *Director General of Fair Trading v Tobyward Ltd* [1989] 2 All ER 266, Ch.
41 SI 1994/3159, Reg 8.

most. For example, if one trader discovers that a commodity is in short supply in one region so that prices have gone up, then with the benefit of this information the trader can purchase the commodity and resell it in the place of short supply. The inducement of profits ensures that the market operates competitively and efficiently, so that goods are quickly moved to those who value them the most. This process would be obstructed, however, if the trader were required to disclose his or her knowledge of market shortage on the initial purchase. Following such disclosure, the information would become public knowledge, permitting others to exploit it. The trader would be prevented from taking advantage of the information, which would in turn discourage him or her from obtaining the information in the first place. Without giving the trader an incentive to acquire the information by promising the trader the commercial benefits of that information, it seems likely that much less information will be produced, leading to inefficiency in the operation of the market. For this reason, it seems inadvisable to require disclosure of commercially valuable information during negotiations for a contract.

The same policy considerations, however, argue for disclosure of the content of the terms of the contract. In an ideal competitive market parties should become fully aware of the proposed terms of the transaction, so that they can compare the relative advantages of different market opportunities. This comparison will enable them to conclude the most efficient contract available on the market. Although these conditions will be satisfied in specially negotiated contracts, in the majority of contracts concluded on standard forms businesspersons and consumers will have neither the time nor the expertise to evaluate the full meaning of all the terms of the contract. To enhance the competitiveness of the market, therefore, the law can require a party relying upon a standard form contract to ensure that the principal terms and any unusual terms are brought to the other party's notice.

This distinction explains the general pattern of the law on disclosure which displays a much greater readiness to require disclosure of the terms of a contract than other kinds of commercially valuable information. But these simple economic models cannot capture the complexity of the issues at stake. The economic model of the operation of commodity markets described above provides an inadequate picture of how markets operate in general. In many instances one person enters into a transaction with another relying upon the other's expertise and superior information. For example, a consumer contracts with a stockbroker for the purchase of some shares relying upon the stockbroker to exercise normal professional skills. If the stockbroker knows or ought to know of information which is about to send the value of the shares plummeting, then the consumer may assert that the failure to disclose this information amounted to a breach of a duty of care owed to him. To deny that such a duty was owed would place the stockbroker in the contradictory position of simultaneously asserting that, on the one hand, it is advisable to make the contract with him or her because of his or her special skill and knowledge, and on the other, denying that the skill and knowledge need be exercised for the benefit of the consumer. What this example shows is that, whilst the law may turn its face against a general duty of disclosure of information, it may discover many situations where, by virtue of the relation of dependence between the negotiating parties, at least some measure of disclosure should be required. The difficulty confronting the law is to identify those situations which justify a departure from the general rule against disclosure.

The concept of a relation of dependence is useful in describing the general pattern of the law governing disclosure of information of facts other than the terms of the contract. The paradigm instance consists of the negotiating relation between a person who regularly conducts the kind of business involved in the transaction and a person who lacks equivalent experience, skill, and knowledge. This relation of dependence will trigger legal duties of disclosure where reasonable reliance has been placed on the exercise of this experience, skill, and knowledge to the extent of disclosure of information. The crucial normative judgement of when it is reasonable to expect disclosure of information must depend, in the absence of explicit legislative guidance, on a careful investigation of the facts of each case.

(1) Disclosure of Terms

The general pattern of the law requires disclosure of the terms of the contract, and failure to do so will render the contract unenforceable either as a whole or in part. The source of this principle lies in the common law, but it is supplemented by numerous statutory requirements aimed at informing consumers of the terms of standard form transactions. With the development of a single European market, these rules are increasingly being harmonized throughout the EC.

The common law's requirement of disclosure derives from a number of particular principles. First, for a standard form to be treated as the terms of the contract, it must be communicated before the contract has been concluded.[42] Secondly, the objective principle for determining the content of the terms of the contract has the effect that confusing or obscure terms should be interpreted by reference to the reasonable promisee's understanding of the terms. Failure to disclose the terms clearly may therefore result in the proposed terms being enforced with a meaning contrary to the profferor's intention or even the conclusion that no binding contract was reached at all.[43] Thirdly, a failure to disclose the full import of the terms of a contract can be treated as a misrepresentation where statements about the content of the terms are made which omit some material element of the proposed contract. This liability for an omission was one of the grounds for the liability of the bank in *Cornish v Midland*

---

42 *Thornton v Shoe Lane Parking Ltd* [1971] 2 QB 163, [1971] 1 All ER 686, CA; *Hollier v Rambler Motors (AMC) Ltd* [1972] 2 QB 71, [1972] 1 All ER 399, CA; *Olley v Marlborough Court Ltd* [1949] 1 KB 532, [1949] 1 All ER 127, CA.
43 *Scriven Bros v Hindley & Co* [1913] 3 KB 564, QB. See chapter 11.

Bank plc.[44] Fourthly, as Dillon LJ stated in *Interfoto Picture Library Ltd v Stiletto Visual Programmes Ltd,*[45]

> If one condition in a set of printed conditions is particularly onerous or unusual, the party seeking to enforce it must show that the particular condition was fairly brought to the attention of the other party.

In that case, under a standard form contract for the hire of some old photographs, there was a provision which imposed heavy charges for late return of the photographs after the period of hire had expired. The Court of Appeal declined to uphold a claim for these heavy charges on the ground that this term in the contract had not been drawn to the attention of the hirer. The sum of all these rules is to require the parties to disclose the terms of a proposed contract in good time for their consideration, clearly, fully, and drawing the other party's attention to any unusual and onerous clauses.

These common law principles are supplemented by legislation with respect to most consumer transactions which imposes more particular duties and incentives for disclosure of information about the terms of a transaction. The objectives of these rules are twofold: to promote a competitive market by making comparisons between contractual terms simple, and secondly to reduce the risk that consumers will enter contracts which are inadvisable in their particular circumstances such as taking out loans which they cannot afford to pay back. These objectives can be served by a huge variety of measures including the requirement of terms which are written down, easily legible, in plain English, with a copy handed to each party to the transaction; the adoption of the same form of words for the terms in every contract of a particular type such as consumer credit transactions; certain terms being highlighted by being printed in a different colour or placed in a conspicuous position; and cooling-off periods during which a consumer has a right to cancel the contract, which permit examination of the terms and comparisons to be made. For example, the Price Marking Order 1991[46] requires retailers to display or mark the selling price of goods in a way which is unambiguous, easily identifiable, and clearly legible.

A general principle governing disclosure of terms in consumer contracts derives from the Unfair Terms in Consumer Contracts Regulations 1994, which in Regulation 6 proposes:

> A seller or supplier shall ensure that any written term of a contract is expressed in plain, intelligible language, and if there is doubt about the meaning of a written term, the interpretation most favourable to the consumer shall prevail.[47]

Although this looks like a rule for interpretation of contracts, in fact a term of written contract which fails to pass the test of being expressed in

44   [1985] 3 All ER 513, CA.
45   [1989] QB 433, [1988] 1 All ER 348, CA.
46   SI 1991/1382, implementing EC Directives 88/314 and 88/315.
47   SI 1994/3159, implementing Directive 93/13, OJ L95/29, 5 April 1993, Art 5.

plain, intelligible language is likely to be regarded as an unfair term and therefore unenforceable. This invalidity creates a strong incentive for traders to rewrite their standard form contracts in a 'user-friendly' style, which in turn should serve the purpose of disclosure of information about the terms of the contract.

In English law the most elaborate provisions of this kind apply to consumers' financial transactions, such as credit arrangements for the purchase of goods or a home. Under EC Directive 87/102,[48] member states must enact legislation to ensure in consumer credit arrangements that they are in writing, that the consumer receives a copy of the agreement, and that the agreement clearly states the annual percentage rate of interest and other essential terms of the contract. The Consumer Credit Act 1974, sections 60–65, enacts these requirements,[49] so that a creditor's failure to comply with these formalities makes the agreement unenforceable against the debtor except by court order.[50] Under these regulations, for instance, the lender is required to describe the cost of borrowing according to a uniform measure, the APR. The objective of this requirement to disclose credit terms in a particular way is to enable the consumer to compare the cost of credit, which in turn should promote a competitive market.[51] It also reflects a view that the APR is the most rational way to compare the cost of credit,[52] even though consumers are likely to measure instead the actual cost of weekly or monthly repayments. The intensity of the controls in this financial sector presumably reflects the sense that the terms of these transactions are likely to be complex and involve concepts with which the ordinary consumer is unfamiliar. In addition, the consequences of breach of these contracts may cause considerable hardship, such as loss of possession of a home, so it is useful to warn the consumer of these risks clearly in advance.

As well as consumer transactions, legislation regulates the disclosure of terms in other standard types of contract. Under EC law, for instance, an employer must provide employees with a written statement of the terms of the contract.[53]

The effectiveness of these legislative provisions for the protection of consumers has been questioned. Even with all this information about the terms of the contract, it must be doubted whether most consumers take the trouble to read the contract, or fully comprehend its implications if

---

48   OJ L42/48, 17 February 1987.
49   Further detailed requirements are contained in Consumer Credit (Agreements) Regulations 1983, SI 1983/1553.
50   Consumer Credit Act 1974, s 127.
51   Report of the Committee on Consumer Credit (Crowther Committee), Cmnd 4596 (1971), para 3.8.3.
52   Whitford, 'The Functions of Disclosure Regulation in Consumer Transactions' (1973) *Wisconsin Law Review* 400, at pp 423–425.
53   Employment Rights Act 1996, s 1; EC Directive 91/533, OJ L288/32, 18 October 1991; Clark and Hall, 'The Cinderella Directive? Employee Rights to Information about Conditions Applicable to their Contract or Employment Relationship' (1992) 21 *Industrial Law Journal* 106.

they do.[54] Nevertheless, provided that a substantial group of relatively sophisticated consumers take advantage of the ability to scrutinize the information and make comparisons, then this is likely to improve the competitiveness of the market overall.[55] The provision of information cannot of course prevent some consumers from entering extremely disadvantageous transactions, but the remedy for this must lie elsewhere in the control over the content of the terms and challenges on the ground of unfairness.

Against these advantages of disclosure requirements to the consumer, however, must be set the costs of compliance to businesses and the expense of enforcement mechanisms. For the most part the disclosure requirements can be satisfied by standard form contracts and printed publicity material at little extra cost. But when regulation goes beyond such easily satisfied requirements, then it seems likely to become unworkable. For example, the regulation of the advertising of credit under the Consumer Credit Act 1974, sections 43–47 seems to deter anything but rudimentary statements, for the costs of full compliance with the regulation would push up advertising costs and lead almost inevitably to unintended breaches of the complex regulations.[56]

(2) Disclosure of Facts
In what circumstances does the law require disclosure of facts other than the terms of the contract?[57] As we have noted, arguments based upon the enhancement of competitive markets favour a general rule against a duty to disclose facts. But these arguments cannot prevail in every case, because markets are permeated with situations where one party relies upon the other to exercise care and skill. Where such a relation of dependence exists then it may be appropriate to impose a duty of disclosure as part of the broad duty to negotiate with care. We examine in this section the situations where such a duty to disclose information will arise. The principal legal techniques for creating such duties of disclosure comprise development of the law of misrepresentation and reliance upon the implication of terms into contracts. These are supplemented in some instances by regulatory offences.

Misrepresentation
In many cases of relations of dependence, the party with superior knowledge or expertise will give advice to the weaker party. We have noted that if this advice is false or misleading, then liability for misrepresentation

---

54   I Ramsay, *Consumer Protection* (London, 1989), pp 330–331, discussing the report of National Consumer Council, *Consumers and Credit* (London, 1980).
55   Schwartz and Wilde, 'Intervening in Markets on the Basis of Imperfect Information: A Legal and Economic Analysis' (1979) 129 *University Pennsylvania Law Review* 630.
56   Ramsay, op cit, at pp 333–334.
57   Nicholas, 'The Precontractual Obligation to Disclose Information' in D Harris and D Tallon (eds), *Contract Law Today* (Oxford, 1989), p 166.

will protect the weaker party. One significant way in which advice may be misleading is that it omits to mention certain material facts. These omissions to disclose information will be treated as a misrepresentation, and the normal rules governing misleading statements will be applied. The test is whether in the circumstances of the case, including any statements made, the fact not disclosed is such that it is impliedly represented not to exist.[58] In *Nottingham Patent Brick and Tile Co v Butler*,[59] during negotiations for the sale of land, the vendor's solicitor stated in response to a question that he was not aware of any restrictive covenants inhibiting the use of the land. The solicitor failed to acknowledge, however, that he had not studied the relevant deeds, so although his statement was true it was misleading by virtue of this omission.

The reasonable expectation of disclosure in a relation of dependence will also arise when a statement is made which, though true at the time it is made, subsequently becomes false prior to the formation of the contract. Having established the relation of dependence through reliance upon the statement, it becomes reasonable to expect disclosure of information which reveals the statement no longer to be true. During negotiations for the sale of a medical practice in *With v O'Flanagan*,[60] the vendor affirmed the current value of the practice, but prior to conclusion of the sale it dropped substantially in value due to the illness of the vendor. The failure to disclose this change in circumstances was treated as a misrepresentation entitling the purchaser to rescind the contract.

The full extent of this potential liability in misrepresentation for omissions was revealed in our earlier discussion of *Crossan v Ward Bracewell*.[61] It will be recalled that the plaintiff visited a solicitor to obtain advice, but after preliminary negotiations decided not to employ the solicitor because of the cost and doubts about the necessity for legal advice. Because the solicitor failed to alert the plaintiff to risks of loss from civil liability, the solicitor was held liable in negligence despite the absence of a concluded contract. The duty of care arose despite the absence of any contract for services, because the advice was given in a relation of dependence.

The same reasoning can apply to cases of misrepresentation by conduct. Covering up and deliberately concealing faults and information can amount to a misrepresentation, if the effect is to imply a false representation. If, for example, the seller of a used car carefully conceals important defects then, unless he or she discloses the true state of the car, he or she will be treated as having made a representation that the car conforms to its appearance. The difficult question here is to determine what implied representations should be inferred from conduct. Should it be inferred, for example, from the fact that a trader offers a used car for sale that he or she impliedly represents that he or she has taken reasonable

58 *Lee v Jones* (1864) 17 CBNS 482, 144 ER 194.
59 (1886) 16 QBD 778, CA.
60 [1936] Ch 575, CA.
61 [1986] *New Law Journal* 849.

care to ensure that the car is safe and free from major defects? The decided cases indicate that perhaps the representation that the trader has taken reasonable care to check that the car is safe is one which can be implied from this conduct, but that the representation that checks have been made to ensure no major defects is too broad.[62] The latter kind of information can lead only to economic loss, and here the argument for enhancing the competitive market by allowing traders to profit from information acquired from the development and exercise of expertise points strongly against imposing a duty of disclosure.

In cases where a duty of disclosure has been established through the law of misrepresentation, the question may arise whether some limited form of disclosure has satisfied the duty. In particular, the person under the duty of disclosure may have made some general declaration purporting to deny that any implied representations have been made and warning the other party to seek independent advice. The courts have permitted such general statements to negative the breach of the duty to disclose information.[63] Such general clauses would now, however, be treated as exclusion clauses subject to a requirement of reasonableness under the Misrepresentation Act 1967, section 3.

Implied Terms

The most important regulation of disclosure of information under the common law derives from the use of implied terms in contracts. In construing a contract a court may imply a term on the ground that it is reasonably necessary to give efficacy to the transaction. This term may constitute a warranty about, for example, the quality of goods and services, or that reasonable care has been taken in the preparation of advice or manufacture of goods. To avoid this potential liability a trader must either seek to exclude such implied terms from the contract by express terms, or alternatively supply information during the negotiations which alerts the other party to the true state of affairs. These implied terms therefore provide an incentive to supply information, with the potential sanction that if information is not given then liability for damages for breach of contract may arise.

In contracts for the sale of goods, for example, the Sale of Goods Act 1979, section 14 implies terms to the effect that a seller acting in the course of business warrants that the goods are of satisfactory quality and are reasonably fit for their normal purpose. These provisions give several incentives for disclosure of information. The seller can avoid liability if any defects are specifically drawn to the buyer's attention before the contract is made, or if the buyer examines the goods and the defects ought to have been apparent. The buyer has an incentive to disclose any particular purpose for which the goods are being bought, for then the

---

62   *Bodger v Nicholls* (1873) 28 LT 441; *Ward v Hobbs* (1878) 4 App Cas 13, HL; *Hurley v Dyke* [1979] RTR 265, HL.
63   *Ward v Hobbs* (1878) 4 App Cas 13, HL; *Hurley v Dyke* [1979] RTR 265, HL.

seller will be held to imply a warranty of fitness for that purpose, except where the circumstances show that the buyer does not rely, or it is unreasonable for him to rely, on the skill or judgement of the seller, that is where there is no relation of dependence. In sales to consumers, these implied terms cannot be excluded by virtue of the Unfair Contract Terms Act 1977, section 6. In other contracts, such exclusions will be subject to a test of reasonableness.

The strength of this incentive to disclose information in order to avoid liability for breach of an implied term of the contract depends upon the extent to which implied terms will be imported into contracts, a topic to be considered in Chapter 11. In sales of land, for instance, there is no established implied warranty akin to the standard of satisfactory quality, which might imply that a house is habitable.[64]

The extent of the incentive to disclose information under implied terms will depend also on the exact meaning of the implied term. Under the sale of goods provisions, for example, goods can be of satisfactory quality even if defective, provided that the seller through any description and the price charged indicates that the goods may be substandard. Similarly, the goods may be of satisfactory quality even though they do not conform to the buyer's expectations, provided that they are fit for the normal purpose for which such goods are intended. In a contract for the supply of professional services, the implied term that reasonable care has been taken to establish the facts on which advice has been given may also fall short of the purchaser's expectation, if the standard of reasonable care which is set by professional customary practice does not require detailed investigations.

Regulatory Offences
To make a crime out of a failure to disclose certain information during negotiations leading to a contract encounters the reluctance in the general criminal law to make omissions a criminal offence. It is not a crime under English law, for instance, to fail to rescue a drowning swimmer, even though a rescue could have been easily effected with no risk. But the dividing line between omissions and acts is hard to draw in the context of misleading statements, for, as we have seen, the failure to give some information whilst giving the remainder can readily give a misleading impression. Thus the regulatory offences which condemn misleading statements can often encompass liability for omissions.

Under the Financial Services Act 1986, section 47, for instance, a person who makes a statement, promise or forecast which he knows or realizes is likely to be misleading, false or deceptive, or dishonestly conceals any material facts, for the purpose of inducing another to enter into an investment, commits an offence. To avoid the commission of this offence an investment broker would have to ensure that any statement about the

---

64   In sales of a new house a builder is liable for latent defects: Defective Premises Act 1972.

investment prospects to a potential investor fully disclosed all material facts, or at least could not reasonably give any false impression.

A similar potential liability for omissions will arise in the context of other consumer protection legislation which we have already considered due to the extensive meaning given to the idea of misleading statements. Because the statement need not be in fact false under section 3 of the Trade Descriptions Act 1968 and section 21 of the Consumer Protection Act 1987, but merely give a misleading impression, then statements which are economical with the truth, which in other words make certain claims but fail to make clear that certain implications which might be drawn from those claims by an unwary consumer should not be drawn, will be caught by the legislation. For this reason, in *Robertson v Dicicco*,[65] the statement that the second hand car was a 'beautiful car', though perhaps literally true since the car had an attractive external appearance, amounted to a misleading statement, for it implied falsely that the car functioned satisfactorily as well.

A more explicit requirement to disclose information arises in connection with unsafe products. A producer of a product sold to consumers is required to provide consumers with the relevant information to enable them to assess the risks inherent in a product throughout the normal or reasonably foreseeable period of its use, where such risks are not immediately obvious without adequate warnings, and to advise them on appropriate precautions.[66] Clear labelling and warnings on products is likely to be the most effective way of complying with this duty of disclosure.

Mistaken Identity

A particular problem for consumers is the difficulty of knowing precisely with whom they are dealing. The problem becomes acute when transactions are conducted by post, as in the mail order business. Regulations require businesses which send out catalogues under which payment is to be made before dispatch of goods to ensure that the catalogue contains in legible characters the true name or registered business name of the person carrying on the business and the address at which the business is managed.[67] In the case of advertisements, it will often be difficult for consumers to ascertain whether or not they are dealing with a business, with all the protection and risks which that creates, or merely another private individual. To put consumers on their guard, advertisements by businesses must reveal their true identity,[68] though this law appears to be widely flouted.

But apart from these limited regulatory interventions, the law provides little protection against mistakes as to the identity of the other transacting

---

65   (1972) 70 LGR 589, DC.
66   General Product Safety Regulations 1994, SI 1994/2328, Reg 8. A Ogus, *Regulation: Legal Form and Economic Theory* (Oxford, 1994) chapter 7.
67   Mail Order Transactions (Information) Order 1976, SI 1976/1812.
68   Business Advertisements (Disclosure) Order 1977, SI 1977/1918.

party. Apart from a deliberate misrepresentation, which will permit rescission of the contract,[69] the consumer must be careful to make diligent enquiries as to the attributes such as credit-worthiness of the person with whom he or she is dealing. There is old authority in *Cundy v Lindsay*[70] which supports the proposition that a contract will be void for the lack of agreement if a person purports to accept an offer which was not made to him but a different person. But the law provides no incentive to disclose information about identity, for the contract will not be voidable for mistake if a genuine mistake as to the identity of the other contracting party has been made.[71]

3. Abuse of Positions of Trust

Numerous positive duties to act in good faith and with care during negotiations for a contract arise from special relationships of trust between the parties. Here the relationship of the parties is distinguished at the outset from the normal market of strangers bargaining at arm's length. Instead, the law identifies a relation of confidence and trust which requires a duty to provide full disclosure of information, to give careful advice, and to avoid any conflicts of interest. The exact boundaries of these relations of confidence and trust have been established in part by the classification of certain types of legal relation, and in part by the examination of particular cases. The classification by reference to types of legal relation takes two forms.

Contracts Uberrimae fidei
One source of classification depends upon the nature of the contract which is being negotiated. Some contracts have been identified as always requiring good faith during negotiations, and these are known as contracts 'uberrimae fidei'. The most important example is a contract of insurance, where the assured has to reveal any facts which he knows, or ought to know, which a reasonable and prudent insurer might regard as material to the estimation of the risk.[72] A failure to disclose such information will entitle the insurer to avoid the contract and refuse to pay any claims under it.

The justification for this special classification of contracts of insurance is that only the insured is in a position to know the facts on which the risk must be estimated. Although this is true, this justification is perhaps inadequate to support the duty of disclosure, for of course it is open to the

---

69 *Car and Universal Finance Co Ltd v Caldwell* [1965] 1 QB 525, [1964] 1 All ER 290, CA.
70 (1878) 3 App Cas 459, HL.
71 *Lewis v Averay* [1972] 1 QB 198, [1971] 3 All ER 907, CA.
72 *Lambert v Co-operative Insurance Society* [1975] 2 Lloyd's Rep 485, CA; *Pan Atlantic Insurance Co Ltd v Pine Top Insurance Co Ltd* [1995] 1 AC 501, [1994] 3 All ER 581, HL.

insurer to ask questions about the risk, and any inaccuracy and omission in the insured's reply could be treated as a misrepresentation. Moreover, the duty placed upon the insured seems excessive, since it assumes that the insured should recognize any features of his or her situation which might affect the insurer's estimate of risk, even though only the insurer possesses this specialized information. For example, a person convicted of robbery ten years before taking out fire insurance for a house was held in *Woolcott v Sun Alliance and London Insurance Ltd*[73] to have failed to have disclosed this pertinent fact so that his fire insurance was invalidated. Here it can be objected that since the insurance company (through its agent, a building society) did not ask any questions bearing on the insured's moral character or criminal convictions, and since it is not immediately obvious why a conviction for robbery could affect the risk of a house catching fire, then the burden of disclosure imposed upon the insured is excessive and unpredictable in its effects.

In response to this criticism, the Association of British Insurance has issued a statement of good practice suggesting that insurers should give clear indication of those matters which the insurers regard as material to the risk, and should not repudiate liability to indemnify an insured on the ground of non-disclosure of a material fact which the insured could not reasonably be expected to have disclosed. This statement of practice, though not altering the strict law, represents a fairer rule for consumers, which might have prevented the avoidance of the fire insurance in *Woolcott v Sun Alliance and London Insurance Ltd.*

The duty to disclose information applies to both parties to a contract 'uberrimae fidei'. The duty of the insurer extends at least to the disclosure of all facts known to the insurer which are material either to the nature of the risk sought to be covered or the recoverability of a claim under the policy which a prudent person seeking insurance would take into account in deciding whether or not to place the risk for which cover is sought.[74]

Fiduciary Relations

The second source of classification comprises the identification of fiduciary relations. It is well established that many commercial relations impose a fiduciary relation between the parties, as in the case of principal and agent, partners in a business, and directors of companies. In any contract between these parties, the fiduciary duties require the highest standards of good faith in dealing, which certainly includes full disclosure of any information. Failure to disclose information will result in the contract being voidable, and may also impose a duty on the party in breach of the fiduciary relation to account for any profits made as a result of the failure to disclose.[75]

---

73   [1978] 1 All ER 1253, QB.
74   *Banque Keyser Ullmann SA v Skandia (UK) Insurance Co Ltd* [1990] 1 QB 665, [1989] 2 All ER 952, CA.
75   *Boardman v Phipps* [1967] 2 AC 46, [1966] 3 All ER 721, HL.

As well as these established instances of fiduciary relations, the equitable jurisdiction to avoid contracts on the ground of undue influence can be employed to identify special circumstances which trigger a duty to disclose information. We saw in *Lloyds Bank Ltd v Bundy*,[76] for instance, how a bank assumed a relation of trust and confidence as a result of dealings for many years with a farmer, so that he came to repose trust in the bank to advise him carefully during negotiations for a contract. The duty imposed on the bank in such circumstances required the bank to ensure that the farmer obtained independent advice and that it disclosed all the information about the transaction to the farmer. Similar relations of trust may arise from the conduct of the parties in many diverse instances, such as the dealings between shareholders in a small family firm,[77] or between the beneficiaries under a Will.[78]

Weaker duties of disclosure arise in connection with particular types of contract, perhaps on account of custom or a perception by the courts that there will otherwise arise a risk of abuse of trust. Here the duty of disclosure does not extend to all material facts, but merely certain facts which are exclusively known to one party and there is a commercial incentive to leaved them undisclosed. For example, a duty is placed on a creditor to explain to a surety any terms in the contract between creditor and debtor which render the surety's obligation materially different in a potentially disadvantageous way from those which the surety might naturally expect.[79] But the duty of disclosure does not extend to the debtor's likely creditworthiness, for the surety is expected to make his or her own enquiries on that point and take the risk of default.

4. Misuse of Confidential Information

During negotiations for a contract, one party may reveal to the other confidential information for the purpose of inducing the other to enter into the contract with him. He may be trying to sell an invention such as a new mechanical system for automobiles,[80] or enter into a joint venture to exploit a discovery such as a seam of gold,[81] and necessarily information about the invention or discovery will have to be disclosed before the other party will be induced to enter a binding contract. Since this information has a commercial value, the risk exists, if the contract is not concluded, that the other party, having become acquainted with the invention or discovery, will then seek to exploit it alone. As part of the duty to negotiate with care, such action will be regarded as a misuse of confidential information, and will give rise to a duty to pay compensation. This aspect

76 [1975] QB 326, [1974] 3 All ER 757, CA.
77 *Coleman v Myers* [1977] 2 NZLR 225, CA.
78 *Greenwood v Greenwood* (1863) 1 De GJ & Sm 28.
79 *Levett v Barclays Bank plc* [1995] 2 All ER 615, QB.
80 *Mechanical and General Inventions Co Ltd v Austin* [1935] AC 346, HL.
81 *LAC Minerals v International Corona Resources Ltd* (1989) 61 DLR (4th) 14.

of the duty serves the valuable purpose of permitting frank negotiations to take place, so that an efficient contract can be concluded.

A number of technical problems make this aspect of the duties during negotiation difficult to state with precision. Given that the parties have never formally entered into a contract, the cause of action must lie either in some form of implied contract or constitute an independent tort. The technique of an implied contract clearly runs directly counter to the traditional law's reluctance to impose contractual obligations during negotiations. But in fact it perhaps most closely accords with the understanding of the parties, which is usually that the information is disclosed on the basis that it will be used for the purpose of considering whether or not to enter the main contract, and not for any other purpose. An implied agreement on these terms should not be difficult to infer from the conduct of the parties. But it is also possible to present the claim as an independent tort of breach of confidence. The disadvantage of the tort claim is that it raises the question of what information should be regarded as confidential. This question is an unnecessary diversion in the context of pre-contractual negotiations, for the point is that the information given has been used for an unauthorized purpose. It should not matter whether the information was secret, or given in confidence. The breach of duty arises from the unauthorized use of the information.

A second technical problem concerns the calculation of an appropriate remedy in damages. In many instances the plaintiff has suffered no direct loss from the misuse of the information. What has occurred rather is that the defendant has been able to take commercial advantage of the information without having to pay for it. The measure of compensation could therefore be formulated as either the commercial value of the information if it had been sold, or the actual profits which the defendant obtained through use of the information. In the Canadian case *LAC Minerals v International Corona Resources Ltd*,[82] the Supreme Court of Canada favoured the latter measure for the remedy, La Forest J arguing that only that measure would deter breach of the obligation to bargain in good faith. In this case the plaintiff had revealed to the defendant the likely presence of gold under a third party's land for the purpose of negotiating a joint venture to purchase the land and mine it. Negotiations broke down and the defendant purchased the land and mined it for its own benefit. The plaintiff succeeded in recovering the stupendous profits made from the mine, which was far greater than the value of the information about the likelihood of a gold seam at the time it was disclosed.

5. Misleading Implied Promises

In stark opposition to the traditional view that during the negotiations for a contract no binding obligations may arise, it is possible for the courts

82 -(1989) 61 DLR (4th) 14.

to infer implied contractual undertakings from conduct and statements made during the negotiations. These undertakings differ from misrepresentations, for they involve a promise to act or refrain from acting in certain ways in the future. Liability for such undertakings may be conceived as either a contract based upon the exchange model supported by consideration, usually in the form of a unilateral contract, or as an estoppel based upon the reliance model. The difference in legal technique depends upon whether or not the court can infer a request to perform an act of detrimental reliance in exchange for the undertaking. If it can, then a contract to perform the undertaking will be found; if not, then the reliance model of estoppel will found the obligation. The difference in the legal technique employed may affect the remedies available to the injured party.

Collateral Contracts
There is nothing anomalous in the idea of a contract preceding another contract. An option to purchase an item in the future acquired for consideration is a typical instance of such a prior contractual undertaking. During negotiations for a major transaction, the parties may wish to secure their position in the meantime against various kinds of opportunism, and they can do so through express contracts. They may make an enforceable agreement to use best endeavours to negotiate an agreement, or an undertaking not to negotiate with any other person for a fixed period of time. What these 'lock-out' agreements seek to achieve is a contractual expression of a duty to bargain with care and in good faith. The validity of such contracts is in general not in doubt, and indeed the courts may imply into such agreements a term to make reasonable endeavours to reach an agreement.[83] But the courts have declined to enforce obligations which they regard as too vague to be policed, such as an undertaking to negotiate for a reasonable period of time or to negotiate in good faith.[84]

In the absence of an express agreement, the courts can also infer a prior contract from the circumstances of the case in order to support the duty to bargain with care. As an example of this contractual approach based upon a finding of consideration, we should consider *Blackpool and Fylde Aero Club Ltd v Blackpool Borough Council*.[85] The defendant owned an airport and granted the right to use the airport for a fee. The defendant invited tenders for such a concession, stating in the invitation that it was not bound to accept all or part of any tender, and that no tender submitted after noon on a specified day would be considered. The plaintiff submitted a tender by posting it by hand an hour before the expiry of the deadline in

---

83   *Queensland Electricity Generating Board v New Hope Collieries Pty Ltd* [1989] 1 Lloyd's Rep 205, PC.
84   *Walford v Miles* [1992] 2 AC 128, [1992] 1 All ER 453, HL; Neil, 'A Key to Lock-Out Agreements?' (1992) 108 *Law Quarterly Review* 405.
85   [1990] 1 WLR 1195, [1990] 3 All ER 25, CA; see also *Harvela Investments Ltd v Royal Trust Co of Canada (CI) Ltd* [1986] AC 207, [1985] 2 All ER 966, HL.

the defendant's letter box. Due to the defendant's oversight, the letter box was not emptied at noon, and subsequently the plaintiff's bid was treated as having been submitted too late for consideration. The defendant then accepted another bid which was lower than the plaintiff's. The plaintiff successfully claimed damages for breach of an implied undertaking by the defendant either that the plaintiff's bid would be considered along with all other bids conforming to the invitation, or that the plaintiff's bid would be considered if other conforming tenders were considered.

Although it is well established that an invitation to tender does not in itself create a contractual obligation, the court found in the particular circumstances of the case an implied contractual obligation to conform to the terms of the invitation. The court emphasized that the implied contract arose because on the facts the defendant had invited the plaintiff to tender (the plaintiff having held the concession until that time), that the defendant was required as a public authority under its rules to conduct the tendering process fairly, and that it had specified in great detail how tenders should be made, not only as to the time, but also by the use of an official envelope to ensure secrecy. This detail in the invitation to tender entitled the plaintiff to go beyond the hope that its tender would be considered, the normal position in tendering cases, and to have a reasonable expectation that a conforming tender would be considered along with the others. This analysis then created an implied contract: the defendant undertook to tenderers to conform to the terms of its invitation, if they in turn submitted bids in conformity with those terms.

The Reliance Model
The alternative legal analysis of these undertakings given during the bargaining process consists of an application of the doctrine of estoppel as in the cases examined under the reliance model such as *Crabb v Arun District Council*.[86] In that case, as a result of the defendant's oral undertaking that the plaintiff would be granted a right of access to a road, the plaintiff sold a portion of his land leaving the remainder inaccessible without the point of access. Subsequently negotiations for the legal conveyance of the right of access broke down, so no formal contract was concluded. Nevertheless, the defendant was held to be bound by the oral undertaking, which had been supplemented by conduct, all of which induced the plaintiff to act to his detriment. The plaintiff's remedy was conceived as one to remedy the injustice which he had suffered, which in this case could only be achieved by granting him the right of access.

In both kinds of legal analysis, whether it be contractual or by estoppel, the courts look for a promise, either express or implied, which induces the other party to change his position on reliance of the promise. The difference between the two analyses is simply that under the contractual

---

86   [1976] Ch 179, [1975] 3 All ER 865, CA.

analysis the change of position has been either expressly or impliedly requested by the promisor, whereas no such request can be implied in the instances of estoppel. Thus in *Blackpool and Fylde Aero Club v Blackpool Borough Council*, the court implied a request to the plaintiff to submit a bid in accordance with the terms of the invitation to tender. In contrast, in *Crabb v Arun District Council*, the court could not find an implied request on the part of the owner of the road for the plaintiff to sell a portion of his land, though certainly such a sale was foreseen as a consequence of the undertaking. But it must be admitted that the implied request which forms the basis of the contractual claim is often artificial. It stretches the facts of *Blackpool and Fylde Aero Club v Blackpool Borough Council* to say that the defendant asked the plaintiff to bid for the concession, rather than simply promising to consider the bids strictly according to the stated terms.

Damages

The need to use the contractual analysis, and therefore to infer requests from all the circumstances of the case, derives from the limitations of the reliance model of liability considered in Chapter 5. In particular, we noted the hesitation of English courts, not shared in other jurisdictions, to extend this basis of liability beyond promises concerning interests in land. In addition, English courts betray a marked reluctance to award damages for breach of these promises under the reliance model, preferring to use traditional equitable remedies for unravelling transactions or completing them. These limitations rendered it more controversial, for example, to use the reliance model as the basis for liability in *Blackpool and Fylde Aero Club v Blackpool Borough Council*. It was difficult to describe the granting of a concession or the promise to conduct a tendering operation fairly and carefully as relating to an interest in land. Even worse, since the concession had already been granted to another organization, then the only practicable remedy available was compensatory damages, a remedy which would have broken new ground under English law.

We observed in discussing the reliance model that other common law jurisdictions have dispensed with these limitations upon the use of estoppel to render promises made during the negotiation process binding. In the Australian case of *Waltons Stores (Interstate) Ltd v Maher*,[87] the company misled the contractor largely by its silence into commencing demolition operations even though it had decided not to proceed with the transaction which had reached the final stage of negotiation. The High Court of Australia held the company to be bound by its implied promise to complete the contract because, knowing that the contractor was incurring expenses by acting on the basis of a false assumption, it was unconscionable for the company to adopt a course of inaction which served to encourage the contractor to incur that detriment. This application of the reliance model

87   (1988) 164 CLR 387 (Aust HC).

is not confined to interests in land, and resulted in an award of damages. This approach seems preferable, because it avoids the fictitious implication of requests, yet leaves the court flexibility with respect to the remedy.

It should not be supposed, however, that the courts will lightly infer such promissory obligations arising during the course of negotiations. One party will often be put to considerable expense and trouble in preparing a bid for a contract, or incur legal expenses in negotiating the terms, but normally these expenses will not be recoverable. What distinguishes the successful claims for compensation is the presence of an express or implied undertaking which makes it reasonable for the promisee to incur those expenses in reliance upon the promise. To avoid this liability, the promisor must take care to avoid giving such a false impression, or, on realizing such an impression has been given, to act promptly to disabuse the promisee of the mistaken assumption. In this sense, this source of liability fits into the general framework of a duty of care during negotiations, the duty comprising one of disabusing the other of mistaken assumptions about intentions which foreseeably will cause the other to act to his detriment.

6. Rationale for the Duty to Negotiate with Care

Having drawn together all these strands in the law which govern duties during the negotiation process, it is time to consider whether these duties can be understood as resting upon some more general principles. The discussion has revealed that the law's analysis of different aspects of the negotiating process differs radically in the concepts employed. Numerous doctrines such as misrepresentation, undue influence, fiduciary duties, estoppel, and implied contracts, together with extensive regulatory provisions, supply a subtle and intricate tapestry by which the law regulates behaviour during negotiations. The complexity of the law combined with the traditional English reluctance to embrace broad principles instead of narrow technical doctrines has so far prevented the emergence and recognition of any general principle which unites these diverse rules governing negotiations.

> In many civil law systems, and perhaps in most legal systems outside the common law world, the law of obligations recognizes and enforces an overriding principle that in making and carrying out contracts parties should act in good faith. This does not simply mean that they should not deceive each other, a principle which any legal system must recognize; its effect is perhaps most aptly conveyed by such metaphorical colloquialisms as 'playing fair', 'coming clean' or 'putting one's cards face upwards on the table'. It is in essence a principle of fair and open dealing ...
>
> English law has, characteristically, committed itself to no such overriding principle but has developed piecemeal solutions in response to demonstrated problems of unfairness.[88]

88   Bingham LJ in *Interfoto Picture Library Ltd v Stiletto Visual Programmes Ltd* [1989] QB 433, [1988] 1 All ER 348, CA.

But if such a principle were to be recognized by the courts as the underlying rationale of their decisions, how should it be described and justified?

A justification for a general principle must commence with a reflection upon the compelling reasons for interfering with the general freedom to enter into negotiations without a binding commitment. This general freedom itself rests upon several possible justifications. In part it depends upon a conception of freedom which allows individuals to act in their own best interests without regard to others. But this is strengthened by considerations of market efficiency. The ability to enter negotiations without commitment permits traders to discover which possible bargain will be the most advantageous, which in turn promotes the goal of wealth maximization. The same ability permits the parties to discuss in advance the details of their proposed relation, which should avoid misunderstandings which might generate costs and opportunistic behaviour later on. 'If the utility of contract as an instrument of self-government is not to be seriously weakened, parties must be free to break off preliminary negotiations without being held to an accounting.'[89] Finally, we have observed that self-interested behaviour must be permitted in order to protect the incentives to acquire information and expertise. Any duty of care towards the interests of the other negotiating party must be constrained so that one who has acquired at some cost or ingenuity better skills or information should be able to reap the rewards of that effort through making advantageous contracts.

But these reasons for rejecting any general principle relating to bargaining duties do not rule out all forms of regulation of negotiations. Considerations of market efficiency can be employed to justify regulation of types of negotiating behaviour which harm the efficiency of the market, as in the case of fraud which induces contracts on the basis of false information. Moreover, bargaining duties may prove necessary in order to ensure that negotiating parties retain the fruits of their efforts, as in the case of disclosure of confidential information. Thus, even on the narrow ground of enhancing the competitive properties of the market, it is possible to justify considerable regulation of the negotiating process. I suggest, however, that this combination of respect for the self-interested exercise of individual liberty, subject to considerations of preserving and enhancing market efficiency, is inadequate to justify the extent to which today the law regulates the parties to contractual negotiations.

At several points in my survey of the law, the full extent of the duties during negotiations for a contract has been explained by reference to the concept of relations of dependence. In these situations the relative skills and knowledge of one party have led to the imposition of a duty to take into account the interests of the other party. In the sale of goods, for example, a seller who is in the business of trading in certain types of goods has imposed on him the duty to warrant that the goods are of satisfactory quality or alternatively to point out the defects to the purchaser. Similarly, when discussing the terms of a contract, one party

---

89   F Kessler, G Gilmore and A Kronman, *Contracts* (Boston, 3rd edn, 1986), p 201.

who is in a better position to understand the legal consequences of the contract will be under a duty to explain the full import of the terms, or else risk liability for misrepresentation. These, and many other instances of relations of dependence, imply that a purely self-interested exercise of freedom during the negotiating process is impermissible where one party stands in a relation of dependence to the other.

This interpretation of the law does not create a direct conflict with the ideal of freedom of contract. It merely interprets the privilege to act in a purely self-interested way within narrower confines. The law never permits self-interested action where it causes direct physical harm to another. The law also protects various economic interests from deliberate or negligent harm, either through actions for breach of contract or the use of the law of torts. In employing the idea of a relation of dependence, the law governing duties during the negotiations for a contract merely expands its conception of when the economic interests of another can be said to have been harmed. The legal duties do not require unlimited altruism, but merely expand the situations when the law requires care to ensure that the economic interests of another are not harmed. In this sense the existence of a law governing negotiating duties does not conflict with the general principle of freedom of contract. Instead, it reinterprets the limits placed upon freedom, narrowing the scope of permitted self-interested action on the ground that it harms the economic interests of others.

Given this justification for the existence of duties during negotiations for a contract, then I suggest that the law can best be interpreted by reference to a duty to negotiate with care. This formulation draws attention to the emphasis in the justification on the protection of the interests of the other party. At the same time, by employing the idea of care, it recognizes that carefulness is a flexible standard, so that the duty becomes stricter as the other party to the negotiations is a person in a relation of dependence, and that the required degree of care will alter between contexts. These features are superior to the alternative formulation of a duty to bargaining in good faith. The latter formulation implies that the law merely requires honesty, which is plainly inaccurate in instances of negligence liability.[90] Moreover, it suggests that the standard is constant, which fails to capture the way in which the legal duties increase in relations of dependence and may vary according to market context.

As we have seen, the pragmatism and doctrinal complexity of English law, born of its system of piecemeal development of the law through precedent decisions, typically resists such generalizations as a duty to negotiate with care as part of the formal fabric of the law. But such generalizations serve the useful purposes of assisting an orderly exposition of the law, revealing its underlying tensions, and articulating the relevant considerations which need to be balanced in a particular case. The principle should not be understood as a rule to be applied according to its terms in

90   For a different interpretation of good faith as co-operation, see: J Adams and R Brownsword, *Key Issues in Contract* (London, 1995) chapter 7.

each case, but as the basic justification for regulation of the bargaining process. With this justification in mind, then anomalies and inconsistences may be avoided.

In particular it is to be hoped that the recognition of a duty to negotiate with care will lead to the elimination of many of the anomalies resulting from the application of different conceptual analyses to similar states of facts. For example, we have noted in the context of implied undertakings during the process of negotiation, that the application of the two organizing frameworks of implied contracts and estoppel leads to inconsistencies of approach to liability and remedies. If a general principle were acknowledged, then a uniform test for liability and a coherent approach to remedies might be achieved.

Similarly, we noted the strange result in connection with the measure of damages for misrepresentation that a plaintiff may gain a higher measure for pre-contractual representations than claims based upon warranties contained expressly in the contract itself. The advantage of a recognition of a general duty to negotiate with care in this context would be to create a distinct species of liability, which is neither precisely contractual nor tortious, so that the courts could develop appropriate principles for the quantification of damages. The measure of damages here should include the losses incurred and the opportunity costs of entering a disadvantageous transaction, since the purpose of the general duty is both to compensate for harm caused and to promote a competitive market. But there should be no need in the context of commercial transactions, apart from perhaps in cases of fraud, for the law to extend liability to non-economic losses such as disappointment and inconvenience, or to remote and unforeseeable risks which are not normally ones which a contract seeks to reallocate.

The underlying problem here is that the failure to develop an independent legal concept of duties existing during the process of negotiation has forced the courts to borrow concepts from other branches of the law which often prove inappropriate. To discover a positive duty in these circumstances, the courts have been compelled to employ the law of tort, which often falls short in describing the kinds of misleading bargaining practices which should be the basis for censure, yet at the same time, when it does apply, suggests a measure of damages remedy which is anomalous in a commercial context. The alternative conceptual framework available to the courts is to treat all these cases as factors which vitiate consent to a contract. The disadvantage of this approach is that it makes little provision for damages beyond restitution, and often a remedy will be barred altogether as a result of the unwitting involvement of innocent third parties or subsequent transactions. The recognition of a duty to negotiate with care as part of the law of contract, yet not comprising contractual obligations based upon the terms of a contract, would solve these conceptual difficulties by filling a black hole at the heart of the common law's regulation of trading practices.

11

Terms

For what does a person make himself contractually responsible? In fidelity to the ideal of individual liberty, which gives rise to a presumption that the parties should be free to choose the terms of their contract, the classical law answers this question by asserting that a party to a contract is bound by those obligations to which he has consented and no others. In short, the terms of the agreement determine the content of the contractual obligations.

This simple principle still provides the first indication of the content of the parties' contractual obligations, but in the modern law it must be substantially modified. In later chapters we will examine the different ways in which the modern law both supplements and controls the terms of contracts, and hence affects the content of the contractual obligations. Those chapters reveal the significant degree to which the freedom to choose the terms has been eviscerated in modern law. This chapter confines its attention to the complicated development of the principle that in the first instance the agreement determines the content of the obligations.

The terms of the contract include both express and implied terms. The express terms comprise written statements of the agreement and any oral agreement. The implied terms have not been mentioned by the parties, but the court nevertheless deems the parties to have agreed to these additional terms. This process of supplementing the express terms is usually justified by reference to the intentions of the parties. It is alleged that the parties intended to include the implied terms, though did not do so expressly either due to lack of time or because the implied terms were so obvious that it seemed unnecessary to state them formally. We shall see, however, that this conventional explanation of the source of implied terms in the intention of the parties wears thin in view of the expansive nature of these implied obligations.

Under the classical law, the express and implied terms are regarded as properly determining the content of the contractual obligations because they conform to the intentions of the parties. This reference to intention provokes a perennial difficulty. If a determination of the content of the terms rests upon the intention of the parties, what happens when there is a dispute about the content or meaning of the terms? If the parties were genuinely at cross-purposes, then it seems that there was no real agreement on the terms. If that is so, then how can the court find that a contract was ever reached between them? The danger is that any dispute over the terms of the contract will be elevated into a dispute about the very existence of the contract in the first place.

It will be recalled that the existence of the contract, the ascription of contractual responsibility, was determined by an objective test. The question posed by the court was not whether a party intended to enter a contract, but rather whether the other party reasonably supposed that he did so intend. The same practice of adopting an objective approach emerges in this context of determining the content of the terms of the contract. The test is not what the promisor intended, but rather what the promisee reasonably supposed that he had been promised. In the case which we used to illustrate the objective test of contractual responsibility, *Smith v Hughes*,[1] a problem of interpretation of the content of the agreement was also raised. As well as arguing that no contract had been reached, the buyer alleged that he believed that one of the terms of the contract was that the oats were warranted to be old, which the seller disputed. If the court had sought the true intentions of the parties, no doubt it would have discovered that the parties were at cross-purposes: the seller only had new oats to sell, so would not have made such a warranty; the buyer, a horse trainer, had no use for new oats, so clearly only wanted to purchase old oats. But the court avoided the issue of intent again, and instead asked whether the buyer reasonably supposed that he had been promised that the oats were old. The reasonableness of such a supposition would depend upon evidence about the seller's statements or conduct.

Once the test for determining the content of a contract shifts to an objective approach, then again we must question whether or not the connection with the intention of the parties is preserved. It is not the intention of the promisor but the reasonable understanding of the promise from the point of view of the promisee. This reasonable understanding must be based on the words of the promise, but it may not correspond with the intention of the promisor. A more radical departure from the idea of intention suggests that the law aims to protect the promisee's reasonable expectations of what the contract contains. These reasonable expectations will be based on the nature of the proposed transaction, the normal terms for such a transaction, and any express refinements or qualifications which have been drawn to the promisee's attention. In the field of consumer standard form contracts, this test of reasonable expectations appears to be the operative principle. Moreover, when we consider the expansive use of implied terms, this practice may best be understood as implementing the reasonable expectations of the promisee.

1   (1871) LR 6 QB 597, QB.

1. Incorporation

The express terms of a contract can comprise not only the oral and written promises given at the time of the contract, but also any documents to which those promises refer. The express agreement may refer to the business's standard terms of business, or the normal trade terms. These standard terms then become part of the contract. For contracts of employment, the employer may issue a short written contract, which then refers to other lengthy documents such as the staff handbook, works rules, and a relevant collective agreement with a recognised union. A short oral agreement can therefore incorporate a lengthy document setting out the rights and obligations of both parties.

A standard form contract is likely to become a statement of the terms of the contract either because the printed document was handed over at the time of the formation of the contract, or because it was incorporated by the express terms of the agreement.

Documents may also be incorporated as express terms of the contract by virtue of custom or a regular course of dealing between the parties. In *British Crane Hire Corpn Ltd v Ipswich Plant Hire Ltd*,[2] the owner of a crane hired it out to a contractor in the same business, without expressly mentioning the intention to enter the contract on the standard trade terms contained in a model supplied by the trade association. But the court inferred that the standard model contract had been incorporated into the contract, these being the customary terms of the trade. A standard set of terms for a contract will also be incorporated automatically into a contract, if there has been a long and consistent course of dealing on those terms between the parties.[3]

For a document to be incorporated into the contract as part of its express terms, however, it must be introduced at the time of the formation of the contract. An attempt to impose a further document containing additional terms after the agreement has been reached will be impermissible, unless this amounts to an agreed variation of the contract. In order to draw this distinction, a court will often have to forge a contrast between a contractual document and a mere receipt or acknowledgment. In *Chapelton v Barry UDC*,[4] the plaintiff hired a deck-chair, and having paid his fee he was given a ticket. The court treated the ticket as a receipt rather than a document containing any express terms of the contract, so the exclusion clause contained in it could not form part of the express terms of the contract.

When both parties to the contract incorporate their standard terms of business into the agreement, there is a danger that the terms may conflict in crucial respects. In these 'battle of forms' cases, it can be argued

---

2   [1975] QB 303, [1974] 1 All ER 1059, CA.
3   *Henry Kendall & Sons (a firm) v William Lillico & Sons Ltd* [1969] 2 AC 31, [1968] 2 All ER 444, HL.
4   [1940] 1 KB 532, [1940] 1 All ER 356, CA.

that the parties never reached an agreement at all, so no contract has been created. In practice, however, the courts will resolve any dispute about the content of the contract by regarding one standard form as the content of the contract. This result can be achieved by interpreting the facts of the case so that one set of terms was impliedly withdrawn or only issued after the formation of the contract. As a last resort, the court will give priority to the last set of terms delivered before the other party commences performance of the contract. Under the objective approach the conduct of performing the contract is regarded as acceptance of the standard form.[5]

2. Oral Agreements

Although oral agreements also determine the content of the express terms of the contract, they can provide fertile terrain for disputes about the content of the contract to flourish. In the absence of a written statement of the terms, there can be endless disagreement about whether a particular warranty was offered or a particular disclaimer made. No doubt for this reason, written terms predominate in business transactions.

Informal Understandings
It seems to be not an infrequent occurrence that in commercial contracts the parties will seek informal understandings between them, which go beyond the written terms of the transaction. Perhaps the lawyers are left to haggle over the details in the formal contract, and the businesses agree informally that the contract should be performed in a particular way or according to a shared understanding. This practice reveals how the parties will often rely upon standards of good faith and co-operation in commercial relations to resolve any issues between them, rather than insist upon strict performance of the contract according to its letter.

Even more frustrating for the lawyers will be the case when the parties deliberately leave the terms of the written contract ambiguous, relying on informal commercial standards to resolve any disputes which may arise.[6] Of course, if the trust reposed in the informal undertaking proves unfounded, then the question must arise whether or not the informal promises were part of the contract so that they can supplement the studied ambiguity of the express terms. In some instances the court will conclude that these informal understandings were not intended to be legally binding commitments, so they will fail the test of legal enforceability. In other instances, the informal understanding may be used to interpret the

---

5 For comparisons with similar developments in other legal systems: see Von Mehren, ' The "Battle of Forms": A Comparative View' (1990) 38 *American Journal of Comparative Law* 265.
6 Thomas, 'Legal Skills and the Use of Ambiguity' (1991) 42 *Northern Ireland Legal Quarterly* 14.

meaning of the contract, as in the case where the performance must be carried out within a reasonable time. A severe difficulty arises when the informal understanding contradicts the written contract.

Formerly the courts applied a rule which excluded such parol evidence of informal understandings which contradicted the written letter of the contract. But the courts now recognise many techniques which remove the force of this rule so that rarely, if ever, will a party to a written contract be prevented from alleging that the terms of the contract were altered by independent oral promises. For example, in *Evans & Son (Portsmouth) Ltd v Andrea Merzario Ltd*,[7] by a written agreement the defendants shipped the plaintiff's goods from Italy to England, but the goods were damaged in transit because they were carried above deck. Under the terms of the contract, the defendants benefited from an exemption clause against damage to the goods and a term which gave them freedom to control the placing of the goods on the ship unless this term was altered by express written agreement. The plaintiff proved, however, that the defendants had given an oral undertaking prior to the formation of the contract that the containers would be shipped under the deck, an undertaking which had induced the plaintiff to agree to the contract. On these facts the English Court of Appeal permitted the plaintiff to claim damages for breach of the oral promise to load the goods under the deck. They held that the oral promise was intended to be legally enforceable. It was either incorporated into the written contract and overrode the contrary written terms, or it constituted a collateral contract, the consideration for which was the plaintiff's entry into the main contract of carriage. Whichever analysis is preferred, the decision in practice eliminates the parol evidence rule from English law.[8]

Informal understandings also run the risk of invalidity for failure to satisfy any statutory requirement of formalities, such as the rule that a contract for the sale of land must be in writing and that the documents must incorporate all the terms.[9] An informal understanding such as a letter may not be incorporated into the contractual documents and therefore unenforceable under the statute. Nevertheless, if the informal understanding can be interpreted as a collateral contract, one which induced entry into the main contract of sale, it may be enforceable as an independent transaction to which the statutory requirement of formalities does not apply.[10]

The practice of the parties during the performance of a contract may also reveal that they placed a particular interpretation on the words of the contract. The courts generally resist the suggestion that evidence of subsequent conduct can be an aid to interpretation of the document.[11] Nevertheless, this conduct can be evidence of an agreement to modify the

7   [1976] 1 WLR 1078, [1976] 2 All ER 930, CA.
8   Law Commission, *The Parol Evidence Rule*, Report No 154 (London, 1986).
9   Law of Property (Miscellaneous Provisions) Act 1989, s 2.
10   *Record v Bell* [1991] 4 All ER 471, Ch.
11   *Schuler AG v Wickman Machine Tool Sales Ltd* [1974] AC 235, [1973] 2 All ER 39, HL.

contract or waiver of breach, which achieves the same effect by a more complex reasoning process.[12]

Rectification

The mirror image of the problem occurs where it is alleged that the written record of the terms of the contract does not conform to the prior oral agreement. Under an action for rectification of a written contractual document, the claim will succeed when the court concludes that the document does not contain the terms which were orally agreed between the parties. This is not an exception to an objective approach to determining the content of the contract, but rather a clarification of the priorities between different sorts of evidence which satisfy the objective test. The action for rectification prevents the written contract from constituting conclusive evidence of the terms where it can be established that the document does not conform to a prior oral agreement.

The narrowness of this claim for rectification is illustrated by *Rose (Frederick E) (London) Ltd v William H Pim Jnr & Co Ltd.*[13] The plaintiff had received an order for 500 tons of Moroccan horsebeans called 'feveroles', but, not knowing what feveroles were, it asked the defendant who said that 'feveroles means just horsebeans'. The plaintiff then orally agreed to buy horsebeans from the defendant, and subsequently entered a written agreement to buy 500 tons of Tunisian horsebeans from the defendant. But the plaintiff's customer rejected these horsebeans on the ground that the beans were a larger, less valuable type known as 'feves', not the feveroles which had been ordered. The plaintiff then sought to have its written contract with the defendant rectified, so that the word 'feveroles' would be substituted for horsebeans. If successful, this claim for rectification would have then put the defendant in breach of contract for supplying the wrong type of horsebeans, so that the plaintiff would be able to recoup its losses resulting from rejection of the goods by the customer. But the action for rectification had to fail, because the written contract with the term horsebeans conformed exactly to the prior oral agreement for horsebeans. As Denning LJ observed:

> Rectification is concerned with contracts and documents, not with intentions. In order to get rectification, it is necessary to show that the parties were in complete agreement on the terms of their contract, but by an error wrote them down wrongly. And in this regard, in order to ascertain the terms of their contract, you do not look into the inner minds of the parties – into their intentions – any more than you do in the formation of any other contract. You look at their outward acts, ie, at what they said or wrote to one another in coming to their agreement, and then compare it with the document which they have signed. If you can predict with certainty what their contract was, and that it is, by a common mistake, wrongly expressed in the document, then you rectify the document. But nothing less will suffice.

---

12 *Panoutsos v Raymond Hadley Corpn of New York* [1917] 2 KB 473, CA; see chapter 15.
13 [1953] 2 QB 450, [1953] 2 All ER 739, CA.

It follows from these principles that a unilateral mistake made by one party about the content of the agreement which is unknown to the other party will not provide the basis for an action for rectification. If, for example, one party does not intend a particular clause to be included in the written contract, but does not communicate this intention and the written contract contains the clause, then the action for rectification will fail.[14]

3. Interpretation

We observed at the outset that the law employs an objective test for determining the content of the contract. But the meaning and implications of this objective test are far from certain.[15] The source of the difficulty lies in a vestigial attachment to the idea that the intentions of the parties should determine the content of the contract. Although this reference to intent fits the idea that the source of contractual obligations depends on the consent of the parties, it cannot provide a practical test for the interpretation of contracts. If the actual intentions of the parties were permitted to determine the content of the agreement, it would always be open to either party to declare that any written agreement did not conform to their true wishes, or that a promise was not intended to be taken literally. These arguments would provide a simple escape route from any contractual obligation which turned out to be unpalatable or inconvenient. An objective test is necessary so that the parties are bound by the terms of their ostensible agreement. Their actual intentions in agreeing to the contract, perhaps supported by evidence of motives, will be regarded as irrelevant.

At the same time, the objective approach insists that it is an investigation of the content of the agreement which took place. It does not permit evidence of the reasonable expectations of the parties when they entered the contract to determine its terms. A consumer purchasing a product will often expect that the printed standard form contract makes provision for dealing with defects in the product. This expectation may be dashed, however, if on close inspection of the terms it appears that the seller has sought to exclude any kind of liability for defects and has abnegated responsibility for any kind of redress. Although these exclusion clauses are now controlled by statute, the control might have proved unnecessary if consumers had been permitted to rely upon their reasonable expectations about the content of the contract as evidence of intent. But the courts treated the standard form contract as the necessary evidence

---

14   *Riverlate Properties Ltd v Paul* [1975] Ch 133, [1974] 2 All ER 656, CA.
15   Howarth, 'The Meaning of Objectivity in Contract' (1984) 100 *Law Quarterly Review* 265; Vorster, 'A Comment on the Meaning of Objectivity in Contract' (1987) 103 *Law Quarterly Review* 276; Farnsworth, 'Meaning in the Law of Contract' (1967) 76 *Yale Law Journal* 939.

of the terms, and ruled out evidence about the expectations of the consumer as incompatible with the objective test. This approach is understandable because it would be impracticable to give effect to an optimistic expectation of the terms of the contract, for then the terms of the contract would depend upon each particular consumer's expectation rather than the seller's written terms. The objective test therefore confines proof of the terms of a contract to the ostensible conduct of the parties, including their words and exchanged documents.

For the interpretation of terms in contracts, the objective test commences with the principle that the meaning of a promise should depend on how it was reasonably understood by the promisee. This interpretation should usually follow the ordinary meaning of the words used by the promisor. But of course the meaning of words can prove indeterminate, and to resolve the ambiguity the courts are likely to appeal to the reasonableness of the outcome, and to resist a construction which favours the party which is relying on its own standard form contract.

> The principles governing the construction of commercial contracts are not in doubt: the more unreasonable the result of a given construction, the readier should the court be to adopt some less obvious construction of the words.[16]

In the last resort, the court must endorse the interpretation placed on the words by the promisee. For example, if two people are standing beside a car which they have just inspected and one offers to sell his car for £1,000 and the other assents, then in the circumstances the purchaser can reasonably understand the promise to refer to the car beside them and not some other wreck belonging to the seller around the corner. This will be true even if the seller does not own the car beside them, for again the purchaser can reasonably understand the seller to be warranting that he owns that car. The reasonable understanding must be based upon the documents and written terms of the contract rather than any other expectations. In a case where the defendant purchased a public house at an auction under the mistaken belief that the lot included a field, the defendant was bound by the contract since the specification of the scope of the property for sale was stated clearly in the particulars which were available for inspection.[17]

The objective approach to interpretation affords some protection to consumers. When they are confronted with a standard form document which is couched in technical and confusing language, they can rely upon their reasonable understanding of the meaning of the terms. But this protection is overtaken by the Unfair Terms in Consumer Contracts Regulations 1994, which provide in Regulation 6:

> A seller or supplier shall ensure that any written term of a contract is expressed in plain, intelligible language, and if there is doubt about the

---

16   Simon Brown LJ, *Lancashire County Council v Municipal Mutual Insurance Ltd* [1996] 3 All ER 545, 552, CA.
17   *Tamplin v James* (1880) 15 Ch D 215, CA.

meaning of a written term, the interpretation most favourable to the consumer shall prevail.[18]

If a standard form contract is riddled with technical language and subordinate clauses, therefore, its objective meaning may not be enforceable against the consumer if the consumer alleges that he or she understood the terms differently.

Although the objective test provides the general guide to the courts' resolution of disputes over the terms of the contract, a number of decisions fit uneasily into this framework. These are cases where it appears that one party to a contract has been able to persuade the court that the ostensible words or conduct did not conform to the true intent, and that as a result either the ostensible contract should not be enforced, or a contract be enforced on terms corresponding to the true intent. One interpretation of these cases suggests that the courts invoke an exception to the objective test which permits an examination of the actual intentions of the parties. The interpretation preferred here, however, suggests that these cases merely display some particular ramifications of the objective approach.

Snapping Up

One type of case occurs where the promisee realises that the promisor's offer does not represent his true intention, but nevertheless purports to accept it. In *Hartog v Colin and Shields*,[19] the defendant offered to sell 3,000 Argentinian hare skins at a fixed price per pound, and the offer was accepted by the plaintiff. The defendant in fact intended to offer the hare skins at the same fixed price per piece, a rather different offer because there are about three pieces to a pound. A crude application of the objective test would have led inexorably to the conclusion that the original contract was binding, because the defendant had not communicated his true intention. But the court rejected the plaintiff's claim for damages for breach of contract, holding that because the plaintiff must have realized and in fact knew that the defendant's offer was a mistake, the plaintiff should not be permitted to enforce the ostensible contract. The plaintiff's knowledge of the mistake, though not admitted, was inferred from the prior verbal negotiations and written letters during which prices had always been discussed per piece. Proof of actual knowledge of the mistake in the terms of the offer is unnecessary. It suffices to show that the mistake in the terms 'would have been obvious to a reasonable person in the light of the surrounding circumstances',[20] or that it was one which the promisee 'could reasonably have known at the time when he accepted it'.[21] This

---

18   SI 1994/3159.

19   [1939] 3 All ER 566.

20   Thompson J, *McMaster University v Wilchar Construction Ltd* (1971) 22 DLR (3d) 9, (aff'd (1973) 69 DLR (3d) 400).

21   Slade LJ, *Centrovincial Estates plc v Merchant Investors Assurance Co Ltd* [1983] Com LR 158, CA. Decisions in cases involving applications for rectification appear to require actual knowledge of the mistake: *Thomas Bates & Son Ltd v Wyndham's*

actual or constructive knowledge of the mistake in the terms of the offer prevents the plaintiff from 'snapping it up'.

What is the legal effect of the finding that an offer has been snapped up? The remedy in *Hartog v Colin & Shields* was merely a rejection of the promisee's action to enforce the apparent contract. When the issue was raised in *Smith v Hughes*, the case concerning the purchase of new oats, the court merely concluded that the seller would not be able to enforce the contract if he knew that the buyer was purchasing under a mistake that the seller had warranted the oats to be old. This remedy appears to imply that no contract had been formed at all, a conclusion which might flow from a fidelity to the idea of consent resting on the actual intentions of the parties. But the remedy is also consistent with the possibility that a contract existed on the terms which the promisor intended and of which the promisee was aware.

Confusing or Ambiguous Offers

A second type of case which apparently qualifies the objective test of the terms of the contract concerns confusing and ambiguous offers. Where an offer is susceptible to different interpretations, and the parties choose different interpretations, which version of the meaning of the terms should govern the case? Where the confusion results from the negligence of one party, then the courts will refuse to enforce the contract according to that party's interpretation. In *Scriven Bros & Co v Hindley & Co*,[22] an auctioneer, acting for the plaintiff, put up for sale lots of hemp and tow, the latter being a less valuable commodity. The defendant bid for one lot, believing it contained hemp, whereas in fact it was tow, offering a high price so his bid was accepted. The reason for the defendant's mistake was that the shipping marks on the lots were all the same, which witnesses explained never happened for different commodities from the same ship. The auctioneer had failed to alert bidders to this unusual circumstance, which had contributed to the defendant's mistake. When sued for the price of the goods, the defendant sought to extricate himself from the apparent contract concluded at the auction. His first argument, that the auctioneer had 'snapped up' the offer failed, for the jury found that the auctioneer did not think that the defendant had made a mistake about the terms of the contract, but merely a mistake about the value of tow. But a second line of defence succeeded. The court decided that the plaintiff could not enforce the contract when his own negligence, or that of his agents, caused, or contributed to cause, the mistake. Thus the auctioneer's failure to alert the defendant to the confusing shipping marks prevented the enforcement of the contract.

Similarly, a court will not enforce a contract which has ambiguous terms at the request of the party who put forward those terms, if the

---

(Lingerie) Ltd [1981] 1 WLR 505, [1981] 1 All ER 1077, CA; though probably suspicion of mistake combined with intention to deceive suffice as unconscionable conduct: *Commission for the New Towns v Cooper (GB) Ltd* [1995] 2 All ER 929, CA.

22   [1913] 3 KB 564.

other party reasonably understood the terms to mean something else. In *Raffles v Wichelhaus*,[23] the seller tried to enforce a contract for the sale of cotton to arrive on a ship called *Peerless* from Bombay. Unfortunately, there were two ships coming from Bombay with the same name, and the defendants claimed that they intended the contract to apply to the ship which arrived three months earlier. Because the plaintiff seller had not been specific about which ship was intended, he was unable to enforce the contract. As we have seen, this principle is extended in the context of consumer standard form contracts by Regulation 6 of the Unfair Terms in Consumer Contracts Regulations 1994 to include terms which, though perhaps precise in their legal meaning, are expressed in language which is not plain and intelligible to the consumer.

Although it is clear that carelessness in formulating the offer will prevent enforcement of it by the offeror if it was reasonably understood by the offeree in a different sense, the full legal effect of this misunderstanding remains in doubt. It could be argued in such cases that there never was a coincidence of offer and acceptance, once the terms are viewed according to the actual intentions of the parties, so that the parties never reached agreement on the same terms. This would result in the contract being void, or rather that it never was concluded. The decisions in *Scriven Bros v Hindley* and *Raffles v Wichelhaus* have often been understood to have decided that no contract existed. The effect would be to prevent the other party from enforcing the contract as well. But it is possible to read the cases as merely preventing enforcement by the party who has negligently caused the mistake, with the effect that the contract is preserved but construed against the negligent party in resolving disputes over the content and meaning of the terms.

Unusual and Onerous Terms

A third illustration of an apparent exception to an objective approach to interpretation concerns contracts containing unexpected terms in small print. Assuming that the printed document has become incorporated into the contract and therefore represents all or part of its express terms, the question arises whether unexpected clauses which the promisee did not intend or expect to be included should be part of the terms of the contract.

The courts have created an exception where a condition of a contract is particularly onerous or unusual. Such a term will not form part of the terms of the contract, unless the party seeking to enforce can demonstrate that the condition was fairly brought to the notice of the other party. In *Interfoto Picture Library Ltd v Stiletto Visual Programmes Ltd*,[24] the defendant advertising agency arranged to hire some photographs from the plaintiff library. The pictures arrived with a delivery note containing the standard terms of hire. It included a term under which the defendants

---

23   (1864) 2 H & C 906, 159 ER 375, Exch.
24   [1989] QB 433, [1988] 1 All ER 348, CA.

were bound to pay a set fee per day per picture hired after the agreed period of hire was over. The defendants did not read the conditions and forgot to return the pictures until they were two weeks overdue. On the basis of the condition, the plaintiff sued for the holding charge which they calculated at £3,783. Although the Court of Appeal found that the delivery note was incorporated as the terms of the contract, it declined to enforce the holding charge on the ground that the plaintiff had not taken all the steps reasonably necessary to draw the condition to the defendant's attention. This approach to onerous conditions apparently qualifies the normal objective test for interpretation, for it permits one party's reasonable expectations to override the express and ostensible terms of the contract unless reasonable steps were taken to disabuse him of that expectation.

It is unclear whether this qualification applies to contracts which have been signed. There is old authority from Scrutton LJ in *L'Estrange v Graucob*[25] to the effect that:

> When a document containing contractual terms is signed, then, in the absence of fraud, or, I will add, misrepresentation, the party signing it is bound, and it is wholly immaterial whether he has read the document or not.

This statement suggests that a signature functions to make the written document a conclusive proof of the content of the contract. But such a principle contradicts the idea that reasonable steps should be taken to draw unusual and onerous terms to the attention of the promisee. Perhaps the two doctrines can be reconciled by limiting the effect of a signature to the ascription of contractual responsibility, rather than to determining the content of the contract as well.

Exceptions to the Objective Approach?

The types of case described above pose a difficulty for the objective approach to interpretation. They display an apparent disposition on the part of the court to permit the actual intention of a party to override the ostensible agreement, at least to the extent of declining to enforce the agreement against him. Do these doctrines reveal exceptions to the objective approach, or even reveal that the objective approach is not the underlying method of interpretation?

If the illustrations are regarded as exceptional instances when actual or subjective intent is permitted to determine the content of the contract, the crucial question then becomes to know how to define the exceptions, which in turn depends on their justification. It is, of course, possible to provide a list of the exceptions, such as 'snapping up', 'confusing offers', and so forth. But this approach cannot tell us whether the list is complete without explaining the justification for the exceptions. The inadequacy of this analysis becomes plain when the textbooks offer lists of exceptions

25 [1934] 2 KB 394, DC.

that differ from one another both in the number and the character of the categories of exception.[26]

The justification proffered for the exceptions is typically grounded in mistake.[27] It is suggested that the mistake negatives the intent to agree to the objectively established terms. The problem with this explanation is that it cannot distinguish between those mistakes which count from those which do not. For example, why did the mistake about the sale of the public house and the inclusion of the field not count, whereas the mistake about hemp and tow defeated the claim for breach of contract? The justification based upon mistake is lacking a crucial ingredient which would explain why some mistakes are effective whereas others are not. The answer plainly lies in the conduct of the parties, that is whether they have acted reasonably and in good faith, but the theory of mistake provides no criteria for determining when conduct should deprive a party from insisting upon the objectively interpreted agreement.

The underlying error of these explanations is to attempt to resuscitate the vestigial attachment to an explanation of the content of contracts by reference to the intention of the parties. It is better to recognize that the objective approach to interpretation always rejected actual intent as the key to determining the meaning of the terms of a contract. But the objective approach proves insufficient to handle all disputes about the content of contracts.

The Duty to Negotiate with Care

The objective approach to interpretation tackles certain types of deceptive practices, such as making a vague promise which could be understood in different ways, as in the earlier example of the sale of a car. But the objective approach needs to be supplemented by aspects of the duty to negotiate with care in order to prevent one party from taking advantage of a misunderstanding which it has induced. On this analysis, the justification for any departure from the objective approach depends upon a breach of a duty to negotiate with care, for which the remedy is to deprive the guilty party of the right to enforce the contract according to the objective approach to interpretation.

Under the objective approach to interpretation, the test is what a reasonable promisee understands to be the terms of the promise. The content of the contract thus turns on what obligations each party reasonably supposed the other had undertaken. The cases on 'snapping up' should be regarded as an application of the objective approach. For example, in *Hartog v Colin and Shields*, the buyer of the hare skins could

---

26 For example, G Treitel, *The Law of Contract* (London, 9th edn, 1995), has three categories of 'operative mistakes', at p 283; E McKendrick, *Contract Law* (London, 1990) has two, plus one unlikely one (at p 14), plus a few more later on (at p 46); P Atiyah, *An Introduction to the Law of Contract* (Oxford, 5th edn, 1995) has one, at p 84.

27 Sometimes the argument is expressed in terms of 'offer and acceptance', though this is unsatisfactory because it suggests that no contract has been made at all.

not reasonably suppose that they were offered per pound in the light of the previous negotiations, so he could not enforce that version of the contract. The difficulty which the objective approach encounters is that if each promise is interpreted objectively from the point of view of the reasonable promisee, we may discover that the parties have been at cross-purposes all along. In *Scriven Bros v Hindley*, the bidder at the auction acted reasonably in believing that the content of the lot (the promise) was hemp rather than tow, yet the auctioneer reasonably believed that he had received a high offer to buy tow. Similarly, the reasonable beliefs of the parties in *Interfoto Picture Library Ltd v Stiletto Visual Programmes Ltd* were almost certainly at cross-purposes. If we allow both parties to rely upon their reasonable beliefs as to the content of the other's promise, then we end up with no agreed terms at all. Instead of declaring that they have failed to reach an agreement, however, the courts investigate the relative fault of the parties in order to determine who is entitled to insist upon their version of the meaning of the contract.

A party to a contract cannot rely upon the objectively interpreted terms, if he has violated the duty to negotiate with care. As we saw in Chapter 10, this duty comprises a set of standards of behaviour which proscribe sharp practice and misleading sales talk during the bargaining process. Since human imagination constantly expands the range of tricks and manoeuvres, no simple rule can encompass the relevant legal regulations. Instead, the general duty to negotiate with care constantly finds new applications and so the precise content of the duty cannot be pinned down. It requires contracting parties to act fairly and reasonably towards each other, but the precise scope of the duty depends upon the kind of abuse which the law seeks to prevent. Once the legal analysis is restated as the application of the set of public standards comprising the duty to negotiate with care, we are not driven to the conclusion that since the parties were at cross-purposes there was no agreement and therefore no contract. The appropriate remedy becomes one to rectify the breach of duty to negotiate with care, which may include a refusal to enforce the contract, the deletion of particular terms, the rectification of a written document, or an award of damages for breach of the duty to negotiate with care. An alternative remedy often makes even better sense: namely to permit the innocent party to enforce a contract on the terms which he supposed constituted the contract.

Where one party misrepresents the content of the agreement, then the other may rely upon that representation to modify the content of the obligations. For example, in *Curtis v Chemical Cleaning and Dyeing Co*,[28] the plaintiff took her wedding dress to the defendant's shop to be cleaned. She was required to sign a contract, which, she was told by an assistant, disclaimed liability for certain specified risks to the beads and sequins which adorned the dress. In fact, the contract contained a clause which exempted the defendant from any damage to the dress whatsoever. The

28   [1951] 1 KB 805, [1951] 1 All ER 631, CA.

plaintiff subsequently sued for damage to her dress comprising a stain of uncertain origin. The English Court of Appeal held that the defendant could not rely upon the full width of the exemption clause on account of the misrepresentation of their employee and permitted the plaintiff's claim for damages. This decision may be explained by stating that, although the ostensible agreement was the signed contract, the defendant could not rely upon the exclusion clause because it broke the duty to negotiate with care by giving misleading information about the content of the terms.

Short of an actual misrepresentation, a party may break the duty to negotiate with care by inducing a mistake as to the consequences of a transaction by representing the terms in a confusing or ambiguous fashion. This breach of duty explains why the seller at the auction in *Scriven Bros & Co v Hindley & Co*, and the seller of cotton off the ship *Peerless* in *Raffles v Wichelhaus*, were unable to enforce the ostensible agreement. The duty to negotiate with care requires that the offeror presents the terms of his offer in a manner which will be properly understood and which avoids ambiguity. The duty can also be expressed as one to refrain from unconscionable conduct, which might include distracting the other party from noting new adverse provisions.[29]

The common law imposes a duty upon the offeror to take reasonable steps to acquaint the offeree with all the terms of the contract, especially those which are unusual or oppressive, as in *Interfoto Picture Library Ltd v Stiletto Visual Programmes Ltd*. This principle has a long ancestry, but the duty to negotiate with care has increased the steps necessary to give reasonable notice of the terms in those cases where the offeree is a consumer or for some other reason is unlikely to be familiar with the normal terms of the trade. For consumer standard form contracts, the principle has been modified by the Unfair Terms in Consumer Contracts Regulations, which suggest that unless the consumer has a real opportunity to become acquainted with the terms of the contract prior to its formation then the terms will be unenforceable against the consumer.[30] An alternative mode for expressing this duty embodied in the American Restatement (Second) of Contracts, section 211(3), disallows any term where the profferor has reason to believe that the other party would not agree to the term if he became aware of it. The obvious disadvantage of this technique for imposing a duty to take reasonable steps to communicate the terms lies in cases where an entire trade or profession employs similar harsh terms so that the profferor has no reason to believe that the other party would reject the contract and seek an alternative. This view of American law suffers from the further disadvantage that it tries to present this aspect of the duty to negotiate with care as merely an interpretative technique, which always runs the risk of permitting skillful draftsmen to eviscerate the public duty by comprehensive standard forms. In practice,

---

29   *Commission for the New Towns v Cooper (GB) Ltd* [1995] 2 All ER 929, CA.
30   1994, SI 1994/3159, Sch 3, para 1(i).

however, the American courts seem to follow closely the approach of the English.[31]

The duty to negotiate with care also places obligations on the offeree. He or she is not permitted to snap up offers which are obviously presented with mistaken terms. This analysis explains why the test does not require actual knowledge of the mistake. The duty to negotiate with care can also encompass those cases such as *Hartog v Colin and Shields*, where it is reasonable to infer that a mistake has been made. In other instances, such as the facts of *Scriven Bros v Hindley* where the terms of an offer are less surprising, only actual knowledge of the mistake would be sufficient to support a finding of a breach of the duty to bargain with care.

Finally, a duty to negotiate with care explains the existence of those cases in which it is suggested that, where one party knows that the other's acceptance of the ostensible terms of the contract is the result of a mistake as to their content, then the ostensible contract cannot be enforced by the party aware of the other's mistake. The duty to negotiate with care extends to this case, because it would be wrong to permit the offeror to take advantage of the objective test when he knows that the other party does not intend to make a contract on those terms. But this breach of the duty to negotiate with care does not necessarily mean that the mistaken party cannot enforce the contract on the terms which he intended. Since the mistaken party has not broken the duty to negotiate with care, in the absence of negligence, it should be possible for the mistaken party to obtain some remedy, if not rectification, at least to cover any loss arising from the breach of duty.

4. Implied Terms

As well as the express terms of a contract, the primary obligations undertaken will be supplemented by terms implied into the contract by the courts. This power to imply terms into contracts is exercised cautiously, for it threatens to interfere with the freedom of the parties to select their own contractual obligations. This caution results in two governing principles for the implication of terms into contracts.

Firstly, terms will not be implied which contradict the express agreement of the parties. This principle reflects the priority attached to the choice of the parties in determining the content of their contractual obligations. But disputes may arise whether or not a proposed implied term contradicts an express term of the contract. In *Johnstone v Bloomsbury Health Authority*,[32] the contract of employment of a junior hospital doctor provided that the employer could require the doctor to work up to eighty hours per week. The doctor contended that this power

---

31   *Weisz v Parke-Benet Galleries, Inc* 67 Misc 2d 1077, 325 NYS 2d 576 (1971).
32   [1992] QB 333, [1991] 2 All ER 293, CA.

was subject to an implied term which limited the exercise of the power for the sake of the health and safety of the doctor and his patients. Although no such limitation was mentioned in the express terms of the contract, the Court of Appeal accepted that the implied term was part of the contract. The court avoided the apparent contradiction by stating that the discretionary power to determine hours of work did not expressly state that it was without any limitation, so that the implied term did not formally contradict the employer's contractual rights.

Secondly, the grounds on which the courts will imply terms into contracts have been circumscribed within three principal categories. The purpose of this limitation of the acceptable grounds for the implication of terms is to avoid the use of a more general power to imply terms into contracts which the courts regard as fair and reasonable, for this power might contradict too directly the freedom of the parties to choose the content of the contract. But in truth the three accepted grounds for implication of terms confer ample discretion upon the courts to shape the terms of contracts, which can be exercised in a way such that the terms of a contract reflect considerations of fairness and reasonableness. The three grounds for the implication of terms will be considered in turn before a concluding examination of the justification for the practice of implying terms into contracts.

(1) Unexpressed Intentions

The first ground for the implication of terms into contracts is that the term represents the unexpressed joint intention of the parties. When articulating the terms of a contract, whether it is concluded orally or in writing, the parties may not state fully all aspects of their agreement. This failure may have a number of causes. The term may be so obvious and essential to the agreement that it was never stated explicitly. Alternatively, the term may be omitted because of shortage of time and the expense of reciting every detail of the proposed agreement. If a court is persuaded that a proposed term does represent the unexpressed joint intention of the parties, then it will imply it as a term of the contract:

> Prima facie that which in any contract is left to be implied and need not be expressed is something so obvious that it goes without saying; so that, if, while the parties were making their bargain, an officious bystander were to suggest some express provision for it in their agreement, they would testily suppress him with a common 'Oh, of course!'.[33]

This colourful 'officious bystander' test leaves unresolved the question of how the courts should infer the intent of the parties. Given that the 'officious bystander' has not in fact intervened, the courts must resort to other evidence from which to infer the intent of the parties. One possibility will comprise the claim that the words used by the parties included, as

33   Mackinnon LJ, *Shirlaw v Southern Foundries (1926) Ltd* [1939] 2 KB 206, [1939] 2 All ER 113, CA.

part of their meaning, the implied term in question. In a contract for the sale of a boat, for example, the use of the word boat by the parties might be held to imply that the object in question floats upon water, for the ordinary usage of the word boat usually refers to something capable of floating. But a more significant source of evidence of intent employed by the courts involves references to the 'business efficacy' of the contract.[34]

By the term 'business efficacy' the courts mean to refer to the commercial purpose of the transaction. They examine the objectives of the parties in entering the transaction, and infer their intent about the terms of the contract in the light of those supposed objectives. The courts will then imply terms which give effect to those objectives, or at least imply terms so that those objectives are not frustrated. In a contract for the sale of a door lock, for instance, a court could easily imply a term to the effect that the seller will also supply a key, for without a key the lock would not serve the purchaser's objective in entering the transaction. This process of inferring the intent of the parties from the supposed business objectives of the parties is not without difficulty, for the parties may be in dispute about the nature of the business objective.

Indeed, we must suspect that if the parties were asked by the officious bystander about a particular provision, in most instances they would not be in agreement at all due to their differing commercial interests. Implied terms are often presented as default rules, that is rules which the parties would agree were the costs of negotiation low or absent.[35] Yet in all probability the parties have not failed to reach agreement on this point because of shortage of time and resources, but have simply not wished to enter into such detailed specification for fear of failure to reach agreement.[36] The attempt to resolve this problem by means of a reification of the purpose of the contract in the business efficacy test only serves to obscure the problem. If the commercial motives of the parties for entering into the contract diverge, as they usually will outside the realm of symbiotic contracts such as partnerships and joint ventures, then the performance of the contract without the implied term might easily satisfy the commercial objective of one party whilst simultaneously frustrating the objective of the other. Although these tests have been hallowed by constant judicial use for over a century, we must doubt whether they make any sense at all.

(2) Importation of General Legal Obligations
The second ground for the implication of terms into contracts involves the application of general civil obligations arising under the law of tort

---

34 The source of this criterion is the judgment of Bowen LJ in *The Moorcock* (1889) 14 PD 64, CA.
35 Goetz and Scott, 'The Limits of Expanded Choice: An Analysis of the Interactions Between Express and Implied Terms' (1985) 73 *California Law Review* 261; Ayres and Gertner, 'Filling Gaps in Incomplete Contracts: An Economic Theory of Default Rules' (1989) 99 *Yale Law Journal* 87.

and unjust enrichment to the obligations of the contracting parties. These obligations could be handled as distinct legal duties arising by operation of law outside the contract. But it has become customary to regard them as implied terms of the contract where the parties have entered into a contractual relation. This incorporation of general legal obligations serves the purpose of ensuring the priority or hierarchy of the express contractual obligations over the residual legal obligations, for under the first principle governing implied terms, they must always give way to contrary express terms.

Under the law of tort the parties to a contract will owe each other a duty of care in various respects. In a contract for services, for example, there is a duty to use reasonable care in the performance of the service. This duty arises even in the absence of a contract for the service under the law of tort, but in the case of contractual services the duty is conceived as an implied term to use reasonable care in the performance of the contractual undertaking. This particular duty has been given statutory force under section 13 of the Supply of Goods and Services Act 1982, which provides that,

> In a contract for the supply of a service where the supplier is acting in the course of a business, there is an implied term that the supplier will carry out the service with reasonable care and skill.

Although the precise content of this duty must depend upon the normal complex balancing of the degree of risk against the cost of precautions applicable to the standard of care in tort,[37] it should normally require conformity to any applicable regulations governing safety standards and practices.[38]

Under the law of unjust enrichment or restitution, one person who has unofficiously conferred a benefit upon another may usually demand compensation for the goods or services provided. In the context of a contractual agreement, this restitutionary duty becomes an implied term to make a reasonable payment for goods or services if no price has been expressly agreed. Again this implied term based upon a restitutionary duty has received statutory backing.[39]

(3) Model Contracts

The third ground for the implication of terms is both more controversial and uncertain in its scope. Here the courts take notice of the fact that many types of contracts have become routine and commonplace. These standard types of transaction, such as contracts of sale, employment, and

---

36   Johnston, 'Strategic Bargaining and the Economic Theory of Contract Default Rules' (1990) 100 *Yale Law Journal* 615.
37   *Bolton v Stone* [1951] AC 850, [1951] 1 All ER 1078, HL; *Haley v London Electricity Board* [1965] AC 778, [1964] 3 All ER 185, HL.
38   *Wilson v Best Travel Ltd* [1993] 1 All ER 353, QB.
39   Sale of Goods Act 1979, s 8; Supply of Goods and Services Act 1982, s 15.

tenancy, normally share many of the same terms. In the absence of a full expression of these terms by the parties, the courts will imply into the contract the standard incidents of such a transaction. These implied terms cannot be justified on either of the previous two grounds, for they are neither essential to the business purpose of the transaction nor a normal obligation arising under the general law of civil obligations. For example, the contract of sale contains an implied term that the goods sold are of satisfactory quality and fit for their normal use, an implication now required by statute.[40] That the goods should satisfy this quality standard is neither essential to the efficacy of a transaction designed to transfer ownership of goods, nor required by the ordinary law of tort and restitution.

This broader power to imply terms involves the court in determining the standard incidents or duties of the respective parties of particular types of contract. The courts select these terms in the light of practical experience, views about the fair allocation of risks between the parties, and customary practices in the trade or business. These implied terms complete the fabric of the contract in the absence of express agreement. This enhances the utility and efficiency of contracts as an economic mechanism, for it saves the parties from having to spend time discussing and agreeing the details of the transaction, provided that it fits into a standard pattern of contractual relation.

A typical example of the way the courts shape the content of contractual relations through the use of implied terms is provided by the contract of employment. Since these contracts were in the past often concluded informally with a brief oral description of the nature of the job and the wages paid, the courts were often called upon to fill out the terms of the agreement. Under these implied terms an employee agrees impliedly to refrain from misconduct, to avoid neglect of the business, to eschew intemperance and insobriety, and to perform the work honestly, obediently, with due diligence, and in a manner loyal to the employer's interests.[41] In recent years the courts have developed commensurate duties upon employers to be implied as terms in contracts, such as the duty not to treat employees arbitrarily, capriciously, or inequitably, to take reasonable care to ensure the safety of employees, and to refrain from acting in a way calculated to destroy mutual trust and confidence.[42] This list of implied terms in the contract of employment is far from complete, but it suffices to illustrate how through the idea of model contracts the courts develop a complete set of terms for a typical contract. These terms will apply to any transaction which the court regards as fitting into a type of employment relation, and in the absence of express terms to the contrary will provide the applicable terms of the contract.

This broader power to imply terms is confined in two ways. In the first place, the transaction has to approximate to a standard type of

---

40 Sale of Goods Act 1979, s 14.
41 *Lister v Romford Ice and Cold Storage Co Ltd* [1957] AC 555, HL.
42 *Woods v W M Car Services (Peterborough) Ltd* [1982] ICR 693, CA; *Lewis v Motorworld Garages Ltd* [1986] ICR 157, CA.

contract. If on the contrary the court is confronted with a unique type of contractual relation, one which is not a matter of settled legal practice, then the courts will confine their interventions to the first and second grounds for the implication of terms.[43] It is important to notice, however, that standard types of transactions need not be commonplace. In commercial relations there may be a settled way of doing business, and, although few people may be involved in the trade, the court will imply the customary terms of the trade into this type of contract. Secondly, the use of the power will be limited to terms which would be generally applicable to this standard type of transaction. A court will not exercise the power to introduce terms which could only apply to a particular instance of this type of contractual relation. In other words, the nature of the terms which a court will imply are only those of general application to the class of contracts, and the power will not be exercised to introduce detailed particularistic terms.[44] In a sale of goods, for example, the general term requiring the goods to be of satisfactory quality is permissible, but the courts would not introduce an implied term which could only apply to a particular type of goods, such as a term that a car should use fuel efficiently.

It should be noted that all three grounds for the implication of terms can operate simultaneously and cumulatively in a particular instance. In *Liverpool City Council v Irwin*,[45] the Council owned a tower block of flats which were let to the tenants. The standard form contract contained extensive provisions regarding the obligations of tenants, but said little about the landlord's obligations. The tenants refused to pay rent by way of a protest against the dilapidation of the premises, and in particular about the failure of the landlord to maintain the common parts of the block of flats, such as the lifts, staircases, and corridors. In the landlord's action for possession resulting from the failure to pay rent, the question was raised whether the landlord was in breach of an implied term of the contract for failure to maintain the common parts of the premises.

What terms could be implied into this transaction? Under the first ground for implication, the House of Lords implied an easement under which the tenants could use the common parts for access, for without such a right of access the lease of a flat would be futile. The landlord itself conceded that under the second ground for implication of terms, it was under the duty imposed on all occupiers of the premises to take reasonable care with regard to the safety of persons entering the premises. The crucial point of the case, however, fell under the third ground for the implication of terms. The court found that in such leases for buildings with multiple occupation, it was an implied term that the landlord owed a duty to take reasonable care to keep in reasonable repair and useability the common parts of the premises. This provision placed the cost of maintenance on

43   *Shell UK Ltd v Lostock Garage Ltd* [1976] 1 WLR 1187, [1977] 1 All ER 481, CA.
44   *Reid v Rush & Tompkins plc* [1990] 1 WLR 212, [1989] 3 All ER 228, CA.
45   [1977] AC 239, [1976] 2 All ER 39, HL.

the landlord, subject to any contrary term in the contract. On the facts of the case, however, the House of Lords concluded that the landlord was not in breach of this obligation.

Notice that this implied term could not be justified on either of the two other grounds for the implication of terms. It could not satisfy the business efficacy test, for, although it was necessary for either landlord or tenant to maintain the common parts in reasonable repair, it could not be said that it was necessary for this duty to fall on the landlord. Similarly, the duty of care in tort could only extend to items which imperilled the safety of the occupants, and would not include such items as keeping the lifts in working order. The implication of the term into the lease in this case therefore depended upon the reasoning that in this class of contract the model should place the cost of reasonable repairs on the landlord. The court no doubt preferred this solution because this seemed to be the most practical and efficient result, since it would be difficult and expensive for the tenants to organize themselves into an effective management company for the premises.

(4) Justifications for Implied T erms

How can we explain and justify the above use of implied terms to supplement contractual obligations? In some instances it is apparent that the reference to the joint intention of the parties, as evidenced by the need to give business efficacy to their transaction, supports the implication of terms on grounds which merely complement the traditional justification of contractual obligations based upon the will of the parties. It is true that the will of the parties was never expressed, but the evidence supporting the claim that the term represents a presupposition or necessary implication of the words used can be so overwhelming that few could doubt that the term represents their original intention. But it is clear that the use of implied terms extends beyond any sort of justification of the type that the term merely states expressly what was silently understood by the parties.

Economic analysis of law suggests a good reason why the courts should provide a set of default rules to govern contractual relations in the absence of express terms. Default rules save transaction costs by permitting the parties to avoid the costs of negotiating every detail of their arrangement every time they make a contract, because they know that the courts will fill in the gaps in the usual way. This makes good sense, but it is far from clear that participants in the market deliberately avail themselves of this opportunity to save transactions costs. On the contrary, the proliferation of the standard form contract suggests that any party with sufficient resources is likely to devise a standard set of express terms to suit his or her purposes exactly. The cases we have discussed so far concerning implied terms, such as *Johnstone v Bloomsbury Health Authority*,[46] and

---

46 [1992] QB 333, [1991] 2 All ER 293, CA.

Liverpool City Council v Irwin,[47] comprise instances where the claim that an implied term exists is used to combat the one-sided standard form contract of the other party.

Nor does the economic analysis suggest a satisfactory account of the grounds for the selection of terms by the courts. Under the efficiency analysis, the court should select those implied terms to which the parties would have agreed but for the presence of transaction costs. Although this criterion makes sense for terms which give a contract business efficacy, it is far from clear that it provides an intelligible guide in other cases. Consider the bargaining situation in *Liverpool City Council v Irwin*. The council was presumably reluctant to agree to an obligation to maintain the common premises, so it would have held out against such an obligation, and, depending upon the local forces of supply and demand for tower block local authority housing, it might or might not have been successful. But even if it had agreed to the obligation, it could have insisted upon an increased rent to cover those costs, so to imply a term requiring a maintenance obligation without adjusting the rent produces a contract to which the parties never would have agreed.

Nor does this economic analysis seem to correspond to the reasons ventured by the courts for the selection of implied terms. What seems to be at the heart of the model reasoning surrounding the implication of terms is the courts' endeavour to structure contracts so that they incorporate a fair and practical allocation of risks. The court imposed the duty to maintain the premises upon Liverpool City Council because this was clearly the most practical and efficient means of achieving the result. In the context of the employment relation, the recent introduction of implied terms which impose obligations upon employers surely reflects changing views about the fair treatment of employees and the risk of losing a job. Similarly, the duty imposed upon professional sellers of goods to ensure that they are of satisfactory quality cannot be justified as the term which would have been agreed in the absence of transaction costs, for sellers would almost certainly seek to avoid such liability for latent defects. The reason for this allocation of risk is surely that it fits both the purpose of consumer protection and it places the risk of defects on the person in a better position to avoid the advent of such risks occurring.

The notion of a default rule is therefore a misleading description of the use of implied terms. Through the implication of terms the courts can achieve what they regard as a fair and practical allocation of risks between the contracting parties, a view which may alter over time as illustrated by the contract of employment. In this process the courts can seek to equalize the obligations of the parties, even in the teeth of express terms of standard form contracts, and so pursue ideas of fairness. The justification for implied terms therefore rests ultimately not on the intentions of the parties but rather the court's view of the reasonable expectations of the parties to the transaction.

47   [1977] AC 239, [1976] 2 All ER 39, HL.

12

Mandatory Obligations

1. The Social Dimension of Markets

The virtue and danger of markets lies in their delegation of power to individuals. The virtue consists in the capacity of individuals to use markets to make choices which contribute to their chosen way of life. Through contracts of employment, sale, hire and so forth, individuals may realize many aspects of a way of life which has meaning for them. The availability of such choices is ensured by a free market in goods and services. The market therefore augments the autonomy of individuals and compares favourably in this respect with the selection of goals for life by political authorities. But this virtue of markets carries with it the danger of subversion of important social goals.

Consider, for example, the problem of the sale of dangerous and defective products to consumers. Under a free market regime such sales would be permitted, with the consumer left to bargain for warranties of quality and compensation for injuries. Under the classical law the seller of such goods would be equally free to insist upon terms in the contract which prevented any liability from arising. Important social policies lead the modern law to reject this type of market. We seek to eliminate dangerous and defective products from markets in order to reduce injuries to consumers. Furthermore, in the event of injuries occurring, we seek to ensure that the consumer receives adequate compensation. More fundamentally, legal guarantees are calculated to augment the confidence of consumers that market transactions will serve to realise their expectations and goals; they increase trust in the market mechanism for the production and distribution of goods and services. These social policies can only be achieved by regulation of the market in ways designed to compel traders to sell only safe and reliable products, and to impose sanctions if they fail to do so. In effect, the modern law imposes a mandatory obligation on businesses to supply safe products free from defects to consumers.

From an economic perspective, these social policies can be described as responses to 'market failures' and a concern for 'externalities'.[1] The market failure problem with dangerous and defective goods arises because the consumer lacks the expertise to determine by inspection whether or not the goods conform to a satisfactory quality. The risk then arises that traders lack an incentive to supply good quality products, for the consumer cannot easily distinguish those products and is therefore likely to select on the basis of price.[2] The concern for externalities consists in the observation that the incentives in individual transactions may not take into account the costs which may be imposed on others. For example, the cost of accidents arising from dangerous products may be borne by others through the insurance system or health care system, so that neither the trader nor the individual consumer will be influenced by those costs when entering particular market transactions. One way to address both market failure and externalities is to impose a compulsory obligation on the trader to supply goods of satisfactory quality. This obligation reduces the trader's incentive to skimp on quality, and forces the trader to include in the price of the goods an allowance to pay for insurance against the risk of accidents.

A wide range of social policies might justify the imposition of compulsory obligations. The protection of consumers' health and safety and their economic interests, which is regarded as a general goal of European Community law,[3] explains the imposition of compulsory obligations in many types of contract, from sales and services, to consumer credit agreements and package holidays. The protection of the environment, the cost of which is frequently treated as an externality, can occasionally be the justification for compulsory obligations, as in the requirement that new cars should use lead-free petrol. A concern for the rights of citizens can lead to compulsory obligations against discrimination in contracts, such as the requirement for an equality clause in every contract of employment which ensures that women receive equal pay for work of equal value. Similarly, a concern to redress the element of subordination inherent in every employment relation leads to the introduction of an inalienable right not to be unfairly dismissed.[4]

As well as these measures designed to protect particular interest groups or to reduce harmful side effects of markets, mandatory obligations may serve to enhance the reliability and calculability of the market itself. Here the argument for a compulsory obligation suggests that under certain conditions it will be advantageous for all parties to eliminate a free market and choice over terms in favour of a non-negotiable standard package with a recognized meaning. These conditions may arise when the cost of negotiating terms deters entry into contracts, or when the uncertainty about the meaning of negotiated terms discourages the formation of

---

1   MJ Trebilcock, *The Limits of Freedom of Contract*, (Cambridge, Mass, 1993).
2   Ackerlof, The Market for "Lemons": Qualitative Uncertainty and the Market Mechanism' (1970) 84 *Quarterly Journal of Economics* 488.
3   Council declaration, OJ C 92 of 25 April 1975, 1; Reich, 'Protection of Consumers' Economic Interests by the EC' (1992) 14 *Sydney Law Review* 23.
4   Employment Rights Act 1996, s 94.

agreements. These conditions may be satisfied, for example, in cross-border trade, where the consumer or small business may be reluctant to make purchases under contracts whose meaning and implications may be unclear. Here a solution may be to remove the freedom to select the terms in favour of a set of compulsory standard obligations. This argument has been used, for example, to justify the development of common rules for consumer contracts in the European Community.[5]

The common theme behind these mandatory obligations consists of a concern to promote a social policy, either in the form of the protection of a group as a class such as consumers, or to protect a social institution such as the market. This theme is distinguishable from a concern about the unfairness of the terms of a particular contract, which might also justify an interference with freedom of contract. In the case of defective and dangerous products, for instance, though it may be the case that a consumer who has purchased an unsafe product has made a poor bargain, the content of the contract would be objectionable no matter how low the price paid by the consumer might have been. Nor do I think that these compulsory obligations are necessarily to tied to any redistributive aims.[6] If a seller of goods is compelled to give a warranty as to the quality of the goods, then the seller is likely to charge a higher price, so there may be no net benefit to consumers. There may be distributional effects if the costs of the social policy cannot be redistributed through the market, but this is not the principal objective of the imposition of mandatory obligations. Interventions on the ground of fairness and for redistributional purposes will be considered in the next chapter.

2. The Use of Compulsory Obligations

Although mandatory obligations may achieve the goals which they are designed to serve, there is a danger that such a blunt interference with the operation of a competitive market will provoke deleterious side-effects. Increased obligations on businesses selling to consumers will presumably drive up the price of the products, which may have the effect of excluding some consumers from the market altogether. If landlords fall under a duty to provide rented accommodation of a minimum standard of 'habitability', then they may opt to increase rents or invest in some other project, with the consequence of a shortage of rented accommodation and a corresponding price increase. Similarly, if workers are awarded an inalienable right not to be unfairly dismissed, then they lose the chance to negotiate with an employer for a higher wage without job security.

---

5   Preamble to the Directive on Unfair Terms in Consumer Contracts, 93/13/EEC, 5 April 1993, OJ L 95/29, 21/4/93; Collins, 'Good Faith in European Contract Law' (1994) 14 *Oxford Journal of Legal Studies* 229.

6   Kennedy, 'Distributive and Paternalist Motives in Contract and Tort Law, with Special Reference to Compulsory Terms and Unequal Bargaining Power' (1982) 41 *Maryland Law Review* 563.

These arguments share the pattern that from an economic perspective the social goods obtained by compulsory obligations can only be obtained at a price, and that the market will adjust prices to a new equilibrium which may not be in the best interests of those groups for whom the protection was initially introduced.

Of course, the market may not work perfectly due to inelasticities of supply and demand, so that the deleterious consequences may not occur. The market for consumer products may prove so competitive that businesses cannot increase prices; landlords may be unable to sell property and reinvest their capital elsewhere; the employer may not be prepared to increase wage costs even to obtain numerical flexibility of labour. Nevertheless, the simple economic model suggests the advisability of caution before imposing compulsory obligations.

This concern leads to a preference in economic analysis of contract law for less interventionist measures. The preferred remedy for market failure, for example, is to increase the information available, so that the purchaser can make an informed choice. On this view there should be no obligation to supply safe products free from defects, but simply a duty to inform the purchaser of the exact details of the product, faults and all. Similarly, the landlord should point out the leaking roof and the broken boiler, draw the prospective tenant's attention to the clause in the contract which absolves the landlord from any duty to make repairs, and then let the tenant bargain for the lowest rent obtainable. This remedy for market failure can never be complete, of course, for the supply of vast amounts of detailed information creates the problem of processing and evaluating this information. Methods for remedying market failure by controlling bargaining practices were considered in the context of the control over coercion and the duty to negotiate with care in Chapters 8 and 10. These methods can certainly be employed to help to achieve the social goals considered in this chapter, but mandatory obligations comprise a distinctive and more effective technique.

As an alternative to compulsory terms or information requirements, the economic perspective suggests that the law should merely provide a set of 'default rules' or implied terms, which the parties to a contract should be free to exclude. The process of negotiating the exclusion of the implied term should then put the parties on notice of the allocation of risks, thereby averting market failure. The flaw in this argument arises from the fact that the process of negotiation is typically truncated by the provision of a standard form contract, so that the reallocation of risks passes unnoticed. The purchaser of goods is asked to sign a document which excludes the implied terms; the tenant signs a lease which absolves the landlord from any responsibilities in technical legal jargon; and the employee is issued with the standard terms of employment.

Against these economic arguments for resisting compulsory obligations, we should place two considerations. First, in the conception of the social market articulated in Chapter 2, we regarded the market not merely as a source of preference satisfaction, but as an opportunity to augment and contribute to the meaning of a person's life. This leads to the view that the law of contract, in regulating and constituting the market order, should channel market opportunities towards those which possess the potential for a genuine contribution to the construction of meaning. Although this involves some difficult subjective judgments, which run the risk of being labelled a form of authoritarian paternalism,[7] we can point to certain types of transactions which seem unlikely to make any worthwhile contribution. The purchase of a dangerous product which is likely to maim or kill the consumer looks unlikely to satisfy the test of making a contribution to the construction of meaning in a person's life. Similarly, the acquisition of a lease on an uninhabitable dwelling will not except in the most extreme circumstances of necessity make a useful contribution towards the establishment of a home. Finally, employment in circumstances where the employer has an unfettered discretion to dismiss at will for any reason creates a degree of subjugation to arbitrary power which presents such a severe sacrifice of autonomy and dignity for the worker that it is likely to impede any endeavour to find meaning through work.

A second consideration which favours the use of compulsory obligations returns to the problem of externalities. Neither a greater disclosure of information nor the provision of suitable default rules in contracts will tackle the problem of deleterious effects on third parties, for the economic incentive to ignore those interests remains the same. The solution to the problem must lie in regulation by the state, though not necessarily by means of compulsory obligations inserted into contractual relations. In some instances, for example, differential taxation can alter incentives, as in the case of lower taxation on lead-free petrol, with the effect of steering behaviour in directions which respect externalities. Other cases may require more elaborate international regulatory agencies which effectively exclude any scope for the negotiation of terms. Nevertheless, for some problems of externalities, the use of compulsory terms in contracts may prove a simple and effective solution.

What seems to be common to the examples of mandatory obligations arising in contractual relations is, first, a sense that criminal sanctions would be inappropriate to these commercial relations; secondly, a belief that control over bargaining practices would not be sufficient to achieve the social purpose, because of the typical inequality of the bargaining power between the parties; and finally, a belief that the compulsory term would function to achieve the social goal, because private enforcement would suffice.

3. Compulsory Terms

Mandatory obligations remove from the parties to a contract the freedom to choose some of the terms for their transaction. The most straightforward

---

7 Kronman, 'Paternalism and the Law of Contracts' (1983) 92 *Yale Law Journal* 763.

example comprises legislation which determines that every contract of a particular type is deemed to include a particular term, regardless of the express terms of the contract and overriding any contrary terms. Under the Equal Pay Act 1970, section 1, for instance, every contract of employment contains an equality clause under which the employer promises to pay a woman employee equal pay to that paid to men in like work or work of equal value. The same effect can be achieved by granting a statutory right which cannot be excluded or qualified by contrary agreement, as in the case of the right of an employee to claim unfair dismissal against an employer.[8]

Statutes do not always contain express prohibitions against terms of contracts designed to subvert rights which the statutes purport to grant. Courts may infer such prohibitions, however, as a necessary concomitant to the statutory scheme of protection. The issue in *Johnson v Moreton* concerned the collective interest in ensuring long-term investment in farming land, such as mechanization and fertilization of soil. Under the Agricultural Holdings Act 1948 Parliament had sought to protect the security of tenure of tenant farmers, so that they had the incentive to make such investments knowing that they could reap the benefits later. The statutory scheme provides that when a landlord serves a notice to quit upon the termination of a lease, the tenant may serve a counter-notice which entitles the tenant to a hearing before a tribunal. The tribunal normally awards the tenant another lease, for it is governed by a presumption in favour of preserving security of tenure. It would have been possible, of course, for the landlord and tenant to have agreed in their contract that a similar option to renew a lease should prevail. Parliament must have determined, however, that tenants were unable to bargain for such terms in the open market, either through ignorance of this possibility, or more likely because of their weak bargaining power. The question in this particular case was whether a term in the contract could provide that the tenant relinquished the right to serve a counter-notice. Although the statute did not expressly preclude such terms, the House of Lords was able to conclude that such a term, if permitted, would quickly subvert the purpose of the statute. Lord Hailsham explained that freedom of contract only permits a person to renounce a right which exists solely for his benefit, but not where a public interest is at stake. The public interest here was the collective interest in investment in farming:

> The truth is that it can no longer be treated as axiomatic that, in the absence of explicit language, the courts will permit contracting out of the provision of an Act of Parliament where that Act, though silent as to the possibility of contracting out, nevertheless is manifestly passed for the protection of a class of persons who do not negotiate from a position of equal strength, but in whose well-being there is a public as well as a private interest.

---

8   Employment Rights Act 1996, s 203; *Midland Electric Manufacturing Co Ltd v Kanji* [1980] IRLR 185, EAT; *Igbo v Johnson Matthey Chemicals Ltd* [1986] ICR 505, CA; *Birch v University of Liverpool* [1985] ICR 470, CA.

The granting of statutory rights and the insertion of compulsory terms as methods of supporting and protecting social goals have the advantage that they minimize collective enforcement costs. If every contract of a particular kind has to include a particular term, then this rule will be largely self-applying by the parties to contracts. At the same time, of course, it shares the endemic weakness which we have already observed in private law remedies, that the term may not be rigorously enforced by private contracting parties because of the costs and uncertainties of litigation.

Under English law the courts have not claimed the power to insist upon compulsory terms without statutory authority. In the absence of a statutory power to declare an exclusion clause invalid, then the express term will override implied obligations. In the United States, however, some courts have developed compulsory obligations in contracts by describing them as tort obligations which arise in contracts in certain types of relationships. These tort obligations cannot usually be excluded by the terms of the contract, so in effect they become mandatory obligations. Examples include the warranty of habitability for new dwellings,[9] and discharge from employment contrary to public policy.[10]

4. Statutory Invalidity

Certain statutes prohibit the use of particular terms in contracts. The purpose of such prohibitions is usually to ensure that the obligations which would otherwise govern the relation between the parties to a contract cannot be excluded or qualified. The statute normally states that a particular type of term shall be invalid, ineffective, or void.

One important provision of this kind in English law is section 2(1) of the Unfair Contract Terms Act 1977, which provides that:

> A person cannot by reference to any contract term or to a notice given to persons generally or to particular persons exclude or restrict his liability for death or personal injury resulting from negligence.

The effect of this prohibition is twofold. It prevents a term in a contract from excluding liability in tort for negligence in causing personal injuries or death. It also prevents the exclusion of implied terms in contracts which would also impose liability for negligently caused personal injuries and death. As an example of this latter kind of case, in *Johnstone v Bloomsbury Health Authority*,[11] a junior hospital doctor persuaded the court that his contract of employment contained an implied term that he would not be required to work such long hours as would foreseeably damage his health. The defendant employer sought to rely upon an express term which

---

9   *Melody Home Manufacturing Co v Barnes* 741 SW 2d 349 (Tex 1987).
10   *Palmateer v International Harvester Co* 421 NE 2d 876 (Ill 1981).
11   [1992] QB 333, [1991] 2 All ER 293, CA.

granted it the discretion to require up to eighty-eight hours of work a week, but this term was regarded as one which potentially contradicted the implied term and could therefore be invalid under section 2(1). In effect this statutory provision ensures that a duty to take reasonable care for the safety of the other party to the contract becomes a compulsory term of contracts where it is appropriate.

The main social objective of this provision is to ensure that the standard of reasonable care is always required with respect to the safety of persons, there being a collective interest in requiring this standard, an externality, which cannot be bargained away by individual contracts. The prohibition also serves the goal of providing compensation to those suffering personal injuries through the negligence of others. But these objectives do not rule out the possibility of contractual terms which allocate the risk of loss through indemnities between the wrongdoer and others, provided that these terms do not prevent the injured party from suing the wrongdoer.[12]

Consumer transactions

The technique of invalidating particular types of terms in contracts applies especially to consumer transactions. In sales by a business to a consumer, for instance, under section 6 of the Unfair Contract Terms Act 1977, the contract cannot exclude the obligation implied by section 14 of the Sale of Goods Act 1979 to supply goods of 'satisfactory quality'. This statutory prohibition therefore has the effect that the duty to supply goods of a 'satisfactory quality' becomes a compulsory term of every consumer sales contract.

The social objective of protecting consumers requires the legislation to classify the nature of the parties to the contracts. The paradigm case consists of a shopper purchasing goods from a retailer in the high street, but the concepts of the seller or supplier acting 'in the course of business',[13] and the purchaser being a 'consumer' pose difficulties of application at the boundaries. In order to identify the seller or supplier as a business, the courts typically look for a degree of regularity in making transactions of this type.[14] The concept of a consumer is normally defined more closely by the relevant legislation, as in section 12(1) of the Unfair Contract Terms Act 1977:

> A party to a contract 'deals as consumer' in relation to another party if –
> (a) he neither makes the contract in the course of a business nor holds himself out as doing so; and
> (b) the other party does make the contract in the course of a business; and
> (c) in the case of a contract governed by the law of sale of goods ... the goods passing under or in pursuance of the contract are of a type ordinarily supplied for private use or consumption.

---

12   *Thompson v T Lohan (Plant Hire)* [1987] 1 WLR 649, [1987] 2 All ER 631, CA.
13   This is the term used in the Sale of Goods Act 1979, s 14, and for the criminal regulation of misleading trading practices: Trade Descriptions Act 1968, s 1.
14   *Davies v Sumner* [1984] 1 WLR 1301, [1984] 3 All ER 831, HL.

Under this definition of a consumer, the purchaser can be a private individual, but not count as a consumer, if the item purchased is a business machine or a heavy goods vehicle. On the other hand, a business company may count as a consumer, if it purchases an item which is ordinarily for private use, such as a saloon car, and it does not trade in cars as part of its normal business operations.[15] In contrast, in European legislation, such as the Directive on Unfair Terms in Consumer Contracts, only a natural person may count as a consumer, and provided he or she is acting outside his trade, business or profession.[16] This definition of a consumer differs because it identifies a consumer by reference to the scope of a person's normal trade rather than the nature of the goods involved. This leaves open the possibility under the European concept of consumer that a small business, trading as a natural person or a partnership, can count as a consumer if the goods purchased, though normally used only in business, are not the kind of goods usually purchased by that particular business.

These differences in statutory concepts of a consumer pose the issue of whether the concept should reflect the actual level of expertise of the purchaser, or whether it should be assumed that all businesses have sufficient resources to acquire expertise whenever necessary. Given that many small businesses lack those resources, then European law assumes that the adoption of the corporate form signals the availability of those resources, but in England, where the corporate form is cheaper and more common for small businesses, such a proxy seems unsatisfactory.

5. Judicial Discretion over Exclusion Clauses

In relation to many types of contractual obligations, however, it is difficult to determine in advance whether a particular term will subvert a social policy and thereby merit statutory prohibition. Short of leaving the matter alone for the sake of achieving certainty with respect to the validity of contractual terms, the legislature must delegate a discretion to the courts or some other agency to distinguish between those cases where a compulsory term is required and those where it is not. The major example of the use of judicial discretion for this purpose in English law is the employment of the test of reasonableness to govern exclusion clauses in some types of contracts under the Unfair Contract Terms Act 1977. A similar jurisdiction emerges in US law with the test of unconscionability under the Uniform Commercial Code.[17] Although these broad tests do

---

15 *R & B Customs Brokers Co Ltd v United Dominions Trust Ltd* [1988] 1 WLR 321, [1988] 1 All ER 847, CA.

16 EC Directive 93/13, OJ L95/29, 5 April 1993, Art 2; implemented by the Unfair Terms in Consumer Contracts Regulations 1994, SI 1994/3159.

17 Art 2-302; Leff, 'Unconscionability and the Code – The Emperor's New Clause' (1967) *University of Pennsylvania Law Review* 485.

not identify with precision any compulsory term which must be included in contracts, their effect in particular instances is to prevent the express exclusion of certain types of liability which would otherwise arise, and so for the parties concerned with this particular contract the law has the effect of compelling them to contract on particular terms. In *Smith v Eric S Bush*,[18] for instance, the question was whether a surveyor and valuer of a house could exclude liability to the purchaser of the house for negligence in making and reporting on the survey and valuation. The House of Lords concluded that such exemption clauses were unreasonable in the context of ordinary home purchases. The effect of this judgment is that it becomes a compulsory term of every home survey and valuation that the surveyor accepts liability for negligence.

In exercising their discretionary power, the courts have to balance the collective interest in a competitive market achieved by freedom of contract against the potential danger to other social values. In balancing these competing interests the question whether or not a particular term which excludes liability offends too greatly against social values may depend upon the weighing of a variety of factors, such as the nature of the parties to the contract, the importance of the social value at stake, and the extent to which the contract term qualifies the obligation. In the case of *Smith v Bush* no doubt important considerations at stake were the protection of the consumer when making a major investment and the concern to ensure that professions comply with a reasonable standard of care when delivering services. In some cases, the factor of the unfairness or imbalance of the terms of the contract also plays a role in influencing the court's exercise of discretion, so that it becomes impossible to draw a sharp distinction between the social policies being pursued and the court's perception of the unfairness of the particular contract under consideration.

The technique of judicial control obviously suffers from several disadvantages. It inhibits contract planning, for the parties will be uncertain whether or not a chosen clause will be regarded as acceptable by a court. It operates retrospectively, so that the parties cannot ascertain the validity of the terms of their contract until the final outcome of litigation is known. There is also a danger of inconsistent judicial decisions, for in the exercise of a broad discretion particular judges may place greater weight on some factors than others. For these reasons the technique of judicial control for the introduction of compulsory terms often proves the least satisfactory.

Some of these objections to judicial control can be addressed in part by the development of clear principles of application of the discretion. As the courts consider numerous cases, then they can develop principles which guide their decisions, and those principles together with reasoning by analogy from decided cases can permit parties to a contract to predict with considerable accuracy the validity of terms which seek to exclude obligations. Another technique for reducing the harmful effects of judicial

18   [1990] 1 AC 831, [1989] 2 All ER 514, HL.

discretion involves what may be called 'grey lists'. Here the legislation indicates to the courts a presumption of how their discretion ought to be exercised in relation to a list of examples of contract terms. The EC Directive on Unfair Contract Terms adopts such a list.[19] If a contract term fits into this list, then it is likely to be held to be unfair, but it remains open to a court to conclude from looking at all the terms of the contract and the circumstances in which it was made that the general test of unfairness is not satisfied, so the potential uncertainty provoked by judicial discretion remains.

(1) The Scope of Judicial Discretion
Despite these concerns about contract planning, the technique of judicial control has been given a prominent position in English law by the Unfair Contract Terms Act 1977. Its key provisions introduce compulsory terms subject to a test of reasonableness. The Act is confined to exemption clauses, that is, terms which purport to exclude, restrict, or limit liability which would otherwise arise under the contract either by express or implied terms.[20] By rendering an exemption clause invalid due to its unreasonableness, the effect is to make the obligation which would otherwise have been excluded a mandatory obligation. Moreover, this mandatory obligation is contrary to the intention of the parties as it is recorded in their written contract.

The test of reasonableness applies in several circumstances, of which the most important are the following.

(A) Section 2(2) brings under the test of reasonableness terms which exclude or restrict liability for damage to property where liability arises from negligence, that is an express or implied term of the contract which requires the exercise of reasonable care with respect to property.

(B) Section 3 addresses principally the situation where an exclusion clause seeks to exclude liability for breach of an express term in a standard form contract, and again this is subject to a test of reasonableness. A typical case under this section would consist of an express promise or guarantee in the standard form contract being subject to other provisions which substantially undermine the extent and worth of the guarantee.

(C) Section 6 states that in contracts for the sale of goods where the purchaser is not dealing as a consumer the implied terms of such contracts required by the Sale of Goods Act 1979 ss 13, 14, and 15, such as the requirement that the goods be of satisfactory quality, cannot be excluded unless the exemption clause satisfies the test of reasonableness.

The Unfair Terms in Consumer Contracts Regulations 1994 also empower courts to review the fairness of exclusion clauses (and other clauses) in consumer contracts. These regulations are more directed towards unfair imbalances in particular contracts, however, so detailed consideration of

---

19 OJ L93/13, 5 April 1993, Art 3(3), Annex; this is replicated in The Unfair Terms in Consumer Contracts Regulations 1994, Reg 4(4) and Sch 3.

20 Section 13 gives an extended meaning to exemption clause.

the rules will be deferred to the next chapter on fairness. Moreover, under these Regulations there is an alternative avenue of enforcement of these provisions through an official agency, which is likely to have much greater practical importance and will be considered below. Nevertheless, as these Regulations based on European law are cumulative to the national English legislation, it is certainly possible that an exclusion clause will be invalid both under the Unfair Contract Terms Act 1977 and under the 1994 Regulations.

(2) The Test of Reasonableness

The courts receive little guidance from the legislation on how the test of reasonableness should be applied. Section 11(1) explains that the test of reasonableness is that:

> the term shall have been a fair and reasonable one to be included having regard to the circumstances which were, or ought reasonably to have been, known to or in the contemplation of the parties when the contract was made.

The statute emphasizes that the court should not use the benefit of hindsight, but must consider what was 'fair and reasonable' according to the circumstances known at the time of the formation of the contract. Section 11(4) indicates that the courts should consider in cases where liability is limited to a specified sum of money whether or not the person liable could have covered his full liability through insurance. If not, then the court may regard the limitation as more reasonable.[21] Finally, Schedule 2 of the Act provides some guidelines for the courts, which must be considered in relation to section 6, but in practice will be taken into account in all cases involving a question of reasonableness. Of particular interest in these guidelines is the stress upon two factors. First, the courts are advised to consider the bargaining positions of the parties relative to each other and to consider whether in fact some alternative arrangement was available which would not have avoided liability. If such an alternative was available and practicable in the circumstances, then the courts are likely to consider the exemption more reasonable. Secondly, the guidelines stress the significance of the customer's knowledge of the terms; if the customer knew or ought to have known of the term, then this fact argues in favour of the reasonableness of the exemption clause.

The statute therefore confines the discretion to be exercised by the courts in invalidating contract terms on the ground of unreasonableness, but it does not eliminate it entirely.[21] The court must weigh up the factors mentioned explicitly in the legislation, together with any other factors which it regards as relevant, before reaching a conclusion. In borderline cases, it will be far from predictable which factors the courts will regard as possessing considerable weight and which way a court will eventually

---

21 Adams and Brownsword, 'The Unfair Contract Terms Act: A Decade of Discretion' (1988) 104 *Law Quarterly Review* 94; Beale, 'Unfair Contracts in Britain and Europe' (1990) *Current Legal Problems* 197.

jump. In reviewing the existing cases which have dealt with this issue, however, I suggest that the social policies pursued by the courts in the course of determinations of reasonableness have become clear, even if their relative weight in a particular instance remains indeterminate. The following considerations constitute the recurrent significant social policies pursued by the courts when assessing questions of reasonableness.

Enforcement of Duties of Care

When the law would normally imply a duty to take reasonable care between the contracting parties, the courts use the test of reasonableness to prevent any derogation from this duty except in unusual circumstances. This liability for negligence itself rests on the proposition that liability will normally be imposed upon the person in the position to avoid the risk at the least cost. The social policy behind negligence liability is therefore to reduce the cost of accidents. The courts accord this policy considerable weight and are reluctant to permit contractual terms to defeat it. Thus in *Smith v Eric S Bush*,[22] Lord Templeman regarded a notice which sought to exempt a surveyor for liability in negligence for an inaccurate valuation of a house as unreasonable primarily on the ground that it would defeat the useful purpose of the general rule imposing negligence liability. For the same reason, a court is unlikely to approve a clause which seeks to exclude liability for both negligence and default for other reasons.[23] Attempts to limit the quantity of liability for negligence may be reasonable if full insurance cover is unobtainable or very expensive, but otherwise limitations of damages for negligence also receive a hostile treatment. When, in *Waldron-Kelly v British Rlys Board*,[24] the railway lost a customer's suitcase through negligence, the limitation of damages clause was held to be unreasonable because it would effectively permit the railway to escape the consequences of its own negligence.

Remedying Market Failure

Of almost equal importance in assessing the reasonableness of exclusion clauses, the courts are concerned to remedy market failure. Here the courts are concerned to challenge uncompetitive markets in an attempt to force traders to offer different and competing terms. Market failures may arise from a number of causes.

One source is consumer ignorance of the terms of contracts apart from key items such as price, so that there is no incentive for traders to compete with respect to the other terms on offer. The statute expressly makes the issue of whether the customer knew or ought reasonably to have known of the existence and extent of the term relevant to the question of

---

22 [1990] 1 AC 831, [1989] 2 All ER 514, HL.
23 *George Mitchell (Chesterhall) Ltd v Finney Lock Seeds Ltd* [1983] 2 AC 803, [1983] 2 All ER 737, HL.
24 [1981] CLY 303, in C Miller and B Harvey, *Consumer and Trading Law Cases and Materials* (London, 1985), p 250.

reasonableness.[25] The courts can deter the use of small print in standard forms and reliance upon incorporated documents which are hard to obtain. But if the trader takes steps to draw the customer's attention to the clause,[26] or it can be shown that the customer was aware of the clause, perhaps as a result of previous dealings,[27] then this knowledge will direct the court towards a finding that the term is reasonable.

Another source of market failure is an effective cartel in a particular trade, so that all traders offer identical or very similar terms. Where the courts detect such a source of market failure, they will normally regard exclusion clauses as unreasonable, with the intended effect of compelling traders to engage in more competitive offers of terms. In *George Mitchell (Chesterhall) Ltd v Finney Lock Seeds Ltd*,[28] for instance, a farmer purchased cabbage seeds from merchants, who limited their liability for supplying the wrong sort of seeds to the cost of the seeds. One important consideration against the validity of the limitation of damages clause was the finding that, 'a similar limitation of liability was universally embodied in the terms of trade between seedsmen and farmers and had been so for many years.'[29] This indicated a market failure caused by an effective cartel. Similarly, there was evidence in *Waldron-Kelly v British Railways Board* that other potential carriers for the suitcase used similar but not identical exemption clauses, so there was no advantage to be gained in 'shopping around'.

The remedy for this market failure which is normally favoured by the courts is that, in the absence of any realistic possibility of renegotiation of terms, traders should offer different sets of terms at different prices which involve different levels of responsibility. In *Woodman v Photo Trade Processing Ltd*,[30] the plaintiff's photographs were lost during processing by the defendant, who sought to limit his liability to the cost of the film as indicated in a notice at the retailers. Such a limitation of liability was standard practice throughout the trade, and of course it helped to keep costs down for the mass of consumers. Nevertheless, the court regarded the limitation of liability as unreasonable. It insisted that the trade should offer two sets of terms to customers, one cheap service with limited liability, and the other option with increased liability which consumers with particularly valuable photographs would choose. The court accepted that it would be reasonable for a trader not to offer the more expensive service itself, provided that it notified customers of the availability of such a service elsewhere.

---

25   Schedule 2.
26   *Woodman v Photo Trade Processing Ltd* (7 May 1981, unreported), in I Ramsay, *Consumer Protection* (London, 1989) p 107.
27   *Waldron-Kelly v British Rlys Board* [1981] CLY 303, in C Miller and B Harvey, *Consumer and Trading Law Cases and Materials* (London, 1985), p 250.
28   [1983] 2 AC 803, [1983] 2 All ER 737, HL.
29   Lord Bridge, [1983] 2 AC 803, [1983] 2 All ER 737, HL.
30   (7 May 1981, unreported), in I Ramsay, *Consumer Protection* (London, 1989) p 107.

Fairness
Under the test of fairness and reasonableness contained in section 11, the courts assess the equivalence of the obligations undertaken by the parties. Where the exclusion clause has the effect of substantially devaluing the promise given by one party with no commensurate reduction in the price paid by the other, the court will invalidate it. This consideration influenced the court in *Woodman v Photo Trade Processing Ltd* in recommending that a two-tier service be offered, an expensive service offering full guarantees, and a cheap service with limited compensation for loss of photographs. But this alternative will not itself satisfy the test of fairness, if the increased cost of full protection is too substantial and in practice prohibitively expensive. A similar set of alternative terms was recognized in *Smith v Eric S Bush* as a possible reasonable market practice, but the alternative offer of a full survey with guarantees was not regarded by Lord Griffith as practicable in that case, because it was prohibitively expensive.

Under this consideration of fairness, the courts have also been impressed by the difference between an agreed limitation of damages clause and the actual loss incurred. In *George Mitchell (Chesterhall) Ltd v Finney Lock Seeds Ltd* for instance, the contract fixed liability at the price of the seeds worth £192, but the actual losses of the farmer for losing a year's harvest were claimed to be £61,000. Similarly in *Waldron-Kelly v British Railways Board* the value of the lost suitcase was £302, but the limitation of damages clause fixed the loss at £27. These disparities are impressive, but I doubt whether they should be relevant in themselves to the question of reasonableness or fairness. The real question is whether, in view of the price paid for the goods or services and the size and likelihood of the risk of loss, the limitation clause was unfair in restricting liability to such an extent. The court should balance the respective obligations of the parties, so that it may be reasonable to restrict liability severely where either the price paid is low or the risks of great loss so high that, for the price paid, it could not be reasonably expected that full liability was undertaken. Customary business practice in a particular trade may prove a useful guide in this respect, provided that there is no suspicion of market failure.

Efficient Allocation of the Burden of Insurance
Most of the losses arising from breach of contract can be insured against, and the costs of this insurance incorporated into the price of the contract. But it may be cheaper for one party to insure against the risk of loss than the other, and the courts will support exclusion clauses where they reflect an agreed and efficient distribution of the burden of insurance. One saving in insurance costs can be achieved by reducing the number of policies taken out. For this reason it was more efficient for the few firms of seedsmen in *George Mitchell (Chesterhall) Ltd v Finney Lock Seeds Ltd* to take out insurance than for the burden to fall on their thousands of customers. On the other hand, the risks at stake may be peculiarly within

the knowledge of one party, and this will tend to make it more efficient for that party to insure against loss. In *Waldron-Kelly v British Railways Board* the railway company argued that only customers knew the exact value of their goods, so that it was reasonable for them to limit their liability to a fixed amount, leaving it to the customer to take out any additional insurance necessary. This argument was not regarded as persuasive in the end, however, perhaps because it would have been more efficient for the railway to take out a single insurance policy and pass on the costs to all customers. It must be admitted that although the courts do pay attention to this factor of the efficiency of insurance arrangements, they have not so far investigated this issue with care, no doubt being hesitant to conduct the complex economic and empirical investigations which this factor really requires. Instead, the courts are likely to assume, in a contract between commercial parties which apparently apportions risk carefully, that the exemption clause should be enforced as appropriate insurance arrangements will have been constructed around it.[31]

Support for Collective Agreement of Terms

The reasonableness test is likely to be satisfied if the terms of the contract have been the product of negotiation between the relevant interest groups. In these circumstances the fears of market failure and the consequent misuse of standard form contracts to achieve unfair bargains disappears, and the courts are likely to find any agreed terms reasonable. Similarly, if there are agreed trading standards set with the approval of the Director General of Fair Trading, then a contract which complies with those terms is likely to be held to be reasonable. If, however, the contract departs from such collectively agreed terms, or fails to conform to standard approved trade terms, then the court is likely to find an exemption clause unreasonable. In *Woodman v Photo Trade Processing Ltd*, for example, the court paid special attention to the Code of Practice for the Photographic Industry which had been promulgated with the approval of the Director General. This Code clearly envisaged that traders would offer a two-tier service, and the failure to conform to this model was probably decisive in the finding that the limitation of liability was unreasonable. Similarly, in *George Mitchell (Chesterhall) Ltd v Finney Lock Seeds Ltd*, the House of Lords indicated that it would have accepted the seedsmen's limitation of liability, if it had been negotiated with a powerful representative of the customers such as the National Farmers Union. This is an unexpected but welcome recognition by the courts of the desirability of encouraging this form of negotiated regulatory control over contract terms.

Control Over Remedial Discretion

One objective of exclusion clauses may be to give the party in breach a range of choices with respect to the redress afforded. By inserting a clause

---

31   *Photo Production Ltd v Securicor Transport Ltd* [1980] AC 827, [1980] 1 All ER 556, HL.

which severely limits remedies for breach, this gives an option to grant greater compensation on an 'ex gratia' basis where commercial considerations may indicate this is advisable. If the dissatisfied customer is a business which frequently purchases the product or requires the service, then, in the interests of preserving this good business relation, it may be desirable for the party in breach to waive the exclusion clause and offer a better remedy in settlement of the claim. The courts have exhibited a hostility to this exhibition of contract power. The House of Lords in *George Mitchell (Chesterhall) Ltd v Finney Lock Seeds Ltd* relied upon evidence which revealed that the seedsmen often gave greater compensation than provided by the limitation clause in the contract in order to justify its conclusion that the limitation was unreasonable.

Undifferentiated Standard Forms

Finally, we can discern signs in the cases that the courts view with suspicion the practice of using an identical standard form contract regardless of the nature of the customer. Evidence which shows that the same terms are proffered regardless of whether the customer is a consumer or a substantial business may indicate that the term is unreasonable in the context of a consumer transaction.[32] Here the policy of support for a social market which differentiates between the types of traders in the market can be realized by insisting upon more flexible contracting practices.

6. Agency Discretion

The great potential advantage of the use of an agency to police the use of exclusion clauses over the court system comprises the potential to regulate in advance the use of terms in contracts. Instead of the parties waiting until trial to discover whether or not a clause is unreasonable and therefore invalid, the issue can be tested in advance by a reference to an independent agency. Many other advantages of agencies exercising this type of discretion should also be noted. The process is usually cheaper and quicker for interested parties. The agency can look at all the contracts used in a particular trade or business and set publicized standards applicable to all traders. The judicial process, in contrast, usually results in an unreported and undiscoverable determination about a particular contract, which is unlikely to have any impact on any other traders' contracting practices.

Under the requirement of the European Directive on Unfair Contract Terms, the English Regulations establish a duty on the Director General of Fair Trading to consider complaints about unfair terms in consumer

---

32 *Waldron-Kelly v British Rlys Board* [1981] CLY 303, in C Miller and B Harvey, *Consumer and Trading Law Cases and Materials* (London, 1985), p 250.

contracts.[33] If the Director considers a complaint to be well founded, then the Director is empowered to negotiate with the business informally for the withdrawal of the unfair terms, and to accept an undertaking from the business to withdraw the clause, or, if no such undertaking is given, to apply to a court for an injunction against any person using or recommending use of such a term. The Unfair Contract Terms Unit established by the Director General to process this new power received 817 cases in its first year of operation.[34] Many of these cases concern instances of unfairness between the parties and will be considered in the next chapter. Here what is relevant is the way in which the Unit has effectively rendered some obligations compulsory in consumer contracts by regarding attempts to exclude or modify the obligations unfair and invalid.

Many of the clauses which the Unit has insisted should be withdrawn comprise prohibited clauses under the Unfair Contract Terms Act 1977. This tends to confirm the hypothesis that a private law remedy backed solely by the judicial sanction of invalidity is unlikely to be effective. The Unit has dealt with clauses in contracts which purport to exclude liability for negligently caused personal injuries, as in this typical notice in a car park:

> Vehicles and their contents are parked at the owner's risk and no liability is accepted for any loss or damage to the vehicle or contents or persons, however caused.

The effect of the Unit's decision in that instance and others like it is that gradually these notices are being taken down across the country. Similarly, the Unit has had to reject as unfair terms which remove the consumer's basic warranty that goods sold in the course of business are of satisfactory quality, an exclusion which is again prohibited by the Unfair Contract Terms Act 1977. An example comes from the terms of a second-hand car dealer:

> No responsibility can be taken by ourselves if the vehicle is not in a roadworthy condition.

Other clauses which the Unit has caused to be withdrawn comprise terms which would have been subject to the test of reasonableness under the Unfair Contract Terms Act 1977. For example, terms which exclude liability for negligently caused damage to property must pass the test of being fair and reasonable in the circumstances. Here the underlying issue is when, if ever, will it be appropriate for a business to avoid the liability which would otherwise arise in tort or under an implied term of the contract to perform work with reasonable care so that no damage is caused to the purchaser's property. In a typical example, the terms of the standard contract used by a company which stripped and reroofed houses excluded liability for damage to the building or its contents however caused.

---

33   The Unfair Terms in Consumer Contracts Regulations 1994, SI 1994/3159, Reg 8.
34   Office of Fair Trading, *Unfair Contract Terms Bulletin*, No 2, September (London, 1996).

The scope of the Unit's powers is unfortunately limited to the investigation of the unfairness of the terms of the particular contract which is the subject of complaint. It lacks the power to issue general regulations applicable to a trade or industry, or to a particular type of standard form contract in common use. The final determination of whether or not a term is unfair is left to judicial decision, so that the Unit's opinions remain advisory and limited to the particular contract. This regulatory framework misses the opportunity to create an agency which might be empowered to approve in advance particular standard form contracts, which could then be used by businesses with the assurance that they are valid and therefore a safe basis for contract planning. This limitation on the Unit's powers reflects a deference to the judicial process for determining contractual rights and the continuation of an assumption that ultimately it must be left to the parties to decide the terms of their contract. Yet this absence of the regulatory power to determine the validity of contracts in advance has the deleterious effect on contract planning that it continues the uncertainty as to the validity of the terms in consumer contracts. Even if the Unit has approved a term in a particular contract, it remains possible that a court will strike it down as unfair under the Regulations.

7. Negotiated Regulation

The obvious remedy for the inefficiency and unpredictability of judicial discretion to introduce compulsory terms consists of increasing the number and specificity of the compulsory terms by means of administrative regulation or delegated legislation. But detailed regulation often shares the same defects, for the sheer quantity of regulatory measures ensures widespread ignorance of their requirements, which makes the law appear unpredictable, and increases the cost of legal advice and other measures to ensure compliance. To compound these problems for the effectiveness of regulation, we must suspect that the law, by seeking to regulate economic activity, may be treated as a cost incorporated into a broader economic calculus guided by the pursuit of profits. If so, then the cost of compliance with detailed regulations may be regarded as too expensive compared to the risk of invalidity of contracts, so that we reach the point of efficient breach of regulations. In the case of a minimum wage law for employees, for instance, employers may regard the risks arising from failure to comply as less costly than the increase in labour costs required by the law, so the rational economic calculus will lead to widespread flouting of the law.

Moreover, detailed regulation of contract terms may create harmful effects on the market. Legal regulation presents the danger that, by neutralizing competitive advantages, it will create disincentives to the provision of an efficient supply of goods and services to the public. Although some regulatory measures can be justified on the ground of their improvements to the efficiency of the market, such as duties of disclosure which supply consumers with sufficient information in order to judge intelligently between products, detailed legal regulation for compulsory terms in pursuit of collective interests may often stifle economic growth and frustrate consumer demand.

In addition, government measures run the risk of merely replacing one set of injustices by another. By replacing the market mechanism for the selection of terms, the legal regulation may achieve priority for one set of collective interests whilst ignoring or devaluing others. The recurring advantage of the market mechanism over legal regulation for determining terms consists in its responsiveness to the choices of all individuals involved in the economic activity. Legal regulation achieved by one pressure group through the political process may exclude the interests of other groups. The regulation simply replaces economic power with political power in the determination of contract terms.

Many of these disadvantages of legal regulation can be relieved by a final technique of regulation for compulsory terms. This method comprises a negotiation between representatives of collective interests resulting in a model set of terms for contracts of a particular type, and prescribed Codes of Practice which govern bargaining practices and avenues for redress of grievances. The model contract then becomes the mandatory standard form contract for transactions made by members of this trading group. The groups involved in negotiation often provide for arbitration of grievances, as opposed to judicial decisions, both because of the greater efficiency of arbitration, and because specialized arbitrators can often supplement negotiated agreements more intelligently in the light of their knowledge of the relevant conflicting interests. The state recognizes the authority of these negotiated model contracts through systems of licensing, provisions encouraging self-regulation and informal adjudication, and ultimately by backing up the codes of conduct and model contracts with legal sanctions including criminal penalties. Within this corporatist pattern, the typical role for the judiciary lies in review of the conduct of groups and bureaucratic administrators rather than adjudication of individual grievances. The purposes of review include checking that groups and administrators do not exceed or abuse their powers, ensuring that the proper level of consultation takes place with affected groups, and guaranteeing that arbitrators conform with the established regulations.[35] These four features of the modern law – negotiated standards, arbitration, state recognition, and judicial review – compose the corporatist or negotiated regulation pattern to which the law of contract increasingly turns.

We discover important examples of this technique in the regulation of many trades. Statutes aimed primarily at consumer protection encourage traders to establish binding Codes of Practice,[36] which then

35   Stewart, 'The Reformation of American Administrative Law', (1975) 88 *Harvard Law Review* 1667.
36   Fair Trading Act 1973, s 124; R Cranston, *Consumers and the Law* (London, 2nd edn, 1984), chapter 2.

sometimes receive legal support through sanctions, including criminal penalties and removal of a licence to trade. International conventions agreed between the relevant countries govern frequent international transactions such as carriage of goods by air or sea. Professions such as medicine and the law often prescribe a code of conduct which is enforced through occupational licensing and some criminal penalties. Special agencies including Ombudsmen also protect investors in banks, company shares, and other securities. The American pattern of labour law shares this corporatist approach, for it approves the market pattern of establishing the terms of the contract of employment by collective bargaining between the employer and a representative union, imposing various penalties upon employers and unions to discourage deviations from this pattern of market relations, and promoting private arbitration of disputes.[37] Occupational licensing schemes apply to many trades and professions, so that breach of approved standards of conduct leads to forfeiture of the licence to trade.

This corporatist pattern alters slightly in the context of consumer protection, because consumers often lack a representative body with which traders should negotiate. State officials such as the English Director General of Fair Trading then assume the burden of negotiating the appropriate standards on behalf of consumers.[38] The final agreement can result in the imposition of delegated legislation, which prohibits in advance certain kinds of terms in standard form contracts or other unsavoury market practices. Moreover, some agencies enjoy the power to use the criminal law process to punish traders who violate the required standards. Together these powers of regulation and enforcement through the criminal law process serve to make up for the weakness of consumers in pursuing their ordinary civil remedies against unscrupulous traders. Indubitably, in some cases the state officials betray the trust reposed in them by failing to represent the interests of consumers forcefully, but this inherent defect in the institutional design of corporatist controls in the context of consumer protection has not prevented it from becoming the prevailing pattern of control.

For similar reasons, self-regulation without effective legal supervision and sanctions should be regarded with suspicion. The regulations are unlikely to be very restrictive and the sanctions against members of the trade association who break the rules often prove illusory in practice. Nevertheless, self-regulation by a trade or profession has become frequent in England. For example, the Advertising Standards Authority sets regulations against misleading advertisements, backed up by the threat of adverse publicity and, if the media co-operate, elimination of the offending advertisement. Insurance companies have also agreed not to take unreasonable advantage of the doctrine of uberrimae fidei and the

---

37   National Labor Relations Act 1947, 29 USC, s 151; similar ideas inspired the British Industrial Relations Act 1971.

38   Cranston, op cit.

harsh provisions of their standard form contracts. In the absence of serious penalties, however, these initiatives have a minimal impact on those inclined to be unscrupulous.

The courts have responded to the advent of corporatist measures by extending their powers of review to all officials and groups who exercise the power of regulating the content of market transactions. The necessary obliteration of the traditional boundaries of public law becomes obvious when the courts take control over trade associations, licensing authorities, and unions by insisting that their powers should not be exercised unreasonably or in bad faith and should not unduly interfere with freedom of contract.

Gathering together these trends in legislation and legal doctrine, we can discern the principal features of this pattern of law for market transactions. Corporatism replaces the old dichotomy of public and private law – that metaphor for a clash between the Welfare State and the free market – with an institutional framework of compulsory associations loosely supervised by bureaucratic and judicial organs of government. Individual traders are bound to observe the approved standards of their compulsory association on threat of criminal penalty or being driven out of business, yet they receive protection against abuse of organizational power through the application of administrative law by the courts. Through this institutional arrangement, a corporatist system counters the danger of an oppressive and inefficient public bureaucratic stranglehold over market transactions. Its participatory and devolved style of government ushers in a procedural transformation which matches more closely the collectivist values which compelled the abandonment of the classical law. At the same time, in the interests of efficiency and securing compliance, each trade association is permitted considerable latitude in devising its regulations and techniques of enforcement.

In the light of these advantages of corporatism for the promotion of the social market, deviations from the pattern of negotiated regulation begin to appear suspect. Bodies which claim the power of regulation without being subject to external review, such as the Law Society or the Stock Exchange in England, experience considerable pressure to submit to some species of state control. Similarly, as we noted above, when courts examine the fairness of the terms of contracts under broad discretionary powers, if a standard form has not been approved by a representative body on both sides of the transaction, it becomes increasingly likely that the court will invalidate the harsher terms.[39]

---

39 Eg *Walker v Boyle* [1982] 1 All ER 634 (standard conditions for sale of property unreasonable because not the product of negotiations between representative bodies).

13

Fairness

A system of contract law committed to freedom of contract must reject controls over the fairness of contracts. No matter that the purchaser has paid an excessive price or the seller received gross undervalue, the principle of freedom to select the terms must prohibit intervention designed to redress the balance of the obligations. At most the law can scrutinize minutely the procedures leading up to the contract to ensure that the freedom of the parties was not restricted by pressure, fraud, abuse of positions of trust, and other factors which interfered with the voluntariness of consent. Tests of procedural propriety are both compatible with and required by the principle of freedom of contract, but any examination of the fairness of the substance of the contract must be forbidden. Accordingly, texts describing the classical law of contract offered no place for a discussion of a requirement of fairness in contracts.

A reluctance to acknowledge the significance of substantive unfairness in contracts as a ground for intervention still characterizes judicial decisions in the common law. A court will stress any elements of procedural impropriety that it can discover rather than address directly the unfairness of the bargain. The substantive unfairness may provide the motive for intervention, but the formal legal reason given for upsetting the contract will be couched in terms of a procedural defect, such as deception, manipulation, or unfair surprise. This approach receives further support from economic analysis of law, since these procedural defects can be regarded as evidence of a market failure which prevented the operation of a competitive and efficient market. To discover the real significance of substantive unfairness in the common law of contract therefore requires an investigation which digs behind the formal reasons given for decisions.

On its own such an investigation could produce ambiguous results. Although it might seem plausible that the courts were concerned about substantive unfairness in a particular case, since their formal reasons for the decision invariably latch onto a procedural impropriety, the case for believing that substantive unfairness was crucial to the decision might be regarded as unproven. The argument is strengthened, however, by reference to a batch of statutory provisions which permit the courts to discuss substantive unfairness openly. Although few common law jurisdictions grant the courts a general oversight of fairness in contracts,[1] a patchwork of legislation governing particular types of contracts provides an impressive array of instruments. Perhaps the most important example of this legislation derives from Article 3 of the EC Directive on Unfair Terms in Consumer Contracts.

> A contractual term which has not been individually negotiated shall be regarded as unfair if, contrary to the requirement of good faith, it causes a significant imbalance in the parties' rights and obligations arising under the contract, to the detriment of the consumer.[2]

When legislation of this kind is combined with the circumstantial evidence from the common law of a concern for substantive fairness, then the significance of intervention on this ground emerges as a major concern of the law of contract.

1.Three Concepts of Fairness

The problem of substantive unfairness arises in a number of contexts which demand different criteria for intervention. The simple case of an excessive or derisory price is in fact the least likely to be regulated. More subtle imbalances of obligations arising from the details of the terms of the contract are controlled more vigorously. Although no difference exists in economic theory between these two types of term, for ultimately each element of the contractual obligation contributes to the cost or price, direct regulation of prices by the courts presents too ostentatious a challenge to the operation of the free market. The difference between the price and ancillary terms is rather that it is much less likely that market failure or procedural impropriety will have caused an unfair price, since this is the term on which the parties will have focused. Even though these market failure considerations are not strictly pertinent to the enquiry into substantive unfairness, they appear to persuade the legislature and the courts to refrain from direct regulation of the price as opposed to ancillary terms. For this reason the Unfair Terms in Consumer Contracts Directive is restricted in its scope by Article 4(2):

> Assessment of the unfair nature of the terms shall relate neither to the definition of the main subject-matter of the contract nor to the adequacy of the price and remuneration, on the one hand, as against the services or goods supplied in exchange, on the other, insofar as these terms are in plain intelligible language.

---

1   An exception is the Contracts Review Act 1980, NSW; *West v AGC (Advances) Ltd* (1986) 5 NSWLR 610, CA; *Dillon v Baltic Shipping Co (The Mikhail Lermontov)* [1991] 2 Lloyd's Rep 155, CA.
2   Directive 93/13 OJ L95/29, 5 April 1993.

One important example of an ancillary term which is regulated both at common law and by legislation is contractual provisions regarding remedies for breach of contract. The controls over agreed remedies will be considered separately in Chapter 16.

When attention is focused on ancillary terms, however, the conception of fairness undergoes a shift. Instead of fairness being measured against a fair price, usually the ordinary market price, the criterion of assessment becomes one of a mixture of balancing reciprocal ancillary obligations and conformity to reasonable expectations. The idea of balance suggests that advantages obtained in ancillary terms, such as an exclusion of liability or a fixed measure of damages for breach, should be matched by corresponding benefits to the other party. Conformity to reasonable expectations suggests that the ancillary terms should not deviate from a reasonable package of terms for transactions of that type unless the parties have expressly negotiated the point.

A further context in which issues of substantive unfairness arise concerns contracts which though apparently fair in their inception are rendered unfair by subsequent unforeseen events. The question which then arises is whether or not the court should terminate or in some other way revise the contract in order to restore substantive fairness. Again the idea of judicial revision on grounds of substantive unfairness clashes with the principle of respect for freedom of contract, but the situation differs because it can be argued that the new circumstances were not anticipated by the parties so that they have not in fact expressed their intentions about the problem in the contract. The topic of judicial revision will therefore be considered separately at the end of this chapter.

This chapter therefore encounters three distinct concepts of substantive fairness. First, in cases involving the fairness of the price, the criterion is likely to be one connected to the market price. Secondly, for challenges to ancillary terms, we discover a combination of the ideas of balance of advantage and conformity to reasonable expectations. Thirdly, in connection with subsequent events which arguably render the contract unfair in its application, the comparison lies with the original balance of advantage at the time when the contract was formed.

2. Fairness in the Common Law

Under the classical conception of contract law, lawyers both asserted the fairness of agreements which satisfied the conditions for the formation of valid contracts, and refused to adopt any explicit measures designed to invalidate unfair transactions. The courts rejected any general test of fairness of the price such as a rule invalidating unconscionable contracts. The central rule remains that a court will refuse to test the adequacy of consideration. Even a peppercorn can provide the consideration for a major capital transaction.

This rule expresses a preference for the distributive outcome achieved by a particular kind of market. It endorses the fairness of voluntary transactions and demonstrates a faith in the ability of individuals to take care of their own interests and to make informed and rational judgements. This faith in individual autonomy and rationality leads to a belief in the fairness of the distributive outcomes of a relatively uninhibited market. Far from refusing to develop a theory of distributive justice and fairness in contracts, the classical conception of contract law states a clear preference for the distributive outcome of a largely uninhibited market.

(1) Instrumentalism

Behind this facade, however, there lurked an understandable reluctance on the part of the courts to be used as instruments of exploitation. When confronted by a manifestly disadvantageous transaction, they could deploy a host of legal doctrines in order to avoid enforcement. Although the doctrines themselves rarely refer to fairness as a relevant consideration, they could be used instrumentally to achieve the outcome of invalidating the contract or a noxious term. Indeed, most of rules governing the formation of contracts could be used instrumentally for this purpose.

Consideration

Although the courts decline to test the adequacy of consideration, the issue of whether or not any consideration existed at all to support the transaction provides fertile territory for instrumental decisions. If an apparent exchange can be described as two unconnected donative promises, because the promises were not given by request, then a court can declare that no contract was established. It might follow this line of reasoning where the promises have a marked imbalance of value.

For example, the legal issue in *Combe v Combe*[3] was whether a husband's promise to his wife during divorce proceedings to pay her £100 maintenance a year was supported by consideration. The Court of Appeal concluded that it was a donative promise because the husband had not requested any action in return for the promise. It would not have been impossible for the court, if it had so wished, to have inferred from the facts of the case an implied request from the husband to the wife to refrain from applying to a court for maintenance. But the court clearly regarded the denial of a remedy to the wife as a just result in this case. Denning LJ observed, 'I do not think it would be right for this wife, who is better off than her husband, to take no action for six or seven years and then come down on him for the whole £600.' This remark reveals that the court regarded the alleged transaction as unfair, for the consideration for the husband's promise would be the sacrifice of a right to maintenance in circumstances where it was unlikely that a court would order maintenance due to the wife's superior income. One may surmise that if the wife had

3   [1951] 2 KB 215, [1951] 1 All ER 767, CA.

shown urgent financial need then the court would have used its ingenuity to imply a request in order to satisfy the doctrine of consideration.

We noted in Chapter 4 when examining the concept of consideration that in fact the courts switch from an abstract exchange model to a concept of benefit and detriment. The move to an evaluation of whether the promise involved a real detriment to the promisor involved a surreptitious deviation from the principle that the court will not test the adequacy of consideration. The reason for switching the concept of consideration is plainly to avoid the enforcement of agreements where the court regards the promise as illusory or without value. This technique is employed, for instance, with respect to variations of contracts where the promisor offers a higher price for exactly the same contractual obligation to be performed. The promisee's promise to perform the existing contractual duty is typically regarded as unsupported by consideration, for it involves no fresh detriment. But this line of reasoning is inconsistent with the principle to refuse to test the adequacy of consideration. Nevertheless the courts can use the doctrine of consideration defined in terms of benefit and detriment in order to invalidate such variations where the court regards them as unfair, or to enforce them on the ground of the presence of real commercial benefit when the court believes the variation to represent a fair outcome.[4]

Incorporation of Terms
In the context of disputes over the terms of the contract, the unfairness of the terms indicates that advantage was taken of the opportunity to sneak into a standard form contract oppressive terms, but the unfairness of the terms is neither an independent ground for relief, nor evidence of the opportunity to take advantage of the bargaining position. What the law requires in cases, such as *Interfoto Picture Library Ltd v Stiletto Visual Programmes Ltd*,[5] is that the more unusual and onerous the terms, the greater the steps required to bring these terms to the actual notice of the disadvantaged party. The logic of this rule is that a party should not be permitted to take undue advantage of the bargaining position gained by insisting upon a standard form contract. The unfairness of the terms and the absence of specific notice of these terms suggests that the opportunity to take advantage of this bargaining position was taken up. It is the risk of abuse of standard form contracts which is the evil which the courts address. The unfairness of the terms merely establishes that the risk to the competitive market materialized.

Undue Influence and Unconscionability
In principle, the issue of whether or not consent was given to a transaction should depend upon the conduct of the parties during the negotiations

---

4 *Williams v Roffey Bros and Nicholls (Contractors) Ltd* [1991] 1 QB 1, [1990] 1 All ER 512, CA; see chapter 15.
5 [1989] QB 433, [1988] 1 All ER 348, CA.

and not on the content of the contract. The absence of agreement or the presence of coercion will negative consent to the contract. Nevertheless, many cases come before the courts where the argument presented suggests that the ostensible consent provided perhaps by a signature on a document was not given voluntarily due to subtle forms of pressure and influence which may or may not be regarded as having negatived consent. These cases are usually considered under the doctrine of undue influence, though the term unconscionability is also used in connection with cases where the victim has a special disability, such as mental infirmity or illiteracy.[6] In order to have the contract rescinded under this doctrine, in the absence of clear instances of pressure, it has to be established that a relation of trust and confidence between the parties presented a danger of abuse of that trust, and that in fact that risk materialized. Although the substantive unfairness of the contract is probably not an essential ingredient of this claim, it clearly provides excellent evidence that the risk of abuse of trust and confidence in fact occurred.

In *National Westminster Bank plc v Morgan*,[7] the bank agreed with a man and wife to a short-term bridging loan of £14,500, secured by a legal charge on a jointly owned matrimonial home, in order to prevent the existing mortgagors from foreclosing and seeking possession of the house, and also to provide finance for the husband's business. Whilst the wife had signed this agreement under some pressure from her husband and the threat of losing her home, the House of Lords declined to rescind the agreement because the bank had not imposed undue pressure or abused a relationship of confidence. Although there was some evidence of undue influence in the form of taking advantage of the wife's business ignorance, the influence had not been abused because the terms of the contract were fair. The rate of interest was comparable to the rate charged for other short-term business loans, and the loan provided a vital material benefit to the wife by allowing her to keep possession of her home.

In contrast, *The Port Caledonia and The Anna*[8] provides an example of a successful proof of abuse of unfair market conditions by reference to the unfair terms of the contract. Bucknill J found that a contract to tow a ship to safety as it was about to collide with another for £1,000 was invalid on grounds which today might be described as economic duress or undue influence in the form of taking advantage of the state of necessity of another, since the tug-boat was the only one in the vicinity. The court reduced the price to £200, which would be the normal commercial charge for such a service. Under this jurisdiction, the unfairness of the terms of a contract is neither an independent ground for relief, nor can it prove that an opportunity to abuse a market position existed. But the unfairness

---

6   *Aylesford v Morris* (1873) 8 Ch App 484; *Fry v Lane* (1888) 40 Ch D 312; *Commercial Bank of Australia Ltd v Amadio* (1983) 151 CLR 447, High Ct of Australia; Green, 'Proof of Mental Incompetency and the Unexpressed Major Premise' (1944) 53 *Yale Law Journal* 272.

7   [1985] AC 686, [1985] 1 All ER 821, HL.

8   [1903] P 184.

of the price is crucial evidence of abuse of market position. Similarly, in *Cresswell v Potter*[9] the sale by a wife to her husband of her interest in the matrimonial home for derisory consideration could be set aside because the husband clearly had the opportunity to take advantage of his wife's business ignorance, and the sale at considerable undervalue without independent advice proved that advantage had in fact been taken.

Although the doctrine of undue influence may be used instrumentally in cases such as these to justify interventions against unfair contracts, the doctrinal reasoning does not regard unfairness as either necessary or sufficient to claim relief. In *National Westminster Bank v Morgan*[10] Lord Scarman suggested that 'manifest disadvantage' was an essential ingredient of claims for undue influence. But this view has been doubted and distinguished. It is certainly not a requirement where there is clear evidence of pressure and deception.[11] It also appears incorrect in principle to add the requirement in cases where a fair price may have been paid, but the victim for independent reasons may not have wanted to sell. Nevertheless, the manifest disadvantage of a transaction must provide compelling evidence that there was abuse of a relation of trust and confidence, or taking advantage of business ignorance.

Equally, evidence of the unfairness of the terms alone will not suffice, for what is required is proof of taking advantage. Thus in *Hart v O'Connor*,[12] an unfair transaction with a person of unsound mind could not be set aside because the stronger party was not aware of the mental infirmity of the weaker party, so he could not have deliberately taken advantage of that weakness. Nevertheless, it appears fairly easy to persuade a court that if a person did suffer from mental infirmity, then the fact that the contract was substantively unfair suggests that the stronger party must have become aware of the infirmity. For example, in *Boustany v Pigott*,[13] an elderly lady granted a lease of business premises on unfavourable terms contrary to the advice of a lawyer present, and the court was able to infer unconscionable dealing from the combination of the disadvantageous bargain and evidence of the woman's past behaviour which suggested mental infirmity.

More generally, the courts require proof of the absence of a competitive market by evidence of the problems arising from a pattern of entrusting choice to another, pressures to compel choice, the opportunity to take advantage of another's business ignorance and the opportunity to take advantage of an effective monopoly position. Having established the

---

9   [1978] 1 WLR 255n, Ch.

10 [1985] AC 686, [1985] 1 All ER 821, HL; *Bank of Credit and Commerce International SA v Aboody* [1990] 1 QB 923, [1992] 4 All ER 955, CA.

11 *CIBC Mortgages plc v Pitt* [1994] 1 AC 200, [1993] 4 All ER 433, HL, overruling *Bank of Credit and Commerce International SA v Aboody* [1990] 1 QB 923, [1992] 4 All ER 955, CA.

12 [1985] AC 1000, [1985] 2 All ER 880, PC.

13 (1993) 69 P & CR 298, PC; *Ayres v Hazelgrove* (9 February 1984, unreported), Ch, discussed in P Birks, *Restitution – The Future* (Sydney, 1992) at p 50.

existence of one or more of these problems at the point of the formation of the contract, the question arises whether in fact this problem occurred to such an extent that a competitive market ceased to exist. At this point evidence of the unfairness of the terms suggests strongly, and perhaps conclusively in the absence of independent advice to the weaker party, that the defect in the market occurred, with the legal consequence that the contract should be made voidable on the ground of undue influence.

Interpretation and Implied Terms

In the course of interpreting contracts, the courts have many opportunities to construct the obligations so that they conform to the reasonable expectations of the parties. During this process the courts do not simply rewrite the terms of the agreement so that they comply with a latent standard of fairness, but they can interpret vague terms and insert implied terms in order to bring the contractual obligations more into balance and to protect reasonable expectations. The idea of reasonable expectations differs from a simple fairness criterion, for its reference is not to an independent standard of a fair price, but rather to the unexpressed intentions of the parties. But the circle becomes almost closed once it is accepted that those intentions are likely to be construed as a desire to enter a contract with a reasonable balance of obligations on both sides.

The criterion of fairness influences, but is not determinative of, the decision to imply a term into a contract. The courts are engaged in seeking a fair and practicable allocation of risks. In *Liverpool City Council v Irwin*,[14] it will be recalled that the court inserted an implied term into a lease for an apartment in a high rise block that the landlord should take reasonable care to keep in reasonable repair and useability the common parts of the premises. I suggested that the court preferred this solution because it appeared the most practical and efficient solution, since it would have been difficult and expensive for the tenants to manage this task themselves. If the criterion of fairness had been used, the court should have considered the level of the rent compared to the services offered by the landlord. But fairness in the sense of balance of obligations and reasonable expectations is relevant here, for no doubt the tenants held the reasonable expectation that the landlords would look after the lifts, corridors, and staircases in the absence of express contrary provision. When this reasonable expectation coincides with a practicable and efficient solution to the handling of a risk, then the implied term can be asserted with confidence.

During the interpretation of terms of contracts, there is also considerable opportunity for the courts to mould the contract to conform with the reasonable expectations of the parties. It can construe exclusion clauses narrowly, so that the normal obligations arising, such as the duty of care, can be protected. It can insist that express terms are subject to a

14   [1977] AC 239, [1976] 2 All ER 39, HL.

requirement of reasonableness, so that a power to terminate a contract must only be exercised on reasonable notice, and a power to insist upon increased performance from employees must be exercised reasonably with regard to the health and safety of employees.[15] Vague terms, such as the requirement of satisfactory quality for goods which are sold, or duties to take reasonable care in the performance of services, also provide the courts with an opportunity to satisfy reasonable expectations and maintain the balance of the obligations. What counts as satisfactory quality will depend upon the price. The buyer is entitled to receive value for money, that is, goods of a quality which reflects the price paid for them,[16] unless the buyer is consciously taking a risk that the goods may not be as valuable as he or she hopes, as where food is reduced in price as it reaches its sell-by date.[17] The purchaser of a new car for a high price can reasonably expect a car without any faults and blemishes, whereas the purchaser of an 'old banger' for £100 can only reasonably expect conformity with basic safety standards. Similarly, what counts as reasonable care will depend in part upon the price being paid for the service.

Mistake

We observed in the discussion of consent in Chapter 7 that the doctrine of mistake occupies an uncertain position. Although there is a superficial logic in regarding a mistake as negativing the intention to enter into a particular contract, this logic cannot be permitted to govern contracts, because it could provide an open-ended excuse to avoid any transaction which turns out to be unpalatable. A better understanding of the doctrine of mistake places it in the context of interpretation of contracts. On this view, certain facts could be regarded as a condition precedent to the obligations arising under the contract. If as a result of a mistake these conditions did not exist, then the contractual obligations should be unenforceable. Whatever the correct interpretation of the doctrine of mistake and its place in English law, there can be little doubt that it provides fertile terrain for a party seeking to escape from a disadvantageous contract.[18]

In *Grist v Bailey*[19] for example, the vendor of a house sold it for £850, rather less than its probable market value of £2,250, under the influence of a mistake that it was occupied by a tenant with tenure protected by statute, whereas in fact the tenant was dead. The English Court of

15 *Johnstone v Bloomsbury Health Authority* [1992] QB 333, [1991] 2 All ER 293, CA.
16 Sale of Goods Act 1979, s 14(2a); *Rogers v Parish (Scarborough) Ltd* [1987] QB 933, [1987] 2 All ER 232, CA.
17 Willett, 'Fairness in Sale of Goods Act Quality Obligations and Remedies', in C Willett (ed), *Aspects of Fairness in Contract* (London, 1996), 123, at 128; *Harlingdon & Leinster Enterprises Ltd v Christopher Hull Fine Art Ltd* [1991] 1 QB 564, [1990] 1 All ER 737, CA.
18 *Patterson*, 'Equitable Relief for Unilateral Mistake' (1928) 28 *Columbia Law Review* 859.
19 [1967] Ch 532, [1966] 2 All ER 875, Ch.

Chancery permitted rescission of the contract on the ground that the parties had made a fundamental mistake, but the court attached a condition to its order which required the parties to make a new contract at the market price for such a house with vacant possession. One cannot doubt that the crucial factor which determined whether or not this mistake was sufficiently fundamental to warrant rescission of the contract was the substantial difference in price between the property with and without vacant possession. A similar interpretation of the doctrine of mistake is applicable to the famous American case, *Sherwood v Walker*.[20] The plaintiff demanded possession of a cow named 'Rose 2d', which he had agreed to purchase for $80. The defendants refused to deliver the cow for that price, on the ground that they had agreed the price on the mistaken assumption that she was barren, whereas she was with calf and worth between $750 and $1,000. The Michigan Court of Appeals reversed the trial court which had enforced the action for possession of the cow. It held that the defendants were entitled to rescission of the contract if the mistake went to the root of the matter, the very nature of the thing. The court held that a barren cow is a substantially different thing from a breeding one, but who can doubt that this judgment was influenced largely by the commercial value of the two kinds of animal rather than their external appearance?

These decisions illustrate how under the doctrine of mistake courts can invalidate contracts which deviate substantially from established market prices. The emphasis on the requirement of a common mistake confines this jurisdiction to instances where neither party is aware of the true state of the facts. This limitation perhaps suggests to the court that neither party has assumed the risk of the facts turning out to be false. If so, then express or implied terms which allocate the risk should prevent the application of the doctrine. The same point can be made by insisting that the doctrine of mistake refers to cases where the parties have agreed by implication that certain fundamental conditions of fact should exist before the contractual obligations arise. What counts as fundamental then depends upon the degree of unfairness of the outcome if the contract were to be enforced according to its terms.

Restraint of Trade

Terms in contracts designed to restrict freedom of trade, such as restrictions on setting up a business or seeking employment, are void under the common law doctrine of restraint of trade unless the term can be justified as reasonable. Although the ostensible purpose of the doctrine is plainly to protect freedom of competition in the market, it can be used instrumentally to invalidate contracts which a court perceives to be imbalanced in its obligations. For example, in *Schroeder Music Publishing Co Ltd v Macaulay*,[21] a composer agreed to give all his song compositions

---

20　66 Mich 568, 33 NW 919 (1887).
21　[1974] 1 WLR 1308, [1974] 3 All ER 616, HL.

to a publisher for a period of five years, renewable at the option of the publisher, in return for royalties but no promise to publish the work. The composer enjoyed considerable success and sought to extract himself from this unfavourable agreement. The House of Lords invalidated the contract on the ground that the weak bargaining position of the composer had led to an unfair agreement under which the publisher undertook minimal obligations in return for total commitment by the composer. Trebilcock correctly observes that this transaction was produced within a competitive market, so that there could be no market failure justification for upsetting the terms of the contract nor any alternative set of terms to be discovered by the technique of market transference.[22] Nevertheless, the court clearly regarded the obligations as out of balance, and so was prepared to extend the doctrine of restraint of trade to avoid the contract.

These examples of instrumental applications of doctrines designed for different purposes, but which can secure the goal of fairness in particular transactions, could no doubt be multiplied almost indefinitely. The constant repetition of this instrumental application of contract doctrines suggests that, though the formal doctrines of the common law may reject a substantive test of fairness for the enforceability of contracts, the courts are capable of implementing such a standard covertly by the instrumental application of the rules available.

(2) *Rationale of the Common Law*
When one puts together all these techniques for ensuring fairness in contracts, and counterposes them to the strict image of the hostility of the classical conception of the law of contract to tests of fairness, a puzzling and complex picture emerges. Whilst the principal doctrines of the classical law expressly rejected any criterion of fairness in contracts, the courts operated many techniques to intervene in cases of perceived hardship. Not every foolish transaction could be invalidated or adjusted, but within the principles governing interpretation and consent the courts could formulate the detailed rules governing market transactions to avoid the worst instances of exploitation. In addition, many other doctrines can be employed in particular instances to achieve the instrumental result of avoiding the enforcement of unfair transactions. How should this legal position be interpreted?

Can we assert, despite the formal rhetorical support for freedom of contract and an uninhibited market, that the courts are in fact operating covertly a criterion of fairness for judging the validity and meaning of contracts?[23] Or should we accept the rationalizations presented by classical lawyers of this practice, that the legal doctrine achieved consistency and integrity, because the rules governing consent merely articulated the

---

22 Trebilcock, 'An Economic Approach to the Doctrine of Unconscionability', in B Reiter and J Swan (eds), *Studies in Contract Law* (Toronto, 1980), p 381.
23 P Atiyah, *Essays on Contract* (Oxford, 1988), chapter 11.

necessary conditions for freedom of contract to be exercised, and the rules governing interpretation merely ensured that the terms of the contract represented the true intentions of the parties? Or should we accept the contention of economic analysis of law that every instance of intervention can be justified on the ground of market failure, so that the purpose of the intervention is to restore competition not to ensure fairness? My discussion of the law reveals that the position is more complex than is suggested by any of these rival interpretations.

The freedom of contract ideal necessarily depends upon a conception of what should count as a competitive market. In describing the situations where a competitive market ceases to exist, the courts must examine all the circumstances which point both to the opportunity to abuse an advantageous market position and to the fact that abuse has taken place. The unfairness of the terms of the contract will inevitably provide crucial evidence of abuse of market position. The rival 'freedom of contract' and 'fairness' interpretations of the common law are therefore much closer than they typically suppose. In articulating a concept of freedom of contract, the courts must be driven to examine the unfairness of the terms of particular contracts. The mistake made by the classical lawyers was to suppose that an examination of the terms of the contract was irrelevant to the protection of freedom of contract.

This mistake seems to have arisen from a number of sources. It was not recognized that the idea of voluntary consent was insufficient on its own to describe the conditions for valid consent without some further specification of the necessary conditions for competitive markets. But when the courts were compelled to describe the conditions for a competitive market through doctrines such as undue influence and the objective test of agreement, they found themselves driven to consider whether or not an abuse of bargaining power had taken place, and the unfairness of the terms proved the determinative evidence on this point. Thus the practical application of the idea of voluntary consent necessarily entails an examination of the fairness of the terms of the contract.

A second mistake of the classical lawyers was to infer from their commitment to the economic analysis of the subjectivity of values, as embodied in the rule against testing the adequacy of consideration, that it was impossible to judge the fairness of terms.[24] This mistake led classical lawyers to suppose that not only was a consideration of the fairness of contracts undesirable but that it was also impossible. A theory of contractual fairness needs both a system of evaluating the obligations undertaken by the parties, and a calculus to determine when the disproportion in value is sufficiently great to justify legal control, for otherwise even the slightest disequilibrium would upset a contract. Classical lawyers assert that it is impossible to devise a suitable two-part theory of valuation. The subjective nature of values prevents the general

24   Gordley, 'Equality in Exchange' (1981) 69 *California Law Review* 1587.

acceptance of any objective criterion of value by which courts may assess unfairness. As Chief Baron Eyre remarked:

> The value of a thing is what it will produce, and admits of no precise standard. It must be in its nature fluctuating, and will depend upon ten thousand circumstances. One man in the disposal of his property may sell it for less than another would; he may sell it under pressure of circumstances, which may induce him to sell it at a particular time. Now, if Courts of Equity are to unravel all these transactions, they would throw everything into confusion, and set afloat all the Contracts of mankind.[25]

By accepting the theory of marginal utility, under which prices are set according to the impulses of supply and demand, the classical lawyers concluded that no objective tests of value exist by which prices can be substituted for what the parties have in fact agreed. Each contract represents a moment in the flow of supply and demand, and, therefore, to hold a contract to be unfair would be merely to substitute another moment in time or another market. Although this might be possible, it would be difficult to imitate the exact conditions under which the contract was made, and furthermore there is no reason to think that a price determined at a later moment or in another context would be any fairer.

The practical objection to a test of fairness has been shown to be false by experience. Whilst it is true that no objective standards of value exist, we can certainly devise mechanisms for determining a fair price which are perfectly rational. Legislation often employs a substitute for a market price, devised according to a calculus which reflects competing policy considerations. Although the ordinary market inhibits intervention, because major adjustments of price may seriously damage supply or demand, mechanisms for setting prices are frequently constructed which introduce marginal adjustments in order to serve distributive goals. For example, rent controls help the position of tenants by reducing the price of accommodation, but the price must be set at a sufficiently high level in order to ensure the continuing supply of adequate quantities of housing. In addition to market substitution by price control mechanisms, it is also possible for the courts to overcome practical difficulties by a technique of market transference. For example, the fairness of a price for consumer goods charged by a door-to-door salesperson can be measured against the market price in retail stores. This device involves a transference of the contract from one market – door-to-door sales – to another – retail stores – and, provided this shift is justifiable, it provides an adequate criterion of fairness for the courts to use. In *Toker v Westerman*,[26] for example, a door-to-door salesman sold a refrigerator-freezer to the defendants at a total price of $1,229 payable in thirty-six monthly instalments. On a claim for an unpaid balance on the account of $574, the defendants proved that the normal retail price in shops for an identical appliance was about $400.

---

25 *Griffith v Spratley* (1787) 1 Cox Eq Cas 383.
26 13 NJ Super 452, 274 A 2d 78 (1970).

The New Jersey Superior Court refused to give judgment for the outstanding balance on the ground that the price was unconscionably high compared to the ordinary retail value. The court's jurisdiction to intervene rested upon the provision concerning unconscionability in the Uniform Commercial Code. In England the jurisdiction might rely upon the special provisions regarding door-step sales, or the equitable jurisdiction of undue influence with the facts indicating a combination of taking advantage of an effective monopoly and the business ignorance of the consumer. In this case the court used the comparable market of retail sales to demonstrate the unfairness of the terms achieved by door-to-door sales.

We choose between the two techniques of market substitution and market transference according to the competence of the adjudicating institution. Typically, special agencies with expertise in economics must be created in order to operate market substitution successfully; on the other hand, courts can manage the market transference technique successfully. It is a mistake, therefore, to suppose that the courts have no practical way of ascertaining a fair price, once one accepts that the fair price is that obtainable in a comparable market which does not contain the defects in competition present in the case to be considered.

These two mistakes of the classical lawyers' rationalizations of the law governing the fairness of contracts persisted because they fitted so closely into the ideal of autonomy celebrated in the slogan 'freedom of contract'. Under the influence of the competitive model of human life derived from evolutionism, and reflecting a concern for the protection of rights of private property, the classical law was drawn to doctrines which insisted that individual freedom could only be realized by an uninhibited market. Any control over the fairness of the terms was regarded as a dangerous distortion of its operation as a competitive system for the distribution of goods and services, and ultimately as a threat to the private property system on which markets were based.

In the modern law of contract, however, it is recognized that we require a more complex idea of the relation between individual freedom and markets. The purpose of markets is to provide worthwhile opportunities to pursue individual goals. Competition in markets is essential for this purpose, but the mere existence of a competitive market does not ensure that any particular transaction has been entered into under conditions of fair competition without an abuse of bargaining position. Similarly, though freedom to select the terms of a transaction usually assists in the process of ensuring that the market provides worthwhile opportunities, we must introduce safeguards so that the terms reflect the reasonable expectations of the parties when there is a danger that the express terms surreptitiously deviate from those expectations. Although this modern interpretation of the connection between individual freedom and contracts, which I have described as the social market, does not require any general rule which invalidates unfair contracts,[27] it does demand that the courts should

---

27   For the contrary argument, Smith, 'In Defence of Substantive Fairness' (1996) *Law Quarterly Review* 138.

eliminate instances where abuse of bargaining position has obtained terms which are out of line with comparable market transactions or where the terms defeat the reasonable expectations engendered by the proposed transaction.

3. Statutory Controls

These modern ideas on the connection between individual freedom and markets have had a much clearer impact on legislation governing contracts. Because legislation lacks the commitment to general principles, but can demarcate interventions by reference to types of transaction and the character of the parties, it can introduce tests of fairness within narrow confines without seeking to impose a general test of the fairness of terms on all contracts. The purpose of these controls over the fairness of terms may imitate the common law's concern for the protection of competitive markets and reasonable expectations. Legislation can introduce tests of fairness of contract terms for quite different purposes as well. The statutes may be concerned with the stabilization of markets or the distributive effects of certain kinds of transactions. We should consider these different aims of legislative control over the fairness of terms of contracts in turn.

(1) Market Stabilization
In most industrialized countries, legislatures impose price controls upon an enormous variety of transactions. Often these controls serve the purpose of stabilizing the market over a period of time in order to encourage investment and ensure adequate supplies. In wartime and during economic crises, national governments proceed so far as to regulate all prices and incomes for brief periods. A typical example of this legislation concerns the regulation of the market for peanuts in the United States. Federal regulations set quotas for the production of peanuts, and farmers who conform to the prescribed limits are entitled to sell to a government purchasing agency at a price determined by a settled formula which takes into account past market prices and the available supply of peanuts. These regulations stabilize the market in peanuts, thereby providing security for producers and incentives to generate an adequate supply of the commodity. Similar methods are employed in the United States and Europe for all basic agricultural products. As a result, farmers enjoy insulation from the detrimental effects of the free market, and public money is expended to distribute income to farmers in times of hardship.

(2) Price Regulation
But legislation can also contemplate broader issues of distributive justice when it seeks to regulate the price of contracts. Since most people acquire

their wealth through market transactions, a legislature may seek to influence the pattern of distribution through control over the terms of contracts. Minimum wage laws and price controls over tenancies represent two common examples of controls over the fairness of terms of contracts with this distributive motive. In some cases, the distributive motive may be entwined with efforts to reduce inflation.

Distributive Justice

The attempt to achieve favoured patterns of distributive justice through contracts sparks particular controversy, because it is feared that such interventions will reduce the success of competitive markets in supplying goods and services. A minimum wage law, for instance, may reduce the number of jobs available because it may diminish an employer's demand for labour in response to the price increase. Similarly, the establishment of fair rents may induce landlords to reduce the supply or quality of tenancies if their profits are reduced.[28] The price of intervention in contract terms for the purpose of distributive justice may therefore be to create disequilibrium in markets, with resulting undesirable side-effects such as higher unemployment or poor quality housing. In some cases the harmful side-effects may even worsen in the long run the position of those classes of people which the intervention was intended to help, by for example creating a shortage of accommodation. For these reasons, it is often preferred to exclude distributive considerations from contract law and instead pursue distributive goals through the tax and social security system, whose effects on the competitive market are less determinate. Even if it is true that the market leads to an unfair distribution of wealth, it is argued that any injustice is best handled by taxation, because it is more efficient than price regulation, tends to interfere less with the market's supply of goods and services, and more accurately pinpoints the incidence of hardship and poverty.

Although these objections to control over the fairness of contracts are powerful, they are invariably overstated. To begin with, the costs of implementation of controls must be considered on a comparative basis.[29] In some cases it is cheaper to regulate contracts than to redistribute wealth through taxation. After all, taxation involves administrative costs just as much as price regulation. In attempts to redistribute wealth, we may discover, for example, that a minimum wage law more efficiently fills the pockets of the poor than does a complex redistributive tax mechanism, because the former is largely self-enforcing. Furthermore, given that the precise effects of any regulation of markets is always difficult to predict because of varying elasticities of supply and demand, it may make sense

---

28   K Hartley, *Problems in Economic Policy* (London, 1977), chapter 8, also in A Ogus and C Veljanovski (eds), *Readings in the Economics of Law and Regulation* (Oxford, 1984), p 275.

29   Kronman, 'Contract Law and Distributive Justice' (1980) 89 *Yale Law Journal* 472.

to chance direct regulation of contracts for distributive ends and test the effects by experience.[30]

But a deeper argument in favour of permitting control over the fairness of terms for distributive motives concerns the degree of risk which citizens should encounter when entering markets.[31] Because of shortage of time and information most contracts occur in imperfect markets. It is likely, however, that contracts will gravitate towards an equilibrium market price due to the cumulative effect of many different transactions taking place after a perfunctory search for market opportunities. But there remains a residual risk that a transaction will be isolated from these market forces, so that a party pays an excessive price or receives derisory consideration. This risk is both inescapable and to some extent desirable. The risk encourages care in comparing market opportunities, which in turn assists the operation of a competitive market. But it is not inconsistent with the acceptance of this risk to recognize that contracting parties should be given, through the law, some limited degree of insurance, so that if a transaction turns out to be significantly disadvantageous compared to alternative market transactions which were available, then this harmful transaction should not be permitted to determine the distribution of wealth. In other words, though it is desirable that contracts should be permitted to distribute wealth, it is far less clear that the law should provide no insurance at all against the possibility that the outcome is unwittingly seriously disadvantageous to one party to the benefit of the other.

The common law takes some steps in this direction through its doctrines of duress and undue influence, but these controls invariably require proof of abuse of market position. Legislation may go further, either by creating a presumption that some markets work so imperfectly as to justify intervention simply on the ground of unfairness, or by providing an insurance against severely disadvantageous contracts even without evidence or suspicion of abuse of bargaining power. The Law Society's control over the prices charged by solicitors to clients may illustrate the former case, where the market for a solicitor's services may be extremely imperfect and the client may not be able to judge the fairness of the charges.

Usury

Statutes against usury provide another common example of market substitution. Where a transaction involves a loan of money or an extension of credit for a period of time, the lender naturally demands interest upon

---

30 Kennedy, 'Distributive and Paternalist Motives in Contract and Tort Law, with Special Reference to Compulsory Terms and Unequal Bargaining Power' (1982) 41 *Maryland Law Review* 563; Leff, 'Economic Analysis of Law: Some Realism about Nominalism' (1974) 60 *Virginia Law Review* 451.

31 Collins, 'Distributive Justice Through Contracts' (1992) 45(2) *Current Legal Problems* 49.

the capital sum to compensate him for the opportunity cost of not investing the capital elsewhere. Although the common law has traditionally permitted interest charges, it has always exhibited suspicion of them on moralistic grounds. The courts reserved a residual power to declare the invalidity of terms providing for excessive interest rates in mortgages on the ground of unconscionability.[32]

In the past, legislation has attempted to impose ceilings on the rate of interest which may be charged. But this method of regulation of fairness is necessarily intricate, because the ceilings must vary according to the type of transaction, the prevailing market rates, and the technique of computing the rate. For example, in the case of a simple loan of money from a bank, the permissible rate of interest may be calculated either by adding up the total finance charges over the period of the loan and analysing them as a percentage of the capital sum, or by the actuarial method of judging the interest payments as a percentage of a declining unpaid balance. The calculation becomes even more complicated in the regulation of interest rates charged upon credit cards, where the balance of the loan is constantly changing, yet all interest charges may be avoided by immediate repayment of the loan. In addition, there is a danger that consumers with poor credit ratings will not be able to obtain a loan at all with fixed rate ceilings.[33] Of course, this paternalistic limitation on the market for credit may not be objectionable if it prevents individuals from taking on loans which they could never afford to repay.[34] Furthermore, by helping to keep interest rates low, the regulation improves the potential of the market to provide access to worthwhile opportunities for purchases to a wider sector of the population, and by reducing the chances of default the regulation may protect family stability.[35] To overcome this complexity of fixing interest rates, the Consumer Credit Act 1974 provides a broad judicial discretion to reopen credit agreements which are extortionate.[36] If the bargain is found to be extortionate, then the court may order a range of remedies for the purpose of relieving the debtor from payment of any sum in excess of that fairly due and reasonable.[37] In determining whether the bargain is extortionate, the court has to find that the payments due are grossly exorbitant or grossly contravene ordinary principles of fair dealing.[38] But in applying this standard, the courts are instructed to examine all the circumstances of the transaction, and in particular to be sensitive to the point that the debtor offered such a poor risk to the creditor that the high interest rate was justified. It is quite

32   *Cityland and Property (Holdings) Ltd v Dabrah* [1968] Ch 166, Ch.
33   Cayne and Trebilcock, 'Market Considerations in the Formulation of Consumer Protection Policy' (1973) 23 *University of Toronto Law Journal* 396.
34   Report of the Committee on Consumer Credit (Crowther Committee), Cmnd 4596 (1971), para 6.6.6.
35   Ramsay, 'Consumer Credit Law, Distributive Justice and the Welfare State' (1995) 15 *Oxford Journal of Legal Studies* 177, 192.
36   Sections 137–138.
37   Section 139(2).
38   Section 138(1).

possible therefore, as illustrated in *Ketley Ltd v Scott*,[39] for a credit agreement in which the interest rate appears well above ordinary market rates, in this case 48% per annum, to be a valid agreement, provided that the creditor can persuade the court that such a high degree of risk of default was attached to the loan that the interest rate was justifiable. The effect of such interpretations of the legislation is to remove its potential as an instrument of redistribution.[40] It cannot protect poor borrowers from high interest rates as long as the risk of default remains high, so the position that poor people pay more for credit is preserved.[41]

(3) Unfair terms in consumer contracts

Legislation designed to protect consumers has the general aims of preserving competitive markets and ensuring that contracts fulfil the reasonable expectations of the parties. The relevance of this legislation to the issue of fairness in contracts lies in the attempts to ensure that contractual obligations conform to the reasonable expectations of consumers. For example, the compulsory term in contracts of sale to consumers that the goods should be of satisfactory quality seeks to ensure that consumers receive value for money, so that the balance of the obligations is roughly equivalent.

Exclusion Clauses under the Unfair Contract Terms Act

We noted in the discussion of the test for the validity of exclusion clauses under the Unfair Contract Terms Act 1977 in Chapter 12 that the courts use as one criterion the equivalence of the obligations undertaken by the parties in the light of the exclusion clause. The extent to which this Act introduces a general requirement of equivalence of obligations depends upon the scope of its coverage. Its central objective is to tackle the exclusion of obligations which would otherwise arise by implied terms and duties of care in tort. But it is possible that the Act can be interpreted to provide a more extensive requirement of equivalence.

The scope of the Act depends crucially on what kinds of terms can be regarded as exclusion clauses and therefore subject to judicial control.[42] The Act determines its range of application in two sections. Section 13, which applies to claims for negligence and breach of implied terms in contracts for the sale or supply of goods, extends the meaning of an exclusion clause to include terms 'which exclude or restrict the relevant obligation or duty'. Section 3(2)(b), which applies to claims under other consumer and standard form contracts, extends the notion of an exclusion clause to encompass terms which permit the defendant to, 'claim to be

---

39 [1981] ICR 241.
40 Bentley and Howells, 'Extortionate Credit Bargains' (1989) *Conveyancer* 164, 234; Wilkinson, 'Unjust Credit Transactions', (1992) (Jan 24) *New Law Journal* 98.
41 I Ramsay, *Consumer Protection* (London, 1989), pp 340–348.
42 Macdonald, 'Exclusion Clauses: the Ambit of s 13(1) of the Unfair Contract Terms Act 1977' (1992) 12 *Legal Studies* 277.

entitled – (i) to render a contractual performance substantially different from that which was reasonably expected of him, or (ii) in respect of the whole or any part of his contractual obligations, to render no performance at all'. The purpose of these provisions is to prevent evasion of judicial control by means of careful drafting of contracts. To evade the Act, a standard form contract might delete express exclusions of liability, and merely state that the positive obligations are extremely limited. In a contract of carriage of goods, for example, the contract may not promise to convey the goods, but merely state that the promisor undertakes to convey the goods to the selected destination if he so wishes. The provisions of the Act recited above are designed to prevent evasions of this type.

But it must be observed that once the meaning of exclusion clauses is extended in this way, it necessarily introduces the idea that the contract should conform to the reasonable expectations of the consumer regardless of the express provisions of the contract in the small print. This provides the opportunity to introduce a standard of fairness, so that the obligations of the trader should conform to what service the consumer reasonably expects in the light of the price being paid. Clauses which substantially detract from such reasonable expectations by confining the obligations of the trader should be tested by reference to the standard of reasonableness and fairness under the Act.

Unfair Terms in Consumer Contracts Regulations
This possibility becomes more clearly realized under the Regulations which enact the EC Directive on Unfair Terms in Consumer Contracts.[43] As we have noted, the Regulations prohibit the courts from directly assessing the fairness of the price of a consumer contract, but they do permit extensive review of the fairness of the ancillary terms of the contract under the test in Regulation 4:

(1) In these Regulations, subject to paragraphs (2) and (3) below, an unfair term means any term which contrary to the requirement of good faith causes a significant imbalance in the parties' rights and obligations under the contract to the detriment of the consumer.

(2) An assessment of the unfair nature of a term shall be made taking into account the nature of the goods or services for which the contract as concluded and referring, as at the time of the conclusion of the contract, to all circumstances attending the conclusion of the contract and to all the other terms of the contract or of another contract on which it is dependent.

(3) In determining whether a term satisfies the requirement of good faith, regard shall be had in particular to the matters specified in Schedule 2 to these Regulations.

(4) Schedule 3 to these Regulations contains an indicative and non-exhaustive list of the terms which may be regarded as unfair.

---

43   Directive 93/13; SI 1994/3159.

In these Regulations, which largely replicate the Directive, the criterion of fairness of ancillary terms must be derived from a combination of the concepts of 'good faith' and 'significant imbalance' together with the illustrative examples in Schedule 3 which describe terms which are presumptively unfair.

Although the 'good faith' concept certainly includes procedural elements, since Schedule 2 draws attention to the relevance of 'the strength of the bargaining positions of the parties' and the extent to which the supplier 'has dealt fairly and equitably with the consumer', it is unlikely that its meaning will be confined to instances of pressure, abuse of trust, and misleading conduct. As the concept derives from European law, it is probable that the European Court of Justice will acknowledge the relevance of the construction placed on the concept of good faith in the various national legal systems. In these jurisdictions, such as Germany and Italy, the idea combines procedural and substantive elements in a way which is similar to the idea of unconscionability deployed in some equity cases in English law. In the context of ancillary terms in consumer contracts, the criterion of reasonable expectation may prove the most useful guide to the interpretation of the concept of good faith, for it describes what the consumer might reasonably expect to be contained in the small print of the contract; if the terms differ significantly in favour of the supplier, then this could be described as inflicting an unfair surprise on the consumer and evidence a lack of good faith on the part of the supplier. The idea of reasonable expectation is not so alien to English law, though it has never functioned directly as a legal principle. As Lord Steyn has observed,

> A theme that runs through our law of contract is that the reasonable expectations of honest men must be protected. It is not a rule or principle of law. It is the objective which has been and still is the principal moulding force of our law of contract.[44]

The second concept of significant imbalance implies a 'mirror image' rule for ancillary terms.[45] This principle suggests that if a supplier inserts into the standard form contract a particular protection or advantage, then a similar or equivalent protection should be afforded to the consumer. The 'grey list' of presumptively unfair terms in Schedule 3 to the Regulations is replete with illustrations of this mirror image rule. For instance, example (f) suggests that a term which authorises the seller or supplier to dissolve the contract on a discretionary basis will be unfair unless the consumer is granted a similar right. Similarly, example (i) concerns clauses which permit the seller to determine the price of goods at the time of delivery are presumptively unfair unless the consumer is

---

44 Steyn LJ, *First Energy (UK) Ltd v Hungarian International Bank Ltd* [1993] 2 Lloyd's Rep 194, CA.
45 Hondius, 'European Approaches to Fairness in Contracts' in C Willett (ed), *Aspects of Fairness in Contract* (London, 1996) 61, 70.

given the corresponding right to cancel the contract if the consumer regards the price as too high. In its practical application of the Regulations, the Unit of the Office of Fair Trading has insisted that simple price variations should be deleted, or they have permitted the variation clause subject to a clause which grants the buyer the right to cancel the contract and receive a full refund if the increase is not acceptable to him.[46]

This last example reveals how close the Regulations come to empowering the courts to upset unfair consumer contracts. Although they are not permitted to declare the contract unfair on the ground of price alone, an ancillary clause which affects the price to be charged is subject to control and will be unfair unless the consumer is granted a discretion to cancel. Similarly, the courts are not permitted to challenge the fairness of a contract on the ground that the main subject matter of the contract represented a poor bargain, but an ancillary term which permits the seller to alter the specifications of the product unilaterally will be regarded as invalid under illustration (k) in the grey list.[47] The reasonable expectation of the consumer will be that the price charged and goods supplied will be those which were stated in the main terms of the contract, and terms which permit deviation will be regarded as contrary to the requirement of good faith unless the consumer is given corresponding rights under the mirror image rule.

If this interpretation of the Regulations is correct, then the principle that the reasonable expectations of consumers should be protected has been enacted as a standard of fairness in consumer contracts. This poses a challenge to the continued use of standard form contracts which seek in their detailed provisions to defeat those expectations through ancillary clauses. If the small print becomes ineffective, then it may not be worthwhile incurring the expense of issuing standard form contracts. There is some evidence to support the view that in the United Kingdom retailers have been abandoning the use of standard forms altogether.[48] The standard form may only remain where the main content of the contract would be unclear without it, as for example in the sale of an insurance policy.[49] Where standard forms continue to be used, then the effect of the reasonable expectation principle will be to invalidate ancillary terms which severely qualify the main obligations of the supplier described in the contract.

This conception of fairness based upon reasonable expectations does not provide unambiguous support for the view that a fairness criterion operates in the law of contract. It can be argued that the consumer's reasonable expectations are effectively the terms to which the consumer in reality was consenting nothwithstanding the small print of the standard

46   Office of Fair Trading, *Unfair Contract Terms,* Bulletin No 2, (London, 1996) p 58.
47   Office of Fair Trading, *Unfair Contract Terms,* Bulletin No 2, (London, 1996) p 57.
48   Micklitz, 'Directive 93/13 in Action: A Report on a Research Project on Unfair Terms in Consumer Sales Contracts' in C Willett (ed), *Aspects of Fairness in Contract* (London, 1996) 77, 78.
49   W D Slawson, *Binding Promises* (Princeton, 1996) 68.

form. Alternatively, it might be argued that the trader could only reasonably infer from the consumer's conduct in signing the standard form unread that consent was given to the main terms of the contract and not unexpected and onerous terms. It is possible, therefore, to view the reasonable expectation principle, as Slawson suggests drawing on the United States experience, as an articulation of the idea of consent applied in the context of consumer standard form contracts.[50] In the European context, however, this view is less convincing when we notice the connection between reasonable expectations and the mirror rule, for the effect of this combination is to permit deviation from reasonable expectations provided the consumer is granted additional rights such as cancellation in order to rectify the imbalance. The focus of the European Directive is better understood as a conception of fairness in contract law.

4. Judicial Revision

During the performance of a contract, the classical rule holds the parties strictly liable for failure to fulfil their obligations. No matter that unexpected events have dramatically altered the costs of one party's performance, the courts have generally insisted upon strict enforcement of the contract. In *Blackburn Bobbin Co Ltd v TW Allen & Sons*,[51] for example, the seller of Finland birch timber found it impossible to import the commodity from Finland as he had intended because of the outbreak of war. Even so, he remained liable to the buyer for breach of contract. He had agreed to deliver the timber, and it was of no concern to the buyer where he acquired the timber. The classical law thus affords little space to arguments seeking relief from bargains in the light of changed circumstances.

This rule of strict liability is not as harsh as it first appears. It provides an incentive for the parties to plan for risks and contingencies, so that if performance becomes more onerous then the contract will provide for some exception or adjustment of the obligations. The price of the contract may be fixed on a 'costs plus' basis, which insulates a contractor against rising prices in materials and secures a fixed percentage rate of profit, or by a formula for tracking market prices.[52] The contract may make provision for price adjustment by means of a neutral arbitrator. Exclusion clauses may absolve one party from his contractual obligations in the event of certain risks materializing, such as bad weather, industrial conflict, and war. Many commercial contracts include a 'force majeure' clause, which excludes liability in the event of performance becoming impossible or

---

50   W D Slawson, *Binding Promises* (Princeton, 1996) chapter 3.
51   [1918] 2 KB 467, CA.
52   Jaskow, 'Price Adjustment in Long-term Contracts: The Case of Coal' (1988) 31 *Journal of Law and Economics* 47.

unlawful. We can expect, therefore, that in carefully planned commercial transactions the rule of strict liability will not lead to severe imbalances in the contractual obligations between the parties, since the contract will make careful provision for contingencies and risks.

Even so, not every contract makes careful provision for contingencies. The events which render the contract more onerous for one party may not have been foreseen, or, if foreseen, the parties may not have been able to reach agreement on an appropriate provision in the contract because of the time and expense involved in negotiations. Here the question arises whether or not the courts should revise the terms of the agreement in order to restore the balance of advantage under the contract.

Judicial revision might take the form of altering a particular term, or more dramatically insisting on the termination of the existing contract and, if the parties wish, its replacement by a new contract. In the case of the supply of timber, judicial revision would raise the price of the timber to a level at which the supplier would make his expected profit on the original contract and still be in a position to deliver the goods, or in the alternative simply terminate the contract. The objective would be to prevent the enforcement of a contract which had become unfair as a result of a change of circumstances which had not been provided for in the terms of the contract.

(1) Objections to Judicial Revision

By stating the implications of judicial revision of contracts in this stark fashion, we can appreciate immediately why most judges and commentators fervently reject it.[53] In the first place, judicial revision undermines the role of the uninhibited market in determining the distribution of wealth. The classical conception of the market imagines a place where individuals use their resources and judgement to strike advantageous bargains. The strict enforcement of contracts provides incentives for the shrewd and calculating to enter the market to increase their wealth, and so to remove those incentives by judicial review would undo the market system itself. In short, if we raised the price of timber in our example, the buyer would be discouraged from entering contracts for supplies in the future, with a consequential detrimental effect upon the whole society, which ultimately depends upon the market for an adequate provision of goods and services.

A second defence of strict liability reminds us that the legitimacy of contractual relations depends in classical law upon the agreement of the parties. On this view, the parties have deliberately allocated the risks of misadventure between themselves in advance. Where the parties remain silent about a particular risk, the law infers that the party on whom the

---

53   Dawson, 'Judicial Revision of Frustrated Contracts: The United States' (1984) 64 *Boston University Law Review* 1; Gillette, 'Commercial Rationality and the Duty to Adjust Long-Term Contracts' (1985) 69 *Minnesota Law Review* 521.

loss will naturally fall has assumed that risk as well. This is not unreasonable, for most contracts fit into standard patterns where by custom the parties allocate the risks in a particular way, and the costs of writing out these terms may not be worth the candle in the long run. Any judicial revision of contracts rewrites the agreed allocation of risks, for even where the contract omits to deal with an eventuality, the law presumes an intended distribution of losses.[54] Thus judicial revision of contracts can be viewed as an illegitimate interference with the joint wishes of the parties. Applying this argument to our example, it is claimed that the seller assumed the risk that war would impede delivery because he failed to include a clause in the contract excusing him from performance in the event of war. Consequently, the temptation to raise the price should be resisted, on the classical view, for the courts should not interfere with the wishes of the parties as expressed in the agreement, since their consent provides the basis for the legitimacy of contractual obligations.

One last objection to judicial revision of contracts predictably raises the issue of the practicability of the exercise. In its simplest form, this objection relies upon the subjectivity of values again, in order to claim that judges cannot impose their own valuation of the obligations upon the parties. But usually the argument more subtly stresses the interdependence of the obligations and objects to piecemeal reform on the ground of fairness. For instance, in our example, it may be that the contract price is higher than normal because the seller has assumed the risk of war and has used his expected profits in part to insure against this eventuality. In these circumstances, to revise the price upwards to compensate the seller for his increased costs would distort the original fairness of the contract. The practical objection to judicial revision states, therefore, that a court should not meddle with the terms because they may already reflect the risks assumed and lead to a fair result.[55]

(2) Unplanned Contingencies

Although these objections to judicial revision suffice to deter the courts from engaging directly in judicial revision of contracts, they possess a number of techniques which can be employed for this purpose covertly. The most important technique consists of construction of the contract so that its apparent harsh effects can be modified by implication. In some cases, the methods of construction have been described as legal doctrines, namely frustration and mistake, which affects the remedies but not the scope of intervention. Although the courts do not acknowledge that they

---

54 Narasimhan, 'Of Expectations, Incomplete Contracting, and the Bargain Principle' (1986) 74 *California Law Review* 1123.
55 For contrary arguments see: Coons, 'Approaches to Court Imposed Compromise : The Uses of Doubt and Reasons' (1964) 58 *Northwestern University Law Review* 750; C Fried, *Contract as Promise* (Cambridge, Mass, 1981), chapter 5; Speidel, 'Court-Imposed Price Adjustments Under Long-Term Supply Contracts' (1981) *Northwestern University Law Review* 369.

are operating a fairness criterion to handle unplanned contingencies, it is hard to believe that the balance of the reciprocal obligations is not the determinative criterion.

Construction of the Contract

Under the oldest method of construction of the contract in the face of unplanned contingencies, the courts depart from their normal practice of ascribing risks to one party or the other according to the principle that the risk is assumed by the person on whom the loss will naturally fall. The courts find instead that some risks are covered by an implied condition which automatically terminates the contract, thereby relieving the parties from any future obligations. Such a condition was regularly implied into contracts of employment, so that in the event of the employee's death or imprisonment, the contract was terminated leaving neither party under any obligations towards the other. Similarly, in *Taylor v Caldwell*,[56] the court terminated a contract for the lease of a music hall when it burnt down, on the ground that the contract contained an implied condition that the hall should continue to exist. The same reasoning invoking an implied condition can be employed in cases of mistakes of fact prior to the formation of a contract.[57]

A second rather metaphysical style of construction argues that the scope of the contract's allocation of risk does not include the events which have arisen. In other words, the courts place limits upon the silent assumption of risk arising from a failure to make express provision for unexpected events. The House of Lords favoured this method in *Davis Contractors Ltd v Fareham UDC*,[58] where, because of labour shortages leading to higher wages and shortages of building materials, a contractor found the job of building a number of houses much more expensive than anticipated. The court reasoned that the contractor was bound by the contract price unless, on its true construction, the contract did not apply to the circumstances which had arisen. On this basis, the court rejected the contractor's appeal, for it regarded the price of labour and the availability of building supplies as one of the risks which had been allocated between the parties in determining the price of the contract. The change of circumstances had not altered the significance of the contractor's obligation, but had merely rendered it more onerous.

The third technique of construction which places limits upon the apparent strictness of contractual liability invokes the metaphor of base and superstructure. Every contract rests upon fundamental assumptions of fact shared by the parties. If these assumptions turn out to be false, then the court concludes that the contract should fall like a building without foundations. For example, in *Krell v Henry*,[59] the defendant rented

---

56   (1863) 3 B & S 826
57   *Associated Japanese Bank (International) Ltd v Crédit du Nord* [1989] 1 WLR 255, [1988] 3 All ER 902, QB.
58   [1956] AC 696, [1956] 2 All ER 145, HL.
59   [1903] 2 KB 740, CA.

a room for two days at an inflated price of £75, paying £25 in advance, in order to view the coronation procession of Edward VII. When the coronation was postponed due to the king's illness, the defendant defeated a claim for the balance of £50, because the occurrence of the coronation was a foundation of the contract, a state of facts without which the contract could not exist. Similar reasoning pervades cases of mistake such as *Sherwood v Walker*.[60] In that case, it will be recalled, the court ruled that it was possible to set aside a contract for the sale of a cow on the ground that both parties mistakenly believed the cow to be barren, a factual assumption at the foundation of the agreement.

Although we have distinguished these three techniques of construction, courts rely upon them cumulatively in many cases and they blend into each other. The need for these elaborate techniques of construction arises because the contingencies which may justify the refusal to enforce the contract must be so unexpected and outside the risks allocated by the contract that the courts are reluctant to assert simply that the exception depends upon an implied term which represents the unexpressed intentions of the parties. Since the contingency was probably never contemplated and was perhaps unforeseeable, to assert that the parties shared any intentions on the matter strikes the courts as an odd and improbable claim. But an elaborate technique of construction of the contract is ultimately vulnerable to the same criticism that it seeks artificially to justify refusal to enforce the contract by reference to the intentions of the parties.

Frustration

Lord Radcliffe suggested in *Davis Contractors Ltd v Fareham UDC* that,

> frustration occurs whenever the law recognizes that, without default of either party, a contractual obligation has become incapable of being performed because the circumstances in which performance is called for would render it a thing radically different from that which was undertaken by the contract.[61]

This view of the doctrine permits frustration of contracts when performance becomes impossible, unlawful, or completely different from what was originally contemplated. If frustration of the contract occurs, then the obligations of both parties are automatically terminated, so that neither is obliged to continue performance of the contract and no liability for breach of contract can arise. In a similar vein, the statutory law of sales cancels further performance of the contract if the goods perish without fault of either party before ownership has passed to the buyer.[62]

In theory there is a profound difference between, on the one hand, legal rules which permit judicial revision of contracts on the ground of frustration, and, on the other, techniques of construction of contracts which

---

60   66 Mich 568, 33 NW 919 (1887).
61   [1956] AC 696, [1956] 2 All ER 145, HL.
62   Sale of Goods Act 1979, s 7; Uniform Commercial Code, s 2-615.

aim to secure the implied intentions of the parties. In practice the rival analyses are hard to distinguish, for elaborate methods of construction of contracts must look suspiciously like legal rules permitting judicial intervention.[63] Similarly, the determination that the contract has been frustrated requires meticulous construction of the contract. For example, the rule that for a contract to be frustrated the performance of one party must have become impossible or impracticable looks like an independent test irrespective of the content of the particular contract. Yet in practice it depends for its application upon the terms of the contract. In our discussion of *Blackburn Bobbin Co Ltd v TW Allen & Sons*,[64] we noted that the contract for the supply of timber was not frustrated by the outbreak of war. The result would have been different, however, if the contract had specified the origin of the timber and performance, according to that requirement, became impossible under wartime conditions. But the contract in question merely provided for the supply of timber, not for the delivery of a specific cargo from Finland, and so performance was not impossible. Similarly, in *Krell v Henry*, the court's conclusion that performance of the contract was no longer possible depended crucially on the interpretation of the contract that it was not simply for the hire of a room, but for hire of a room to watch the coronation procession. Indubitably, the courts are tempted to reify the concept of an event rendering performance impossible in order to distinguish frustration from techniques of construction, but in practice a determination that performance has become impossible depends upon the construction of the terms of the contract to discover what performance is actually required.

The difference between the techniques of construction and frustration arises from the effects on the contract. Whereas frustration discharges the parties from further performance under the contract, the technique of construction imagines that the parties have made a provision for the events which have occurred so that the risk has been allocated onto one party.

Common Mistake

The doctrine of mistake, which has already been considered in Chapter 7, applies in this context to suggest that, if the parties enter into a contract on the basis of a mistaken assumption of fact and that fact is fundamental to the contract, then a court may hold the contract to be void or voidable, provided that neither party assumed the risk of the mistake under the express and implied terms of the contract. The relevance of this doctrine here is that the mistake may only come to light during performance of the contract. Again it is hard to distinguish this technique from construction of the contract, since the determination that the mistake of

---

63   Atiyah and Bennion, 'Mistake in the Construction of Contracts' (1961) 24 *Modern Law Review* 42; Slade, 'The Myth of Mistake in the English Law of Contract' (1954) 70 *Law Quarterly Review* 385.
64   [1918] 2 KB 467, CA.

fact was so fundamental to destroy the entire transaction depends upon an examination of the terms of the contract itself. For instance, the court had to decide whether the contract in *Sherwood v Walker* concerned a barren cow, any cow, or simply Rose 2d, whether or not she was barren, in order to identify the fundamental assumption of fact on which it was based. The court decided, no doubt after close inspection of the price, that if the contract concerned the sale of a barren cow, as seemed likely, then the presence of a fertile cow would destroy this fundamental assumption of fact.

If mistake and frustration are regarded as independent doctrines for judicial revision of contracts, then the principal difference between them lies in the time at which the unexpected event occurred. Mistake applies to events existing at the moment of the formation of the contract; frustration applies to subsequent events. In practice, it can prove difficult to disentangle the two categories. In *Sherwood v Walker*, the happy fact that the cow was fertile was a continuing one, which only became known after the formation of the contract, though the court dealt with it as a mistake of fact existing prior to the formation of the contract. But this difference in the timing of the unexpected event should not lead to different results. On facts very similar to those of *Krell v Henry*,[65] the coronation case, Wright J held in *Griffith v Brymer*[66] that the contract to hire a room to view the coronation was void for mistake, since the agreement had been reached unwittingly a few minutes after the Palace had announced the cancellation of the procession. It certainly would be strange if the accident of whether the contract was formed a few minutes before or after the cancellation of the procession would have made a difference to the legal result.

Fairness

Although the courts prefer to describe their practices as either construction of the contract in order to fulfil the intentions of the parties or as independent rules of law named mistake and frustration which are concerned with impossibility, neither of these accounts appears strongly persuasive. If the intervention is described as merely construction of the contract, then, given that the parties did not foresee and have any clear intentions towards the events which have occurred, we must suspect that the courts use a further criterion for determining the intent of the parties. The best interpretation of this standard is one which takes fairness in the sense of the preservation of the balance of advantage of the contract as the unacknowledged but vital guide to interpretation. Alternatively, if the intervention is described as the application of the rules of prior and subsequent impossibility, then again the decision whether an unexpected event renders an obligation impossible must depend upon a judgment as

---

65   [1903] 2 KB 740, CA.
66   (1903) 19 TLR 434.

to whether to continue to insist upon performance would upset the balance of advantage contained in the contract. On this interpretation, the real issue in *Blackburn Bobbin Co Ltd v TW Allen & Sons Ltd*[67] was not whether supplies of Finnish timber could be obtained any longer, but rather whether to impose this obligation upon the seller after the outbreak of war would upset the balance of advantage of the contract. Here the court took the view that the parties to a commercial agreement had allocated the risk of this eventuality in their contract, and that the materialization of the risk did not upset the balance of the obligations.

The relevance of fairness is often betrayed when a court finds an excuse to deny that a contract has been frustrated on the ground either of attributing the insuperable difficulty to the fault of the party in breach or by denying that performance has become impossible. For example, in *Tamplin SS Co Ltd v Anglo-Mexican Petroleum Co*,[68] a ship hired under a five-year time charter was requisitioned by the government during the war in 1915 after three years of the charter. Normally a court would find that the requisitioning of a ship would frustrate a time charter, but in this case the House of Lords declined to hold that the contract had been frustrated on the dubious ground that the war might be over in time to permit further use of the charter. In reality, by this decision the court tried to achieve fairness between the parties, for the person entitled to use the ship would benefit from government compensation which was higher than the charge under the agreed hire. In this case the owner of the ship was attempting unsuccessfully to escape from his contract so that he would receive the superior level of income from the government. Similarly, the legislative provisions on sales can be avoided by implying a duty to supply a lesser quantity of goods at the option of the buyer.

Although many judges deny that fairness is relevant to the question of whether or not a contract is frustrated or can be rescinded for mistake, in increasing numbers they have been admitting that a notion of fairness underlies their decisions. The courts usually avoid the terminology of fairness, however, preferring the concept of justice and injustice to express the scope of the doctrine. In a representative description of the doctrine of frustration, Bingham LJ states:

> The object of the doctrine was to give effect to the demands of justice, to achieve a just and reasonable result, to do what is reasonable and fair, as an expedient to escape from injustice where such would result from enforcement of a contract in its literal terms after a significant change in circumstances...[69]

These references to injustice, or as we prefer to say unfairness, require further elucidation.

The process of judicial revision is not so simple as to compare the obligation of one party before and after the unexpected event in order to discover whether the event has substantially increased the cost of

---

67 [1918] 2 KB 467, CA.
68 [1916] 2 AC 397, HL.
69 *J Lauritzen AS v Wijsmuller BV, The Super Servant Two* [1990] 1 Lloyd's Rep 1, CA.

performance of his obligation. The criterion of fairness must also be sensitive both to the sophistication of the parties when they established their contract and the precise allocation of risks by the contract. Where the parties enjoyed comparable resources for devising a complex commercial transaction and exercised those resources in order to create a contract which attempted to allocate all the risks between the parties, then it is unlikely except in calamitous circumstances that the courts will be prepared to accept that unexpected events have created any imbalance in the obligations. If, on the other hand, either one or both parties lack these skills, then the contract is less likely to be regarded as a presumptively fair allocation of the burdens of unforeseen and unprovided for eventualities. In these cases, the courts will countenance judicial revision in order to restore the expectations of the parties with respect to the balance of advantage contained in the contract.

The contrast between *Amalgamated Investment and Property Co Ltd v John Walker & Sons Ltd*[70] and *Grist v Bailey*[71] illustrates this differential treatment. In the former case, the plaintiffs sought to avoid a contract for the purchase of a building intended for redevelopment when, shortly after signing the agreement, it emerged that the government had designated the building one of special architectural or historical interest which immediately reduced the market value of the property. In *Grist v Bailey* the vendor of a house claimed rescission of the contract on the ground that he had mistakenly believed that it was occupied by a tenant with statutorily protected tenure which reduced the price. Whereas the English Court of Appeal in the former case gave short shrift to the plaintiffs' argument that they should be relieved from their calamitous contract on the ground that the government order was just one of those risks which purchasers of property take, the High Court in *Grist v Bailey* bent over backwards to permit the vendor, who was an ordinary house owner with no special skills, to rescind the contract because of his mistake about vacant possession. These cases may be distinguished on a number of grounds. Most commentators would point out that the mistake in *Grist v Bailey* existed at the time of the contract, whereas in *Amalgamated Investment and Property Co Ltd v John Walker & Sons Ltd* the administrative order was only finally issued after the contract had been signed. But if this distinction should make a difference, which I doubt, then it should argue in favour of precisely the opposite outcome, for the courts may be justifiably more reluctant to set aside contracts on the grounds of unexpected events when it was possible for the parties to have discovered the truth of the matter before committing themselves. Alternatively, it might be asserted that the mistake in one case was more fundamental than the other, though in monetary terms this is a tough argument to present since the drop in value in *Amalgamated Investment and Property Co Ltd v John Walker & Sons Ltd* was from £1,710,000 to approximately £200,000. It is more realistic, however, to acknowledge that, whereas the parties in one case were commercial enterprises, aware of the risks of property development, the parties in the other were ordinary householders and relatively naive about the risks associated with their transaction. The courts adopt a criterion of fairness which discriminates between types of contractors, forcing commercial enterprises to shoulder more risks of misadventure than ordinary individuals.

This interpretation of the techniques of construction and the application of the doctrines of mistake and frustration suggest that the common law is edging towards what Wilhelmsson calls 'social force majeure'.[72] He suggests that in Nordic consumer contract law, there is a unifying thread in statutory interventions and judicial interpretation of contracts which relieves a consumer from contracts when they prove oppressive as a result of a serious change in the consumer's fortunes, due perhaps to illness or unemployment. The similarities with English law become more striking when we add statutory interventions designed to protect the consumer. The key legislation is the Consumer Credit Act 1974, which gives a court considerable powers to revise a consumer credit agreement. If a court regards it as just to do so, it can reschedule debts or payments of interest in the light of the debtor's likely ability to pay, so that the consumer may receive a breathing space.[73] The costs of such deferrals of payments will raise the cost of credit to consumers in general, so that the risks of temporary inability to repay loans will be dispersed. Increasingly, creditors also offer consumers an insurance policy against the risk of inability to repay a debt through illness or unemployment, which has the same effect of dispersing the costs of default. This is perhaps a more efficient way of handling the problem of social force majeure, though it has the flaw that the insurance policy is not compulsory.

72   Wilhelmsson, 'Social Force Majeure – A New Concept in Nordic Consumer Law' (1990) 13 *Journal of Consumer Policy* 1, also in T Wilhelmsson, *Twelve Essays On Consumer Law and Policy* (Helsinki, 1996) 226; T Wilhelmsson, *Critical Studies in Private Law* (Dordrecht, 1992) chapter 8.
73   Section 129. The court is unlikely to make a time order if there is no reasonable prospect of repayment in the future: *First National Bank plc v Syed* [1991] 2 All ER 250, CA.

14

The Range of Liability

1. Privity of Contract

A contract can neither impose additional obligations on nor give any enforceable rights to a person who was not a party to the contract. Lawyers call this rule governing the range of liability the doctrine of privity of contract. Under the traditional law of contract, the principle of privity was believed to follow logically from the principle that contractual responsibility arises only from agreement or voluntary consent; it followed that a contract could not affect the rights and obligations of those who were not parties to the agreement. Even if Peter and John agree under a legally enforceable contract that Peter should hand money over to Mavis, Mavis possesses no legal right to sue Peter for the money unless she is a party to the contract.

This severe limit on the range of contractual liability does not apply to other branches of the law of obligations. Claims based upon ownership interests in property do not depend upon the establishment of a contract between plaintiff and defendant. If Mavis could establish a proprietary interest in the money, perhaps because Peter and John had established a trust in her favour, then Mavis could assert her right to her money without the need to claim rights under the contract. Similarly, under the tort of negligence, a claim for personal injury or damage to property may arise without any contractual link between plaintiff and defendant. When a houseowner contracts with a builder to construct an extension, and the builder subcontracts the electrical work to an electrician, if through negligence the electrician causes the whole house to burn down, the houseowner may sue the electrician in the tort of negligence for the damage to his property even though the houseowner had no direct contract with the electrician. But the tort of negligence does not normally permit recovery for pure economic loss as opposed to damage to property, so if the houseowner's grievance against the electrician is merely that the electrical work was done poorly so that rewiring is required, then the houseowner has no claim against the electrician either in contract or tort for the cost of rewiring. Since the different branches of the law of obligations may overlap and apply simultaneously to particular cases, the effect of the doctrine of privity of contract can be that the third person possesses non-contractual rights which supplement or even subvert the contractual arrangements.

These complex implications of the doctrine of privity of contract compel us to examine the principle under four headings.

(1) Burden of Positive Obligations

A person who is not a party to the contract cannot have obligations to perform acts imposed upon him by the contract without his consent. It would plainly be a serious invasion of the liberty of the individual if a person could be subject to additional obligations merely by virtue of an agreement between others without his consent. Such an invasion of liberty would occur, for instance, if the parties to a contract agreed that a third person should run a marathon. The doctrine of privity of contract wisely denies the parties to the contract the right to sue the third person for refusing to run the race.

(2) Burden of Disability

A person who is not a party to the contract cannot have his rights arising under other branches of the law of obligations reduced or eliminated by the contract without his consent. A contract which purports to appropriate a third person's proprietary rights or to exclude a third person's rights to claim compensation for injury in tort is ineffective in imposing a disability on the third person.

We observed in Chapter 7, however, that consent may be inferred from conduct. Although the courts will rarely infer consent to positive obligations without express indications, the inference may be more quickly drawn in respect of disabilities within networks of contracts. The case of *Morris v CW Martin & Sons*[1] illustrates how consent to a disability contained in a contract to which the plaintiff was not a party can be inferred from the plaintiff's conduct. It will be recalled that the plaintiff agreed with a furrier that her mink stole should be sent to the defendant specialists for cleaning, but her claim against the defendant for the loss of the stole was obstructed by a term in the furrier's contract with the defendant. Although the plaintiff was not a party to the agreement between the furrier and the defendant, she was held bound by its terms when she brought a claim in tort against the defendant. Lord Denning MR inferred her consent to this disability from her agreement that the stole should be sent to the cleaner on the normal terms of the trade. In effect this reasoning discovers a direct contractual link between plaintiff and defendant, a collateral contract which includes the term limiting the defendant's liability.

---

1   [1966] 1 QB 716, [1965] 2 All ER 725, CA.

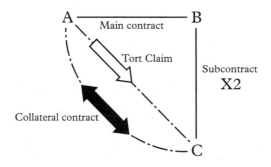

In the diagram, the plaintiff A has an implied collateral contract with the defendant C, which includes the exclusion of liability X2 contained in the subcontract between the furrier B and the defendant. The case does not contradict this aspect of the doctrine of privity of contract, but it reveals how easily the courts may infer consent to a disability.

(3) *Beneficial Positive Rights*
The doctrine of privity prevents a third person from being able to sue upon a contract made for his or her benefit. In a simple illustration, if a son contracts for renovations to be carried out to his father's home by a builder, the father cannot bring a claim against the builder for failure to carry out the renovations. In *Beswick v Beswick,* [2] a nephew promised his uncle that in return for transfer of the uncle's coal business, the nephew would pay his aunt an annuity after his uncle's decease. The nephew failed to keep his promise, but his aunt had no legal right to claim the annuity. Similarly, in an English case, *Jackson v Horizon Holidays Ltd,*[3] where a man bought a package holiday for himself and his family from a tour operator,and the tour operator broke the contract by providing an unpleasant holiday, by virtue of the doctrine of privity, his wife and children were unable to sue the tour operator directly for damages, since they were not parties to the agreement, but merely third persons intended to benefit from the contract.

This limitation on the rights of third parties intended to benefit under contracts would perhaps not matter much but for the normal rule in the law of damages that a plaintiff may only recover for his or her own losses. If the losses arising from a breach of contract fall on a third party, then as a general rule the promisee cannot recover compensation for those losses.

---

2   [1968] AC 58, [1967] 2 All ER 1197, HL.
3   [1975] 1 WLR 1468, [1975] 3 All ER 92, CA.

Under this rule, for instance, it seems unlikely that the uncle's estate in *Beswick v Beswick* could have obtained more than nominal damages, since only the aunt suffered loss resulting from failure to pay the annuity. Similarly, it should not have been possible for the husband in *Jackson v Horizon Holidays Ltd* to obtain compensation for the losses incurred by his wife and family. The principle was affirmed in *Woodar Investment Development Ltd v Wimpey Construction UK Ltd*,[4] but some of the harsher effects of this rule may be avoided by taking a broad view of the plaintiff's loss. In the case of a family holiday, for instance, the husband's loss may be described as including his inconvenience and disappointment resulting from his family's unpleasant experience, and on this basis the majority of the court in *Jackson v Horizon Holidays Ltd* determined that the husband's loss included the suffering of his family, and so awarded an augmented measure of damages. Some doubt has been cast on the general rule prohibiting the recovery of substantial damages where the plaintiff has suffered no loss in circumstances where the plaintiff transferred ownership in goods[5] or land[6] after entering into a contract involving the performance of work and that contract was broken after the transfer of the asset. It is possible that this exception might be extended to cover the case of the son contracting for renovations to his father's home, thereby permitting the son to obtain substantial damages for breach of the building contract.

Again the privity rule which prevents third parties from claiming benefits conferred under a contract would matter rather less if the parties to the contract could obtain specific performance, that is an order from a court to perform the contract. In general, however, the courts are reluctant to order specific performance of contracts except those involving interests in land. Nevertheless, this approach was successful in *Beswick v Beswick*. The estate of the deceased uncle succeeded in obtaining an order of specific performance which required the nephew to pay the annuity to his aunt. In order for this technique to circumvent this aspect of the doctrine of privity of contract more widely, however, it would be necessary to follow the Australian law that contracts for the benefit of third parties are normally ones for which damages will be an inadequate remedy and where justice requires an order for specific performance.[7] There are signs that such a development is taking place.[8]

Yet these devices for evading the effect of privity by giving the promisee the right to sue for the benefits which should have been conferred on the third party remain subject to serious disadvantages. In the first place, the promisee may be unwilling or unable to bring an action for damages

---

4   [1980] 1 WLR 277, [1980] 1 All ER 571, HL.

5   *The Albazero* [1977] AC 774, [1976] 3 All ER 129, HL.

6   *Linden Gardens Trust Ltd v Lenesta Sludge Disposals Ltd* [1994] 1 AC 85, [1993] 3 All ER 417, HL; *Darlington Borough Council v Wiltshier Northern Ltd* [1995] 1 WLR 68, [1995] 3 All ER 895, CA.

7   *Coulls v Bagot's Executor and Trustee Co Ltd* (1967) 119 CLR 460 (Aust HC).

8   *Co-operative Insurance Society Ltd v Argyll Stores (Holdings) Ltd* [1996] Ch 286, [1996] 3 All ER 934, CA; overruled on other grounds [1997] 2 WLR 898, HL.

or specific performance, and the third party cannot compel the promisee to litigate in the absence of a fiduciary relation between them. It was fortunate in *Beswick v Beswick* that the aunt was the administrator of the estate, for if the nephew had held this role, then it seems unlikely that he would have been concerned to enforce his uncle's contract against himself personally. Secondly, it is unclear whether the promisee who obtains substantial damages is under a legal duty to hand over this compensation to the third party.

(4) Beneficial Immunities
When a contract purports to give a third person a legal immunity, such as an immunity from claims brought in tort by a party to the contract, then the third person cannot rely upon that exclusion of liability. The doctrine of privity indicates that the third person should not be able to enforce the promised immunity by way of a defence to the claim by the promisor, since the third person cannot obtain any rights from a contract to which he is a stranger.[4] A leading English case on the doctrine of privity, *Scruttons v Midland Silicones Ltd*,[9] illustrates this rule. Under a contract for the carriage of goods in the form of a bill of lading, the owner of the goods agreed to a limitation of liability for damage to the goods which purported to cover not only the other party to the contract, the carrier, but also any bailee, that is a person entrusted with the goods. When one company which was arguably a bailee, the stevedores, damaged the goods, they were unable to rely upon the promised immunity as a defence to the claim in the tort of negligence, since they were not a party to the bill of lading.

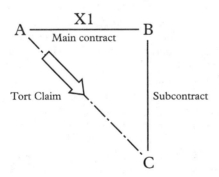

In the diagram, the owners of the goods A were able to sue the stevedores C in the tort of negligence for damaging the goods, and the stevedores were unable to set up as a defence the exclusion clause X1 in

---

9   *Scruttons Ltd v Midland Silicones Ltd* [1962] AC 446, [1962] 1 All ER 1, HL; for criticism of this logic, see Andrews, 'Does a Third Party Beneficiary have a Right in English Law?' (1988) 8 *Legal Studies* 14.

the contract between the owner A and the carrier B since the stevedores were not a party to that contract.

Although the doctrine of privity prevents a defendant third person from relying on the benefit of an immunity directly by enforcing the contract, the immunity may affect the main cause of action. In the tort of negligence, for instance, liability depends upon the court discovering that the defendant owed the plaintiff a duty of care to avoid the harm which occurred. A duty of care may be negatived or modified by reference to their conduct, including consent to a restriction of liability. A court may conclude that in cases where the plaintiff has consented in the contract to a restriction upon the duty of care that in the circumstances it would not be 'just and reasonable' to impose a duty of care.[10] This argument succeeded in *Norwich City Council v Harvey*.[11] Under a construction contract for a swimming pool, the plaintiff had agreed with the main contractors to accept any risk of loss or damage by fire to the building. Unfortunately the defendant sub-contractors set fire to the building while using a blowtorch. But the plaintiff's action for negligent damage to the building against the defendant failed. Although the defendant would normally owe the plaintiff a duty of care to avoid burning down the building, the court regarded the contractual arrangement governing the allocation of the risk of fire between the plaintiff and the main contractor as demonstrating that it would not be just and reasonable to impose the duty in this case. The underlying argument in favour of this result is that the plaintiff undertook to accept the risk of fire and obtained suitable insurance cover, and that the defendant sub-contractor when accepting the work reasonably relied upon this arrangement. In general, however, the courts will be reluctant to decide that a negligent third party which causes damage to the promisor's property owes no duty of care in tort.

Where the promisor brings a contractual claim against the third person, despite having agreed in a contract with another party not to make the claim, again in principle the doctrine of privity of contract prevents the third person from claiming an immunity. In a simple case a father pays off the debts of his son owed to the plaintiff in return for the plaintiff's promise not to pursue his claim in debt against the son. If the plaintiff nevertheless brings his claim against the son, the doctrine of privity of contract appears to prevent the son from taking advantage of the defence offered by his father's contract. Such a result appears unjust, both because it practises a deceit on the father and because it may permit the plaintiff double recovery. The courts seem likely to reject the plaintiff's claim in the circumstances, either on the ground that the debt has been extinguished, or that the action represents a type of equitable fraud against the father which a court should prevent.[12]

10   *Caparo Industries v Dickman* [1990] 2 AC 605, [1990] 1 All ER 568, HL; *Marc Rich & Co AG v Bishop Rock Marine Co Ltd, the Nicholas H* [1996] AC 211, [1995] 3 All ER 307, HL.
11   [1989] 1 WLR 828, [1989] 1 All ER 1180, CA.
12   *Hirachand Punamchand v Temple* [1911] 2 KB 330, CA.

2. Parties to the Contract

Since the doctrine of privity of contract restricts the rights and obligations arising from the contract to the parties, it becomes vital to know who the courts will regard as parties. As well as the general principles determining who are parties to a contract, special rules such as agency can extend who will be deemed to be parties.

(1) The General Principle

Perhaps surprisingly English law remains confused on the determination of the parties to the contract. One view suggests that all persons expressly named as parties will enjoy the rights and obligations arising under the contract. An alternative theory suggests that the doctrine of consideration applies to this issue, so that only persons who have supplied some consideration under the contract count as parties. The difference between the views arises when two persons, perhaps a husband and wife, both promise to sell property which is in fact owned by the husband alone, and then the question arises whether the wife can bring a claim against the promisee for the agreed payment. On the former view, the wife can claim the sum due as an express party to the contract, whereas on the latter only the husband can sue because he alone provided consideration.

The second view that the doctrine of consideration provides the test of who are parties to the contract receives considerable support from the frequent repetition of the adage 'consideration must move from the promisee'. Unfortunately this phrase is ambiguous, for it usually means no more than an enforceable promise requires consideration, but it can be understood as determining the range of persons who may sue upon the promise, in other words who are the parties to the contract.

It is surely a mistake, however, to confound the question of which promises are legally enforceable with the issue of who are parties to the contract with the right to sue upon it. Furthermore, it is surely undesirable to introduce a complication into the determination of the parties to a contract by searching behind the formal document in order to check that both promisees provided consideration.

Despite frequent reference to the adage that 'consideration must move from the promisee', the courts appear to determine the question of the parties to the contract by a careful examination of the facts of the case and the intentions of the parties. In some instances, although a person may be named in a contract, the court regards that person as a third person who cannot enforce the contract. In other cases, the court interprets the arrangement as one where the third person is a joint promisee, so that the parties intended all three to be parties to the contract, with the effect that all three obtain rights under the contract.[13]

---

13 *Coulls v Bagot's Executor & Trustee Co Ltd* (1967) 119 CLR 460 (High Ct of Australia); Law Commission, *Privity of Contract: Contracts for the Benefit of Third Parties*, Report 242 (London, 1996) 70.

(2) The Extension of Parties

Many rules permit the extension of the parties to a contract. On the death of a party to a contract, the contractual rights pass to the executors or administrators of the deceased's estate. Negotiable instruments, such as cheques and bills of exchange, provide commonplace instances where a third party may claim rights under a contract, for the rights created by these instruments can usually be transferred to third parties by means of a simple endorsement. Similarly, under many types of contracts, such as leases and money debts, the original parties frequently assign their rights to third parties, and, with certain safeguards, the law recognizes that a written or verbal transfer of rights effectively substitutes the third party as a party to the contract.[14] In addition, the common law permits wide relations of agency where a principal may gain rights under a contract made on his behalf by his agent.

In each of these examples, the legal reasoning shares an identical pattern: by virtue of a legally recognized technique, such as endorsement or written assignment, a third party is added or substituted as the holder of the rights under a contract. This reasoning deftly avoids a direct challenge to the doctrine of privity, whilst creating simple legal methods for providing third parties with benefits under a contract. It is therefore unusual these days for the doctrine of privity to lead to much injustice and frustrated expectations, for often with no more than trivial precautions the original parties can make certain that the third party gains rights under the contract.

Agency

The principles of agency apply to many routine transactions. If a consumer purchases goods in a supermarket, although the transaction takes place superficially between the sales assistant and the consumer, the legal analysis describes the sales assistant as an agent for the supermarket, so that the only parties to the contract are the consumer and the supermarket. It is even possible for a person to enter a contract simultaneously as a party and as an agent for a third person, provided that this dual status is clearly expressed. The formation of contracts through agents provides a method for circumventing the doctrine of privity of contract.

When one of the parties to the main contract simultaneously enters into a collateral contract acting as an agent for a third person, then two contracts have been created, one of which gives the third person legal rights. This analysis applied in *New Zealand Shipping Co Ltd v Satterthwaite & Co Ltd (The Eurymedon)*.[15] The plaintiff's goods were damaged due to the defendant stevedore's negligence during unloading from a ship. Under the plaintiff's contract of carriage with the carrier in the form of a bill of lading, the plaintiff had agreed that liability for damage

---

14　The common law principles are supplemented by statute to achieve this effect: Landlord and Tenant Covenants Act 1995.

15　[1975] AC 154, [1974] 1 All ER 1015, PC.

to the goods should be limited. The contract recited that this promise was made not only to the carrier, but also that for this purpose the carrier acted as an agent for any employees, agents, or independent contractors. The Privy Council accepted that this agency clause permitted the stevedores, as independent contractors of the carrier, to rely upon the immunity conferred by the bill of lading.

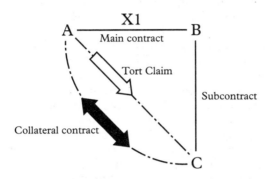

In the diagram, the plaintiff A has agreed with the carrier B to a limitation of liability X1, which defeats the plaintiff's claim in tort against the stevedores C by virtue of the collateral contract created between A and C by means of B acting as C's agent for this purpose. Although similar on its facts to *Scruttons Ltd v Midland Silicones Ltd*, the creation of an express agency relation in the terms of the bill of lading permitted the court to discover a collateral contract between the plaintiff and the stevedores under which the stevedores benefited from an exclusion of liability. This method for circumventing the doctrine of privity only works when the technical agency relation between the promisee and the third person can be established, though by relying on the ostensible authority of an agent and subsequent ratification by a principal the method has a potential wide field of application.[16]

3. Rationale of Privity

Numerous justifications have been advanced for the doctrine of privity. None of them entirely succeed in justifying the current legal rules excluding third parties from taking the benefit under contract. But they do reveal that some constraints upon actions brought by third parties are necessary. We should consider three of the principal justifications for the doctrine.

---

16 *Port Jackson Stevedoring Pty Ltd v Salmond and Spraggon (Australia) Pty Ltd (The New York Star)* [1981] 1 WLR 138, PC; see also Lord Goff, *The Mahkutai* [1996] AC 650, [1996] 3 All ER 502, 512, PC.

(1) Autonomy

Under the principles governing the ascription of contractual responsibility, only consent to an agreement engenders contractual responsibility. Without consent to the agreement, the third party should not obtain rights and obligations under it. In other words, contractual rights and duties remain personal to those who create them; all contracts resemble a marriage in so far as no third party can claim the right to share the intimate relations established between the spouses. This argument justifies the restriction of the range of responsibility to the parties to the contract.

This argument overlooks the distinction between the issue of how a person becomes bound by contractual obligations with the separate question of who may obtain rights under a contract. It is perfectly consistent to say out of respect for the autonomy of individuals that only persons who have consented to an agreement should be bound by the contract, but at the same time permit another to claim rights under the contract if the contract purports to confer a benefit on this third party. The purpose of entering contracts is to restrict the freedom of the parties in certain ways for their mutual advantage, and if they choose to give a legal right to a third person this is no greater interference with their autonomy than any other term of the contract.

This rebuttal of the argument based on respect for autonomy must be qualified in one respect. In some circumstances, to permit third parties to sue upon a contract would interfere with the autonomy of the original parties to the contract by preventing them from terminating or modifying it by agreement. But this consequence does not follow automatically. The parties to the contract could be permitted to terminate or modify it, in which event the third party would lose any rights under it, except perhaps the right to claim damages for any detrimental reliance on the basis of a claim under the reliance model. Alternatively, sufficient protection for the autonomy of the contracting parties could be achieved by declaring that the right to modify or vary the agreement is lost when either the third party materially changes his position in justifiable reliance on the promise or when the third party manifests his assent to the contract at the request of the promisor or promisee.[17]

(2) Mutuality of Rights

The doctrine of privity is also justified by the argument that since the third party provides nothing in return for the promised benefit and cannot be liable for breach of contract, it is inequitable to give the third party the right to sue upon the contract. This moral argument that the law of contract should always insist upon a mutuality of rights and liabilities became confused with the doctrine of consideration. It was suggested that

---

17   See Restatement (Second) of Contracts, s 311(3); *Wiley v Berg*, 282 Or 9, 578 P 2d 384 (1978).

the rule was that only a person who has provided consideration may enforce a promise.[18] Of course, the doctrine of consideration deals with the quite separate question of what types of agreement should be enforced by the state. It should have no application to the different question of which persons should be entitled to claim rights under a contract.[19]

Yet the moral argument in favour of privity based upon mutuality of rights, unencumbered by references to the doctrine of consideration, has greater substance. If third parties were granted rights to sue upon a contract, but not being parties themselves could not be sued, then this would create an imbalance of rights. This argument only works, however, on a superficial analysis of the situation. In a typical case, the promisor ensures that his remedies against the promisee under the contract are adequate so that there is no need to acquire additional rights against the third party. If such additional rights are required then they can be sought through such devices as guarantees and indemnities.

Indeed the promisor often has obtained full performance of the contract from the promisee already, so that the equity of rights idea is quite unrealistic. In *Beswick v Beswick*,[20] for instance, an elderly coal merchant sold his business to his nephew in return for a promise of an annuity, which would be payable to his widow after his death. After his uncle's death, the nephew declined to make any further payments to his aunt. Although it may be said of this case that, since the nephew could not sue his aunt, it would be wrong to grant her a cause of action, this argument overlooks the point that the nephew has already received in full his expected benefit under the contract, so he has no need of any remedy. On the contrary, to deny the aunt a remedy must promote unjust enrichment of the nephew, in the sense that he has acquired the coal business without having had to pay the agreed price for it. Similarly, in *Jackson v Horizon Holidays Ltd*,[21] it is true that the tour operator cannot sue the man's family for the price of the holiday, but it can sue the husband directly, and has almost certainly required payment in advance. In these circumstances, the tour operator enjoys full protection, but the law of privity prevents third party beneficiaries from gaining a corresponding level of security.

On closer inspection, therefore, the moral argument concerning the equity of rights rarely carries any weight, for promisor and third party are not in equivalent positions. The moral argument concerning equity between the parties often in fact points in the opposite direction: since the promisor's rights have been fully vindicated, either a contracting party should be entitled to claim damages on behalf of intended beneficiaries,

---

18   Flannigan, 'Privity – The End of an Era (Error)' (1987) 103 *Law Quarterly Review* 564.

19   This view of the separation of consideration and privity has often been questioned: Coote, 'Consideration and the Joint Promisee' (1978) *Cambridge Law Journal* 301; Law Revision Committee, Sixth Interim Report (Statute of Frauds and the Doctrine of Consideration), Cmd 5549, paras 37, 41.

20   [1968] AC 58, [1967] 2 All ER 1197, HL.

21   [1975] 1 WLR 1468, [1975] 3 All ER 92, CA.

or more simply third parties should receive equivalent rights, for otherwise there is a risk of unjust enrichment to the promisor.

The moral argument concerning the mutuality of rights can also be weakened by reference to the intentions of the promisor. If the promisor has agreed to an arrangement under which he accepts liability to perform a promise, even though the beneficiary of the promise will incur no obligation, then it could be insisted that for the promisor to go back on his word is to undermine the intentions of the parties to the contract. The promisor no doubt took the opportunity to secure his interests in other ways, and this denial of a right vested in the third party is in reality an attempt to revise the contract without the consent of the promisee.

(3) Indeterminate Range of Liability

A much more substantial objection to an abolition of the rule that third parties cannot sue upon a contract points out that the numbers of third parties interested in suing may be considerable and engender unexpectedly enormous liabilities. The ever present danger of introducing third party rights is the possibility of exposing the promisor 'to a liability in an indeterminate amount for an indeterminate time to an indeterminate class'.[22] If such broad liability to third parties could be created by contracts, then this would certainly discourage entry into transactions, with the consequence of serious harm to the market system for the creation of wealth as a whole.

The American case, *Martinez v Socoma Companies Inc*,[23] illustrates this problem well. Under the Economic Opportunity Act of 1964 (as amended) the United States Congress designated certain neighbourhoods which had large concentrations of low income persons and unemployment as Special Impact Areas and made federal funds available for government contracts with local private industry. The defendants entered into such a contract with the government and undertook to train and employ a specified number of local residents. The plaintiffs were members of the class intended to benefit from legislative aid who alleged that the company had failed to comply with its contractual obligation to hire and train the required number of local residents. The plaintiffs claimed a right to sue the company as intended beneficiaries under the contract. The California Supreme Court denied their claim on the ground that from the terms of the contract it did not appear that the government intended to make a gift to the plaintiffs or to confer on them a legal right against the defendants. The plaintiffs were simply incidental beneficiaries of the contract, and the company's responsibility did not extend so far. It is evident that the court feared to extend rights to such a wide class of beneficiaries, that is, all the poor and unemployed persons in the Special Impact Area, and that this fear provided the reason for preserving a modified privity rule. To make the company liable to the poor and

---

22   Per Cardozo CJ, *Ultramares Corpn v Touche* 174 NE 441 (1931) at 444.
23   11 Cal 3d 394, 521 P 2d 841 (1974).

unemployed persons in the neighbourhood certainly would have provided a vigorous incentive for the company to comply with the terms of the government contract and the policy of the legislation, but, in the long run, to impose such liability might deter companies from accepting federal aid and ultimately thwart the purpose of the law. Thus even in jurisdictions which do not follow the strict doctrine of privity, the courts must balance the interests of third parties who indirectly depend upon proper performance of the contract against the danger that worthwhile transactions will be discouraged by the threat of liability to a wide range of persons.

The law of tort encounters the same problem of limiting the range of liability. Suppose that under a contract for the carriage of goods by road the driver of the lorry negligently crashes and destroys the load. The driver or his employer will be liable for breach of contract, but there is also the prospect of potential liability to anyone affected by the damage to the goods. We may imagine that the intended recipient of the goods is a factory which is forced to shut down temporarily until fresh supplies can be obtained, which in turn leads to loss of wages for employees at the factory, which in a further ricochet effect reduces the turnover of local shops. The law of tort shrinks from the prospect of rendering the driver liable to all these potential claimants, even though it is possible to trace a causal link between the negligent driving and these losses. For this reason, the law of negligence generally prohibits claims for pure economic loss, that is claims not based on damage to the plaintiff's property. This restricts claims in tort in the example to the owner of the goods at the time when they are damaged. Here the law of tort responds to the same problem that liability to an indeterminate number of plaintiffs would discourage any market transactions.

The most significant justification for the doctrine of privity thus boils down to the simple point that the law of contract must draw a line at some point to set limits to the range of liability to third parties. English law established the line firmly at the point where a person was a party to the agreement. But many other possibilities could have been recognized. These possibilities can be illustrated by a series of circles which progressively expand the range of liability from the smallest group of potential plaintiffs, the parties to the contract as in the rule governing privity of contract, to the widest group, which might be anyone whose economic loss was caused as a result of justifiable reliance upon the defendant.

The test for the range of liability could have been any person explicitly named as an intended beneficiary of the contract. A slightly broader circumference of liability would have included all those persons intended to benefit from performance of the contract. For instance, American courts recognize an exception which provides that, where the contract expressly mentions third parties as intended beneficiaries of the contract, they will be permitted to claim the envisaged benefits. The facts of the previous examples concerning the rights of beneficiaries of a contract for a package holiday and of the intended recipient of a sum of money probably fit within the exception. Furthermore some American courts proceed so far as to permit intended beneficiaries who were not expressly mentioned in the contract to claim rights under it. For example, a downstream landowner successfully sued a chicken processor for breach of its contract with the local city not to oversaturate its sewage treatment facilities, since the purpose of the agreement plainly included the protection of those drawing water from the creek.[24] These results indicate that the doctrine of privity enjoys a precarious existence in modern American law.

All of these tests have been used in different jurisdictions, so the question which must be addressed in English law is whether or not there is a good justification for setting the range of liability so narrowly. Although the problem of remote third parties requires a limitation upon the range of liability, it is far from clear that the line drawn by the English law of contract by reference to consent to the contract achieves satisfactory results.

4. Objections to Privity

Does the law of privity cause injustice? It can be criticized on three grounds. One concerns the frustration of the intentions of the contracting parties; another seeks to provide relief from justifiable detrimental reliance incurred by the third party resulting from reliance upon the contract; and the third concerns the possibility of unjust enrichment to the promisor. We will consider these objections in turn.

(1) Intentions of the Parties
The doctrine of privity of contract may defeat the intentions of the parties to the contract. Under their contract it may have been their joint intent to confer a benefit on the third party, either by way of a gift of property or the conferral of an immunity from suit by the promisee. If the third party cannot vindicate this right, then there is a danger that the law of contract will deviate from its role in supporting transactions through enforcing them according to their terms.

24　*Ratzlaff v Franz Foods*, 250 Ark 1003, 468 SW 2d 239 (1971).

The strength of this argument depends considerably on the ease by which the parties to the contract can evade the doctrine of privity by invoking some legal mechanism through which the third party can acquire enforceable rights. We have noted how this may be done, either through the establishment of an agency relation between promisee and the third party, or the assignment of rights to the third party. More complex legal arrangements such as trusts can also achieve the same effect. But these techniques all require a degree of legal skill, and it must be questioned whether the law of contract serves its purpose of buttressing market transactions adequately when it requires traders to secure the services of a lawyer before they can give effect to their joint intentions. It would have been possible, for example, for the uncle in *Beswick v Beswick*[25] to have achieved the desired result of conferring the benefit of an enforceable annuity upon his wife by means of a trust or an assignment, but it is doubtful whether the law should erect such hurdles to such simple transactions.

Even in those cases where the parties are guided by lawyers, it may not always be possible to devise a contract which secures the interests of third parties adequately. This problem arises where the identity of the third parties cannot yet be known at the time of the formation of the contract. In the case of construction contracts, for instance, the main contractor may not have fixed upon all the sub-contractors for the work, and indeed their identity may depend upon subsequent nomination by the promisor. If the main contractor seeks to confer any benefit upon these sub-contractors, such as protection under an insurance policy, then without being able to name the sub-contractors as insured persons under the contract, it may not be possible to give the sub-contractors enforceable rights against the insurance company.[26]

This objection to the doctrine of privity points to the need for modest reform. The intentions of the parties could be fulfilled in two ways. First, third parties could be granted the right to sue for a benefit or claim an immunity if the contract intended to benefit them in this way and identified them clearly either by name or by intended function, as in the case of sub-contractors. Alternatively, the promisee could be granted the right to sue upon the contract in order to obtain the benefit intended to be conferred upon the third party, but then be under an obligation to transfer that benefit to the third party.

(2) Justifiable Reliance

A broader objection to the doctrine of privity insists that the law of contract should seek to protect persons engaged in commerce from incurring losses resulting from justifiable reliance upon the words and conduct of others.

---

25 [1968] AC 58, [1967] 2 All ER 1197, HL.
26 *Trident General Insurance Co Ltd v McNiece Bros Pty Ltd* (1988) 165 CLR 107 (Aust HC).

We have already noted the significance of this principle both under the reliance model of the test of enforceability, and as part of the duty to bargain with care. Here the principle suggests that those third parties who have acted in reliance upon the proper performance of the contract by the promisor, either by incurring expense or by failing to take steps to safeguard their position, should be protected if that reliance was justifiable.[27] Although this principle, if adopted, would deal a lethal blow to the doctrine of privity of contract, we should observe that the elements of this idea have provided a crucial theme in pushing the courts towards circumventing the doctrine of privity by alternative legal techniques.

One example of how the idea of justifiable reliance influences the development of routes around the doctrine of privity concerns the device of collateral contracts. In the leading example of this device, *New Zealand Shipping Co Ltd v AM Satterthwaite & Co Ltd (The Eurymedon)*,[28] the Privy Council found a collateral contract between the owners of goods and stevedores who unloaded the goods under a contract with a carrier. The terms of this collateral contract provided that in return for unloading the goods the owner would accept certain limitations upon his rights to sue the stevedores in tort for negligent performance of their work. The court found its justification for the imposition of a collateral contract from the fact that, in the contract between owner and carrier, the owner expressly promised to respect certain limitations of his rights against the sub-contractors of the carrier. The strength of the stevedores' claim to be protected by the exemption clause surely stems in part from the fact that it was eminently foreseeable that stevedores would rely upon the exemption clause when unloading the goods. Suppose, for instance, that the damage to the goods had been committed not by the stevedores but by a building contractor who happened to be working for the carrier on the dock. Although the terms of the owner's promise encompassed all independent contractors of the carrier, surely the court would have been much less willing to allow the builder to take advantage of this clause, because such reliance would not be justifiable.

In the United States, where the reliance model for the test of enforceability is more firmly established, the courts can use the idea of promissory estoppel to protect third parties under this principle. In *Hoffman v Red Owl Stores Inc*[29] the liability of the franchise company extended not only to the man whom they had strung along during their negotiations, but also to his wife, who, as joint owner of their assets, foreseeably acted on the faith of the representations made to her husband. Similarly, a bank's promise to a businessman to approve a loan could lead to foreseeable reliance by other creditors of the businessman, who might

---

27   G Gilmore, *The Death of Contract* (Columbus, Ohio, 1974), pp 87–96; Reiter, 'Contracts, Torts, Relations and Reliance' in B Reiter and J Swan (eds), *Studies in Contract Law* (Toronto, 1980), pp 288–310.
28   [1975] AC 154, [1974] 1 All ER 1015, PC.
29   26 Wis 2d 683, 133 NW 2d 267 (1965).

extend credit in the expectation of repayment out of the bank's loan. If the bank then failed to produce the loan, the creditors might be able to claim compensation for their misplaced reliance upon the bank's promise to grant a loan, even though the promise was not made to them.[30]

In English law, the development of this principle of justifiable reliance has been undertaken primarily by the law of tort. Because the duty of care is not confined to contractual relations, it is open to the courts to discover a duty of care between the promisor and the third party. When the third party has suffered physical damage or personal injuries, then normally such a duty of care will be discovered provided that the parties were in a proximate relation. The law of tort developed this protection in the context of consumers who purchased defective products which caused personal injuries or damage to property. For the sake of consumer protection and to improve the safety of products put on the market by manufacturers, the courts permitted the consumer to sue the manufacturer direct for negligence. This jurisdiction has now been largely overtaken by a statutory regime of strict liability in the Consumer Protection Act 1987, Part 1, which gives effect to the EC uniform regime throughout the single market area of Europe.[31] Under these rules, a consumer who suffers personal injury or minor property damage due to a defective product may claim compensation directly from the manufacturer or producer.

The principle of protecting justifiable reliance runs headlong into the worry that indeterminate numbers of remote plaintiffs may claim compensation for their economic losses. Here the law of tort restricts the potential range of liability by excluding claims for pure economic loss except within relations of close proximity. The relevant principles in English law may be gleaned from inspecting two leading decisions. The defendants in *Caparo Industries plc v Dickman*[32] were auditors of a company under a contract with the company. It was alleged that the defendants were negligent in certifying that the accounts showed a true and fair view of the company's financial position. If this allegation were true, then clearly the auditors would be liable for breach of contract to the company for failure to provide the service with reasonable care, subject to any exclusion of liability in the contract. The question addressed by the court was whether other groups of people who had relied upon the auditors performing the service carefully could also claim damages for the losses which they had incurred when the accounts proved misleading under an action for negligence in tort. Since the audited accounts become a published document available for anyone to inspect, the court regarded

---

30   *Alaska v First National Bank of Ketchikan* 629 P 2d 78 (1981), where the argument failed on the facts.

31   Product Liability Directive EC 85/374. See Stapleton, 'Products Liability Reform – Real or Illusory?' (1986) 6 *Oxford Journal of Legal Studies* 392; Clarke, 'The Consumer Protection Act 1987' (1987) 50 *Modern Law Review* 614. Compare, J White and R Summers, *Handbook of the Law under the Uniform Commercial Code* (St Paul, Minn, 2nd edn, 1980), pp 398–411.

32   [1990] 2 AC 605, [1990] 1 All ER 568, HL.

the problem of remoteness as severe, and so ruled out any possibility of general liability towards third parties. But the court did consider that some classes of third parties might have a sufficiently proximate relation to be entitled to claim in tort. The test for the existence of this proximate relation required that the defendant should know that the accounts would be communicated to the plaintiff, and that to the defendant's knowledge the plaintiff would use those accounts for the purpose of deciding whether or not to enter a transaction of a particular kind or adopt some other particular course of action to the plaintiff's detriment. Under this test the court regarded it as possible that the shareholders as a group could sue the accountants, if the shareholders could demonstrate that the false accounts had failed to alert them to the need to exert their powers to replace the directors of the company. The shareholders' claim to fall within a proximate relation was strengthened by the point that the company's statutory duty to submit to audit was designed for the protection and information of shareholders in the running of the company. But the plaintiff in this case, who had relied on the accounts to purchase shares in the company and to mount a successful takeover bid, was found not to be in the requisite proximate relation. The auditors owed no duty of care to potential investors in the company in the absence of direct communication between the parties with the intended investment expressly drawn to the auditor's attention.[33] This test of proximity was satisfied, however, in *Smith v Eric S Bush*,[34] where the purchaser of a house relied upon an inaccurate survey and valuation which was arranged under a contract between the surveyor and the mortgage lender. Not only was the surveyor aware in this case that the survey would be given to and relied upon by the intended purchaser, but also the purchaser had in effect paid for the survey in her contract with the mortgage lender.

A second leading authority, *White v Jones*,[35] appears to take the protection of justifiable reliance much further when no problem of indeterminate liability is present. Here a solicitor who had undertaken to draw up a Will failed to do so prior to the client's death, with the result that the plaintiffs who were intended to benefit under the Will did not receive their expected bequest. The plaintiffs successfully sued the solicitor for negligence. This claim differs from the case of *Caparo v Dickman*, since the solicitor had not made representations which he knew would be relied upon by the plaintiffs. One way of explaining the decision is to say that in undertaking the work the solicitor assumed an obligation of responsibility not only to the client but also the intended beneficiaries. Such a broad principle would, however, permit the law of tort to be employed to protect the justifiable reliance of many third parties. It might revive the principle in the earlier discredited case of *Junior Books Ltd v*

---

33   *Morgan Crucible Co plc v Hill Samuel & Co Ltd* [1991] Ch 295, [1991] 1 All ER 148, CA.
34   [1990] 1 AC 831, [1989] 2 All ER 514, HL.
35   [1995] 2 AC 207, [1995] 1 All ER 691, HL; McBride and Hughes, 'Hedley Byrne in the House of Lords: an Interpretation' (1995) 15 *Legal Studies* 376.

Veitchi Co Ltd,[36] where a sub-contractor produced faulty work in laying a floor under a contract with a building contractor. The owner of the building successfully sued the sub-contractor directly for the negligent performance of the contract, even though he was not a party to a contract with the sub-contractor.

The underlying difficulty for the courts in developing protection for justifiable reliance through the law of tort is that whether or not reliance is justifiable depends on several crucial considerations. Not only is it relevant that the defendant was aware of the degree and type of reliance, and not only is there the concern to avoid the deterrence to commerce from the potential risk of indeterminate liabilities, but also the agreed allocations of risk will be pertinent. Reliance should not be regarded as justifiable if it in effect renders nugatory a contractual provision designed to allocate risks in other ways. If, for example, the owner of the building in *Junior Books Ltd v Veitchi Co Ltd* had agreed with the main contractor not to make any claims against the subcontractor for negligent work, then this agreement should count against any claim based upon reliance.

The test for existence of a duty of care includes the element that the duty must be just and reasonable in the circumstances. Increasingly courts refer to the contractual allocations of risk pertinent to the case in order to determine whether either that the imposition of a duty of care would upset the contractual allocation of risk, or that it would in fact fill in a gap in the economic arrangements between the parties. It was this kind of reasoning which led the court in *Norwich City Council v Harvey*[37] to deny the existence of a duty of care, even in a case where the defendant had seriously damaged the plaintiff's property by fire, on the ground that it was just and reasonable in view of the contractual allocation of risk of fire agreed by the promisor to absolve the defendant from a duty of care.

(3) Unjust Enrichment

The third objection to the doctrine of privity is that it can lead to unjust enrichment. By the phrase unjust enrichment, it is not intended to refer to the precise rules governing restitutionary claims, but rather the general concept that one person has unjustifiably obtained a benefit at another's expense. This defect of the doctrine of privity emerges clearly in those cases such as *Beswick v Beswick*, where the promisor receives valuable property in return for an unenforceable promise to benefit a third party. But the problem of unjust enrichment will occur whenever the promisor has received the consideration under the contract and is seeking to avoid the reciprocal obligation to confer a benefit on the third party. Here the promisee under the contract has suffered no loss, so cannot claim substantial damages, but the third party cannot claim the intended benefit.

---

36   [1983] 1 AC 520, [1982] 3 All ER 201, HL; cp *Sears, Roebuck & Co v Jardel*, 421 F 2d 1048 (3d Cir 1970).
37   [1989] 1 WLR 828, [1989] 1 All ER 1180, CA.

An analogous problem arose in the Australian case *Trident General Insurance Co Ltd v McNiece Bros Pty Ltd*.[38] The insurance company had agreed to provide liability insurance against claims for personal injuries to the owner of a site, and under the policy the insured person was defined to include not only the owner but also its independent contractors and their sub-contractors engaged on the construction project. An employee of a sub-contractor was injured on the site and successfully claimed damages for personal injuries against the main contractor. The main contractor then sought an indemnity under the owner's insurance policy. The doctrine of privity blocked this claim, because the main contractor was not a party to the contract of insurance, and nor had the owner contracted as an agent for the main contractor. Nevertheless the claim succeeded, though the court gave different reasons for its decision, ranging from direct assaults on the doctrine of privity to a more limited exception governing insurance policies. Under English law, apart from special rules governing liability insurance,[39] the claim would fail for want of privity of contract.[40] The underlying objection to the application of the doctrine of privity in this case is surely that the insurance company had received the premiums under the policy which had been calculated on the basis of the risk of having to indemnify all contractors on the site, yet now it was seeking to keep those premiums but not pay out under the policy when a claim contemplated by the contract of insurance was brought.

Of the three arguments for reform of the law of privity of contract, this concern with the unjust enrichment of the promisee is surely the most compelling. But it would not address all the problems created by the doctrine of privity, such as the creation of immunities for third parties.

5. Reform

There is widespread acceptance of the need for reform of the English law of privity of contract in order to remove the injustice which it occasions. In addition, proponents of reform suggest that it would have the advantages of reducing the need for complex contractual arrangements to circumvent its unwanted effects, and also bring English law into harmony with other European legal systems.[41] The hurdle confronting any reform will be to meet all three objections to privity of contract, namely that it thwarts the intentions of the parties, it leaves justifiable reliance unprotected, and that it leads to unjust enrichment of the promisor.

---

38   (1988) 165 CLR 107 (Aust HC).
39   Road Traffic Act 1988, s 148(7); Third Parties (Rights Against Insurers) Act 1930.
40   *Vandepitte v Preferred Accident Insurance Corpn of New York* [1933] AC 70, PC.
41   Law Commission, *Privity of Contract: Contracts for the Benefit of Third Parties*, Report No 242, Cm 3329 (London, 1996) pp 41–43.

The English Law Commission has proposed in its report entitled *Privity of Contract: Contracts for the Benefit of Third Parties*,[42] to introduce a statutory provision granting novel legal rights to some third parties, whilst leaving any existing claims through the law of tort or under specific statutes untouched.[43] The new legal right for a third party to enforce the contract occurs either if the contract expressly confers the right or if a term of a contract purports to confer a benefit on a third party unless on the proper construction of the contract it appears the contracting parties did not intend to grant the right. The third party can be designated either by name, class, or a description. The reform also proposes that the parties to the contract should retain the right to vary or cancel the contract until either the third party has communicated his assent to the contract, or the promisor is aware that the third party has relied on the contract, or where the promisor should reasonably have foreseen that reliance which has in fact occurred. In effect the proposal creates a presumption that contracts designed to confer a benefit on third parties will afford the third party the right to enforce it subject to contrary indications in the contract.

This proposal for reform clearly addresses the objection that the current English law thwarts the intentions of the parties. It also removes the problem of unjust enrichment, for the third party can claim the intended benefit. The position in *Beswick v Beswick*, for instance, would be reversed, for the widow could claim that the contract purported to confer a benefit upon her. The position created by the proposed reform with respect to justifiable reliance, however, remains more complex.

Although the reform may protect some instances of justifiable reliance, it will not encompass those cases where it cannot be said that the contract purports to confer a benefit on the third party, but merely is likely to benefit the third party. On the facts of *White v Jones*, for instance, the contract with the solicitor to draft a Will was likely to result in benefits to the beneficiaries, but it could not be said that this contract itself purported to confer a benefit on them. Similarly, on the facts of *Junior Books v Veitchi Ltd*, a subcontractor on a construction project will enter a contract for work which will benefit the owner of the building, but the subcontract itself is unlikely to be framed in the form of conferring a benefit on the owner as third party. The extent to which the proposed reform tackles instances of justifiable reliance by third parties will depend crucially on how the idea that the contract purports to confer a benefit on the third party will be interpreted.

It is perhaps understandable that these instances of justifiable reliance should be left to the common law of tort, because the issue of when reliance

---

42 Law Commission, Report No 242, Cm 3329 (London, 1996); Adams, Beyleveld, Brownsword, 'Privity of Contract – the Benefits and the Burdens of Law Reform' (1997) 60 *Modern Law Review* 238; the proposed reform is similar to the New Zealand Contracts (Privity) Act 1982.

43 Law Commission, op cit, p 138.

is justifiable depends upon numerous factors which have to be weighed. It is not possible to create a simple rule which grants enforceable rights to third parties when such rights may turn on such issues as whether the right might upset the allocation of risks in a network of contracts or the right might extend to an indeterminate number of third parties. Yet the failure to tackle these issues as part of the law of contract merely displaces them into tort, where further irrelevant considerations such as proof of negligence serve merely to complicate matters. The simple issue at the heart of both *White v Jones* and *Junior Books v Veitchi Ltd* was whether a third party who had relied upon a contract could sue for its breach. The answer to that question should not depend upon proof of negligence, but whether or not the contract had been broken, and whether the third party had justifiably relied upon performance. In turn the issue of justifiable reliance should not turn on whether or not the contract purported to confer a benefit on the third party, but rather on whether the contract would foreseeably benefit the third party, whether the third party had in fact relied upon performance, and whether the reliance was justifiable in the light of the potential range of liability and the surrounding contractual allocations of risk. It is noticeable that the Law Commission was prepared to envisage that these considerations should be taken into account both when rebutting the presumption that a contract which purported to confer a benefit on a third party should not in fact give the third party a right, and also when removing the right of the parties to vary or cancel their contract. Yet the Commission was unable to see that its proposed reform would necessarily prove incomplete unless it tackled the problem of justifiable reliance directly.

But the fundamental advantage of employing the principle of justifiable reliance as the standard for reform of the law is that it addresses directly the problems created by the doctrine of privity for the organization of relations of production through networks of contractual relations.[44] Here three or more parties are engaged in a productive enterprise. It is time-consuming and expensive to ensure that all parties enter into direct contractual relations with each other. Normally the absence of direct contracts provokes few problems, for if the parties foresee difficulties they will seek contractual arrangements to govern them. Nevertheless, it always remains possible for an economic relation not governed by contract to cause loss to one of the parties. What the courts need to achieve here is to fill in the gaps in the economic relations constituting a network, so that the business relations provide a coherent pattern of incentives and risks between the parties. The underlying strength of the stevedores' claim in *New Zealand Shipping Co Ltd v AM Satterthwaite & Co Ltd (The Eurymedon)* rests upon the good sense of the business practice that the owner of the goods should insure against loss or damage, because that person knows best the value of the goods and thus insures efficiently. It

---

44 Adams and Brownsword, 'Privity and the Concept of a Network Contract' (1990) 10 *Legal Studies* 12.

therefore made sense for the Privy Council to supplement the arrangements of this network for the transportation of goods by discovering a collateral contract in order to protect the stevedores' justifiable reliance upon the promised immunity. The principle of justifiable reliance has sufficient flexibility to be used in this role, for it can supplement these economic relations with additional duties to protect the economic interests of members of the network who lack direct contractual claims, in particular employees of contractors, whilst at the same time suppressing potential liability where this would subvert the scheme of risk allocation implicit in the network.

15
Co-operation

In most transactions, co-operation simply requires performance according to the terms of the contract. A shopkeeper hands over the goods in return for payment by the customer, or a solicitor drafts a Will and then is paid for the service by the client when it has been completed. This co-operation takes place largely as a result of the economic self-interest which led the parties to enter the transaction in the first place. The incentive for co-operation is strengthened in competitive markets by the recognition that each party has the opportunity to enter similar transactions with others for the goods or services. These incentives ensure that most contracts are self-enforcing without the need to invoke the law.

In accordance with this model of co-operation in contracts, the classical law limited its regulation to two principles. The first involved a commitment to support co-operation by enforcement of the terms of contract agreed by the parties. The second set the conditions under which one party might terminate the contract in the face of breach by the other. The right to terminate the contract was essential, so that the injured party could take up the opportunity to acquire the goods and services elsewhere. Under the classical law, there was no further general obligation to co-operate, to assist each other, to perform in good faith, or to make the contract a success for both parties. Such additional mandatory duties not only appeared unnecessary to secure co-operation, but also they threatened to breach the principle that the parties must consent to contractual obligations.

The flaw in the classical law's approach to co-operation consists in its assumption that all contracts fit into the pattern set by an isolated sale of goods or the performance of a finite service. As soon as the context shifts to long-term commercial relations, such as a business partnership, it becomes readily apparent that co-operation requires considerable obligations of loyalty and mutual assistance in order to make the transaction a success. Indeed, a strict insistence upon the terms of the contract or a threat to terminate the contract for a minor breach would almost certainly destroy co-operation between the parties and lead to dissolution of a business relation such as a partnership. For some categories of business relation, such as partnership and agency, the classical law responded to this context by supporting co-operation through the imposition of equitable fiduciary duties of good faith and loyalty. Outside these special categories of business relation, however, the traditional approach persisted.

In the modern law, however, we can detect an increasing willingness of the courts to recognize that for many transactions support for co-operation between the parties requires the recognition of supplementary obligations. Consider the case of an employment contract, where the employee insists upon a 'work to rule', that is, strict performance of the contract according to its terms. Unless the employer has foreseen every eventuality, and so tightly constrained the discretion of workers that they must perform as automatons under the terms of the contract, then the employees will necessarily enjoy a degree of discretion in how they carry out their tasks. They could quickly frustrate the employer's business objectives by a 'work to rule' in which they withdraw goodwill, that is fail to act in a co-operative manner, taking into account the interests of the employer. Performance according to the terms of the contract would render the contract unworkable and destroy its commercial purpose for the employer.

Contracts of employment illustrate a type of contract which is incomplete by design. The terms of the contract do not seek to fix in detail the obligations of each party. Instead, the contract gives a degree of discretion to both parties as to how performance should be achieved; the employer retains a discretion to direct or manage employees, and the employee retains a discretion over the details of how the work is to be completed. Contracts which are incomplete by design often contain their own dispute resolution mechanism, so that minor disagreements about how discretion should be exercised can be resolved by arbitration or further negotiation. Neither party wishes disagreement to escalate into termination of the economic relation. Similarly, business format franchises and the relation between manufacturer and distributor are incomplete by design, for they leave discretion to the parties to determine the details of performance.[1] For example, the franchisor or the manufacturer will commit themselves to advertising the product, but the manner and extent of advertising will be left to their discretion. At most, the contract may specify that the discretion should be exercised in good faith or that 'best efforts' should be employed.

There are many reasons why contracts are left incomplete by design. The parties recognise that adjustments to their obligations will have to be made in order to respond to changing market conditions. By leaving the details indeterminate, these adjustments can be effectuated without the cost and delay of a renegotiation of the contract. Another important reason for incompleteness is that this type of contract can take better advantage of the division of labour by granting to each party the discretion

---

1   Beale, Harris, and Sharpe, 'The Distribution of Cars: A Complex Contractual Technique', in D Harris and D Tallon (eds), *Contract Law Today* (Oxford, 1991).

to utilise its skills and knowledge in the best way to achieve performance of the objective of the contract.[2] This discretion can also tap into the potential of both parties for innovation and creativity, which may lead to greater profits for both parties. In a business format franchise for a restaurant, for instance, the franchisee may discover that the local market favours a particular variation of the product such as a fishburger, and this innovation may then be disseminated by the franchisor throughout the franchise operation to the mutual benefit of franchisor and franchisees.

These potential advantages of contracts incomplete by design will only be realized if the parties co-operate in ways which go beyond performance according to the strict terms of the contract. The parties must display trust towards each other, both in the sense of respecting the exercise of discretion and more fundamentally in assisting each other as far as possible in the effective use of that discretion. Where such a relation of trust permeates the business relation, then the contract can be left radically incomplete as merely a framework document thereby permitting adjustment to cope with shifts in demand; the parties can dispense with detailed monitoring of each other's performance; and the parties can exchange knowledge and expertise in order to improve the competitiveness of the product.[3] The normative standards will be supplied by the more general sense of good faith dealing and customary standards in the trade or business. This style of business relation based upon trust has been constructed in many business contexts, as in the example of 'supplier partnerships' between automobile assemblers and their component suppliers.

The problem which the law must address is how to differentiate between types of contracts in order to respond appropriately to the unwritten expectations of co-operation. In some contexts, such as an isolated sale of goods, the appropriate response will normally be to insist upon strict observance of the terms of the contract. In other contexts, however, an insistence upon the strict terms of the contract will undermine the trust required for achievement of the objectives of the contract. In order to achieve this differentiation, the key insight is to recognise that the long-term business interests of the parties may be at variance with a short-term insistence upon performance of the contract according to its letter.[4] These long-term business interests may be used as a criterion to interpret the obligations under the contract, to constrain the discretion

---

2   Schanze, 'Symbiotic Contracts: Exploring Long-Term Agency Structures between Contract and Corporation' in C Joerges (ed), *Franchising and the Law* (Baden-Baden, 1991) p 67.

3   Deakin and Wilkinson, 'Contracts, Co-operation and Trust: The Role of the Institutional Framework' in D Campbell and P Vincent-Jones, *Contract and Economic Organisation* (Aldershot, 1996) p 95.

4   Campbell and Harris, 'Flexibility in Long-term Contractual Relationships: The Role of Co-operation' (1993) 20 *Journal of Law and Society* 166.

in contracts incomplete by design, and to validate informal adjustments to the obligations contained in the contract.

Respect for the requirements of co-operation does not therefore require the courts to believe that the parties have suddenly been overcome by altruistic concerns. Nor does the idea suppose that the parties share a common interest in performance of the contract which differs from their individual interests.[5] It is no doubt likely that their co-operation will be guided in part by standards other than those of their strict economic interests, such as a desire to remain on friendly terms with the other party in order to sustain personal relationships of trust.[6] But a court can focus on the criterion of long-term economic interest as a guide to the requirements of co-operation in each particular contract. This approach is compatible with a commitment within a social market of fostering worthwhile economic opportunities. If such opportunities can only be realized by the law respecting unwritten expectations of co-operation, then the law must construe the obligations of the parties so that the expectations can be protected.[7]

This chapter examines how the law supports co-operation between the parties. The discussion is divided into three parts: obligations arising during performance of the contract; the handling of adjustments and modifications to contracts; and finally, the rules governing the right to terminate performance of the contract in response to breach of contract.

1. Performance

Duties of co-operation can be introduced into contracts through processes of construction of the terms and the development of implied terms. The interpretation of the contract can supplement the express terms with further implied obligations which support co-operation, such as the requirement in contracts for services that the service will be provided with reasonable care and skill.[8] Implied terms may qualify the express contract terms in such a way that strict insistence upon those express rights will itself amount to a breach of contract. The construction of the contract can also emphasize the incentives for the parties to perform their obligations in full and in good time.

---

5   For this suggestion, see Brownsword, 'From Co-operative Contracting to a Contract of Co-operation' in D Campbell and P Vincent-Jones, *Contract and Economic Organisation* (Aldershot, 1996) 14.
6   Collins, 'Competing Norms of Contractual Behaviour' in D Campbell and P Vincent-Jones, *Contract and Economic Organisation* (Aldershot, 1996) 67.
7   Macneil, 'The Many Futures of Contracts' (1974) 47 *Southern California Law Review* 691.
8   Supply of Goods and Services Act 1982, s 13; Farnsworth, 'On Trying to Keep One's Promises: The Duty of Best Efforts in Contract Law' (1984) 46 *University Pittsburgh Law Review* 1.

(1) ImpliedTerms

These techniques of construction and interpretation remain faithful to the basic tenets of the classical law of contract, by justifying the imposition of obligations by reference to the implied intentions of the parties. English law lacks a more general principle of law that the parties should perform the contract in good faith, which is common in many other European and common law systems. In the United States, for instance, the Uniform Commercial Code, section 1-203 decrees that, 'Every contract or duty within this act imposes an obligation of good faith in its performance or enforcement'.[9] The apparent contrast is misleading, however, since English courts can achieve similar results on the basis of the interpretation of particular contracts.

The most common justification for implied terms, that they are necessary to give business efficacy to a contract, illustrates this process well. We can understand the idea of business efficacy to mean that, without the supposed implied duty, then one party would be prevented from obtaining the full value of his expectation under the contract, because the other party is insisting upon limiting his obligations to a strict interpretation of the express terms of the contract. In Chapter 9 we illustrated this style of interpretation of contracts by the decision in *Liverpool City Council v Irwin*.[10] In that contract for the tenancy of a flat in a high rise apartment block, the landlord resisted the implication of a term requiring it to take reasonable steps to keep the common parts such as staircases and lifts in good repair. The court's acceptance of this term as reasonably necessary to give business efficacy to the contract reveals a disposition to introduce a duty of co-operation. In theory either the landlord or tenant could have arranged for the repair of common parts, but it would obviously be simpler and more efficient (by saving transaction costs) for the landlord to undertake the burden.

As well as the business efficacy test, other implied terms reflect a concern to promote a duty to co-operate during performance of a contract. If, for example, an employee insists upon a 'work to rule', then a court will discover that, far from this constituting performance according to the terms of the contract, it in fact constitutes a breach of an implied term of the contract. The implied term will require the employee at least not to frustrate the business objectives of the employer, and perhaps go further to require the exercise of good faith in deploying any discretion in the performance of work.[11] The introduction of the implied term supports the duty to co-operate, which in turn ensures that the contract itself does not become an obstacle to the maximization of the joint values of the parties to it. Similarly, in another type of incomplete contract, the requirements contract under which the purchaser agrees to buy all requirements for a particular product from the other party, the courts

9   Summers, 'Good Faith in General Contract Law and the Sales Provisions of the Uniform Commercial Code' (1968) 54 *Virginia Law Review* 195.
10 [1977] AC 239, [1976] 2 All ER 39, HL.
11 *Secretary of State for Employment v ASLEF (No 2)* [1972] ICR 19, CA.

interpret the buyer's duty to include a determination of its requirements in good faith, that is honestly, for that was the expectation of how the discretion would be exercised.

(2) Incentives and the Order of Performance
Where the performance required from each party to a contract takes place on different occasions or over a period of time, in the absence of explicit contractual provisions, the courts must determine the order in which each party should perform, and the duties impliedly undertaken. In a contract of employment, for example, as a rule the employee must carry out his work before the employer's duty to pay wages arises, which obviously encourages an employee to perform his obligations under the contract of employment. At the same time, however, the modern law balances this duty upon the employee to perform first by placing obligations upon the employer to avoid interference with performance of the contract by, for example, failing to supply the employee with work and suitable tools. In this case, provided that the employee is ready and able to work, he is entitled to payment of wages. Through this interplay of ordering performance and implied duties, the modern law reinforces the incentives created by the contract for performance and thereby establishes a co-operative spirit in which each party assists the other's aims and helps to satisfy expectations.

In determining the order of performance, the courts employ a bewildering variety of conceptual distinctions including the division between unilateral and bilateral contracts, the implication of conditions precedent, and the distinction between entire and severable obligations. Whatever the terminology, at bottom a court strives to establish duties of co-operation appropriate to the needs of the parties and the nature of the transaction. By insisting that one party's performance should be completed substantially before the other party falls under a duty to commence performance, the court can ensure that full performance is effected by both sides to the transaction.

Unilateral Contracts
In a unilateral contract, by definition the promisee must perform his duties first before payment becomes due. In contrast, no set rule governs the ordering of performance in bilateral contracts. Hence judicial classification of contracts into unilateral and bilateral categories often conceals instrumental reasoning aimed towards establishing principles for the timing of performance conducive to completion of the obligations. In the case of agents working for a commission on sales of a product, for example, the classification of the contract as unilateral relieves the agent from any duty to seek a purchaser, for his entitlement to a commission arises only if he chooses to achieve a sale. Yet at the same time, the agent knows that no payment falls due until a sale has been achieved,[12] which provides the

---

12 *Luxor (Eastbourne) Ltd v Cooper* [1941] AC 108, [1941] 1 All ER 33, HL.

agent with a strong incentive to solicit customers. The incentive becomes even stronger if the employer is entitled to cancel the agency at any time, which is the effect of classifying the contract as unilateral, for until the agent has performed by finding a customer, the agent has not provided consideration for the seller's promise. A similar result can be achieved by a bilateral contract in which the agent is placed under an express or implied obligation to use his best efforts to achieve sales, but the seller may find the threat of complaining about breach of this term less efficacious in achieving full co-operation from the agent than the threat of withholding any remuneration.

Conditions Precedent and Entire Obligations

In bilateral contracts, the courts represent their determinations of the order of performance as a process of construction. They purport to search for conditions precedent, that is express or implied terms which make it clear that the performance by one party is a condition precedent to the duty upon the other to perform. Another way of describing the process of construction uses the classification of entire and severable obligations. When a court concludes that in order to achieve the necessary incentives for co-operation one party ought to complete his performance before obligations on the other party fall due, then the court describes his obligation as entire. Under either classification, until the promisor satisfies the condition precedent or completes his entire performance, the promisor is entitled to neither payment nor damages.

The instrumental character of this conceptual reasoning reveals itself in cases where the courts employ it in order to protect consumers from defective performance. For example, following a credit agreement for the purchase of a car, a buyer avoided liability for default upon his repayments on the ground that the seller's duty to supply the legal documents evidencing change of ownership was a condition precedent to the buyer's performance of his obligations under the credit agreement.[13] Similarly, a contractor who had agreed to install central heating into the defendant's house, failed to recover the agreed price on the ground that his work was so unsatisfactory that in reality he had failed to complete the contract, and that fulfilment of the entire obligation was essential before any payment fell due.[14] In both instances, the court manipulates the order of performance to strengthen the position of a consumer/purchaser and to ensure proper performance of the contract.

(3) Disclosure of Information

In order to obtain the full benefits of a long-term business relation, the parties will often need to exchange information, ideas for innovation, insights of fresh market opportunities, and suggestions for improvements

---

13   *Bentworth Finance Ltd v Lubert* [1968] 1 QB 680, [1967] 2 All ER 810, CA.
14   *Bolton v Mahadeva* [1972] 1 WLR 1009, [1972] 2 All ER 1322, CA.

in efficiency. Early disclosure of information about risks to the joint enterprise can also avoid or reduce the effects of adverse changes in circumstances. In Chapter 8 we observed that the law is reluctant to impose obligations to disclose information during the formation of contracts. This general stance can be justified by the need to provide incentives for the discovery of commercially valuable information. Unfortunately, this reluctance to require disclosure of information seems to extend to the performance of contracts, when the efficiency considerations point in the opposite direction, especially in contracts incomplete by design.

It is possible that the disclosure of information acquired during performance of a contract might prevent the party in possession of the information from taking commercial advantage of it in another transaction, thereby reducing the incentive to acquire the information. Yet if the provision of the information improves the return on the investment in the long-term business relation, then efficiency considerations indicate that disclosure should be required. For this reason, some contracts such as partnership and agency will be classified for this purpose as fiduciary in character, so that information pertinent to the success of the project must be disclosed. The problem for the courts is to differentiate other types of business relation where a duty to disclose information would enhance the joint value of the venture without removing the incentive to acquire the information.

The classical law of contract normally rejected any duty of disclosure. The courts viewed such a term as in conflict with a more basic right of every individual to go about his business as he chooses, even where the exercise of that right obstructs successful performance of existing contracts.[15] In addition, the courts reject a duty of disclosure where the information can only be obtained at considerable cost.[16] At most, the courts were prepared to imply a duty to disclose information where that information was exclusively in the possession of one party and, without it, the other party could not perform a central obligation under the contract. If a seller of goods has to acquire an export licence, for instance, it will be an implied term that the buyer must co-operate by telling him the destination of the goods and other information which is required to obtain the licence.[17]

Where the express terms of the contract reveal an obligation to disclose information, the courts give full effect to the provisions. Express terms of this kind will be inserted into contracts where one party is likely to acquire information which substantially alters the risk undertaken by the other. In a contract of insurance, for instance, the insured may become aware of

---

15 *Mona Oil Equipment Co v Rhodesian Railways Ltd* [1949] 2 All ER 1014, QB; *Luxor (Eastbourne) Ltd v Cooper* [1941] AC 108, HL; Burrows, 'Contractual Co-operation and the Implied Term' (1968) 31 *Modern Law Review* 390.
16 *Reid v Rush and Tompkins Group plc* [1990] 1 WLR 212, [1989] 3 All ER 228, CA.
17 *Pound & Co Ltd v Hardy & Co Inc* [1956] AC 588, HL.

a new serious risk, and under the policy the insured will be under a duty to disclose the information. Similarly, where security is given for a loan, the contract may require the lender to be notified of risks to the value of the security.[18]

There are recent signs that the courts are reconsidering their restrictive attitude towards implied duties of disclosure of information.[19] In contracts of employment, for instance, both employer and employee owe limited duties of disclosure. An employer must advise employees on safety matters and give proper instructions on how to adopt safe methods of work.[20] The employer must also keep employees informed of any changes in the terms of the contract of employment, such as alterations in the occupational pension scheme.[21] On the other side, the employee has a duty to disclose information concerning breaches of contract by subordinate employees,[22] though the implied duty of loyalty does not extend to a duty to disclose information about the employee's own breach of contract.[23] Similarly, if there is a contractual relation between doctor and patient, the doctor will be required to disclose to the patient information concerning treatment such as surgery and its likely effects.[24] In a contract of insurance the pre-contractual duty of disclosure, which arises because this is classified as a contract requiring the utmost good faith during negotiation, can persist by implication during the performance of the contract.[25] These duties of disclosure of information have been developed so far in particular contexts often for the purpose of buttressing other statutory safeguards such as safety standards at work, but their proliferation suggests that the courts will be disposed to recognize implied duties of disclosure in a wide range of contractual relations.

One interest of the developing duty of disclosure during performance of contracts is that it reveals the courts trying to grasp the nature and dynamics of contracts which are incomplete by design. The imposition of a duty of disclosure may be regarded as a legal response to the perception that for such business relations to work successfully both parties must

---

18   Both examples are illustrated in *Bank of Nova Scotia v Hellenic Mutual War Risks Association (Bermuda) Ltd (The Good Luck)* [1991] 3 All ER 1, [1991] 2 Lloyd's Rep 191, HL.

19   Collins, 'Implied Duty to Give Information During Performance of Contracts' (1992) 55 *Modern Law Review.*

20   *General Cleaning Contractors Ltd v Christmas* [1953] AC 180, [1952] 2 All ER 1110, HL.

21   *Scally v Southern Health and Social Services Board* [1992] 1 AC 294, [1991] 4 All ER 563, HL.

22   *Sybron Corpn v Rochem Ltd* [1984] Ch 112, [1983] 2 All ER 707, CA.

23   *Bell v Lever Bros Ltd* [1932] AC 161, HL; *Horcal Ltd v Gatland* [1984] IRLR 288, CA; Freedland, 'High Trust, Pensions and the Contract of Employment' (1984) 13 *Industrial Law Journal* 25.

24   *Sidaway v Bethlem Royal Hospital* [1985] AC 871, [1985] 1 All ER 643, HL; *Thake v Maurice* [1986] QB 644, [1986] 1 All ER 497, CA.

25   *Black King Shipping Corpn v Massie (The Litsion Pride)* [1985] 1 Lloyd's Rep 437; *Banque Keyser Ullmann SA v Skandia (UK) Insurance Co Ltd* [1990] 1 QB 665, [1989] 2 All ER 952, CA.

co-operate and build up reciprocal trust. A duty of disclosure in performance is an elementary ingredient in such relationships, one which will be expected according to the informal norms of that business relation, which the law can then endorse in the event of disputes.[26]

Where a court finds that there has been a breach of a duty of disclosure during performance of a contract, the available remedy depends upon the source of the obligation. If the obligation arises from the breach of an implied term of the contract, then this should permit an award of damages for the resulting losses, and in serious cases may permit termination of the contract. If the failure to disclose information amounts to a breach of the duty of care in tort, then again this will permit a remedy in damages. But if the duty to disclose information during performance of the contract arises because the parties are held to be in a fiduciary relation, or because the contract is one like insurance which requires utmost good faith, then breach of the duty merely entitles the injured party to avoid the contract and seek restitution for any benefits conferred under the contract.[27] The duty to disclose information may also arise where one party seeks to rely upon the other's breach of contract to terminate the contract, whilst being aware that the breach of contract is unknown to the party in breach, with the effect that the failure to disclose this information prevents a remedying of the breach. Here the remedy will lie in disallowing termination of the contract on the ground of estoppel or waiver.[28]

2. Modification

In the light of changing market conditions or fresh information, the parties to a contract may wish to vary their obligations under it. In the absence of a contractual discretionary power to make minor adjustments, one party should not be permitted to do so unilaterally, for this would permit opportunistic variations in its favour. For example, an employer is not permitted to reduce the wages of employees unilaterally.[29] Even when an express power to vary the terms is granted by the contract, the power is likely to prove invalid in consumer contracts under the Unfair Terms in Consumer Contracts Regulations 1994.[30] But there is no objection in principle to any kind of consensual variation. On the contrary, in a long-term business relation mutual adjustments of obligations will almost certainly be necessary in order to maximize the opportunities presented

---

26 For discussion of analogous problems: Hadfield, 'Problematic Relations: Franchising and the Law of Incomplete Contracts' (1990) 42 *Stanford Law Review* 927.
27 *Banque Keyser Ullmann SA v Skandia (UK) Insurance Co Ltd* [1990] 1 QB 665, [1989] 2 All ER 952, CA.
28 *Tradax Export SA v Dorada Cia Naviera SA (The Lutetian)* [1982] 2 Lloyd's Rep 140.
29 *Rigby v Ferodo Ltd* [1988] ICR 29, HL.
30 Schedule 3, para 1 (j), SI 1994/3159, see chapter 13.

by the business relation.[31] A refusal to renegotiate prices in the light of altered market circumstances may be regarded as a breach of trust and lead subsequently to a damaging decision to terminate all future business dealings.[32] But the classical law placed considerable obstacles in the way of modification of contracts.

It viewed with suspicion any claim that the original contractual agreement was not binding on the parties. The ground for this suspicion was the observation that debtors are frequently inclined to avoid their contractual obligations by suggesting that some understanding or accommodation has been reached which exculpates them from strict performance of the original contract. Moreover, even if the debtor could prove the existence of such an agreement to modify the original contract, there remained the doubt whether the creditor had truly consented to the variation, or, as often proved the case, the creditor had been forced to consent because of commercial pressure or concern about the debtor's creditworthiness. In response to these justified concerns about modifications of contracts, the classical law developed a test for their validity which proved unnecessarily obstructive to genuine consensual variations of contracts.

(1) Obstructions to Modification

The classical law decided to judge the validity of modifications of contracts by reference to the same rules as those governing formation of contracts. It insisted that variations could only be binding if they satisfied the requirements of agreement and consideration, and, if necessary, they complied with any requirements of formalities for the formation of contracts, such as the need for the contract to be in writing.[33] In addition, any further grounds for the invalidity of contracts such as misrepresentation, duress, and undue influence, were also applied to modifications of existing contracts. Although these strict requirements for the enforceability of modifications of contracts could be complied with, so that variation was possible, they set a series of traps for the unwary, which often served merely to frustrate the intentions of the parties to the contract. Even worse, the legal rules could become the instrument of fraud in the sense that one party might employ the rules opportunistically in order to invalidate a perfectly consensual adjustment.

Agreement

The classical law normally requires an express agreement for any modification of contractual obligations. This serves as an important

---

31   Macneil, 'Contracts: Adjustment of Long-Term Economic Relations under Classical, Neoclassical, and Relational Contract Law' (1978) 72 *Northwestern University Law Review* 854; Goldberg, 'Relational Exchange' (1980) 23 *American Behavioral Scientist* 337.

32   Goldberg and Erickson, 'Quantity and Price Adjustment in Long-term Contracts: A Case Study of Petroleum Coke' (1987) 30 *Journal of Law and Economics* 369, 396.

33   Stoljar, 'The Modification of Contracts' (1957) 35 *Canadian Bar Review* 485.

bulwark against unilateral variations which detrimentally affect the other party to the contract. The problem which occurs with the requirement of an express agreement between the parties to modify their obligations is that often there will be a degree of informality and paucity of communication between the parties, so that it becomes impossible to say that agreement was reached, even though both parties acted as if an understanding were in place. This informality will often occur when one party commits a technical breach of the contract, but the other, knowing of breach, does not object, but rather continues to act as if the contract was being properly performed. For example, in *Panoutsos v Raymond Hadley Corpn of New York*,[34] the seller agreed to make several deliveries of flour in return for the buyer paying for each shipment by a confirmed banker's credit (that is, an irrevocable credit arrangement which the seller can draw upon at the buyer's bank). The buyer in fact paid for each shipment, but failed, to the seller's knowledge, to open the necessary credit arrangement. The seller continued to perform the contract for a time, but subsequently purported to terminate the contract on the ground of the buyer's breach of this term of the contract. In these circumstances the court could not find that any modification of the contract had been agreed, so that it was compelled to conclude that the original contract stood.

Fortunately the court prevented this opportunistic reliance upon the legal requirement of an express agreement by drawing upon the doctrine of waiver of breach or affirmation of the contract. This permitted the court to imply from the seller's conduct a promise not to rely upon the breach, on which promise the buyer had acted, so that in conclusion the court could deny the seller's right to terminate the contract for breach. But this instrumental use of the doctrine of waiver of breach should not disguise the point that in effect the court modified the contract on the basis of an informal understanding which was little more than an implied promise that had been acted upon.

Consideration

A similar pattern emerges in connection with the requirement of fresh consideration to support the variation. Although in many instances a modification of a contract will result in a mutual adjustment of obligations, with the consequence that the doctrine of consideration is satisfied because each party expects to gain something from the alteration, this will not always be the case. In some instances, one party may agree to pay more for what he or she is already entitled to under the contract. In other cases, one party may agree to receive less than full contractual performance. In either case, it will be difficult to satisfy the benefit and idea in detriment behind the doctrine of consideration, for it appears that the party whose rights have been altered has received nothing in return: he or she either receives less for the same price, or the same performance for an increased

---

34 [1917] 2 KB 473, CA.

price.

No doubt with the aim of creditor protection in mind, the courts usually concluded in such cases that the modification of the contract was unenforceable because of the absence of fresh consideration. In *Stilk v Myrick*,[35] which involved a claim by a sailor for extra wages on the faith of a promise by the captain during the ship's voyage, Campbell's report of the case, which has since been treated as authoritative, states that the court rejected the claim on the ground that the captain's promise to pay more was unsupported by fresh consideration in the form of additional duties to be performed by the sailor. Similarly, with respect to a promise to accept less, the case of *Foakes v Beer*[36] has been treated as firm authority that a creditor's promise to accept less money than is due will also be unenforceable for want of consideration.

These decisions frustrate the intentions of the parties in cases of genuine adjustments of obligations. The promise to pay more may reflect a recognition that the original contract price was based upon a mistake about the burdens entailed, or an error in drafting the terms of the contract so that they do not fully accord with the intentions of the parties, or it may be a response to changing circumstances which render performance more onerous. Although there is no obligation to pay more, there may be many reasons why such a promise might be made. The disadvantageous promise may be given by the promisor in anticipation of future advantageous transactions which may come his way, especially if the variation serves to keep a valued customer. The agreement to modify the contract may also reflect a reluctance to drive the other party out of business, if that might harm the promisor's business in the long run, as in the case where the contract envisages a long-term production relation such as a franchise or a requirements contract. Moreover, if the promisor is in a position to pass on increased costs, the variation in the contract price may not cause any significant disadvantage; this may explain a disposition to be flexible about the price, provided that due performance is completed on time. Similarly, the decision to accept a lesser payment may be the result of a wise commercial calculation of long-term business interests and business reputation, combined with a realistic assessment of the chances of being paid in full without considerable legal costs. For all these reasons, even disadvantageous variations may be perfectly fair and sensible in commercial transactions.

Some techniques were available for avoiding the potential for opportunism presented by the requirement of fresh consideration. Trivial alterations in the contractual obligations could be regarded as amounting to fresh consideration. A valid modification could be effected by an alteration in the time or place of payment, or the mode of payment such

---

35   (1809) 2 Camp 317, 6 Esp 129. Halson, 'The Modification of Contractual Obligations' (1989) *Current Legal Problems* 111.
36   (1884) 9 App Cas 605, HL.

as by cheque rather than cash. But the courts will not always be drawn into such absurdities except for the purpose of defeating opportunism. In *D & C Builders Ltd v Rees*, the Court of Appeal was not persuaded that the plaintiff builder's agreement to accept a cheque for a lesser sum than the debt owed, instead of payment in cash, could be described as fresh consideration to support a promise to accept less, no doubt because the facts of the case revealed coercion rather than a consensual agreement. A more complicated technique for discovering fresh consideration asserts that the original contract has been terminated by agreement, and that a completely new contract with different terms has replaced it. Although this analysis overcomes any problems of consideration, it often amounts to an improbable interpretation of the simple facts of the case, where all that has happened is that one party has agreed to a disadvantageous modification of one of the terms of the original contract. The doctrine of consideration as a test for the enforceability of modifications proved a blunt instrument by which to distinguish between instances where the debtor was compelling the creditor reluctantly to agree to an inferior deal, and those where the creditor was genuinely willing to arrange some accommodation.

Formalities
The classical law also insisted upon the application of any requirements of formalities to modifications as well as formation of contracts. This presented a serious trap for the unwary, for if the law required a contract to be in writing, then an orally agreed modification could have no effect. The only exception to this rule which the courts endorsed was that an oral agreement could terminate or rescind a contract entirely. A typical example of this trap and the absurd consequences which it produced is found in *Morris v Baron*.[37] This case concerned a contract for a sale of goods which at that time had to be evidenced in writing. Following a dispute between the parties, they reached an oral settlement on slightly different terms. But the court declared that this oral modification was unenforceable. Either the oral variation was ineffective to change the original contract because of the absence of writing, or the oral agreement was effective to rescind the original contract, but it could not create any new binding agreement because of the absence of formalities. Thus, the court concluded that either the original contract was binding still, or, and this was the final outcome in the House of Lords, there was no contract at all.

This astonishing result exemplifies the problem of the application of the rules requiring formalities in the formation of contracts to subsequent modifications. Because these modifications will often be agreed informally, without regard to legal niceties, the parties will often end up with their whole transaction confounded and invalidated by the courts.

37 [1918] AC 1, HL.

Duress

The classical law also applied the other normal requirements for validity of contracts to modifications, so that to be enforceable they had to be free from the taint of duress, undue influence, and misrepresentation. The important issue here is whether a modification agreed only as a result of severe commercial pressure can be avoided on the ground of duress. As we have seen, the danger presented by modifications is that a debtor may in effect coerce a creditor into forgoing rights by threats of default or defective performance. Where the creditor has no viable commercial option but to proceed with the original contracting party, then the debtor will be able to take advantage of this bilateral monopoly in an opportunistic manner by demanding higher payment or a reduction of contractual obligations.

But the classical law of duress proved inadequate to cope with these situations. Although a few cases seem to have used duress as a ground for invalidating coerced modifications, as for example in the Espinasse report of the decision in *Stilk v Myrick*,[38] the doctrine of duress was normally regarded as being more strictly confined to cases where the coercion involved the commission of a tort, either a threat to the person or property.[39] It seemed to follow that a mere threat to break a contract, which was the coercive technique usually employed to gain advantageous modifications, could not usually amount to duress at common law. The absence of duress as a tool for invalidating coerced modifications probably then led the courts to rely upon the doctrine of consideration to perform the same function, though, as we have seen, this was a clumsy tool for it invalidated uncoerced disadvantageous modifications as well.

(2) *Modern Flexibility*

The classical law governing modification reveals a series of obstructions calculated to defeat the genuine intentions of the parties and to create the potential for opportunism. The underlying mistake of the classical law was the failure to realize that long-term business interests could lead rational self-interested parties to agree informally to disadvantageous adjustments. Commercial contractors expect a degree of 'give and take' during performance. They will offer indulgences, refrain from pedantic insistence upon strict contractual rights, and seek genuine accommodations in cases of difficulty. They do so in order to co-operate, so that the contract is performed, and to preserve goodwill in long-term informal commercial relations. This mistake then led to the insistence that any modification should comply with the rules governing formation of contracts, which were designed to ensure that the variation complied with short-term economic interest.

---

38 (1809) 6 Esp 129.
39 Beatson, 'Duress as a Vitiating Factor in Contract' (1974) *Cambridge Law Journal* 97.

In the modern law, however, we can observe a series of adjustments to the law which permit the courts to differentiate between cases where the requirement of co-operation demands strict observance of the original contractual rights and those where the parties have modified their agreement with a view to long-term business interests. The traditional obstacles to modification have been evaded or diluted in these latter cases. The law appears complex and even inconsistent until it is appreciated that this process of differentiation requires divergent handling of cases of modification.

Consent and Change of Position

In a business relation which is sustained by trust, where the parties undertake incomplete obligations, they expect minor adjustments to obligations. In some instances the variation will be the result of a deliberate agreement, but in others it may be arranged casually or even evolve out of an alteration of practice without either party being aware that it involves a breach of the original contract. A seller may be lulled into believing that the buyer does not object to a minor alteration in the type of goods or method of delivery, especially if this practice continues for some time without objection. Similarly, a unilateral increase of wages by an employer is unlikely to be met by a formal letter of acceptance by the employee, but rather the employee indicates assent by the conduct of continuing to work without raising objection. Instead of seeking an express agreement to the variation, the modern law can be satisfied by either an express promise which is acted upon or conduct which can reasonably be interpreted to indicate an implied promise and a corresponding acceptance of a change in the contractual relation through conduct involving a change of position. This flexibility in detecting consent to a variation is achieved either by a dilution of the traditional requirements of offer and acceptance, or by the use of the doctrine of equitable estoppel.

For express promises to vary the contract which are then acted upon, the courts can either find agreement through conduct or determine the case under the principles of equitable estoppel. The latter principles were adopted by Denning J in *Central London Property Trust Ltd v High Trees House Ltd*.[40] The landlord made an express promise to accept a reduced rent for a period of time, and, since this was acted upon by the tenant by paying the reduced rent, it was unnecessary to point to an express acceptance of the landlord's offer.

In the absence of an express promise, the courts may still with difficulty infer agreement from the conduct of the parties or seek to vindicate the modification through estoppel. The danger here is that the construction of implied modifications runs the risk of unilateral imposition of opportunistic variations. In the leading case on implied agreements,

---

40   [1947] KB 130, KB.

Paal Wilson & Co A / S v Partenreederei Hannah Blumenthal (The Hannah Blumenthal),[41] the contract for the sale of a ship contained an arbitration clause which governed any disputes. The buyers, dissatisfied in some respects with the ship, initiated arbitration proceedings in 1972. Apart from some exchanges of letters, however, little happened until 1980 when the buyers purported to fix a date for the arbitration proceedings. The sellers then sought to establish before the court (amongst other points) that the contract had been modified to the extent that the buyers had agreed to abandon their claim and the arbitration proceedings. The obstacle to this argument was the absence of any express agreement to abandon the claim. The sellers had to rely upon the conduct of the buyers, or more precisely their inactivity for eight years, in order to establish the modification. The sellers failed to establish the modification on the facts of the case, because there was evidence indicating that the sellers knew that the buyers were still intending to proceed with the claim. But the tests of modification employed by the House of Lords indicate an acceptance of a less formal test of agreement. It was sufficient, said Lord Brandon, that:

> the conduct of B, as evinced towards A, has been such as to lead A reasonably to believe that B has abandoned the contract, even though it has not in fact been B's intention to do so, and that A has significantly altered his position in reliance on that belief.

The emphasis in this judgment lies upon the three elements of (i) conduct which implies a promise to modify; and (ii) which induces a reasonable belief in such a promise to modify; and (iii) which is acted upon by the promisee. The conduct may consist almost entirely in a failure to act, as in the case of a failure to complain within a reasonable time about late deliveries or minor defects,[42] though mere silence alone can only be treated as equivocal.[43]

Similar principles apply to cases such as *Hughes v Metropolitan Rly Co*[44] which are decided on the basis of equitable estoppel. Here a landlord gave the tenant of his property six months' notice to effect repairs as it was entitled to do under the lease. The parties then entered into negotiations for sale of the property. But when these negotiations failed, the landlord then purported to exercise a forfeiture clause under the lease to evict the tenant on the ground that the repairs had not been carried out in the six-month period. The House of Lords gave relief from forfeiture on the ground that the negotiations for sale of the property led the tenant reasonably to believe that the contractual right to forfeiture would not be

41 [1983] 1 AC 854, [1983] 1 All ER 34, HL.
42 *Société Italo-Belge pour le Commerce et l'Industrie SA v Palm and Vegetable Oils (Malaysia) Sdn Bhd (The Post Chaser)* [1982] 1 All ER 19, [1981] 2 Lloyd's Rep 695, QB.
43 *Allied Marine Transport Ltd v Vale do Rio Navegacao SA (The Leonidas D)* [1984] 1 WLR 1, [1983] 3 All ER 737.
44 (1877) 2 App Cas 439, HL.

enforced. In effect the court found that the landlord had made an implied promise which had been acted upon by the tenant failing to complete repairs pending negotiation of the sale. By negotiating for the sale of the land to the tenant, the court was able to infer from this conduct that the strict contractual rights of the landlord and tenant relation were temporarily suspended, for there was no point in the tenant effecting the repairs if he was shortly to acquire the property himself.

The reasonable belief criterion makes it clear that the conduct need not in fact be based upon an intention to modify the contract. What is necessary is that it is reasonable for the other contracting party to interpret that conduct as amounting to an implied promise to modify the agreement. It did not matter, therefore, that neither the landlord in *Hughes v Metropolitan Rly Co*, nor the buyer in *Paal Wilson & Co A/S v Parten-reederei Hannah Blumenthal, (The Hannah Blumenthal)*,[45] intended to modify the contract; the crucial issue was whether the other party had formed a reasonable belief that such an implied promise was being made. In the former case, the tenant did have reasonable grounds for belief in the implied promise, but in the latter case the buyer had sufficient indication from the intermittent correspondence that the claim was not abandoned to prevent it from reasonably supposing that an implied promise of abandonment had been made.

A test of enforceability?

A question which remains unsettled in the development of the modern law governing modification concerns the extent to which it requires a test of enforceability in addition to the diluted requirement of agreement described above. In other words, is there still a requirement of consideration before a modification will be enforceable?[46] The importance of the question in practice should not be exaggerated. In most instances the test of consideration will be satisfied, because both parties give up or gain some rights. In addition, some modifications amount to a rescission of the original contract and its replacement or abandonment, and here again no doubts arise about consideration. But in the cases highlighted earlier of promises to pay more for the same performance, and promises to accept a lesser sum for the same contractual obligations, the difficulty created by the classical law of finding consideration persists. The legal doctrine seems to have taken an unnecessarily complex and even absurd turn in these contexts. It divides the problem into two parts and deals with them quite separately.

With respect to promises to pay more for the same contractual performance, the cases stick to the test of consideration in order to determine the enforceability of the modification. But the definition of

---

45   [1983] 1 AC 854, [1983] 1 All ER 34, HL.
46   Hillman, 'Contract Modification under the Restatement (Second) of Contracts' (1982) 67 *Cornell Law Review* 680; Uniform Commercial Code, s 2-209 dispenses with the requirement of consideration.

consideration has become subtly altered in order to take into account the long-term commercial advantages of superficially adverse variations. In *Williams v Roffey Bros and Nicholls (Contractors) Ltd*,[47] the plaintiff carpenter agreed with the defendant building contractor to perform work on the refurbishment of twenty-seven flats in return for a fixed sum of £20,000. The plaintiff fell behind schedule in the work, which concerned the defendant because under the main contract for the building works a clause reduced payment for late completion. The defendant, partly out of recognition that the original price was too low for the plaintiff to be commercially viable, and partly as an inducement to speed up the work, promised to pay the plaintiff an extra amount of £10,300, at the rate of £575 per completed flat. The plaintiff completed work on eight flats, but the defendant only paid £1,500 more, so the plaintiff sued for the balance under the modified contract. The Court of Appeal overcame the objection that the promise to pay the additional sum was not supported by consideration because the plaintiff did not undertake any new obligations, by arguing that the defendant had secured other commercial benefits through the promise. These benefits included changing work practices so that at least some of the flats were completed, avoiding or reducing the penalty for delay, and avoiding the expense and difficulty of having to make alternative contractual arrangements. Once the courts acknowledge these commercial factors as constituting consideration, then the doctrine ceases to be a bar to enforceability in those cases where the promisor has good commercial reasons for agreeing to a modification. Although the old rule of *Stilk v Myrick*[48] remains formally intact, it will cease to obstruct genuine commercial modifications, for these will always be motivated by long-term business interests.

The courts have treated promises to accept less in return for the same performance rather differently. Since the decision in *Central London Property Trust Ltd v High Trees House Ltd*,[49] it has been accepted that a promise to make such an indulgence will be enforceable if acted upon. Thus the doctrine of consideration is held to be irrelevant in such cases. The promise by the landlord to accept a reduced rent for a period of time was binding, Denning J suggested in that case, because the tenants had acted upon it, not because they had provided consideration for it. Now that the flats were full, however, the condition of the promise was satisfied, so that the landlords could insist upon reversion to the original higher rent on reasonable notice. To justify this evasion of the requirement of consideration for modifications of contracts, Denning J relied upon the doctrine of equitable or promissory estoppel. But in so doing he stretched that doctrine considerably. In particular, estoppel had usually been confined to statements of fact which were relied upon rather than promises with respect to the future. In addition, estoppels are normally binding

---

47   [1991] 1 QB 1, [1990] 1 All ER 512, CA.
48   (1809) 2 Camp 317, 6 Esp 129.
49   [1947] KB 130, KB.

only if they induce detrimental reliance, but in this case the tenants could not realistically claim they had suffered any detriment from being permitted to pay a lower rent. But Denning J was content to brush these difficulties aside in order to circumvent the application of the doctrine of consideration to modifications of contracts, where such application would clearly defeat the intentions of the parties in the pursuit of their long-term business interests.

This bifurcation of approach leaves the law in an unwelcome complicated position. Is there a justification for this radically different treatment of the two kinds of modification: promises to pay more on the one hand, and on the other promises to accept less? The justification, such as it is, claims that the idea of promissory estoppel in the *High Trees* case must be confined to defences to claims rather than itself constitute a new cause of action. This limitation is insisted upon, for otherwise the principle of promissory estoppel would indirectly abolish the requirement of consideration in the formation of contracts. The limitation is often described metaphorically by stating that promissory estoppel only functions 'as a shield and not a sword'.[50] Accordingly, it is suggested that, whereas in the context of promises to accept less, the enforcement of the promise merely functions as a defence to a claim under the original contract, in the case of promises to pay more, promissory estoppel is not available, for this would be to use it as a sword to enforce a new claim for money or additional performance.

In my view, however, this justification lacks any real merit. We should recognize that in both instances, the issue is one of the modification of contracts, for which the doctrine of consideration is not properly suited. In an important sense all cases of contractual modification concern defences to a cause of action, that is, enforcement of the original contract, so that to distinguish between the different types of modification as if there is some principle at stake is wholly misleading. If any test of enforceability is required other than the presence of an express or implied agreement, then this test should reflect the reasons why such modifications are agreed and should be binding. We have noted that collateral commercial advantages lie at the heart of the reasons for agreeing to these modifications. The test should look for advantages, such as the preservation of a commercial relationship because of mutual economic dependence, the possibility of continuing contractual relations with a valued customer, the avoidance of possible harms such as loss of confidence or reputation and contingent financial penalties under other contracts. The revised doctrine of consideration in *Williams v Roffey Bros and Nicholls (Contractors) Ltd* examines these matters and so should be preferred and applied to all modifications, if a test of enforceability is required at all. It is certainly more appropriate than the approach contained in the *High Trees* case, which looks for action in reliance upon

50   Birkett LJ, *Combe v Combe* [1951] 2 KB 215, [1951] 1 All ER 767, CA.

the promise. This idea of reliance, I argued above, is in fact an element of the test of an informal agreement rather than an independent test of enforceability. The action in reliance confirms that the promisee accepts the modification, for it is important to prevent unilateral alteration of terms of contracts.

But surely it would be better to drop this requirement of a test of enforceability altogether and concentrate instead on the questions of whether there was an express or implied agreement, and if so, was it invalidated on the ground of economic duress? For as we shall see below, the doctrine of economic duress, as it has been developed, examines the question of whether such collateral benefits or long-term business interests exist much more closely, and infers from their absence that the modification was coerced. Any further test of enforceability is unnecessary in the context of modifications, for by definition the parties have already entered a binding legal transaction with due caution. The question posed for the courts is not whether there is a binding contract, but what are its current terms in the light of subsequent modifications? The question of content should be judged by reference to the express or implied agreement. The question of the validity of this agreement should be considered in the light of the normal factors which vitiate consent such as fraud and duress, together with an expanded doctrine of economic duress to cope with the problems of bilateral monopolies, described above.

To summarize these points on the test of enforceability: the rules governing modifications should consist solely of the two requirements of agreement and factors which vitiate consent such as misrepresentation and especially economic duress. The additional requirement currently imposed by the courts, a test of enforceability in the form of the doctrine of consideration or its substitutes, such as promissory estoppel and waiver of breach, serves no useful function once the doctrine of economic duress has been established, so it should be eliminated completely. In cases of informal or implied agreements, however, it will be necessary to preserve the requirement of action in reliance upon the express or implied promise, such as paying a lower rent or accepting a higher salary, not as some kind of substitute for the doctrine of consideration, but simply as an indication of acceptance of the modification in order to avoid the danger of unilateral variation.

Economic Duress

Although the doctrine of economic duress applies in principle to the formation of contracts as well, the potential for opportunism is greatly enhanced in the context of modifications, since there is often a real danger of exploitation of a bilateral monopoly. Once a party has become locked into a particular agreement, and perhaps performed a substantial part of the contractual undertaking, then he or she may be vulnerable to coercive claims for additional advantages because the costs of terminating the contract far exceed the additional demands. This will occur especially when the character of performance requires a particular kind of investment unique to the customer, so that the only way in which these 'sunk costs' can be recovered is through performance by the customer. Similarly, the customer may become peculiarly dependent upon the supplier where no other sources of supply are available in the time available. For example, in *North Ocean Shipping Co v Hyundai Construction Co (The Atlantic Baron)*,[51] the buyers under a shipbuilding contract had in anticipation of performance leased the ship from a certain date, so that, when the shipbuilders demanded additional payment before delivery (in order to compensate them for devaluation in the currency of payment), the buyers were compelled to agree to the higher price since they could not find a substitute ship of the same specifications in the short time available. Another example occurs when a consumer has a valid claim for payment against a business, as in the case of a claim on an insurance policy, and the insurer uses its advantage of business skills to compel a disadvantageous settlement.[52] These examples indicate that apparent modifications of contracts need to be invalidated where these characteristics of a bilateral monopoly exist, in order to prevent opportunistic advantage-taking, but in the absence of such factors, there should be no reason to doubt the validity of the agreed modification.

The task confronting the courts is to distinguish between genuine, co-operative accommodations during the lifetime of an agreement, and coerced modifications which seek to exploit a strong bargaining position. The law of economic duress has developed rapidly in recent years, yet it remains unequal to this task, because it has failed to make explicit all the relevant considerations to making this distinction.

The leading case, *Pao On v Lau Yiu Long*,[53] however, makes a useful start in the right direction. The plaintiffs sold their company to the defendants' company in exchange for shares in the defendants' company, but the plaintiffs agreed not to sell 60% of those shares for a year in order to avoid a sudden drop in value of those shares. In a collateral agreement the defendants in person agreed to buy back 60% of the shares at or before the end of the year for a fixed price, so that the plaintiffs would not suffer from any drop in the value of the shares. Subsequently the plaintiffs realized that, if the shares rose in price, they would not be able to take advantage of this, because the collateral agreement was effectively a future sale at a fixed price. So the plaintiffs refused to proceed with the main contract, unless the collateral agreement was cancelled and replaced by a promise of an indemnity if, at the end of the year, the shares were sold below a fixed price. The question before the court was whether the indemnity, which was agreed, was a binding contract. The Privy Council made extraordinarily heavy weather over the difficulty of finding consideration, apparently missing the point that the consideration

---

51   [1979] QB 705, [1978] 3 All ER 1170, QB; cf *Atlas Express Ltd v Kafco Ltd* [1989] QB 833, [1989] 1 All ER 641, QB.
52   *Dillon v Baltic Shipping Co (The Mikhail Lermontov)* [1991] 2 Lloyd's Rep 155 (CA NSW).
53   [1980] AC 614, [1979] 3 All ER 65, PC; cf *Atlas Express Ltd v Kafco Ltd* [1989] QB 833, [1989] 1 All ER 641, QB.

supporting the indemnity could be found in the agreement to cancel the collateral contract, a common technique in cases of modification as we have noted. But then came the crucial question of whether the plaintiffs had only secured the indemnity by means of impermissible economic duress by threatening not to proceed with the main contract for the sale of their company. In deciding that no economic duress had occurred, Lord Scarman stated the doctrine of economic duress in the following terms:

> Duress, whatever form it takes, is a coercion of the will so as to vitiate consent ... In determining whether there was a coercion of the will such that there was no true consent, it is material to inquire whether the person alleged to have been coerced did or did not protest; whether, at the time he was allegedly coerced into making the contract, he did or did not have an alternative course open to him such as an adequate legal remedy; whether he was independently advised; and whether after entering the contract he took steps to avoid it.

We must doubt, for reasons discussed in Chapter 8, whether it is helpful to conceive of duress as causing an involuntary act rather than forcing a choice between two unpalatable courses of action. But it is clear that Lord Scarman does not take the idea of an involuntary act too seriously, for the factors which he lists as relevant, such as the absence of an adequate legal remedy, merely highlight the extent to which the choice was constrained.

What I suggest is the crucial factor in this case, and one which can be defended in principle, is a situation equivalent to a bilateral monopoly, combined with evidence of advantage being taken of this superior bargaining position.[54] The failure of the claim of economic duress in this case can be accounted for in part because of the absence of a strong degree of bilateral monopoly, but mostly because the plaintiffs did not seek to take undue advantage of their position. To some extent the defendants were constrained in their bargaining position, for they were worried that if the main contract was cancelled or broken then there might be a loss of business confidence in their company. But even if this concern was enough to provide the plaintiffs with the occasion for opportunism, it could not seriously be argued that they had sought to take advantage of it. In reality they had made a mistake about the initial form of the collateral contract, which did not accord with their intentions. The replacement indemnity contract fitted their original intentions, and at the same time did not expose the defendants to any greater risk of loss. Indeed, as events turned out, the shares did drop in price, so that ironically the original collateral agreement would have satisfied the plaintiffs' interests, and so they need not have created all the legal problems which their simple modification engendered. What influenced the Privy Council decisively against a finding of economic duress was, I suggest, the simple fact that the modification

---

54   This is a way of describing what is called in economic analysis opportunism or strategic behaviour: Aivazian, Trebilcock, Penny, 'The Law of Contract Modifications: The Uncertain Quest for a Benchmark of Enforceability' (1984) 22 *Osgoode Hall Law Journal* 173.

did not impose any additional losses on the defendants and so no advantage had been taken of them.

I am suggesting, therefore, that, for economic duress to invalidate modifications of contracts, the court should, and probably does without stating so explicitly, ascertain first, whether the situation amounts to a bilateral monopoly in effect, and, secondly, whether or not that bargaining position was exploited opportunistically for gain at the expense of the other party. These criteria will explain how in other cases the court reached the different conclusion that economic duress had been exercised.

For example, it will be recalled that in *North Ocean Shipping Co v Hyundai Construction Co (The Atlantic Baron)*,[55] the shipbuilders demanded an extra ten percent payment to compensate them for devaluation of the currency of payment. Because ships take a considerable time to build and they may not be readily available on the open market with the right specifications, there was certainly a possibility that the shipbuilders were in a strong bargaining position. On the other hand, the buyers might have had good reason to agree to a higher price in order to keep the favourable charter which they had arranged for the vessel, and in order to preserve amicable relations for future dealings, much like the main contractors in *Williams v Roffey Bros and Nicholls (Contractors) Ltd*,[56] where no economic duress was established. But what was decisive against the shipbuilders was the clear gain which they had seized against the buyers by increasing the price. They transferred the risk of currency fluctuations onto the buyer, despite having agreed initially to accept this risk by a fixed price contract in a particular currency. This fact distinguishes *The Atlantic Baron* from *Williams v Roffey Bros and Nicholls (Contractors) Ltd*, for in the latter case there was evidence that the main contractors realized that the original price was unrealistically low, and that they were prepared to make some accommodation to avoid driving the sub-contractor out of business.

Similarly, an agreement to accept lesser payment will not necessarily be evidence of economic duress, for there may be good reason to reduce the price. In the *High Trees* case, for example, the landlord's motive for reducing the rent was inextricably tied up with the fact that the tenant was a wholly owned subsidiary company of the landlord company, so there would be no commercial advantage to the group of companies as a whole to insist upon the original rent. But it will often be the case that an agreement to accept a lesser sum will have been extracted through exploitation of a strong bargaining position. Hence in *D & C Builders Ltd v Rees*,[57] the English Court of Appeal declined to enforce an agreement between a small firm of builders in financial straits and a wealthy creditor for whom they had done work to accept £300 instead of the £480 due under the original contract in the face of a threat of being paid nothing at

---

55 [1979] QB 705, [1978] 3 All ER 1170, QB.
56 [1991] 1 QB 1, [1990] 1 All ER 512, CA.
57 [1966] 2 QB 617, [1965] 3 All ER 837, CA.

all, which would have forced them into insolvency. Lord Denning MR justified this decision on the ground that it would be inequitable to enforce the modification. The result might have been different, however, if the court found evidence that the original agreement was overpriced, or that the builders had good commercial reasons to wish to benefit the creditor.

To conclude this discussion of economic duress, we must recognize its central importance to the law of modifications. Without it, the flexibility of the modern law would run the risk of permitting opportunistic gains during the performance of contracts. Although it is correct in a sense to view economic duress as a factor which vitiates consent, for we have seen that express or implied consent by both parties is the essential requirement for effective modification, it is wrong to confine economic duress to instances of involuntary acts as Lord Scarman seems to suggest. Behind this rhetoric of the 'coercion of the will' lies in fact a flexible analysis of the situation in which the modification was agreed. The crucial issues are whether the agreement was both coerced in the sense that one party had an effective bilateral monopoly and that this position was exploited to the detriment of the other party. It is only these factors which can account for the different results in the cases we have considered.

(3) Incentives to Modify Contracts

The preceding discussion highlights the way the modern law facilitates modifications of contracts by removing many of the obstacles imposed by the classical law. The necessary safeguards against unilaterally imposed variations and opportunistic advantage-taking have been established despite more relaxed tests of agreement and the effective abandonment of the traditional doctrine of consideration in this context. This flexibility of the modern law encourages co-operation between the parties, recognizing that often a measure of 'give and take' will be expected and appropriate in contractual relations during performance. But the modern law goes further than simply recognizing the effectiveness of the parties' intentions and reasonable expectations with regard to co-operation during performance. To some extent, it also provides incentives to renegotiate contracts. We noted above the special advantages of such incentives in the case of long-term contracts where it is often difficult to plan for all eventualities, and so the parties may expect to alter and give greater specificity to their agreement over time.

One incentive for adjustment derives from the courts' practice of inserting an implied term into long-term contracts that they can be terminated on reasonable notice. They have even been prepared to do so in the teeth of apparently contrary express terms, as in *Staffordshire Area Health Authority v South Staffordshire Waterworks Co*,[58] where under a contract for the supply of water the price was fixed 'at all times hereafter', but the court construed the contract to contain an implied term permitting

---

58   [1978] 1 WLR 1387, [1978] 3 All ER 769, CA.

termination on reasonable notice. The possibility of such an implied term then reduces the chance that the parties to the contract will be able to insist upon its original terms. Instead, in order to combat the threat to terminate the contract on reasonable notice, the other party will have an incentive to consider the option of renegotiating the terms of the agreement so that it may continue.

Another incentive to adjust the contract springs from the duty to mitigate loss arising from breach of contract. A party to a contract who refuses to accept a modification may of course claim damages if the original contract is imperfectly performed, but this tactic encounters the risk that a court may reduce the measure of damages in the light of his failure to co-operate on the ground of failure to mitigate loss. If a purchaser of a ship refuses to accept late delivery, as for example in *The Solholt*,[59] his damages may be reduced to nil where the cheapest and most reasonable method for reducing his losses resulting from the breach of contract would have been to accept late delivery with some alteration in the price to reflect the costs of delay and changes in market conditions. In effect, the doctrine of mitigation, which requires the injured party to take reasonable steps to reduce losses resulting from breach, also creates an incentive in many instances to renegotiate a contract if this is the most cost-effective means of reducing loss.

4. Termination for Breach of Contract

Apart from the anomalous doctrine of frustration, even a serious breach of contract does not terminate it.[60] The common law insists that the injured party should enjoy the choice of either terminating the contract or affirming it. The language of choice reflects the classical law's attempt to attribute every legal consequence to the agreement of the parties,[61] but more pressing considerations dictate this approach. In part this choice protects the injured party from an attempt by the party in breach to rely upon his own wrongful breach of contract to escape from his remaining obligations. At the same time this right preserves the contract intact so that the parties might be encouraged to find a compromise. It expresses the duty of co-operation by requiring the party in breach to fulfil his obligations whenever the injured party desires it.[62] In reality, no doubt, the injured party frequently has little choice but to terminate the contract in the face of a serious breach or an absolute refusal to proceed. Yet this right aids the injured party where he perceives some ancillary benefits

59   [1983] 1 Lloyd's Rep 605, CA.
60   *Decro-Wall International SA v Practitioners in Marketing Ltd* [1971] 1 WLR 361, [1971] 2 All ER 216, CA; *Photo Production Ltd v Securicor Transport Ltd* [1980] AC 827, [1980] 1 All ER 556, HL.
61   Williston, 'Freedom of Contract' (1921) 6 *Cornell Law Review* 364.
62   Gabel, 'Intention and Structure in Contractual Conditions: Outline of a Method for Critical Legal Theory' (1977) 61 *Minnesota Law Review* 601.

from prolonging the life of the contract. For example, when employees go on strike in breach of contract, the employer is entitled to terminate their contracts, but he or she is unlikely to do so in the interests of promoting a quick settlement, reducing the damage to harmonious industrial relations, and retaining his or her skilled labour force.

We noted at the outset that the right to terminate the contract in response to a breach provides a powerful incentive to perform the obligations. If minor breaches can be punished by termination of the contract, so that the party in breach loses the whole commercial benefit of the transaction, then there is a strong incentive to comply with the contractual obligations. Yet a right to terminate the contract even for trivial breaches may put the injured party in a position to take opportunistic advantage of changes in market conditions.[63] Where a fixed price contract becomes unattractive due to a change in the ordinary market rates, then the injured party may be tempted to point to a minor breach in order to escape the transaction and make a better deal either by renegotiation or by seeking a new contractual partner. In order to promote co-operation and to discourage opportunism the courts must in general support the right to terminate the contract for breach, but qualify this stance in cases of minor breaches.

The general test for determining whether the right to terminate the contract was stated by Diplock LJ:

> does the occurrence of the event deprive the party who has further undertakings still to perform of substantially the whole benefit which it was the intention of the parties as expressed in the contract that he should obtain as the consideration for performing those undertakings?[64]

In short, to justify termination the party in breach must have substantially deprived the injured party of the benefits of performance of the contract. This principle invokes a test of degree, which requires the court to examine the facts in order to determine what the effects of the breach have been and how much less than proper performance of the contract has been received by the injured party. In order to give greater specificity to this underlying principle, the courts developed further doctrines. We will consider in particular the concept of repudiation, express termination clauses, and the distinction between conditions and warranties.

(1) Repudiation
One set of facts which normally satisfies this test of substantial failure of performance occurs when one party indicates through his words or conduct that he no longer intends to be bound by the contract. In this instance, the injured party may respond to a complete repudiation of the contract by terminating it. When the refusal to perform relates to one aspect of

---

63   Reynolds, 'Discharge by Breach as a Remedy' in P Finn (ed), *Essays on Contract* (Sydney, 1987), chapter 6.
64   *Hong Kong Fir Shipping Co Ltd v Kawasaki Kisen Kaisha Ltd* [1962] 2 QB 26, [1962] 1 All ER 474, CA.

the contract, however, the court cannot escape from making a discretionary judgment concerning the degree to which the injured party will be deprived of the benefit of correct performance. A repudiation may take place even before any performance under the contract has become due, a situation often given the confusing name of 'anticipatory breach'. In whatever form the repudiation takes place, the other party to the contract enjoys the normal choice of either accepting the repudiation, thereby terminating the contract, or affirming the contract by his words or conduct and awaiting further negotiations.

(2) Express termination clauses
In order to avoid the uncertainty surrounding the exercise of judicial discretion in cases of partial breach of contract, in commercial transactions the parties usually agree express provisions governing minor breaches. The contract states that breach of a particular provision or the occurrence of a particular event will entitle one party to terminate the contract. These clauses will normally be valid, subject to specific statutory prohibitions. When a party has the right to terminate under the contract, the action of declaring the contract terminated will not count as a repudiation, but rather a permitted form of performance. If, however, one party exercises the contractual right to rescind improperly and in bad faith, then the purported termination is regarded as repudiation.[65]

(3) Conditions and Warranties
As well as explicit termination clauses, it became established through precedent that certain phrases used in contracts signalled that breach of that term would give rise to the right to terminate the contract. A common phrase of this kind is 'time is of the essence', which has the effect that lateness, no matter how trivial, entitles the other party to terminate for delay.[66] The most important phrase was to describe a term as a 'condition', in contrast to a 'warranty', for it became established that breach of condition gave the right to terminate the contract. Indeed, the courts tended to classify all terms of contracts into either conditions and warranties. Once a particular term had been classified as a condition or a similar code phrase signalling that breach would entitle the injured party to terminate the contract, then the precedent force of the decision would mean that in subsequent disputes involving the same term in a different contract the court would be bound to give it the same effect. Draftsmen of contracts found it a convenient technique to pre-determine the results of breach by carefully labelling each term in the contract as either a condition or a warranty.[67] Similarly, the Sale of Goods Act 1893 (now 1979) adopted

---

65 *Woodar Investment Development Ltd v Wimpey Construction (UK) Ltd* [1980] 1 WLR 277, [1980] 1 All ER 571, HL.
66 *Bunge Corpn v Tradax SA* [1981] 1 WLR 711, [1981] 2 All ER 513, HL.
67 *Bentsen v Taylor, Sons & Co (No 2)* [1893] 2 QB 274, CA.

the terminology of conditions and warranties, in order to express the effects of the statute as precisely as possible. The implied terms as to the quality, quantity, and conformity to sample were earmarked as conditions, so that any breach entitled the buyer to reject the goods and terminate the contract.

The advantages of the classification of terms in this way go beyond the benefits of certainty and the avoidance of disputes and delays. By characterizing obligations as conditions, the parties provide a strong incentive to perform the contract according to its terms, thereby promoting co-operation. Moreover, the seller of goods will usually be in a better position than the buyer to dispose of them at the least cost in the market, especially when the buyer is a consumer, so that the costs of breach can be reduced by permitting the buyer to reject the goods.[68]

At the same time, however, the classification of terms may permit opportunism. A buyer may be able to point to a trivial defect in order to escape the transaction in a falling market. In a contract for services, the purchaser can effectively enjoy the right to terminate the contract at will if the contract specifies that even trivial deviations from the contract count as breach of condition. For example, in *Schuler AG v Wickman Machine Tool Sales Ltd*,[69] a company of sales representatives agreed to market a German product in Britain, and, as a condition of the contract, undertook to pay weekly visits to the major regular customers, the six largest motor manufacturers, during the four and a half year lifetime of the contract. On a literal reading of the contract, a single failure to visit a customer out of the contemplated 1,400 visits would have entitled the German producers to terminate the contract. The value of co-operation therefore points to the introduction of a limitation on the right to terminate the contract for breach of conditions.

The courts and then the legislature have responded to the problem by reintroducing the criterion of the seriousness of the breach. In some cases, the courts argue that the parties could not have intended by their use of the term condition that even trivial breaches should trigger the right to terminate the contract. As an interpretation of the facts in a case such as *Schuler AG v Wickman Machine Tool Sales Ltd*, this may appear unconvincing, for the producers no doubt wanted to have the clause in reserve in order to keep the sales representatives on their toes. Nevertheless, this interpretation does reinsert the value of co-operation into the contract by forbidding reliance on the term as a pretext. Another approach used by the courts is to claim that some terms which have not been expressly labelled will be regarded as neither warranties nor conditions, but rather as falling into a third category of innominate terms. In this category the test for the entitlement to terminate depends upon

---

68   Priest, 'Breach and Remedy for the Tender of Non-conforming Goods' (1978) 91 *Harvard Law Review* 960.
69   [1974] AC 235, [1973] 2 All ER 39, HL; cf *Arcos Ltd v Ronaasen* [1933] AC 470, HL.

whether or not the breach is fundamental,[70] which permits a reinsertion of the test of the seriousness of the breach.

In exercising this discretion, the courts take into consideration a variety of factors. The difference between the performance contemplated in the contract and the actual performance provides the main criterion. For example, where one party delivers defective goods as a result of unsuitable conditions during carriage, the court examines the difference in market value between the goods delivered and those specified in the contract and whether the goods are still fit for their intended purpose, in order to determine whether there has been a fundamental breach of the contract of carriage.[71] In addition, the courts examine the position in which the injured party has been placed as a result of the breach. They ask whether damages would be an adequate remedy or whether the injured party needs to be able to terminate the contract in order to safeguard his economic position. In some cases, the injured party may be so short of time that he has no option but to terminate the contract, for otherwise he will be left with goods on a falling market or miss other profitable opportunities or suffer severe losses as a result of an adverse financial predicament. Here a court is likely to decide that timing was of the essence to the contract, and that even a short delay will entitle the injured party to terminate the contract. Where those factors are absent, on the other hand, a court may find that any attempt to terminate the contract is premature.

An alteration in the Sale of Goods Act 1979 has now applied this more flexible approach to the breach of the implied terms regarding quality and quantity in the sale of goods. Where the breach of one of these conditions is 'so slight that it would be unreasonable' to reject them, then a court may regard the breach as only giving rise to a right to damages.[72] Following the recommendation of the Law Commission,[73] this flexibility does not apply to purchases by consumers, who remain entitled to reject goods for minor breaches of quality standards.

(4) Loss of the right to terminate

The right to terminate a contract for breach supplies a key incentive for performance and co-operation. The right may be lost, however, where the injured party has indicated by words or conduct that it wishes to continue with performance of the contract. This conduct is described as 'affirmation of the contract' or 'waiver of breach'. The principles applicable here mirror the modern rules used in relation to informal modifications, since they

---

70 *Cehave NV v Bremer Handelsgesellschaft mbH (The Hansa Nord)* [1976] QB 44, [1975] 3 All ER 739, CA.
71 Ibid.
72 Sale of Goods Act 1979, s 15A(1), as amended by the Sale and Supply of Goods Act 1994, s 4.
73 Law Commission, *Sale and Supply of Goods*, Report No 160, Cm 137 (London, 1987).

are designed to prevent the kind of opportunism where a party first indicates that a variation has been agreed and then seeks to renege on that commitment.

In clear cases of the loss of the right to terminate, the injured party demands further performance or sues for specific performance. Short of express demands or unambiguous legal action, however, the courts must look at the conduct of the injured party to discover whether he has acted in such a way as to evidence either that he has resigned himself to the termination of the contract, or that he continues to await and expect further performance. For example, if an employer imposes a wage cut on employees without their consent but the employees continue to work as normal, their conduct has to be construed as either acceptance of the breach resulting in termination and the formation of a new contract, or alternatively the employees' conduct may be construed simply as an affirmation of the original contract so that they can continue to claim the original wage rates.[74] The election to terminate the contract is likely to be found from any change of position which indicates that the injured party does not expect to proceed with the transaction.[75]

(5) Incentives to Renegotiate

The right to terminate not only provides an incentive to perform the contract, but also it can give the parties an incentive to renegotiate the terms of the contract in the light of changed circumstances and unplanned contingencies. The long-term business interests of the parties may dictate a renegotiation rather than the conclusion of business relations. For instance, in *Staffordshire Area Health Authority v South Staffordshire Waterworks Co*,[76] these two government agencies, a water supplier and a hospital, made a long-term contract for the supply of water at a fixed price. After more than sixty years had passed, the price was plainly unrealistic due to inflation. Although the terms provided that the contract was to be binding 'at all times hereafter', the English Court of Appeal implied a term permitting the supplier to terminate the contract upon reasonable notice. The effect of the implied term was to force the hospital authority back to the bargaining table to renegotiate the cost of water supplies up to a more economic price.

The difficult question is whether a right to terminate the contract best serves the purpose of encouraging co-operation in the form of renegotiation to handle unexpected contingencies.[77] An alternative consists in permitting the courts to revise contracts in the manner of judicial revision to secure fairness considered in Chapter 13. Where the

---

74   *Rigby v Ferodo Ltd* [1988] ICR 29, [1987] IRLR 516, HL.
75   *Société Italo-Belge pour le Commerce et l'Industrie SA v Palm and Vegetable Oils (Malaysia) Sdn Bhd (The Post Chaser)* [1982] 1 All ER 19, [1981] 2 Lloyd's Rep 695, QB.
76   [1978] 1 WLR 1387, [1978] 3 All ER 769, CA.
77   J Bell, 'The Effect of Changes in Circumstances on Long-Term Contracts' in D Harris and D Tallon (eds), *Contract Law Today* (Oxford, 1989), chapter 5.

courts possess such a power, then there would be an incentive to renegotiate the contract on terms comparable to those likely to be imposed by the court. This approach has the advantage over the right to terminate the contract in that neither party is given the option to walk away from the contract altogether, which avoids the possibility of opportunism in the light of changed circumstances. As we have seen, English law does not grant the courts an express power to revise contracts, though techniques of construction can achieve comparable results in some cases. In the United States some courts have experimented with judicial revision, most famously in *Aluminum Co of America v Essex Group*.[78] Under a sixteen-year contract with an option to renew for an additional five years, ALCOA agreed to convert alumina supplied by Essex into molten aluminium. The contract contained detailed provisions designed to raise the price in line with the wholesale price index, but this index failed to account for the sharp rise in the cost of energy to ALCOA, so the contract became increasingly unprofitable to them. The Federal District Court declared that the contract had gone awry because of a mistake in formulating the pricing mechanism to account for inflation. So the court set aside the contract and imposed a new pricing formula. The parties subsequently renegotiated the contract in the light of this judicial revision of the contract.[79]

78 499 F Supp 53 (WD Pa 1980).
79 Campbell and Harris, 'Flexibility in Long-term Contractual Relationships: The Role of Co-operation' (1993) 20 *Journal of Law and Society* 166.

16

Agreed Remedies

The terms of contracts normally make provision for the remedies available to the parties in the event of breach of contract. The terms may specify the amount of compensation payable, or arrange for some guarantee of payments due under the contract, or even determine that any disputes be resolved outside the ordinary courts by an arbitrator. If no such provisions have been agreed, then the courts supply judicial remedies such as an order for compulsory performance (specific performance or injunctions) or an order to pay compensation (damages). These judicial remedies will be considered in Chapter 17. Most written contracts, however, pay considerable attention to agreed remedies. A majority of the terms of a standard form contract will in all likelihood seek to augment, structure, and confine the claims available to each party in relation to the breach of contract. In short, the normal remedy for breach of contract is that provided in the contract itself.

Indeed, the whole nature of a transaction may be devised with the remedial aspect in mind. A hire-purchase contract (or conditional sales contract), for example, can only be understood from this perspective. Instead of a finance company making a loan to a consumer who wishes to purchase some goods, such as a car, the finance company purchases the car itself and then rents it out to the consumer for a period of time in return for hire charges. At the end of the period of hire the consumer has a contractual right to purchase the car for a nominal sum. The major purpose of this elaborate arrangement is to give the finance company a security for repayment of the loan by distributing property rights in a particular way. By retaining ownership of the car, in the event of the consumer's default on payments, the finance company can bring the hire arrangement to a close, sell the car, and recoup its money, without having to rely upon the consumer's ability to pay damages. The agreed remedy of the finance company, namely the right to sell the goods in order to satisfy the consumer's debt, is central to the whole structure of this artificial contractual edifice.

The reasons for the deployment of agreed remedies are not hard to seek. Lawyers can create an advantage to their client by improving on the normal judicial remedy for breach of contract, which comprises compensatory damages. By devising a more reliable remedy, such as a security interest or a guarantee from a bank, the lawyer greatly increases the chances of the legal system providing an effective remedy against breach. This increases the threat available to the injured party, which is important both in the discouragement of breach and in obtaining beneficial settlements of claims.

The significance of agreed remedies is therefore not merely that they represent the normal remedy for breach of contract, but also that they often provide a different kind of remedy by changing the nature of the right being claimed from a personal right to a proprietary right. This aspect of contractual practice greatly facilitates the use of 'self-help' as a sanction for breach of contract.

1. Freedom and Control

These contractual practices rely on the general rule that agreed remedies will be enforced by the courts. An agreed measure of compensation, for instance, will be regarded as a debt which is owed, which can be claimed quickly through the courts' procedures for seizure of goods to the value of the debt. Similarly, the courts will decline jurisdiction over a contractual dispute governed by an arbitration clause. This support for contractual determination of remedies rests on cogent policy considerations.

In the first place, agreed remedies may considerably reduce the costs and uncertainties arising from contractual disputes. Instead of the parties engaging in prolonged debates about the measure of loss arising from the dispute, the fixed measure of compensation will be payable. Similarly, where a creditor has taken security against a debt, such as a deposit, the creditor can simply retain the deposit rather than seeking compensation in the courts. This first advantage of agreed remedies brings with it another: it reduces the cost to the public purse of the adminstration of justice. At a deeper level, the power to agree remedies for breach facilitates a whole range of market transactions which otherwise might be stifled. For example, few would be prepared to loan another a large sum of money without some kind of guarantee or security for repayment. Otherwise lenders naturally fear that their money will disappear without trace, or that the borrower will become insolvent and be unable to repay the loan. A hire-purchase agreement, despite the considerable advantages gained for the finance company, may be socially beneficial if it provides the necessary mechanism for consumer purchases to be bought on credit. Yet these crucial benefits deriving from respect for the agreed remedies in the contract do not rule out all regulation and control, for these terms, like other aspects of freedom of contract, pose the danger of the abuse of contractual power and can threaten the integrity of other valuable institutions of the market economy.

Complete freedom of contract with respect to remedies for breach could never be tolerated. It might permit terms granting the creditor the right to imprison, beat, or commit immoral acts against the debtor. Any agreed remedy of this type would certainly be unenforceable as immoral or contrary to public policy. However, the dangers of abuse of contractual power need not be as obvious as Shylock's demand for a pound of flesh. More commonly we find attempts to secure a scale of financial compensation for breach of contract which exceeds any loss incurred by the injured party. Alternatively, the party in breach will have used a standard form contract to minimize any compensation payable by reference to a fixed sum or a limitation of damages clause. As well as fixing the quantity of compensation payable to their advantage, purveyors of standard form contracts will often seek to enhance the reliability of their remedy by the acquisition of property rights. In what is known as a 'catching bargain', for instance, the lender of money may arrange, in the event of a failure to repay instalments on time, that the lender acquires title not only to the goods purchased by the debtor with the loan, but also all the other goods of the debtor. Not only will this provide the debtor with a strong incentive to repay, but also it improves the reliability of any remedy on default. To gain such proprietary rights over all the debtor's assets as a result of failure to pay a small sum of money may be regarded, however, as an abuse of bargaining power and unconscionable transaction.

Agreed remedies can also pose an indirect threat to the institution of the market as a whole. Two dangers should be highlighted at this point. First, there is the danger that an agreed choice of forum will prevent a fair and impartial determination of disputes. This will be an affront to the public system of justice and the civil rights of individuals, as well as perhaps leading to unfair results. We consider how this problem has been addressed in the final section of this chapter.

Secondly, many agreed remedies distribute property entitlements, not only in order to provide a security for performance, but also to ensure priority over other creditors, so that even in the event of the debtor's insolvency a substantial remedy will be available to the creditor.[1] The danger which this practice poses to the market is that it often leads to confusion and uncertainty over the exact allocation of proprietary rights. The apparent owner of a television under a hire-purchase agreement is of course the consumer, though in reality title remains vested in the finance company. Third parties may assume that the apparent owner is the true owner, enter contracts with the consumer on that false assumption, and incur loss as a result.[2] Public systems of registration of proprietary interests can reduce this problem, by making it possible to ascertain ownership of proprietary interests before entering into transactions. But not every kind of proprietary interest need be registered, so there remains

---

1   The question of the fairness of creditors' priorities is beyond the scope of the discussion here.
2   This particular problem is governed by Hire-Purchase Act 1964, s 27 (as amended by Consumer Credit Act 1974, s 192(3)) and protects the innocent private purchaser by giving him or her title to the television.

the risk that the widespread divergence between ostensible ownership and legal ownership will deter entry into market transactions. For this reason the law may not give full effect to unregistered proprietary interests, particularly when they are used against third parties who are justifiably ignorant of those rights.

The legal regulation of agreed remedies therefore consists of a balance between respect for freedom of contract and controls against abuse of contractual power. We will consider how this balance is struck in relation to the principal types of remedial provisions, namely, fixed measures of compensation, security interests in property, guarantees, and arbitration clauses.

2. Fixed Measure of Compensation

A common agreed remedy fixes the measure of compensation payable for breach of contract. A variety of terms achieve this effect. The term may state the sum due either as an expression of the price of the contract or as damages. The term may seek to augment or restrict the measure of damages. The fixed measure of compensation may be combined with a security interest, as in the case of a deposit, which both fixes the measure of compensation and gives the creditor a proprietary right over a sum of money. The general purpose of legal controls over these terms is to frustrate attempts to secure greater compensation for breach of contract than might be obtained from judicial remedies.[3] This purpose contains a conception of fairness, one which is not concerned with the fairness of the bargain, but one which insists that the remedial arrangements should not cause a redistribution of wealth which provides the injured party with either greater or lesser compensation than his actual losses. But the incidence and tightness of these legal controls over fixed measures of compensation varies according to the form of the term and the nature of the parties to the contract.

(1) Agreed Price
Under an action for debt or an agreed sum of money, the plaintiff relies upon the term fixing the price of the goods or services to set the measure of compensation payable. The rules of civil procedure of the courts enable the plaintiff to adopt a quick and truncated legal process by which the claim for the price may be pursued. Unless the defendant offers a defence that the sum is not due, then the plaintiff can proceed to enforce the claim by using the court's process of seizure and sale of goods to the value of the debt. There is no requirement that the plaintiff should prove the

---

3 Macneil, 'Power of Contract and Agreed Remedies' (1962) 47 *Cornell Law Quarterly* 495.

amount of the loss suffered provided that the debt has fallen due. Nor is there in general any duty to mitigate any losses resulting from the breach of contract. On the other hand, no claim can be made for additional losses such as interest on the money while awaiting payment. Because of the simplicity of the action for debt, whenever the breach of contract consists of a failure to pay an agreed sum of money, this will be the most common means of pursuing a remedy.

In this action for debt, the primary obligation which determines the price also fixes the scale of compensation. This coincidence explains why the courts are unwilling to control actions for debt. To do so would inevitably clash with their stance against testing the adequacy of consideration and their general unwillingness to intervene to invalidate or rewrite harsh bargains. Although direct controls on grounds of the unfairness of the price are not generally available, the courts have devised a number of protections for the debtor in such cases.

Due Date of Payment

The main protection consists of an insistence that the payment should have fallen due. The due date may be set by the contract itself, as in the case of an advance payment.[4] In consumer contracts, express terms which seek to order performance so that the consumer has to pay in full in advance may be regarded as unfair and invalid under the Unfair Terms in Consumer Contracts Regulations.[5] In the absence of express provision fixing the due date, the courts must construe the agreement. In a sale of goods, for instance, payment will not generally fall due until the vendor has transferred ownership of the goods under the contract and is ready and willing to tender delivery of them in exchange for the price.[6] In the case of provision of services, the contract will normally be interpreted to require full or substantial performance of the service to a reasonable standard before the debt falls due.[7] In a long-term service contract, such as a contract of employment, payments of wages will fall due periodically according to the terms of the contract, as in the case of wages payable monthly in arrears.

The courts have been able to construe the contract in order to fix the due date for payment in ways to protect consumers from claims for money where the performance of the contract has proven unsatisfactory. In *Bolton v Mahadeva*,[8] the plaintiff agreed to instal a central heating system into the defendant's home for £560. The system proved defective in several respects, including inadequate heat in some rooms and noxious fumes in

---

4　Sale of Goods Act 1979, s 49(2).
5　SI 1994/3159, Sch 3, para 1(o) 'obliging the consumer to fulfil all his obligations where the seller or supplier does not perform his'.
6　Sale of Goods Act 1979, ss 28, 49(1). R Goode, *Commercial Law* 2nd edn (London, 1995) pp 423–425.
7　*Hoenig v Isaacs* [1952] 2 All ER 176, CA.
8　[1972] 1 WLR 1009, [1972] 2 All ER 1322, CA.

others, and required £174 of repairs. The defendant successfully resisted an action for the full price of the work under the original contract (subject to a set-off for the defects), on the ground that payment did not fall due until the plaintiff had substantially fulfilled his obligation. This is described as an 'entire obligation', that is, one which must be substantially performed before payment falls due. The test of whether substantial performance has been provided depends for its application upon the nature of the defects and the proportion between the cost of rectifying them and the original contract price. In *Bolton v Mahadeva*, there was no substantial performance since the cost of repairs amounted to nearly a third of the contract price, but the result would probably be different if the repairs cost less than ten per cent of the contract price.[9]

Set-Off
Another escape route from an action for an agreed price is to claim the right to set off against the price any sums due to the debtor from the creditor. This is a common express provision in commercial contracts,[10] but the right to set-off exists in equity without the need for an express term. Thus in *Bolton v Mahadeva* the defendant offered the full price minus the cost of repairs to the plaintiff in full satisfaction of the debt. Equally a debtor may set off against an action for an agreed price debts owed by the creditor to him under other contracts,[11] provided that it would be manifestly unjust to enforce the debt without taking into account the debtor's counter-claim.[12] Courts tend to regard the right to set-off as a fundamental principle of fairness with respect to agreed remedies, so they have little hesitation in regarding attempts to exclude the right as unreasonable and therefore void under the Unfair Contract Terms Act 1977.[13] This control is strengthened in relation to consumer contracts, where the Unfair Terms Regulations instance as an unfair term one which prevents consumers from exercising a right of set-off against a seller.[14]

Anticipatory Breach
If a debtor repudiates the contract before performance has commenced, can the creditor nevertheless perform the contract and claim the price? Suppose that the debtor agrees to purchase some goods at a future date, but before that date states that he no longer wishes to be bound by the contract. Can the vendor nevertheless offer to deliver the goods on the due date and then claim full payment? The traditional rule of English

---

9   For example *Hoenig v Isaacs* [1952] 2 All ER 176, CA.
10   R Goode, *Commercial Law* 2nd edn (London, 1995), p 657.
11   But the right to set-off may not be available against an insolvent creditor, for this might subvert the rules ensuring fairness between unsecured creditors.
12   *Federal Commerce & Navigation Co Ltd v Molena Alpha Inc* [1978] QB 927, CA; S R Derham, *Set-Off* (Oxford, 1987), pp 11–20.
13   *Stewart Gill Ltd v Horatio Myer & Co Ltd* [1992] QB 600, [1992] 2 All ER 257, CA.
14   SI 1994/3159, Sch 3, para 1(b).

law laid down in *White and Carter (Councils) Ltd v McGregor*[15] permits the vendor to complete performance, if this can be done without the co-operation of the debtor, and to succeed in a claim for the price in these circumstances. In that case the defendant agreed to pay a fixed price to have his business advertised by the plaintiff on litterbins for three years, but later the same day repudiated the contract. The plaintiff nevertheless carried the advertisements for three years and successfully claimed the agreed price. Here the defendant received the benefit of the advertisements for the price, but perhaps he placed no value on them, and indeed perhaps they served no useful purpose, so considerations of efficiency might have pointed against enforcing the agreed price.

This traditional rule may rest on the assumption that the debtor can dispose of unwanted goods as efficiently as the vendor, though this seems unlikely for consumer purchasers. The rule may also be influenced by the principle that the debtor acquires ownership of the goods on the due date of performance, since the repudiation has not been accepted by the vendor, which has the effect that the vendor may not be able to give good title to a third party.[16] The rule may be criticised because it appears to lead to inefficient results when the goods or services have no commercial value either to the debtor or a third party, as in *White and Carter (Councils) Ltd v McGregor*. Suppose that a fixed price is agreed for the painting of a portrait by using photographs. If the debtor announces before the artist has begun work that he no longer wants the portrait, should the artist be entitled to proceed and sue for the price when the picture has been completed? Assuming that the picture has little or no value to anyone else, the debtor has little chance of recouping his loss if he has to pay the price. On the other hand, the artist could have reduced her loss by seeking alternative employment.

English courts have recently qualified the rule, however, in cases where the creditor is behaving wholly unreasonably and has no legitimate interest in performing the contract. The scope of this qualification remains uncertain, since it is impossible to know how it can ever be wholly unreasonable to perform a contract and ask for the agreed price. Given the uncertainties and additional expense of claiming damages, a claim for the agreed price will almost invariably represent a sensible choice. Nevertheless, this exception has been applied in *Clea Shipping Corpn v Bulk Oil International Ltd (The Alaskan Trader)*.[17] Under a time charter for hire of a ship for two years, engine failure took the ship off-hire for several months and the charterers indicated that they wished to repudiate the contract since the cost of chartering ships had fallen. Nevertheless, the owners had the ship repaired and then anchored the vessel off Piraeus with a full crew ready to sail until the charter expired, and then sold the

15   [1962] AC 413, [1961] 3 All ER 1178, HL. Compare *Clark v Marsiglia* 1 Denio 317 (NY 1845).
16   See: Sale of Goods Act 1979, s 48(2); Torts (Interference with Goods) Act 1977, s 12.
17   [1984] 1 All ER 129, [1983] 2 Lloyd's Rep 645, QB.

vessel for scrap. The charterers succeeded in recovering the hire charges which they had paid from the time the vessel was repaired, on the ground that the owners had 'no legitimate interest' in continuing performance of the contract,[18] or that continued performance was 'wholly unreasonable' and damages would be an adequate remedy.[19] The charterers persuaded the court that it was wholly unreasonable for the owners not to have sought alternative employment for the ship, or lay it up without a crew, or have sold it for scrap without repairs.

These arguments describe what would have comprised the duties to mitigate loss if the owners had accepted the repudiation and merely sought damages, which suggest that economic efficiency considerations colour this qualification. Perhaps the court was also impressed by the futility and waste of resources in repairing the ship and then selling it for scrap.[20] On the other hand, it must be observed that the owner acted in a way which saved it the trouble of suing for damages for the difference in hire charges, and was able to keep its crew in full employment. Nor could it be said that the charterers had no commercial use for the vessel, for their failure to use it resulted from their choice to break the contract and make alternative arrangements at lower cost.

Fairness
The underlying problem for judicial control over the action for an agreed price concerns the characterisation of the claim. If the creditor's claim is regarded simply as an enforcement of a primary obligation under the contract, then the judicial reluctance to rewrite bargains and test them for fairness discourages any scrutiny of the reasonableness of the claim. But once the action for an agreed price is classified, as it should be, as a form of agreed remedy, then the courts can employ standards which prevent oppression, waste of resources, and excessive compensation. The courts have used the devices of 'entire obligations', set-off, and 'legitimate interest in performance' to serve this purpose of controlling these claims.

(2) *Limitation of Damages*
A simple and common term for specifying the measure of compensation consists of fixing an upper limit to compensation payable in an action for damages in the courts. An alternative is to specify the exact amount payable for breach of contract at a level which falls below the ordinary measure of compensatory damages.[21] Limitation of damages clauses in commercial contracts often serve a useful function in setting the limits of

---

18 The test suggested by Lord Reid in *White & Carter (Councils) Ltd v McGregor* [1962] AC 413, [1961] 3 All ER 1178, HL.
19 The test suggested by Kerr J in *The Odenfeld* [1978] 2 Lloyd's Rep 357, QB.
20 See also: *Attica Sea Carriers Corpn v Ferrostaal Poseidon Bulk Reederei GmbH (The Puerto Buitrago)* [1976] 1 Lloyd's Rep 250, CA, where the cost of repairs to the ship was twice its market value when repaired.
21 *Cellulose Acetate Silk Co Ltd v Widnes Foundry (1925) Ltd* [1933] AC 20, HL.

potential liability in advance, so that appropriate insurance arrangements can be taken out.

As a form of exclusion clause, these limitation of damages clauses are subject to a test of fairness and reasonableness under the Unfair Contract Terms Act 1977.[22] In *George Mitchell (Chesterhall) Ltd v Finney Lock Seeds Ltd*,[23] for instance, the contract fixed the maximum liability at £192 which was the price of the seeds being sold, whereas the plaintiff claimed losses of £61,000 as a result of planting the wrong seeds. The House of Lords found the limitation of damages clause unreasonable and invalid. One important consideration operating here was the gross disparity between the fixed measure of compensation and actual measure of loss. In addition, however, the control also rested on a perception that the plaintiff lacked equality of bargaining power, so that limitation of damages clauses between substantial commercial entities might prove enforceable even if they lead to substantial undercompensation. Those limitation of damages clauses which fall outside the scope of the 1977 Act will normally be enforceable according to their literal meaning, the courts believing that the dangers of oppression and unfairness will not exist in these circumstances.[24]

In consumer contracts, limitation of damages clauses will also be subject to the Unfair Terms in Consumer Regulations, where the relevant illustration of a presumptively unfair clause speaks of 'inappropriately' limiting the legal rights of the consumer in the event of breach of contract.[25] A limitation of damages clause in a consumer contract may prove valid under the general good faith and fairness standard, however, if the consumer received an inducement to agree to the term or perhaps if the clause fitted into otherwise fair insurance arrangements between the parties.

(3) Liquidated Damages and Penalties

A more ambitious type of clause in a contract which sets a level of agreed compensation fixes in advance the sum of money which will be payable in the event of breach of contract. These liquidated damages clauses serve the valuable purpose of reducing the uncertainties and expense entailed in claims for damages, for they can be enforced as an action for an agreed sum in debt. A fixed level of compensation also has the attraction of determining precisely the potential scale of the financial risk, and of allocating the risk of loss in advance, so that worries about unexpected claims will not deter entry into contracts. They can also ensure that the injured party receives full compensation for losses incurred, even though these might not be fully recoverable in an ordinary action for damages

---

22   Section 13(1)(b) provides that the controls over exclusion clauses apply also to any term which restricts any remedy in respect of liability.
23   [1983] 2 AC 803, [1983] 2 All ER 737, HL.
24   *Ailsa Craig Fishing Co Ltd v Malvern Fishing Co Ltd and Securicor (Scotland) Ltd* [1983] 1 WLR 964, [1983] 1 All ER 101, HL.
25   SI 1994/3159, Sch 3, para 1(b).

because of difficulties of proof of actual loss. Liquidated damages clauses also benefit from the advantage of employing an action for an agreed sum in securing a simplified legal process for claiming fixed sums of money through the courts. The threat of such an action may help to put pressure on a contractor to reduce delay and may facilitate agreed settlements of compensation payable for breach.[26]

Equitable Control
The courts have, however, devised strict controls over liquidated damages clauses which exceed the normal level of compensatory damages for breach of contract. Unless the clause sets a level of compensation which is a genuine pre-estimate of the loss, then the term will be dubbed a 'penalty clause' and will be unenforceable if the court regards it as unconscionable. The court will replace the agreed compensation with a sum of money representing an accurate assessment of a fair measure of compensation for the injured party's loss, which can then be enforced as a debt.[27] The measure of compensation will be calculated by reference to the ordinary measure of damages payable for that type of breach of contract.

There can be no clear dividing line between agreed price clauses and agreed compensation clauses. Indeed, to avoid judicial control over penalty clauses there is every incentive for a party to attempt to present the fixed sum as a primary obligation under the contract, as the agreed price rather than compensation. In *Interfoto Picture Library Ltd v Stiletto Visual Programmes Ltd*[28] the contractual terms stated that there would be a fixed hire charge per day after the due date for return of the photographs. These terms sought to present a penalty clause as merely an agreed rate of hire, and, though the court left the issue undecided, it seems likely that the jurisdiction over penalty clauses could have been applied. The courts have often revealed little hesitation in cutting through such shams and controlling the disguised penalty clause. In *Willson v Love*[29] a lease provided for the increase of rent in the event of a breach of covenant, but the court treated this as a penalty clause. This makes sense if the purpose of the jurisdiction is to ensure fairness between the parties by controlling the terms of the contract, but is inexplicable if the courts are merely concerned to prevent oppressive remedies from interfering with individual freedom. Yet the courts have proved reluctant to drop the barrier to the jurisdiction to give relief from penalty clauses which requires that the sum of money should be payable on breach of contract.[30] The reason for

26 Beale and Dugdale, 'Contracts between Businessmen' (1975) 2 *British Journal of Law and Society* 45, at p 55.
27 *Beckham v Drake* (1849) 2 HL Cas 579; *Bridge v Campbell Discount Co Ltd* [1962] AC 600, [1962] 1 All ER 385, HL; *Jobson v Johnson* [1989] 1 WLR 1026, [1989] 1 All ER 621, CA.
28 [1989] QB 433, [1988] 1 All ER 348, CA.
29 [1896] 1 QB 626, CA.
30 *Export Credits Guarantee Department v Universal Oil Products Co* [1983] 1 WLR 399, HL; but compare Lord Denning in *Bridge v Campbell Discount Co Ltd* [1962] AC 600.

this reluctance is that dropping this requirement would enable them to test the fairness of the price in all actions for an agreed sum, a jurisdiction which they have systematically declined, no doubt because they believe that it would interfere too greatly with freedom of contract, and weaken the utility of the quick remedy for debt.

This invalidity of penalty clauses does not prevent the level of agreed compensation from being set above an ordinary award of damages. The legal test requires the agreement to contain a genuine pre-estimate of loss, which may in the events which happen deviate from the actual loss. With the benefit of hindsight it may be possible to see that the agreed compensation was excessive, but, provided that the court is convinced that the agreement did try to estimate the likely loss accurately, it will enforce the clause as permitted liquidated damages.[31] A strict rule against agreed levels of compensation above ordinary damages would render liquidated damages clauses almost always vulnerable to attack, since at the time of the formation of the contract the parties will not have complete foresight of the consequences of a breach of contract. The courts therefore permit some latitude in the fixing of agreed remedies.

The approach to testing the validity of higher levels of compensation can be described as 'risk averaging'.[32] The degree of tolerance extends to agreed remedies which fix a sum of compensation which represents an average of probable losses resulting from different breaches of the same contract. For example, in *Dunlop Pneumatic Tyre Co Ltd v New Garage & Motor Co Ltd*,[33] the manufacturer of tyres required under its contracts with distributors a payment of £5 for every tyre sold to the public below list price, or sold after tampering with the manufacturer's markings, or supplied to prohibited persons, or exported. The defendant dealer sold to the public below list price, which created the risk to the manufacturer that its other dealers would either demand reduced prices or go to other manufacturers. Although the fixed sum of compensation might have exceeded the manufacturer's loss in any particular breach of contract, since the loss springing from a more competitive market was in any case difficult to assess, the court enforced the fixed sum by way of liquidated damages as a genuine attempt to predict it. The £5 charge was not an extravagant measure of compensation for any of the potential breaches of contract. It was a prediction of the average probable loss resulting from each breach of contract.

This latitude does not extend to cases where the obligation which has been broken merely involves the payment of money or the transfer of ascertained property. In cases involving an obligation to pay money, as in the case of a loan, the courts will simply examine the question of whether the agreed compensation exceeds the creditor's loss. Whenever the agreed

---

31   *Clydebank Engineering and Shipbuilding Co v Castaneda* [1905] AC 6, HL.
32   Collins, 'Fairness in Agreed Remedies' in C Willett (ed), *Aspects of Fairness in Contract* (London, 1996) 97, 116.
33   [1915] AC 79, HL.

compensation exceeds the sums due to the creditor by way of return of principal and payment of interest, the court will scale down the penalty clause. This will be true even if the creditor suggests that his possible losses, as foreseen at the time of the formation of the contract, might have exceeded the repayment of principal and interest. Similarly, where the agreed compensation is described in the form of a transfer of a property right, if the value of the property exceeds the injured party's loss, then the court can order the debtor to sell the property and deliver to the injured party that part of the proceeds which amounts to the sum of the injured party's loss.[34]

Consumer Contracts

The origins of the equitable jurisdiction to give relief from penalty clauses lay in loan agreements. Creditors inserted into the loan agreement a term under which the debtor in default agreed to pay a fixed sum greatly in excess of the loan and interest. The creditor would then seek to enforce this 'penal bond' in an action for an agreed sum. But courts of equity prevented these actions on the ground that the loan agreement constituted an unconscionable bargain, and insisted that the only sum recoverable by the creditor was the principal and interest on the loan. In most cases such agreements would now be regulated by the Consumer Credit Act 1974, sections 137–140, which permits a court to reopen and revise an extortionate credit bargain, but the common law jurisdiction could still be applicable outside the field of consumer protection.

Prior to the 1974 Act, the jurisdiction to give relief from penalty clauses was used to regulate transactions such as hire-purchase, as in *Bridge v Campbell Discount Co Ltd*.[35] Under this contract for the hire and purchase of a car from a finance company, the terms provided that as compensation for depreciation of the value of the car the finance company should be entitled to retain any instalments paid and also claim the remainder of the payments to the sum of two-thirds of the hire-purchase price. The debtor returned the car after having paid only a few instalments and was then sued for the sum representing the balance of two-thirds of the hire-purchase price. The House of Lords refused to enforce this term for agreed compensation, on the ground that it could not represent a genuine pre-estimate of the creditor's loss, since the sum payable for depreciation in the value of the car actually decreased over time rather than increased. At bottom this contract was objectionable because it sought to guarantee interest on a loan which could far exceed market rates, since the finance company could be sure under the terms of the agreement of gaining both the value of the car at the date of breach of contract and the value of two-thirds of the instalments. This amounted to unjust enrichment of the finance company.

---

34 *Jobson v Johnson* [1989] 1 WLR 1026, [1989] 1 All ER 621, CA.
35 [1962] AC 600, [1962] 1 All ER 385, HL. The current law governing this case is contained in Consumer Credit Act 1974, ss 99–103.

This strict legislative control over fixed measures of compensation in consumer contracts has been expanded under the Unfair Terms in Consumer Contracts Regulations.[36] For example, Schedule 3, para 1(e) illustrates a type of term which is presumptively unfair as one which requires a consumer in breach of contract 'to pay a disproportionately high sum in compensation'.

These Regulations also appear to introduce a novel principle derived from European civil law systems. The Regulations imply in the illustrations of terms which may be regarded as unfair contained in Schedule 3 a principle that the seller's advantages obtained in agreed remedies should be mirrored by identical or equivalent remedial advantages afforded to the consumer. For example, illustration (d) creates a presumption of unfairness and therefore invalidity for a term:

> permitting the seller or supplier to retain sums paid by the consumer where the latter decides not to conclude or perform the contract, without providing for the consumer to receive compensation of an equivalent amount from the seller or supplier where the latter is the party cancelling the contract.

This illustration suggests that while sellers may insist upon advance payments and deposits as security, these terms will only be effective if the consumer receives an equivalent financial assurance of performance from the seller.

Fairness

The equitable and legislative controls over excessive measures of agreed compensation invoke a standard of fairness. Dillon LJ has observed that the courts do not claim a 'general power not to enforce any agreement which the courts regard as unconscionable and extravagant...but rules which evolved as to the types of cases in which relief would be given, and one of those rules, not too entrenched to be challenged, is the equitable rule against penalties'.[37] Other justifications for the control over penalty clauses appear less convincing.

One justification is that a penalty clause represents a form of private punishment for breach of contract which is objectionable in the relations of civil society in the market. While this justification is true and explains why terms contrary to moral standards will be invalid on grounds of public policy, an obligation to pay compensation does not constitute punishment except in the sense that it provides for a greater measure of compensation than the ordinary law of damages. Another justification for control over penalty clauses is that they constitute an attempt to pressurize a person to perform a contract, which is an invasion of freedom of the individual and which should therefore be strictly controlled and administered by the courts. This criticism certainly makes sense if, for example, in a contract of employment where the weekly wage is £200

36   SI 1994/3159.
37   *Jobson v Johnson* [1989] 1 WLR 1026 at 1032, CA.

the employee agrees to pay £1,000 compensation for any day's absence. But this objection to penalty clauses rarely applies to a carefully constructed commercial agreement. The application of the equitable jurisdiction to such commercial agreements also undermines the possibility of justifying the control on the ground of coercion or oppression during the bargaining process.[38]

The standard of fairness explains better why the courts examine the precise details of the level of compensation provided in commercial agreements. The concept of fairness at stake is one which compares the agreed remedy with the ordinary measure of damages. Attempts to increase the measure of compensation will be invalidated. But this concept of fairness is qualified by respect for the parties' attempts to plan the consequences of breach. This leads to the tolerance of the 'risk averaging' approach under which the agreed compensation may exceed actual loss provided the fixed level represents a genuine estimate of the probable loss arising from a number of possible breaches of contract.

The equitable jurisdiction to give relief from penalty clauses has been criticised on the ground that it interferes with freedom of contract and inhibits the use of contracts for wealth maximization.[39] For example, Rea argues that a party to a contract will charge a higher price if it risks a penalty clause in the event of breach of contract; so the penalty clause is paid for by the higher price for the contract; and the contract is worth more to both parties than a contract without a penalty clause.[40] By invalidating the penalty clause, not only does a court prevent the maximization of wealth through contracts, but the court also causes unfairness by refusing to enforce a promise (the liability to pay a penalty) which has been paid for (by a higher contract price). This argument assumes that the ancillary remedial clauses in contracts will form part of the bargaining over the price, which is unlikely in the case of consumer standard form contracts, so that the controls over consumer contracts will not be vulnerable to this criticism. Indeed the 1994 Regulations appear to agree with the point in the mirror principle, which insists that the consumer should be awarded an equivalent right. Another criticism of the courts' control over penalty clauses is that the agreed remedy may achieve a remedy for an item of loss which might not be compensated

---

38 Goetz and Scott, 'Liquidated Damages, Penalties and the Just Compensation Principle' (1977) 77 *Columbia Law Review* 554; Harris, 'Incentives to Perform, or Break Contracts' (1992) 45(2) *Current Legal Problems* 29; Muir, 'Stipulations for payment of an Agreed Sum' (1983-85) *Sydney Law Review* 503; some support for the relevance of procedural unfairness is given by Mason and Wilson JJ in *AMEV-UDC Finance Ltd v Austin* (1986) 162 CLR 170 (High Court of Australia) at p 193.

39 A penalty clause may deter efficient breach of contract, but this seems unlikely if there is post-breach bargaining between the parties: Clarkson, Miller and Muris, 'Liquidated Damages v Penalties: Sense or Nonsense' (1978) *Wisconsin Law Review* 351; Goetz and Scott, 'Liquidated Damages, Penalties and the Just Compensation Principle' (1977) 77 *Columbia Law Review* 554.

40 Rea, 'Efficiency Implications of Penalties and Liquidated Damages' (1984) 13 *Journal of Legal Studies* 147.

under the ordinary law of damages.[41] This observation is correct, but the courts appear sensitive to this point, as in *Dunlop Pneumatic Tyre Co Ltd v New Garage and Motor Co Ltd*, where one reason for upholding the validity of the £5 charge was that the losses were unpredictable and in many respects speculative, so that the plaintiff's claim for damages might have failed for want of proof of loss.

In some jurisdictions the fairness principle leads to the invalidity of all clauses which fix a level of compensation above the normal level of damages for breach of contract.[42] This approach has the advantage that the parties can appy it themselves in order to test the enforceability of the agreed remedy, but it suffers from the problem that the parties cannot always foresee the likely losses at the time of the formation of the contract. The English Law Commission, however, has rejected any change to the approach of requiring the parties to make a genuine pre-estimate of loss which then permits what we have called risk averaging.[43]

3. Security

Under the terms of a contract a creditor may seek to acquire an interest in property so that, in the event of breach of contract, the creditor can use the proprietary interest in order to satisfy the debt. This form of agreed remedy has the obvious advantage to the creditor that it provides a security against the debtor's performance of his contractual obligations; the debtor is more likely to perform if he risks some property interest, and if he fails to perform then the creditor can realize the value of the asset in order to ensure compensation for any loss. The creditor's remedy is also likely to be cheaper and quicker, since the creditor can help himself to the proprietary right rather than seek an award of damages through the courts. Some proprietary rights will also accord the creditor priority over other creditors in the event of the debtor's insolvency, so that the risks associated with the debtor's insolvency are greatly reduced. The enormous advantage of these types of secured transactions to a market system should be obvious. Without the facility of taking security, credit arrangements would be far less common, with a substantial diminution in transactions overall. The law permits considerable flexibility to the parties to determine the precise scope and incidents of these types of proprietary security.

The nature of a proprietary right can range from absolute ownership to a much lesser interest such as possession. We have noted, for instance,

---

41   Goetz and Scott, 'Liquidated Damages, Penalties and the Just Compensation Principle' (1977) 77 *Columbia Law Review* 554.

42   See The International Institute for the Unification of Private Law (Working Group for the Preparation of Principles for International Commercial Contracts) *Principles for International Commercial Contracts* (1992) 40(3) *American Journal of Comparative Law* 703, Art 7.4.14.

43   Law Commission, *Penalty Clauses and Forfeiture of Monies Paid*, Working Paper No 61.

that in a hire-purchase contract the finance company retains ownership of the goods, merely giving the debtor possessory rights under a contract of hire. The positions can be reversed. Under a lien, for instance, the debtor retains title to the goods, but the creditor enjoys the right to possess the goods until the debt has been paid. English law has developed a remarkably subtle system of proprietary rights, so that it can distribute many different types of interests in property such as ownership and possession to different persons at the same time. This permits the parties to a contract to shape the agreed remedies in a host of ways which distribute the proprietary interests in numerous patterns.

Although the complexity of the different patterns and species of proprietary interests which may be distributed between creditor and debtor prevents any comprehensive and simple classification of these contractual arrangements, it is possible to provide a preliminary guide to the principal types of proprietary distributions adopted as agreed remedies. We can divide proprietary rights into four basic forms: full title (which includes both legal and equitable proprietary interests in property); bare legal title; equitable proprietary interests; and mere possessory rights. These four basic categories of proprietary interests can be distributed between creditor and debtor by a contract, which results in four basic patterns as illustrated by the following table.

	Creditor's Right	*Debtor's Right*	*Example*
1	*Full title*	*Possessory right*	*hire-purchase*
2	*Legal title*	*equitable interest*	*lease*
3	*Equitable interest*	*legal title*	*home loan, floating charge*
4	*Possessory right*	*full title*	*lien*

A common example of (1) is the hire-purchase contract, where the creditor retains full ownership of the goods, but grants the debtor a contract of hire which entitles the debtor to use the goods. Breach of contract by the debtor leads to loss of the possessory right. The arrangement in (2) is typified by a lease of property under which the tenant (debtor) acquires an equitable proprietary interest, but the landlord retains legal ownership of the property. Failure to pay rent or breach of some other covenant leads to forfeiture of the tenant's equitable proprietary interest.

Under arrangement (3), the creditor is granted an equitable charge over property owned by the debtor, as in the typical case of a home loan, so that, on the debtor's failure to repay the loan, the creditor may rely upon the charge to secure possession of the property and sell it and use the proceeds to satisfy the debt. A particularly startling and sophisticated device of this kind is the 'floating charge' over the assets of a company. This charge gives a creditor of a company the right to seize and sell all the assets of the company subject to the charge through a receiver in the event of breach of the credit arrangement, but prior to the breach the management of the company is left at liberty to use and dispose of the assets as it sees fit.

The arrangement in (4) corresponds to the lien, where the creditor is entitled to retain possession of the goods until the debt has been paid. A vendor of goods, for instance, can arrange to retain possession of the goods until full payment has been received. In the absence of express provision in the contract, by law the vendor of goods is given an implied lien which permits the vendor to retain possession of the goods until payment is made.[44] The lien does not give the right to sell the goods, though a power of sale after certain procedures have been followed is provided for by statute.[45] Similarly, a pawnbroker enjoys the right to possession of the goods which have been pledged until he receives repayment of the loan. Of course, these rights to retain possession and to sell the goods in the event of default can be combined. In the case of a pawnbroker, if the pawn is not redeemed within six months or a longer period provided for by contract, then in general the pawnbroker may sell the pawn after giving the statutory prescribed notice.[46]

It should be stressed, however, that these four broad patterns of the distribution of property rights conceal considerable subtleties in the varieties of agreed remedies. The parties to a contract may divide the incidents of ownership between them in a myriad of ways, according to such considerations as the need for strong proprietary security, avoidance of taxation, and simplicity such as avoidance of registration requirements. Nor is it easy to fit every type of contract into these four basic categories.

It is difficult, for instance, to classify the practice of giving deposits of money as advance payment for goods and services. If, for example, a person pays ten per cent of the price of a holiday in advance, by way of security or earnest of future performance, then this payment will be classified as a deposit.[47] On receipt of the payment from the debtor, the creditor receives legal title to the money, but it seems that the creditor is under an obligation to devote the money towards satisfaction of the debt. If the debtor fails to pay the balance of the debt, then the money is forfeited to the creditor. This arrangement fits most closely the pattern in (2), but it is not clear from the cases that the debtor enjoys an equitable interest in the money. The position seems to be that the debtor merely enjoys a contingent claim to repayment in the event of the creditor's breach of contract, a claim which is regarded simply as return of money on the ground of unjust enrichment. A deposit differs from an advance payment or a payment of an instalment, because the deposit will be forfeited on breach of contract, whereas other types of pre-payment will be recoverable if there has been no consideration received for them.[48]

---

44   Sale of Goods Act 1979, s 39. A lien also arises in favour of the repairer of goods, and proves an effective security even if the owner of the goods did not make the contract for repairs: *Green v All Motors Ltd* [1917] 1 KB 625, CA.
45   Torts (Interference with Goods) Act 1977, s 12.
46   Consumer Credit Act 1974, ss 114–121.
47   *Howe v Smith* (1884) 27 Ch D 89, CA.
48   *Dies v British and International Mining and Finance Corpn* [1939] 1 KB 724; *Hyundai Shipbuilding & Heavy Industries Co Ltd v Papadopoulos* [1980] 1 WLR 1129, [1980] 2 All ER 29, HL.

What interests us here, however, is not a taxonomy of all the types of agreed distributions of proprietary interests, but rather the nature and extent of the controls exercised by the law over the freedom of the parties to create such proprietary remedies. The question is whether any clear principles can be discerned for limiting the freedom of the parties to contracts to agree any type of distribution of proprietary interests between them. There are three principal grounds for control over this type of agreed remedy which should be considered in turn: promoting certainty of proprietary rights, protection of possessory interests, and prevention of unjust enrichment arising from excessive compensation.

(1) Certainty of Proprietary Rights
As indicated in the introduction to this chapter, a complex division of proprietary interests poses a threat to the institution of the market. Uncertainties about the location of ownership and rights to dispose of property can deter beneficial transactions. Here the position of third parties is the crucial concern. If a third party wishes to deal with goods or assets which are subject to a complex division of proprietary interests, then it will be difficult for the third party to be sure whether he will acquire the desired form of proprietary rights over the goods. The legal principle that no one can sell a proprietary right which they do not own has an attractive logic, but it renders the position of third parties dealing with persons who are the apparent owners, but who in fact enjoy lesser rights, rather precarious.

One solution to this difficulty lies in systems of registration of interests in property. Once a system of registration has been established, then a failure to register a particular kind of interest can be used as a ground to protect a third party who acquires an interest in property without notice of another's prior claim. Two important systems of registration in England are the compulsory registration of interests in land,[49] and proprietary interests in the assets of companies.[50] Proprietary interests in goods, such as a mortgage of a ship, created by individuals are also registrable under the Bills of Sale Act (1878) Amendment Act 1882. This complex and patchy scheme of registration is certainly due for reform, to ensure that it becomes simplified in its coverage of security interests.[51] Yet systems of registration are objectionable because they are expensive and time-consuming, so that compulsory registration of interests should be used as sparingly as possible.

Another solution is to permit ostensible ownership arising from possession of property to confer certain powers to make contracts with respect to the property, so that the third party dealing in good faith

---

49   Land Registration Act 1925.
50   Companies Act 1985, Part XII, as amended by Insolvency Act 1985 and Companies Act 1989.
51   Diamond, 'The Reform of the Law of Security Interests' (1989) *Current Legal Problems* 231.

acquires good title. In the case of hire-purchase, for instance, by statute the consumer can give good title over goods to a third party.[52] Obviously this solution cannot be available frequently, for otherwise it would render the security afforded to creditors of proprietary interests in the debtor's property illusory, which in turn would deter entry into these secured credit arrangements.

Retention of Title Clauses

A good illustration of these competing policy concerns and how the courts have sought to reconcile them arises in the context of commercial contracts of sale containing retention of title clauses. The pattern of the creditor retaining full legal and equitable proprietary interests and merely conferring possessory rights on the debtor has a long history. This is the form of a hire-purchase contract and other conditional sales. It is also the underlying structure of a mortgage agreement, under which the debtor transfers title to property in return for a loan and a right to repurchase the property on repayment of the loan. By virtue of his ownership, the creditor can sell the property in the event of the debtor's default, realize the value of the asset, and secure repayment of the debt from its proceeds. In principle this scheme of retention of title can apply to any type of property except money (where ownership is normally tied to possession). Under the Sale of Goods Act 1979, section 19, the law leaves it to the parties to the contract to choose at what point in time ownership of the goods passes between them.

In recent years creditors have favoured the strategy of retention of title in the context of the sale of goods between commercial parties in order to secure priority in the event of insolvency. With repeated and deep economic recessions and credit squeezes, this has perhaps been an inevitable response by creditors. Under these contracts, known as Romalpa Clauses after a leading case,[53] a seller of goods includes a term in the contract to the effect that legal title to the goods remains the seller's until the debtor has paid for the goods in full. This allows the debtor to acquire goods on credit without having to seek a loan from a bank to pay for them, whilst at the same time affording the protection of a proprietary right to the creditor. These Romalpa Clauses have the advantage to the creditor that they fall outside any requirement of registration, since the debtor does not receive any proprietary interest until full payment has been made. As a consequence, the proliferation of retention of title clauses in commercial sales results in considerable uncertainty with respect to the rights of ownership in goods. A third party cannot be sure whether or not goods on sale by a person in possession of them in fact belong to the possessor or a third party.

---

52   Hire-Purchase Act 1964, s 27 (as amended by Consumer Credit Act 1974, s 192(3)).
53   *Aluminium Industrie Vaassen BV v Romalpa Aluminium Ltd* [1976] 1 WLR 676, [1976] 2 All ER 552, CA; the technique was accorded validity initially in *McEntire v Crossley Bros Ltd* [1895] AC 457, HL.

These Romalpa Clauses create especially severe difficulties when the purchaser uses the goods in a production process, so that they become mixed up with other goods which the debtor owns. For example, in *Clough Mill Ltd v Martin*,[54] the vendor sold yarn to a buyer which used the yarn to manufacture fabrics which were then sold on to third parties. Under the contract for sale of the yarn the seller retained ownership of the yarn, even if it had been mixed up with other goods to make a fabric, until full payment had been received. The contract also provided, however, that the purchaser of the yarn could sell the made-up material. Some of the difficult questions which may arise in such situations are: will the third party who receives the material receive good title to it? who owns the proceeds of such sales, the seller or the buyer of the yarn?[55] who owns the fabric after it has been manufactured if all the suppliers of goods to the manufacturer have insisted upon a retention of title clause?[56]

The answer to these perplexing questions at present turns on the terms of each contract and how it is construed by a court. The question in *Clough Mill Ltd v Martin* was whether the seller owned the yarn when the buyer became insolvent and went into receivership, and, if so, whether the seller could obtain damages against the receiver for using the yarn after the seller had given notice that it sought return of its property for breach of contract. The Court of Appeal upheld the seller's claim, stating that the seller had retained full ownership of the yarn so there was no need for it to have registered its proprietary interest. On the other hand, in so far as the yarn had become mixed up with other goods and made into fabric, then the seller had lost full ownership of the yarn, so its proprietary interest became less than full ownership and needed to be registered in order to be valid in the event of insolvency. This puzzling result under which legal ownership changes hands as workers on the shop floor open up bundles of yarn and mix them into a fabric reveals how retention of title clauses can provoke considerable confusion in markets.

This need for limitations upon freedom of contract with respect to retention of title clauses becomes all the more apparent when they are employed in an oppressive manner. One striking illustration of oppression even in commercial transactions is where the creditor insists upon retention of title of goods sold until not only full payment for those goods have been received, but also any other debts owed by the debtor to the creditor or members of the creditor's group of companies have been satisfied. If the parties to the contract of sale have long-term business relations with frequent contracts, then such a provision will have the effect that the debtor will never acquire title to any goods unless all outstanding credit has been paid off. The creditor can thus achieve a

---

54   [1985] 1 WLR 111, [1984] 3 All ER 982, CA.
55   *Aluminium Industrie Vaassen BV v Romalpa Aluminium Ltd* [1976] 1 WLR 676, [1976] 2 All ER 552, CA. Despite elaborate contractual provision, the proceeds of a sub-sale will be owned by the buyer, leaving the seller with a registrable charge: *Compaq Computers Ltd v Abercorn Group Ltd* [1991] BCC 484, QB.
56   *Borden (UK) Ltd v Scottish Timber Products Ltd* [1981] Ch 25, [1979] 3 All ER 961, CA.

dominant position over the debtor by means of this 'catching bargain'. Nevertheless, the House of Lords in *Armour v Thyssen Edelstahlwerke AG*[57] has accepted the validity of such agreements, relying simply on the idea that the parties should be free to set the terms on which property interests in goods will pass.

This striking adherence to freedom of contract with respect to retention of title clauses overlooks the danger which this commercial practice poses to markets. Although the courts may be bound to observe the logic of these retention of title arrangements with respect to the distribution of proprietary interests, the absence of the normal protection afforded to third parties by systems of compulsory registration of interests requires some measure of reform. Either a system of registration for such contractual arrangements should be introduced, or it might be possible to restrict the kinds of retention of title clauses which may be used effectively against third parties.

(2) *Protection of Possessory Interests*

Under most of these schemes for the distribution of property rights, the debtor risks losing possession of the goods or property in the event of breach of contract. This right to repossess provides one of the principal securities for the creditor against the debtor's default. In practice a creditor is likely to prefer to negotiate a settlement such as a rescheduling of repayments under a loan in order to avoid the costs of a forced sale. But clearly the creditor's proprietary interest provides him with a powerful bargaining chip in securing a favourable settlement. Although the common law invariably respects this right to repossess under a forfeiture clause in a contract, an equitable jurisdiction and various statutory measures have been developed to protect the debtor's possessory interest.

Equitable Relief from Forfeiture

The reason for this protection of the debtor's possessory interest reveals a realistic interpretation of the purpose of forfeiture clauses. The purpose of the clause is to provide a security against payment by the debtor. The creditor is unlikely to wish to acquire the property for himself, and will almost certainly on repossession seek to divest himself of the property. In contrast, the debtor will often have a strong interest in maintaining possession of the property. In a contract for a lease, for instance, the debtor or tenant normally wishes to continue occupation of the land. If the lease is forfeited because of failure to pay rent or breach of some other covenant, then the landlord can repossess the property and evict the tenant, resulting in great inconvenience to the tenant. Similarly, under a contract of hire-purchase, a consumer will normally wish to retain possession of the car

---

57   [1991] 2 AC 339, [1990] 3 All ER 481, HL; Bradgate, 'Retention of Title in the House of Lords: Unanswered Questions' (1991) 54 *Modern Law Review* 726.

or television set, though this will be forfeited on failure to pay the hire charges. The courts of equity recognized that the creditor did not usually have any interest in possession of the property. The purpose of the forfeiture clause was rather to provide a deterrence against default and a way of securing the debt.

On the basis of this realistic interpretation of forfeiture clauses, equity devised a mechanism for the protection of the debtor's possessory interest. It provided relief from forfeiture on condition that the debtor paid any sums of money owing to the creditor plus interest on the money for late payment. Provided the debtor can produce this sum of money within the time which the court is prepared to allow,[58] then the debtor has a complete defence to an action for repossession of the property.[59] This equitable relief from forfeiture is routinely available, for instance, to tenants in arrears of rent.

But the exact scope of the protection of a debtor's possessory interest provided by the equitable jurisdiction remains controversial. Lord Wilberforce in *Shiloh Spinners Ltd v Harding* observed that:

> we should reaffirm the right of courts of equity in appropriate and limited cases to relieve against forfeiture for breach of covenant or condition where the primary object of the bargain is to secure a stated result which can effectively be attained when the matter comes before the court, and where the forfeiture provision is added by way of security for the production of that result.[60]

The courts have subsequently defined the limits to this jurisdiction by reference to two criteria.

The first criterion concerns the urgency of the debtor's performance. If the contract expressly provides that with respect to the debtor's performance 'time is of the essence', then the courts infer that the parties have agreed that the delays envisaged by the jurisdiction to relieve from forfeiture are inappropriate. Thus in *Scandinavian Trading Tanker Co AB v Flota Petrolera Ecuatoriana (The Scaptrade)*,[61] the House of Lords declined to give relief to a charterer of a ship under a time charter when the owner of the vessel sought repossession of the vessel for failure to pay the charges due on time, on the ground that the contract expressly stated that prompt payment was of the essence of the charterer's obligations. To give relief from forfeiture in these circumstances would be to permit the charterer much greater flexibility in the date of payment without fear of losing possession of the ship, whereas under the contract the charterer had expressly agreed to make prompt payments. In short, the courts will not exercise the jurisdiction to relieve from forfeiture where this would undermine the express agreement between the parties on the need for

---

58 *Starside Properties Ltd v Mustapha* [1974] 2 All ER 567, CA.
59 *In Re Dagenham (Thames) Dock Co* (1873) 8 Ch App 1022, CA; *Kilmer v British Columbia Orchard Lands Ltd* [1913] AC 319, PC.
60 [1973] AC 691, at 723, [1973] 1 All ER 90, at 101, HL.
61 [1983] 2 AC 694, [1983] 2 All ER 763, HL.

prompt payment, even if payment is only ten minutes late,[62] at least if this express agreement has been reached between commercial parties dealing at arm's length.

The second criterion for limiting the scope of relief from forfeiture concerns the nature of the debtor's proprietary or possessory interest. Lord Diplock in *The Scaptrade* insisted that the jurisdiction to relieve from forfeiture was confined to certain proprietary and possessory rights. He concluded that the jurisdiction could not apply to a time charter, because he characterized the arrangement as merely a contract for services under which the ship owner provided a vessel and crew in return for a hire charge, rendering the contract analogous to the hire of a taxi. The equitable jurisdiction appears to have been confined further by the House of Lords in *Sport International Bussum BV v Inter-Footwear Ltd.*[63] Here the debtor's interest was in the right granted under a contractual licence to use the creditor's trademark in the sale of footwear. The debtor breached the contract, not by failing to pay sums due, but by failing to arrange for a bank guarantee of payment by a set date. For this technical breach of contract which caused the creditor no delay in payment, the creditor purported to terminate the licence to use the trademark, thus ruining the debtor's business. The court upheld this termination, partly on the ground of the first criterion that time was of the essence in securing the bank guarantee, but also on the ground that the contractual licence to use a trademark was not the kind of possessory interest for which relief from forfeiture would be given. This is a striking limitation on the jurisdiction, for the possesory interest in the trademark was of the highest commercial interest to the debtor.

The decision contrasts sharply with the acceptance of jurisdiction to grant relief from forfeiture in *BICC plc v Burndy Corpn*,[64] where the proprietary interest at stake was a joint interest between the parties in certain patent rights. Although it is possible to draw a distinction between joint ownership and a mere contractual licence, there is little difference between them from the point of view of the commercial function, for in both cases the point of the transaction is to permit another to exploit a particular form of intellectual property.

Instead of utilizing these formal distinctions concerning the nature of the debtor's proprietary interest in order to define the scope of the equitable jurisdiction to give relief from forfeiture, it would be better if the courts asked themselves three questions. First, does the debtor have a real commercial or consumption interest in retaining possession of the property? Secondly, was the forfeiture clause merely designed to ensure payment rather than to establish a conditional sale of a proprietary interest? Thirdly, have the parties through the terms of their contract, either expressly or impliedly, indicated that prompt payment is an

---

62   *Union Eagle Ltd v Golden Achievment Ltd* [1997] 2 All ER 215, PC.
63   [1984] 1 WLR 776, [1984] 2 All ER 321, HL.
64   [1985] Ch 232, [1985] 1 All ER 417, CA.

essential feature of the contract, thereby negativing the possibility of delays afforded by applications for relief from forfeiture? If the answer to the first two questions is affirmative, and to the last negative, then normally relief from forfeiture should be available.

Statutory Relief

In many specific instances, the power to give relief from forfeiture has been accorded to the courts and regulated by statute. Forfeiture of leases for non-payment of rent is governed by the Common Law Procedure Act 1852, sections 210–212, and forfeiture of leases for other breaches of covenant is regulated by the Law of Property Act 1925, section 146. In consumer credit transactions, the Consumer Credit Act 1974 protects the consumer's interest in possession of property being acquired under a conditional sale agreement or hire-purchase in two ways. First, the creditor must follow a statutory procedure under sections 87–89 for giving notice or warning to the debtor that the default in payments risks the creditor's repossession of the goods. Secondly, the court has a general power under section 129 to allow the debtor time to make good any missing payments, if the court regards it as just to do so.[65] This latter power of making time orders goes beyond the equitable jurisdiction, because it gives the court much greater flexibility, so that in effect it can reschedule the payment of debts.

(3) Unjust Enrichment by Over-Compensation

The third ground on which a court may control an agreed distribution of property rights as a remedial device contained in a contract is to prevent unjust enrichment of the creditor. For consumer contracts, any device designed to achieve disproportionate compensation is likely to be regarded as an invalid unfair term.[66] Moreover, the mirror principle may require consumer contracts to grant equal or equivalent proprietary interests to both supplier and consumer, so that a deposit without an equivalent assurance to the benefit of the consumer may invalidate an attempt to retain the deposit.[67] Outside statutory protections, however, the existence of a power to prevent excessive compensation is both controversial and uncertain in its scope.[68] But it is clearly analogous to, and overlaps with, the jurisdiction to control penalty clauses, and doubts about its existence should be put aside. The purpose of the jurisdiction is to ensure that the

---

65 The court is unlikely to make a time order if there is no reasonable prospect of repayment even after rescheduling: *First National Bank plc v Syed* [1991] 2 All ER 250, CA.

66 The Unfair Terms in Consumer Contracts Regulations 1994, SI 1994/3159, Schedule 3, para 1(e).

67 The Unfair Terms in Consumer Contracts Regulations 1994, SI 1994/3159, Schedule 3, para 1(d).

68 Beatson, 'Discharge for Breach: The Position of Instalments, Deposits and Other Payments Due Before Completion' (1981) 97 *Law Quarterly Review* 389.

creditor does not receive a remedy which far exceeds his loss resulting from the debtor's breach of contract. The forfeiture of valuable property rights can risk this result just as much as a contractual penalty clause which specifies high levels of compensation.

Unjust Enrichment as a Defence

Where the creditor seeks to enforce an agreed distribution of property rights by applying for a court order to convey or transfer those rights, then the court may decline to make such an order on the ground that this compensatory arrangement is unconscionable, though it will require the debtor to compensate the creditor fully. In *Jobson v Johnson*,[69] for instance, the contractual remedy for breach provided that the debtor should transfer to the creditor some valuable shares in a company owning a football club. The court ordered that if the value of the shares exceeded the loss to the creditor, then an order of specific performance would be refused, and instead the court would replicate the technique of scaling down penalty clauses by ordering sale of the shares and payment of the debt out of the proceeds. Similarly, in, *BICC plc v Burndy Corpn*,[70] the court decided that specific performance of the assignment of the patent rights would not be ordered in any event, since the debt owed by the defendant to the plaintiff was less than the amount of money owed by the plaintiff. Here the right of set-off was used to defeat the proprietary remedy, for otherwise this would result in unjust enrichment to the plaintiff.

In these cases it was easy for the court to detect the risk of over-compensation for the creditor. In other instances, the issue will often be more difficult to assess. Consider, for example, the pattern of commercial contracts known as commercial leases. In recent years leases have been used widely as a form of commercial finance. The finance company purchases the goods selected by the debtor, and then leases them for a fixed term to the debtor in return for periodic payments of rent. This differs from a hire-purchase both in the absence of the debtor's right to purchase the goods, and in the way that the cost of credit or rate of interest is concealed in the price of the rent. This arrangement may prove attractive as a means of financing a purchase if the value of the goods will quickly depreciate, as in the case of a computer, for then the security provided by ownership of the goods will prove minimal. Under the terms of the lease, the rental payments will continue to be payable during the period of the lease, regardless of the fact that the lessee returns the goods or the lessor repossesses them for breach. There is a danger for the lessor that a court may regard the term requiring payment of all future rent for the term of the lease as a penalty clause,[71] but it is far from clear that the rent represents anything more than a genuine pre-estimate of the loss, especially if allowances are made for acceleration of payments and the

---

69   [1989] 1 WLR 1026, [1989] 1 All ER 621, CA.
70   [1985] Ch 232, [1985] 1 All ER 417, CA.
71   *Lombard North Central plc v Butterworth* [1987] QB 527, [1987] 1 All ER 267, CA.

resale value of the goods. In any event, as illustrated by *Lombard North Central plc v Butterworth*,[72] a case concerning the commercial lease of a computer to an accountant, the lessor will be able to claim damages as a secondary obligation for the loss of the bargain amounting to close on the whole amount of rental payments due for the term of the lease. At first sight this may appear to leave the lessor over-compensated, for it receives most of the rent and return of the goods prior to the end of the term of the lease, but once one recognizes that the goods may not have any commercial value so that the lessor cannot mitigate its loss, then this contractual measure of compensation does not result in unjust enrichment.

Restitutionary Claim

The courts have shown themselves more circumspect in providing relief from unconscionable measures of compensation through contractual distributions of proprietary rights when the debtor has already transferred the property and now seeks to claim a sum of money to remedy the unjust enrichment of the creditor. This reluctance is understandable, since the court is not merely being asked to refuse an order for specific performance of a contract, but is required to make a positive order for the creditor to pay money to the debtor because of the over-compensation. In the case of deposits for the purchase of interests in land, this jurisdiction has statutory backing, which gives a court the discretion to order repayment of a deposit.[73] This jurisdiction appears to reflect a more general equitable jurisdiction to provide relief from deposits if the sum forfeited far exceeds the loss and is unreasonable.[74]

A similar protection is afforded to the debtor under transactions regulated by the Consumer Credit Act 1974. Here the general rule is that the creditor cannot repossess the goods being purchased on credit once the debtor has paid to the creditor one-third or more of the total price of the goods without a court order.[75] In making an order, the court then has broad discretionary powers to attach conditions to the order,[76] and may strike it down as an extortionate credit bargain.[77] In addition, under a hire-purchase agreement where the owner recovers possession, the court enjoys broad powers to order the return of any money paid in respect of the goods by the debtor, if it appears just to do so.[78] But can a restitutionary claim be used more generally for return of money and property forfeited under the terms of a contract?

---

72 [1987] QB 527, [1987] 1 All ER 267, CA.
73 Law of Property Act 1925, s 49(2); *Universal Corpn v Five Ways Properties Ltd* [1979] 1 All ER 552, CA.
74 *Public Works Comr v Hills* [1906] AC 368, PC; *Workers Trust and Merchant Bank Ltd v Dojap Investments Ltd* [1993] AC 573, [1993] 2 All ER 370, PC.
75 Section 90.
76 Section 136.
77 Section 137.
78 Section 132.

The question of whether or not this jurisdiction exists was answered affirmatively by a majority of the Court of Appeal in *Stockloser v Johnson*.[79] Under a contract for the sale of machinery, the price was payable by instalments. The contract provided that in the event of breach by the purchaser, the seller was entitled to retain instalments already paid. This forfeiture of instalments was held to be valid on the facts of the case, since in view of the risks accepted by the seller and his losses the retention of the instalments was not unconscionable. But the majority of the court recognized the possibility of a restitutionary claim for return of all or part of the instalments, if the forfeiture clause led to unjust enrichment. Romer LJ, dissenting, denied the existence of any such equitable jurisdiction, arguing that it would give the courts a power to rewrite contracts by dispensing with forfeiture clauses altogether.

But this criticism overlooks the analogous power to control penalty clauses, and misses the point that the aim of judicial control is merely to prevent unjust enrichment through agreed remedies and not to rewrite the terms of contracts in general. The only difference between penalty clauses and these instances of forfeiture of property is that in the latter the creditor has already secured through the contract a proprietary interest representing the agreed compensation. This puts the creditor in a stronger position than a simple claim for agreed compensation, and there may be a case for respecting this choice of the parties in the contract by restricting equitable intervention to severe cases of unjust enrichment caused by forfeiture of deposits and other proprietary interests, but this should not prevent the equitable jurisdiction from operating to give relief from unconscionable agreed remedies.[80] 'This argument leads towards the conclusion that, since a promised penalty cannot be claimed, a penalty which has already passed into the other's hands should be recoverable.'[81]

4. Guarantees and Indemnities

A contract of guarantee provides an agreed remedy against a third party. Subject to the precise terms of the contract, the guarantor promises to a creditor either to procure performance of a debtor's obligations under a contract or to fulfil those obligations himself.[82] A director of a company may, for example, give a personal guarantee of his company's contractual performance to a creditor such as a bank. If the debtor company breaks the contract with the bank, then the bank may enforce the guarantee

---

79   [1954] 1 QB 476, [1954] 1 All ER 630, CA; see also *Cornwall v Henson* [1900] 2 Ch 298, CA, Collins LJ at p 302.
80   This view prevails in Australia: *McDonald v Dennys Lascelles Ltd* (1933) 48 CLR 457 (Aust HC); and in the USA: Corbin, 'The Right of a Defaulting Vendee to the Restitution of Instalments Paid' (1931) 40 *Yale Law Journal* 1013.
81   P Birks, *An Introduction to the Law of Restitution* (Oxford, 1985), p 215.
82   *Moschi v Lep Air Services Ltd* [1973] AC 331, [1972] 2 All ER 393, HL.

against the director as guarantor, as if the guarantor were the primary debtor. This is a valuable technique for facilitating market transactions where the debtor cannot offer any valuable proprietary security to the creditor. A performance bond is a type of guarantee under which a bank guarantees a fixed measure of compensation in the event of the defendant's breach of a contract to perform a service, though the plaintiff will only be able to retain under the performance bond an amount equal to the extent of its loss caused by the defendant's breach of contract.

A contract of indemnity performs a similar function to a guarantee. Here the third party normally promises that he will meet any loss suffered by a creditor as a result of contracting with the debtor. This is an independent contract between the third party and the creditor, so that unlike a guarantee its content and enforceability do not depend upon the validity of the contract between the debtor and the creditor.[83] In particular, a contract of indemnity could extend to cover the debtor's tortious liability to a creditor, whereas a contract of guarantee merely promises to meet the debtor's contractual obligations to the creditor. Thus an indemnity not only serves the purpose of encouraging credit transactions, but can also provide a risk allocation device between three parties. It is not an exclusion clause which limits liability, but merely determines which of the three parties should eventually meet the cost of losses incurred during business.[84]

A guarantee is only valid if evidenced by a note or memorandum in writing signed by the guarantor.[85] No formalities are required, however, for a contract of indemnity. The consideration to support the enforcement of both a guarantee and an indemnity is usually discovered in the creditor's entry into a contract with the debtor.

The guarantor, if called upon to perform, then enjoys implied rights of indemnity against the debtor except in so far as these are qualified by contract. Thus the director, if called upon to perform the personal guarantee, could then claim an indemnity against the company. Because the guarantor's right to claim an indemnity is his only security, any agreement between the creditor and debtor which alters or extinguishes the value of this indemnity is likely to be held to discharge the guarantor from liability. Unlike a guarantee, a contract of indemnity given by a third party does not give rise to a similar implied contract of indemnity against the debtor, though of course such an additional indemnity might be agreed as well.

Outside commercial transactions, the risk posed by contract of guarantee is that the debtor may persuade a friend to give a guarantee when the friend does not fully appreciate the potential extent of liability and the nature of the risk. To reduce this danger, the Consumer Credit

---

83 R Goode, *Commercial Law* 2nd edn (London, 1995), pp 821–825.
84 *Thompson v T Lohan (Plant Hire) Ltd* [1987] 1 WLR 649, [1987] 2 All ER 631, CA.
85 Statute of Frauds (1677), s 4. *Elpis Maritime Co Ltd v Marti Chartering Co Inc (The Maria D)* [1991] 2 Lloyd's Rep 311, HL.

Act 1974 requires guarantees for consumer credit transactions to be in writing according to a prescribed form and also requires the details of the transaction to be given in writing to the guarantor.[86] This is a slim protection, for it assumes that information is a sufficient bulwark against foolish transactions. In contrast, under section 4 of the Unfair Contract Terms Act 1977, a person dealing as a consumer is protected by the test of reasonableness from giving foolish indemnities against his own or another's breach of contract or negligence.

5. Forum

Under the terms of a contract the parties may agree that any disputes arising between them should be resolved by a forum other than a public court. International business transactions often prefer private arbitration. Many industries dealing with consumers also prefer to set up an arbitration system or an Ombudsman. Some use of arbitration also occurs in the collective arrangements between management and unions. An arbitration agreement can normally be enforced by an injunction, which will prevent a party to the contract from going to a public court without first using the arbitration system agreed in the contract.

The attractions of private arbitration are numerous. The parties can select an arbitrator who is familiar with the nature of the business and who has their confidence. Arbitration proceedings may prove quicker and more convenient, though they are often more expensive since the parties have to pay the arbitrator. The arbitrator may also be more willing to act as mediator between the parties and help them to reach a settlement. These advantages may prove particularly significant in long-term relational contracts, where the parties wish to avoid any breakdown in the economic relationship, yet need a method of dispute resolution to govern the occasional unforeseen divergence of interest. A simple example is the contract of employment, where many employers have established internal arbitration for the grievances of individual employees to be heard and for disciplinary sanctions to be imposed.

The use of arbitration is controlled by legislation for two purposes. In the first place, the legislation reserves to the courts the power to ensure that the arbitration acts within the substantive jurisdiction conferred on it by the parties.[87] Beyond this issue of jurisdiction, however, the parties are free to agree to exclude review by the courts. A second reason for legislative control concerns the risk that a party dealing with consumers will seek to impose through a standard form contract a biased system of arbitration as the forum for resolving disputes. The bias may lie either in the choice of arbitrator or more simply in hurdles of procedure and expense

---

86   Sections 105–112.
87   Arbitration Act 1996, s 67.

which will deter consumers from ever making claims.[88] The Arbitration Act 1996 gives limited protection to consumers against this form of oppression by declaring arbitration clauses in consumer contracts involving small claims invalid as unfair terms contrary to the Unfair Terms in Consumer Contract Regulations 1994.[89] In those Regulations, Schedule 3, para (q) indicates that an example of an unfair term may be one:

> excluding or hindering the consumer's right to take legal action or exercise any other legal remedy, particularly by requiring the consumer to take disputes exclusively to arbitration not covered by legal provisions, unduly restricting the evidence available to him or imposing on him a burden of proof which, according to the applicable law, should lie with another party to the contract.

Short of an agreed forum such as arbitration, a contract may provide an alternative optional avenue of redress to litigation. There is no objection on the ground of fairness to such arrangements for they merely augment avenues of redress for consumers and do not detract from any legal rights. In recent years many industries dealing with consumers have established through their trade associations ombudsmen as a relatively informal and inexpensive means by which consumers may seek redress against large organizations such as banks, insurance companies, and building societies.[90] An ombudsman offers the consumer the possibility of a thorough investigation of a complaint, an opinion about the merits of the case without necessarily being tied to the strict contractual terms of a standard form contract, and as a last resort a binding decision against the member of the trade association. As the existence of these ombudsmen have become known to consumers, they have been swamped by complaints. Although the trade associations exclude many issues from the purview of ombudsmen, this alternative dispute resolution mechanism seems likely to become a key ingredient in providing a more effective remedy for consumers' complaints about breach of contract.

---

88   Thomas, 'Consumer Arbitration Agreements Act 1988' (1991) *Arbitration* 48.

89   Arbitration Act 1996, s 91; SI 1994/3159. This protection does not appear as detailed or as favourable to consumers as the Consumer Arbitration Agreements Act 1988, which was repealed by the Arbitration Act 1996.

90   Wilkinson, 'Complaining to Ombudsmen' (1992) (2 October) *New Law Journal* 1348.

17

Judicial Remedies

In the absence of any contractually agreed remedies, a party injured by a breach of contract can seek judicial remedies. The courts offer compensatory damages as the principal remedy for breach of contract. In some circumstances, it is also possible to obtain an order for compulsory performance, either in the positive form of an order for specific performance of the contractual obligations, or in a negative form of an injunction against breach of contract.

Other judicial remedies might apply to actions for breach of contract in particular cases, such as an order to deliver goods to the injured party,[1] or an order to carry out those formalities known as completion which are necessary to effect a legal transfer of ownership of land, or the appointment of a receiver and manager of property in order to carry out positive obligations under a contract.[2] A breach of contract may also provoke insolvency proceedings against a defendant company, resulting in the court's appointment of an administrator or receiver.[3]

Failure to comply with judicial orders for remedies for breach of contract results in the application of further coercive measures. If an award of damages is not paid by the defendant, then the plaintiff may invoke a court procedure for the seizure and sale of the defendant's goods to the value of the outstanding sum owed. The effectiveness of this remedy, of course, depends upon the plaintiff being able to locate the defendant's assets, the existence of such assets, and the speed at which the court's process operates before the defendant's assets are moved and dispersed. The coercive mechanism backing up orders for specific performance and injunctions differs because these orders have their origins in the equitable jurisdiction of the courts. If the defendant defies an order for compulsory performance, then the plaintiff may invoke the sanctions for civil contempt

---

1   Torts (Interference with Goods) Act 1977, s 3.
2   *Hart v Emelkirk Ltd* [1983] 1 WLR 1289, [1983] 3 All ER 15, Ch; *Parker v Camden London Borough Council* [1986] Ch 162, [1985] 2 All ER 141, CA; A Burrows, *Remedies for Torts and Breach of Contract* (London, 1987),p 413.
3   Insolvency Act 1986.

of court. If the court determines that the defendant has committed contempt by failing to comply with its order, then it may impose the sanctions of fines or imprisonment in order to coerce performance from the recalcitrant defendant.

1. Settlements

Before these judicial remedies will be required, however, the parties are most likely to engage in bargaining towards a settlement of the dispute. The vast majority of litigation terminates as a result of a settlement or compromise before any court order is required.

A settlement comprises a species of contract under which both parties agree that the litigation or dispute should be terminated in return for the payment of any agreed compensation or return of property. This contract will normally satisfy the ordinary requirements of agreement and consideration. Mere payment of a sum of money to the plaintiff does not amount to a settlement of the claim unless the plaintiff agrees that the sum has been accepted in full settlement, or, in a phrase commonly used, in accord and satisfaction.[4] A promise not to enforce existing legal rights in return for compensation counts as good consideration even when these rights are invalid or turn out to be unenforceable.[5] There is clearly a danger that fraudulent and dishonest threats to litigate upon spurious claims will be encouraged, so the courts have refused to find consideration where the person offering to refrain from litigation knows that the claim is invalid or spurious.[6] This exception is hard to square with the rule that the courts will not test the adequacy of consideration, for in principle it should be left to the promisee to determine whether the surrender of an invalid claim has any value to him. Clearly the courts were unwilling to permit the device of settlements to be used as an instrument of fraud. A settlement may also be impugned on the ground of economic duress under the principles described in Chapter 15.

The time and expense of litigation normally provide sufficient incentives for the parties to want to arrange a compromise if at all possible. But the available judicial remedies for breach of contract affect the nature of this bargaining process. The likely outcome in court provides the benchmark against which the parties reach a settlement. In crude terms, a party injured by breach of contract will not agree a settlement unless it accords roughly with what remedy might be provided by a court discounted by the risk of not being able to establish the claim and minus the likely costs of litigation. If the defendant is teetering on the edge of insolvency, then the injured party may be persuaded to accept an extremely

---

4   *Ferguson v Davies* [1997] 1 All ER 315, CA.
5   *Haigh v Brooks* (1839) 10 Ad & El 309, Ex; *Cook v Wright* (1861) 1 B & S 559, 121 ER 822, QB.
6   *Wade v Simeon* (1846) 2 CB 548.

disadvantageous settlement for fear of being left without any substantial remedy as an unsecured creditor. For these reasons, the most important impact upon the market of judicial remedies is the way they determine in part the relative bargaining strength of the parties in post-breach settlements.

Two crucial variables in judicial remedies play a major role in determining this bargaining strength of the parties in settlement of disputes. One variable consists in the likely measure of damages or compensation to be awarded by a court. The greater this potential liability, the higher the financial settlement to which the defendant must agree. To the extent that the measure of compensation falls below the value which the injured party places upon performance of the contract, which often proves to be the case in practice, then any settlement is likely to be disadvantageous to the injured party. The second variable concerns the incidence of orders for compulsory performance. If the injured party can obtain an order for specific performance or an injunction, then this threat increases his or her bargaining power in seeking an advantageous settlement. The availability of compulsory performance gives the injured party something analogous to a property right in the performance of the promise.[7] Since the injured party may ultimately threaten the defendant with the sanctions for contempt of court, the injured party may insist upon a settlement which is equal to the value which he or she places upon performance of the contract. Notice how the bargaining position of the injured party is enhanced by the potential availability of an order for compulsory performance.

One final crucial factor affects the practice of reaching settlements. Representation by a lawyer with expertise in respect of the disputed issue can improve the bargaining strength of a party. A sophisticated lawyer can raise numerous technical problems, dubious legal points, and procedural hurdles in order to dissuade a plaintiff from pursuing a claim. For this reason consumers and employees find themselves generally at a disadvantage against businesses and their employers. A business which is a constant employer of legal expertise, such as a liquidator of companies, is likely to be able to extract an unusually favourable settlement.[8]

2. Considerations Shaping Judicial Remedies

A general aim of the law of contract is no doubt to support the practice of entering market transactions. But it does not follow from this general aim that the courts should necessarily order the defendant to keep the contractual obligation according to its precise terms. Several important

---

7   Calibresi and Melamed, 'Property Rules, Liability Rules, and Inalienability: One View of the Cathedral' (1972) 85 *Harvard Law Review* 1089; J Coleman, *Markets, Morals and the Law* (Cambridge, 1988), chapter 2.

8   S Wheeler, *Reservation of Title Clauses* (Oxford, 1991).

considerations dictate that the courts should confine awards of compulsory performance and limit the measure of compensatory damages awarded.

Avoidance of Deterrence
In the first place, the courts must bear in mind that stiff penalties for breach of contract might deter parties from entering contracts in the first place. If due performance of the contract lies in the future, then uncertainty about market conditions and possible unexpected impediments to performance may deter the formation of the contract when the risk of substantial potential liability looms. The remedy available to the injured party must therefore not be so immense as to deter the creation of binding contracts. A balance must be struck between provision of a remedy which supports the reliability of contractual undertakings whilst not being so great as to discourage the formation of binding commitments.[9]

This consideration leads the courts both to confine the measure of damages by doctrines such as remoteness of damage, and to limit the availability of orders for specific performance and injunctions. The purpose of the rule denying recovery for remote losses is the same as the doctrine of privity of contract. It avoids the deterrence to enter into contracts which might result from the scope of potential liability. In the case of privity of contract, the risk arises from the potential number of plaintiffs injured by breach of contract. In the case of remoteness of loss confining the measure of damages, the rule prevents the single plaintiff's measure of damages from becoming a potential deterrent to the formation of contracts.

Minimizing Social Cost
Secondly, the courts are concerned to limit the social costs of breach of contract. These costs include the administration of justice, the costs of bargaining towards settlements of claims for breach of contract, and the waste of resources following breach of contract. The costs of administration of justice can be reduced to the extent that the parties can be induced to settle the claim out of court. This consideration argues against the use of specific performance and injunctions, which necessarily require a court order, and in favour of damages, for a financial settlement will achieve the same result without the use of the courts. Against this it must be observed, however, that once the parties are in court, then the equitable remedies are often awarded speedily and cheaply by interlocutory proceedings.[10] The consideration of the costs of the administration of justice also supports the enforcement of settlements as binding contracts regardless of the justice achieved, subject perhaps to safeguards against fraud and duress.[11] Various rules of civil procedure also induce settlements.

---

9   Goetz and Scott, 'Enforcing Promises: An Examination of the Basis of Contract' (1980) 89 *Yale Law Journal* 1261.
10   For conflicting views: R Posner, *Economic Analysis of Law* (Boston, 4th edn, 1992), p 131; P Atiyah, *Essays on Contract* (Oxford, 1990), p 157.
11   J Coleman, op cit, pp 202–215.

In particular, if the defendant pays into a court a sum of money prior to the court hearing and this sum proves equal to or greater than the eventual award of damages, then the plaintiff cannot recover the costs of litigation from the defendant.

The costs of bargaining towards settlement of claims can be reduced in a number of ways. The best method is for the courts to provide an easily reckonable method for ascertaining the likely measure of a judicial award of damages. The greater the certainty of the outcome of the court process, the more likely that the parties will be able to agree a settlement for they will be bargaining under conditions of relative certainty. It is difficult to predict whether or not the potential for an award of compulsory performance will reduce or increase the costs of bargaining towards a settlement. Although an injured party entitled to an award of specific performance may be tempted to hold out for an advantageous settlement of any claim, this manoeuvre and its associated costs may not prove any worse in terms of transaction costs than the bickering between the parties over a final settlement of a claim for damages.[12] The costs of bargaining over settlements may also be reduced by the introduction of a neutral conciliator or mediator who will bring the parties together. This method has been used in specialized areas such as an employer's breach of the contract of employment,[13] and the search for an efficient reduction of social costs may lead to the spread of such alternative dispute resolution mechanisms for breach of contract claims across a broader field of contractual disputes.

With respect to the third aspect of social cost, the waste of resources, this tends to argue against the use of awards of compulsory performance and towards the imposition of duties upon the parties to minimize the losses resulting from breach. The objective of the law should be to reduce the total costs resulting from breach of contract. The most common way in which this result may be achieved is to encourage the injured party to seek contractual performance from an alternative source. This will prevent losses arising from delays. For this reason the injured party is under a duty to take reasonable steps to reduce the losses resulting from breach of contract, which is known as the duty to mitigate loss. In addition, this consideration of minimizing social cost argues against the availability of orders for compulsory performance, for such a right would remove the incentive for the injured party to seek alternative sources of supply, which might be available at a lower cost than the cost to the defendant of performance of the contract. The argument against compulsory performance becomes even greater when the injured party no longer has any use for the goods or services acquired under the transaction.

12   For conflicting views: R Posner, op cit; Schwartz, 'The Case for Specific Performance' (1979) 89 *Yale Law Journal* 271.
13   Industrial Tribunals Act 1996, ss 18–19 ; P Lowry, *Employment Disputes and the Third Party* (London, 1990).

Efficient Breach of Contract

We should also consider why parties to a contract choose to break it. Many breaches of contract will not be intentional, but result from negligence or an unforeseen latent defect. Here the purpose of remedies must include the deterrence of negligence and the allocation of risk onto the person in the best position to avoid or reduce the cost of losses. In these instances it will be too late for an award of specific performance of the original contract, but the courts can provide incentives for the defendant to reduce the losses resulting from breach by duties of repair and replacement. In the case of consumer purchases of defective goods, for instance, the consumer may reject the goods, leaving the seller with a duty to mitigate loss, which often points to the supply of a substitute. Breaches of contract may also result from calculated business decisions.

Assuming the validity and enforceability of the contract, the main reasons for deliberate breach are likely to comprise either a recognition that performance has become uneconomic, or that a greater profit can be gained by breach of contract and an engagement with another person for contractual performance involving the same object. Two important factors would have to be included in such an efficiency calculation carried out by a party contemplating deliberate breach of contract. In the first place, the party in breach would have to consider the possible harm arising from deliberate breach of contract to business reputation and to long-term business relations. Secondly, the cost/benefit analysis would have to include the potential liability in damages to the injured party from breach of contract. If this liability exceeds either the potential losses on an uneconomic contract or the profits on an alternative deal, then there will be no economic incentive to break the contract. But even with these two factors included in the efficiency calculus, in some instances deliberate breach of contract may prove the most advantageous course of action. The question in such cases boils down to whether or not the law should discourage or support the deliberate breach of contract.

A wealth maximizing criterion of justice supports the view that the law should permit efficient breaches of contract. This view holds that the wealth of the society will be increased in total by the breach of contract. With the receipt of damages for breach of contract the injured party should be at least no worse off than before, and the defendant should, if his calculations prove correct, be better off. The breach of contract will move goods to those who value them most, without any party being worse off than before, which complies with the standard of Pareto efficiency. The law should therefore support efficient breach of contract.[14] If this wealth maximizing criterion of justice does guide the law in its determination of judicial remedies, what practices does it require?

---

14   R Posner, op cit, pp 117–119. This analysis leaves out transactions costs which are likely to be increased by breach: Friedman, 'The Efficient Breach Fallacy' (1989) 18 *Journal of Legal Studies* 1, 6.

It suggests that orders for compulsory performance should not be generally available. If the injured party can insist upon performance of the contract, then this may prevent the defendant from making an advantageous profitable transaction elsewhere. If the effect of the availability of compulsory performance is merely to change the bargaining strengths of the parties, then it will result in the injured party being able to acquire a greater proportion of the profits which the defendant gains by the alternative contract, and this in turn may discourage the defendant from seeking such alternative wealth-enhancing contracts. If the reason for the defendant's breach is simply that the contract has ceased to be an economic proposition, then again compulsory performance may be undesirable, for it seems likely (if the defendant has calculated correctly) that the injured party will be able to acquire the performance elsewhere at less cost than performance would cost the defendant. In contrast, an award of damages leaves the defendant free to seek an alternative beneficial transaction simply on payment of compensation to the injured party. In the case of disadvantageous contracts, the losses to the defendant are minimized by refusing an award of compulsory performance. Awards of damages therefore better support the wealth maximizing properties of markets.

The theory of efficient breach of contract also indicates how the measure of the damages remedy should be calculated. In order to ensure that the injured party is no worse off as a result of the breach of contract, the defendant must pay damages at a level set to ensure that outcome. But an ambiguity plagues this principle, for it is unclear whether the injured party's position should be judged as it was prior to the formation of the contract with the defendant, or as the injured party expected it to be following proper performance of the contract. Advocates of the theory of efficient breach of contract assume that the latter measure is the correct one, but in fact the former measure seems more likely to promote efficient breach of contract. The need to permit efficient breach of contract does rule out firmly the possibility of compensation based upon, not the losses to the injured party, but the gains to the defendant achieved by breach. If these profits were the measure of damages, then the defendant could never be better off as a result of deliberate breach of contract, which would obliterate the incentive to search for better market opportunities.

Social Market
Whatever the precise consequences of the theory of efficient breach, our discussion leaves open the issue whether or not efficiency or wealth maximization should count as a relevant consideration determining the shape of and access to judicial remedies. The problem with this criterion is surely that it assumes that the motive for entering contracts can be reduced to one concerned with wealth, so that the law can afford to be indifferent as to the means by which this wealth is acquired, either through performance of the contract or payment of damages. This analysis may serve well enough in most commercial transactions, but throughout this

book I have argued that the field of contract law extends across a wide variety of voluntary undertakings, which cannot always be reduced to a simple analysis of wealth enhancement or preference satisfaction. In a contract of employment, for instance, the employee no doubt enters the contract in the pursuit of wealth in the form of wages, but in addition the employee may seek to acquire status, friendship, skills and training, and the satisfaction achieved by giving meaning to one's life through work. When the theory of efficient breach is applied in this context, we can see its dangers. It suggests that the employer should be entitled to terminate the contract in order to replace the employee by a worker who is either prepared to accept lower wages or who has greater productivity. Although this might prove the efficient result, it ignores the claims of the incumbent employee with respect to those social interests in job security which cannot be reduced to money damages.

This objection to the theory of efficient breach and its reductionism returns us to the theme of the social market and the perception that markets serve a greater purpose than mere preference satisfaction. The judicial remedies for breach of contract should also be guided by the recognition that contracts distribute wealth, establish power relations, and provide opportunities for the realization of meanings for one's life. These considerations may run against the grain of the efficiency arguments. In the case of the dismissed employee, for instance, whereas the efficient result may be to restrict the employee to a claim for damages, the result required by policies informed by the social market may indicate the appropriateness of compulsory performance in some cases so that the employee keeps his or her job. At the same time, concern for freedom of the individual may prompt a refusal of specific performance at the behest of the employer. Similarly, the remedy for a tenant facing an eviction in breach of contract may require more than damages, for the premises may represent the tenant's home and the basis of security for the tenant and his or her dependants. In some instances damages may prove the sole practicable remedy, but consideration of the power relation and the risk to important interests and rights of the injured party may indicate that greater compensation than usual should be available, even though this might not prove the efficient outcome.

The social market will also be concerned with the fairness of the outcomes of judicial remedies for breach of contract.[15] Unjust enrichment of the defendant at the expense of the injured party will be avoided. The courts will be reluctant also to order compulsory performance of a contract which is severely disadvantageous to the defendant. We will also consider the possibility that the interests of third parties become important to the formulation of remedies as part of more general policies to control the operation of markets.

---

15   Vernon, 'Expectancy Damages for Breach of Contract: A Primer and Critique' (1976) *Washington University Law Quarterly* 179.

In the following discussion of the remedies of damages and compulsory performance, we will examine how these conflicting considerations direct the shape and availability of judicial remedies for breach of contract. But this discussion should be prefaced with a warning. The variety of the subject matter of contracts for which judicial remedies are sought makes it difficult to establish any firm general rules. When this variety combines with the competing policy considerations described above, then it becomes almost impossible to state any general principles applicable to the field of judicial remedies. At best we can only hope to indicate the outline of how these remedies are constructed in the light of the relevant considerations.

3. Damages

Damages is the normal remedy for breach of contract, in the absence of agreement or the availability of an action for the price. This rule applies to contracts supported by consideration or contained in a deed. The position with respect to obligations arising from detrimental reliance encouraged by the promisor remains more ambiguous for, as we noted in Chapter 5, English courts have so far been reluctant to award damages for breach of such obligations, but have achieved various measures of equitable relief instead. In jurisdictions in the United States, which have accepted the availability of damages for promissory estoppel, the rules governing quantification have gradually been assimilated to those governing any breach of contract.[16] Given the primacy of consideration as the test of enforceability in English law, it is true in general that an award of damages is the normal remedy for breach of contract. As Oliver Wendell Holmes observed in a famous essay:

> The duty to keep a contract at common law means a prediction that you must pay damages if you do not keep it – and nothing else.[17]

Although this dictum exaggerates the extent to which orders for compulsory performance are excluded from actions for breach of contract, it does indicate how damages are quite frequently the sole option for the injured party. The question to be addressed here is how an award of damages is calculated.

(1) The Compensatory Principle
Damages are designed to compensate the injured party for losses flowing from the breach of contract rather than to punish the defendant. The injured party must prove the items of loss which are claimed and demonstrate that they were caused by the defendant's breach of contract.

---

16   Slawson, 'The Role of Reliance in Contract Damages' (1990) 76 *Cornell Law Review* 197.
17   Holmes, 'The Path of the Law' (1897) 10 *Harvard Law Review* 457, 462.

The injured party must also demonstrate that the losses were unavoidable or at least reasonably incurred. Even when these requirements have been satisfied, however, the courts further restrict claims in light of the considerations discussed above.

Cost of substituted performance

In many instances of breach of contract, the claim for compensation coincides with the cost of substituted performance. The injured party seeks the additional cost of buying the goods or services elsewhere. Where a seller of goods fails to deliver all or some of the goods specified by the contract, or the provider of services fails to perform all or some of the services which he has undertaken, the measure of damages under the compensatory principle amounts to the difference between the contract price and the market cost of the substitute goods or services which the injured party is obliged to seek. The injured party recovers sufficient compensation to pay for substitute goods and services at no extra cost to himself. Similarly, where the goods or services supplied prove defective, the injured party may claim the cost of rectifying the fault. We noted, for instance, in the case of *Bolton v Mahadeva*,[18] that the defective installation of a central heating system rendered the defendant liable to pay the cost of curing the defects. In addition, the injured party may claim the costs involved in finding a substitute contracting party.

Since the underlying criterion is the net loss to the injured party, no damages may be claimed at all, or merely nominal damages claimed, if the sum of the market price, that is, the price which he is forced to pay to obtain a substitute, plus any transaction costs, is lower than the original contract price.

Wasted Expenditure

If the option of substituted performance is unavailable, then the injured party can claim for losses representing any wasted expenditure. Where the injured party has already wasted expenditure in performance of his own obligations under the contract, the costs of that work can be recouped, including incidental expenditure such as the cost of the journey to arrive at the appointed place of performance of the contract. In *McRae v Commonwealth Disposals Commission*,[19] for instance, where the plaintiff incurred expense seeking a sunk tanker for salvage sold to it by the defendant, when it subsequently emerged that no such tanker existed, the plaintiff recovered this wasted expenditure. The recoverable expenses extend to the costs of preparing for performance of the contract, even where those expenses were incurred prior to the formation of the contract.[20]

18 [1972] 1 WLR 1009, [1972] 2 All ER 1322, CA.
19 (1950) 84 CLR 377 (Aust HC).
20 *Anglia Television Ltd v Reed* [1972] 1 QB 60, [1971] 3 All ER 690, CA.

Compensation will also be payable for any money paid or goods transferred to the defendant, subject to any counterclaims for compensation or set-off.

It is also possible to recover money paid through an action in the law of restitution. This is known misleadingly as recovery of money for 'total failure of consideration'. Here consideration means performance, so that the action is only available where the plaintiff has not received any of the promised contractual performance. This situation may arise either where the defendant has failed to perform his side of the bargain, such as the delivery of goods or the performance of a service, or where the contract is itself void for reasons of illegality, public policy, or ultra vires. The claim is based on an entitlement to the money rather than the breach of contract, but the defendant may resist the claim on certain grounds such as 'change of position'.[21]

Cost of Repair

The breach of contract may have caused damage to the plaintiff's property. For example, the negligent installation of electrical wiring may cause a fire in the plaintiff's premises. The costs of repairing the damage can be recovered as well as the cost of substituted performance in having the wiring properly installed.

Notice that the cost of repair is only recoverable where the defendant's breach caused the damage or defect. It will not apply, for instance, where the breach of contract merely failed to alert the injured party to the need for repairs or further work. In *Watts v Morrow*,[22] a negligent survey report failed to alert the purchaser of a house as to its many defects such as the need for a new roof and specialist woodworm treatment. Although this work when completed cost about £34,000, the surveyor was held liable only for £15,000 representing the difference between the contract price for the house and its actual market value with the latent defects.

Losses to third parties

A breach of contract may cause losses to third parties. Their property may be damaged or they may fail to receive a benefit which should have been supplied by the contract. The compensation principle appears to deny any claim to the party to the contract for such losses, since the losses have fallen exclusively on the third party. In *Beswick v Beswick*,[23] for instance, where the uncle sold his coal business to his nephew in return

---

21   *Lipkin Gorman v Karpnale Ltd* [1991] 2 AC 548, [1992] 4 All ER 512, HL; *Woolwich Building Society v IRC* [1993] AC 70, [1992] 3 All ER 737, HL; *Westdeutsche Landesbank Girozentrale v Islington London Borough Council, Kleinwort Benson Ltd v Sandwell Borough Council* [1994] 1 WLR 938, [1994] 4 All ER 890, CA; *Kleinwort Benson Ltd v Birmingham City Council* [1997] QB 380, [1996] 4 All ER 733, CA.
22   [1991] 4 All ER 937, CA.
23   [1968] AC 58, [1967] 2 All ER 1197, HL.

for various promises including the payment of an annuity to his widow after his death, the uncle's estate was unable to recover damages to cover the loss to the widow, since she was not a party to the contract. The plaintiff can recover substantial damages for breach of a contract intended to benefit a third party, however, if that breach then renders the plaintiff liable to pay compensation to the third party himself.

The problem with this derivation from the compensatory principle of damages is that in many instances, as a result of the principle of privity of contract, the third party also will be unable to claim compensation for breach of contract. The third party must bring a claim in tort or perhaps establish a direct collateral contract with the defendant in order to claim damages. Where such claims are unavailable, as in a claim for pure economic loss in negligence, there is a danger that neither the party to the contract nor the third party who has suffered loss will be in a position to claim for compensation. The courts have displayed a reluctance to follow the logic of the compensation principle when it leads to the conclusion that the party in breach of contract will not be required to pay damages to anyone for the losses caused.

The cases which reveal this qualification to the compensatory principle lack any clear basis in principle. In *Jackson v Horizon Holidays Ltd*,[24] where a man purchased a holiday for his wife and children and the holiday turned out disastrously, the court suggested that this kind of case could represent an exception to the ban on recovery for the losses of third parties, and awarded the husband damages for the losses suffered by his family. But the scope of the exception was not defined.[25] In commercial contexts the courts have created exceptions to cope with complexities caused by the transfer of ownership of an asset between the formation of the contract and performance. In a contract for the carriage of goods, the owner of the goods may sell them before a breach of the contract which damages or delays the goods. If the new owner cannot sue for breach of contract because rights under the contract of carriage have not been assigned, then the original owner can claim substantial damages.[26] Similarly in a contract for building work, if the owner sells the building before breach of the construction contract, unless the new owner is entitled to claim damages for the cost of substitute performance under an exception to the doctrine of privity such as assignment, then the original owner can claim substantial damages.[27] These decisions reveal a striking willingness to ignore the logic of the compensatory principle where otherwise no compensation for the breach of contract could be obtained by either the party to the contract or the third party.

24 [1975] 1 WLR 1468, [1975] 3 All ER 92, CA.
25 *Woodar Investment Development Ltd v Wimpey Construction (UK) Ltd* [1980] 1 WLR 277, [1980] 1 All ER 571, HL.
26 *The Albazero* [1977] AC 774, HL.
27 *Linden Gardens Trust Ltd v Lenesta Sludge Disposals Ltd* [1994] 1 AC 85, [1993] 3 All ER 417, HL. This was described as the principle of 'transferred loss' in *White v Jones* [1995] 2 AC 207, [1995] 1 All ER 691, HL.

There must be another principle at work in these cases which overrides the dictates of the compensatory principle. One possibility is that the courts realize that one of the basic functions of the law of contract is to support transactions by providing the threat of sanctions for breach, and that where the compensatory principle removes the sanction entirely, it has to be overridden. Another possibility is that the courts recognize that the party in breach in these cases will be unjustly enriched in the absence of substantial damages, since the breach may have reduced costs without a commensurate reduction in the price paid. A third possibility, which comes to the fore in relation to specific performance as we shall see below, suggests that the interests of third parties become a relevant consideration in the award of damages as part of broader social policies designed to regulate the social market.

Net Loss

The general approach of the compensatory principle is to award the injured party its net loss as a result of the breach of contract. If the original contract was disadvantageous in the first place, then the injured party may receive no compensation at all, since the cost of substitutes will be less than the contract price. The courts avoid putting the injured party in a better position than if the contract had been correctly performed.

In a claim for wasted expenditure during performance of a contract, this principle can prevent the recovery of these costs if they exceed the benefits which would have accrued from the defendant's performance of the contract.[28] For example, if the injured party undertakes to perform work for a fixed price but incurs a greater expenditure than the contract price, the claim for compensation is limited to the price. Similarly, where the result of repair of damage to property is an increase in the value of the property, such as new building which is worth more than the old one, then the damages for the cost of repair will be reduced to reflect that increase in value.

(2) Loss of Profits

In a commercial contract, the objective of the parties is likely to include the opportunity to make a profit from the transaction. The goods acquired may be resold at a profit. Alternatively, raw materials may be used in a factory for making products to be resold at a profit. Breach of the contract to supply goods in both instances will lead to a loss of profits unless substituted performance can be obtained in time. Loss of profits may also result from breach of contracts of carriage of goods, as where the carrier delivers a vital component late with the effect of halting production at a factory. Similarly damage to the plaintiff's property caused by breach of

28   *C & P Haulage v Middleton* [1983] 1 WLR 1461, [1983] 3 All ER 94, CA; *CCC Films (London) Ltd v Impact Quadrant Films* [1985] QB 16, [1984] 3 All ER 298, QB.

contract can lead to a loss of profits if the property was a productive asset such as a factory or a machine.

In principle the courts permit claims for loss of profits in such circumstances. It is argued that this implements the objective of putting the injured party in as good a position as if the contract had been properly performed.

> The rule of the common law is, that where a party sustains a loss by reason of a breach of contract, he is, so far as money can do it, to be placed in the same situation, with respect to damages, as if the contract had been performed.[29]

But the courts are aware that claims for profits can amount to sums out of all proportion to the original value of the contract, which creates the risk that parties will be deterred from entering into contracts for fear of incurring indeterminate amounts of liability to pay compensation. A carrier who transports a component for £100, but who delays delivery resulting in a loss of profits of many thousands of pounds, may be reluctant to enter such contracts in the future. Similarly, the electrical contractor who burns down a factory may incur liability for loss of profits on the factory's production. These concerns can be met by adequate liability insurance cover, but the costs of this insurance against indeterminate amounts of liability may prove considerable.

For these reasons, the courts tend to restrict claims for loss of profits. They insist first of all that the injured party should be able to prove the loss, and then, secondly, many claims for loss of profits are denied on the ground that they are too remote.

Proof of loss

Although the injured party need not prove the lost opportunities to make a profit with absolute certainty, the courts require demonstration that the profits were easily reckonable. For example, an author's claim for loss of royalties resulting from a failure by the publisher to publish his book will fail unless the court is reasonably sure that the author would have earned royalties from the publication of the book by another publisher. In *McRae v Commonwealth Disposals Commission*,[30] where it will be recalled a salvor wasted money fruitlessly searching for a non-existent wreck of an oil tanker, the claim for profits expected from a successful salvage was dismissed as far too speculative.

For the seller of goods who manages to sell the goods elsewhere, the normal measure of damages will be the difference between the two contract prices. If the seller is in the business of trading in this commodity, then the seller may seek to claim a loss of profits resulting from lost throughput, that is a reduction in the number of sales with the effect of a reduced

---

29 Parke B, *Robinson v Harman* (1848) 1 Exch 850.
30 (1950) 84 CLR 377 (Aust HC).

profit. Such a claim failed in *Lazenby Garages Ltd v Wright*.[31] The seller of a used car claimed damages from a buyer who repudiated the contract. The seller managed to dispose of the car to a second customer for £100 more. The seller claimed loss of profit for the loss of opportunity to sell two cars rather than one, but this claim for lost throughput was rejected by the English Court of Appeal as too speculative. The seller therefore received no damages for breach of contract, since the second sale at a higher price covered its wasted expenditure.

Remoteness of loss
The test of remoteness of loss derives from *Hadley v Baxendale*,[32] a case concerned with delays in the transport of a mill-shaft causing temporary idleness of a mill. The rule prevents compensation unless the losses were:

> such as may reasonably be supposed to have been in the contemplation of both parties, at the time they made the contract, as the probable result of the breach of it.

In the case, the carrier was held not liable for the consequential loss of profit resulting from delay in the delivery of the mill-shaft. The court argued that the loss of profits should only be recoverable if the millers had communicated to the carrier the urgency of their need and the loss of profits which would arise from delays; from the mere request to transport the mill shaft, the carrier could not reasonably have foreseen that delays would cause the loss of profits, since the miller might have possessed another mill-shaft.

The courts frame the test of remoteness in terms of whether the parties to the contract at the time of its formation foresaw the probability of this kind of loss resulting from breach as a serious possibility. In a modern statement of the doctrine, Lord Reid explained that:

> The crucial question is whether, on the information available to the defendant when the contract was made, he should, or the reasonable man in his position would, have realised that such loss was sufficiently likely to result from the breach of contract to make it proper to hold that the loss flowed naturally from the breach or that loss of that kind should have been within his contemplation.[33]

But this test proves misleading, for the issue turns not so much on the probability of the loss of profits, but on the implicit allocation of the risk

---

31   [1976] 1 WLR 459, [1976] 2 All ER 770, CA.
32   (1854) 9 Exch 341. Danzig, '*Hadley v Baxendale*: A Study in the Industrialisation of the Law' (1975) 4 *Journal of Legal Studies* 249; Barton, 'Contractual Damages and the Rise of Industry' (1987) 7 *Oxford Journal of Legal Studies* 40; Bishop, 'The Contract-Tort Boundary and the Economics of Insurance' (1983) 12 *Journal of Legal Studies* 241.
33   *Koufos v C Czarnikow Ltd, The Heron II* [1969] 1 AC 350, 385, [1967] 3 All ER 686, 691. See also Sale of Goods Act 1979, s 53(2) 'The measure of damages for breach of warranty is the estimated loss directly and naturally resulting, in the ordinary course of events, from the breach of warranty'.

of that loss between the parties. The courts search for a case where in effect the defendant has assumed the responsibility of an insurer against such losses. This in turn depends upon both the defendant's knowledge of the purposes for which the plaintiff enters the contract and any allocation of risks within the contract. If the defendant has no knowledge of the plaintiff's purpose in entering the transaction, then the defendant may not be held liable for even certain consequential losses. On the other hand, if the defendant is familiar with the plaintiff's expectations, then, in the absence of an express contractual allocation of risk, the defendant may be held liable for even improbable consequential losses.

If, for example, the carrier benefits from a broad liability insurance policy, the costs of which he transfers to customers through higher charges for his services, then a court will lean towards imposing liability for those opportunity costs amounting to loss of profits. Similarly, if the carrier was informed of the urgency and possible financial implications of any delay, and he accepted the contract at an unusually high price in the knowledge of this degree of financial dependence, then again a court may infer an assumption of liability for a broad range of opportunity costs and consequential losses. In an unusually favourable decision for the plaintiff, in *Jackson v Chrysler Acceptances Ltd*,[34] a purchaser of a new car on hire purchase, which turned out to be seriously defective and not of satisfactory quality, succeeded in a claim not only for the defects in the car, but also for the loss arising from a spoiled holiday in France due to the breakdown of the car, because the plaintiff had informed the car dealer of his intention to use the car for that purpose shortly after its purchase.

Short of precise information available to the defendant about likely consequential losses, however, the courts must infer the allocation of risks between the parties from the nature of the business transaction. If the contract concerns the sale and delivery of business machinery, then the court can infer that the seller accepts the risk of the buyer's loss of profits due to late delivery. In *Victoria Laundry (Windsor) Ltd v Newman Industries Ltd*,[35] for instance, the defendant delivered a boiler late to a commercial laundry. The defendant was held liable for the plaintiff's loss of usual business profits, but escaped liability for unusually high profits which the plaintiff had expected to gain from a particularly lucrative contract.

With respect to carriers of goods, the difficulty for the court is to know how much knowledge of the business objectives of the owner of the goods should be attributed to the carrier. In a controversial decision of this type, *Koufos v C Czarnikow Ltd (The Heron II)*,[36] the House of Lords allowed recovery for anticipated profits where a carrier regularly transported a commodity from one location to another under instructions from a business which, as the carrier knew, made its profits by moving goods promptly to

34   [1978] RTR 474, CA.
35   [1949] 2 KB 528, [1949] 1 All ER 997, CA.
36   [1969] 1 AC 350, [1967] 3 All ER 686, HL.

locations where the price was highest. On account of the carrier's delay in arriving in port, competition had lowered the price of the commodity, thereby reducing profits from resale. The court held the carrier liable for the loss of profits resulting from delay, despite the absence of clear evidence that the carrier had assumed the burden of these losses from the outset. Instead, the court inferred from the nature of the trading relationship that the carrier should bear this responsibility. This case can be distinguished from *Hadley v Baxendale* on the ground that the carrier had greater knowledge of the owner's business purposes, and therefore had had the opportunity to allocate the risk of delay through the contract.

But mere knowledge of the plaintiff's business and the likely losses resulting from breach of contract should not suffice to render the loss recoverable. The court must also allocate the risk of this loss in the light of the implicit understanding between the parties. In *Parsons (H) (Livestock) Ltd v Uttley Ingham & Co Ltd*,[37] the manufacturers and suppliers of a pig food hopper were held liable to a farmer for the death of his pigs from disease which was caused as a result of negligent installation of the hopper, but not for the loss of possible profitable sales expected by the farmer. The farmer could recover the value of the pigs when they died from disease, since that was an unavoidable loss caused by a breach of contract, but the anticipated profits failed the test of remoteness because the manufacturers of the hopper had not assumed implicitly the position of an insurer against such losses when agreeing to supply the hopper. The hopper was merely one method of feeding the pigs, not an essential tool of the farmer's business like the boiler for a laundry, so that it could not be supposed that the supplier had undertaken to be responsible for the farmer's business profits resulting from rearing the pigs and taking them to market.

Like any test which depends upon the hypothetical intentions and knowledge of the parties, the remoteness rule conceals the real policy considerations at stake. The rule can be explained by reference to efficiency considerations. An objective of the rule is to encourage the efficient allocation of risks under the contract. The injured party is given an incentive to disclose the risks of loss resulting from breach, so that the defendant can either agree to accept these risks with a commensurate price increase or exclude this liability in return for a reduced price. Although the rule provides this incentive to make efficient allocations of risks, when the courts apply the rule to particular cases, of course, this incentive has not worked, for the parties have not agreed an allocation. In these circumstances it may be argued that the courts are effectively imposing terms which the parties ought to have agreed in view of the standard of efficient allocation of risk.

Unfortunately, a rigorous application of the efficiency standard would probably not fit the cases. For example, it would almost certainly be cheaper for the farmer to insure against the loss of his pigs than for the

37   [1978] QB 791, [1978] 1 All ER 525, CA.

supplier of the hopper to incur the cost of liability insurance. Although these considerations of efficient risk allocation may play a role in fixing the extent of liability for loss of profits, it seems likely that the courts are also concerned about the possible deterrent effect on market transactions if they were to award routinely damages for full loss of profits.

(3) Avoidable Losses

The compensatory principle for the assessment of damages disallows any claim where a court finds that the injured party could have avoided the loss by preventative action after the breach of contract. The reason for this general rule probably depends heavily on the aim to reduce the social costs arising from breach of contract. There is a social interest in providing incentives for efficient use of resources at all times. But this reason is further supported by the aim of encouraging co-operation between the parties. The losses may be reduced by an agreed modification of the contract, and if this is the least costly way of handling the breach, the injured party will be required to reach such an agreement on pain of losing damages for the increased loss.[38] The courts may also regard it as unfair to require compensation to be paid to an injured party for losses which in part are attributable to his own choices after the breach of contract. Four doctrines consolidate this general principle which denies recovery for avoidable losses.

Time of Assessment

To begin with, courts normally assess the measure of loss at the date when it was first reasonable for the injured party to find substitute performance or take remedial action. The injured party cannot sit back while the costs of substitute performance escalate as a result of inflation or shortages and then claim the higher measure of recovery. The normal time for the assessment of loss is the date of breach of contract, but this will not be true, for example, where either the injured party discovers the breach subsequently,[39] or where it is reasonable to wait to see if the defendant remedies the breach,[40] or where no remedial action is immediately possible, such as when the injured party is prevented from taking steps to minimize the damage through his own impecuniosity and inability to obtain credit.[41] In these exceptional cases, the court will determine another appropriate date at which damages should be assessed.[42]

---

38 *Payzu Ltd v Saunders* [1919] 2 KB 581, CA. Goetz and Scott, 'The Mitigation Principle: Toward a General Theory of Contractual Obligation' (1983) 69 *Virginia Law Review* 967.

39 *Cehave NV v Bremer Handelsgesellschaft mbH (The Hansa Nord)* [1976] QB 44, [1975] 3 All ER 739, CA.

40 *Radford v De Froberville* [1977] 1 WLR 1262, [1978] 1 All ER 33, Ch.

41 *Wroth v Tyler* [1974] Ch 30, [1973] 1 All ER 897, Ch.

42 *Johnson v Agnew* [1980] AC 367, [1979] 1 All ER 883, HL.

Causation

A second method by which courts prevent recovery for avoidable losses is to hold that the loss resulted not from the breach of contract, but was caused by the injured party's own negligence. For example, the purchaser of a defective product who is injured by it may find that the court holds that his injury was caused not by the defect, but by his own foolishness in using the machine once it was apparent that it was defective. In *Lexmead (Basingstoke) Ltd v Lewis*,[43] a purchaser of a trailer coupling continued to use it even after it was clearly defective, and this resulted in serious personal injuries to a third party. The seller was held not liable to the purchaser for the consequential losses of liability for personal injuries resulting from the defective coupling, since the accident had been caused by the purchaser's act rather than the defect in the product.

Although this argument is framed in terms of causation, it should be clear that it departs from the normal attitude to causation found in the common law. In the law of tort and crime, a person will be held to have caused an event if his actions provided the occasion for the accident and constituted a continuing source of the danger. A murderer cannot escape responsibility, for example, merely by demonstrating that better medical care would have avoided the fatality following the infliction of stab wounds. Where the injured party carelessly adds to his injury or through his negligence increases his risk of harm, in tort his contributory negligence reduces the measure of damages but does not eliminate it entirely. In the law of contract, however, the courts often hold that any unreasonable or careless act on the part of the injured party between breach of contract and loss breaks the chain of causation and thus they deny the claim for damages.[44]

Contributory Negligence

This sharp, all-or-nothing result produced by the doctrine of causation has been relieved in recent years by the application of the doctrine of contributory negligence to negligent breaches of contract. Under the Law Reform (Contributory Negligence) Act 1945, section 1(1), subject to contrary contractual agreement,

> Where any person suffers damage as the result partly of his own fault and partly of the fault of any other person or persons, a claim in respect of that damage shall not be defeated by reason of the fault of the person suffering the damage, but the damages recoverable in respect thereof shall be reduced to such extent as the court thinks just and equitable having regard to the claimant's share in the responsibility for the damage.

Although this provision for apportionment of blame and reduction of damages was designed to reform the law of tort, its terms can also encompass at least cases where a negligent breach of contract also

---

43   [1982] AC 225, [1981] 1 All ER 1185, HL.
44   *Quinn v Burch Bros (Builders) Ltd* [1966] 2 QB 370, [1966] 2 All ER 283, CA.

constitutes grounds for an action in tort.[45] But there is a case for extending the coverage of the legislation, so that it excludes the all-or-nothing reasoning of causation when the case involves purely contractual obligations which impose a duty of care.[46] Such a reform would not alter the result in *Lambert v Lewis*, however, for the retailer's obligation was one of strict liability under the Sale of Goods Act 1979, section 14.[47]

Mitigation of loss
The injured party cannot recover damages for losses where it is shown that by seeking substitutes in the market he could have avoided or reduced the losses. The purchaser of goods can usually find a suitable alternative in the market, and in the absence of unusual circumstances, any unreasonable failure to take advantage of this opportunity will result in the reduction of his damages to the level of unavoidable loss. Once again, special circumstances may prevent the injured party from minimizing his loss. For example, his impecuniosity and inability to borrow money may prevent him from taking immediate steps to find a substitute or cure the damage. Someone who purchases a new house on a large mortgage and then discovers defects in the foundations may not be able to take remedial steps until the builder has paid damages for breach of contract, because until that time the homeowner lacks the means to finance the building work.

The duty to mitigate loss requires the injured party to take reasonable steps to reduce loss. These reasonable steps may include incurring additional costs with respect to one item of recovery in order to reduce the losses under another heading. In *Harbutt's Plasticine Ltd v Wayne Tank and Pump Co Ltd*,[48] the plaintiff's factory was destroyed by a fire caused by the defendant's breach of contract. In principle the plaintiff could recover for the cost of repairing the factory and the consequential loss of profits from the factory being shut down. The plaintiff built a new factory, which was worth substantially more than the old one, and succeeded in a claim to recover the cost of the new factory. At first sight this result breaches the compensatory principle, for the plaintiff receives a more valuable factory than it has lost. But the court reasoned that by building a new factory the plaintiff was taking reasonable steps to reduce the measure of consequential loss of profits, for without a new factory the plaintiff would have been able to claim loss of profits for an indeterminate number of years.

---

45 *Forsikringsaktieselskapet Vesta v Butcher, Bain Dawles Ltd* [1989] AC 852, [1988] 2 All ER 43, [1989] 1 All ER 402, CA, HL. The statute also applies to claims for misrepresentation: *Gran Gelato Ltd v Richcliff (Group) Ltd* [1992] Ch 560, [1992] 1 All ER 865, Ch.
46 Law Commission, *Contributory Negligence as a Defence in Contract*, Report No 219 (London, HMSO, 1993).
47 *Barclays Bank plc v Fairclough Building Ltd* [1995] QB 214, [1995] 1 All ER 289, CA.
48 [1970] 1 QB 447, [1970] 1 All ER 225, CA.

(4) Waste of Resources

An important qualification to the compensation principle concerns the waste of resources. For the sake of the welfare of the whole community, courts will not award damages amounting to the cost of curing defects in performance where the cost of repair is grossly disproportionate to the value of the benefits gained. In one typical case, when building a large house, the contractor used pipes manufactured by a different firm from those specified in the contract, though in all other respects the pipes were identical. The owner of the house claimed damages for the cost of rebuilding the house with the correct pipes, but the New York Court of Appeals declined to give more than nominal damages since there was no diminution in the value of the house. Cardozo J expressed the correct principle in these terms:

> The owner is entitled to the money which will permit him to complete, unless the cost of completion is greatly out of proportion to the good to be attained. When this is true, the measure is the difference in value.[49]

We should recognize, however, that not all judges are as forthright as Cardozo J. They disguise the refusal to award damages for the cost of curing a defect on the ground that it would be a waste of resources under a variety of arguments, such as the claim that there is no loss, or that the cure would be an unreasonable way to mitigate loss.

In *Ruxley Electronics and Construction Ltd v Forsyth*,[50] a builder had agreed to construct a swimming pool 7ft 6in deep, but in breach of contract the finished pool was only 6ft deep. The defendant refused to pay the builder the contract price, and counterclaimed a sum in excess of the contract price to have the pool reconstructed to the agreed depth. The court accepted evidence that the finished pool had the same value as a pool of greater depth, since both were safe for off-the-side diving. It would clearly be a waste of resources to reconstruct the pool. The House of Lords permitted the builder's claim for the contract price and refused the counterclaim for reconstruction on the ground that it would be unreasonable to reconstruct the pool.

Especially difficult problems arise with respect to waste of resources in cases where the work which has not been undertaken in breach of contract is designed to improve the environment, for no doubt some regard all environmental endeavours as a waste of resources. Courts will be tempted to confine the measure of recovery to the diminution in the value of the asset, rather than award compensation to cover the costs of the environmental work. Although in *Radford v De Froberville*[51] the court permitted a claim for the cost of the environmental work where the injured party sought the cost of building a wall around his garden, in *Tito v Waddell (No 2)*[52] the court dismissed a claim to enforce a promise to restore a

---

49   *Jacob and Youngs v Kent* 230 NY 239, at p 244, 129 NE 889, at p 891 (1921).
50   [1996] AC 344, [1995] 3 All ER 268, HL.
51   [1977] 1 WLR 1262, [1978] 1 All ER 33, Ch.
52   [1977] Ch 106, [1977] 3 All ER 129, Ch.

Pacific island to its idyllic state prior to extensive phosphate mining, though doubts about the likely success of the relandscaping also contributed to defeat the claim.

(5) Non-pecuniary losses
The rules governing the assessment of compensation described so far have focused on the pecuniary losses resulting from breach of contract. In many types of contract, however, the purpose of entering the contract includes dimensions which include the expectation of enjoyment, satisfaction, and the construction of meaning in life. Examples might include the purchase of a theatre ticket, a package holiday, a swimming pool, or a holiday home. Breach of these contracts will result not only in a financial loss, which the compensatory principle can rectify, but also disappointment, vexation, and worry. The classical law routinely refused compensation for such items of loss, taking an entirely financial perspective on the purpose of entry into contracts.[53] In the modern law, a differentiation between types of contracts is occurring, so that in appropriate cases the courts will offer compensation for such items of loss.

One way in which this differentiation has been accomplished is by asserting that the contract contains an express or implied term to the effect that the promisor undertakes to relieve the promisee from distress or to give the promisee an enjoyable time by the provision of services. If such a term can be inserted, then a claim for compensation for its breach will succeed. Claims for mental distress resulting from breach of contract have succeeded, for example, in the case of a disappointing package holiday,[54] and an undertaking by a firm of solicitors to take legal action to prevent a man from molesting his wife.[55] But a similar claim failed in a case of a negligent survey of a house, in *Watts v Morrow*,[56] when the purchaser was disappointed in the expectation of acquiring a trouble-free second home for holidays. It was not part of the terms of the surveyor's contract to provide a guarantee that the home would be enjoyable. It is possible, however, to recover compensation in such a case for the physical inconvenience and discomfort caused by the breach of contract when the defects are repaired. In the case of contracts of employment, the traditional rule appears still to deny recovery to an employee who suffers distress, frustration and vexation resulting from an employer's breach of contract.[57]

This technique of discovering an implied term may, however, not be necessary in future. In *Ruxley Electronic and Construction Ltd v Forsyth*,[58] the House of Lords, it will be recalled, refused a claim for the cost of reconstructing a swimming pool to the depth specified in the contract.

53 *Addis v Gramophone Co Ltd* [1909] AC 488, HL.
54 *Jarvis v Swans Tours Ltd* [1973] QB 233, [1973] 1 All ER 71, CA.
55 *Heywood v Wellers* [1976] QB 446, [1976] 1 All ER 300, CA.
56 [1991] 1 WLR 1421, [1991] 4 All ER 937, CA.
57 *Bliss v South East Thames Regional Health Authority* [1985] IRLR 308, CA.
58 [1996] AC 344, [1995] 3 All ER 268, HL.

Nevertheless the court permitted a claim for compensation for 'loss of amenity'. The court seems to have inferred from the subject matter of the contract that its purpose included enjoyment. The result is puzzling, however, since the evidence suggested that the shallower pool should be equally enjoyable. The court seemed to recognize that in cases where the injured party had placed a personal, subjective and non-pecuniary value on performance according to the terms of the contract, compensation should be permitted to meet that interest. This greater flexibility in the differentiation of contracts may lead to the recognition that in many types of personal contracts the injured party may have suffered non-pecuniary losses.[59] Such losses are sometimes described as the 'consumer surplus', that is the value placed on performance above the contract or market price.[60] If this value is recognized more liberally in consumer contracts, as in *Ruxley Electronic and Construction Ltd v Forsyth*, then perhaps it will extend to other fields such as employment, where certainly many employees attribute a value to their job above the wages that they receive.

At the borderline between pecuniary and non-pecuniary loss, there are interests in reputation. One effect of a breach of contract may be that the injured party discovers that its reputation with other traders has been damaged because the injured party has been forced to default on other contracts. Damage to reputation may also occur to an employee, for a wrongful dismissal may impede future chances of employment with other employers who may take the view that there is no smoke without fire. Given that business reputation can be a vital force in determining selection of contracting parties and in providing incentives for co-operation, it seems appropriate that compensation should be awarded under this heading. It has been acknowledged as a suitable item for compensation where a bank wrongfully dishonoured a cheque causing damage to the reputation of its customer, though the measure of damages will be confined by the rules governing remoteness of loss to the ordinary losses resulting from injury to a person's credit rating.[61] An equivalent claim for employees who suffered reduced employment prospects resulting from their former employer's fraud on customers has succeeded,[62] and similarly claims by businesses for damage to reputation which is likely to reduce sales have been accepted.[63]

(6) Punitive Damages
As a general rule, the compensatory principle of damages excludes the possibility of punitive damages for breach of contract, that is, a measure

---

59   J Wightman, *Contract: A Critical Commentary* (London, 1996) p 98.
60   Harris, Ogus and Phillips, 'Contract Remedies and the Consumer Surplus' (1977) 95 *Law Quarterly Review* 179.
61   *Kpohraror v Woolwich Building Society* [1996] 4 All ER 119, CA.
62   *Malik v BCCI* [1997] 3 All ER 1, HL.
63   *Aerial Advertising Co v Batchelors Peas Ltd (Manchester)* [1938] 2 All ER 788, QB; *Evans Marshall & Co v Bertola SA* [1973] 1 WLR 349, [1973] 1 All ER 992, CA; Enonchong, 'Contract Damages for Injury to Reputation' (1996) 59 *Modern Law Review* 592.

of compensation which exceeds the injured party's loss. Moreover, as we have seen in Chapter 16, the courts generally prevent the parties from enforcing an agreed remedy, such as a penalty clause which provides a greater measure of compensation than is available under the compensatory principles. But in some circumstances the courts award a measure of compensation which exceeds loss.

Punitive damages alter the incentives for efficient breach of contract, so that rarely can a defendant profit from a deliberate breach. In this respect they are similar to orders for compulsory performance, but they have the advantage that they overcome some of the obstacles to specific performance, such as the concern for individual liberty and the costs of supervising performance. The general rule against punitive damages makes sense within the framework of the pursuit of a fair distribution of loss resulting from a breach of contract, but punitive damages can be justified from the perspective of both improving the competitiveness of markets and satisfying the requirements of the social market.

Competition
Punitive damages can be used to deter the exploitation of a position of domination derived from an effective bilateral monopoly. In some jurisdictions in the United States, the courts have experimented with the use of punitive damages by recategorizing the breach of contract as a tort for which punitive damages may be awarded.[64] Typical cases involve deliberate procrastination and evasion by insurers in settling claims under insurance policies and refusals by retailers and manufacturers to repair consumer goods properly contrary to an agreed warranty. These decisions concern instances of an effective bilateral monopoly, where the consumer becomes heavily dependent upon the supplier because no substitutes are available in the market. The client of an insurance company must rely heavily upon the good faith of the company in processing the claim, and the purchaser of a consumer product depends upon the retailer or manufacturer to carry out the warranty of service. In the absence of these conditions, such as a bad faith discharge of an employee who can gain employment elsewhere, the US courts have recently become reluctant to extend the ambit of punitive damages.[65] In English law punitive damages have not yet been awarded in similar circumstances. Some protection may be afforded to consumers by invalidating disadvantageous settlements

---

64 Sullivan, 'Punitive Damages in the Law of Contract: The Reality and the Illusion of Legal Change' (1977) 61 *Minnesota Law Review* 207; Chutorian, 'Tort Remedies for Breach of Contract: The Expansion of Tortious Breach of the Implied Covenant of Good Faith and Fair Dealing into the Commercial Realm' (1986) 86 *Columbia Law Review* 377. The Canadian position has also moved towards punitive damages: Chapman, 'Punitive Damages as Aggravated Damages: The Case of Contract' (1990) 16 *Canadian Business Law Journal* 269.

65 *Foley v Interactive Data Corpn* 47 Cal 3d 654 (1988).

of such claims on the ground of economic duress or an intervention on the ground of unfairness.[66]

Punitive damages could also be used in a complementary fashion to criminal offences in order to deter misleading trade practices, where the compensatory principle provides insufficient incentive for ordinary plaintiffs such as consumers to pursue litigation. In the discussion of damages for misrepresentation in Chapter 10, we observed a move in this direction by the application of the measure of damages for fraud to cases of negligent misrepresentation under section 2(1) of the Misrepresentation Act 1967. This measure removes the limit of remoteness of damage to the claim, so that the full range of opportunity costs are recoverable. The courts may also augment covertly the measure of damages for breach of contract in response to notorious and persistent breaches of contract. The discretion in calculating the measure of compensation may have been exercised in this fashion in *Jarvis v Swan's Tours*,[67] where damages considerably in excess of the contract price were awarded against a company providing package holidays, when a booked holiday turned out to be an unpleasant experience as a result of multiple failures to comply with the lavishly illustrated brochure's ecstatic promises. This result should be seen against the background of numerous press reports of misleading and unreliable holiday brochures. The potential for employing punitive damages openly to deter scandalous trade practices has still to be realized, and the English law has perhaps already chosen to follow a different path by employing the regulatory offences discussed in previous chapters.

Social Interests

English statutes make some provision for punitive damages in order to protect individuals against invasion of fundamental civil liberties through breach of contract. For example, an employer who dismisses an employee for a reason connected with the employee's membership (or non-membership) of a trade union will be required to pay a punitive measure of compensation.[68] The measure of compensation for intentional sex and race discrimination in breach of contract (or negotiations for a contract) also permits aggravated and exemplary damages for injury to feelings and insulting treatment.[69] These adjustments to the normal compensatory principles for breach of contract reflect dimensions of the social market which reject the image of the market as an institution for preference satisfaction, and instead insist upon its importance as an opportunity for citizens to bring meaning to their lives, an opportunity which must be afforded to citizens equally.

---

66   *Dillon v Baltic Shipping Co (The Mikhail Lermontov)* [1991] 2 Lloyd's Rep 155 (NSW CA). The Unfair Contract Terms Act 1977 may not apply to settlements: *Tudor Grange Holdings Ltd v Citibank NA* [1992] Ch 53, [1991] 4 All ER 1, Ch.
67   [1973] QB 233, [1973] 1 All ER 71, CA.
68   Trade Union and Labour Relations (Consolidation) Act 1992, ss 152, 156–158.
69   *Alexander v Home Office* [1988] 2 All ER 118, [1988] ICR 685, CA; *Bradford City Metropolitan Council v Arora* [1991] 2 QB 507, [1991] IRLR 165, CA.

A type of punitive damages can also be awarded to condemn a breach of a fiduciary relation. If the fiduciary breaches its obligations of loyalty and good faith, then the court may render it liable to account for any profits. The measure of compensation is therefore not the plaintiff's loss but the fiduciary's gain. This applies, for example, when the director of a company diverts business from the company to a personal transaction.

Apart from fiduciary relations, the extent of the possibility to bring a claim for the disgorgement of profits remains controversial.[70] The claim is available where the defendant makes the profit from the unauthorized use of the plaintiff's property.[71] The types of property could include intellectual property such as copyright material or trade secrets. The remedy may also be available to recoup profits made from the unauthorized use of confidential information.[72]

One other instance where punitive damages may prove appropriate for breach of contract concerns instances where the normal remedy of an injunction against breach must be withheld for some pressing reason, but the court nevertheless wishes to ensure that the defendant cannot take full advantage of the breach. In *Wrotham Park Estate Co v Parkside Homes Ltd*,[73] the defendant ignored a covenant not to build without the plaintiff's prior consent. The court refused to make an order for the destruction of the fourteen houses which had been built and occupied for reasons connected with the waste of resources. But the plaintiff could not prove any loss from the buildings resulting from a diminution of the value of its own land. Nevertheless the court awarded substantial damages representing the hypothetical price at which the plaintiff would have consented to the building development. These damages vindicated the proprietary right to control building development, and for this reason were not tied to the plaintiff's actual loss. But this decision has been interpreted narrowly, for a claim for the value of the fee for waiving the covenant not to build was rejected in *Surrey County Council v Bredero Homes Ltd*.[74] Steyn LJ reasserted the principle that this restitutionary measure of disgorgement of profits is only available for the misuse of the plaintiff's proprietary interests.

---

70 Smith, 'Disgorgement of the Profits of Breach of Contract: Property, Contract and 'Efficient Breach' (1994–5) 24 *Canadian Business Law Journal* 121; Law Commission, *Aggravated, Exemplary and Restitutionary Damages*, Consultation Paper No 132 (1993).

71 *Penarth Dock Engineering Co Ltd v Pounds* [1963] 1 Lloyd's Rep 359; *Strand Electric and Engineering Co Ltd v Brisford Entertainments Ltd* [1952] 2 QB 246, [1952] 1 All ER 796, CA.

72 *LAC Minerals Ltd v International Corona Resources Ltd* [1989] 2 SCR 574, 61 DLR (4th) 14.

73 [1974] 1 WLR 798, [1974] 2 All ER 321, Ch. Approved in *Jaggard v Sawyer* [1995] 1 WLR 269, [1995] 2 All ER 189, CA, but regarded as an application of the compensatory principle.

74 *Surrey County Council v Bredero Homes Ltd* [1993] 1 WLR 1361, [1993] 3 All ER 705, CA.

A particularly difficult social interest to compensate under the ordinary law of damages consists of the performance of a service to the public. With the increasing use of sub-contracting of services provided to the public, the issue of the appropriate measure of compensation for breach becomes more pressing. Under such contracts the services to be delivered may range from street cleaning, the cleaning of public buildings such as hospitals and schools, the guarding of prisoners, or the provision of a fire service. The problem for assessing the measure of damages for breach is that the provision of a defective service may cause no loss to the public authority. If the streets are a little dirty, the schools untidy, the fire service and the prison service undermanned, then the contractor may be saving money, but the public authority may suffer no loss. The contract may provide an agreed remedy of compensation for deviation from quality standards, but there is a risk that this will be held to be invalid as a penalty clause. An alternative measure of damages would consist in the expenditure saved by the contractor, which could also be described as the additional profit achieved through breach of contract. This would be a type of punitive damages, described as disgorgement of profits, which might be the only way to provide a legal remedy in such cases. At present, the effective sanctions are those provided by monitoring and agreed penalties in the contract (often in the form of performance bonds or guarantees), which the contractors do not challenge since presumably they wish to keep the business in the long term.[75]

4. Compulsory Performance

Courts seldom issue an order to perform a contract or to refrain from breach of it. In practice, the injured party rarely asks for this remedy, for it is usually possible to locate an alternative source of supply for the goods or services which are available without the costs and delays associated with litigation. Alternatively, if the right to obtain compulsory performance is clear, then this will induce negotiations towards a favourable settlement for the plaintiff. But even where the injured party seeks compulsory performance, the common law rarely permits the remedies of specific performance and injunctions.

(1) Inadequacy of Compensation
A series of historical accidents deformed the legal principles governing the award of orders for compulsory performance, thereby rendering it almost impossible to discern the rationale behind the modern law. The

---

75   P Vincent-Jones and A Harries, 'Limits of Contract in Internal CCT Transactions: A Comparative Study of Buildings Cleaning and Refuse Collection in "Northern Metropolitan"' in D Campbell and P Vincent-Jones, *Contract and Economic Organisation* (Aldershot, 1996) 180.

general rule is normally stated to be that courts will only order specific performance or an injunction where damages would be inadequate to compensate the plaintiff's loss. This looks a puzzling rule, since the law of damages should compensate the plaintiff's loss in most respects unless the defendant is insolvent. The origins of the rule lie in a political accommodation between the common law courts and the king's court of Chancery, under which the latter confined its intervention to cases where the common law failed to provide an adequate remedy. Hence the Chancery courts advanced the rule that specific performance and injunctions would only be granted for breach of contract where common law damages were inadequate.[76]

This rule then raises an embarrassing question: when can damages be inadequate, given that they compensate the injured party for all his losses? One suggestion is that damages prove inadequate when a claim involves those interests which are excluded from compensation, such as remote losses, avoidable losses, and waste of resources.[77] An order for specific performance, if it could be made in time, would give the injured party his expected profits or would prevent non-pecuniary losses from arising. But then the question becomes, why should we wish to subvert these limitations on awards of damages, which rest on important policies such as the minimization of social cost, by introducing compulsory performance as an available remedy?

The argument based upon the inadequacy of damages may prove more convincing, however, where the claim is likely to be defeated for being too speculative. Here the court can avoid the risk of overcompensation or under-compensation, not by denying any damages at all, but by ordering specific performance.[78] A common kind of case where compulsory performance is ordered for this reason involves transactions for the transfer of an asset which will provide an opportunity to earn an uncertain income. If the injured party cannot prove his losses with sufficient certainty to satisfy the compensatory principle, a court may order specific performance. For example, an injured party may be able to enforce a sale of shares which would give him control over a corporation, because damages for his loss of the right to control the corporation are too speculative to be compensatable. Similarly, the loss of the right to be an exclusive distributor of a product may lead to the loss of goodwill and trade reputation, items which are hard to quantify under the compensatory principle, but which can be protected by an injunction. The fundamental problem here is not that damages are inadequate to cover these kinds of losses but that the losses cannot be proven, and, in order to overcome these evidentiary difficulties, the courts are prepared to order compulsory performance where this will lead to a fair distributive consequence.

---

76 Dawson, 'Specific Performance in France and Germany' (1959) 57 *Michigan Law Review* 495.
77 Harris, Ogus and Phillips, 'Contract Remedies and the Consumer Surplus' (1977) 95 *Law Quarterly Review* 581.
78 Kronman, 'Specific Performance' (1978) 45 *University of Chicago Law Review* 351.

In practice it has become well established that the only type of contract which will be routinely enforced by an order for specific performance is one concerning the transfer of an interest in land. This practice is hard to square with the rule that damages must be inadequate. Given that the purchaser of a house is likely to be able to discover a satisfactory substitute fairly quickly, then it is hard to see how damages could be inadequate. Even more strangely, the vendor of property can also obtain specific performance, though his claim will only be one for payment of money. The general rule therefore encounters the difficulty of explaining the major case where it is invariably satisfied.

Another instance where it is often suggested that specific performance will be routinely ordered concerns unique goods.[79] One possible reason why damages may prove inadequate here is because the uniqueness of the goods prevents a clear market price from being established. But this argument appears weak, for it should be possible to obtain a reliable estimate of the current market value for even a rare work of art. In fact the courts do not rely upon this category of uniqueness frequently, but assume that satisfactory substitutes can be obtained in the market, so that damages will be an adequate remedy.[80] The argument based upon the uniqueness of the goods seems likely to succeed only when the plaintiff can persuade the court of a particular personal reason for seeking possession of that particular item, that it has a sentimental value or significance which cannot be replaced by a substitute.

Although the courts still repeat the rule that damages must be inadequate before they will award an order for compulsory performance, the rule has been subtly modified in recent years. In *Beswick v Beswick*,[81] an elderly and ailing coal merchant sold his business to his nephew in return for various promises including a promise to pay his widow £5 per week after his death. When the nephew refused to pay, the widow in her capacity as administratrix of her husband's estate claimed specific performance of the contract. Since the estate had lost nothing by the nephew's breach of contract, because the payments were owed to the widow personally, it was likely that the measure of damages would be nominal. The House of Lords ordered specific performance of the contract even though an award of nominal damages would have covered all the losses of the estate. The court made the award of compulsory performance because they thought that it achieved a just result, for otherwise the nephew would have been unjustly enriched by being entitled to hold onto his uncle's business without paying his aunt a penny. The modern judicial test asks the question: is it just in all the circumstances that the plaintiff should be confined to his remedy in damages?[82] This test squarely raises the issue

---

79   *Falcke v Gray* (1859) 4 Drew 651, Ch.
80   *Société des Industries Métallurgiques SA v Bronx Engineering Co Ltd* [1975] 1 Lloyd's Rep 465, CA.
81   [1968] AC 58, [1967] 2 All ER 1197, HL.
82   Sachs LJ, *Evans Marshall & Co Ltd v Bertola SA* [1973] 1 WLR 349, [1973] 1 All ER 992, CA.

of describing the circumstances which induce a court to find the award of the remedy of specific performance more just than damages.

The key to the law of compulsory performance lies in recognizing that such a remedy is not designed to compensate the injured party for the losses, but to force performance of the contract. Normally a court declines to order performance because damages provide a sufficient incentive to complete most contracts except where the defendant hopes to achieve unusual economic benefits from breach, in which case to compel performance would only serve to discourage contracts and to reduce the combined wealth of the contracting parties. A remedy of compulsory performance therefore deliberately overrides these normal considerations governing remedies in order to serve different policies. Two policies which are central to the use of orders of compulsory performance are to resist exploitation of relations of domination and to protect solidarity rights, but the courts' discretion is sufficiently broad to permit such orders whenever the courts regard them as appropriate in all the circumstances.

(2) Oppression

In transactions which are performed over a period of time, such as output and requirements contracts or distributorships, because of transaction costs and opportunity costs one party may become heavily dependent upon the other for proper performance of the contract. For example, the retailer of petrol under a franchise agreement may be closely tied to one oil company because he is bound to satisfy all his requirements from it. If the oil company refuses to deliver petrol to satisfy his requirements, then the retailer must make the difficult choice between either going out of business or terminating the contract and seeking a new franchise and sources of supply, which may not be readily available and may appear unreliable. In these circumstances, the relation of dependence may be counterbalanced by an order to the oil company to perform its side of the requirements contract.[83] In other words, having forged a relation of domination through freedom of contract, the oil company makes itself vulnerable to orders for compulsory performance to achieve a more even balance in the transaction. Notice that damages could be a sufficient compensatory remedy in this case, for the oil company would be liable for the full range of opportunity costs and expenses. The principal reason for ordering compulsory performance is not to compensate economic loss or indeed to compensate anything at all, but to control the exercise of power established through contractual agreement by requiring that power to be exercised fairly in the light of the interests of the subordinate party. The courts adjust the rules governing termination of contracts by insisting that considerations based on the value of co-operation should override the ordinary principles governing judicial remedies in order to strengthen the hand of the dependent party.

---

83   *Sky Petroleum Ltd v VIP Petroleum Ltd* [1974] 1 WLR 576, [1974] 1 All ER 954, Ch.

This pattern of transaction which justifies the use of specific performance can be glimpsed in many other instances. In the contract of employment, an employee may invest a considerable amount of time and effort in acquiring skills specific to the employer's enterprise. This investment of human capital in the job makes the employee peculiarly vulnerable to threats of dismissal, for he may not be able to command the same wages and status in life elsewhere, so he must relinquish any control over his behaviour which the employer desires. These considerations create a strong case for specific performance of many contracts of employment in order to relieve the intensity of the subordination of the employee.[84] The pattern of domination which can be relieved by specific performance repeats itself in some consumer transactions. Where a consumer purchases a product, which, by virtue of its complexity and mechanical parts, can only be maintained and repaired by skilled contractors trained by the manufacturer, then again the service contractor enjoys a relation of domination over the consumer which can be effectively constrained by orders of compulsory performance of express promises to repair the product. Though on a refusal to perform the servicing operation the consumer may affirm the contract and sue the contractor for damages under the normal principles governing termination of contracts, the judicial order to perform the contract for repairs and the threat of seeking such an order strengthen the bargaining position of the consumer considerably.

The origins of the routine enforcement of contracts for the sale of interests in land may also lie in this purpose of preventing oppression. Some of these contracts do fit the pattern of relief from domination since, between the contract and the formal legal conveyance of the property, both parties are heavily committed to the transaction in terms of expenditure and opportunity costs, so that the threat of compulsory performance removes the potential for domination and opportunism by, for example, demands for a higher price or a delay in completion. Where none of these considerations apply to a sale of land, however, as in the case of a sale of one among many identical apartments by a developer, some American decisions have refused specific relief to the vendor.[85]

(3) Solidarity Rights

Orders of compulsory performance can also protect the interests of third parties. Under the doctrine of privity of contract, these third parties have no claim at all, even though they expected to benefit from performance of the contract and may have relied upon its performance. A court can recognize the force of these interests without granting the third parties

---

84   Eg *Powell v Brent London Borough Council* [1988] ICR 176, [1987] IRLR 466, CA; *Hughes v Southwark London Borough Council* [1988] IRLR 55, QB.

85   Van Hecke, 'Changing Emphases in Specific Performance' (1961) 40 *North Carolina Law Review* 1.

rights by ordering performance of the contract. We may describe this kind of protection of the interests of remote parties as the recognition of solidarity rights.[86]

This motive for ordering specific performance clearly lay at the heart of the decision in *Beswick v Beswick*. The justice of the case required the protection of the widow's interest in receiving her annuity, even though she lacked a direct contractual claim to enforce this interest against her nephew. By ordering specific performance of the contract to provide an annuity, the court was able to protect the widow's interest.

In a more commercial context, a similar justification explains the decision of the Court of Appeal in *Co-operative Insurance Society Ltd v Argyll Stores (Holdings) Ltd*.[87] The plaintiff landlords owned a shopping centre and leased the largest unit to the defendant supermarket chain for 35 years including a covenant that the supermarket should be kept open for the usual hours of business. Other units in the shopping centre were leased to separate business tenants who clearly benefited from the presence of the supermarket in attracting customers. After 15 years the supermarket was running at a loss, so the defendants closed it without finding a suitable assignee for the lease. The plaintiffs succeeded in obtaining an order for specific performance of the lease and its covenant. The court noted that the plaintiffs would encounter difficulty in proving their loss, for the real risk was to the diminished value of all the leases. Perhaps more significantly, the court also insisted upon compulsory performance in order to prevent losses to the other tenants, which would otherwise be irrecoverable under the doctrine of privity of contract except to the extent that rents might be reduced.

(4) Limitations

Although the courts possess a broad discretion to make compulsory orders for performance when appropriate, they observe a number of important limitations on the exercise of this jurisdiction.

Waste of Resources

One limitation upon compulsory performance which is common to this branch of remedies as well as damages is that the courts will not countenance a waste of resources. Just as they will not award damages to pay for remedying a defect where the work is pointless or wholly disproportionate to the resulting benefit, so too no court would order specific performance of a wasteful enterprise.

In the past, the courts have often hidden behind the pretence that they were unable to supervise such works and so could not properly order performance. But since the court may always appoint agents, such as

---

86 R Unger, *False Necessity: Anti-Necessitarian Social Theory in the Service of Radical Democracy* (Cambridge, 1987) p 535.
87 [1996] Ch 286, [1996] 3 All ER 934, CA; revsd on other grounds [1997] 2 WLR 898, HL.

receivers, to act for it, these days this argument concerning the difficulties of supervision is seldom heard.

> Where it is necessary, and in my opinion right, to move away from some 19th century authorities, is to reject as a reason against granting relief, the impossibility for the courts to supervise the doing of work.[88]

The point is rather that the costs of performance far exceed any worthwhile benefit emerging from proper performance of the contract. Thus in *Tito v Waddell (No 2)*,[89] the court declined to order specific performance of the mining company's promise to restore the land to its former state, partly on the ground that it considered the venture unlikely to succeed and partly on the ground that the benefits of restoration were uncertain. The same concern to avoid a waste of resources led the court in *Wrotham Park Estate Co v Parkside Homes Ltd*[90] to decline to order the destruction of fourteen homes in order to enforce a covenant. Similarly, an order to continue with a business, as in the case of the order to run a supermarket, may be rejected if it is likely to cause substantial losses to the defendant without clear benefit to the plaintiff. The assessment of these possible losses should be approached cautiously, however, for the effect of the order for compulsory performance will be to strengthen the plaintiff's bargaining position in achieving a settlement, and will not necessarily lead to the expected waste of resources.

Liberty

A second limitation upon orders for compulsory performance concerns the protection of individual liberty. A court will be reluctant to order performance of a contract involving the personal performance of services on the ground that this restricts the freedom of an individual too severely. By statute the courts are prevented from making such orders against employees.[91] At one time this limitation was thought to preclude orders for compulsory performance of any contracts involving personal service. But the rule has become more refined. An injunction may be ordered against an employee to prevent breach of a negative covenant in the contract of employment, such as a promise not to work for certain competitors of the employer.[92] A court can also enforce a contractual promise to appoint a person to a particular job, such as an undertaking to provide a porter for a building.[93] In recent years injunctions have also been routinely issued against breach of disciplinary procedures by employers, in which case the order does not require the employer to keep

---

88   Lord Wilberforce, *Shiloh Spinners Ltd v Harding* [1973] AC 691, 724, [1973] 1 All ER 90, 102, HL.
89   [1977] Ch 106, [1977] 3 All ER 129, Ch.
90   [1974] 1 WLR 798, [1974] 2 All ER 321, Ch.
91   Trade Union and Labour Relations (Consolidation) Act 1992, s 236.
92   *Warner Bros Pictures Inc v Nelson* [1937] 1 KB 209, Ch; Stevens, 'Involuntary Servitude by Injunction' (1921) 6 *Cornell Law Quarterly* 235.
93   *Posner v Scott-Lewis* [1987] Ch 25, [1986] 3 All ER 513, Ch.

on the employee, but simply to comply with the agreed remedial procedure under the contract.[94]

The crucial remaining issue with respect to this limitation concerning personal services is whether a court will issue an injunction simply restraining an employer from dismissing an employee.[95] Given the social market considerations which suggest that the employee has vital interests in a job going beyond the mere income which it produces, the claim of employees for specific performance appears strong. The courts have traditionally resisted such orders, however, on the ground that the order would be impracticable given the breakdown of trust and confidence between the parties. Recent cases have overcome this bar to compulsory performance, by discovering instances where the trust and confidence between employer and employee has not broken down.[96] The modern test of whether or not an injunction will be awarded against dismissal of an employee appears to be whether the order is workable.[97]

Fairness

A third special limitation on awards of compulsory performance insists that contracts not only be fair in their inception, but that also it would be fair to enforce them at the date of judgment. In *Patel v Ali*,[98] for example, after the defendant had agreed to sell her house, she suffered an injury requiring amputation of her leg. She became pregnant and her husband was judged bankrupt and sent to prison. Despite the normal practice of awarding specific performance for sales of land, the court declined to order compulsory performance on the ground that it would inflict on the vendor hardship amounting to injustice.

Mutuality

The final special limitation upon compulsory performance, which is known as the mutuality rule, requires the court to check that by ordering specific performance it does not replace one relation of domination with another. Unless the interests of the defendant are adequately secured, by forcing him to perform the contract, he may be left then with no reliable remedy against the plaintiff. For example, if the defendant refuses to perform a contract for services because he reasonably believes that the plaintiff cannot afford to pay him for his work, a court will decline to order compulsory performance unless the plaintiff either pays in advance or provides adequate security for performance.[99]

---

94   *Jones v Lee* [1980] ICR 310, CA; *McClaren v Home Office* [1990] IRLR 338, CA.
95   Ewing and Grubb, 'The Emergence of a New Labour Injunction?' (1987) 16 *Industrial Law Journal* 145.
96   *Hill v CA Parsons & Co Ltd* [1972] Ch 305, CA; *Powell v Brent London Borough Council* [1988] ICR 176, [1987] IRLR 466, CA.
97   *Robb v Hammersmith and Fulham London Borough Council* [1991] IRLR 72, QB.
98   [1984] Ch 283, [1984] 1 All ER 978, Ch.
99   *Price v Strange* [1978] Ch 337, [1977] 3 All ER 371, CA.

Index

Acceptance,
    battle of forms, 155-6, 163
    communication, 152, 157, 322
    conduct, 151, 152, 321
    correspondence, 151
    counter-offer compared, 151, 156, 157
    cross-offers, 152
    estoppel, 159, 164, 321
    modification, 316-7, 321, 326
    postal, 157-8, 163
    reliance, 153-4, 326
    self-service store, 160-1
Accord and satisfaction, 369
Account for profits, 196, 198, 393
Adhesion contracts 3, 112
Administrative injunction, 185, 246
Advertisements, 114-5, 185, 190, 194, 249
Agency, 120-2, 179, 290-1, 306, 311-2, 313
Alternative dispute resolution, 19, 45, 245,
    366-7, 372
Anson, 154, 156-7
Anticipatory breach, 333, 343-5
Arbitration, 45, 94, 248, 307, 322, 339, 366
Assignment, 290
Atiyah, 68, 69
Atomization, 104
Autonomy, 29, 101-2, 105, 129, 292, 375

Bailment, 287
Battle of forms, 155-6, 163, 166, 208-9
Bill of Exchange, 19, 44, 50, 290
Bill of Lading, 50, 287, 290-1
Bill of Sale, 355

Capacity, 109-110, 257
Catching bargain, 340, 358
Classical law of contract, 3-7, 129, 147, 148
Code of practice, 248
Collateral contract, 115, 121, 127, 163, 181,
    199-200, 210, 284-5, 290-1, 298, 305

Collective agreement, 99, 133
Commercial lease, 362
Commodification, 4
Common mistake, see Mistake
Competition, 35, 130, 145-7, 170, 172, 177,
    186, 189-90, 391
Compulsory terms, 26-27
Conditions, 333-5
Condition precedent, 117-9, 312
Confidential information, 197-8, 393
Consent,
    agreement, 150, 321
    common mistake, 116-9
    intent, 112, 117
    modification, 113, 321-3
    objective test, 111-6, 119, 143
    reliance, 116, 153-4
    remote parties, 119-124, 292
    role of, 108-111
    signature, 111, 148
    silence, 113
    subject to contract, 114
    tender, 114, 115
    voluntary, 129, 131-2
Consideration,
    adequacy, 58, 253, 262, 342, 369
    benefit and detriment, 57, 63, 68, 72,
        76, 93, 255, 317, 324
    conditional promise, 60
    estoppel, 81-2
    executory contract, 67
    fairness, 24, 57, 58, 62, 64, 254-5
    family contracts, 91
    implied request, 61-2, 68, 75-6, 201
    modification, 317-9, 323-6
    negotiable instruments, 44-5
    past, 63
    parties to contract, 289, 293
    pre-existing duty, 58, 93, 318
    rationale, 44, 54, 66-70

Consideration–*contd*
  settlements, 369
  total failure of, 378
  unilateral contract, 60
Constructive notice, 141
Consumer,
  arbitration, 366-7
  credulous, 176
  defective product, 299
  disclosure of terms, 220
  exclusion clauses, 40
  formalities, 50
  inequality in expertise, 31, 35, 170, 188
  limitation of damages, 346
  litigation, 184
  misleading trade description, 176
  penalty clause, 349
  pressured sales, 141
  regulation, see Regulatory offences
  statutory definition, 236-7
  time order, 361
  unfair terms, 270-3
Consumer credit, 50, 141, 188-90, 230,
    268, 282, 338, 349-50, 361, 363, 366
Consumer surplus, 390
Contempt, 368-9, 370
Contingency fee agreements, 52
Contractualization of social relations, 48,
    55, 89-90, 101-6
Contributory negligence, 386-7
Co-operation,
  ascription of responsibility, 33-4, 150,
    165
  contracts incomplete by design, 307-8,
    314-5
  employment, 307, 310
  incentives, 28, 330-1, 336-7
  long-term contract, 17, 33, 306, 397
  modification, 209, 315, 320, 385
  performance, 306, 309-15, 397
  requirements contract, 310-1
  termination, 306, 334, 397
Corporatism, 248
Counter-claim, 343, 378
Credible commitments, 19

Damages,
  aggravated, 392
  avoidable losses, 385-7
  causation, 386
  compensatory principle, 376-80
  consumer surplus, 390
  contributory negligence, 386-7
  cost of repair, 378
  estoppel, 84-5, 201, 376
  disappointment and distress, 183, 205,
    286, 389-90
  disgourgement of profits, 374, 393, 394

Damages–*contd*
  limitation clause, 345-6
  liquidated, 346-52
  loss of profits, 380-5
  misrepresentation, 181-4
  mitigation, see Mitigation of loss
  net loss, 377, 380
  punitive, 390-4
  remoteness of loss, 183-4, 371, 382-5,
    390, 392, 395
  reputation, 390
  social cost, 371, 385, 395
  social market, 374-6, 380
  speculative, 352, 381-2, 395
  substituted performance, 377, 387
  third party loss, 285-6, 378-80
  throughput, 381-2
  time of assessment, 385
  wasted expenditure, 377, 380, 382
  waste of resources, 388-9
Debt, 341-5, 347, 349
Deed, 53
Defective product, 299
Deposit, 19, 339, 341, 354, 361, 363
Detrimental reliance, 76-7
Director General of Fair Trading, 40, 185,
    244, 245-7, 249
Disclosure of information,
  contracts incomplete by design,
    314-5
  doctor, 314
  during performance, 312-5
  economic analysis, 185-7, 232
  employment, 314
  facts, 190-5
  fiduciary, 196
  labelling, 194
  regulatory offences, 193-4
  relation of dependence, 187, 190
  terms, 187-90
  undue influence, 197
Distributive justice, 11-14, 20, 23-4, 89-90,
    94, 106-7, 231, 254, 256-7
Donative promises, 54, 67, 69, 254
Door-to-door sales, 141, 263
Disclaimer, see Exclusion clauses
Due date of payment, 342
Duress, 132-6
  affirmation, 143
  economic, 133-4, 143, 256, 320, 326-30,
    392
  fairness, 267
Duty of care, 126-7, 148, 166, 170, 241,
    288, 295, 301

Economic analysis,
  agreed remedies, 339, 344
  breach, see Efficient breach

Economic analysis–*contd*
    compulsory terms, 229-32
    consideration, 68-9
    disclosure, 185-7
    economic duress, 328
    estoppel, 86-7
    externalities, 96-8
    implied terms, 227-8
    market failure, 26-7, 96-7, 229-32, 251
    measure of damages, 374
    penalty clauses, 351-2
    pre-contractual obligations, 168, 185-7, 203
    procedural fairness, 251
    remedies, 371-2
    remoteness of loss, 384
    wealth maximization, 25-6, 68-9, 86-7
Efficiency, 25-6, 96, 373
Efficient breach, 373-4, 391
Entire obligation, 312, 342-3, 345
Equality, 23, 31, 33, 102, 230, 234, 392
Equity, 42, 73, 84, 136
Estoppel,
    American Restatement, 73, 74, 84
    Ancillary reliance, 164-5
    Australia, 74, 77
    ascription of responsibility, 116, 125-6
    classification as contract, 54, 80-5
    consideration, 72-3, 81-2
    damages, 84-5, 166, 201
    detrimental reliance, 76-77
    economic analysis, 86-7
    encouragement, 75-6
    modification, 292, 321-3, 324-5
    pre-contractual responsibility, 199, 200-1
    privity, 298-9
    proprietary, 82-3
    rationale of reliance model, 85-8
    reasonable reliance, 77-9
    remedy, 84-5
    unconscionability, 79-80
European Community, 14, 42-3, 130, 187, 189, 230, 231, 239, 240, 299
Exclusion clauses,
    consumer sales, 40, 193, 236
    fairness, 243, 269-70, 346
    interpretation, 123
    limitation of damages, 345-6
    misrepresentation, 192
    judicial discretion, 237-45
    negligence liability, 235-6, 241, 246
    third party, 287-8
    reasonableness test, 239-45, 366
    set-off, 343
    statutory definition, 239, 269-70
    unfair term, 246
Executory contract, 67, 70

Express terms,
    battle of forms, 155-6, 209
    course of dealing, 208
    incorporation, 208-9, 216-7, 255
    informal understanding, 209
    oral, 210
    receipt, 208
    standard form, 208,
    termination clause, 333
    unusual and onerous terms, 216, 220
Externality, 96, 230, 233
Extortionate credit bargains, 31, 32, 268-9, 349, 363

Fairness,
    adequacy of consideration, 62, 253, 262
    agreed remedies, 341, 345, 347
    ancillary terms, 252-3, 270-2
    balance of advantage, 253, 280-1
    classical law, 6-7, 24
    compulsory terms, 231
    disability, 110, 256-7
    duress, 135-6
    exclusion clause, 243
    frustration, 280
    implied terms, 228, 258
    incorporation of terms, 255
    interpretation, 258-9
    judicial revision, 253, 280-1
    limitation of damages, 243, 346
    mistake, 259-60, 279, 281
    penalty clause, 347, 350-2
    price, 252, 257, 263, 348
    procedural, 32-3, 251, 271, 351
    reasonable expectations, 253, 270, 272
    restraint of trade, 261
    social force majeure, 282
    social market, 28, 32-3
    specific performance, 401
    terms, see Unfair terms
    unconscionability, 256-7, 264
    undue influence, 137, 255-8
Family relations, 91-4, 102, 104-5
Fiduciary, 138, 196, 307, 313, 393
Firms, 11, 121
Floating charge, 353
Force majeure, 273
Forfeiture, 322, 353, 354, 358-61, 364
Formalism, 5, 37-8, 44
Formality, 47, 48, 49-50, 53, 188-9, 210, 319, 365
Franchise, 11, 307, 318
Fraud, 110, 118, 139, 141, 181, 183, 288, 392
Freedom of contract, 22, 25, 262, 339-40
Fried, 69
Frustration, 42, 277-8, 280, 331
Fuller, 87-8

Globalization, 41-45
Good faith, 17, 39, 44, 85-6, 103, 109, 136,
    150, 169, 196, 199, 202, 270-1, 307,
    310
Grey list, 239, 271, 343
Guarantee, 19, 50, 118, 121, 293, 339, 364-
    6, 394

Harmonization, 14, 43
Hire-purchase, 338, 339, 340, 349, 353,
    356, 358, 363
Hobbes, 15
Hohfeld, 144
Holmes, 376

Illegality, 51-3, 95, 98, 340, 378
Immorality, 47, 92, 340, 350
Implied terms,
    business efficacy, 223, 226-7, 310
    condition, 276
    conflict with express term, 221-2, 309,
        330
    default rules, 223, 227-8, 232
    economic analysis, 227-8
    employment, 225, 276, 390, 401
    general legal obligations, 223-4, 227
    incentive for disclosure, 192-3
    intent, 206, 222-3
    justification, 227-8
    mistake, 119, 276
    model contracts, 224-8
    officious bystander, 222
    reasonable care and skill, 224
    reasonable expectations, 207, 228, 258
    reasonable price, 224
    safety, 224, 226
    sale of goods, 192, 193, 225, 226, 236,
        259
    sale of land, 193
    services, 193, 224
    termination on reasonable notice,
        330-1
    tort obligations, 224
Inalienable property, 95
Incomplete contracts, 26, 225, 307-8, 313,
    314-5
Incorporation of terms, 208-9
Indemnity, 236, 293, 327, 364-6
Injunction, 366, 370, 371, 394-401
Insolvency, 340, 352, 356, 368, 369
Insurance, 195-6, 240, 243-4, 272, 313-4,
    391
Intention to create legal relations, 54, 64-
    6, 78, 91, 99, 209
Interpretation,
    ambiguity, 215-6
    conduct, 210
    co-operation, 309

Interpretation–*contd*
    duty to negotiate with care, 218
    exclusion clause, 123
    intention, 212, 215, 217, 277
    misrepresentation, 173
    objective approach, 187, 207, 212
    plain language, 188, 213-4, 216
    reasonable expectations, 207, 212, 217,
        258-9
    reasonable understanding, 213, 218
    risk, 276
Invitation to treat, 162

Judicial Revision, 253, 273-5, 336-7

Letters of intent, 99
Lex Mercatoria, 45
Lien, 353-4
Long-term contracts, 103, 306, 308-9, 313,
    315-6, 336-7, 366

Macaulay, 15
Mail order, 194
Malinowski, 15
Market failure, 26-27, 28, 35, 96
Market stabilization, 265
Materialization of law, 39, 41
Misleading statements,
    descriptions of products, 176
    due diligence, 178-9
    negligence, 178
    omission, 187
    price, 172, 173, 177, 179
    regulatory offences, 184-5
    vicarious liability, 179-80
Misrepresentation,
    burden of proof, 177-8
    conduct, 191-2
    damages, 181-4, 205
    exclusion clause, 192
    mere puff, 174-7
    omission, 187, 190-2
    negligence, 177-80, 191
    rescission, 177-8, 180,
    statements about contractual terms,
        173, 219
    statements of future intentions, 174
    statements of law, 172
    statements of opinion, 174-6
Mistake, 42
    common mistake, 116-9, 260, 278-9
    identity, 194-5
    fairness, 259-60, 277
    negligence, 119
    unilateral, 212, 214-5, 218, 221
Mitigation of loss, 331, 342, 345, 372,
    387
Model contracts, 9, 31, 224-7, 248

Modification, 58, 68, 113-4, 133-4, 210, 292, 315-331
Mortgage, 19
Mutuality, 401

Negligence, 34, 283, 295, 299-301
Negotiable instruments, 45, 50, 290
Networks, 304-5

Offer, 149-50
    invitation to treat, 160-1, 162
    revocation, 162-3, 164
    termination, 151
Ombudsman, 367
Opportunity cost, 174, 182-3

Parol evidence, 210
Parties to contract, 289-91
Paternalism, 100, 233, 268
Penal bond, 349
Penalty clause, 347-52, 362, 391, 394
Performance,
    bond, 365, 394
    co-operation, 309
    good faith, 310
    legitimate interest in, 344
    order of, 311-2
Plain language, 188
Pollock, 65
Power, 11-12, 28, 30-2, 375, 397
Price marking, 188
Privity , 78
    agency, 120-2, 290-1
    assignment, 290
    benefit, 285-7
    burden of contract, 119-124, 284
    collateral contract, 284, 290-1, 298, 305
    concept, 283-8
    indeterminate range of liability, 294-6
    intentions of the parties, 297, 303
    negligence liability, 287-8, 295, 299-301, 304
    networks, 304-5
    product liability, 299
    proprietary interests, 124, 283
    rationale, 291-6
    reform, 302-5
    reliance, 298-301, 303-4
    specific performance, 398-9
    trust, 297
    unjust enrichment, 301-2, 303
Product safety, 194
Proprietary estoppel, 50
Proprietary rights, 124, 352-3
Public law, 32, 94-5
Pure economic loss, 295

Quantum meruit, 125, 167

Rea, 351
Reasonable expectations, 207, 212
Receiver, 368
Rectification, 211-2
Regulation, 247-8
Regulatory competition, 43
Regulatory offences, 184-5, 193-4, 392
Regulatory trilemma, 2
Regulation by negotiation, 247-50
Rejection of goods, 335, 373
Relation of dependence, 170, 186-7, 203-4
Remoteness, see damages
Repudiation, 332-3, 343-4
Reputation, 16, 46, 133, 150, 318, 332-3, 373, 390
Requirements contract, 16, 157, 310-1, 318, 397
Rescission,
    affirmation, 143, 180
    bars, 142-3, 180
    damages in lieu, 180-1
    lapse of time, 180
    misrepresentation, 180, 195
    mistake, 195
    restitution, 143, 180
    third parties, 143, 180
Reservation of title clause, 19
Restitution, 63, 88, 108, 125, 166-7, 205, 363-4, 378, 393
Restraint of trade, 24, 28, 260-61
Retention of title, 356-8
Risk, 116, 123, 158, 273-5, 280, 305, 365, 382-4

Salvage, 135, 256
Security,
    charge, 49, 353
    deposit, 354
    disclosure of information, 197, 314
    lien, 353-4
    mortgage, 356
    pawn, 354
    possession, 353, 354, 358-61
    purpose, 19, 338-9, 352
    registration, 340-1, 354, 355, 356, 357
    retention of title, 356
    third parties, 355, 357
    undue influence, 141-2
Self-help, 15, 18-19, 150
Self-regulation, 40, 185
Settlements, 59, 347, 358, 369-70, 371-2, 392, 400
Set-off, 343, 362
Slawson, 273
Snapping up, 214, 218, 221
Social force majeure, 282

Social market, 30, 43, 69, 101, 170, 232-3, 245, 264, 309, 374-6
Solidarity rights, 398-9
Specific performance, 84, 124, 286, 362, 370, 371, 372, 374, 375, 394-401
Standard form contracts, 2-3, 44, 112, 122, 173, 186, 187, 207, 212, 214, 232, 245, 272-3
State, contracts with, 94-5, 110, 200, 394
Strict liability, 273-5, 299
Subject to contract, 114
Summers, 169
Surrogacy, 105-6
Symbiotic contracts, 11, 223, 308

Tender, 114, 115, 162, 164, 199-200
Termination,
    adequacy of damages, 335
    affirmation, 331, 333, 335-6
    conditions and warranties, 333-5
    consumer, 335
    co-operation, 306, 331-2, 336-7
    express term, 333
    formality, 319
    for breach, 332
    innominate term, 334-5
    modification, 317
    reasonable notice, 330, 336
    sale of goods, 334-5
Teubner, 2
Time of the essence, 359
Tort,
    consent, 108, 126-7, 133, 288
    pre-contractual liability, 166
    pure economic loss, 299-301
Total failure of consideration, 378
Transaction costs, 26, 96-7, 112
Transformation thesis, 21
Transplants of legal rules, 42

Uberrimae fidei, 195, 249, 314
Uncertainty, 162
Unconscionability, 79-80, 81, 86, 139, 140, 220, 237, 256-7, 268, 347, 362
Undue influence, 33, 136-142
    bars to rescission, 142-3
    constructive notice, 141-2
    disclosure of information, 197
    fairness, 255-7, 267
Unfair terms,
    arbitration, 367
    deposit, 350, 361
    exclusion clauses, 269-70
    good faith, 271, 346
    limitation of damages, 346
    limits on ostensible authority, 122
    mirror principle, 271, 350, 351, 361
    modification, 315
    payment in advance, 342
    penalty, 350, 351, 361
    reasonable expectation, 271
    set-off
    unfair contract terms unit, 246-7, 272
Unilateral contract, 60, 81, 158-9, 163-4, 199, 311-2
Unique goods, 396
Unjust enrichment, see Restitution
Usury, 267-69

Variation, see Modification

Waiver of breach, 317, 335-6
Walzer, 106
Warranty, 59, 110, 117, 118, 333
Waste of resources, 345, 372, 388-9, 399-400
Weber, 103
Welfarism, 36
Wilhelmsson, 282